PRINCIPLES OF DIGITAL IMAGE SYNTHESIS

THE MORGAN KAUFMANN SERIES

IN COMPUTER GRAPHICS AND GEOMETRIC MODELING

Series Editor, Brian A. Barsky

Principles of Digital Image Synthesis
Andrew S. Glassner

Radiosity & Global Illumination
François X. Sillion and Claude Puech

Knotty: A B-Spline Visualization Program
Jonathan Yen

User Interface Management Systems: Models and Algorithms
Dan R. Olsen, Jr.

Making Them Move: Mechanics, Control, and Animation of Articulated Figures
Edited by Norman I. Badler, Brian A. Barsky, and David Zeltzer

Geometric and Solid Modeling: An Introduction
Christoph M. Hoffmann

An Introduction to Splines for Use in Computer Graphics and Geometric Modeling
Richard H. Bartels, John C. Beatty, and Brian A. Barsky

VOLUME ONE

Andrew S. Glassner

PRINCIPLES OF DIGITAL IMAGE SYNTHESIS

MORGAN KAUFMANN PUBLISHERS, INC.   SAN FRANCISCO, CALIFORNIA

Sponsoring Editor   Michael B. Morgan
Production Manager   Yonie Overton
Assistant Editor   Douglas Sery
Assistant Production Editor   Julie Pabst
Composition   Ed Sznyter, Babel Press
Illustration   Tech-Graphics
Cover, Text, and Color Insert Design   Carron Design
Copyeditor   Gary Morris
Indexer   Steve Rath
Proofreaders   Bill Cassell, Ken DellaPenta, and Mary Gillam
Color Separation   Color Tech
Printer   Quebecor Printing

Morgan Kaufmann Publishers, Inc.
Editorial and Sales Office
340 Pine Street, Sixth Floor
San Francisco, CA 94104-3205
USA
Telephone   415/392-2665
Facsimile   415/982-2665
Internet   mkp@mkp.com

Library of Congress Cataloging-in-Publication Data
Glassner, Andrew S.
    Principles of digital image synthesis / Andrew S. Glassner.
        p.   cm.
    Includes bibliographical references and index.
    ISBN 1-55860-276-3 (v. 1: hardcover)
    1. Computer graphics. 2. Image processing–Digital techniques.
I. Title.
T385.G585   1995
006.6–dc20   94-36565

To the inspiration of Leonardo da Vinci: artist, musician, writer, and bold explorer of the imagination

Those who fall in love with practice without science are like a sailor who enters a ship without a helm or a compass, and who never can be certain whither he is going.

Leonardo da Vinci

CONTENTS

VOLUME II (UNITS III, IV, AND V)

III MATTER AND ENERGY   541

Inspiration begins with imagination and the spirit to create. Then comes the need to communicate, to share an idea or thought. Grab a pencil and you can make it real: a *picture*, abstraction made concrete, ideas preserved in time. Our hearts and minds are moved to tell stories, to teach what we think and feel to others and learn the same from them.

Of all the visual media, computer graphics is one of the newest. The computer is a powerful amplifier—it can take terse descriptions of the world and create pictures of that world, using any rules you choose. If we choose the classical rules of light, then we can make pictures that can pass for photographs; other rules explore other ways of seeing.

The field of *image synthesis*, also called *rendering*, is a field of transformation: it turns the rules of geometry and physics into pictures that mean something to people. To accomplish this feat, the person who writes the programs needs to understand and weave together a rich variety of knowledge from math, physics, art, psychology, physiology, and computer science. Thrown together, these disciplines seem hardly related. Arranged and orchestrated by the creator of image synthesis programs, they become part of a cohesive, dynamic whole. Like cooperative members of any complex group, these fields interact in our minds in rich and stimulating ways.

I find each of these disciplines inherently interesting; together they are fascinating. Understanding the interplay of such diversity and exploring the connections is exciting, and with the understanding of such elegant ideas comes a deep satisfaction. That's why I love computer graphics: it's stimulating to the intellect and rewarding to the heart.

I couldn't find a book that presented image synthesis as a complete and integrated field of study, encompassing all of the topics I just mentioned. But I love to write. And so this book was born.

The big idea in this book is to lay out the rules that tell a computer how to take 3D shapes and lights and create a picture—one that would pass for a photograph of that scene if it existed. So our driving problem is the simulation of Nature's illumination of a scene, the capturing of that illumination on film, and its presentation to an observer. Sometimes we bypass the film idea and just imagine an observer in the scene. We often make it easy and pretend the observer has only one eye, so we can ask, "Given this scene, what picture do I show to the observer to make her think that she's viewing the real scene?" We use all the disciplines I listed earlier to answer this question, since our goal is not merely to create an image, but to create a perceptual response in the viewer.

It's all a trick! Like any visual medium, computer graphics creates illusions. Fred Brooks [65] has observed that our job as image synthesists is to create an illusion of reality—to make a picture that carries our message, not necessarily one that matches some objective standard. It's a creative job.

This book is not about how to write specific programs, or how to implement particular algorithms. The history of computer graphics is like any discipline of thought: tried-and-true ideas are constantly challenged by new ideas, and sometimes the older ones, once seemingly invulnerable, are found somehow deficient and fade away. So it is with rendering algorithms; our marketplace of ideas is a noisy and bustling place right now.

But there are some ideas that I believe are fundamental, that come from the basis of our discipline and lie at the heart of all we do. Those are the ideas in this book. I have included many examples from current practice, but I rarely go into their details. There are lots of references, and you can find a wealth of implementation information in the literature. My purpose here is to discuss the underlying principles—the ideas that have slowly emerged as the core of our discipline.

There are three such basic fields: human vision, signal processing, and physics. These are not independent disciplines; as I've said, much of the fun of image synthesis is seeing how these fields fit together. But here I have chosen to give each of these topics its own day on the stage, in the form of a unit of the book. The fourth unit pulls the first three topics together and shows how they combine to make rendering algorithms. I look at two of today's most popular techniques, hierarchical radiosity and distribution ray tracing, as examples to illustrate the principles. Finally, the fifth unit contains several appendices with short topic summaries, historical notes, and reference data.

I make a general argument in this book. To design and implement a computer system for creating synthetic digital images for people to view, you need to understand the physics of the world you are simulating, the appropriate methods for simulating those physics in the computer, and the nature of the human visual system that ultimately interprets the image.

The following few paragraphs describe the structure of the book and show how the discussion has been arranged to provide an accumulating body of mathematical, physical, and physiological information that culminates in a modern image rendering system. There's too much information here for a one-semester course on image synthesis. Teachers may choose to present in detail only some of the information in this book, covering the rest at a higher level; deciding where to dig deeply and where to summarize lightly will depend on the instructor, the course, and the students. The only material that ought not be skipped is the section on notation in Chapter 4. With suitable summaries from the instructor to cover the gaps, students can work sequentially, skipping material as desired. Since the book is cumulative, I don't recommend hopping back and forth.

In Volume 1, Unit I covers the human visual system, the effects of displays on images, and the representation of color. The idiosyncrasies of the human visual system are endless; it's a finely tuned physical and neurological system of great complexity, which we are only beginning to understand in a quantified way. But there are some large-scale features that we do understand and that are important to computer graphics: those are the topics I stress in Chapter 1. I discuss some of the ways of representing color in Chapter 2, so that you can write programs that manipulate color information correctly. In addition, Chapter 3 considers the effect of a display on an image, since the transformation of a mathematical ideal into a physical reality inevitably includes a change in the message.

Unit II addresses digital signal processing. In a digital computer, we transform the smooth signals of everyday life into digitized, or sampled, representations. For example, we usually compute the color of an image only at a finite number of points on the display (the pixels), rather than at every infinitely small point on the image. This simple operation has profound repercussions, which often clash with an intuition born of our experience in the physical world. To ignore these effects is to invite a flood of visual and numerical problems, from "jaggies" or stairsteps in an image to an incorrect simulation with splotchy illumination and other ugly artifacts. To understand these issues, Chapter 4 discusses the nature of digital signals, and then Chapter 5 introduces the Fourier transform, which is a mathematical tool that reveals some of the internal structure of a signal. Like listening to an orchestral symphony and then looking at the complete score, taking the Fourier transform of a signal lets us isolate different components of the signal for closer study. A related tool is the wavelet transform, which is presented in Chapter 6. With these tools we can find ways to efficiently and accurately compute the integrals of functions. This is an essential part of image synthesis; in fact, much of image synthesis can be seen as nothing but numerical integration of various types. Chapter 7 covers the basic ideas of Monte Carlo integration, which is a powerful tool for handling this complex type of problem.

With these analytic and comparative tools available to guide the discussion, I turn to more practical issues involved in rendering images. Chapter 8 discusses uniform sampling, which is the process of taking a continuous signal and turning it into a digital representation by taking evenly spaced measurements. This process, though conceptually simple, introduces a Pandora's box of unexpected problems. An alternative is nonuniform sampling, addressed in Chapter 9, which offers a different blend of advantages and disadvantages. Unit II ends with Chapter 10's survey of the signal-processing methods that have proven of most use in image synthesis in recent years.

Unit III, which opens Volume 2, turns to the physics of the real world. We begin with a study of the nature of light in Chapter 11, and then move on in Chapter 12 to quantify the movement of energy through the world using the tools of energy transport. Chapter 13 presents the field of radiometry, which offers us terms and units for discussing the quantities and qualities of light present in different parts of a scene. Chapter 14 covers the physics of materials, so we have some understanding of how they interact with the light striking them. This leads us to Chapter 15's study of the large-scale simulation of light-matter interaction, known in computer graphics as shading. The equations that describe how the shading on one object affects the shading on another involve integrals, so we look at the mathematical methods for manipulating and solving such integral equations in Chapter 16. By Chapter 17, we've learned enough to gather these ideas into a single equation known as the radiance equation, which gives the basic structure for how light moves through an environment. This is the single most important equation in image synthesis, and every digital image based on geometrical optics is always an approximate solution of it.

The presentation of the radiance equation crowns the theoretical development covered in this book. Rendering practice is largely involved with finding ways to accurately and efficiently solve this equation. Because a complete analytic solution appears impossible in any but the most trivial environments, we must cut corners, simplify, and otherwise approximate everything involved in image-making, from the geometry of the scene to the physics of the simulation. The methods of digital signal processing give us the tools to understand which approximations are reasonable and what their effects will be, so we can choose our simplifications in a principled way.

Unit IV demonstrates how the ideas in the first three units may be combined to make a complete rendering algorithm. I present the popular techniques of radiosity and ray tracing in Chapters 18 and 19 by applying different sets of assumptions and simplifications to the radiance equation. Chapter 20 returns to the themes of Unit I and discusses how displays affect the perception of a computed image. I present some ideas for compensating for this distortion. The unit ends with Chapter 21, in which I offer a few opinions about where I think image synthesis is headed.

Unit V consists of seven appendices. Appendices A–D offer reference material on linear algebra and probability, some historical discussion of reflection and refraction, and a catalog of analytic form factors for computing radiation exchange. Appendix E provides a summary of useful constants and units, Appendix F an interpretation of the two most popular standards for describing real physical lighting instruments, and Appendix G measured spectral emission and reflectivity data for a wide variety of materials. For your convenience, the bibliography and index are printed at the end of each volume.

The language of geometry, signals, and physics is largely written in mathematics. So there are mathematics in this book, because that's the best way people have found for expressing clearly, simply, and precisely what are usually very simple and elegant ideas. I've tried to use the most straightforward math possible at all times. This may mean I've used some notation that's unfamiliar to you. It's all explained, and I hope it's not at all tricky. There's lots of discussion about the equations and what they mean, and it builds slowly. If you flip through the book now and something looks daunting, don't be concerned: by the time we reach the complex-looking stuff it won't be complex at all, because you'll know how to read it.

If you know something about linear algebra (vectors and matrices), and you remember the basic ideas of calculus (what integrals and differentials are, even if you're rusty on the mechanics), then you have everything you need to get through this book. There's a short appendix on probability if you're unfamiliar with that field; everything we use in the text is covered there. The occasional forays into other areas of math are well-paved. I encourage you to consult standard math texts when you want to, but I hope that you will infrequently need to.

This book does not consider all of computer graphics—such a book would be a huge undertaking. I address only image synthesis: the job of converting a scene description into a picture. There are many other important subfields in computer graphics, including implicit and explicit modeling, motion control, compositing, lighting, and more. You can find discussions of these topics and pointers to more literature in the general textbooks. A good introductory text is Hearn and Baker [199]. More encyclopedic and detailed discussions are available in Foley et al. [147] and Watt and Watt [473]. A general introduction without math may be found in my book for artists and designers [159].

If you're studying on your own, make use of the references; there's a world of alternate explanations of almost everything in here. If you can study with a friend, I encourage you to do so; it's easier and often much more pleasant than working on your own. I have always learned at least as much from my colleagues as I have from my teachers.

I hope that this book is useful both to the student studying independently and the student in the classroom. There are some exercises at the end of each chapter. These ask mostly for prose descriptions and discussions, rather than mathematical manipulation; the goal is to think about what the math represents, not the mechanics of how it accomplishes the representation. If the ideas are in place, the mechanics will come; going in the other direction is much harder.

I enjoy computer graphics. I like math and I like art, and image synthesis stimulates me analytically and emotionally. This book shares with you what I feel are the most important and rewarding ideas in image synthesis.

Acknowledgments

Nobody can write a book of this magnitude alone. It gives me great pleasure to acknowledge and thank all those people who have generously given to me their time, energy, and support. I cannot list everyone who has helped me; such a list would fill another volume! I have singled out below those people who have been especially helpful over the three years that I have been working on this project.

This book was written while I was a member of the research staff at the Xerox Palo Alto Research Center (PARC), where my colleagues offered me stimulation, encouragement, and support. Lisa Alfke of the PARC Technical Information Center was my librarian *extraordinaire*. She tracked down and obtained hundreds of papers, theses, and reports, many obscure and out of print. My thanks go also to the rest of the helpful and widely resourceful TIC staff. My managers, Eric Bier, Frank Crow, Per-Kristian Halvorsen, and Maureen Stone, all offered a supportive and encouraging atmosphere.

Many members of the Xerox PARC research staff made themselves available for discussions, help, and moral support; I thank Marshall Bern, Dan Bloomberg, Jules Bloomenthal, Ken Fishkin, John Gilbert, Don Kimber, Ralph Merkle, Les Niles, Dan Russel, and Maureen Stone. Kim Brook and Kathleen Dunham provided secretarial support and helped with countless daily tasks. Thanks to Brian Tramontana and Natalie Jerimijenko, photographer and subject, respectively, for Natalie's photograph used in Unit II.

The final stages of the book's production were carried out while I was a Researcher at Microsoft Research. My thanks go to my manager, Dan Ling, and my colleagues at Microsoft for their support.

This book has been brewing for several years. Thanks to Jeff Hultquist for helping to shape the book and to Brian Barsky for getting it on the road to reality. Deep thanks to Mike Morgan for his brave and enthusiastic support of this project through delays and dramatic changes. I appreciate the wind in my sails offered by Jim Arvo, Dan Bloomberg, Eric Braun, Lakshmi Dasari, Eric Haines, Pat Hanrahan, Jeff Hultquist, Mike Morgan, Peter Shirley, and Maureen Stone. They encouraged me, at different times and in different places, to continue with this project when I was ready to quit.

Many computer graphics people generously gave time to answer questions about their work and to provide supplementary materials. Thanks to Rob Cook, Ken Fishkin, Steven Gortler, Eric Haines, Pat Hanrahan, Paul Heckbert, Masa Inakage, Eric Jansen, Jim Kajiya, Jean-Luc Maillot, Don Mitchell, Sumant Pattanaik, Rich Redner, Holly Rushmeier, David Salesin, Peter Schröder, Peter Shirley, François

Sillion, Maureen Stone, Sam Uselton, Greg Ward, and Jack van Wijk. Particular thanks go to Jim Arvo for generously allowing me to use his unpublished notes on integral equations and transport theory.

This manuscript has benefited greatly from the suggestions made by volunteers who reviewed drafts of various chapters. For their advice I thank Dan Bloomberg, Ken Fishkin, Marc Levoy, David Marimont, David Salesin, Peter Schröder, Maureen Stone, Greg Turk, and Greg Ward. In particular, Eric Haines and Peter Shirley have read almost all of the manuscript in some form and some chapters in several forms—surely a Herculean task. Any errors that remain are purely my responsibility.

The production of this book presented many challenges, but it was executed with great skill and cheerfulness by Yonie Overton and Julie Pabst. My thanks to both for their imagination, precision, and, most of all, care for this project.

Where you work affects your mood and influences the final result. Three particularly pleasant places deserve special mention: Farley's in San Francisco, where I developed most of the first half of the book with cups of hot chocolate in hand, and Hobee's and Printers, Inc. in Palo Alto, where almost all of Unit III was developed from behind cups of hot tea.

It would have been easy to get burned out on a project of this size. Gary Marks and Jennifer Youngdahl kept my musical soul alert and creative even when I was too busy to practice. My parents, Bertram and Roberta Glassner, and my siblings, Adriana, Bruce, and Marshall, offered encouragement and support. Eric Braun and Chuck and Pam Mosher helped me stay on the big path. Lakshmi Dasari provided moral support in numerous large and small ways.

To those who are about to learn image synthesis, I extend my hopes that you find the process rewarding and exciting. Image synthesis is a field that can fire the imagination and stimulate the intellect, satisfying heart and mind. I hope you find the journey illuminating.

Andrew S. Glassner
Seattle, Washington

SUMMARY OF USEFUL NOTATION

Notation	Meaning	Section where defined
$\mathcal{R}_\mathcal{V}$	The visual band	1.3
$\mathcal{R}$	The real numbers	4.3.1
$\mathcal{Z}$	The integers	4.3.2
$\mathcal{C}$	The complex numbers	4.3.5
$\bar{z}$	The complex conjugate of z	4.3.5
$\otimes$	Cartesian product	4.3.4
$\oplus$	Cartesian sum	4.3.4
$\sum_k, \sum_{k \in Z}$	Summation over all integers	4.3.7
$\sum_{k \in [N]}$	Summation over $[d, d + N - 1]$	4.3.7
$\int dt$	Integration over $[-\infty, \infty]$	4.3.7
$\langle f \,\vert\, g \rangle$	Inner product of $\bar{f}$ and g	4.3.9
$f * h$	Convolution of f and h	4.5
$H(\omega)$	System response	4.5.3
$\mathcal{F}\{x\}$ $\overset{\mathcal{F}}{\longleftrightarrow}$	Fourier transform	5.12
$(\mathcal{K}x)(t)$	Kernel integral operator on x	16.3
$(\mathcal{L}x)(t)$	Composite integral operator on x	16.3
$\psi, \psi_k, \psi_k', \psi_2$	Fourier basis functions	4.3.8
$\delta(t)$	Dirac impulse distribution	4.4.1
$b_W t, b_W[n]$	Box functions	4.4.2
$\mathrm{III}_T(t), \mathrm{III}_T[n]$	Impulse trains	4.4.3
$\mathrm{sinc}(x)$	$\sin(x)/x$	4.4.4
$v(\mathbf{r}, \vec{\omega})$	Visible-surface function	12.12.2
Q	Energy	13.5
Φ	Power (flux)	13.5
I	Intensity	13.5
M, B	Exitance (radiosity)	13.5
E	Irradiance	13.5
L	Radiance	13.5

THE HUMAN VISUAL
SYSTEM AND COLOR

I cannot forbear to mention among these precepts
a new device for study which, although it may
seem but trivial and almost ludicrous, is
nevertheless extremely useful in arousing the mind
to various inventions. And this is, when you look
at a wall spotted with stains, or with a mixture of
stones, if you have to devise some scene, you may
discover a resemblance to various landscapes ...
or strange faces and costumes, and an endless
variety of objects, which you could reduce to
complete and well drawn forms.

Leonardo da Vinci

INTRODUCTION TO UNIT 1

In this unit we will discuss color images and their perception by human beings. I believe it is important that creators of images understand how people see, and how they react to what they see.

There are two principal reasons to create a synthetic image: for analysis by a computer, or for display to a person. If we are creating an image for a computer, then we don't even need to actually display the image; we need only create a set of color values and give them to an analysis program.

But when we present an image to a person, our task is much more difficult. No matter what specific purpose has brought us to create a picture, our primary and essential desire is to *communicate* something to another person. We want to get an idea into someone else's head, and we are going to do it through that person's sense of vision. Anything in our image that doesn't make it through the visual system will be imperceptible by the viewer; we have wasted our time generating such information. The human visual system is complex and loaded with idiosyncrasies: for example, we sometimes see edges where there are none, or assume an object is concave or convex depending on the direction from which it is being illuminated. When we look at a picture, we see not just the image displayed and computed, but all the artifacts added in by the visual system. The problem with these artifacts is that they become part of the message, and augment or distort the message we intend.

If we don't wish to waste time computing useless information, and we want to avoid visual artifacts that will change our message, we need to understand how the visual system works, at least in a basic way. The problem of the *representation* of information is the job of the designer of the image, who must plan for the *perception* of the image.

My goal in this unit is not to cover everything interesting about the visual system (that would take volumes), nor even to cover everything that might be taught in an undergraduate vision course. Rather, I have attempted to isolate those features and phenomena that I feel are most important to computer graphics.

We are a long way from fully understanding the human visual system (new theories are still being developed). But today's theories provide a strong basis for our new work, and it is that basis we cover in Chapter 1.

Chapter 2 addresses the description of color and its perception. We will discuss color because our computer programs need to calculate with color, adding and subtracting color representations to determine the amount of light bouncing around a scene and ultimately displayed to a viewer. Our goal is to understand how to describe colors in a way that allows us to discuss them abstractly and objectively, yet still correlates to how they will be perceived. As with the visual system, new color systems are still being introduced.

Compared to vision and color, the field of display technology is moving very fast, and entirely new devices and principles are constantly replacing old standbys. We must say something about displays in order to have at least a feeling for how important the mechanics of the display process are to the presentation of an image, but the field is too broad and changing too quickly for us to hope to cover the field even superficially. Therefore in Chapter 3 I have chosen to pick just one common, representative sample, the CRT display, and discuss that in some detail to give an idea behind some of the thinking that goes into the trade-offs involved in designing and intelligently using a particular display. Note that the term *display* includes any presentation medium, including ink or paper or lasers projected onto granite cliffs.

I discuss displays in this part of the book to emphasize their relationship to the visual system and image fidelity. We can think of image synthesis as a process that ends when a file of color values has been computed, so that display of this file is a separate problem. But the job of image synthesis isn't complete until the image can actually be viewed by someone, and that requires dealing with the limitations and restrictions of real displays. Thus we discuss the CRT in this section as a representative of the types of issues involved when designing and using a real system for display of images to the human visual system. New hardware and software technologies are giving image creators increased control over the mechanisms of display, and their interaction with each other and the visual system is important to the effective display of an image.

The mind is the real instrument of sight and observation, the eyes act as a sort of vessel receiving and transmitting the visible portion of the consciousness.

Pliny (A.D. 23–79)

1

THE HUMAN VISUAL SYSTEM

1.1 Introduction

The human visual system is composed of two major components: the eyes and the brain. A great deal is known about the physiology of the eye, including the operations of various sets of cells that seem to work in concert. Much less is understood about the brain, but it would be a mistake to neglect the brain as part of the visual system. All experiments in which an observer is asked to report on visual sensation implicitly include the brain's processing of the visual signal. In this book we will not venture into philosophical distinctions between "brain" and "mind"; for us, the brain will serve as the agent of all abstract perception and reasoning.

We will start with a review of the structure of the human eye, since it acts as the initial perceptual filter: signals not perceived by the eye cannot be further refined by the brain. We will then survey some of the important features of the human visual system as a whole.

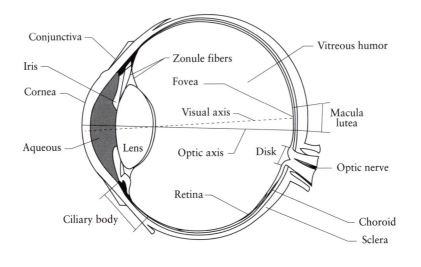

FIGURE   1.1

Physiology of the human eye, shown in cross section.

1.2   Structure and Optics of the Human Eye

An overview of the physiological structure of the human eye is shown in Figure 1.1. A "schematic eye" has been developed to facilitate high-level quantitative and structural discussions of the eye; Gullstrand's simplified (number 2) schematic eye is shown in Figure 1.2 [123]. Some numerical values for that schematic are given in Table 1.1. A more complete, though more complex, schematic eye has been introduced by LeGrand [489].

Our discussion of the eye will include two common optical terms: the *diopter* and the *visual angle*.

The *diopter* (abbreviated D) is one measure of the power of a lens. It is defined as the reciprocal of the focal length of the lens measured in meters. Thus a lens with a focal length of .1 m (100 mm) has an equivalent power of 10 diopters.

Another important optical measure is the *visual angle*. This is the angle subtended by some structure when seen from the *nodal point* inside the eye, as shown in Figure 1.3.

The most important structural elements in the optical path are the *cornea, iris, pupil, lens,* and *retina.*

The *cornea* is a clear coating over the front of the eye. The cornea has two purposes: it serves as a protection mechanism against physical damage to the internal

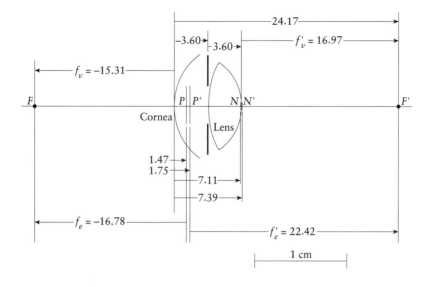

FIGURE 1.2

Gullstrand's simplified (number 2) schematic eye.

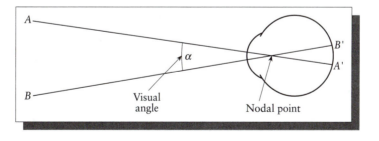

FIGURE 1.3

Visual angle is measured from the nodal point.

		Unaccommodated	Accommodated 8.62 D
Radii of curvature	Cornea	$r_1 = +7.80$ mm	$+7.80$ mm
	Lens anterior	$r_2 = +10.00$ mm	$+5.00$ mm
	Lens posterior	$r_3 = -6.00$ mm	-5.00 mm
Refractive indices	Air	$\eta_1 = 1.000$	1.000
	Aqueous	$\eta_2 = 1.336$	1.336
	Lens	$\eta_3 = 1.413$	1.413
	Vitreous	$\eta_4 = 1.336$	1.336
Axial separations	Anterior chamber	$d_1 = 3.60$ mm	3.20 mm
	Lens	$d_2 = 3.60$ mm	4.00 mm
	Vitreous	$d_3 = 16.97$ mm	16.97 mm
Surface powers	Cornea	$F_1 = +43.08$ D	$+43.08$ D
	Lens anterior	$F_2 = +7.70$ D	$+15.40$ D
	Lens posterior	$F_3 = +12.83$ D	$+15.40$ D
Equivalent powers	Lens	$+20.28$ D	$+30.13$ D
	Eye	$+59.60$ D	$+68.22$ D
Equivalent focal lengths	Anterior	$f = -16.78$ mm	-14.66 mm
	Posterior	$f' = +22.42$ mm	$+19.58$ mm

TABLE 1.1

Gullstrand's simplified (no. 2) schematic eye. *Source:* Data from Davson, ed., *The Eye,* 4:103.

structure, and it provides initial focusing and concentration of the incoming light. A typical human cornea has an optical power of about 40 diopters, due to its curvature and the refraction (or bending of light) that occurs when the light passes from air into the corneal tissue. The cornea is the strongest focusing element in the eye.

The *iris* is a colored annulus behind the cornea but before the lens. The iris contains radial muscles that allow it to change the size of its inner hole, the *pupil*. Only light passing through the pupil proceeds further into the eye.

Light passing through the pupil opening then strikes the transparent *crystalline lens*. The lens is surrounded by a set of muscles called the *ciliary body*, which can pull at the sides of the lens. When the ciliary muscles are relaxed, the lens is stretched radially, flattening it and reducing its optical power; the light entering the eye is now brought to a focus as far from the lens as possible. The ciliary muscles may be tensed to exert a compressive force on the lens: its diameter shrinks, the lens becomes thicker, the optical power increases, and the focal point moves closer to the lens. Thus when the muscles are relaxed, the lens has its longest focal length. When the muscles tense, the lens is focused on nearer objects.

The ability of the lens to stretch in reaction to the pressure from the ciliary body is called *accommodation*. The range of accommodation is a function of elasticity, which diminishes with age. In a young child the lens typically has a range from 10 to 30 diopters. Past age 45 the lens has usually lost most of its elasticity, and remains in a rigid, slightly stretched state [123].

Light focused by the lens falls on the *retina*, a thin but extensive layering of cells covering about 200° on the back of the eye. The retina contains two types of photosensitive cells: *rods* and *cones*. Cones are primarily responsible for color perception; rods are limited to intensity, though they are typically ten times more sensitive to light than cones. Rods are also physically smaller structures than cones, so more of them may be packed into any given space, improving spatial resolution.

Although most of the retina is photosensitive, there is a small region at the center of the visual axis known as the *fovea*, which subtends only 1 or 2° of visual angle. The structure of the retina is roughly radially symmetric around the fovea. The fovea contains only cones, and it is here that we find the densest collection of cones on the surface of the retina: linearly, there are about 147,000 cones per millimeter.

In contrast, the soaring hawks (buteos) have as many as 1 million receptors in the same area [412]. Because their optics are also somewhat specialized, hawks may have vision as much as eight times better than ours; they can see a small object on the ground at a distance from which we could not even see the bird in the sky.

Moving outward from the fovea, rods begin to appear among the cones, and at the edge of the fovea there are more rods than cones, as shown in Figure 1.4. Traveling further on a radial path from the fovea, the rods begin to form rings around each increasingly infrequent cone, as shown in Figure 1.5 (color plate). The highest density of rods appears at about 20° from the fovea. In total, the human eye contains about 120 million rods and 6 million cones. Since the optic nerve contains only about 1 million fibers, the eye must perform a lot of processing before the visual signal ever reaches the brain.

There are two important aspects of Figure 1.4 that deserve mention. The first is that the number of photoreceptors diminishes as we work our way outward from the fovea. This would suggest that we have our greatest visual acuity in the region in the center of our visual field, and less precision as we work our way out. The second feature of the graph is the *blind spot*, where the optic nerve meets the retina and there are no photoreceptors at all.

Figure 1.4 is based on classic work performed by Østerberg in 1935, and represents photoreceptor counts only along one radial line through the retina. A more recent series of studies has produced a far more detailed set of maps of the dis-

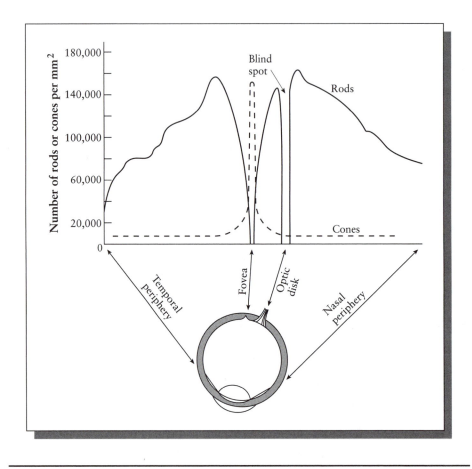

FIGURE 1.4

Density of receptors. Redrawn from DeValois and DeValois, *Spatial Vision*, fig. 3.4, p.60.

tribution of photoreceptors in the retina. Curcio et al. [112] have measured the population of rods and cones and produced the map of Figure 1.6 (color plate). In these color-coded maps of the retina, the fovea is always at the center, and the orientation is consistent (though the scale factor with respect to the center changes). The color scales indicate the number of thousands of cells per square millimeter.

Figure 1.6(a) shows the density of cones in the fovea, over the entire retina. A close-up of the fovea is shown in (b). Parts (c) and (d) show the same regions but plot rod density; a close-up of the rod density near the fovea is shown in (e).

These figures confirm our earlier statements. From Figure 1.6(a) we see that there aren't very many cones in the outer portions of the retina, but that the number jumps suddenly when we reach the fovea. In (b) we see that this increase is quite abrupt. Rods, however, are numerous in the retina outside the fovea, and from Figure 1.6(c) we can see that at about 6 mm from the center there is a particular high-density annulus called the *rod ring*. The density of rods falls off slowly as we approach the fovea, and then drops off suddenly; this drop-off can be seen in more detail in panel (d). An even closer view in (e) shows that the rod density drops to zero right in the center of the fovea in the *rod-free zone*. Note that the rod-free zone in (d) is precisely where the cones are densest in (b).

The change in photoreceptor density is directly related to a change in our perceptual acuity in the image falling on that part of the retina. To demonstrate the changing acuity in our gaze, consider Figure 1.7. Close one eye, and hold this image about arm's length directly in front of your open eye. Stare fixedly at the center. Because the larger numbers are projected onto the less populated region of the retina, they will be fuzzier, though the smaller numbers will be sharper. So all of the numbers in the figure should be equally legible.

There are many ways to demonstrate the blind spot, but we must be careful to distinguish the purely physical effect from additional psychological effects. Sometimes the visual system will "fill in" information that is logical, but not explicitly presented in a scene; such filling in processes are known collectively as *completion* phenomena. We must then be sure that in attempting to demonstrate a physical effect, we isolate it as much as possible from further layers of processing. It can be difficult to prevent all completion phenomena, since our experience tells us that we seem to see a complete visual field all the time. Given that there is a region of the retina where there are no photoreceptors, we must be filling in information all the time; otherwise we would see a constant black spot everywhere we look.

To demonstrate your blind spot, look at Figure 1.8. Close your left eye, and hold the figure about arm's length away from your right eye. Stare fixedly at the cross on the left. You may need to move the figure toward or away from you, but at some distance the black dot should seem to disappear; at this position the dot is falling on the blind spot, and the visual system is completing the white background in this region.

Returning to the anatomy of the eye, the combination of cornea and lens provides a total optical power ranging from +60 to +80 D, which translates to a focal length from about 16 to 12.5 mm. A typical human eye is about 24 mm from cornea to retina, which requires an optical power of about 42 D. Thus there is some extra focusing power available in the system to compensate for imperfect shaping of the eye, in addition to the flexibility of optical power required to focus on objects from very near to very far.

As an example of the variation in the shape of the eye, consider *eccentricity*, one of the most common structural defects in the human eye. An eccentric eye is

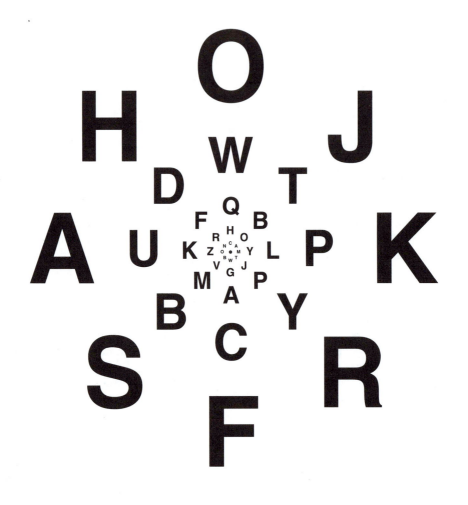

When you look at the center dot in this figure with one eye, all the letters should be equally legible. Redrawn from Sekuler and Blake, *Perception*, fig. 3.20, p. 88.

✕
Fixation cross

●

A diagram for demonstrating the blind spot.

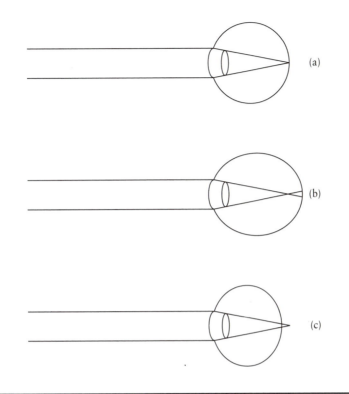

FIGURE 1.9

Eye geometry. (a) A normal (emmetropic) eye. (b) A myopic eye. (c) A hyperopic eye.

either too long or too short. If the focal length of the resting eye's optical system converges at the retina, the eye is called *emmetropic*, and the lens has sufficient power to focus on objects both near and far (Figure 1.9(a)). Note that an eye need not be physiologically ideal to be emmetropic; if the eye is too long but the lens is correspondingly weak, the focus can still be brought to the retina, and vision is normal.

   If the lens is normal but the the eye is too long, then the eye is *myopic*; people with a myopic eye structure are often called *nearsighted*. When the muscles around the lens are at rest, then light is focused at a point in front of the retina (Figure 1.9(b)). Tensing the ciliary muscles only increases the optical power of the lens, which brings the focal point yet closer to the lens, making the problem worse, not better. Until objects are very near, the lens cannot bring them into focus, because the lens can only increase its optical power. Corrective lenses are the most common means for helping people with myopia achieve normal vision.

The opposite problem occurs if the eye is too short, called a *hyperopic* eye. When this eye is at rest, the focal point of the lens is behind the retina (Figure 1.9(c)). Objects at infinity may be brought to focus by accommodative effort; hence the term *farsighted*. However, when an object gets too close then the lens cannot compress any more, and objects closer still will be out of focus, even though the lens is at its maximal optical power. In effect, there is extra, useless optical power left over to bring into focus objects "beyond infinity." Corrective lenses also help hyperopic eyes achieve a normal range of accommodation.

Although we have not said so explicitly, Figure 1.9 describes only a single color of light at a time. Recall that a prism breaks up white light into a rainbow because of *refraction*: different colors of light are bent by different amounts when they pass from one medium to another. This is also true when the light passes through the lens of the eye, so that a sharp white circle is in fact spread out by the time it reaches the retina into a little circular rainbow; this inevitable effect is called *chromatic aberration* in the lens.

This suggests one reason why artists think of red as an "advancing" color and blue as a "receding" one [360]. Because the different colors bend slightly differently as they pass through the lens, we must exert effort to change the shape of the lens to bring the various colors to focus on the retina. To bring a red object to focus requires the same action needed to bring a near object to focus, while blue focusing is like focusing on a distant object.

1.3 Spectral and Temporal Aspects of the HVS

The human visual system involves much more than just the eye. Once the light has been focused on the retina, many layers of physiological and psychological systems process the information, rejecting some pieces of information, emphasizing others, and shaping the signal into something that we can then interpret, often as representative of physical structures.

There is a distinct band of electromagnetic energy to which the eye is sensitive, usually called the *visual range* or *visual band*. Although the range of sensitivity extends into both the infrared and ultraviolet range (albeit at very low sensitivities), for practical purposes the visual range is usually defined to include light with wavelengths from 380 to 780 nanometers (1 nanometer = 1 nm = 10^{-9} m). We will defer a detailed discussion of the nature of light and the meaning of wavelength until Chapter 11. For now, the term *wavelength* may be thought of as corresponding to a particular pure (or *spectral*) color, such as that produced by a laser. Throughout this book we will indicate the range 380 to 780 nanometers with the symbol $\mathcal{R}_\mathcal{V}$. A visual signal is often represented as a plot of intensity versus wavelength, as in

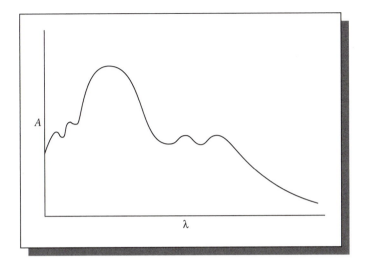

FIGURE 1.10
An example of a power-versus-wavelength curve.

Figure 1.10. This is called a *spectral radiant power distribution*, a *spectral plot*, or sometimes simply a *spectrum*.

Such a plot may be used to measure how much light is absorbed (rather than radiated) per wavelength by a material. In this case the vertical axis is usually the percentage of absorption.

The photosensitive cells of the eye are not uniformly responsive to all wavelengths in the visible range, and the processing that comes after the eye serves to further refine the ultimate importance of various regions of the spectrum to an interpretation of the image.

The first step in processing light information is the reception of the light signal by the photosensitive cells on the retina. Although most of these cells have a long, thin structure, they are not packed into the retina parallel to each other. Rather, they are tilted toward the center of the pupil. The result is a directional sensitivity known as the *Stiles-Crawford effect*, in which cones are more responsive to light arriving straight on than at an angle through the edge of the pupil [123].

Once light has managed to reach the photosensitive material in a rod or cone, it causes a chemical action that results in a neural signal. The chemical at the heart of this process has the generic name *photopigment*. The particular photopigment found in rods, *rhodopsin*, has been studied extensively. It has been found that

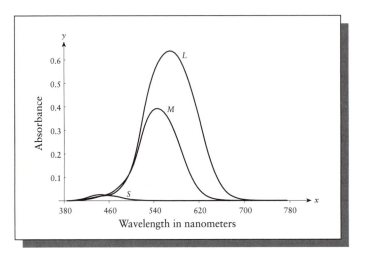

FIGURE   1.11

Photopigment absorption.

rhodopsin reacts to light in a bell-shaped curve, centered at about 500 nm. This is in agreement with the sensitivity of the human visual system during night vision, when there is not enough light to stimulate the cones, making the rods the dominant sensor. Cone photopigments have rarely been extracted from primates, but many psychophysical, psychological, and microspectrophotometric studies have been run on primate and visual observers. The results of these experiments have yielded consistent information that is probably a reliable description of cone sensitivity. This information is summarized below.

There are three types of cones in the human eye, typically called S, M, and L (named respectively for their peak response to relatively short, medium, and long wavelengths), with peaks located at roughly 420, 530, and 560 nm, as shown in Figure 1.11. The response curves for these cones (as well as the rods) are asymmetrical; the drop-off at the high-frequency side is sharper than at the low-frequency side. Thus the shorter wavelengths are more readily absorbed than the longer wavelengths for all three ranges. Both rods and cones may be considered the ultimate in visual sensitivity: a single photon carries enough energy to produce the chemical reactions that change the electrical potential at the cell's membrane, signaling the arrival of light at that cell.

The signal carried by the change in membrane potential makes up the entire message sent by a photoreceptor to the rest of the visual system. Thus the only message sent by a rod or cone is that light has arrived and stimulated the photopigment; there is no information transmitted describing the wavelength of the photon. This effect is called the *principle of univariance* [123]. The likelihood of absorption of a photon by a particular cell is a function of the spectral sensitivity of the receptor and the intensity of the incoming light (e.g., if the receptor is 30% sensitive at some wavelength, any particular photon may not be absorbed, but about 30 of every 100 will). The time-averaged output of a photoreceptor is related to the number of photons received over some recent interval, but there is no way to determine the frequency distribution of these absorbed photons. It is only by combining the results of many photoreceptors with different spectral sensitivities that the visual system is able to reconstruct intensity and color descriptions of the incoming signal; this reconstruction is believed to happen at a very early stage in visual processing.

The principle of univariance may at first seem puzzling: why should the visual system have developed in such a way that the very first step in processing throws away information that then must be re-derived? The answer is probably similar to the reasoning behind the process of *dithering*, used in graphics when a display cannot provide as many colors or gray levels as an image demands [445]. Suppose that the eye contained many distinct color sensors with different, narrowly defined bands of absorption. Although they might be as close-packed as cones, the number of sensors for any particular frequency band in a fixed region would necessarily be fewer than if only three types of cones occupied the space, thereby sacrificing spatial color resolution. The human eye has evolved with a compromise of three sensors, which gives good color sensor density in the retina and a sufficient amount of color information to recompute the spectral information of the incident signal. Either the number of sensors or their density could be theoretically increased at the expense of the other. In fact, the density trade-off can be found in the very center of the human fovea. Here there are no S cones to be found at all, so M and L cones are able to pack even more tightly [463]. At the other extreme, some birds have five to seven different color receptors (produced by a combination of the photoreceptors themselves and a layer of oil) [412].

Not so easily explained is the curious structure of the retina itself. Surprisingly, the photosensors are not the innermost layer of cells on the inside of the retina. Rather, there are several layers of interconnecting cells on top of the photoreceptors, blocking the light from the lens. The overall density of these cells is quite low, so most of the incident light gets through. Even more surprising is the fact that the photoreceptors themselves are oriented so that they face the *back* of the eye rather than the pupil, so light must travel through the body of the photoreceptor before it reaches the photopigment that will trigger a response [123]. These two pieces of physiology have suggested to some that the retina appears to have evolved "inside-out" from the structure that we would probably think most efficient. What forces caused the eye to evolve this way? Are there indeed advantages that we don't yet appreciate? Although many people now believe that the retina is simply the result of an early, mysterious evolutionary preference, these puzzles continue to interest researchers in the physiology, structure, and function of the visual system.

This seemingly reversed structure of the visual system is common to all vertebrates [412]. It suggests that, for vertebrates, eyes are actually part of the brain and represent an outgrowth from it. In fact, the cells of the retina are formed during development from the same cells that generate the central nervous system; the retina truly is part of this essential structure [463]. In contrast, invertebrate eyes come from an invaginated bubble in the skin. The photoreceptors in invertebrates all face toward the lens, while in all vertebrates they face away from the lens and toward the brain. Spiders are unique in that they have both forms of eyes [412].

So far we have only discussed the response of the eye to a single photon. In fact, the chemical processes that occur inside a photoreceptor last several milliseconds, and additional photons that strike the receptor during that time add to the overall response. Thus the output of a receptor is really a time-averaged response, an effect called *temporal smoothing*. In effect, the sensors impose a low-pass filter over their time response, though the cutoff frequency of that filter changes with respect to the background light level: when there is little light arriving, there is little smoothing.

The effect of temporal smoothing leads to the way we perceive light that blinks, or *flickers*. When the blinking is slow, we perceive the individual flashes of light. Above a certain rate, called the *critical flicker frequency* (or CFF), the flashes fuse together into a single continuous image. Far below that rate we see simply a series of still images, without an objectionable sense of near-continuity.

Under the best conditions, the CFF for a human is around 60 Hz [389]. In contrast, a bee has a CFF of about 300 Hz. We note that as with most other visual phenomena, the *flicker rate* (that frequency at which flicker becomes noticeable) is dependent on many factors, such as ambient light, size of the visual target, and duty cycle between the length of time the image is displayed and the blank time (if any) between images. For one set of conditions, Figure 1.12 shows the sensitivity of the eye to different frequencies of flicker. Very early movies flickered because there were not enough frames displayed per second to cause the eye to integrate the images; they were perceived as a flickering series of still photos.

We saw earlier that a sensor reacts to an incoming photon with a chemical change, which is then communicated to the neural circuitry in the eye by a change in electric potential at the cell's membrane. There is an additional complication, however, that enables the eye to respond to enormous variations in levels of incoming light. The phenomenon of *adaptation* gives the system great sensitivity when the overall illumination is low, and some (though less) sensitivity when the overall illumination is high [123]. Although maximum sensitivity over all illumination ranges would be best, this appears to be a difficult problem for any receiving system. Given the need

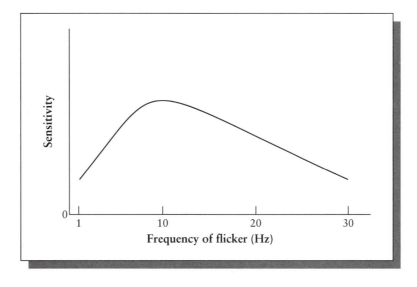

FIGURE 1.12

Flicker sensitivity. Redrawn from Sekuler and Blake, *Perception*, p. 254.

to compromise, it seems very desirable to have the most sensitivity at low light levels where small variations carry a great deal of information.

The range of adaptation is extremely large. Figure 1.13 gives the average *luminance* of background against which we often view the world [355]. The luminance is measured in *candelas* per square meter, which may be considered the light generated by a typical candle (a more formal definition is given in Appendix E).

Because rods are about ten times as sensitive as cones, they are most useful for night (or *scotopic*) vision, when ambient light levels are low. Figure 1.14 shows the response of rods to different levels of incident light, and thus different levels of adaptation. At low levels of light (L_A), rods in their "normal" state are sensitive in terms of both amplitude and wavelength; a small number of photons is likely to produce a signal, and a change in the average wavelength will produce a change in response. At higher light levels (L_B), the intensity-response curve has begun to flatten out, and rods are less sensitive to both the number of photons and changes in wavelength. Beyond a certain intensity (L_C), the rods are *hyperpolarized*, or completely saturated, and release no synaptic chemicals, and thus do not contribute to vision. This saturation typically occurs at daylight levels of illumination.

In daylight (or *photopic*) levels of illumination, it is the cones that are the most

Background	Luminance (candelas per square meter)
Horizon sky	
Moonless overcast night	0.00003
Moonless clear night	0.0003
Moonlit overcast night	0.003
Moonlit clear night	0.03
Deep twilight	0.3
Twilight	3
Very dark day	30
Overcast day	300
Clear day	3,000
Day with sunlit clouds	30,000
Daylight fog	
Dull	300–1,000
Typical	1,000–3,000
Bright	3,000–16,000
Ground	
Overcast day	30–100
Sunny day	300
Snow in full sunlight	16,000

FIGURE   1.13

Luminance of everyday backgrounds. *Source:* Data from Rea, ed., *Lighting Handbook 1984 Reference and Application*, fig. 3-44, p. 3-24.

useful detectors of light information. When a cone has adapted to a particular level of light intensity, it performs just like the rods: light intensities beyond a particular level will cause the cone to hypersaturate and stop sending neural signals. For example, in Figure 1.14 a cone that is adapted to light level L_C will not be able to distinguish light levels L_D and L_E. However, if we assume that the incident light is at level L_D for some time, the cone will adapt, shift its response curve to center at that point, and thus be able to distinguish light levels L_D and L_E.

You may augment the frequency response information discussed above with the

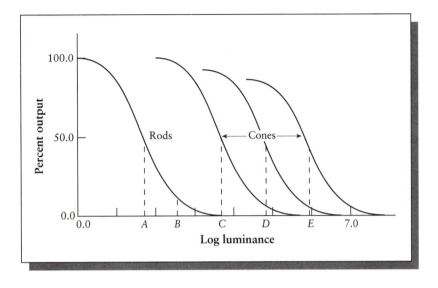

Rod and cone adaptation. Redrawn from DeValois and DeValois, *Spatial Vision*, fig. 3.14.

further processing carried out by the rest of the visual system by performing psychological and neurophysiological experiments. In the final analysis, you may distill the results into a final set of curves that provide the overall frequency sensitivity of the human visual system at some particular level or range of illumination. Often two curves are presented: one for low-level (scotopic) illumination, where the rods provide the most information, and the other at high-level (photopic) illumination, where the cones predominate. Typical scotopic and photopic *luminous efficiency functions* are given in Figure 1.15.

Note that there is a shift in the frequency of peak sensitivity due to the different photopigments of rods and cones. You can experience this change in peak perception, called the *Purkinje shift*, by watching a red or yellow flower with dark green leaves at sunset. When the sun is still above the horizon, your cones are active, and the yellow flower will appear lighter than the leaves because yellow is closer to peak of the photopic sensitivity curve than dark green. When the sun has set and light levels are lower, your rods are the principal sensors. The scotopic sensitivity curve is more responsive in the shorter wavelengths, so the green leaves will now appear relatively lighter than the yellow flower, though both will of course be much darker due to the lower amount of incident light.

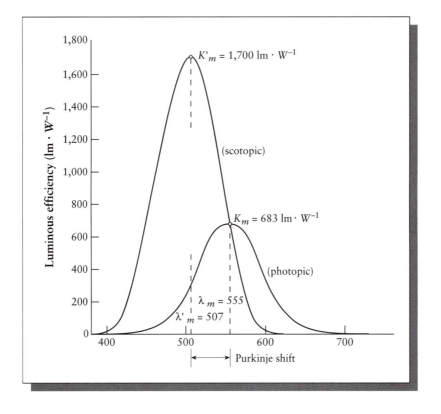

FIGURE   1.15

Luminous efficiency curves. Redrawn from Wyszecki and Stiles, *Color Science*, fig. 2(4.3.2), p. 258.

Rods and cones can only respond to the light that reaches them. As we mentioned earlier, the light must pass through the inner layers of the retina, which can absorb some light. The light must also pass through the eye itself, going through the lens and the other components of the eye. For example, the lens in the human eye changes color with time, becoming increasingly yellow as a person ages [489]. Thus, the lens acts as a yellow filter, which obviously affects the spectral distribution of light striking the retina. Measurements of the transmissive characteristics of the eye have been carried out by Boettner and Wolter [52]; their data are summarized in Figure 1.16. Note the transmission curves are both of high magnitude and flat within the visual band.

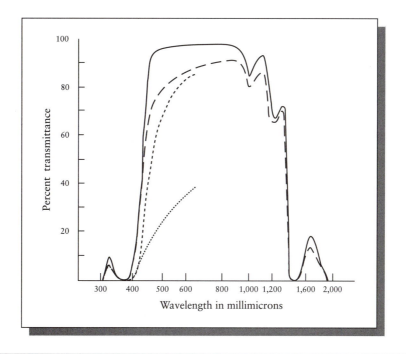

FIGURE 1.16

Transmittance of the human lens. Solid curve = total transmittance of a 4-1/2-year-old lens. Long-dashed, short-dashed, and dotted curves = direct transmittance of 4-1/2-, 53-, and 75-year-old lenses, respectively. Redrawn from Boettner and Wolter in *Investigative Opthalmology*, fig. 7, p. 781.

1.4 Visual Phenomena

The human visual system is sufficiently complex that much of our understanding comes from trying to understand intriguing phenomena that are revealed by physical experiments. Some of these are familiar in computer graphics because we produce images that tend to exaggerate these effects; others are less well known in the graphics community.

We present here a short summary of some of these phenomena.

1.4.1 Contrast Sensitivity

Suppose that an observer is shown a sheet of paper with reflected intensity I, and inside there is a smaller sheet with a slightly different intensity $I + \Delta I$, as in Fig-

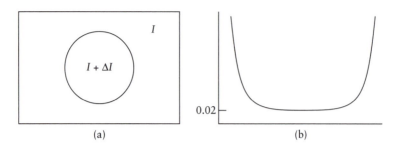

FIGURE 1.17

A contrast sensitivity experiment. (a) A small region in a larger one. (b) The just-noticeable-difference curve.

ure 1.17(a). We would like to find the smallest *just noticeable difference* (or *jnd*) ΔI such that the observer will report that the inner region is of a different intensity than the outer region. Over a wide range of intensities, the ratio $\Delta I/I$ (called the *Weber fraction*) is nearly constant with a value of about 0.02, as shown in Figure 1.17(b) [345]. This curve is known as the *contrast sensitivity function*, or *CSF*.

The curve of Figure 1.17(b) suggests that the human visual system is responsive to *ratios* of intensities, not absolute values. We note that dI is the limit of ΔI, and that $d[\log(I)] = dI/I$. This suggests that there is a constant k such that increasing the logarithm of a signal by k corresponds to a just-noticeable difference in the intensity.

We can also measure contrast sensitivity with respect to a signal of changing or constant frequency. A common such signal is a *grating*, which is simply a series of vertical bars. If the bars have sharply defined edges, a horizontal profile through the image would look like a square wave; a smoother transition would have a profile more like a sine wave. The frequency of a grating is measured by the number of cycles per millimeter on the retina; our response to different gratings is called the *contrast sensitivity function* (CSF). The response of a human adult to sine-wave gratings of different frequencies is shown in Figure 1.18. Note that for each frequency a certain amount of contrast is required to perceive the grating; if the contrast is lower than this amount, we see only a flat gray field. For a particular contrast, there is some frequency of sine wave which we are best able to detect. For frequencies that are higher and lower than that peak, we require more contrast in order to see the variation.

Our contrast sensitivity is also dependent on whether we are using our rods or cones. Figure 1.19 shows the difference in our CSF for scotopic (night) and photopic (day) vision.

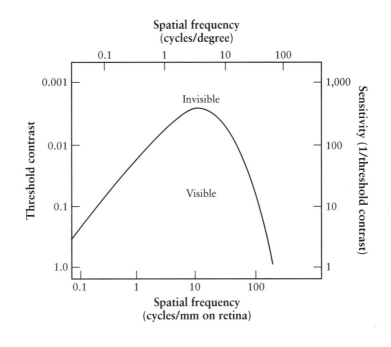

FIGURE 1.18

Contrast sensitivity for sine waves. Redrawn from Sekuler and Blake, *Perception*, fig. 5.18, p. 155.

Adaptation plays an important part in our contrast sensitivity. When the eye has adapted to a particular frequency, the sensitivity to information at and near that frequency is decreased, as shown in Figure 1.20.

Figure 1.21 shows the CSF for a human infant and an adult. Notice that our sensitivity increases with age. An important implication of this curve is that infants cannot see high-frequency information as well as an adult. To an infant, the world beyond a short distance appears blurry, as with extreme myopia. As the child ages through its first year, its nervous system becomes more complex and capable of encoding the high-frequency information that is striking its retina. As its ability to transmit high-frequency information matures, the world comes into sharper focus.

As we age beyond about 20, our sensitivity to high frequencies begins to drop off, as shown in Figure 1.22. This decrease in sensitivity probably comes from a decrease in the pupil size of the eye [389], which decreases the amount of light arriving at the retina.

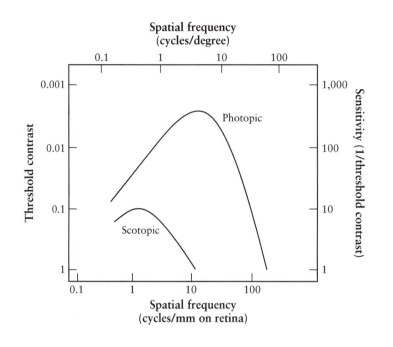

FIGURE 1.19

CSF for day and night. Redrawn from Sekuler and Blake, *Perception*, fig. 5.19, p. 157.

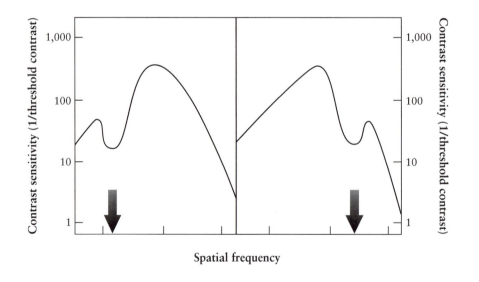

FIGURE 1.20

CSF in response to frequency adaptation. Redrawn from Sekuler and Blake, *Perception*, fig. 5.28, p. 167.

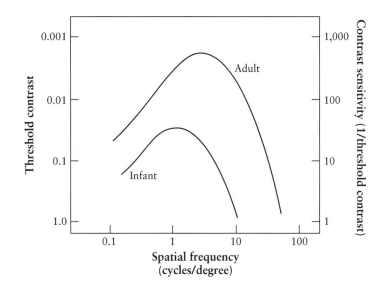

FIGURE 1.21

CSF for an adult and an infant. Redrawn from Sekuler and Blake, *Perception*, fig. 5.24, p. 162.

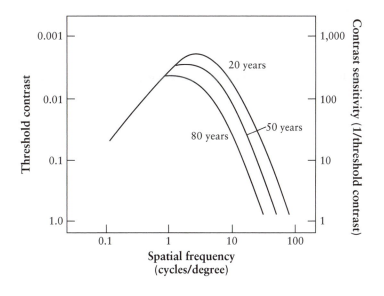

FIGURE 1.22

CSF for an adult from about 20 to 80. Redrawn from Sekuler and Blake, *Perception*, fig. 5.26, p. 164.

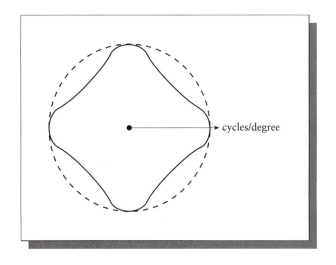

FIGURE   1.23

The CSF with respect to orientation. Redrawn from Bouville et al. in *Proc. Eurographics '91*, fig. 1.

This response depends on direction. Our ability to resolve a grating of a given frequency and contrast is best when that grating is horizontal or vertical [433] as shown in Figure 1.23.

A full discussion of the CSF could easily fill a chapter; interested readers are encouraged to consult the references in the Further Reading section.

1.4.2 Noise

Many human senses are tolerant of *noise*. For now, we will simply consider noise to be a signal that seems to have a strong random component that is added in to the signal we care about. An example from the audio domain is *tape hiss*, which is the sound made by blank audio tape. A visual example is static on a television signal, where colors are occasionally wrong and there is a sprinkling of white or black spots.

As long as this noise isn't too extreme, the human visual system tends to be very good at ignoring it [218]. This is probably the result of how the photoreceptors are distributed on the inside of the retina [479, 496]. This relative acceptance of noise will prove to be of great value to us when we discuss the phenomenon of *aliasing* and ways to control it, in Units II and III.

1.4.3 Mach Bands

People who make Gouraud-shaded polygonal images are familiar with *Mach bands*. Named for the Austrian physicist Ernst Mach, Mach bands are an illusion that variously emphasizes edges or suggests edges in a picture where the intensity is in fact changing smoothly.

Figure 1.24 shows a set of vertical gray bars. Beneath them is a plot of their gray values. Look near the boundary between any two bars. Although the intensity is constant across each bar, the right side of each bar appears a bit darker than the middle of the bar, and the left side appears a bit lighter. The transition from one bar to another is emphasized by these illusionary changes in the intensity.

This sort of figure prompts the folklore theorem in computer graphics that Mach bands arise where the first derivative of the intensity is discontinuous. In this case, we have Mach bands around spikes in the first derivative.

In Figure 1.25 we have a smooth gray transition, yet we still see vertical bands where the intensity changes quickly. Here all the derivatives of the intensity signal exist and are smooth, so our folklore isn't a complete predictor of the problem.

The origin of Mach bands is not completely understood, but a reasonable explanation involves the *retinal ganglion cells* [388]. In a simplified model of the eye, these cells act as weighted integrators of the intensity signal coming from the photoreceptors. The integration is organized spatially; the geometric arrangement of the photoreceptors is part of how they are interpreted. The type of retinal ganglion cell we will consider integrates over a small circular region on the retina. These cells sum the photoreceptor response in the center of this region, and subtract the photoreceptor signal in the annulus outside this disk but within the region of integration. The effect of some cells reducing the response of nearby cells is sometimes referred to as *lateral inhibition*.

Figure 1.26 shows four of these cells overlaid on a pair of bars. Cell A is completely covered by the darker bar and cell D by the lighter one. The additive center of cell B is on the darker bar but its subtractive outer annulus is partly on the lighter bar. Because not as much signal is subtracted from B as from A, cell B will report a slightly darker value. Similarly, the additive center of cell C is in the lighter area, but its subtractive annulus is partly in the darker bar; more is subtracted away from the center of C than the center of D, so C will report a lighter value than D. Since this happens at all points along the boundary, and the effect increases as we get nearer to the boundary, the left edge of the boundary looks darker and the right edge lighter than the centers of the respective bars.

This analysis is probably too simple, but it suggests that we are likely to see Mach bands in regions where the intensity is changing quickly; thus, a "large" first derivative is sufficient (though not necessary) to predict the perception of a Mach band. The interpretation of "large" depends on the context of the image, the viewing conditions, and the viewer.

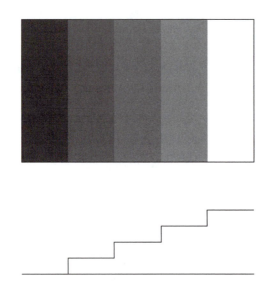

FIGURE   1.24

Gray wedges in equal increments of intensity.

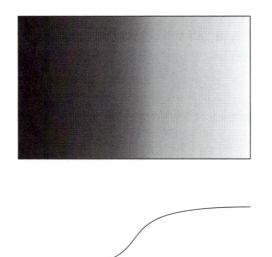

FIGURE   1.25

A smooth gray transition.

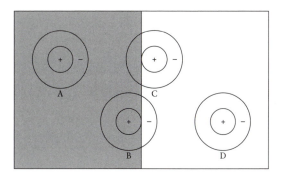

FIGURE 1.26

Neural analysis of Mach bands.

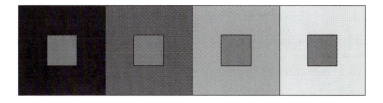

FIGURE 1.27

Lightness contrast. All of the interior regions are the same gray value.

1.4.4 Lightness Contrast and Constancy

The phenomenon of *lightness contrast* (also called *simultaneous contrast*) is illustrated in Figure 1.27. Here we have a patch of a given gray value surrounded by a number of other patches of different gray values. The apparent lightness of the patch seems to depend on the surrounding gray value; the darker the surrounding gray value, the lighter the patch appears.

This phenomenon makes it difficult for us to pick two intensities (or, with suitable extensions, two colors) at random and expect them to behave in predictable ways throughout an image. For example, a typical shorthand for representing a nighttime scene is a horizontal wash of color, light at the bottom (to represent the light from the setting sun) and dark at the top (to show the night sky), as in Figure 1.28.

Suppose we have a flying object in this scene, such as a bird or flying saucer, that is not shaded in three dimensions (3D) but rather has a constant shading. As the

FIGURE 1.28

A horizontal wash sometimes used as a background for a night scene.

object moves vertically in the scene, it will appear to get lighter and darker. If you spot-check a few frames of the animation, you may see this change in lightness and be concerned, but the phenomenon is a normal part of our experience and does not need correction. When the change in the surrounding lightness is dramatic, some compensation may make the scene appear more natural.

The phenomenon of *lightness constancy* allows us to accept a scene as the same in both day and night, when the level of illumination is very different. For example, suppose you are reading at your desk one evening. The book in front of you is printed on white paper that reflects, say, 40% of the incident light, and the black ink of the printing reflects only 5%. Now you turn on another lamp which doubles the illumination in the room. The black print is now reflecting twice as much light energy back to you, but the print doesn't appear twice as bright. This is because the white page is also twice as bright, so the *ratio* has remained the same.

Lightness constancy is a powerful feature of the visual system and is one of the phenomena that makes it possible for us to maintain a consistent mental image of the world, despite dramatic changes in the level of illumination. We can explain both lightness contrast and lightness constancy on a general level using the same ideas of retinal ganglion cells we used for Mach bands [389].

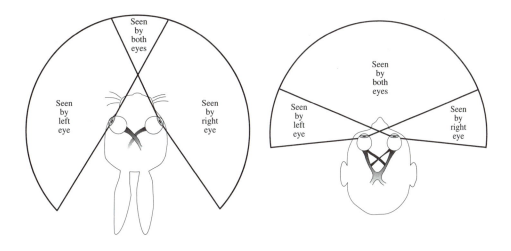

FIGURE 1.29

Eye placement for a rabbit and a person.

1.5 Depth Perception

The human visual system is capable of constructing a 3D view of the world. This ability, called *depth perception*, comes from many different kinds of visual information, some of which may be gathered from one eye alone, and some of which requires two eyes.

To see how two eyes work together, consider the placement of the eyes on the heads of a rabbit and a person, as in Figure 1.29. The rabbit has almost 300° of vision, though only a small amount of the visual field is seen by both eyes. The human has a smaller total field of view, but the two eyes overlap in a much larger region. Other examples of eye placement are the snail, which has eyes on the ends of flexible stalks so that the regions of visibility and overlap may be changed at will, and the whale, which has eyes so far apart on the sides of its head that it is completely blind straight ahead [412]. Spiders and scorpions have clusters of at least six eyes, and some have eight; there is a significant amount of field overlap.

In general, predatory animals have their eyes near the front of the head with a lot of overlapping field, for better depth estimation when going after prey. Conversely, animals that are preyed upon have their eyes far apart, the better to see more of the environment and respond to potential attacks. For example, the owl's eyes have a very large region of overlap. The woodcock is a bird that eats small mud worms by sticking its long, sensitive bill deep into the mud to seek out the unseen worms. The

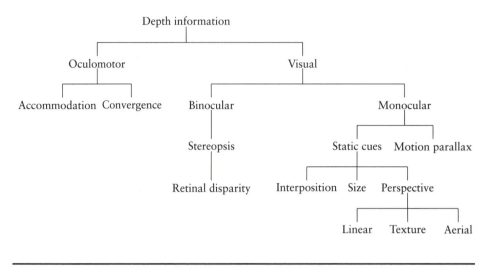

FIGURE 1.30

Types of depth information. Adapted from Sekuler and Blake [389].

woodcock's eyes are perched on the extreme sides of its head, so the bird can see all around and behind itself while immersed in mud [340].

The types of depth information we gather from our visual field are summarized in Figure 1.30. We will discuss these cues one by one below; much of the discussion is based on material in Sekuler and Blake [389].

1.5.1 Oculomotor Depth

Oculomotor effects come from the muscular adjustments in our eyes. When you look at something, you use the muscles surrounding your eye to *converge* them, or physically rotate them to bring the point of attention, or *fixation point*, to fall on the fovea. You also *accommodate* by changing your focus, tensing or relaxing your ciliary body to adjust the thickness of the crystalline lens inside your eye.

Neither of these effects is a particularly robust or accurate indicator of depth information, since they only relay useful information for objects very nearby. When you are looking at an object more than about 6 meters away, the ciliary body is at its most relaxed state, and your eyes are effectively converged on infinity (looking straight ahead). Thus, for 6 meters and beyond there are basically no oculomotor cues that contribute to depth perception.

The other major category of depth cues are the *visual* cues, which are distinguished into the *binocular* and *monocular* classes, depending on whether they involve two eyes or one.

1.5.2 Binocular Depth

When two eyes are involved in a vision task, it is termed a *binocular* activity. The ability to make depth judgements based on information from binocular vision is called *stereopsis*. Stereopsis can provide very precise information on the depth of objects in a scene.

For example, suppose you hold two pencils vertically about 1 meter from your eyes. Stereopsis makes it possible for you to see a 1-mm disparity in the distances of those two pencils; that's a rather remarkable precision of 1 unit in 1,000.

To perceive depths based on binocular information, the visual system needs to perform two tasks that are (at least conceptually) distinct. The first is to *match features* in the two images, followed by a calculation of their *retinal disparity*, or relative displacement in the retinal images.

We can imagine that feature matching begins with *feature extraction*, or finding significant objects in both images, followed by *feature correspondence*, which identifies like features in the two images. An example of this is suggested by looking at a room full of books; the first stage of processing would identify each book-shaped blob in each image as a "book." Two red books may then be put into correspondence. Though it seems reasonable, this theory can be easily disproved.

This famous demonstration makes use of a *random-dot stereogram*, as shown in Figure 1.31. When you view these images as suggested in the caption, directing one image only to each eye, neither eye sees any of the other image. Since the images are made simply of black and white dots, there are no common features to extract and then merge; any black dot could match any other black dot. Yet when properly viewed, a very distinct 3D structure with two layers is revealed. The experiment may be repeated with more complex shapes and a larger number of identifiable layers.

The random-dot stereogram puts to rest the idea that the visual system first extracts features from the individual images at the eyes, and then later matches those features in the brain. After all, there are no features in these drawings to be matched! The identification process must be somewhat more complex. It may be interesting to note that infants as young as four months, as well as monkeys, cats, and falcons, appear able to see the effect. A variant on the random-dot stereogram is the *single-image random-dot stereogram* (SIRD). A SIRD is a repeating band of vertical texture, where the dots have been displaced horizontally as a function of their depth. Some people can deliberately cross their eyes and line up adjacent copies of the bands, so that dots shifted in one band appear over unshifted dots in another band; the brain

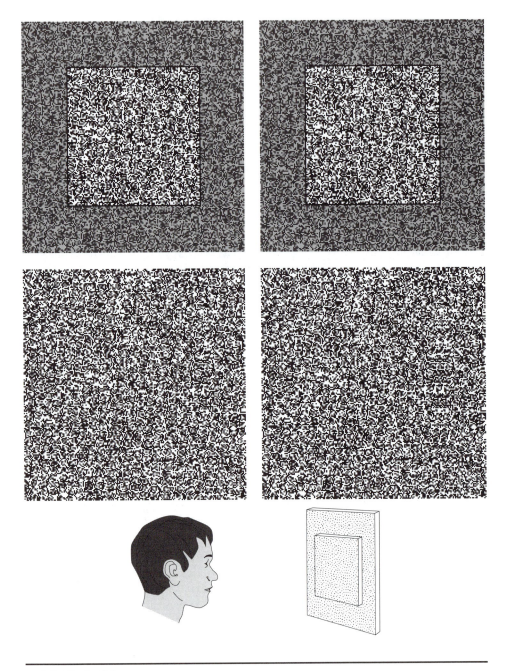

FIGURE 1.31

Random-dot stereograms. To see the stereogram, it may help to place a piece of paper between your eyes, so that each eye sees only one image. Try to illuminate both sides equally. Relax your focus and attempt to fuse the two images. You'll find that a part of the image appears to float in front of the background.

interprets these shifts as changes in depths as in the regular random-dot stereogram and a depth pattern encoded into the shifts can be made to emerge.

The principal characteristic distinguishing the images in the two eyes is *retinal disparity*. This refers to the *lateral separation* of the two images—the fact that some features are shifted on one retina with respect to other features. Although we have seen that features are not extracted and then matched, there must be some sort of matching process going on in the visual system, since we do perceive one complete, 3D world, rather than two similar views at all times.

The complete explanation of depth perception and binocular image combination is not known, but it appears that the physiology of the visual system and the brain plays a very large role in resolving retinal disparity to create a unified image of the world. There seem to be cells that are specifically designed to find matches between particular parts of each retina. When these cells find a match, the depth of the point of fixation may be used to help determine whether the object under scrutiny is closer or farther than the focus point.

As with the rest of the visual system (and the entire human body), stereopsis is both remarkably robust and fragile. If any of the many steps involved in stereopsis are not satisfied, then a person is said to be *stereoblind*. Rather than tolerate two competing or unresolved images, the visual system seems to select one image for presentation to the rest of the brain, and suppresses the information coming from the other eye. The choice of which eye's image to process may be fixed, or may change, depending on the individual.

1.5.3 Monocular Depth

Several depth cues can be extracted from a single image; these are known as *monocular* depth cues. There are two general categories of such cues: *static* cues that can be extracted from a single scene, and *dynamic* cues that require several images over a period of time. We will look at static cues first.

Interposition

The first cue we will examine is known in the vision community as *interposition*, and in computer graphics as *visibility*. Computer graphics has a tradition of generating this cue using *hidden-surface removal* techniques. The simplest of these techniques, the *painter's algorithm*, simply renders all the objects in the image one by one, working from the farthest to the nearest, overwriting any previous information in the image. The interposition cue is how we understand such a scene: if object A occludes object B, we assume that A is nearer than B. Interposition is very powerful; if in an experiment a subject is shown a scene in which retinal disparity and interposition cues contradict each other, the interposition cues will win out.

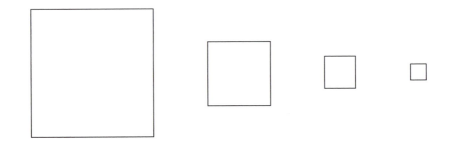

FIGURE   1.32

An example of the size cue.

Size

The cue called *size* summarizes our experience that larger objects seem closer than smaller ones. Even in an abstract set of objects, such as the squares in Figure 1.32, the largest object appears to be closer than the others. We also seem to have a notion of *familiar size*; if you see a friend's face, you can quickly estimate how far away that person is because you know roughly the actual size of his or her face.

Size may be responsible for the famous *moon illusion*. For a person on Earth looking directly at the moon without additional optical instruments, the moon may be considered to always have a fixed radius and a constant distance from Earth. Therefore the visual angle subtended by the moon is a constant, and we might imagine that the moon should always appear the same size. For thousands of years observers have reported that the moon *appears* bigger when it is near the horizon than when it is high in the sky [72]. This phenomenon seems to be common to all cultures and ages. A complete answer to the moon illusion is still elusive, but it probably depends on a number of perceptual cues being combined unconsciously to cause different estimates of the moon's size in different surrounding situations. The heart of the problem is that when the moon is low to the ground and visible behind common objects, we interpret it as part of that scene and apply our normal experience of Earth-based vision to interpreting the distance of the moon. That is, we mistake the size of the moon when it is near the horizon because it appears in close proximity to many other, familiar objects.

The argument is based on the idea that when the moon is high in the sky, we have no reference points, and because our normal range of visibility is typically only a few kilometers or less, we unconsciously assume the moon is at about this distance, underestimating its actual distance. Since we know that things appear smaller as they get farther away, we then underestimate the size of the moon to make it agree

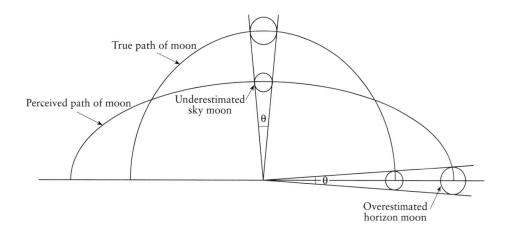

FIGURE 1.33
The moon illusion.

with our underestimate of its distance. When the moon is on the horizon, we can compare it to familiar objects such as buildings and trees, and we unconsciously revise our distance estimate so the moon is farther away. But the retinal image of the moon hasn't changed size. So if the moon is farther away, but its image is not smaller, the moon itself must be larger, as in Figure 1.33.

This explanation is far from the last word on this long-standing illusion [72], but it suggests that some distance and depth cues may involve a sophisticated blend of experience and judgment.

Perspective

The depth cues classified as *perspective* phenomena all deal with perceived changes of physical structures with distance. Perspective is a natural result of the small pupil that acts as the entry gate to our visual system. You could think of the pupil as a point through which all light must pass, creating a *perspective projection*. Perspective is not the only way to project a 3D world onto a 2D surface, but it is the one with which we are most familiar in our daily lives.

Perspective may be used to fool us deliberately. Across the United States there are some famous tourist attractions that advertise themselves as located on "gravitational anomalies" or "physical impossibilities" [30]. Generally, the visitor is taken on a tour through one or more buildings where balls appear to roll uphill, people become

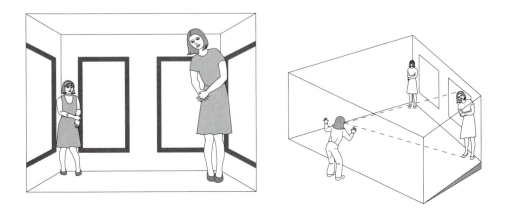

FIGURE 1.34

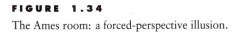

The Ames room: a forced-perspective illusion.

shorter and taller as they walk from one door to the next, and trees seem to grow at an angle. These are almost always *forced-perspective* illusions, where the normal visual cues of perspective are amplified and distorted so that we are presented with a consistent visual argument that defies our previous experience. Perhaps the most famous example of such an illusion is the *Ames room*, shown in Figure 1.34. Many science museums have an Ames room in which you can experiment; it is fascinating that even when you know exactly how the illusion is constructed and the principles on which it is based, the visual argument is still compelling.

Linear perspective is the geometric variety of perspective that is most familiar in computer graphics. It is the phenomenon whereby objects appear to get smaller as they get farther away. The diminishing size of railroad track ties as they recede is the classic example of this effect.

Texture gradient perspective tells us about depth by the change in the size, color, and spacing of objects with distance. Figure 1.35 shows an abstract example of this type of perspective. Sharp discontinuities in the texture field can suggest edges and corners.

Aerial perspective (or *atmospheric perspective*) accounts for the effects of intervening media such as fog and smoke, which are more pronounced upon the image of an object as that object recedes. As light from an object is scattered through the medium, it loses saturation and can be hue-shifted; contours and sharp edges are also diffused. Objects that are farther away are seen less clearly than those nearby.

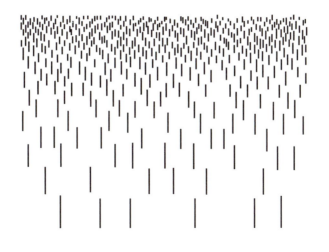

FIGURE 1.35

An example of texture gradient.

1.5.4 Motion Parallax

The last cue we will examine depends on motion. As we move our heads, the relative position of objects appears to move as well; this is called *motion parallax*.

The field of apparent motion is not uniform. To see this, fix your gaze at some point not too far away and then move your head to the right. Objects nearer than the fixation point will appear to move to the left; those farther away will appear to move to the right, as in Figure 1.36.

In general, objects closer than the fixation point will move in the opposite direction of your head motion and those farther than the fixation point will move in the same direction as your head. In both cases, the apparent speed of the motion increases with distance from the fixation point. You can confirm this easily by closing one eye, holding up two fingers at different distances, fixating on one and then moving your head.

Motion is relative, and motion parallax will occur if your head is still but the object is moving. A simple but very effective demonstration uses a large tree. View the tree with one eye when the air is calm, around noon when there are few horizontal shadows and the trunk appears to be a flat shade of brown; the tree will appear flat. But when the wind picks up and the leaves move, suddenly the tree will acquire an easily perceived depth.

These two types of parallax are sometimes distinguished with the terms *head-motion* parallax and *object-motion* parallax.

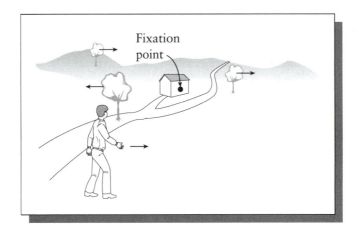

FIGURE 1.36

The apparent visual flow in head-motion parallax.

Note that motion parallax and retinal disparity seem to present the same information in two different ways. Why should we have two such sensitive means for determining depth? One answer may come from the different times when these skills are useful. Motion parallax is useful when a predator is moving quickly, chasing after moving prey. When a predator is searching for prey, it may be useful to stay as still as possible; in this case retinal disparity would be very useful.

1.6 Color Opponency

It is interesting to consider how color information is propagated from the photoreceptors to the brain. Just as we saw the effect of the surround on lightness contrast above, there is a phenomenon called *color contrast* that causes us to see colors in different ways, depending on their surround.

This is not a new idea. Consider what Leonardo da Vinci [113] had to say about it around A.D. 1500:

> Of several colours, all equally white, that will look whitest which is against the darkest background. And black will look intense against the whitest background.
> And red will look most vivid against the yellowest background; and the same is the case with all colours when surrounded by their strongest contrasts.

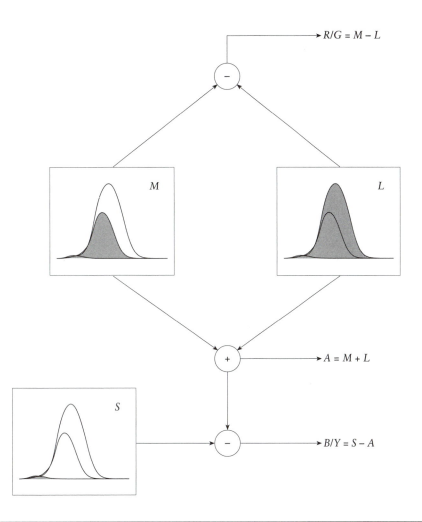

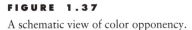

FIGURE 1.37

A schematic view of color opponency.

This observation is described by a theory called *color opponency*. The model for this theory is sketched in Figure 1.37.

The basic idea is that color information is transmitted from the eye to the brain along three nerve bundles, or *channels*. The information along each channel is not simply the values of the three retinal photoreceptors. Rather, each channel carries a sum or difference of the color information derived from the photoreceptors. The sum of the responses from the M and L cones is transmitted along the *achromatic* channel $A = M + L$; this carries only black-and-white (or intensity) information.

It has been suggested [472] that early, primitive sea creatures developed this achromatic channel first, as a basic intensity-only response to light. As animals became more complex, a chromatic channel developed, primarily to differentiate sky and water from earth and vegetation. A second channel then developed to provide a further refinement in the ability to distinguish colors.

One chromatic channel carries the difference between the M and L cones. Since these correspond roughly to green and red, this is called the *red-green* chromatic channel. In symbols, $R/G = M - L$ (note that the channel's conventional name, R/G, does not imply the ratio of R to G).

A second chromatic channel makes use of the S photoreceptors. This carries the difference between the S information (roughly in the blue region) and the achromatic channel (roughly yellow). So this second channel is called the *blue-yellow* chromatic channel: $B/Y = S - A$.

This suggests that colors get transmitted in a 3D space with axes of intensity, red-green, and blue-yellow. This is why a color may be reddish yellow, but never reddish green. This is easily verified: if you project red light onto a white screen, and add green light, the sum appears yellow, not greenish red.

This theory also suggests why some colors appear more saturated than others; for example, a yellow appears less saturated than a red or blue [389]. This comes about because a hue will appear desaturated if it creates a strong achromatic response, and at least some response in one of the chromatic channels: it's the ratio of the chromatic to the achromatic response that predicts how saturated a color will appear.

This is only a rough description of color contrast and color opponency, but it should suggest that our perception of color depends on many factors, such as the color of the surrounding environment, and that our visual system doesn't allow us to perceive certain color combinations.

These observations have important implications when we design and choose colors for image synthesis. The surrounding field of every color must be considered if we want to present a particular color.

1.7 Perceptual Color Matching: CIE XYZ Space

As we have seen above, the response of the visual system to incident light depends on the different adaptations made by the physical components of the eye. In fact, that is barely the tip of the iceberg: the many additional layers of physical and psychological processing each have their own mechanisms for reacting to different forms of light input and image structure, and thereby affect the overall response of the visual system.

Although a further study of the human visual system is fascinating and rewarding, we will not need to explore this field deeper for this book. But keep in mind that there are many factors to be considered when evaluating how an observer will react to a particular visual input. Some of the additional problems include: the frequency distribution and intensity of the background illumination, the size of the target (or image), the intensity and frequency of recent stimuli, fatigue, age of the observer, and even nutrition.

Given the complications, it may seem hopeless to attempt to find some single way to describe "color" in terms of human perceptual response. We may be able to create a laser that radiates at 555 nm, and call it "red," but how do we determine if an observer would call it "red"? And given the enormous range of influences on the visual system and its response, might someone call this laser "red" today but "green" tomorrow?

As we know from experience, the situation is not that bad. In practice, most people have no trouble differentiating "red" from "green" on a reliable basis; achieving this consistency is probably the purpose of many of the correction and adaptation mechanisms we have discussed. But a single objective standard would be a very useful context in which to discuss color. We could then discuss different observers with respect to how they differ from an objective, *standard observer*.

A set of standard conditions for measuring human response to color was decided upon by the CIE (Commission Internationale d'Eclairage). Under these test conditions, a number of color matching experiments were performed.

One result of these experiments was the observation that any perceived color could be generated by some combination of three well-chosen light sources. This is almost certainly a result of the fact that our eyes contain three different types of cones, each sensitive in a different frequency range.

Conceptually, the experiments proceeded as follows. Three particular light sources were chosen and projected on the left side of a white screen, so they overlapped and their colors added together, as in Figure 1.38. Subjects were seated in front of this screen, and given a knob to control the intensity of each of the three sources. Then on the right side of the screen a single "target" color was shown, and the subject was asked to adjust the knobs of the three sources until the mixed color matched the target color. The lights were arranged so that the intensity of each of the three source lights could be dialed to any number between +1 and −1. At +1 the light was fully on, at 0 it was fully off, and at −1 the color was "subtracted" from the composite; this was achieved by instead adding it to the target (this was necessary in order to match all colors). This matching experiment was run for every spectral color, and the three source values were recorded. The results of this experiment for one set of source lights, simply called *r*, *g*, and *b*, are shown in Figure 1.39. These three lights were almost *monochromatic*, that is, almost completely made up of a single pure wavelength; in this case $r = 700\,\text{nm}$, $g = 546.1\,\text{nm}$, and $b = 435.8\,\text{nm}$ [489]. Although each person's responses are different, after enough trials we can

FIGURE 1.38

The CIE color-matching experiment.

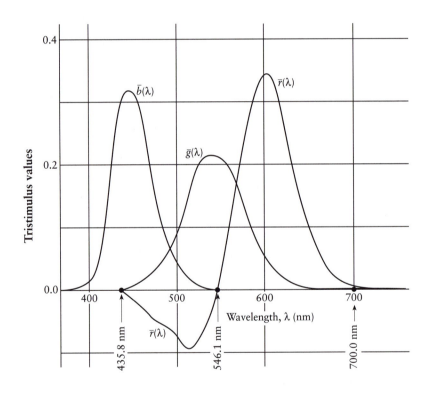

FIGURE 1.39

The r, g, and b color-matching curves. Redrawn from Wyszecki and Stiles, *Color Science*, fig. 4, p. 124.

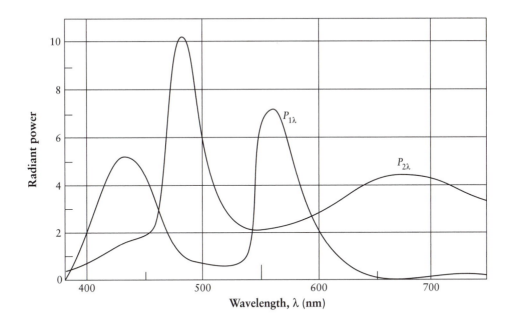

FIGURE 1.40

Two different spectra that appear the same. Redrawn from Wyszecki and Stiles, *Color Science*, fig. 6, p. 126.

average the results and attribute them to a hypothetical standard observer. This has been a very simplified account of color matching; more details are available in many reference texts, such as Wyszecki and Stiles [489].

One surprising result of the color matching experiments is that very different spectra can evoke the same perceived color. Figure 1.40 shows two spectra, each of which cause observers to report the same perceived color. Different spectra that give rise to the same perceived color under some set of conditions are called *metamers*. In fact, any perceived color may be matched by an infinite number of different metamers. This has important implications for image synthesis: if we wish to represent the arbitrary color of one or more objects in a synthetic scene with a spectral energy distribution, we may choose from the infinite possibilities any metamer we like. Often this will be the one most convenient for storage and computation.

Because of the practical difficulties in working with control values that are sometimes negative, the CIE defined three new hypothetical light sources, with spectra

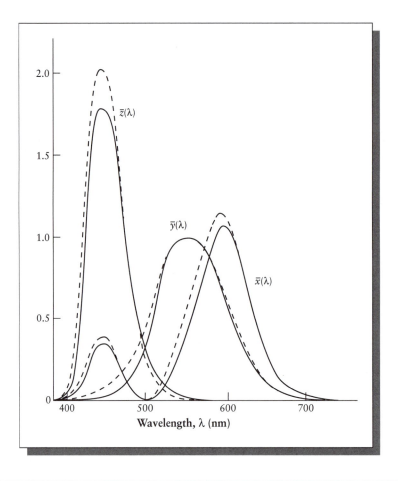

FIGURE 1.41

The $\overline{x}(\lambda)$, $\overline{y}(\lambda)$, and $\overline{z}(\lambda)$ color-matching functions for the 2° standard observer (solid curve) and the 10° standard observer (dashed curve).

designated $\overline{x}(\lambda)$, $\overline{y}(\lambda)$, and $\overline{z}(\lambda)$. The matching curves for these functions across the spectrum are shown in Figure 1.41; note that all values are always positive.

To predict how much of each source would be needed to match an arbitrary input color $C(\lambda)$, you add together the necessary amount of each component at each wavelength. Mathematically, this is simply the integral of the input and the source. In other words, to "match" the color $C(\lambda)$, we find how much of each of the three standard sources we need to add together to create a color perceptually equivalent to $C(\lambda)$. Thus to match $C(\lambda)$ using

$$C(\lambda) = X\,\overline{x}(\lambda) + Y\,\overline{y}(\lambda) + Z\,\overline{z}(\lambda) \tag{1.1}$$

we find the weights X, Y, and Z from

$$X = \int_{\lambda \in \mathcal{R}_v} C(\lambda)\,\overline{x}(\lambda)\,d\lambda$$

$$Y = \int_{\lambda \in \mathcal{R}_v} C(\lambda)\,\overline{y}(\lambda)\,d\lambda$$

$$Z = \int_{\lambda \in \mathcal{R}_v} C(\lambda)\,\overline{z}(\lambda)\,d\lambda \tag{1.2}$$

(recall that $\int_{\lambda \in \mathcal{R}_v}$ stands for $\int_{\lambda=380}^{780}$ when the visual band is taken to be 380 to 780 nm).

In effect, this standard defines a 3D linear space of colors, with respect to a particular coordinate system called CIE *XYZ* space. This 3D color space is awkward to work with directly. It is common to project the space onto the plane $X+Y+Z=1$. This results in a 2D space known as a *chromaticity diagram*. Figure 1.42 shows this plane including the 3D *XYZ* locus for visible colors, demonstrating the projection of the solid onto the *XY* plane. The coordinates in this projected 2D plane are usually called x and y, derived from the 3D values by the relations

$$x = \frac{X}{X+Y+Z}$$

$$y = \frac{Y}{X+Y+Z}$$

$$z = \frac{Z}{X+Y+Z} = 1 - x - y \tag{1.3}$$

The plane of Figure 1.42 is shown in Figure 1.43. The curve in Figure 1.42 is based on using targets that subtend a 2° angle from the observer; this is often called the xy triangle for the 2° standard observer. Since the three $\overline{x}(\lambda)$, $\overline{y}(\lambda)$, and $\overline{z}(\lambda)$ matching functions are all positive, all colors lie within the convex shape created by the horseshoe curve forming the top two legs of the "triangle." We may then simply draw a line connecting the two ends of the horseshoe, and thereby define a closed convex shape which contains all colors. The dashed triangle in the figure shows the subset of colors that may be displayed on a typical CRT monitor.

The standard observer is a useful myth. In practice, each person has a slightly different response to color, influenced by many environmental and psychological factors.

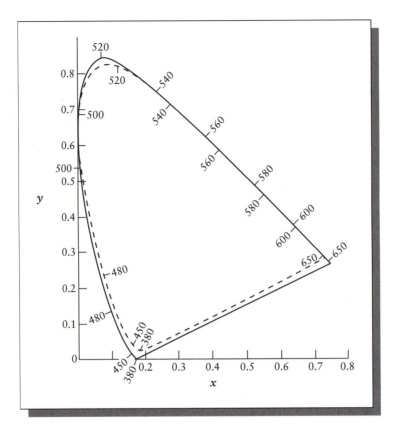

FIGURE 1.42

A chromaticity diagram. Redrawn from Silverstein, *Color and the Computer*, fig. 2-4, p. 33.

Perception may also be altered deliberately. During World War II, the United States Navy wanted to use infrared signal lights to send signals that would be invisible to everyone but the intended recipient. Unfortunately, United States seamen were as blind to infrared as everyone else, so the signals were useless [389]. To overcome this, Navy scientists observed that all retinal photopigments include vitamin A. They hypothesized that by feeding the sailors a diet containing a chemical form of vitamin A different from that in a normal diet, they might be able to influence the character of the photoreceptive cells. For several months volunteers were fed a diet low in the usual form of vitamin A but rich in an alternative chemical form. The experiment appeared to be working, but an electronic device capable of sensing infrared was

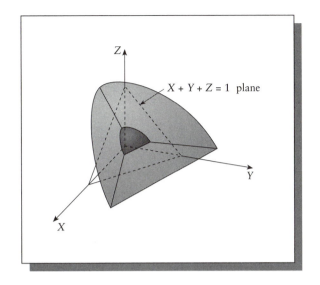

FIGURE 1.43
The spectral locus.

developed at about the same time, and the Navy cancelled the dietary experiment. Nevertheless, the results show that a change in diet can influence the perception of color.

1.8 Illusions

Optical illusions have contributed a lot to our understanding of the visual system. They serve to isolate and demonstrate effects and phenomena that we usually either take for granted or are unaware of. The classic compendium of visual illusions is Luckiesh [277]. More recent catalogs of illusions may be found in the references in the Further Reading section.

We present a few illusions here to illustrate that there can be a large disparity between the mechanistic description of an image and its perception. It can be easy to forget this when working in computer graphics; there is a temptation to believe that if one performs an accurate physical simulation of light physics, with appropriately stable numerical methods and signal processing, then the final result is an "accurate" image. The definition of accurate in this case does not include the

FIGURE 1.44
Subjective contours.

observer, since people often "see" objects, contours, and relationships in images that are not explicitly part of the image.

For example, consider Figure 1.44. In these images most observers perceive a triangle whose corners are suggested by the cutaway black dots. The visual system fills in the rest of the contours of the triangle, even if the edges are not straight; these are called *subjective contours*.

Many famous illusions place equal-size objects in different contexts, with the result that they appear unequal. The Müller-Lyer illusion in Figure 1.45 shows two horizontal lines of equal length, one bracketed by inward-pointing arrows, the other by outward-pointing arrows. The line enclosed by inward-pointing arrows usually appears longer. One explanation of this effect is that the arrows appear to suggest two intersecting planes. The inward-pointing arrows suggest an angle that is concave from our point of view; for example, we are looking into the junction between a wall and a ceiling from inside a room. The outward-pointing arrows suggest a convex

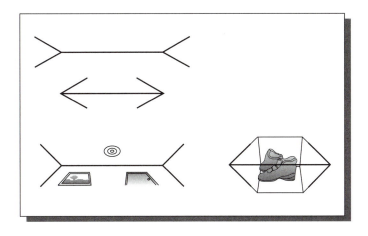

FIGURE 1.45

FIGURE 1.45

The Müller-Lyon illusion. Both horizontal lines are the same size.

angle; the outside of a box, for instance. Observers perhaps assume that the concave intersection is farther away than the convex one, since it appears to be receding. Since both horizontal segments have the same length, we "know" from perspective that the farther-away line must therefore be larger [389]. This argument is not certain, but it suggests the type of high- and low-level phenomena that probably combine to create some illusions.

A similar illusion is shown in Figure 1.46; the two inner circles are the same size, though they usually don't appear that way. The explanation for this illusion is even more tenuous.

Humans tend not to be particularly good at estimating absolute quantities, particularly the magnitudes of angles. In general, small angles tend to be overestimated and large angles underestimated [358]. Professional magicians know that these errors in judgement can be enhanced by additional visual cues; thus, a magician's assistant may "disappear" from a clear tank that is sitting on a base that is "obviously" too small for the assistant to have curled up into. Our perception of the size of the base is misguided by color and shape cues that are carefully designed to force us to underestimate its true size and shape.

Other classic illusions include "impossible figures," where we are presented with a planar projection of a 3D shape that is locally logical but globally inconsistent. Famous examples include Penrose's impossible tribar and endless staircase, in Figure 1.47.

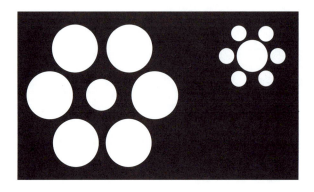

FIGURE 1.46

The two inner circles are the same size.

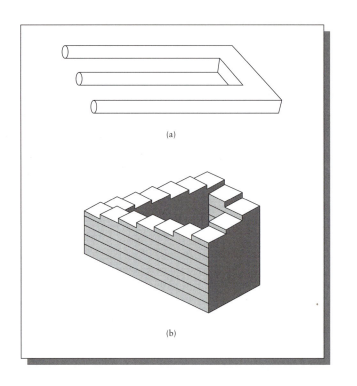

FIGURE 1.47

Two illusions found by Roger Penrose. (a) The impossible tribar. (b) The endlessly ascending (or descending) staircase.

1.9 Further Reading

Much more on the human visual system may be found in standard textbooks and advanced research works. In particular, Sekuler's textbook [389] is a good source for a general introduction, and Wandell's textbook [463] provides more detail and some basic mathematical structure. There is a lot of classic wisdom in Leonardo da Vinci's notebooks; an excellent low-cost, unabridged, and illustrated two-volume translation is available from Dover [113]. Further information on the anatomy of the visual system may be found in volumes 2 and 4 of Davson [117, 118]. An excellent brief survey of the visual system may be found in the IES lighting handbook [355]. Resnikoff presents a look at perception from an information-theory point of view [358]. Some numerical information on the various parts of the physical system are given by Wyszecki and Stiles [489].

A discussion of impossible-figure illusions and a great variety of examples may be found in Ernst [137]. Discussions of illusions in general appear in Luckiesh [277], as well as Lanners [257], Gregory [171], and Sekuler [389]; the latter two contain modern descriptions of the theories that have been put forth to explain some illusions. Gregory in particular presents a very interesting discussion on the relation between perception and awareness.

A description of the many processes involved in spatial vision may be found in DeValois and DeValois [123]. The visual systems of other animals are surveyed in detail in a lavishly illustrated volume by Sinclair [412]. A general discussion of the visual system and some philosophy about its relation to our development may be found in Gregory [171].

The dependence of the visual system on the direction of a grating was originally reported by Taylor [433]. The classic paper on the implications of photoreceptor packing patterns on the retina is Yellot's paper of 1983 [496] on the monkey retina. The work of Williams and Collier on the human retina [479] suggests that there may be similarities between the monkey and human retina. The particular types of noise that the human visual system is willing to tolerate were studied and characterized by Huang [218].

1.10 Exercises

Exercise 1.1

Fire trucks used to be painted red. Now many new fire trucks are yellow-green. Why?

Exercise 1.2

If you open your eyes underwater, it is difficult to see well, even if you have normal

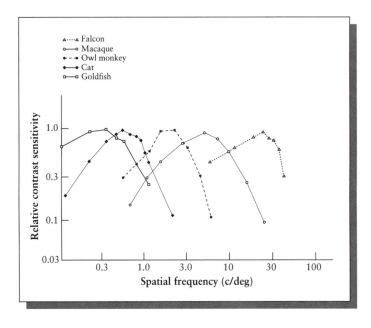

FIGURE 1.48

CSFs for different species. Redrawn from DeValois and DeValois, *Spatial Vision*, fig. 5.2, p. 150.

vision. But if you put on a face mask before diving, your vision is about as good as it is out of water. Why?

Exercise 1.3

Consider the variety of contrast sensitivity functions shown in Figure 1.48. Suppose you were part of a psychology team preparing images to be shown to falcons. What are the implications for your rendering system? Considering the CSF as the only change between falcons and humans, could you produce images more quickly, or would it take more time? How about for a goldfish?

Exercise 1.4

One common method for printing 3D figures is to print two different pictures on top of each other, one each in red and green inks. Then a pair of glasses is supplied, with a red transparent filter over one eye and a green filter over the other. Thus the eye covered with the red filter perceives only the green part of the drawing, and the other eye perceives the red. If the two figures are drawn as though seen from the two eyes, a properly adapted viewer will see a 3D figure. Why do you think red and

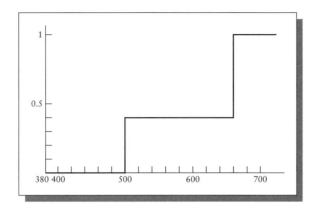

FIGURE 1.49

An absorption curve that's 0 in blue, about 1/3 in green, about 1 in red.

green are the most common choice of colors for the inks? Why are the same colors used for the filters? Would other colors work as well, or better?

Exercise 1.5

What evolutionary factors do you think may have been involved that led to the eye focusing at infinity when at rest ?

Exercise 1.6

Design some images where different depth cues are inconsistent. Determine a relative ranking for the importance of different cues to the human visual system.

Exercise 1.7

Colored glasses are popular both in mythology and in practice.

(a) Would image synthesis be easier or faster if everyone wore rose-colored glasses?

(b) Some firms sell sunglasses (sometimes called "blue-blockers") that block ultraviolet and even some visible-blue light. Would you expect these glasses to actually improve any aspect of your vision in any specific and measurable ways? Explain.

Exercise 1.8

Suppose you had a sheet of plastic with the response curve given in Figure 1.49. How would the daytime world look through a sheet of this material? How about through two sheets? Three?

If the resolution of our vision were as poor as the resolution of our olfaction, when a bird flew overhead the sky would go all birdish for us for a while.

Daniel C. Dennett
("Consciousness Explained," 1991)

2

COLOR SPACES

2.1 Perceptually Uniform Color Spaces: $L^*u^*v^*$ and $L^*a^*b^*$

The XYZ color space is not a very intuitive space. It is difficult to interpret the meanings of the values for X and Z, though Y was designed to represent the brightness of a color. In addition to an intuitive interpretation of the axes, an "ideal" color space would be perceptually linear: the distance between any two points measures how "alike" they look. Such a space can make some computations easier.

For example, consider interpolation. If we wish to interpolate from color A to color B, we might write $C = (1 - \alpha)A + \alpha B$ and sweep α from 0 to 1. This is the typical way that Gouraud and Phong shading are implemented. We would probably like equal increments of α to result in steps of C that were of perceptually equal sizes. Unfortunately, this does not happen in XYZ space: equal steps along the path from A to B do not produce perceptually equal steps in the color of C. Figure 2.1 shows this phenomenon. It shows the results of a color-matching experiment. Conceptually, two colors of equal luminance were shown to observers and then one was changed. The observer was asked to report when the change was visible. Each ellipse is a region of constant color (the ellipses are magnified for visibility). The important observation here is that the ellipses are not the same size or in the same orientation.

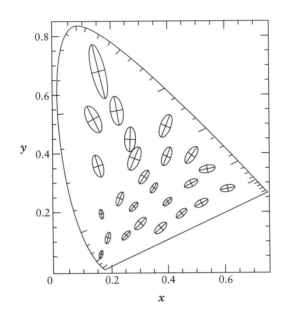

FIGURE   2.1

The MacAdam ellipses. Redrawn from Pratt, *Digital Image Processing*, fig. 3.7-2(a), p. 86.

Thus, a particular magnitude of shift in color space at one point may be undetectable, but the same shift applied to a different color would be quite visible.

To overcome this problem the CIE defined two new, alternative color spaces, called $L^*u^*v^*$ and $L^*a^*b^*$. Both of these spaces, based on the XYZ space, were designed to be perceptually uniform. Figure 2.2 shows the result of the ellipses in the u^*v^* plane. Note that they are much more uniform than in Figure 2.1, though they are still not perfect.

Another nonlinear transformation has been proposed [139] to make the color space even more uniform; the MacAdam ellipses in this space are shown in Figure 2.3. Though the uniformity is much better, the computation is much more complex than for the $L^*u^*v^*$ or $L^*a^*b^*$ systems, as discussed in Pratt [345].

Each space is defined with respect to a *reference white* color (X_n, Y_n, Z_n). Usually the reference white is one of the CIE standard illuminants, scaled so the Y_n value is 100. Both spaces use the same definition of L^*:

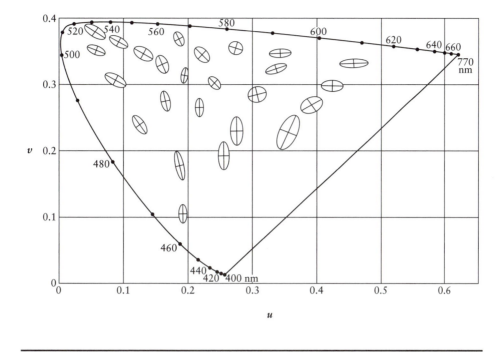

FIGURE 2.2

MacAdam's ellipses in a perceptually linear space. Redrawn from Pratt, *Digital Image Processing*, fig. 3.7-2(b), p. 86.

$$L^* = \begin{cases} Y/Y_n \geq .008856 & 116\left(\dfrac{Y}{Y_n}\right)^{1/3} - 16 \\ Y/Y_n \leq .008856 & 903.3\left(\dfrac{Y}{Y_n}\right) \end{cases} \tag{2.1}$$

Note that $L^* = 100$ for the reference white, when $Y = Y_n$. In fact, L^* may be considered to measure the "lightness" of the color. The conversion between XYZ and $L^*u^*v^*$ is given by Wyszecki and Stiles [489]:

$$u^* = 13L^*(u' - u'_n)$$
$$v^* = 13L^*(v' - v'_n) \tag{2.2}$$

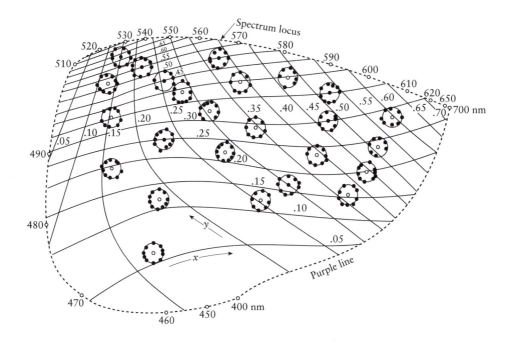

FIGURE 2.3

MacAdam's ellipses in Farnsworth's nonlinear transformation. Redrawn from Pratt, *Digital Image Processing*, fig. 3.7-3, p. 87.

The variables in Equation 2.2 are given by

$$u' = \frac{4X}{X + 15Y + 3Z}$$
$$v' = \frac{9Y}{X + 15Y + 3Z}$$
$$u'_n = \frac{4X_n}{X_n + 15Y_n + 3Z_n}$$
$$v'_n = \frac{9Y_n}{X_n + 15Y_n + 3Z_n} \tag{2.3}$$

A plot of the spectral colors in $L^*u^*v^*$ space is shown in Figure 2.4. The solid in the center is the region occupied by the colors reflected by objects that are illuminated

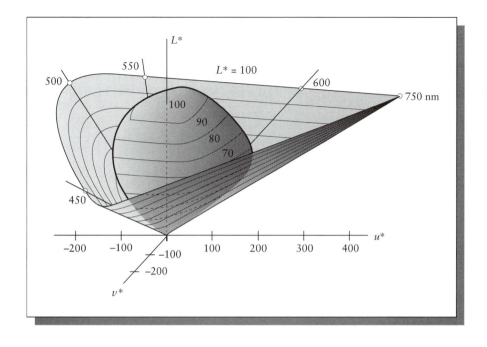

FIGURE 2.4

Sketch of the $L^*u^*v^*$ color space. Redrawn from Wyszecki and Stiles, *Color Science*, fig. 1(3.3.9), p. 166.

by the CIE standard illuminant D_{65}; it is the region within which the distance formula in Equation 2.10 is intended to be valid [489].

The $L^*a^*b^*$ space is another perceptually based color system that is sometimes used instead of $L^*u^*v^*$. The $L^*a^*b^*$ space is based on ANLAB(40), a color system in wide use in the textile industry. The value for L^* is the same as in Equation 2.1. The other variables are given by

$$a^* = 500L^* \left[f\left(\frac{X}{X_n}\right) - f\left(\frac{Y}{Y_n}\right) \right]$$
$$b^* = 200L^* \left[f\left(\frac{Y}{Y_n}\right) - f\left(\frac{Z}{Z_n}\right) \right] \tag{2.4}$$

A plot of the spectral colors in $L^*a^*b^*$ space is shown in Figure 2.5. As in the $L^*u^*v^*$ picture, the solid in the center is the region occupied by the colors reflected by objects that are illuminated by the CIE standard illuminant D_{65}; it is the region

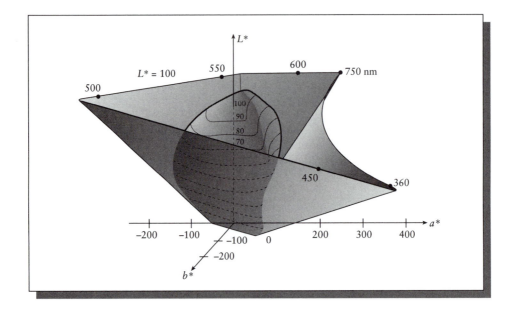

FIGURE   2.5

Sketch of the $L^*a^*b^*$ color space. Redrawn from Wyszecki and Stiles, *Color Science*, fig. 2(3.3.9), p. 167.

within which the distance formula in Equation 2.10 is intended to be valid [489]. Note that the spectral color curve has a kink at around 570 nm.

Each of the ratios given above is passed through a function f before it is used. The function usually takes the cube root of its input. For numerical precision and stability, values below a certain threshold are approximated linearly:

$$f(r) = \begin{cases} r \geq .008856 & r^{1/3} \\ r < .008856 & 7.787r + 16/116 \end{cases} \tag{2.5}$$

Just as L^* corresponds to lightness (or the value transmitted along the achromatic channel in the visual system), the a^* axis corresponds to the red-green channel and the b^* axis to the blue-yellow channel.

To recover the XYZ coordinates of a color from either $L^*u^*v^*$ or $L^*a^*b^*$ requires an inversion of the mapping process. The inverse relation for Y is the same in both spaces:

$$Y = \frac{Y_n}{100} \left(\frac{L^* + 16}{116} \right)^3 \tag{2.6}$$

To recover X and Z from u^* and v^*, we first define a few temporary variables Q, R, and A to help decouple the relations:

$$Q = \frac{u^*}{13L^*} + u'_n \qquad R = \frac{v^*}{13L^*} + v'_n \qquad A = 3Y(5R - 3) \tag{2.7}$$

With these definitions, we find

$$Z = \frac{(Q - 4)A - 15QRY}{12R} \qquad X = -\left(\frac{A}{R} + 3Z\right) \tag{2.8}$$

Note that if $L^* = 0$, then X and Z are undefined. It is traditional in such cases to set $X = Z = 0$.

Recovery of X and Z from a^* and b^* is rather more direct:

$$X = X_n \left[\left(\frac{Y}{Y_n}\right)^{1/3} + \frac{a^*}{500}\right]^3$$

$$Z = Z_n \left[\left(\frac{Y}{Y_n}\right)^{1/3} + \frac{b^*}{200}\right]^3 \tag{2.9}$$

Neither of these two color spaces is perceptually completely uniform, though they are close. Work continues on developing more uniform spaces. The choice of which of these two spaces to use probably doesn't matter as much as making sure one of them is used consistently.

By design, the Euclidean distance between any two colors A and B in either perceptual color space may be computed from the magnitude of the vector between the colors:

$$E^*_{uv} = \sqrt{(L^*_A - L^*_B)^2 + (u^*_A - u^*_B)^2 + (v^*_A - v^*_B)^2}$$

$$E^*_{ab} = \sqrt{(L^*_A - L^*_B)^2 + (a^*_A - a^*_B)^2 + (b^*_A - b^*_B)^2} \tag{2.10}$$

One particularly important feature of these spaces is that two pairs of colors with the same distance metric are almost perceptually equally similar or different.

These spaces do admit an intuitive interpretation. Think of either space as a cylindrical coordinate system, with L^* acting as the main axis of the cylinder, and the other coordinates representing a point in the plane perpendicular to this axis. The L^* axis represents the "lightness" of a color. Given a value of L^*, the plane through the color point perpendicular to the L^* axis defines a 2D system based on (u^*, v^*) or (a^*, b^*). Intuitively, the angle around this plane represents the hue of the color, and the distance from the L^* axis represents the saturation. More formally, h, the CIE 1976 *hue-angle*, is given by Hunt [219]:

$$\begin{aligned} h_{uv} &= \tan^{-1}(v^*/u^*) \\ h_{ab} &= \tan^{-1}(b^*/a^*) \end{aligned} \tag{2.11}$$

and C^*, the CIE 1976 *chroma*, is given by

$$C^*_{uv} = \sqrt{(u^*)^2 + (v^*)^2}$$
$$C^*_{ab} = \sqrt{(a^*)^2 + (b^*)^2}$$

$$(2.12)$$

Much of the color computation in computer graphics has historically been done in *RGB* space (discussed in more detail in the next chapter). For example, Gouraud shading blends the color at the vertices across the face of a polygon. Typically this blending is carried out by linearly interpolating the *RGB* coefficients of the colors separately. Although this technique was chosen for convenience and speed rather than theoretical accuracy, it usually seems to work acceptably well. This may be somewhat surprising when we recall two of the problems that the perceptually uniform spaces were designed to cure: equal steps in *RGB* space are not perceptually equal color steps, and we might pass through colors on the way from one point to another that intuitively don't seem to be "in between" the two endpoints.

Figure 2.6 (color plate) shows the equal-step linear interpolation of two colors in *RGB* space and the corresponding colors in *XYZ* and *L*u*v** space. We show these points plotted in both *RGB* and *L*u*v** spaces in Figure 2.7.

2.2 Other Color Systems

Many applications of computer graphics require the use of accurate color representations of natural objects. A blade of grass, a piece of obsidian, and a tin can all have specific reflectivities that may be carefully measured. The best way to describe these colors is probably with some form of spectral radiant power distribution (i.e., a complete spectrum). Each material is described by much more than simply a single color; we will consider more complete material descriptions in Chapter 15.

There are also times when it is useful to create a new color: for example, when creating textures to apply to surfaces or images that depart from reality. It is useful to have access to convenient color representations for color design in such situations.

As mentioned above, the *XYZ* system, though a useful reference, is not an intuitive space in which to design colors.

The *RGB* (red-green-blue) color cube, shown in Figure 2.8(a), is not much better than the *XYZ* space for color calculations. It is difficult to find any particular color, and once located, it is difficult to adjust that color. Classic examples of both of these problems are to ask a user to find brown, and then once found, make a lighter shade of brown.

The *L*u*v** and *L*a*b** spaces have an intuitive interpretation as a roughly cylindrical color space. In effect, the *L** axis controls the lightness of the color. Each cross section is a polar coordinate system with the angle controlling hue and radius controlling saturation. A user may be given control over each of the three values.

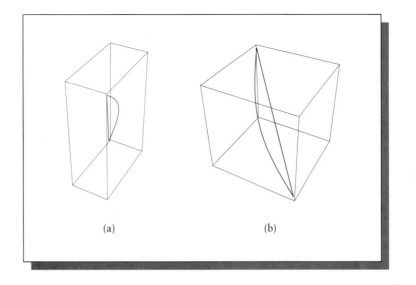

FIGURE 2.7

The interpolation of two colors in equal steps in *RGB* and $L^*u^*v^*$ color spaces. (a) In *RGB* space. (b) In $L^*u^*v^*$ space.

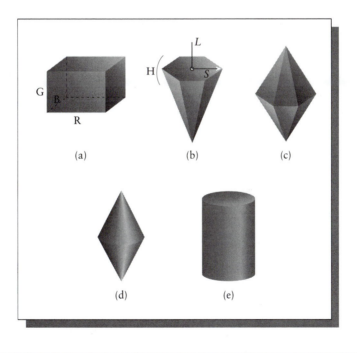

FIGURE 2.8

Several different color spaces. Redrawn from Hall, *Illumination and Color in Computer Generated Imagery*, fig. 3.1, p. 46.

Formulas for converting between these spaces and XYZ are given above. Interactive navigation through one of these spaces is not easy.

The next four color spaces are very similar to each other and the perceptually uniform spaces just mentioned. Each has a lightness axis and represents saturation by distance from that axis and hue by angle around the axis. Each is defined with respect to the particular monitor's RGB. Thus, when communicating a color designed with one of the following systems, you must specify the monitor's phosphor chromaticities in order to interpret the coefficients. It is probably better to convert the RGB values to XYZ, since that provides a universal, device-independent representation.

The HSV (hue, saturation, value) hexcone is shown in Figure 2.8(b). The central axis carries the gray values from black at the bottom to white at the top. The conversion between RGB and HSV is a short procedure [147, 181].

The HSL (hue, saturation, lightness) double hexcone is shown in Figure 2.8(c). Its difference from the HSV hexcone is that the level of maximum available saturation is at $L = 0.5$ rather than $L = 1.0$. The HSL double cone in Figure 2.8(d) is similar to the HSL double hexcone, except that the cross section is circular rather than hexagonal. The HSL cylinder in Figure 2.8(e) is like the HSL double cone, except that the complete radius is available at all points along the L axis.

2.3   Further Reading

More information on color descriptions may be found in the standard text on color systems written by Wyszecki and Stiles [489]. An extensive table for converting among different color standards used in image processing and broadcast is presented in Pratt's book on image processing [345]. Hall [181] has much to say about color systems and their effective use, and provides source code for converting between color systems. Foley et al. [147] summarizes some of these and presents algorithms for converting between color spaces.

2.4   Exercises

Exercise 2.1

Build a color picking system using the $L^*a^*b^*$ or $L^*u^*v^*$ color space. How easy it is to use? Compare it to an RGB system.

Exercise 2.2

Mixing light is an additive color system (red + green + blue = white), rather than a subtractive system. Why do you think this is so?

Exercise 2.3

(a) Interpolate the color $C_1 = (.2, .3, .3)$ to $C_2 = (.8, .9, .7)$ in RGB space in ten equal steps. Convert the RGB value at each step to $L^*a^*b^*$, and find the distance between each successive pair of points in $L^*a^*b^*$ space.

(b) Convert C_1 and C_2 to $L^*a^*b^*$, and interpolate them in ten equal steps in that space. Convert each interpolated $L^*a^*b^*$ value to RGB, and find the distance between each successive pair of points in RGB space.

(c) Discuss your results. Suggest two situations where RGB interpolation is appropriate, and two where it is not.

Exercise 2.4

Many of the intuitive color systems in this chapter use a cylindrical or conical coordinate system. Design an intuitive model based on a spherical system. What does it mean to interpolate colors in your system? Can you come up with a good distance metric? Do you think a color system built on a toroidal coordinate system would be a good idea? Why or why not? Do any other geometries suggest themselves to you for color selection?

*The portrait had altered. ... That such a
change should have taken place was incredible
to him. And yet it was a fact. Was there some
subtle affinity between the chemical atoms, that
shaped themselves into form and colour on the
canvas, and the soul that was within him?
Could it be that what that soul thought, they
realized?—that what it dreamed, they made
true?*

Oscar Wilde
("The Picture of Dorian Gray," 1891)

3

DISPLAYS

3.1 Introduction

The principal display devices in use today are *light-emitting* and *light-propagating*.
The distinction resides in where the light comes from: either the display itself or elsewhere. Light-emitting displays include CRT and LED displays. Light-propagating
displays include print media, transparencies (including slides), and LCD panels.
Each type of display has many variations, and new alternatives are being developed
rapidly. In this section we will focus our attention on the CRT because it is one of
the most common devices used for creating images.

Each type of device also has many variations in the geometry of its component
color elements. For our CRT discussion we will emphasize the triangular lattice of
phosphors, though alternatives abound [298].

3.2 CRT Displays

A typical color CRT (*cathode-ray tube*) is shown in schematic form in Figure 3.1. At
the neck of the tube are three *electron guns*, each of which emits a narrow stream of

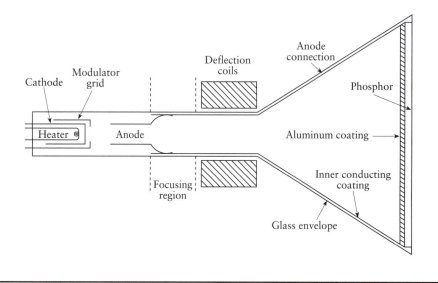

FIGURE 3.1

A schematic view of a CRT.

electrons. Each stream passes through a pair of deflection coils that exert an electrical force on the electrons and bend the beam from side to side and up and down.

The inside of the front face of the tube is coated with a pattern of blobs of three different types of chemicals known as *phosphors*. A phosphor is a chemical material that radiates light of a characteristic color when struck by electrons. Up to a material-determined limit, striking a phosphor with more electrons causes it to glow brighter. Many different types of phosphors that emit different colors have been discovered. Most CRTs use red, green, and blue phosphors, which can form a basis for a useful region of color space. We will have much more to say about phosphors in Chapter 14.

The arrangement of the phosphors on the inside of the tube varies, but one common setup is to place one small dot of each phosphor on the vertex of an equilateral triangle, as shown in Figure 3.2 [298]. Phosphors are usually described not just by color but also by *persistence*: how long they continue to glow after absorbing a burst of electrons. A *long-persistence* phosphor will glow for a longer period of time than a *short-persistence* phosphor. If you have seen television tubes that appear to leave a "streak" behind fast-moving objects, this is probably due to overly long phosphor persistence.

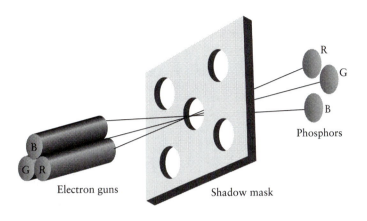

FIGURE 3.2

The arrangement of electron guns and phosphors.

Typically, each of the three guns is dedicated to creating an electron beam that only strikes phosphors of a single color. So although each gun is simply an electron emitter, they are often called the red, green, and blue guns, identifying the color of phosphor that the electron beam eventually strikes. Since the three beams are deflected in unison, they are sometimes referred to as "the beam," the three components being distinguished only when necessary.

To ensure that each beam strikes the correct phosphor in each triplet, a *shadow mask* is usually placed just behind the phosphors. The mask is an opaque screen that has holes only where the beam needs to pass through to reach a phosphor. The mask and the geometry of the beam angle serve to limit the beam to the intended phosphor.

To create an image, the beam is deflected in unison to sweep the entire face of the tube. Starting at the upper left (viewed from outside of the front face), the beam is moved across the screen to the upper right. As the beam moves into position to strike a particular triplet, the video signal coming into the monitor input specifies the color to be displayed at that point as a linear combination of red, green, and blue intensities, matching the phosphors on the screen. The intensity of the electron beam at each gun is modulated to match the specified intensity, which in turn causes each of the three phosphors struck by the beam to glow with the specified intensity. Then the beam is moved to the next triplet, the correct color intensities are fed to the guns from the video signal, and the process repeats.

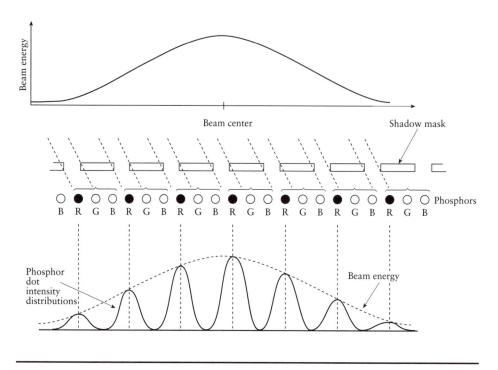

FIGURE 3.3

Beam spread illuminates several phosphors.

Although in this discussion we spoke of "the triplet" to which a beam is aimed, in fact the beam is typically much wider than a single phosphor triplet. The beam itself has a profile as shown in Figure 3.3, so the phosphors near the beam center will glow most brightly and those to the sides less so [298]. The granularity of the dot spacing on the shadow mask (called the *pitch* of the mask) is typically in the range of 0.2 to 0.6 mm. The shadow-mask pitch is usually not the limiting factor on CRT resolution; this is usually due to the electron optics or the bandwidth of the video signal.

Many factors can cause the beam to stray from perfect alignment with the phosphors. These include assembly variations, stray magnetic fields from the environment, or the effect of heat inside the tube causing various parts to expand. To reduce the required precision, some CRTs are designed so that the phosphor dot is larger than the expected projection of the electron beam, as in Figure 3.4(a). The beam thus has some tolerance for both horizontal and vertical movement, and the energy will

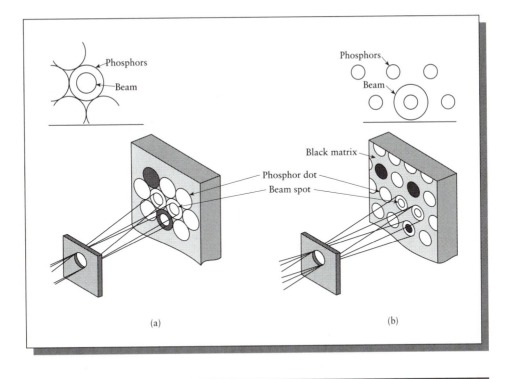

FIGURE 3.4

The idea of the guard band. (a) Conventional CRT. (b) Black matrix CRT. Redrawn from Merrifield in *Color and the Computer*, fig. 3-11, p. 72.

land on the desired phosphor. If the beam moves too far, then a nearby phosphor of another color will be illuminated, reducing the precision of displayed edges.

In some environments, there may be enough ambient light in the room where the CRT is viewed that the image on the screen will appear faded and the colors less pure. Solutions to this problem generally involve somehow increasing the perceived contrast. This may be accomplished with directional viewing screens, or *angle-restrictive filters*, which can take the form of a thin or thick honeycomb placed over the front of the CRT. This blocks ambient light from the side from reflecting off the face of the CRT, but it also propagates that ambient light that impinges on the screen. Another solution is to reduce the size of each phosphor and place it on some light-absorbing material such as carbon black, as in Figure 3.4(b); typically, the mask aperture is enlarged slightly at the same time. The beam now surrounds the phosphor and again there is some margin for misplacement. Everywhere on the face of the tube where there is no phosphor, the background material will absorb the ambient illumination. The amount of light each phosphor can put out is reduced because of its smaller size, but the gain in contrast is sometimes worth the trade-off [298].

Other contrast enhancement relies on the optical properties of various materials. For example, phosphors may be impregnated with pigments that absorb light near the phosphor's emission range and absorb all other light, effectively absorbing the ambient illumination. This of course reduces the light emitted of the phosphor, since some of its energy is being absorbed inside its own material, but the relative proportions of the materials may be adjusted over a wide range to achieve a desired contrast [267]. Another approach to increasing contrast involves a *neutral-density filter*. This is a filter placed over the front of the CRT that uniformly reduces the energy of all wavelengths of light passing through it. The reason this improves contrast is because the intensity of the ambient light is usually much lower than the intensity of the emitted light from the CRT, so reducing them both eliminates the ambient light while still leaving a fraction of emitted light. The environment, filter choice, and intended use of the display determine what fraction of attenuation is called for. Finally, a *selective filter* may be placed over the screen. Figure 3.5 shows the spectrum for didymium glass, along with the emission bands for some generic red, green, and blue phosphors. Dymidium glass passes these wavelengths better than others, so it works to attenuate some background radiation.

In general, monochromatic CRTs are capable of sharper focus, thinner lines, and brighter output than color CRTs. This is because the shadow mask blocks most of the beam energy in a multispectral tube, so that its achievable luminance is about 10 to 20% of that achievable from a high-output monochromatic CRT [298].

3.3   Display Spot Interaction

There are many types of phosphor geometries used for CRTs. We will use as an example a triangular lattice of clusters, where each cluster contains one phosphor each of red, green, and blue, as in Figure 3.6.

3.3.1   Display Spot Profile

We further assume that each piece of phosphor may be modeled as a point-source of light, with a circularly symmetrical emission p that assumes a Gaussian form. That is, the intensity p at each point (x, y) on the screen (when the illumination is at the origin $(0, 0)$) is given by

$$p(x, y) = e^{-(x^2+y^2)} = e^{-r^2} \tag{3.1}$$

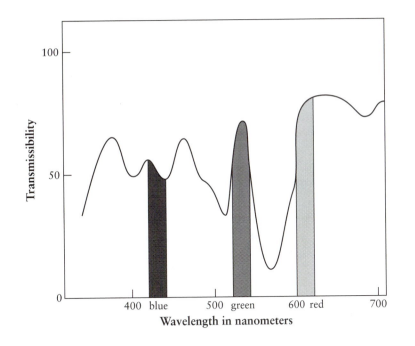

FIGURE 3.5

The spectrum of didymium glass. Redrawn from Merrifield in *Color and the Computer*, fig. 3-15, p. 75.

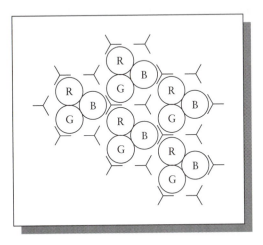

FIGURE 3.6

A triangular phosphor geometry.

It will be useful to define R as that radius where $p(R) = 0.5$. Then

$$p(r) = e^{-R^2} \tag{3.2}$$

or, solving for R,

$$R = \sqrt{-\ln(0.5)} \tag{3.3}$$

3.3.2 Two-Spot Interaction

We are interested in the sum of many display spots on the screen. Following the ideas in Castleman [77], we consider each spot p_i to have center C_i. Then for any point $P = (x, y)$, we may write the cumulative intensity $D(P)$ as

$$D(P) = \sum_i p_i(P - C_i) \tag{3.4}$$

Equation 3.4 requires finding the contribution of every dot on the screen. The Gaussian $p(r)$ decreases monotonically with r, so we expect that at some cutoff radius $r = r_c$, we can consider the contribution from a given spot to be negligible. For any threshold $\tau = p(r_c)$, we find $r_c = \sqrt{-\ln(\tau)}$. We will suppose that a contribution of 1% is small enough to be negligible. When the spot drops to an intensity of $\tau = 0.01$, we find $r \approx 2.15$. Thus if spots are closer together than about 2.15 times the radius of the Gaussian, they will sum with each other. We will consider spots farther away than 2.15 times the radius from any point to have a negligible contribution at that point. Call the interspot distance d. As d increases, two adjacent spots interact less.

Figure 3.7 shows the value of $D(d/2)$ for two fully on spots as d increases from 0 to $4R$; that is, we are looking at how much light comes from a point midway between the centers of the two spots as one moves away. We would like our field of white to have value 1.0 everywhere, so we watch the sum of the dot contributions at this particular point arbitrarily and find the distance where the two spots sum to 1; we get a value of $D(r) = 1$ at $d = 2R$.

This suggests that an interspot spacing of $d = 2R$ may be the most desirable, since we would like a flat field of fully on spots to have the value 1 everywhere. Figure 3.8 shows the amplitude of the field from one spot center to the next at this spacing. The total intensity at each point x measured from one center is given by $D(x) = p(x) + p(2R - x)$. At $x = 0$ and $x = 2R$, $D(0) = D(2R) = 1.0625$. The lowest value is at $x = R$, where $D(R) = 1$, as expected. So the response isn't quite flat, though the variation is only 6.25% of the amplitude we would prefer.

This analysis has only considered the interaction of two spots. We will get a better idea of how spots interact if we consider the entire local neighborhood for several different patterns. We will do this now.

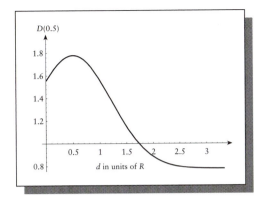

FIGURE 3.7

The field $D(0.5)$ halfway between two spots versus their distance d.

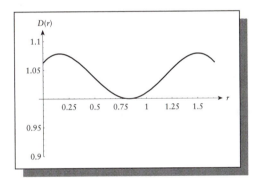

FIGURE 3.8

The field $D(r)$ between two spots for different r using $d = 2R$.

3.3.3 Display Measurement

In the next few sections, we will look at the *contrast*, C, of several different patterns. Contrast may be defined as

$$\text{contrast} \triangleq \frac{\max - \min}{\max + \min} \tag{3.5}$$

(other definitions include $\max/\min$ and $(\max - \min)/\min$).

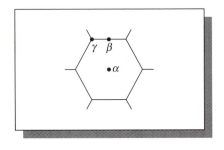

FIGURE 3.9

Positions for α, β, and γ points.

To determine the contrast for different spot patterns, we will examine the brightness of the field at three points: the center of a spot (which we call an α-type point), a point midway between two spots (a β-type point), and a point midway between three spots (a γ-type point), as in Figure 3.9.

To find the amplitude at each of these points, we need to find all the spots that contribute some light to that point. Recall our cutoff above of 2.15 radii; thus, we need only concern ourselves with spots that have centers within this radius of the point being evaluated.

The analysis is based on the geometry of the phosphor pattern. Figure 3.10 shows the geometry for an α-type point, positioned directly over a spot center. Working our way outward, we find that because of symmetry there are only four unique types of phosphor centers that contribute: the spot the test point is on (S), and those labeled A, B, and D in the figure. Since we have set our interspot spacing to $d = 2R$, the cutoff for contribution by a spot to this test point is $2.15d$. The circle in the figure is drawn at $r = 2.15d$. We also include one layer of centers outside the circle to confirm that we have included all the appropriate centers. Table 3.1 gives the distances.

Thus the brightness for spot α may be written by summing the Gaussian response from each spot (using Equation 3.3 evaluated at the correct distance). For each pattern, each contributing spot will have an associated weighting factor $w(S_i)$ of either 0 (if cell S_i is off), or 1 (if it's on). We can write the final intensity of α (that is, $D(\alpha)$) as

$$D(\alpha) = w(S) + \sum_{i=1}^{6} w(A_i)p(d_A) + \sum_{i=1}^{6} w(B_i)p(d_B) + \sum_{i=1}^{6} w(D_i)p(d_D)$$

$$= w(S) + \sum_{i=1}^{6} w(A_i)e^{-d} + \sum_{i=1}^{6} w(B_i)e^{-4d} + \sum_{i=1}^{6} w(D_i)e^{-3d} \qquad (3.6)$$

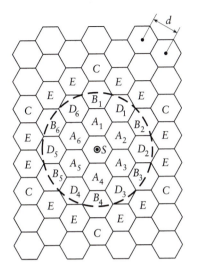

FIGURE 3.10

Geometry for centered spot.

Spot type	Distance (units of d)	Significant?
S	$d_S = 0$	$\checkmark$
A	$d_A = 1$	$\checkmark$
B	$d_B = 2$	$\checkmark$
C	$d_C = 3$	
D	$d_D = \sqrt{3} \approx 1.732$	$\checkmark$
E	$d_E = \sqrt{7} \approx 2.646$	

TABLE 3.1

Spot distances for α.

We can carry out the same analysis for the other two patterns. The distances for β and γ, shown in Figures 3.11 and 3.12, are given in Tables 3.2 and 3.3.

We use the same capital letters in all three patterns for convenience; because each analysis has a unique number of elements, there should be no confusion about which position is intended by which letter.

The corresponding equations for β and γ spots are given by

$$D(\beta) = \sum_{i=1}^{2} w(A_i)p(d_A) + \sum_{i=1}^{2} w(B_i)p(d_B) + \sum_{i=1}^{2} w(D_i)p(d_D)$$

$$+ \sum_{i=1}^{4} w(E_i)p(d_E) + \sum_{i=1}^{4} w(F_i)p(d_F)$$

$$= \sum_{i=1}^{2} w(A_i)e^{-d/4} + \sum_{i=1}^{2} w(B_i)e^{-9d/4} + \sum_{i=1}^{2} w(D_i)e^{-3d/4}$$

$$+ \sum_{i=1}^{4} w(E_i)e^{-7d/4} + \sum_{i=1}^{4} w(F_i)e^{-13d/4} \tag{3.7}$$

and

$$D(\gamma) = \sum_{i=1}^{3} w(A_i)p(d_A) + \sum_{i=1}^{6} w(B_i)p(d_B) + \sum_{i=1}^{3} w(C_i)p(d_C) + \sum_{i=1}^{6} w(F_i)p(d_F)$$

$$= \sum_{i=1}^{3} w(A_i)e^{-d/3} + \sum_{i=1}^{6} w(B_i)e^{-7d/3} + \sum_{i=1}^{3} w(C_i)e^{-4d/3} + \sum_{i=1}^{6} w(F_i)e^{-13d/3}$$

$$\tag{3.8}$$

3.3.4 Pattern Description

Each pattern of on-and-off phosphors may be described by a characteristic *cell*, or cluster, which is a small group of pixels that is simply translated across the screen to generate the pattern. Because we are interested in the contrast ratios for different patterns, we will only consider black (off) and white (fully on) pixels. Each pattern will be characterized by a value τ, defined as the ratio of the number of white to black pixels in the cell that describes that pattern:

$$\tau = \frac{\text{number of white pixels}}{\text{number of black pixels}} \tag{3.9}$$

We will consider values of τ from 0 to 1.

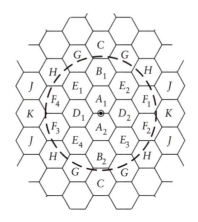

FIGURE 3.11

Geometry for β-type points.

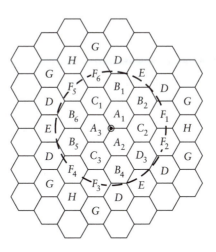

FIGURE 3.12

Geometry for γ-type points.

Spot type	Distance (units of d)	Significant?
A	$d_A = 1/2 = 0.5$	$\checkmark$
B	$d_B = 3/2 = 1.5$	$\checkmark$
C	$d_C = 5/2 = 2.5$	
D	$d_D = \sqrt{3}/2 \approx 0.866$	$\checkmark$
E	$d_E = \sqrt{7}/2 \approx 1.323$	$\checkmark$
F	$d_F = \sqrt{13}/2 \approx 1.803$	$\checkmark$
G	$d_G = \sqrt{19}/2 \approx 2.179$	
H	$d_H = \sqrt{21}/2 \approx 2.291$	
J	$d_J = \sqrt{31}/2 \approx 2.784$	
K	$d_K = 3\sqrt{3}/2 \approx 2.598$	

TABLE 3.2
Spot distances for β.

Spot type	Distance (units of d)	Significant?
A	$d_A = \sqrt{1/3} \approx 0.577$	$\checkmark$
B	$d_B = \sqrt{7/3} \approx 1.528$	$\checkmark$
C	$d_C = \sqrt{4/3} \approx 1.155$	$\checkmark$
D	$d_D = \sqrt{19/3} \approx 2.517$	
E	$d_E = \sqrt{16/3} \approx 2.309$	
F	$d_F = \sqrt{13/3} \approx 2.082$	$\checkmark$
G	$d_G = \sqrt{28/3} \approx 3.055$	
H	$d_H = \sqrt{25/3} \approx 2.877$	

TABLE 3.3
Spot distances for γ.

3.3.5 The Uniform Black Field ($\tau = 0$)

The uniform black field is shown in Figure 3.13(a). In this trivial pattern, every point (x, y) has the same intensity of 0: $D(\alpha) = D(\beta) = D(\gamma) = 0.0$. This is a perfect response for this pattern; all three of our samples accurately display the pattern intensity 0.0.

3.3.6 Clusters of Four ($\tau = .25$)

A fundamental cell of four pixels, with one white pixel, is shown in Figure 3.13(b); it has a density of $\tau = 1/4 = .25$. There are four cells in the pattern, so there are four different places to put an α-type test point. These four choices are shown in the left-hand column of Figure 3.14. Similarly, there are four places to put a β-type point (in the middle column) and four places for a γ-type point (right column). The weights for the various spots around each center are given in Table 3.4.

Using the weights in Table 3.4 and Equation 3.6, we can write the intensity for each center:

$$
\begin{aligned}
D(\alpha_0) &= 1 + 6e^{-4d} \\
D(\alpha_1) &= 2e^{-d} + 2e^{-3d} \\
D(\alpha_2) &= 2e^{-d} + 2e^{-3d} \\
D(\alpha_3) &= 2e^{-d} + 2e^{-3d}
\end{aligned}
\tag{3.10}
$$

The last three positions of α are equivalent, since they have similar neighborhoods. Ideally, $D(\alpha_0)$ should be one and the other three should be zero.

We can make the same analysis for the β positions; there are again four of them. The weights are summarized in Table 3.5. Using the weights in Table 3.5 and Equation 3.7, we can write the intensity for each center:

$$
\begin{aligned}
D(\beta_0) &= e^{-3d/4} + 2e^{-7d/4} \\
D(\beta_1) &= e^{-3d/4} + 2e^{-7d/4} \\
D(\beta_2) &= e^{-d/4} + e^{-9d/4} + 2e^{-13d/4} \\
D(\beta_3) &= e^{-d/4} + e^{-9d/4} + 2e^{-13d/4}
\end{aligned}
\tag{3.11}
$$

Again we notice that, due to symmetry, the expressions for β_0 and β_1 are equal, and so are those for β_2 and β_3.

Finally, we can carry out the same analysis for the γ class of points. The weights are summarized in Table 3.6. With Equation 3.8 and Table 3.5 we can write the values for each position of the γ points:

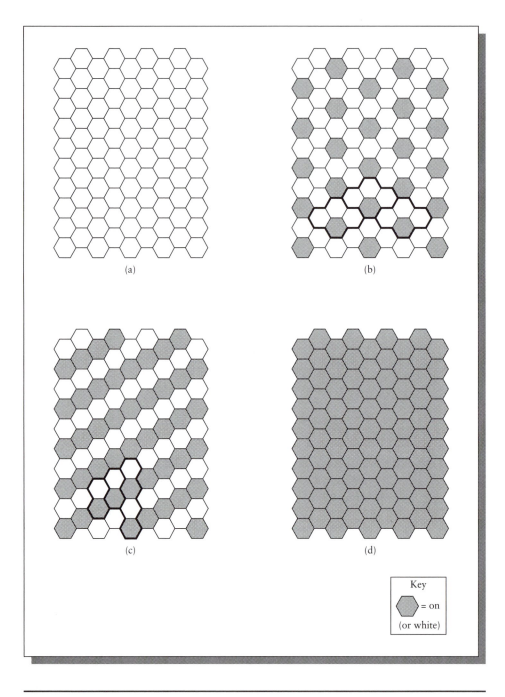

FIGURE 3.13

Contrast and average test patterns. (a) The uniform black field, $\tau = 0.0$. (b) Clusters of four, $\tau = 1/4 = 0.25$. (c) Clusters of two, $\tau = 1/2 = 0.5$. (d) The uniform white field, $\tau = 1.0$.

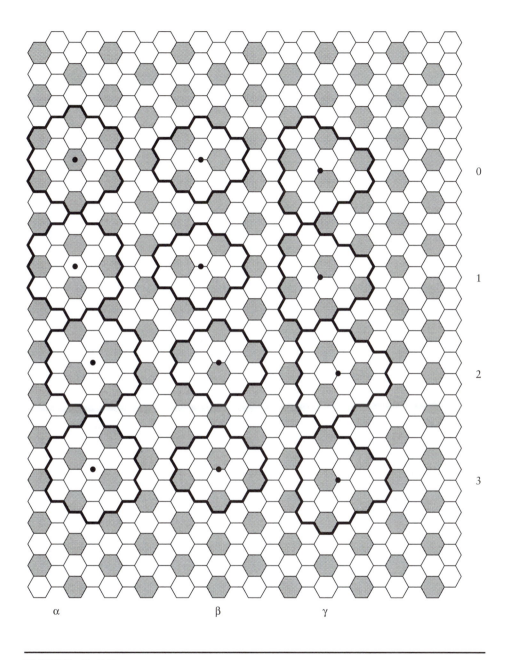

FIGURE 3.14

Centers for the clusters of four. α-type points are in the left column, β-type points are in the middle column, and γ-type points are in the right column.

Center	S	A_1	A_2	A_3	A_4	A_5	A_6	B_1	B_2	B_3	B_4	B_5	B_6	D_1	D_2	D_3	D_4	D_5	D_6
α_0	1	0	0	0	0	0	0	1	1	1	1	1	1	0	0	0	0	0	0
α_1	0	1	0	0	1	0	0	0	0	0	0	0	0	0	1	0	0	1	0
α_2	0	0	1	0	0	1	0	0	0	0	0	0	0	0	0	1	0	0	1
α_3	0	0	0	1	0	0	1	0	0	0	0	0	0	1	0	0	1	0	0

TABLE 3.4
α weights for each cluster of four.

Center	A_1	A_2	B_1	B_2	D_1	D_2	E_1	E_2	E_3	E_4	F_1	F_2	F_3	F_4
β_0	0	0	0	0	0	1	1	0	0	1	0	0	0	0
β_1	0	0	0	0	1	0	0	1	1	0	0	0	0	0
β_2	0	1	1	0	0	0	0	0	0	0	1	0	0	1
β_3	1	0	0	1	0	0	0	0	0	0	0	1	1	0

TABLE 3.5
β weights for each cluster of four.

Center	A_1	A_2	A_3	B_1	B_2	B_3	B_4	B_5	B_6	C_1	C_2	C_3	F_1	F_2	F_3	F_4	F_5	F_6
γ_0	0	1	0	1	0	0	0	0	1	0	0	0	1	0	0	1	0	0
γ_1	1	0	0	0	0	0	1	1	0	0	0	0	0	1	0	0	1	0
γ_2	0	0	0	0	0	0	0	0	0	1	1	1	0	0	0	0	0	0
γ_3	0	0	1	0	1	1	0	0	0	0	0	0	0	0	1	0	0	1

TABLE 3.6
γ weights for each cluster of four.

$$D(\gamma_0) = e^{-d/3} + 2e^{-7d/3} + 2e^{-13d/3}$$
$$D(\gamma_1) = e^{-d/3} + 2e^{-7d/3} + 2e^{-13d/3}$$
$$D(\gamma_2) = 3e^{-4d/3}$$
$$D(\gamma_3) = e^{-d/3} + 2e^{-7d/3} + 2e^{-13d/3} \tag{3.12}$$

We can now compute various intensities on the screen for this test image for different values of d. Figure 3.15 shows the values for the four different α-type points as d varies from R to $3R$. Similarly, Figures 3.16 and 3.17 show the variation for β and γ points for the same range of d.

We can now compute the contrast on the screen with respect to this set of positions. For each value of d, the brightest and darkest points are the minimum and maximum of Figures 3.15, 3.16, and 3.17. These are shown in Figure 3.18, along with the contrast value computed from them.

Notice that the contrast improves as the spot spacing increases. This argues that for the best contrast, the spot centers should be as far apart as possible.

Our calculations allow us to compute some other interesting properties as well. Consider the average intensity of the image. The ideal would be a value of 25%. If we average the four values for just the α positions, we find a range of averages shown in Figure 3.19.

3.3.7 Clusters of Two ($\tau = .5$)

A striped pattern may be generated by a fundamental cell of two pixels, with one white pixel. One example is shown in Figure 3.13(c); it has a density of $\tau = 1/2 = .5$.

We will now apply the same analysis as above to this pattern. Figure 3.20 shows the cell neighborhoods. There are only two of each type of point in this size cluster.

The weights for the two α-type spots are given in Table 3.7.

Using the weights in Table 3.7 and Equation 3.6 we can write the intensity for each center:

$$D(\alpha_0) = 1 + 2e^{-d} + 6e^{-4d} + 2e^{-3d}$$
$$D(\alpha_1) = 4e^{-d} + 4e^{-3d} \tag{3.13}$$

The weights for β-type points are summarized in Table 3.8.

Using the weights in Table 3.8 and Equation 3.7 we can write the intensity for each center:

$$D(\beta_0) = e^{-d/4} + e^{-9d/4} + e^{-3d/4} + 2e^{-7d/4} + 2e^{-13d/4}$$
$$D(\beta_1) = e^{-d/4} + e^{-9d/4} + e^{-3d/4} + 2e^{-7d/4} + 2e^{-13d/4} \tag{3.14}$$

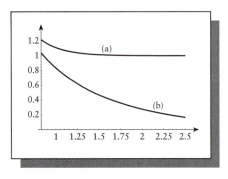

FIGURE 3.15

The intensity of α points with respect to changing d for the cluster of four. (a) $D(\alpha_0)$. (b) $D(\alpha_1)$, $D(\alpha_2)$, and $D(\alpha_3)$.

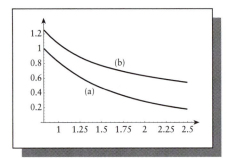

FIGURE 3.16

The intensity of β points with respect to changing d for the cluster of four. (a) $D(\beta_0)$ and $D(\beta_1)$. (b) $D(\beta_2)$ and $D(\beta_3)$.

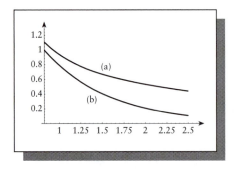

FIGURE 3.17

The intensity of γ points with respect to changing d for the cluster of four. (a) $D(\gamma_0)$, $D(\gamma_1)$, and $D(\gamma_3)$. (b) $D(\gamma_2)$.

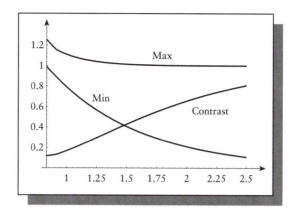

FIGURE 3.18

Min, max, and contrast for the cluster of four for different values of d.

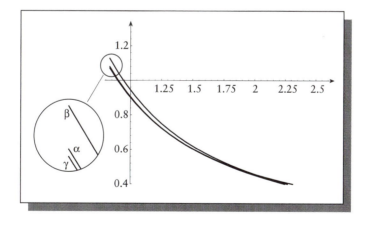

FIGURE 3.19

The average intensity of the cluster of four for different values of d.

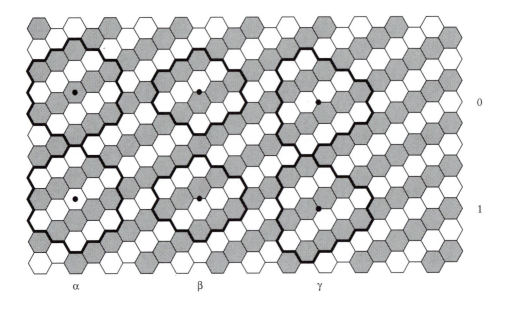

FIGURE   3.20

Centers for the clusters of two.

Again we notice that, due to symmetry, both expressions are equivalent.

Finally, we can carry out the same analysis for the γ class of points. The weights are summarized in Table 3.9.

With Equation 3.8 and Table 3.8 we can write the values for each position of the γ points:

$$D(\gamma_0) = e^{-d/3} + 2e^{-7d/3} + 3e^{-4d/3} + 2e^{-13d/3}$$
$$D(\gamma_1) = 2e^{-d/3} + 4e^{-7d/3} + 4d^{-13d/3} \tag{3.15}$$

The corresponding intensity plots for this pattern are shown in Figure 3.21 for α-type points and Figures 3.22 and 3.23 for β and γ points.

As before, we can now compute the contrast on the screen with respect to this set of positions. For each value of d, the brightest and darkest points are the minimum and maximum of Figures 3.21, 3.22, and 3.23. These are shown in Figure 3.24, along with the contrast value computed from them.

Again, notice that the contrast improves as the spot spacing increases.

The ideal average intensity of this image would be a value of 50%. If we average

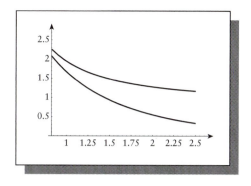

FIGURE 3.21

The intensity of α points with respect to changing d for the cluster of two.

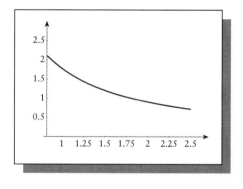

FIGURE 3.22

The intensity of β points with respect to changing d for the cluster of two.

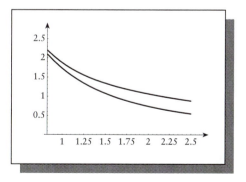

FIGURE 3.23

The intensity of γ points with respect to changing d for the cluster of two.

Center	S	A_1	A_2	A_3	A_4	A_5	A_6	B_1	B_2	B_3	B_4	B_5	B_6	D_1	D_2	D_3	D_4	D_5	D_6
α_0	1	0	1	0	0	1	0	1	1	1	1	1	1	0	0	1	0	0	1
α_1	0	1	0	1	1	0	1	0	0	0	0	0	0	1	1	0	1	1	0

TABLE 3.7
α weights for cluster two.

Center	A_1	A_2	B_1	B_2	D_1	D_2	E_1	E_2	E_3	E_4	F_1	F_2	F_3	F_4
β_0	0	1	1	0	0	1	1	0	0	1	1	0	0	1
β_1	1	0	0	1	1	0	0	1	1	0	0	1	1	0

TABLE 3.8
β weights for cluster two.

Center	A_1	A_2	A_3	B_1	B_2	B_3	B_4	B_5	B_6	C_1	C_2	C_3	F_1	F_2	F_3	F_4	F_5	F_6
γ_0	0	1	0	1	0	0	0	0	1	1	1	1	1	0	0	1	0	0
γ_1	1	0	1	0	1	1	1	1	0	0	0	0	0	1	1	0	1	1

TABLE 3.9
γ weights for cluster two.

the four values for just the α positions, we find a range of averages as shown in Figure 3.25.

3.3.8 The Uniform White Field ($\tau = 1$)

The uniform white field is shown in Figure 3.13(d). In this field every pixel is on. There is only one position for each type of point. We can write the equations for the

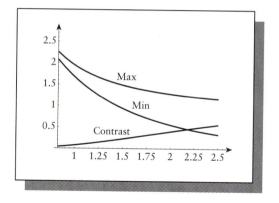

FIGURE 3.24

Min, max, and contrast for the cluster of two for different values of d.

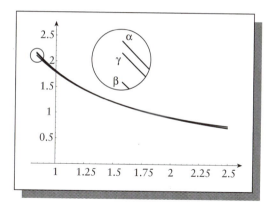

FIGURE 3.25

The average intensity of the cluster of two for different values of d.

different spot positions by inspection.

$$D(\alpha) = 1 + 6e^{-d} + 6e^{-4d} + 6e^{-3d}$$
$$D(\beta) = 2e^{-d/4} + 2e^{-9d/4} + 2e^{-3d/4} + 4e^{-7d/4} + 4e^{-13d/4}$$
$$D(\gamma) = 2e^{-d/3} + 2e^{-7d/3} + 2e^{-4d/3} + 4e^{-13d/3}$$

$$(3.16)$$

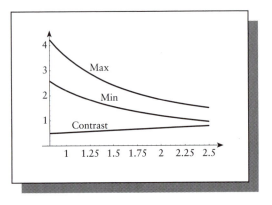

FIGURE 3.26

Min, max, and contrast for the white field for different values of d.

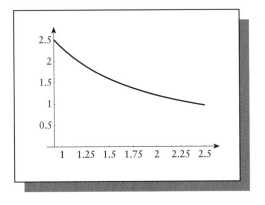

FIGURE 3.27

The average intensity of the white field for different values of d.

Contrast and average curves are shown in Figures 3.26 and 3.27. Notice that in this case we want the contrast to be as low as possible, since we want a flat, white field where every point in the image is identical.

3.3.9 Spot Interaction Discussion

The essential point to notice from the above discussion is that there is a natural tension on the distance between dots. To achieve a flat, uniform white image the dots should be close together, so there is very little black space between dots. But for high contrast, the dots should be far apart, so that one does not bleed into the next, and a spot that should be off has an intensity near zero.

This tension must be balanced by the designer of the display; different choices may be appropriate for different images. Although hardware manufacturers set the dot spacing for CRTs, many tools for printing allow the user to set dot spacing and other parameters as part of the imaging process.

The interdot spacing sets an upper limit on the precision with which we can represent detail in an image. The *apparent* dot spacing is a function of the physical spacing on the device and the distance between the device and the viewer, discussed in more detail below.

3.4 Monitors

Earlier we presented a description of the physical construction of a CRT. We now enlarge our view to include the driving electronics that control the beams; the composite device is called a *monitor*.

Recall that the beam is swept top to bottom, left to right. When the beam reaches the upper-right corner of the screen at the end of the first row, or *scan line*, it moves back to the left side of the screen to start the next *horizontal sweep*. During this interval, called the *horizontal retrace*, the beam is *blanked*: the electron emission is set to zero, so no phosphors are affected. This interval is needed so that the deflection circuitry can have time to update its charge, so the beam will be appropriately positioned when it is turned on again. When the deflectors have settled to aim the beam at the far left, it is turned on and the sweeping from left to right starts again.

If the monitor is *noninterlaced*, then the second scan line swept out is directly beneath the first. Thus if the monitor displays pictures with a vertical resolution of 525 lines, then the order of lines swept out is 1, 2, 3, ..., 525, as shown in Figure 3.28(a). When the beam reaches the bottom right, it is again blanked and then moved back to the upper left, during the *vertical retrace*. In the United States, a complete video image is usually swept out in about 1/30 second.

On the other hand, if the monitor is *interlaced*, then the image is built up by first displaying all of the odd scan lines, then all the even, so the order of lines would be 1, 3, 5, ..., 525, 2, 4, 6, ..., 524, 1, as shown in Figure 3.28(b). This requires an additional vertical retrace for each picture after the final odd scan line. The first set of lines is called the *odd field*, the second the *even field*. Most

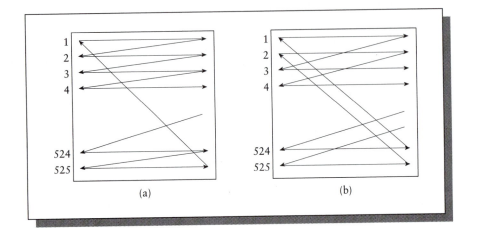

FIGURE 3.28

Two raster scan patterns. (a) Noninterlaced. (b) Interlaced.

commercial monitors in the United States display images in interlaced format, since commercial broadcasts use the NTSC standard, which specifies an interlaced signal. Some industrial monitors offer both modes, with the choice controlled by a switch or a computer signal.

An advantage of interlaced display is that the likelihood of *flicker* is reduced. As we saw in Chapter 1, a rule of thumb is that under most viewing circumstances, the flicker rate is about 30 frames per second, so a noninterlaced monitor will often appear to flicker (consider a scan line 1/3 of the way down the screen; it is only refreshed every 1/30 second). Of course, an interlaced monitor also displays only 30 complete frames per second, but alternating the fields effectively doubles the display rate. To see this, again consider a scan line 1/3 down the screen: although after it is swept it will not be swept again for 1/30 second, the scan lines immediately above and below it are drawn 1/60 second later. Since we saw earlier that phosphors are typically close enough to affect each other, we do not see a set of black bands where the scan lines are at their oldest (almost 1/30 of second). The persistence of the phosphor also helps sustain the steady emission of light from that scan line until it is revisited.

Most monitors provide a pair of controls called *brightness* and *contrast* for the user to adjust. Figure 3.29 shows a diagram of how these controls affect the signal driving the electron guns. Figure 3.30 is a curve showing the intensity of emitted light plotted against the voltage applied to the guns. Note that below a cutoff voltage

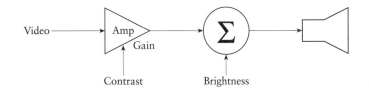

FIGURE 3.29

What contrast and brightness controls do.

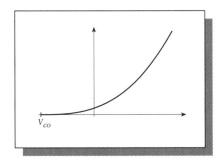

FIGURE 3.30

The phosphor light emission plotted as a function of input voltage.

V_{co}, no light is emitted by the tube. For voltages V greater than the cutoff, the light intensity follows an exponential curve of the rough form $k(V - V_{co})^{\gamma}$. The exponent γ is usually between 2 and 3; we will have more to say about it in a moment.

The contrast control adjusts the amount of amplification of the signal; the more the signal is amplified, the brighter it will appear on the screen. The brightness control is a *bias* adjustment, adding some fixed voltage into the video signal before it reaches the guns. Note that this moves the response curve left and right, not up and down; this is important. The brightness setting then simply changes the minimum amount of video signal necessary to cause the screen to emit light. The brightness control is normally set to $-V_{co}$, so that 0 volts of signal is black, but any positive signal is visible. It is the control normally called "contrast" that adjusts the overall brightness of the image by boosting the intensity of the visible parts of the signal.

Typically we desire a monitor's response to be linear with input signal: if we double the signal, we would like to double the energy of the emitted light (notice that we are discussing radiant energy, and not brightness perceived by a human observer; the latter has its own nonlinearities). For example, if we compute one pixel to have a gray value of 100, and another a gray value of 200, we would expect the latter pixel to emit twice as much light as the former. But as we saw a moment ago, the intensity response curve is exponential, rather than linear, so doubling the input intensity does not double the output light. Symbolically (and assuming that brightness is set to $-V_{co}$), $2k(V^\gamma) \neq k(2V)^\gamma$. To compensate, we typically adjust the input signal before sending it to the monitor. Since the nonlinear response of the monitor is described by the exponent γ (gamma) in the response curve, this compensation is usually called *gamma correction*. Thus instead of sending V to the monitor, we send $V^{1/\gamma}$; then $2k\left(V^{1/\gamma}\right)^\gamma = k\left((2V)^{1/\gamma}\right)^\gamma$. In broadcast video, gamma correction is performed before the signal is transmitted, so most monitors expect the signal to already be corrected.

The usual range of gamma for color receivers is 2.8 ± 0.3. Typically for video display, full gamma correction is not applied; instead, the video signal V is usually raised to about $1/2.2$. The result is that the final image has an increase in gamma over the original input signal by a factor of about 1.27. This intentional error is introduced to compensate for the reduction in apparent contrast caused by the dim surround conditions in which a monitor is normally viewed. Unfortunately, this also causes colors to increase in purity and shift in their dominant wavelength. The increase in purity may be beneficial in some circumstances, when it serves to compensate for an apparent decrease in saturation of the colors due to the dim surround conditions. Unfortunately, the shift in dominant wavelength will cause small shifts in hue, as shown in Figure 3.31.

In modern display systems the gamma is often fine-tuned by setting a compensation curve into the color map [78], though this must be done carefully [181]. Alternatively, the pixel values themselves may be precorrected [50].

The colors displayed on a monitor can be affected by many different phenomena, only some of which can be controlled [62, 78]. Even the magnetic field of the Earth can affect the focusing and deflection of the electron guns [146], to the extent that moving a monitor from the Northern to the Southern Hemisphere can cause a shift of as much as 3 mm in the display's center. Several manufacturers align their monitors in different magnetic field environments depending on the destination of the CRT. Even rotation within the field can cause a change in deflection; one company always calibrates its monitors while facing east [146].

3.5 *RGB* Color Space

In Chapter 2 I stated that red, green, and blue (RGB) are often used in computer graphics as the basis of a color space. This is an important observation that has many practical results. The most obvious result here is that we can create any color

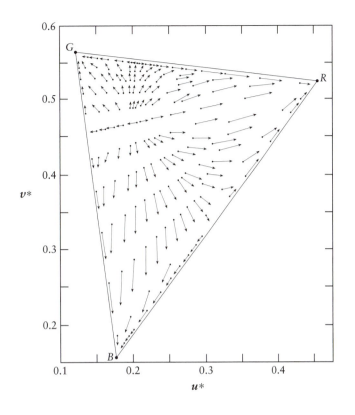

FIGURE 3.31

The shift in x, y coordinates due to gamma correction. Redrawn from Hunt, *Reproduction of Color*, fig. 19.10, p. 395.

by an appropriate combination of red, green, and blue. This is why those particular types of phosphors are used in the construction of CRTs.

But "red" is an imprecise specification of a color. Precisely what "red" is used in a CRT? The choice of phosphors must be carefully considered by a monitor builder. For example, people are very sensitive to skin colors. If the broadcaster specifies a particular color at some point on the screen to represent a skin tone, this cannot just be specified by some combination of "red, green, and blue"; one manufacturer's choices of which colored phosphors to use may differ significantly from another manufacturer's, resulting in very different final colors on the screen. In practice, most phosphor sets used in CRTs today are similar but not identical, and

	x	y
r	0.670	0.330
g	0.210	0.710
b	0.140	0.080
w	0.313	0.329

TABLE 3.10

x, y coordinates for standard CIE phosphors and D_{6500} white point. *Source:* Data from Hall, *Illumination and Color in Computer Generated Imagery.*

they can vary even within sets of the same model produced with different shipments of phosphors.

Referring back to Figure 1.42, the dashed triangle shows the subset of colors that can be represented by a monitor with a particular set of phosphors. The phosphors are at the triangle vertices and can generate anything inside by various linear combinations. Note that there are huge patches of color space that aren't inside the triangle; these are colors we can perceive that are simply not available for display on this type of device. By choosing other phosphors, you may define different triangles and try to include more of the space. However, phosphors are complex compounds that must meet many conflicting criteria, such as x, y chromaticity, purity, persistence, stability, toxicity, and cost [267].

Recall from Chapter 2 that a color may be objectively described in the CIE XYZ color space as a linear combination of the three $\overline{x}(\lambda)$, $\overline{y}(\lambda)$, and $\overline{z}(\lambda)$ matching functions. In effect, this is a 3D linear space with a particular choice of axes. We may choose any three mutually orthogonal nonzero vectors to form an orthogonal set of axes (or *basis*) in this space. We may then specify a color with respect to these new vectors, and a linear transformation will take us from this set of coordinates to XYZ coordinates, or vice versa.

The principal observation that supports the design of current CRTs is that most sets of red, green, and blue phosphors form a roughly orthogonal (or at least non-degenerate) basis in a linear color space.

When a broadcaster creates a video signal, the color information is described as though all monitors used a particular set of *standard phosphors*. Thus, from the broadcaster's point of view, the precise meaning of "red, green, and blue" is exactly the spectral response of the standard phosphors bearing those names. The chromaticities of these phosphors are given in Table 3.10 along with the white point for the CIE standard D_{6500} illuminant.

If a particular monitor was not constructed out of the standard phosphors, then the displayed color will be different from what was intended. Whether this distortion is acceptable depends on the amount by which the particular phosphors used differ from the standards, and the desired accuracy of the match. Some receivers have internal circuitry to map the incoming signal (assumed to be with reference to the NTSC primaries) to the particular phosphors in that tube [181]. Most industrial *RGB* monitors do not include this circuitry.

The main point here is that it is meaningless to speak of "*RGB* values" without explicit reference to which phosphors you are discussing. Nevertheless, you often hear computer graphics people speak of a color in terms of *RGB* without reference to a phosphor set. They are usually implicitly referring to the *RGB* signal intensities that they feed into some particular monitor to achieve the desired color. If they do not specify their phosphors, then they are really not telling you much; if you use those *RGB* values on another monitor, you will probably get something like what they had, but you may be rather far off; there is certainly no need for much care or precision in matching such a loosely specified color.

The mechanism for converting from a standard color space to the particular *RGB* phosphors in some monitor is straightforward. The following discussion will show the procedure with respect to *XYZ* color space, since transformations to and from that space are well known for most color descriptions.

Our goal is to find a matrix **M**, which will take a three-element vector representing an *XYZ* color and transform it to an equivalent *RGB* vector for some particular monitor. We will compute **M** by finding **N** (the transform from *RGB* to *XYZ*) and then inverting the matrix.

The first step is to find the chromaticities of the phosphors and white point of the target monitor. We will call the white spot (w_x, w_y), and the red, green, and blue phosphors, respectively, (r_x, r_y), (g_x, g_y), and (b_x, b_y). The corresponding z value for each color may be found from $z = 1 - x - y$.

From the phosphor triplets the matrix **K** in Equation 3.17 is built, and from the white-spot triplet the *XYZ* vector **W** is built; the latter is the color corresponding to the white point (X_n, Y_n, Z_n) scaled so that the luminance Y_n has the value 1.0. We will also have use for the *RGB* white point $\mathbf{F} = (1\ 1\ 1)$.

$$\mathbf{W} = \left[\begin{array}{ccc} \dfrac{X_n}{Y_n} & 1 & \dfrac{Z_n}{Y_n} \end{array} \right]$$

$$\mathbf{K} = \left[\begin{array}{ccc} r_x & r_y & r_z \\ g_x & g_y & g_z \\ b_x & b_y & b_z \end{array} \right]$$

$$\mathbf{V} = \left[\begin{array}{ccc} G_r & G_g & G_b \end{array} \right]$$

$$\mathbf{G} = \begin{bmatrix} G_r & 0 & 0 \\ 0 & G_g & 0 \\ 0 & 0 & G_b \end{bmatrix}$$

Observe that $\mathbf{N} = \mathbf{GK}$ (the *RGB*-to-*XYZ* matrix is given by the matrix of the phosphor *XYZ* chromaticities, differentially scaled so that the white-point luminance Y is set to 1.0). Since $\mathbf{N}$ relates the *XYZ* white $\mathbf{W}$ to the *RGB* white $\mathbf{F}$, we can write $\mathbf{W} = \mathbf{FN}$. Substituting the previous expression for $\mathbf{N}$ into this equation, we find $\mathbf{W} = \mathbf{F}(\mathbf{GK})$, so $\mathbf{WK}^{-1} = \mathbf{FG}$. Observing that $\mathbf{V} = \mathbf{FG}$, rewrite this as $\mathbf{V} = \mathbf{WK}^{-1}$. We now have $\mathbf{V}$, and from that we can build $\mathbf{G}$. With this, find $\mathbf{N} = \mathbf{GK}$, and from that result find $\mathbf{M} = \mathbf{N}^{-1}$. In summary, the steps are as follows:

1 Build $\mathbf{W}$ and $\mathbf{K}$ from the monitor white spot and color phosphor chromaticities.

2 Compute $\mathbf{V} = \mathbf{WK}^{-1}$.

3 From the vector $\mathbf{V}$, build the matrix $\mathbf{G}$.

4 Compute $\mathbf{N} = \mathbf{GK}$.

5 Compute $\mathbf{M} = \mathbf{N}^{-1}$.

Now, to convert any *XYZ* space color vector $\mathbf{C}_{XYZ}$ into the appropriate *RGB* color $\mathbf{C}_{RGB}$ for this monitor, just post-multiply $\mathbf{C}_{XYZ}$ by the *XYZ*-to-*RGB* matrix $\mathbf{M}$: $\mathbf{C}_{RGB} = \mathbf{C}_{XYZ}\mathbf{M}$. Similarly, if you have designed a color $\mathbf{C}_{RGB}$ you like on your monitor and you want to know its *XYZ* coordinates $\mathbf{C}_{XYZ}$, use the inverse matrix: $\mathbf{C}_{XYZ} = \mathbf{C}_{RGB}\mathbf{M}^{-1}$. The matrix $\mathbf{M}$ for a monitor with standard NTSC phosphors and a white point given by the phosphors in Table 3.10 is

$$\mathbf{M} = \begin{pmatrix} 1.967 & -0.955 & 0.064 \\ -0.548 & 1.938 & -0.130 \\ -0.297 & -0.027 & 0.982 \end{pmatrix} \tag{3.17}$$

3.5.1 Converting XYZ to Spectra

One problem shared by all these systems is that the resulting color does not have an intrinsic spectral representation. We will find it important in later sections to describe colors as functions defined with spectral representations, providing an amplitude at each wavelength. We saw earlier the equations to convert such a color, $C(\lambda)$, into *XYZ* coordinates. But the color systems mentioned above provide only the *XYZ* coordinates; from these three numbers we wish to build a corresponding spectrum $C(\lambda)$.

There are several techniques that may be used, each with advantages and disadvantages. These are discussed in Glassner [155]. If you know the phosphor curves for your monitor, then you may simply represent any color by the appropriate weighted sum of those three phosphor curves. Another reasonably useful method synthesizes a color by weighting the first three Fourier basis functions.

Specifically, choose a flat spectrum $F_1(\lambda)$, a single cycle of a sine curve $F_2(\lambda)$, and a single cycle of cosine $F_3(\lambda)$. Since these functions form a basis for all spectra and the conversion from spectra to RGB is linear, we may match an RGB with the transformed values of the spectra and use the same weights to create a new spectrum. In this case, build the three functions each from 380 to 780 nm:

$$F_1(\lambda) = 1.0$$
$$F_2(\lambda) = \frac{1}{2}\left[1 + \sin\left(2\pi\frac{\lambda - 380}{400}\right)\right]$$
$$F_3(\lambda) = \frac{1}{2}\left[1 + \cos\left(2\pi\frac{\lambda - 380}{400}\right)\right] \tag{3.18}$$

We now wish to find the three weights $\mathbf{W} = [w_1\ w_2\ w_3]$ with which to scale these spectra to build the new spectra. To find these weights we will find the RGB coefficients of each spectrum and store them in a matrix $\mathbf{D}$. We build $\mathbf{D}$ from the XYZ components of the three spectra:

$$\mathbf{D} = \begin{pmatrix} \int_{\lambda \in \mathcal{R}_\mathcal{V}} F_1(\lambda)\overline{x}(\lambda)\,d\lambda & \int_{\lambda \in \mathcal{R}_\mathcal{V}} F_1(\lambda)\overline{y}(\lambda)\,d\lambda & \int_{\lambda \in \mathcal{R}_\mathcal{V}} F_1(\lambda)\overline{z}(\lambda)\,d\lambda \\[2mm] \int_{\lambda \in \mathcal{R}_\mathcal{V}} F_2(\lambda)\overline{x}(\lambda)\,d\lambda & \int_{\lambda \in \mathcal{R}_\mathcal{V}} F_2(\lambda)\overline{y}(\lambda)\,d\lambda & \int_{\lambda \in \mathcal{R}_\mathcal{V}} F_2(\lambda)\overline{z}(\lambda)\,d\lambda \\[2mm] \int_{\lambda \in \mathcal{R}_\mathcal{V}} F_3(\lambda)\overline{x}(\lambda)\,d\lambda & \int_{\lambda \in \mathcal{R}_\mathcal{V}} F_3(\lambda)\overline{y}(\lambda)\,d\lambda & \int_{\lambda \in \mathcal{R}_\mathcal{V}} F_3(\lambda)\overline{z}(\lambda)\,d\lambda \end{pmatrix}$$
$$\tag{3.19}$$

Each component of $\mathbf{D}$ is the result of integration of one of the basis functions with one of the CIE matching functions. For example, $F_1(\lambda)_X = \int_{\lambda=380}^{780} F_1(\lambda)\overline{x}(\lambda)\,d\lambda$. Since $\mathbf{D}$ represents the XYZ coordinates of the spectra, the composite matrix $\mathbf{DM}$ represents their RGB values, where $\mathbf{M}$ is the XYZ-to-RGB matrix built in the preceding section. Recall that $\mathbf{M}$ is different for each monitor's unique set of phosphors. Some set of weights $\mathbf{W}$ on these RGB values will match the RGB color $\mathbf{R} = (r\ g\ b)$ we have designed:

$$\mathbf{W}(\mathbf{DM}) = \mathbf{R} \tag{3.20}$$

We may now easily solve for $\mathbf{W}$:

$$\mathbf{W} = \mathbf{R}(\mathbf{DM})^{-1} \tag{3.21}$$

The spectrum $C(\lambda)$ we desire is thus $C(\lambda) = w_1\,F_1(\lambda) + w_2\,F_2(\lambda) + w_3\,F_3(\lambda)$. This spectrum is smooth and continuous, but it may contain negative values.

A drawback of this process is that the curves have little relation to the monitor. The connection may be made stronger by using real spectra as the matching functions if they are available, either from the monitor's phosphors for output, or the scanner's response if we are digitizing a photograph. Although they are more closely tied to the color being matched, these spectra are often far from smooth.

Color calculations with intuitive meaning are best performed in $L^*u^*v^*$ or $L^*a^*b^*$. Referring back to our earlier example of linear interpolation, equal parametric steps in this space will result in perceptually equal steps of color. Other color calculations, such as finding the center of gravity of a collection of colors, filtering a set of colors, or even simply finding the color halfway between two extremes, are all best performed in one of these perceptually uniform spaces if the results need to be perceptually consistent and there is sufficient processing power available.

3.6   Gamut Mapping

Consider again Figure 1.42; it shows the triangle of colors representable on a CRT for a given set of three phosphors. The range of displayable colors for any particular device (i.e., monitor, printer, film) is called the device *gamut*.

Unfortunately, not all displays share the same gamut. When some of the colors in an image lie outside the colors available on a particular device, we must somehow get the colors in the image gamut to all lie within the device gamut. This process is called *gamut mapping*.

Gamut mapping is difficult since it involves somehow distorting the original picture in order to make it displayable.

A chromaticity diagram for a typical monitor and printer is shown in Figure 3.32 (color plate). The monitor gamut is marked with the triangle, and the printer is the colored region in the center. Notice that the white points of the two devices do not line up. Also notice that there are colors available to the printer that the monitor cannot represent; an image designed on a monitor is unlikely to take advantage of these colors. Far worse from today's computer graphics standpoint is that there are many colors available on a CRT that are simply unprintable. There are missing regions in the greens and reds, and a great deal of unavailable color space in the blues.

Proper gamut mapping for a given image is still an art [181, 420]. Hall [181] distinguishes two types of out-of-gamut colors: those that have a chromaticity that cannot be matched by the device, and those that can be matched in chromaticity but not intensity. The first set of colors, when mapped to a CRT device, gives *RGB* values less than 0; the second set gives *RGB* values greater than 1. Most gamut-mapping methods assume that the input is an image that has already been converted to *RGB* for a particular monitor.

Most gamut-mapping methods seem to fall into one of two general categories:

global and *local* approaches. A *local* approach examines each pixel individually and adjusts only those pixels that are out of gamut. A *global* approach applies information gathered from the entire picture when considering what to do with each pixel, including those within gamut.

Local methods operate on each pixel independently, typically only processing those that are out of gamut. Some local methods involve projecting the *RGB* values into another color system, operating on the pixel there, and then returning to *RGB*. Some of these methods include the following:

■ Scaling the pixel *RGB* components uniformly until it is within the device gamut.

■ Scaling the intensity of the pixel but leaving its chromaticity unchanged.

■ Desaturating the pixel leaving the hue and intensity unchanged.

■ Clipping the pixel to the range $[0, 1]$.

■ Scaling the pixel nonuniformly even if it is within gamut.

The problem with all local approaches is that they can introduce a type of error we call *limit errors*. Limit errors appear when an object suddenly changes in appearance from one pixel to the next due to an abrupt decision to apply a local transformation. For example, consider a simple clipping operation that takes any color component beyond 1 and sets it to 1. Figure 3.33(a) shows the color profile of the desired green component of a sphere across a scan line, and (b) shows the result of clipping. In effect, the bright part of the sphere becomes a flat sea of saturated green, and the object will no longer look spherical at all. Even a smooth local operation, such as the one shown in (c), changes the shading so that the object is no longer shaded like a sphere. All local approaches share these sorts of problems.

Global approaches look over the entire picture before doing any processing. Some global methods include these:

■ Finding the smallest color component in the picture (that is, the smallest value of R, G, or B) and calling it a. Similarly, find the largest color components and call it b. Display each pixel i as

$$\left(\frac{R_i - a}{b - a}, \frac{G_i - a}{b - a}, \frac{B_i - a}{b - a}, \right) \tag{3.22}$$

■ Similar to the above, but compressing only that part of the input range for each color component that is out of range, as in Figure 3.34. Using s and d from Table 3.11, display each pixel as

$$(d + s(R_i - a), d + s(G_i - a), d + s(B_i - a)) \tag{3.23}$$

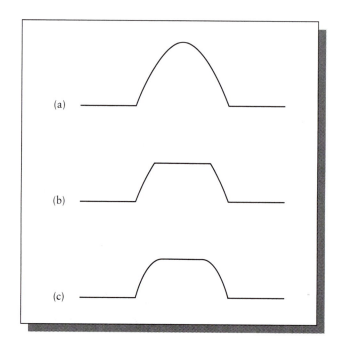

FIGURE 3.33

Local gamut mapping. (a) A desired profile for a sphere. (b) The clipped profile. (c) A less drastic transformation.

■ Scanning the image and gathering statistics on all out-of-gamut pixels. Select a local or global technique based on this information.

Global approaches don't introduce the sort of limit errors created by local methods, but they have their own drawback: they introduce *semantic inconsistency errors*. Consider Figure 3.35, which shows a red ball reflected in two different mirrors. For convenience, we will assume that the ball is a uniform bright red color, so from any angle it appears as a flat disk. The left mirror is 25% and the right mirror 50% reflective. Suppose that the brightest parts of the ball map to a red component of 3 units (the monitor can only display values 0 to 1). So the pixels representing the visible ball have red value 3, pixels displaying the ball in the left mirror have a red value of 3/4, and pixels showing the image of the ball in the right mirror have a red value of 1.5.

If we only adjust the pixels that are out of gamut, then we will affect the pixels showing the ball and the pixels in the right-hand mirror, but not those in the left-hand

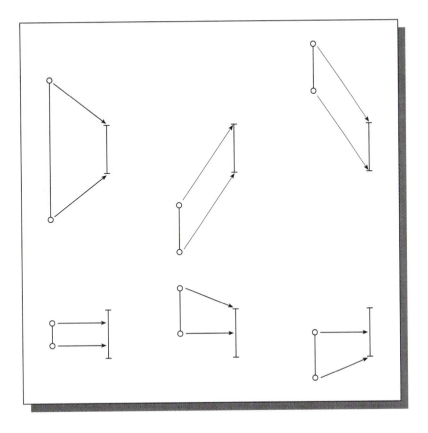

FIGURE 3.34

The six possibilities for range compression.

	$a \in [0, 1]$	$a \notin [0, 1]$
$b \in [0, 1]$	$d = a, \quad s = 1$	$d = 0, \quad s = \dfrac{b}{b - a}$
$b \notin [0, 1]$	$d = a, \quad s = \dfrac{1 - a}{b - a}$	$d = 0, \quad s = \dfrac{1}{b - a}$

TABLE 3.11

Selecting d and s for partial range compression.

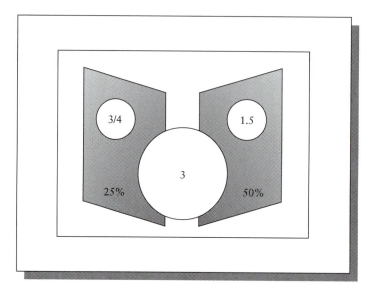

FIGURE 3.35

A ball reflected in two different mirrors with different colored reflectivities.

mirror. This is an example of a violation of semantic consistency: the picture no longer represents what it originally was meant to represent. The red ball is darker, the reflection in the right mirror is darker, and the reflection in the left mirror is unchanged. If no other objects in the scene are out of gamut, and are reflected off of these mirrors, then we have a strange situation where almost everything in the scene is telling us about the reflectivity of these mirrors, but the images of the ball act differently.

A local method to mapping this picture would also fail. Suppose we simply clip; then the red ball and its right reflection are both at red value 1, and the left reflection is at 3/4. Suddenly the right mirror seems to be reflecting all of its light for the red ball, while reflecting only half of the light for everything else in the scene.

When all we have to work with is a grid of *RGB* values, there may be no best solution. Stone et al. [420] suggest that a gamut-mapping technique should satisfy five criteria, whose importance is based on the image and the destination gamut into which we are mapping:

1 The gray axis of the image should be preserved.

2 Maximum luminance contrast is desirable.

3 Few colors should lie outside the destination gamut.

4 Hue and saturation shifts should be minimized.

5 It is better to increase than to decrease the color saturation.

If the goal is to display synthetic images, then we can use information gathered during the rendering step to help in the gamut mapping, or even guide the rendering process so that explicit gamut mapping can be avoided altogether, preventing any limit or semantic inconsistency errors [160].

One approach is to change the renderer so that it creates not just *RGB* values at each pixel, but also a complete *symbolic expression* that completely specifies which colors were used to create that pixel and how they were combined [160]. Returning to our mirrored ball example, pixels in the right-hand mirror reflecting the ball would contain an expression that combines the emission of the light source and the reflectivities of the ball and mirror. If we have this information for every pixel, we can go back to the scene and adjust the scene colors until the resulting image is completely in gamut, effectively rerendering the image with new colors for one or more lights or objects.

The resulting image is not identical to the original picture, but any gamut-mapping algorithm must change the picture since the original cannot be displayed. The advantage of this approach is that the resulting picture is entirely self-consistent: the image is rendered using adjusted colors, so for that set of object and light spectra, the image displays the rendered results, not just a displayable distortion. Another advantage is that the same scene may be processed several times for different gamuts, so a scene designed on a monitor could have its colors adjusted so that the resulting image includes those colors unavailable on the monitor but within the printer gamut. For example, a dark blue wall may become desaturated because the printer can't handle that blue (thereby changing the effect of that wall on the rest of the scene), but a green carpet might become somewhat brighter because the printer has that color available. Note that the colors of some objects and lights in the scene may not be directly visible in the final picture, but they also may be adjusted to cause the entire image to come into gamut. This process may be run automatically, or a designer may exert manual control over which objects may change color and which may not. We will return to this idea in Chapter 20.

3.7 Further Reading

A good discussion of color and many of its applications to computer display may be found in Durrett's book [133]. In particular, Merrifield's chapter [298] contains a lot of information about CRTs, and Silverstein's chapter [411] discusses many issues related to the human visual system. The chapter by Andreottola [10] surveys color hard-copy devices, which have very different characteristics than CRTs.

An extensive discussion of almost every aspect of phosphorescence and phosphors is offered by Leverenz [267], who includes chemical information, glow curves, and even some manufacturing suggestions.

Colormap correction for gamma compensation was first presented to the graphics community by Catmull [78]. The presentation there is carried on in Hall's book [181] and Blinn's 1989 column [50]. The problem of gamut mapping is discussed by Hall [181], who offers some suggestions; more recent work is discussed by Stone et al. [420].

One of the first papers to consider the display as an integral part of the computer graphics process was presented by Kajiya and Ullner in 1981 [238].

3.8   Exercises

Exercise 3.1

Perform the Gaussian spot analysis for a rectangular grid. Use the center of a cell, the center of an edge, and the corner of a cell as the three points of analysis.

   (a) Identify the spot centers that contribute significantly to each type of point, using the definition in the text.

   (b) Compute the values at these three points for an all-white signal.

   (c) Compute the values at these three points for an all-black signal.

   (d) Compute the values at these three points for a perfect checkerboard signal.

Exercise 3.2

Write a program to compute spectra for a given RGB using the monitor matrix in Equation 3.17 and the first three Fourier basis functions. Transform the colors $(.2, .4, .13)$ and $(.8, .55, .45)$ into spectra from 400 to 700 nm in 5-nm increments.

Exercise 3.3

   (a) Implement gamut mapping using clipping.

   (b) Implement gamut mapping using global scaling.

   (c) Implement gamut mapping using partial range compression of Equation 3.23.

   (d) Try out all three methods on a few pictures that are out of gamut; how do the results compare? Is any method fully acceptable?

Exercise 3.4

Analyze the contrast and average properties for the two fundamental cells shown in Figure 3.36.

   (a) is a fundamental cell of three pixels, with one white pixel. It has a density of $\tau = 1/3 = 0.\overline{3}$.

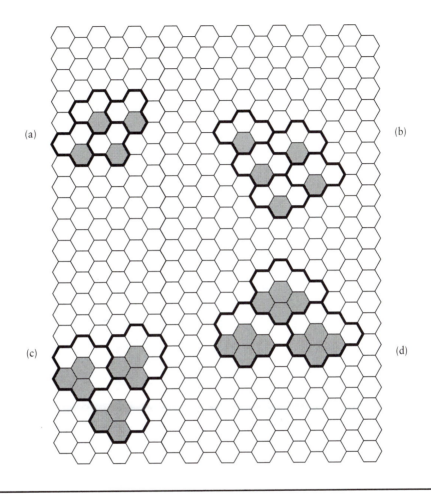

FIGURE 3.36

Figure for tiling exercise. (a) A fundamental cell of three spots. (b) A different tiling of a four-spot cell. (c) A fundamental cell of seven spots. (d) A fundamental cell of eight spots.

(b) is the same fundamental cell we analyzed earlier, but with a different tiling pattern. It has a density of $\tau = 1/4 = .25$.

(c) is a fundamental cell of seven pixels, with three white pixels. It has a density of $\tau = 3/7 \approx .429$.

(d) is a cell of eight pixels, with four white pixels. It has a density of $\tau = 4/8 = .5$.

Exercise 3.5

(a) Look very closely at the front of a color monitor and draw the pattern of phosphors you see there. Suggest why they are arranged this way.

(b) Render on that monitor an image that is all black except for a single one-pixel-wide vertical white line, and view it from at least arm's length on that monitor. What does the image look like? Look close up at the phosphor pattern and describe how the phosphors are being illuminated. If the phosphors are not lined up vertically in perfect columns, do you see a jagged line when at arm's length? If not, why not?

(c) Repeat step (b) for a horizontal line.

Exercise 3.6

Suggest a function for a local gamma-correction operation that is continuous in the first and second derivatives.

Exercise 3.7

Kajiya and Ullner [238] model a Gaussian bump as

$$g(x) = \frac{1}{\sigma\sqrt{2\pi}} \exp\left[-x^2/\sigma^2\right] \tag{3.24}$$

and suggest that the best value of σ for an interdot spacing of 1 unit is $\sigma = 0.66$.

(a) Plot the function $f(x) = g(x) + g(1 - x)$ between two dots in the domain $x \in [0, 1]$ for $\sigma = 0.66$ and $\sigma = 0.55$.

(b) Numerically integrate to find the RMS flat-field error

$$E = \int \left[1 - f(x)\right]^2 \, dx \tag{3.25}$$

between the two dots for $\sigma = 0.66$ and $\sigma = 0.55$.

(c) Use your results from (b) to find the minimum for E as a function of σ, and plot the resulting field as in (a) using the same scale. Compare the shape of this curve and its values to your results from (a).

(d) In (b) we computed E using a nominal flat-field value of 1. Was this a good idea? Would it be better or worse to use a nominal flat-field value of $g(0) + g(1)$?

(e) Test your answer to (d) by finding the RMS flat-field error

$$E_d = \int \left[d - f(x)\right]^2 \, dx \tag{3.26}$$

where $d = g(0) + g(1)$ for $\sigma = 0.66$ and $\sigma = 0.55$. How do the results compare?

(f) Use your results from (b) and (e) to find the minimum for E_d as a function of σ, and plot the resulting field f as in (a) using the same scale. Compare the shape of this curve and its values to your results from (a).

II

SIGNAL PROCESSING

I came to the mouth of a huge cave before which I stopped for a moment, stupefied by such an unknown thing. I arched my back, rested my left hand on my knee, and with my right shaded my lowered eyes; several times I leaned to one side, then the other, to see if I could distinguish anything, but the great darkness within made this impossible. After a time there arose in me both fear and desire—fear of the dark and menacing cave; desire to see whether it contained some marvelous thing.

Leonardo da Vinci

INTRODUCTION TO UNIT II

What is an image? If we're scanning the world with our eyes, then the visible world is projected onto our retinas, where photoreceptors convert the light information into electrical and chemical information. The photoreceptors are densely packed on the retina, but there are only a finite number of them. So the information leaving the retina is really only a description of a bunch of individual colored dots.

This hardly seems possible; the image of the world in our mind's eye appears to be a smooth and continuous picture, and hardly a collection of colored dots. In fact our visual system is doing a lot of processing both before and after the transformation of the light into dots, not the least of which is to fuse our individual visual images into a coherent whole. This remarkable process creates a mental image that for the most part is free of the dots imposed by the photoreceptor pattern.

Image synthesis also produces a set of colored dots: these are the color values on a frame buffer or other display. Because the same static image is visible for a prolonged period of time (as opposed to the fleeting images on our retina), side effects caused by this discrete representation become much more visible and thus more important. Many of these side effects are known collectively as *aliasing*. Even when the individual images are fine, we can experience aliasing in time for an animated sequence, since each frame of the sequence represents its own (discrete) slice of time.

A synthetic image computed on a digital computer is a *digital signal*. We usually imagine it to be a discrete approximation of some smooth function that provides a color at every point on the image. The image inside a computer is necessarily digital by nature; the computer can only store numbers and (usually) can only compute with finite precision.

To understand the nature of digital signals, we need to discuss the field of *digital signal processing*, which involves the creation of digital signals from smooth ones, the transformation of those digital signals, and the process of eventually smoothing them out again.

The worst problem that arises when we convert a smooth signal into a digital one is *aliasing*. The mere word can conjure up visions of jaggies, motion strobing, moiré patterns, popping, and many other objectionable artifacts in images and animations. It is important that any rendering system suppress aliasing effects as much as possible.

The first step in controlling aliasing effects is to understand the problem. Aliasing is a direct result of the fact that in computer graphics we work on a digital computer, which stores continuous signals as a collection of samples. Intuitively, it seems reasonable to believe that if you have enough samples of a signal (such as the variation of color across a scan line), you should have a pretty good description of the thing that was sampled. Aliasing comes about when we don't have enough samples for the object under consideration.

Aliasing effects are prevalent in computer graphics. Like crabgrass in the manicured lawn of a rendering system, aliasing shows up everywhere you don't explicitly address it. To suppress aliasing requires a good understanding of its sources. The best way to understand aliasing is to understand what happens to a signal when it is sampled; the Fourier transform is a mathematical tool that allows us to see this effect most clearly. It also gives us the vocabulary and related tools to discuss aliasing problems.

We will see that while in general it is impossible in practice to remove aliasing effects from our images, we usually can contain them or change their character so they are less annoying.

This unit of the book presents material from the field of signal processing that is relevant to computer graphics. Our goal will be to develop an understanding of aliasing, both in the time and frequency domains. Our principal tool in this analysis will be the Fourier transform.

In this part, I include most of the steps in various derivations and transformations. If you get lost between some pair of equations, a good technique is to expand everything out in both equations, and look for the simplifications that turn one into the other. When a transformation goes beyond basic manipulation by using an identity or other powerful tool, I will always mention it. I have also included several tables of useful identities and properties to which we will refer throughout the book.

The traditional signal processing we cover in this chapter is a well-understood body of knowledge. It is quite clean and elegant from a mathematical point of view, once you get past the sometimes daunting notation. I have tried to make the notation as straightforward as possible in this chapter, but much of the heart of signal processing comes about from transformations on equations that seem to inevitably contain a lot of subscripts, superscripts, limits, and other necessary clutter. The equations are typographically complex, but most are simple in concept.

There are many books on digital signal processing listed at the end of these chapters. What I have tried to do here is to select and present just the parts that are most important to rendering. I have tried to be as clear as possible in the discussion and the derivations, but I have not always been rigorous. For example, continuity, integrability, and other necessary conditions are often assumed, but not proven. The goal in these chapters is to present the general ideas behind digital signal processing in a way that makes them useful for computer graphics.

Before we begin, it may be helpful to take a bird's-eye view of the entire process. This is presented in Figure A for a 1D signal, and in Figure C for a 2D signal (or image). The general idea is that we start with some 1D function (say $a(t)$) that is defined for all values of its argument t, and eventually end up with something that we present to an observer (using a CRT or other output device), labeled k in the figure. What happens in between is the subject matter of this unit.

Let's look at the general flow of information; all of these steps will be examined in much more detail in the chapters in this unit. The general goal is that we want signal k to look as much like signal a as we can. But we're frustrated in that desire because we assume that we are only allowed to gather *point samples* of a, represented in c. The goal then is to somehow get something like a out of c. Anticipating the basic ideas of this unit, we will use the words "signal" and "function" interchangeably. We will also be a bit informal with the rest of our terms; we'll sharpen them considerably as we move through the book. We will sometimes think of the function as a picture we want to show; think of it as a grey-level image so we don't get bogged down with questions about color right now.

We begin with a, which is defined at all points t; this might be any kind of function or procedure. We begin by gathering *samples* of a at particular points that are given by b, which is a row of pulses that are so narrow they select just a single value from a. If we multiply together these two functions we get c, which is 0 everywhere except where there's a pulse in b; at those places, c has the value of a. This is the process of *sampling*, and it's typically implemented in a rendering system by a ray-tracer, z-buffer scan coverter, or similar visibility algorithm.

Now we only constructed c in this way because we assumed that we were forced to (that is, a was so complicated the only information we could get out of it was a set of point samples). The signal c doesn't look much like a at all; it's basically a flat function with a few spikes. It may seem reasonable to simply connect the spikes to approximate a, and in fact that's one way to go. But we will see that theoretically the best way to look at this is to *convolve* c with a *filter* given by d. In this case, that means we place one (reversed) copy of d on top of each spike in c, scaling that copy of d so it has the same height as c at the spike. This act of *convolution* (symbolized by a star ($*$)) results in e. In this case, d serves to simply connect the spikes, but a different choice of d would combine the spikes in a different way.

Now we will suppose that we want to show the signal on a display device that can only switch between color values at a finite number of places. For example, on color hardcopy devices this is the smallest blob of ink the printer can make. Typically the printer lays down a blob of ink of a certain color, and then moves the print head just

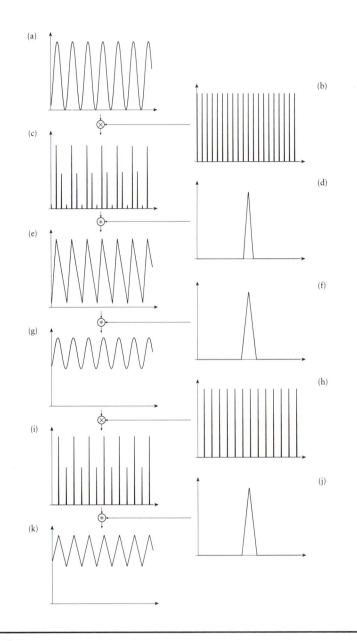

FIGURE A

The general flow of a 1D signal from definition to display. (a) The input signal a. (b) A set of equally spaced sampling pulses b. (c) The product signal ab, formed by multiplying the two signals (or *sampling* signal a). (d) A *reconstruction filter*. (e) The signal $c * d$, formed by *convolving* signal c with the filter d. (f) A *low-pass filter*. (g) The result of convolving e with f. (h) A new set of sampling pulses. (i) The product gh. (j) The *display reconstruction filter*. (k) The displayed signal $i * j$.

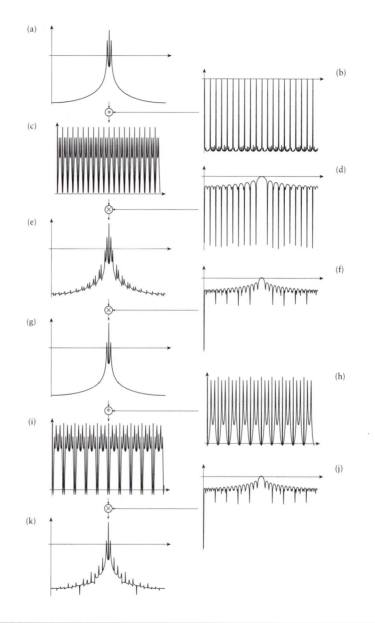

FIGURE B

The Fourier transform of the general flow of the 1D signal in Figure A from definition to display.

a bit in order to lay down the next blob. We have no control over what happens between the blobs; the inks combine or not as they may. A CRT is similar; we can choose what color we want to display at a finite number of locations on the screen, but what happens between them depends on the physical device. For a given density of display samples, there will be some signals we can't show. For example, if we can display a maximum of 100 dots per inch, then we just won't be able to show a sine wave with a frequency of 1,000 dots per inch. So we *filter* the signal before sampling it, this time trying to get rid of any wiggles in the signal that might be happening between our samples.

We smooth out the signal in *e* by convolving it with another filter, shown in *f*. The convolution is a little trickier to see in this case since we place a (reversed) copy of *f* over *every* point in *e*. We actually did this with *d* before, but because most of *c* was zero, we never saw those copies. The result is the signal *g*.

Now we're ready to figure out what to display. We make up another set of samples represented by *h* to stand for the frame buffer memory locations and multiply that with *g*; that gives us *i*. Each spike of *i* corresponds to a color we will show. If the pulses in *h* correspond to pixel centers, then each pulse in *i* gives the intensity at that pixel.

But we're not done quite yet. Recall that once we've displayed a color in a frame buffer, or printed it on a page, the color bleeds or the ink smears, depending on the output device. Mathematically, what's happening is that our signal *i* is getting convolved with a function like *j* that tells how the device spreads around each of our samples when it's displayed. The resulting convolved signal is shown in *k*. This is the signal that actually gets displayed.

The exact same process is shown for images in 2D. Here the original signal *a* is the ideal function that represents the world that we want to render. Signal *c* is the result of ray-tracing or scan-converting the scene, and *i* is what we store in the frame buffer or output file. Signal *j* is the characteristic response of the monitor or printer, so what we end up seeing is signal *k*.

The whole trick of signal processing is to get each of these steps just right: we want to pick the right places to sample (that is, place the pulses in *b*), and we want to use just the right filters in *d* and *f* to process the signal. We want to do this all efficiently and accurately.

In this unit we will spend a lot of time designing the sampling signal shown in *b*. We will be guided by what we call The Sampler's Credo: *every sample is precious*. This is motivated by the fact that rendering is often very expensive; in scenes with millions of objects, every sample can take a long time to compute and involve many visibility and shading calculations. We don't want to waste even one, and we don't want to compute even one that we don't really need. To make sure we get enough samples, we have to use every bit of knowledge we can about *a*, even to the point of building up that knowledge as we sample.

We need to choose our *reconstruction filter* in *d* so that we recover a good approximation to a in signal c (joining the dots together with straight lines is easy, but not very smooth; we can do better). Then we need to choose a good *low-pass filter* in f so that we get rid of the quickly varying parts of the signal that we can't display. Typically, we're given the sampling density in h as a characteristic of the hardware and we can't do anything about it. So we have to smooth out the inappropriate quickly changing parts of e prior to its resampling by h with as little damage as possible to the parts that we can represent.

The multiplication steps in this diagram are straightforward, but the convolution steps may seem pretty weird. It turns out that they're easy to understand if we take the *Fourier transform* of the various signals. This gives us a similar but different version of each function. The steps where we convolve functions then become multiplications of the Fourier representations, which have a very intuitive interpretation. For reference, the Fourier transform for Figure A is shown in Figure B, and the Fourier transform for Figure C is shown in Figure D. Notice that the multiplication operators have been replaced by convolution, and vice versa. This duality of multiplication and convolution is an important part of Fourier analysis.

The goal of this unit of the book is to introduce those parts of digital signal processing that are necessary to understand these figures, because they represent what has to happen inside a rendering program. Sometimes one or more of these steps is left out or ignored, and sometimes that's justifiable; often, though, it isn't, and the result is that we get artifacts in our pictures.

It's my opinion that a good understanding of rendering requires a good understanding of this flow of information, and that requires a good intuitive feeling for the Fourier transform. Chapter 4 starts the unit with the definition of signals and systems. We then build to the Fourier transform in Chapter 5 (and in Chapter 6 we discuss its more recent cousin, the wavelet transform). The convolution operation can be performed as an integration, which can be performed efficiently for very complex signals (such as those in graphics) using *Monte Carlo* methods; we discuss these in Chapter 7. We then lock down the interpretation of Figure A with a few fundamental theorems in Chapter 8 that tell us exactly how to build our filters in d and f given the sampling patterns in b and h under some specific conditions. Chapter 9 takes a look at the more complicated problems that arise when the samples are not uniformly spaced; that is, the pulses in b are not all the same distance apart. After building up all this theory, we turn to practice in Chapter 10 where we survey the algorithms people have developed to turn this theory into efficient and practical rendering techniques.

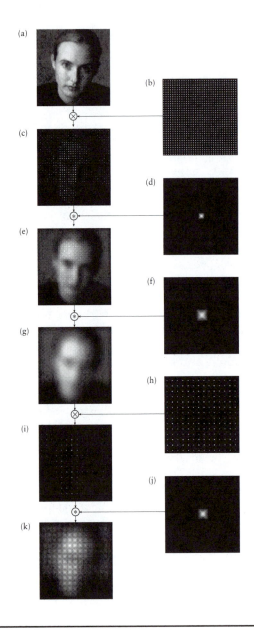

FIGURE C

The general flow of a 2D signal from definition to display. (a) The input signal a. (b) A set of equally spaced sampling pulses b. (c) The product signal ab, formed by multiplying the two signals (or *sampling* signal a). (d) A *reconstruction filter*. (e) The signal $c * d$, formed by *convolving* signal c with the filter d. (f) A *low-pass filter*. (g) The result of convolving e with f. (h) A new set of sampling pulses. (i) The product gh. (j) The *display reconstruction filter*. (k) The displayed signal $i * j$.

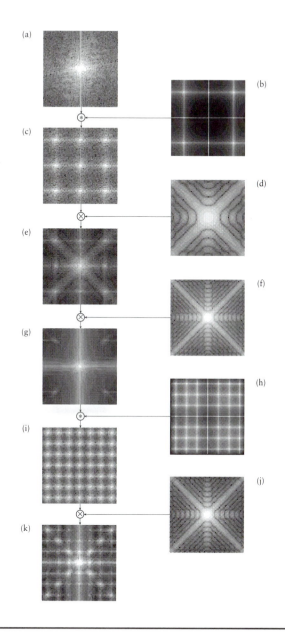

FIGURE D

The Fourier transform of the general flow of the 2D signal in Figure C from definition to display.

Far more important than the nomenclature are the underlying concepts. We introduce nomenclature only in order to be able to talk about the concepts.

F. E. Nicodemus et al.
("Geometrical Considerations and Nomenclature for Reflectance," 1977)

4

SIGNALS AND SYSTEMS

4.1 Introduction

In this book we will think of synthetic images as multidimensional *signals*. This chapter presents the basic tools for defining and discussing signals and the systems that modify them. We will present several different types of signals and the different types of information they can represent. We will also discuss the concept of different *spaces* for representing signals. We show some notation that will prove useful later in the book, and present a short catalog of useful idealized signals that we will use as canonical examples.

We will discuss a fundamental technique for characterizing systems, and show which signals pass through a system unchanged except for scale.

4.2 Types of Signals and Systems

For our purposes, a *signal* is any parametric function, of any number of input and output dimensions, for which we would like to find individual values, or average

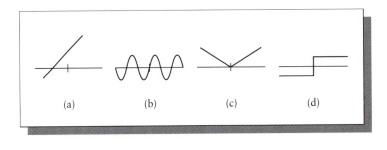

FIGURE 4.1

(a) $y(x) = 2x + 3$ is smooth and continuous. (b) $y(x) = \sin(x)$ is smooth and continuous. (c) $y(x) = |x|$ is not smooth, but continuous. (d) $y(x) = \text{sgn}(x)$ is neither smooth nor continuous.

values, within some range of the arguments. For example, signals include the distribution of light on a screen, the light falling on a point on a surface or in space, or the description of a reflection function on a surface. Since both signals and mathematical functions have only one value for any set of parameters, we use the terms *signal* and *function* interchangeably.

4.2.1 Continuous-Time (CT) Signals

The conceptual side of computer graphics often deals with *continuous-time* (CT) (or *analytic*) signals. These have a symbolic representation that enable us to evaluate them for any parameter value; examples include $y(x) = 2x + 3$ and $y(x) = \sin(x)$, which are plotted in Figure 4.1(a) and (b). An analytic signal need not be *smooth* (i.e., differentiable everywhere), or *continuous* (i.e., unbroken).

The term "continuous-time" is unfortunate, because it implies that the parameter to the function is a time value. In fact, this parameter (or *argument*) may represent anything, including time, so perhaps "continuous-parameter" would be a better term. But the term "continuous-time" is firmly established in the literature, so we will use it here.

The concepts of a *continuous-time* signal and a *continuous* signal are distinct; the former term only refers to the analytic representation of the function. Figure 4.1(c) and (d) show plots of the functions $y(x) = |x|$ and $y(x) = \text{sgn}(x)$; the former is not smooth, and the latter is neither smooth nor continuous, but both are continuous-time signals, since they can be evaluated for any value of their parameter x.

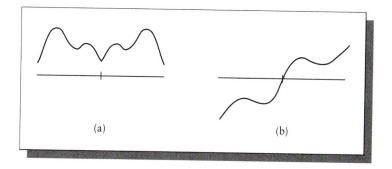

FIGURE 4.2

(a) An even function $f(x) = f(-x)$. (b) An odd function $f(x) = -f(-x)$.

The term "continuous" is often used in the signal processing literature when the more precise term "continuous-time" is meant. The appropriate meaning is usually clear from context. When there is possible confusion, I will use the full term "continuous-time" (or its acronym CT).

We will write analytic signals with parentheses around the index, as $f(x)$. The index will typically be x or t, referring to spatial position or time. These letters may be considered generic indices; the arguments will apply equally well for any interpretation of the parameter. Our arguments to analytic functions will typically be either real or complex vectors of one or more components. We will sometimes write $f(t)$ simply as f for convenience.

We say a signal is *even* if it is symmetrical about the origin; that is, for all x, $f(x) = f(-x)$, as illustrated in Figure 4.2(a). A signal is *odd* if it is antisymmetrical about the origin; that is, for all x, $f(x) = -f(-x)$, as illustrated in Figure 4.2(b). One mnemonic for this definition is to remember that x^2 is even (2 is even) and x^3 is odd (3 is odd). Another common example that will be valuable to us later is that cosine is even and sine is odd.

4.2.2 Discrete-Time (DT) Signals

The practical side of computer graphics usually deals with *discrete-time* (DT) signals, also called *discrete* or *sampled* signals. These are signals that are only defined at particular, discrete locations (typically integer values of the index parameter).

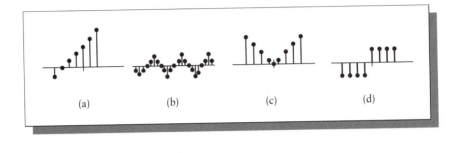

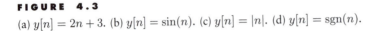

FIGURE 4.3

(a) $y[n] = 2n + 3$. (b) $y[n] = \sin(n)$. (c) $y[n] = |n|$. (d) $y[n] = \mathrm{sgn}(n)$.

Sampled counterparts of Figure 4.1 are shown in Figure 4.3. Notions of smoothness and continuity do not have analogs in discrete signals.

We will write discrete signals with brackets around the index, as $f[n]$. The index will typically be i, k, m, or n, referring generically to any integer.

Because computers store real numbers with finite precision, signals are usually *quantized* when they are evaluated. Sometimes we can avoid this problem by storing our samples in a symbolic form (e.g., $\sqrt{3}/2$ instead of 0.866), but most often we store the results numerically, and thus surrender to the limited precision of the computer. Although floating-point numbers are notoriously nonuniform in the quality with which they can represent real values, even naïve programming seems to perform surprisingly well in general. A careful analysis of the quantization error in a computer program is notoriously difficult [3, 353]; for the most part we will ignore this issue in this book and assume that our floating-point number representations are perfect.

4.2.3 Periodic Signals

A signal is *periodic* if there exists some real number T, called the *period* of the signal, such that for all x, $f(x + T) = f(x)$, as shown in Figure 4.4. If a function is not periodic, then it is *aperiodic*. By convention, T is positive; this saves us from needing some absolute-value signs later on. The most common form of aperiodic signal in practice is one that is everywhere 0 to the left and right of some interval. Any signal that is zero outside of some finite fixed interval (called the *active interval*, the *support interval*, or the *region of support*) is said to have *compact support*. We encounter signals with compact support all the time in computer graphics. For example, an

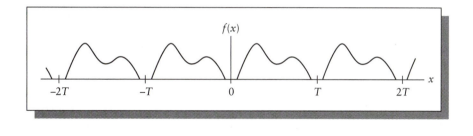

FIGURE 4.4

A periodic function with interval T: $f(x + T) = f(x)$.

image is 0 beyond the boundary of the raster, light starts streaming into a scene at some time and then stops some time later, and objects are at rest, then move, and then come to rest again. These are all aperiodic signals with fixed support.

We will often form periodic signals by repeating an aperiodic signal. To make a periodic signal $g(t)$ with period T from an aperiodic signal $f(t)$, we write

$$g(t) = \sum_{k=-\infty}^{+\infty} f(t - kT) \tag{4.1}$$

Because this notational fragment will recur frequently in this book, it is worth spending a moment now to become familiar with this idiom. It is most common in the case where $f(t)$ has compact support; that is, $f(t) = 0$ for all $|t| > t_f$, as in Figure 4.5(a).

Equation 4.1 builds a new signal $g(t)$ from $f(t)$ by repeating it every T units (for the moment, we assume $T > 2t_f$, so the copies don't overlap). Suppose we know the value of $f(s)$ for some real number $-T/2 < s < T/2$. Then $g(s) = \cdots + f(s-T) + f(s) + f(s+T) + \cdots = f(s)$, since only the value at $f(s)$ is nonzero. Now suppose we want the value of $g(s + T)$. Using Equation 4.1 we find that

$$
\begin{aligned}
g(s+T) &= \cdots + f((s+T)+T) + f((s+T)) + f((s+T)-T) + f((s+T)-2T) + \cdots \\
&= \cdots + \quad f(s+2T) \quad + \quad f(s+T) + \quad\quad f(s) \quad\quad + \quad f(s-T) \quad + \cdots
\end{aligned}
\tag{4.2}
$$

All these values are 0 except $f(s)$; thus, $g(s+T) = f(s)$, so $g(t)$ is a periodic version of $f(t)$ with period T, as shown in Figure 4.5(b). If $T \leq t_f$, then the repeated copies of $f(t)$ will overlap and sum together, as in Figure 4.5(c).

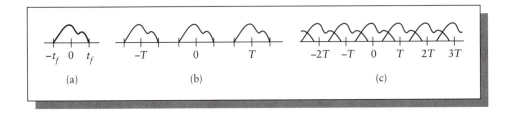

FIGURE 4.5

(a) The signal $f(t)$, which is zero for all $|t| > t_f$. (b) The signal $g(t) = \sum_k f(t - kT)$. This repeats the input signal every T units. (c) When $T \leq t_f$, the copies of f will overlap.

4.2.4   Linear Time-Invariant Systems

Anything that alters a signal may be considered a *system*. For example, a concert hall may be considered a system. In this case, think of the sound of a violin as a signal represented by the amplitude of sound with respect to time. So a concert hall changes an input signal (a violin played on stage) to an output signal (the particular sound you hear at some particular seat). In computer graphics, our systems will typically be programs, acting either as models of physical systems or in more abstract settings. For example, a program to calculate reflection is often based on a physical reflection model, while color-space transformations are abstract operations.

The easiest class of systems to understand are *linear* systems. For example, suppose we have a system $\mathcal{L}$ that *maps* (or transforms) some input $x(t)$ to an output $y(t)$. We write $y(t) = \mathcal{L}\{x(t)\}$; in mathematical terms, $\mathcal{L}$ is an *operator*. An operator may be imagined as a device that takes in some object as an argument and returns some new object, which is not necessarily of the same type as the input. In this case $\mathcal{L}$ takes as input a function $x(t)$, and returns a new function $y(t)$. When we drop the explicit argument, we write $\mathcal{L}\{x\}$, which we often abbreviate simply as $\mathcal{L}x$. To return the argument into this last form, we parenthesize the new operated-upon function, writing $y(t) = (\mathcal{L}x)(t)$.

We say that $\mathcal{L}$ is *linear* if, for any two scalars a and b, and any two signals $f(t)$ and $g(t)$, the following is true:

$$\mathcal{L}\{af + bg\} = a\mathcal{L}\{f\} + b\mathcal{L}\{g\} \tag{4.3}$$

This important definition, diagrammed in Figure 4.6, is actually two definitions in one. The first states that if we scale an input to the system, the output is an equally scaled version of the output to an unscaled version of the input. In symbols,

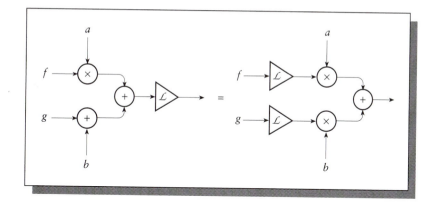

FIGURE 4.6

$\mathcal{L}\{af + bg\} = a\mathcal{L}\{f\} + b\mathcal{L}\{g\}.$

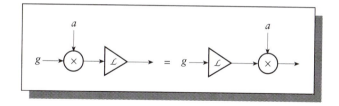

FIGURE 4.7

$\mathcal{L}\{ag\} = a\mathcal{L}\{g\}.$

$\mathcal{L}\{ag\} = a\mathcal{L}\{g\}$; this is diagrammed in Figure 4.7. The second property states that the response to the sum of two signals is equal to the sum of the responses to the individual signals; in symbols, $\mathcal{L}\{f + g\} = \mathcal{L}\{f\} + \mathcal{L}\{g\}$. This is diagrammed in Figure 4.8. These properties are at the foundation of many simplifying assumptions that make linear systems easy to analyze and describe. In most of this book, we will discuss only linear systems.

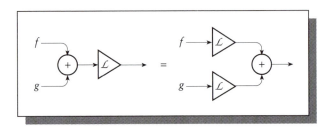

FIGURE 4.8
$\mathcal{L}\{f + g\} = \mathcal{L}\{f\} + \mathcal{L}\{g\}.$

Our definition of a linear system includes many operators with which we are familiar. Addition and multiplication are linear, as are summation and integration, though the functions square root and floor are not.

If a system obeys Equation 4.3 for real numbers a and b, we say the system is *real-linear*. If it also holds when a and b are complex numbers (discussed below), we say the system is *complex-linear*.

One property we will often exploit is that since integration and summation are linear operators, we can move another linear operator $\mathcal{L}$ through them:

$$\mathcal{L}\left\{\int f(t)\,dt\right\} = \int \mathcal{L}\{f(t)\}\,dt$$

$$\mathcal{L}\left\{\sum_{k=-\infty}^{+\infty} f[k]\right\} = \sum_{k=-\infty}^{+\infty} \mathcal{L}\{f[k]\} \tag{4.4}$$

We will use linearity properties often in this book.

In addition to linearity, we will further restrict our attention to *time-invariant* systems. These are systems that respond the same way no matter when the signal arrives. For example, consider an idealized concert hall, where properties such as temperature and humidity are constant. If you clap your hands in such a hall, you create a sudden pulse of sound that reverberates through the space in a particular way characteristic of that room. If you clap your hands again a minute or two later, the response is the same; the time you applied the signal is not relevant. This is an example of a *time-invariant* system. In symbols,

$$\text{if } y(t) = f(x(t)), \text{ then } y(t - \tau) = f(x(t - \tau)) \text{ for any } \tau \tag{4.5}$$

No real-world physical systems are truly time-invariant. As an example of a system that is not time-invariant, consider the energy required to make a pot of cold water boil. Initially the pot is cold, so you must not only heat the water but the pot as well. Once the water is boiling, you can pour it out and replace it with new cold water. Since the pot is already hot, you need less energy to bring this new pot of water to a boil than you needed for the first pot. So the same input (a fresh pot of cold water) produces different results, depending on what has gone before. The output of a time-invariant system to a given signal is always the same, while the output of a time-variant system to the same signal depends on the signals that have come before.

A discrete system obeying the similar rule

$$\text{if } y[n] = f(x[n]), \text{ then } y[n - m] = f(x[n - m]) \text{ for any } m \qquad (4.6)$$

is called *shift-invariant*. These terms are usually written as acronyms, so the linear, time-invariant property is written LTI, and similarly, a linear, shift-invariant system is an LSI system.

In most of this book we will discuss only LTI and LSI systems. Systems that are either nonlinear, time-variant, or both are usually much more difficult to analyze and understand, though chaos, fuzzy logic, and complexity theory are making fascinating progress [2, 161, 226, 227, 253].

4.3 Notation

In this section we present some pieces of notation and terminology that will simplify the discussions throughout the book.

4.3.1 The Real Numbers

The set of all real numbers is denoted by $\mathcal{R}$. To indicate that any particular number r is real, we write it as a member of this set: $r \in \mathcal{R}$. The symbol for the reals is sometimes used to indicate the *domain* (or set of possible inputs) for a function. If a function f takes a real number to another real (e.g., $f(x) = 3x$), we say that f *maps* the reals into the reals. We say the same thing symbolically as $f \colon \mathcal{R} \mapsto \mathcal{R}$.

In computer graphics we often deal with spaces with more than one dimension. A vertex V of a polygon, for example, may be specified by three real numbers. We say that V is drawn from a space built from three reals by writing $V \in \mathcal{R}^3$. A matrix $\mathbf{M}$ that transforms the vertices of a polygon from one 3D orientation to another may be said to map $V \in \mathcal{R}^3$ to $V' \in \mathcal{R}^3$, or $\mathbf{M} \colon \mathcal{R}^3 \mapsto \mathcal{R}^3$.

4.3.2 The Integers

The set of integers is denoted by $\mathcal{Z}$. Thus if we write $k \in \mathcal{Z}$, we are saying that k can take on any negative or positive integer value, including 0. The canonical integers are denoted by letters from i to n, inclusive (although j will always stand for the square root of -1, as discussed in more detail below).

A function $f[n]$ which maps an integer to a real, such as $f[n] = \sqrt{n}$, can be written $f \colon \mathcal{Z} \mapsto \mathcal{R}$.

An important subset of the integers are the *integers mod N*. The word *mod* stands for modulo arithmetic; the value of $a \bmod b$ is the remainder when a is divided by b. For example, $2 \bmod 3 = 8 \bmod 3 = 2$. We write the set of integers modulo some number N as $\mathcal{Z}/N$. For example, $\mathcal{Z}/5 = \{0, 1, 2, 3, 4\}$, and the binary group $\mathcal{Z}/2 = \{0, 1\}$. Anyone who has worked with integers on a computer has had experience with modulo arithmetic. An 8-bit register can hold the integers from 0 to 255. Thus, in $\mathcal{Z}/256$, the sum $255 + 1 = 0$. We will write this $255 + 1 = 0 \ (\bmod\ 256)$, when the nature of the arithmetic isn't clear from the context. In general, the set $\mathcal{Z}/N = \{0, 1, 2, \ldots, N - 1\}$.

4.3.3 Intervals

An *interval* is a range of real or integer values. Explicitly, if a is bounded by two values a_0 and a_1 such that $a_0 \le a_1$, then the interval of all a satisfying $a_0 \le a \le a_1$ is written $[a_0, a_1]$. If a is not intended to actually include its *lower bound* a_0, then we use a round parenthesis for the left extreme: $a \in (a_0, a_1]$. Similarly, we can exclude the *upper bound*, $a \in [a_0, a_1)$, or both.

This notation is motivated by the problem of partitioning an interval. Suppose we have an interval $A = [a, c]$, where $a < b < c$. Then we can partition A into two pieces $A_1 = [a, b)$ and $A_2 = [b, c]$. Together, $A_1 \cup A_2 = A$, as in Figure 4.9(a). If we defined A_1 to include b at its upper limit and A_2 to include b at its lower limit, then we would have b represented twice when the sets were combined as in Figure 4.9(b). This notation allows us to place b in only one set, avoiding the problem. Two sets with no common elements are *disjoint*.

A single scalar a may be represented by a *degenerate* interval $[a, a]$. Sometimes it is useful to specify just the size of an interval without fixing it to a particular starting value. We call this a *free interval* and write it as $[a]$. Thus $[a]$ represents the interval $[g, a + g]$ for any g. We will often see $[N] = [0, 1, \ldots, N - 2, N - 1]$. In general, when we write $k \in [N]$, we mean any sequence $[k, k + 1, \ldots, k + N - 2, k + N - 1] \bmod N$. So $[5] = [0, 1, 2, 3, 4]$, though we could interpret it as $[5] = [2, 3, 4, 0, 1]$, since where we start doesn't matter.

In this book, we will represent intervals with capital Greek letters (e.g., Γ and Λ).

If an interval is restricted to the integers, then there are only a finite number of values in that range. For example, the *integer interval* $[0, 5]$ is $[0, 1, 2, 3, 4, 5]$, while

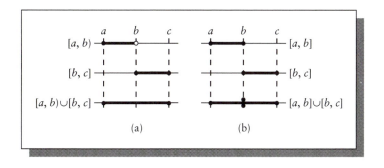

FIGURE 4.9

(a) $[a, b) \cup [b, c]$. (b) $[a, b] \cup [b, c]$ duplicates b.

the *real interval* $[0, 5]$ contains an infinite number of values. We can distinguish these types of intervals by writing $\Gamma \in \mathcal{Z}$ or $\Gamma_{\mathcal{Z}}$ for an integer interval, and similarly $\Gamma \in \mathcal{R}$ or $\Gamma_{\mathcal{R}}$ for a real interval.

4.3.4 Product Spaces

It is often convenient to bundle up two or more spaces into one composite space. For example, the function $f(a, k) = ak$ multiplies together a real number $a \in \mathcal{R}$ and an integer $k \in \mathcal{Z}$. So the domain of this function is both the set of reals and the set of integers. We combine these two individual domains with the operator $\otimes$, which is called the *Cartesian product operator*, so the resulting space is called a *Cartesian product space*. The resulting space is a combined space; if we form the Cartesian product of the integers and the reals, we get a new space that has an integer component and a real. An element of this space would be a pair of numbers, say an integer k and a real a: $(k, a) \in \mathcal{Z} \otimes \mathcal{R}$. We would write f as taking an argument from the product space and returning a real: $f : \mathcal{R} \otimes \mathcal{Z} \mapsto \mathcal{R}$, indicating that it takes a real and an integer and returns a real.

As another example, consider the function $g = a\mathbf{U}$, which scales a 3D vector $\mathbf{U}$ by a real number a. The domain is thus formed by the Cartesian product of the real numbers $\mathcal{R}$ and the 3D vectors $\mathcal{R}^3$, so $g : \mathcal{R} \otimes \mathcal{R}^3 \mapsto \mathcal{R}^3$.

A related idea is the *Cartesian sum*, written $\oplus$, which forms the union of two spaces. Since the reals contain the integers, the Cartesian sum of the reals and the integers is just the reals: $\mathcal{Z} \oplus \mathcal{R} = \mathcal{R}$, and the Cartesian sum of the reals and the reals

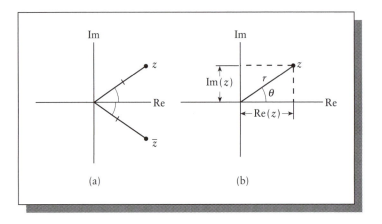

FIGURE 4.10

(a) The Argand diagram for a point z and its conjugate $\bar{z}$.   (b) A point $z = (x, y) = (r\cos(\theta), r\sin(\theta))$.

is just the reals again: $\mathcal{R} \oplus \mathcal{R} = \mathcal{R}$. For example, if we had a (admittedly strange) function that accepted as arguments only the integers mod 5 and the reals, we would write its input domain as $[5] \oplus \mathcal{R}$ (or $\mathcal{R} \oplus [5]$, since union is commutative).

4.3.5 The Complex Numbers

A *complex number* is a pair of real numbers: $z = (a, b)$. Complex numbers may be interpreted in a variety of ways. One common approach is to write the number as the sum of *real* and *imaginary* components.

Imaginary numbers involve the square root of -1. In this book I adopt the electrical engineer's notation and use j for this value: $j^2 = -1$. The other common choice for this symbol is the letter i. I chose j because it is widely used, and because i is a canonical integer index in much of computer science and this book. So we can *define* $z = a + jb$. We write the real part of z as $\mathrm{Re}(z) = a$ and the imaginary part as $\mathrm{Im}(z) = b$. The set of all complex numbers is represented by $\mathcal{C}$.

Complex numbers are often plotted on an *Argand diagram*, shown in Figure 4.10. This is a standard 2D grid, with the x axis identified with the real component of z and the y axis identified with the imaginary component. Thus a point (x, y) corresponds to the complex number $x + jy$.

The *complex conjugate* of any real number z is written as $\bar{z}$ or z^*; we will use the former notation in this book. The complex conjugate is found by negating the imaginary component (or, graphically, by reflecting the point across the x axis). Thus $\bar{z} = a - jb$, as in Figure 4.10(a).

An alternative to the Cartesian system of the Argand diagram is the polar coordinate system. Here each point (r, θ) is expressed by its radius r and angle θ measured counterclockwise from the x axis. The two systems are related by $(x, y) = (r \cos \theta, r \sin \theta)$, as in Figure 4.10(b).

In a 2D coordinate system such as Figure 4.10, the distance from the origin to any point P with coordinates (P_x, P_y) is found by $\sqrt{P_x^2 + P_y^2}$. By analogy, we can write the squared *magnitude* of a complex number z as $|z|^2 = z\bar{z} = (a + jb)(a - jb) = (a^2 + b^2)$. We say the *phase* or *angle* of a complex number is given by its angle in the polar interpretation, so the phase of a complex number z is given by the inverse tangent of the angle θ in Figure 4.10(b): $\angle z = \tan^{-1}[\text{Re}(z)/\text{Im}(z)]$.

Since every real number a may be considered a complex number $a + 0j$, we say that the real numbers are a subset of the complex numbers: $\mathcal{R} \subset \mathcal{C}$. In this chapter we will see continuous functions $f(z)$, which map complex numbers to new complex numbers. We often say that the domain $\mathcal{C}$ is mapped onto itself, or that the function maps the complex numbers onto themselves. We say that f is a *complex-valued complex function* if $f : \mathcal{C} \mapsto \mathcal{C}$. Note that such a class of functions includes the *real-valued real functions* $f : \mathcal{R} \mapsto \mathcal{R}$, the *real-valued complex functions* $f : \mathcal{C} \mapsto \mathcal{R}$, and the *complex-valued real functions* $f : \mathcal{R} \mapsto \mathcal{C}$ as special cases. For all functions $f : \mathcal{A} \mapsto \mathcal{B}$, we call $\mathcal{A}$ the *domain* of f, and $\mathcal{B}$ the *range*.

Another handy feature of real numbers is that they are their own complex conjugates: $a + 0j = a - 0j$. So if we have a function $f(x) \in \mathcal{R}$, then for all x, $\overline{f(x)} = f(x)$. This will prove useful when writing formulas later on, particularly with the *braket notation* discussed below.

A *Hermite* function $f(t)$ is one that is symmetrical about the origin except for conjugation; that is, it satisfies $f(t) = \overline{f(-t)}$.

If a system $\mathcal{L}$ is linear, then its real and imaginary parts are processed independently. That is, $\mathcal{L}\{z\} = \mathcal{L}\{\text{Re}(z)\} + j\mathcal{L}\{\text{Im}(z)\}$. So to transform a purely real signal, we can attach any imaginary part, do the transform, and then ignore the imaginary.

4.3.6 Assignment and Equality

The symbol $\overset{\triangle}{=}$ is used in this book to indicate a *definition* (some authors use $\equiv$ or simply $=$).

The equal sign $=$ is often used in computer languages to indicate *assignment* to a variable. In pseudocode we will use the left arrow ← to indicate assignment. The equal sign will be used only to express equality between two expressions.

4.3.7 Summation and Integration

We will often write summations and integrations over the reals or the integers. To reduce notational clutter, we will define shorthand forms for these operators.

For infinite summations, we will indicate the index k over the range $[-\infty, \infty]$ either by $k \in \mathcal{Z}$, or simply with the argument k:

$$\sum_{k} \stackrel{\triangle}{=} \sum_{k \in \mathcal{Z}} \stackrel{\triangle}{=} \sum_{k=-\infty}^{+\infty} \tag{4.7}$$

For infinite integrals, the integrand is in the argument, so we write

$$\int dt \stackrel{\triangle}{=} \int_{-\infty}^{+\infty} dt \tag{4.8}$$

We will often sum over the integer interval $[0, N) = [0, N-1] = [N]$ for some N. We define

$$\sum_{k \in [N]} \stackrel{\triangle}{=} \sum_{k=0}^{N-1} \tag{4.9}$$

4.3.8 The Complex Exponentials

A famous identity due to Euler is

$$e^{j\theta} = \cos\theta + j\sin\theta \tag{4.10}$$

where e is the base of the natural logarithm; $e \approx 2.71828$ [458]. This type of complex-valued function is called a *complex exponential* or *complex sinusoid*. Proof of the identity can be found by writing out the Taylor series for e^t, and noticing its relationship to the Taylor series for sine and cosine.

Euler's identity can be used to generate many other identities that will come in handy when we perform symbolic manipulations on complex numbers. Table 4.1 lists many of these identities, along with the definition above and some standard results on exponentials from trig, algebra, and calculus. They are labeled E1 through E21 so that we can later refer to different properties efficiently, though several are simple variations on another. Some of the less obvious but useful identities are left as exercises. We will use some of the more powerful identities later on to simplify

E1	$e^{j\alpha} = \cos(\alpha) + j\sin(\alpha)$
E2	$\text{Re}(e^{j\alpha}) = \cos(\alpha)$
E3	$\text{Im}(e^{j\alpha}) = \sin(\alpha)$
E4	$e^{j\alpha}\,\overline{e^{j\alpha}} = 1$
E5	$|e^{-j\alpha}| = 1$
E6	$e^{-j\alpha} = \overline{(e^{j\alpha})}$
E7	$e^{j\alpha_1}e^{j\alpha_2} = e^{j(\alpha_1+\alpha_2)}$
E8	$e^{j\alpha}e^{-j\alpha} = 1$
E9	$e^{j2\pi k+\alpha} = e^{\alpha}$ for $k \in \mathcal{Z}$
E10	$\dfrac{d}{dx}\left(e^{u}\right) = e^{u}\dfrac{du}{dx}$
E11	$\displaystyle\int e^{\alpha t}dt = e^{\alpha t}/\alpha$
E12	$\dfrac{e^{j\alpha} - e^{-j\alpha}}{2j} = \sin(\alpha)$
E13	$\dfrac{e^{j\alpha} + e^{-j\alpha}}{2j} = \cos(\alpha)$
E14	$1 - e^{-j\alpha} = e^{-j(\alpha/2)}\left[e^{j(\alpha/2)} - e^{-j(\alpha/2)}\right]$
E15	$\displaystyle\sum_{m=0}^{W} e^{-j\alpha m} = e^{(-j\alpha W/2)}\dfrac{\sin\left(\frac{\alpha}{2}(W+1)\right)}{\sin\left(\frac{\alpha}{2}\right)}$ $\qquad \alpha \neq k2\pi, k \in \mathcal{Z}$
E16	$\displaystyle\sum_{m=-W}^{W} e^{-j\alpha m} = \dfrac{\sin\left(\frac{\alpha}{2}(2W+1)\right)}{\sin\left(\frac{\alpha}{2}\right)}$ $\qquad \alpha \neq k2\pi, k \in \mathcal{Z}$
E17	$e^{j2\pi k} = 1$ for $k \in \mathcal{Z}$
E18	$e^{0} = 1$
E19	$\dfrac{e^{j\alpha} - e^{-j\alpha}}{e^{j\beta} - e^{-j\beta}} = \dfrac{\sin(\alpha)}{\sin(\beta)}$ $\qquad \beta \neq k\pi, k \in \mathcal{Z}$
E20	$\displaystyle\int e^{-\pi u^2}du = 1$
E21	$\displaystyle\int_{-W}^{W} e^{-j\alpha t}dt = 2W\,\text{sinc}(\alpha W/\pi)$

TABLE 4.1
Some properties of the complex exponentials.

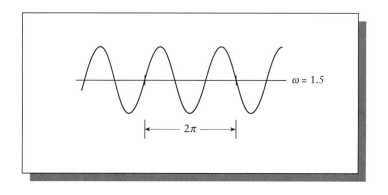

FIGURE 4.11

A sinusoid passes through ω cycles in a time period of 2π.

taking forward and inverse Fourier transforms. The sinc function in E21 will be introduced in Section 4.4.4.

We can see from Euler's relation that a complex exponential is a sum of sine and cosine terms. Since each of these is periodic with period 2π, the whole complex exponential is also periodic with period 2π. It is common to write the exponential with a mixed exponent involving both *frequency* ω and *time* t, as in $e^{j\omega t}$, and associate with it a period T:

$$T = 2\pi/\omega \qquad (4.11)$$

The frequency is determined by ω, while t typically sweeps out the complex sinusoid of that frequency. These terms are motivated by a picture such as Figure 4.11, where a sine wave passes through ω cycles in a time interval of 2π. One cycle takes up a width of T on the time axis. Here again standard notation uses the word "time" and index t in these functions, but any parameter would do as well.

To see that these functions are periodic with interval T, we write the value of any such function at times t and $t + T$ as

$$\begin{aligned}
e^{j\omega t} &= e^{j\omega(t+T)} \\
&= e^{j\omega(t+2\pi/\omega)} \\
&= e^{j\omega t}e^{j\omega 2\pi/\omega} \\
&= e^{j\omega t} \qquad (4.12)
\end{aligned}$$

using E17 with $k = 1$.

An *eigenfunction* is any function that passes through a system unchanged except for a constant scaling of its amplitude. Thus, for any $f(t)$ that is an eigenfunction of a system $\mathcal{S}$, $\mathcal{S}\{f(t)\} = sf(t)$ for some (perhaps complex) constant s. That value of s for a particular function $f(t)$ is called the *eigenvalue* for that eigenfunction. These terms come from the German word *eigen*, meaning "same."

The complex exponentials are very important to us in this book because they are the *eigenfunctions* for any LTI system, and the scaling factors are the associated *eigenvalues*. We will prove this below when we discuss convolution. This property forms the heart of the Fourier transform, which we discuss in detail later.

Shorthand Complex Exponentials

We will use complex exponentials often in this book. Sometimes we need to have all the exponents available in order to carry out a calculation or derivation, but often they are just clutter that gets in the way of an intuitive interpretation.

To reduce this clutter, we will sometimes use a shorthand notation for the complex exponentials. We will use primarily four types of these functions in this book, which we define as

$$\psi = e^{j\omega t}$$
$$\psi_k = e^{jk\omega t}$$
$$\psi'_k = e^{jk(2\pi/N)n}$$
$$\psi_2 = e^{(\mu x + \nu y)} \tag{4.13}$$

We have already seen ψ and ψ_k; the other functions will be discussed when they are encountered.

4.3.9 Braket Notation

The physicist P. A. M. Dirac introduced a notation called the *bra-and-ket* or *braket* notation primarily to simplify some common expressions in quantum mechanics. These expressions are of the same form as the Fourier expressions, which will occupy much of our attention in this unit, so this notation is well suited to our needs.

The full definition of this notation can be derived from some basic ideas in group and measure theories. Building up to the definition is straightforward, but would take us far afield from our subject matter; a nice derivation may be found in Reid and Passin's book [357]. We will not be using this notation in its full generality; the exposition below is limited just to what we will need.

There are two pieces to this notation. The first piece we consider is the one called a *ket* (rhymes with bet). A ket is based on a function g, and is written $|g\rangle$. Note that the delimiters $|$ and $\rangle$ are not absolute-value and greater-than signs, but form a single entity along with g; the right bracket $\rangle$ is also narrower than the greater-than sign $>$. In general, we will consider kets to be *objects* in some space.

Typically, kets are objects without a coordinate system attached to them. For example, given two points A and B in space, a ket could represent $A - B$. Note that $A - B$ completely specifies a measurable, precise quantity, though we haven't defined this difference with respect to any particular coordinate system (e.g., standard Euclidean, polar, cylindrical, and so on).

To turn a ket into a number, we typically use a *projection operator*, which maps the object into some particular coordinate system. In this text, this abstract idea boils down to multiplying a ket by a *bra* (rhymes with la). A bra is also built from a function: for the function f the bra is written $\langle f|$.

Multiplying a bra and a ket together yields a *braket*, written $\langle f | g \rangle$. If f and g are both complex-valued functions on a continuous space (such as $\mathcal{R}$), then the braket is defined as

$$\langle f | g \rangle \triangleq \int \overline{f(t)} g(t) \, dt \tag{4.14}$$

Note that the domain of integration is not specifically mentioned in the braket; it must be understood from context.

If f and g map the integers to the real or complex numbers, then the braket is defined as

$$\langle f | g \rangle \triangleq \sum_n \overline{f[n]} g[n] \tag{4.15}$$

An example of the braket is the familiar Euclidean dot product of two real vectors $\mathbf{A}$ and $\mathbf{B}$:

$$\langle \overline{\mathbf{A}} | \mathbf{B} \rangle = (A_x B_x + A_y B_y) = \mathbf{A} \cdot \mathbf{B} \tag{4.16}$$

Note that we have used $\overline{\mathbf{A}}$ in the braket, since the braket conjugates its first argument. Because of this interpretation, the braket can often be considered very similar to the dot product. When the first argument is real, it doesn't matter if it's conjugated or not, since a real is its own conjugate. In this case $\langle \mathbf{A} | \mathbf{B} \rangle = \langle \overline{\mathbf{A}} | \mathbf{B} \rangle$ is often pronounced "A dot B."

The power of the braket notation is that it lets us think about objects such as $|g\rangle$, and ways to measure them such as $\langle f|$, without getting bogged down in the details of the representation and the measurement. This is the same reason we write $\mathbf{A} \cdot \mathbf{B}$ rather than $\sum_{i=1}^{N} A_i B_i$; they both mean the same thing, but the former is more succinct and general.

The reason for defining the braket this way has to do with the types of formulas we will encounter later on. In this book you can usually think of $\langle f | g \rangle$ as the projection of a vector g on a vector f, where we will sometimes use functions rather than vectors.

The reason for conjugating the first argument in a braket is simply to make the result easier to use. Because our functions are generally complex-valued, if we take the conjugate of one, then the result will be the integral of the square value of the function:

$$\langle f | f \rangle = \int \overline{f(t)} f(t)\, dt$$

$$= \int [a(t) - jb(t)][a(t) + jb(t)]\, dt$$

$$= \int [a^2(t) + b^2(t)]\, dt$$

$$= \int f^2(t)\, dt \tag{4.17}$$

Note that we may use a constant z_c for either a bra or ket; simply interpret it as a function $f(z) = z_c$. Also, observe that because the definition of the braket involves taking the complex conjugate of the first function, if this is a real number then its conjugate is itself.

The braket is not completely uniform in its properties. Let's examine linearity. For any three functions f, g, h, and any two complex constants a, b, the ket is complex-linear:

$$\langle f | ag + bh \rangle = a \langle f | g \rangle + b \langle f | h \rangle \tag{4.18}$$

so this is satisfied for $a, b \in C$. But the bra is only real-linear:

$$\langle ag + bh | f \rangle = \overline{a} \langle g | f \rangle + \overline{b} \langle h | f \rangle \tag{4.19}$$

so linearity only holds when $a = \overline{a}$ and $b = \overline{b}$; that is, $a, b \in \mathcal{R}$.

However, the braket is symmetrical under conjugation:

$$\langle f | g \rangle = \overline{\langle g | f \rangle} \tag{4.20}$$

The braket notation is unusual in signal processing, and you won't find it used in too many books on the subject (an exception is Reid and Passin's book [357]). I use it here because the standard notation of Fourier transforms (and the derivations leading to them) involves integrals of complex exponentials—such equations involve limits and exponents that clutter up the formulas and make them look more complex and daunting than they are. It requires some effort and determination to plunge into a complex expression and decipher each symbol and its relation to the whole; the fewer symbols, the less effort is required. Furthermore, simpler equations are easier to understand. If the concepts are understood, and the notation is matched to the concepts rather than the mechanics, then we can express relationships among objects in a natural way. For signal processing, the braket notation is well matched to the concepts we will use, and allows us to write simpler and more intuitive formulas.

The braket notation is not always appropriate for performing mechanical transformations on functions and equations, so we will often drop back into explicit functional form for such operations. We will also write some important formulas in both representations so that they will appear familiar when encountered in other texts.

Sometimes we will want to restrict the limits of the integration of a braket to something less than infinity. We can accomplish this by subscripting the braket with the desired interval. Thus, for CT functions f and g, if $\Gamma = [a, b]$,

$$\int_a^b f(t)g(t)\,dt = \left\langle \overline{f} \,\middle|\, g \right\rangle_{[a,b]}$$
$$= \left\langle \overline{f} \,\middle|\, g \right\rangle_\Gamma \tag{4.21}$$

When no domain of integration is explicitly listed, often we imply the domain of the first function; as mentioned earlier, this is usually the interval $(-\infty, \infty)$.

A more general definition of the braket involves a weighting function $w(t)$ that gives different importance to different regions of the domain being integrated. The braket with weighting function is then

$$\langle f \,|\, g \rangle = \int \overline{f(t)}g(t)w(t)\,dt \tag{4.22}$$

which may be written $\langle f \,|\, g \rangle_w$. In this book we generally set $w(t) = 1$, so most of the time we can safely leave out an explicit weighting function.

4.3.10 Spaces

The Fourier transform may be considered a technique for converting the definition of a signal back and forth between two forms. We often speak of these forms as the *signal-space* and *frequency-space* representations.

The terminology of referring to representations of numbers, functions, and other objects as members of a *space* is quite intuitive once you get used to it, but it can be confusing at first, particularly if you begin by imagining some actual physical space. In signal processing, the word "space" is used in an abstract way to refer to a style of description.

For example, consider a publisher who prints sheet music for popular songs. Most sheet music include the words, melody, and *chords* of the song. Chords are clusters of notes that carry the harmonic structure of the song. There are several different ways to represent chords, and a music publisher must pick one (or more) to use in the sheet music. Consider the "B-flat-seven" chord, written $B\flat^7$. One option is simply to write out the four notes of the chord: $B\flat^7 = B\flat, D, F, A\flat$, as in Figure 4.12(a). This is rather bulky and rarely used; music notation allows us to represent the same four notes more compactly as four black dots on a staff, as in Figure 4.12(b). A third common option is to draw a small picture of a guitar neck,

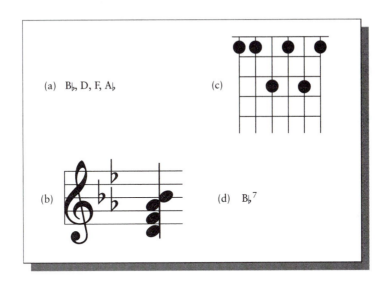

FIGURE 4.12

Chord spaces for $B\flat^7$. (a) Listing the chord notes in text. (b) Listing the chord notes on the staff lines. (c) A picture of a chord for guitar. (d) Simply name the chord.

and place black dots where the fingers ought to go, as in Figure 4.12(c). A fourth option is to simply name the chord in standard notational style, as in Figure 4.12(d).

A guitar student who knows no music theory can follow the picture in (c) and get the right results; a more advanced musician may read the chord notes in (b) and play them as written, or interpret the chord name in (d) as a suggestion from the composer, which may be altered to fit the mood of an improvisational performance.

There are other choices, but we can stop here. The point is that each of these representations of a chord carries the same information as the others, but in a different way. We can speak of (a) as the *text-space* representation of the chord, and similarly, (b) is the *staff-space* representation, (c) is the *picture-space* representation, and (d) is the *name-space* representation. We may think of the chord itself as an abstract object, made up of a collection of notes, which is *projected* into one of the *spaces* so that we may actually play it. In this case we can easily write the rules for transforming from the representation in any space to any other.

The power of using alternate spaces to represent some object is that sometimes it is easier to understand some characteristic of that object in a space other than the one in which it was handed to you. To a learning musician, two consecutive chord pictures might mean nothing more than mechanical instructions for how to change one's fingers on the guitar neck. Another musician given the same pictures may first figure out their names (i.e., project the chord from picture space into name space) and thereby understand their relationship.

The purpose of the next chapter is to define and discuss the *frequency-space* representation of a signal and its implications. The *Fourier transform* is the recipe for converting a signal back and forth between *signal space* and *frequency space*. Understanding the characteristics of this transform gives us insight into the nature of frequency space itself and how it mirrors objects and actions in signal space.

A synonym for space is *domain*. For example, we will sometimes speak about the representation of a signal in the frequency domain, rather than in frequency space. The word domain is overloaded in signal processing, since it is also used to represent the allowable inputs to some function, whose output is the *range*. Normally the correct interpretation is clear from context.

4.4   Some Useful Signals

Several signals will prove useful to us for examples and calculations. We summarize them below.

4.4.1   The Impulse Signal

One particularly useful "signal" is unusual in that it isn't technically a signal at all. Conceptually, an *impulse signal* is zero everywhere but 0, where it has an infinite value. It is an infinitely narrow spike of infinite height, but which integrates to a value of 1.0. Strictly, we should call this a *distribution*. We *define* the impulse signal, written $\delta(t)$, also called the *Dirac delta function* [151], as the distribution that modulates a continuous function f such that

$$\delta(t) = 0 \quad \text{if } t \neq 0$$

$$\int_{-\infty}^{\infty} \delta(t)\, dt = 1$$

$$\int_{a}^{b} \delta(t - c) f(t)\, dt = f(c) \quad c \in [a, b] \tag{4.23}$$

To get another view of the impulse function, consider the *unit step* $u(t)$:

$$u(t) = \begin{cases} 0 & t < 0 \\ 1 & t > 0 \end{cases} \tag{4.24}$$

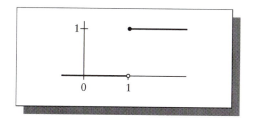

FIGURE 4.13

The unit step function.

which is shown in Figure 4.13. Note that this function is discontinuous at $t = 0$.

The unit step may be expressed as the integral of the impulse function [327]:

$$u(t) = -\int_{-\infty}^{t} \delta(\tau)\, d\tau \tag{4.25}$$

In other words, the impulse is the derivative of the unit step:

$$\delta(t) = \frac{du(t)}{dt} \tag{4.26}$$

Now because $u(t)$ is discontinuous at $t = 0$, Equation 4.26 doesn't satisfy the conditions for differentiation. But we can think of $u(t)$ as the limit of functions that are continuous, and we can see what happens as those functions approach $u(t)$.

To that end, consider the *ramp function* $r_w(t)$ defined by

$$r_w(t) = \begin{cases} 0 & t < 0 \\ t/w & 0 \le t \le w \\ 1 & t > w \end{cases} \tag{4.27}$$

as shown in Figure 4.14. This function is 0 to the left of 0, 1 to the right of w, and a step from 0 to 1 in the region from 0 to w. The ramp is a continous function.

Now we can find the derivative of this function without getting into any formal difficulty. We call the result δ_w, and it is plotted in Figure 4.15.

Now δ_w is a box of width w and height $1/w$, so its area is 1 for every value of w. As $w \to 0$, δ_w gets narrower and narrower, but it must become taller and taller to maintain unit area. In the limit,

$$\delta(t) = \lim_{w \to 0} \delta_w(t) \tag{4.28}$$

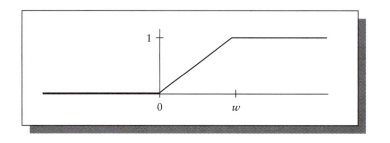

FIGURE 4.14

The ramp function $r(w, t)$.

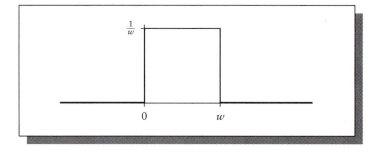

FIGURE 4.15

The derivative δ_w of the ramp r_w.

giving us an infinitely thin, but infinitely tall box. So although the *value* of $\delta(t)$ at $t = 0$ is infinite, it has a finite area of exactly 1.

In particular, we will find it useful to note that

$$\int f(t)\delta(t)\, dt = f(0) \tag{4.29}$$

The Dirac delta function is plotted in Figure 4.16(a). We will sometimes call this the *impulse signal*, *impulse function*, or just *impulse*. It is typically drawn with a thin

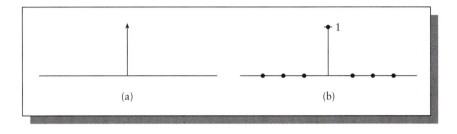

FIGURE 4.16
(a) The continuous impulse function $\delta(t)$. (b) The discrete impulse function $\delta[n]$.

arrow at $t = 0$, to indicate infinite height, as in the figure. Here the height of the arrow is irrelevant.

The delta function behaves in an unusual way when the argument is scaled. Specifically,

$$\delta(at) = \frac{1}{|a|}\delta(t) \tag{4.30}$$

To see this, suppose we have an arbitrary function $f(t)$. We set $at = \tau$, so $t = \tau/a$ and $dt = (1/a)\,d\tau$, and write

$$
\begin{aligned}
\int \delta(at)f(t)\,dt &= \frac{1}{a}\int \delta(\tau)f\left(\frac{t}{a}\right)d\tau \\
&= \frac{1}{|a|}f(0) \\
&= \frac{1}{|a|}\int \delta(t)f(t)\,dt \\
&= \int \left[\frac{1}{|a|}\delta(t)\right]f(t)\,dt \tag{4.31}
\end{aligned}
$$

The introduction of the modulus sign in the second line is motivated by observing that because the delta function is defined to integrate to 1, scaling the function should not change the sign of the integration. The last line proves Equation 4.30. This behavior of the delta function must be kept in mind when one scales its argument during a calculation. Because of the absolute-value sign, $\delta(x) = \delta(-x)$.

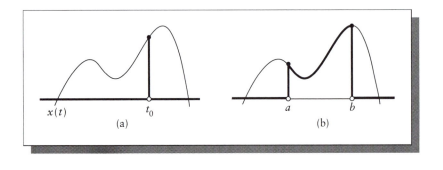

FIGURE   4.17
(a) The sifting property for a point t_0. (b) The sifting property for an interval $[a, b]$.

The discrete-time version of the impulse, $\delta[n]$, may be written

$$\delta[n] = \begin{cases} 1 & n = 0 \\ 0 & \text{otherwise} \end{cases} \tag{4.32}$$

and is plotted in Figure 4.16(b). Although the continuous-time impulse $\delta(t)$ has the rather unusual properties listed in Equation 4.23, the discrete-time impulse $\delta[t]$ is a much more conventional function, which is simply 0 everywhere except at $n = 0$, where it has the value 1.

Note that to place an impulse at any value k, we may simply shift the signal so that k is the new origin; an impulse at k is given by $\delta(t - k)$.

The functional definition of the impulse in Equation 4.29 gives rise to the *sifting property* of the impulse signal. For any function $x(t)$ and any value t_0, we can make a signal which is zero everywhere but t_0, where it has the value $x(t_0)$. We make this signal by multiplying $x(t)$ with an impulse at t_0.

$$x(t_0) = \int \delta(t - t_0) x(t) \, dt \tag{4.33}$$

This is diagrammed in Figure 4.17(a). This may seem a roundabout way of writing $x(t_0)$, but by sliding the impulse through some domain, we can pick out just the part of the signal we're interested in, without explicitly writing each sample individually.

For example, we can sweep t through the entire interval $(-\infty, +\infty)$ and end up with $x(t)$ itself:

$$x(t) = \int \delta(t - \tau) x(\tau) \, d\tau \tag{4.34}$$

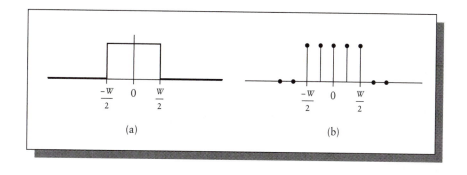

FIGURE 4.18
(a) The continuous box $b_W(t)$. (b) The discrete box $b_W[n]$.

We can write a similar relationship for discrete signals:

$$x[n] = \sum_k \delta[n-k]x[k] \qquad (4.35)$$

Alternatively, we may restrict τ or k to some other interval (or even several disjoint intervals). So the piece of $x(t)$ lying between a and b is

$$\int_a^b \delta(t-\tau)x(\tau)\,d\tau = \begin{cases} 0 & t < a \\ x(t) & a \le t \le b \\ 0 & b < t \end{cases} \qquad (4.36)$$

This is diagrammed in Figure 4.17(b). We use the sifting property often when calculating Fourier transforms and their inverses.

4.4.2 The Box Signal

The continuous-time *box function*, written $b_W(t)$, has the value 1 within some interval of width W centered at $t = 0$, and is 0 outside:

$$b_W(t) = \begin{cases} 1 & |t| < W/2 \\ 0 & \text{otherwise} \end{cases} \qquad (4.37)$$

It is plotted in Figure 4.18(a).

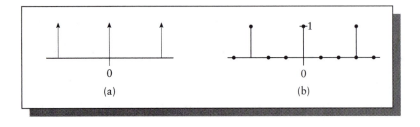

FIGURE 4.19

(a) The infinite continuous impulse train $\text{III}_T(t)$. (b) The infinite discrete impulse train $\text{III}_T[n]$.

Its discrete-time counterpart $b_W[n]$ is similarly defined:

$$b_W[n] = \begin{cases} 1 & |n| \leq W/2 \\ 0 & \text{otherwise} \end{cases} \tag{4.38}$$

This is plotted in Figure 4.18(b).

4.4.3 The Impulse Train

A very useful periodic function involving the impulse signal is the *impulse train*, sometimes also called a *comb* or *shah* function. This is simply an infinite repetition of impulses at equal intervals. Writing the interval as T, the continuous impulse train $\text{III}_T(t)$ may be written

$$\text{III}_T(t) = \sum_k \delta(t - kT) \tag{4.39}$$

The notation III is meant to remind us of a row of vertical spikes, representing the impulses. The discrete-time case $\text{III}_t[n]$ is similar:

$$\text{III}_T[n] = \sum_k \delta[n - kT] \tag{4.40}$$

Equations 4.39 and 4.40 are plotted in Figure 4.19(a) and (b).

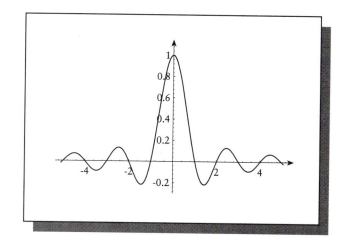

FIGURE 4.20

The sinc function $\sin(\pi x)/(\pi x)$.

4.4.4 The Sinc Signal

A notational convenience is provided by the *sinc* (pronounced "sink") signal, $\mathrm{sinc}(x)$:

$$\mathrm{sinc}(x) \equiv \frac{\sin(\pi x)}{\pi x} \tag{4.41}$$

plotted in Figure 4.20.

A couple of particular values for the sinc will prove useful later. We *define* $\mathrm{sinc}(0) \overset{\triangle}{=} 1$. We also note that $\mathrm{sinc}(k) = 0$ for all integers $k \neq 0$. Finally, we observe

$$\int \mathrm{sinc}(x)\,dx = 1 \tag{4.42}$$

4.5 Convolution

One of the most useful operations in signal processing is *filtering*. A *filter* may be considered any system which modifies a signal; we say that a particular system *filters* the signal, or that the signal has been *processed through a filter*, or simply *filtered*.

Recall that the sifting property of the impulse function allows us to write any signal as a continuous sum of scaled impulses:

$$f(t) = \int f(\tau)\delta(t - \tau)\, d\tau \tag{4.43}$$

Suppose we send this signal through a linear system $\mathcal{L}$:

$$\mathcal{L}\{f(t)\} = \mathcal{L}\left\{ \int f(\tau)\delta(t - \tau)\, d\tau \right\}$$
$$= \int f(\tau)\mathcal{L}\left\{\delta(t - \tau)\right\}\, d\tau \tag{4.44}$$

We call the signal $h(t,\tau)$ *defined* by $h(t,\tau) \overset{\triangle}{=} \mathcal{L}\{\delta(t - \tau)\}$ the *impulse response* of the system $\mathcal{L}$. It describes how the system responds to an impulse signal $\delta(t - \tau)$, which is simply an impulse at $t = \tau$. Equation 4.44 may be interpreted as telling us that if we know how the system responds to an impulse for each value of t, we can find that system's response to any input by breaking the input into impulses and summing together the system's response to each impulse, weighted by the value of the signal at that time. This is an important idea; it is illustrated in Figure 4.21(a).

If $\mathcal{L}$ is time-invariant, then the system responds the same way no matter when the input is applied; thus, $h(t,\tau)$ does not change for each value of τ, but is rather a single function $h(t - \tau)$, valid for every τ. This is illustrated in Figure 4.21(b). We may then write

$$\mathcal{L}\{f(t)\} = \int f(t)h(t - \tau)\, d\tau \tag{4.45}$$

We *define* the *convolution operator* $*$ to represent this operation:

$$f(t) * h(t) \overset{\triangle}{=} \int f(t)h(t - \tau)\, d\tau \tag{4.46}$$

where

$$h(t) = \mathcal{L}\{\delta(t)\} \tag{4.47}$$

The convolution operator is an *infix* operator; like the addition operator $+$, it appears between its arguments.

Equation 4.46 defines the operation of *convolution*. We say that $g(t)$ is the result of *convolving* $f(t)$ and $h(t)$, or that $f(t)$ and $h(t)$ are *convolved* to produce $g(t)$. The asterisk $*$ is often used as the infix convolution operator, though some authors surround the asterisk with a circle, as in $\circledast$.

The essential point here is that we have defined one method that allows us to find the response of any LTI system to any input signal. To review, because of the sifting property of impulses, we can write any signal as a (perhaps continuous) sum

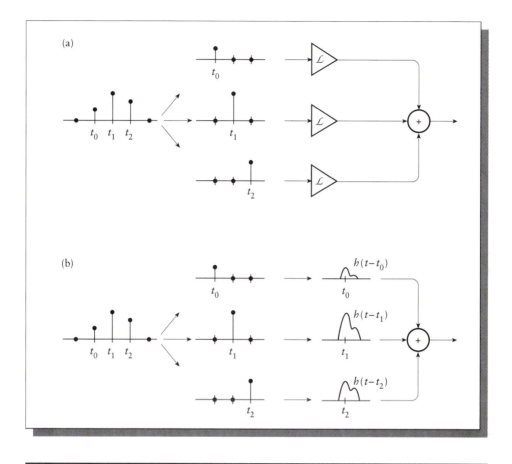

FIGURE 4.21

(a) A system's response in terms of impulse responses. (b) The impulse response is the same at all values of t.

of scaled impulses. Since the system is linear, its response to the sum of impulses can be found by summing its response to each individual impulse. Since the system is time-invariant, it has the same response to an impulse no matter when the impulse arrives.

To use the impulse response of a system to find its response to any input, compute the convolution of the impulse response $h(t)$ with the input $x(t)$ and sum, as in Equation 4.46. This means to find the value of $f(t) * h(t)$ at some point t, a scaled and reversed copy of the impulse response $h(t)$ is placed at t, multiplied with f, and

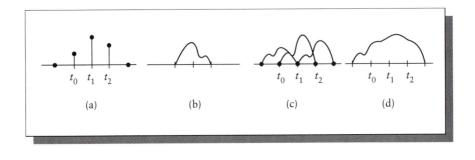

FIGURE 4.22

An example of convolution. (a) The input signal $x(t)$. (b) The impulse response $h(t)$. (c) The response of the system to $x(t_0)$. (d) The product of $x(t)$ and $h(t)$ is integrated to find the convolution at t.

the resulting product integrated, as in Figure 4.22. The impulse response is reversed because of the negative sign in the definition.

When the input signal is just a sequence of impulses, we can simply place a reversed copy of the impulse response $h(t)$ at each impulse and scale it accordingly. If the impulses arrive sufficiently slowly, and the impulse response has finite support, then the responses will not add to each other. As the impulses arrive more quickly, the responses move closer together, and after a certain point they begin to overlap and sum together. This phenomenon is shown in Figure 4.23.

As an example of this behavior, recall the description of clapping your hands in a concert hall. If you clap once and then wait, the sound will echo through the room and then (for all practical purposes) eventually fade out to nothing. The sounds of successive claps, followed by long pauses, will not add together because each one will fade out before the next arrives. But if you clap repeatedly and quickly, so that each new clap is made while the sound of previous claps is still reverberating, the sounds will add to each other and will be harder to distinguish. The response of the system to each input event hasn't changed, but each response is harder to isolate from the others.

Consider the effect of convolving a finite-support signal $f(t)$ with width W_f with a shah function $s(t)$ with period T:

$$y(t) = f(t) * s(t) = \int f(\tau) \sum_k \delta(\tau - kT)\, d\tau \qquad (4.48)$$

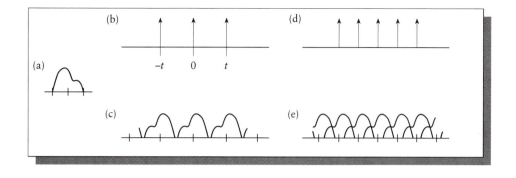

FIGURE 4.23

(a) An impulse response $h(t)$ with finite support. (b) An input signal $x_1(t)$ of impulses. (c) The output $x_1(t) * h(t)$; note that the responses are independent. (d) An input signal $x_2(t)$ of closer impulses. (e) The output $x_2(t) * h(t)$; note that the responses overlap.

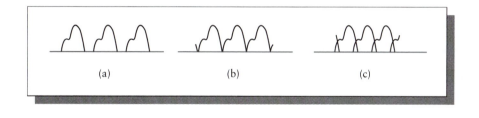

FIGURE 4.24

(a) The convolution result when the period of $s(t)$ is larger than the width of $f(t)$. (b) The convolution result when the period of $s(t)$ is equal to the width of $f(t)$. (c) The convolution result when the period of $s(t)$ is smaller than the width of $f(t)$.

This is illustrated in Figure 4.24(a). The result is that a copy of $f(t)$ is placed at each of the impulses in $s(t)$. When the period T matches the width W_f, the copies touch each other, as in Figure 4.24(b). When the period is smaller than the width, the copies overlap and sum together, as in Figure 4.24(c).

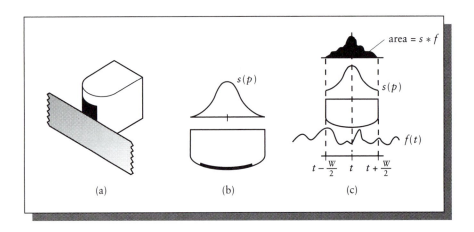

FIGURE   4.25

(a) A piece of magnetic tape and a tape head. (b) The sensitivity of the head $s(p)$ varies with p over the head. (c) The physical convolution of the tape head and a piece of tape.

Convolution is important because it tells us how to use a system's impulse response to find the output of the system to a given input. This is useful when we need to write computer programs to implement linear systems, such as camera lenses or reflecting surfaces. We may directly implement convolution as the algorithm to carry out a simulation of any linear system operating on any signal, given only the signal and that system's impulse response.

4.5.1   A Physical Example of Convolution

Let's consider a physical example of convolution as described in Bracewell [61]. Figure 4.25(a) shows part of an ordinary tape recorder. We assume a signal $f(t)$ has been recorded on a magnetic tape, where the mapping from time to position is linear and monotonic: the signal $f(t)$ is placed on the tape at position $x = t$, where $x = 0$ is the physical start of the tape. Upon playback, the tape is pulled at a uniform speed over the playback head, which reads the magnetic field off the tape and converts that information into an electrical signal that is then amplified. The tape head has a finite width W, and its sensitivity $s(p)$ varies over its width as a function of position p on the head; we place $p = 0$ at the center of the head, as shown in Figure 4.25(b).

At any given moment t, the head is placed over some section of tape centered at x, so the head is in contact with a section of the tape from $[x - W/2, x + W/2]$, as shown in Figure 4.25(c). We will assume that each part of the head responds only to the field on the piece of tape immediately in front of it. So the response $y(t)$ of the head may be written as an integral of the signal on the piece of tape times the response of the head at each point:

$$y(t) = \int_{t-W/2}^{t+W/2} f(t - \tau)s(\tau)\, d\tau \tag{4.49}$$

The convolution integral in Equation 4.49 says that the response at every moment is the product of the signal on the tape over some width times the responsivity of the head at each point. As the tape streams over the head, different sections are integrated, though the response $s(p)$ remains constant.

In computer graphics, we convolve every time we display an image. As shown in Figure C at the start of this unit, the display device takes the signal that we compute and combines it with the response of the hardware to create a displayed image. On a CRT, each dot we compute is convolved with the Gaussian blob representing the footprint of the beam on the fact of the tube; generally this blob is large enough that the footprints overlap and the displayed response of each dot is at least partly influenced by nearby dots.

To evaluate a convolution manually requires summing together as many scaled impulse responses as there are values in the input signal. When the input signal is discrete, or is made up of impulses itself, we can imagine manually placing and summing the finite number of impulse responses to find the output of the system. But when the input signal is continuous, we cannot compute the convolution directly by such a brute-force strategy. We will see later that Fourier transforms offer an alternative.

Convolution of discrete signals can be an expensive operation; if a discrete input has N samples and the convolution filter has M samples, then we require about MN multiplies and additions to implement the equations above. For 2D signals, N might represent the pixels of a 512×512 image (so $N = 2^{18}$), and M might span a 5×5 grid of pixels, requiring 25×2^{18} floating-point operations; this may be too expensive for some applications (and is probably an overly conservative estimate for today's rendering densities). We will see later that the Fourier transform also provides an alternative way to compute convolutions that may be less expensive in some situations.

4.5.2 The Response of Composite Systems

Convolution has several useful properties. For convenience, we will leave off the function argument in the following list, since the properties are true for both CT and

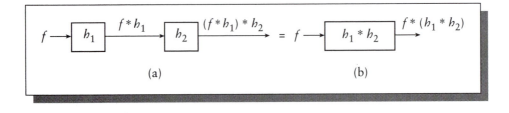

FIGURE 4.26

(a) A serial system h_1 followed by h_2. (b) An equivalent system.

DT signals. For any three functions x, h_1, and h_2, convolution is

commutative: $x * h = h * x$

associative: $x * (h_1 * h_2) = (x * h_1) * h_2$

distributive: $x * (h_1 + h_2) = (x * h_1) + (x * h_2)$ (4.50)

These properties allow us to characterize the response of a wide variety of systems. The latter two properties, in particular, simplify *series* and *parallel* arrangements, which are the fundamental building blocks of many more complex systems.

Consider a pair of systems h_1 and h_2, connected in a *series* network as in Figure 4.26(a). The output of the first system is $f * h_1$. The output of the second system is $(f * h_1) * h_2$. By the associative property, this is equivalent to a single, combined system with impulse response $(h_1 * h_2)$:

$$(f * h_1) * h_2 = f * (h_1 * h_2)$$ (4.51)

as shown in Figure 4.26(b). So we can precompute $h_s = h_1 * h_2$ and replace two convolutions with one.

A parallel network is shown in Figure 4.27(a). Here two independent systems receive the input f, and their results are summed together. By the distributive property, the sum of the outputs may be represented by a single system with impulse response $(h_1 + h_2)$:

$$(f * h_1) + (f * h_2) = f * (h_1 + h_2)$$ (4.52)

as shown in Figure 4.27(b). Again, precomputing $h_p = h_1 + h_2$ lets us save a step and clarify our understanding of the system.

Keep in mind that the term *system* may be interpreted as a *program* or *procedure* for many computer graphics applications. Thus two systems in a series may be modeled by two procedures A and B, where the input of B is the output of A. In computer graphics, we cascade systems in this way all the time. For example, to

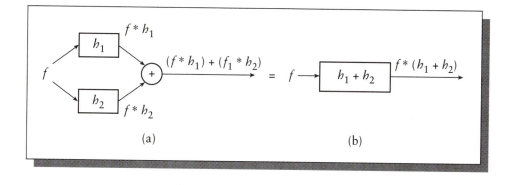

FIGURE 4.27

(a) A parallel system h_1 and h_2. (b) An equivalent system.

render a polygonal scene using z-buffering, we take a polygon as input and transform it into a rectangular grid of color values and depth using the scan-conversion program A. Then this grid is combined with the existing z-buffer and color grid by the visibility resolving program B. The complete image may be smoothed to reduce jaggies by a postprocessor C. The point is that we can often decompose a complex task into simpler ones (a popular principle of software engineering); when these are signal processing tasks, there is a direct correlation to decomposing a system into a set of simpler systems.

4.5.3 Eigenfunctions and Frequency Response of LTI Systems

We mentioned earlier that the complex exponentials are *eigenfunctions* of LTI systems; that is, they pass through such systems unchanged except for scaling by a (perhaps complex) constant. We will prove that assertion now.

Suppose we have an input signal $x(t) = e^{\omega t}$, $w \in C$. Let's find the response of any LTI system to this signal.

We write the response $y(t)$ as the convolution of the input signal $x(t)$ with the system's impulse response $h(t)$; we will make no assumptions about $h(t)$.

$$y(t) = \int h(\tau)x(t - \tau)\,d\tau$$

$$= \int h(\tau)e^{\omega(t-\tau)}d\tau$$

$$= e^{\omega t} \int h(\tau) e^{-\omega \tau} d\tau$$

$$= e^{\omega t} H(\omega) \tag{4.53}$$

The third step is justified because the system is linear and $e^{\omega t}$ is a constant with respect to τ.

The complex value $H(\omega)$ is called the *frequency response* (or *system transfer function*) of the system. It is a complex constant defined by

$$H(\omega) \triangleq \int h(\tau) e^{\omega \tau} d\tau \tag{4.54}$$

So an input of frequency ω passes through the system unchanged except for a scaling factor $H(\omega)$. Recall we made no demands upon the system except that it was LTI. Thus for any LTI system, $e^{\omega t}$ is an eigenfunction with associated eigenvalue $H(\omega)$ given by Equation 4.54.

This fact reveals that one of the easiest types of functions to study with respect to LTI systems are the complex exponentials, since they pass through such systems unchanged except for complex scaling. If we can represent an input signal as a sum of these functions, then we can find the response of the system to each exponential individually, and then sum the responses together. The Fourier series and transform provide precisely the tools that decompose a signal into a sum of exponentials.

4.5.4 Discrete-Time Convolution

The discrete-time version of convolution follows from the continuous version with almost no changes, except that the integrals are replaced with summations.

We write the response of a discrete-time system to an impulse at time k as $h_k[n]$. We may then find the output $y[n]$ of a system $\mathcal{L}$ to an input $x[n]$ from

$$y[n] = \sum_k x[k] h_k[n] \tag{4.55}$$

If the system is also *shift invariant*, then it doesn't matter when the impulse arrives; an isolated impulse at time n will produce the same response as one at time $n - k$ for any k. If the impulse response lasts for more than one sample, the copies will sum together, but each response is effectively independent of the others. In this case we can drop the sample-identification subscript k and write $h_k[n] = h[n]$.

We can now rewrite Equation 4.55 as

$$h * k \triangleq \sum_k x[k] h[n - k] \tag{4.56}$$

Equation 4.56 is the definition of the *discrete-time convolution sum*, usually written with the infix operator $*$.

4.6 Two-Dimensional Signals and Systems

The techniques presented earlier in this chapter may be generalized to higher dimensions; we will discuss the 2D signal as a useful special case. Two-dimensional signals are important in image rendering. For example, the 2D plane of an image, and the 2D hemisphere which integrates light arriving at a point, are both 2D signals. A signal's two dimensions need not be spatial. For example, some filtering techniques work in time and one spatial dimension. Thus, we could write a function $f(x, y)$ or $f(x, t)$ to distinguish these two cases.

The most general notation is probably $f(x_1, x_2)$, which avoids any particular interpretation of the arguments and allows for easy generalization to higher dimensions. This notation is somewhat awkward, however, so we will use $f(x, y)$ below. Keep in mind that these two arguments, however, can have different physical interpretations.

This section will briefly review the generalizations of the preceding discussions about two dimensions. We will be mostly concerned with showing the nature of the generalization, the appropriate notation, and some examples. Most of the principles of 1D signals and systems generalize in similar ways, so we don't need to review every property individually.

4.6.1 Linear Systems

We begin by reviewing some of the properties of linear, time-invariant systems in two dimensions. The property of time invariance is sometimes called *spatial invariance* when the signal is defined over spatial dimensions. A 2D system $\mathcal{L}$ is linear if for two functions $f(x, y)$ and $g(x, y)$, it satisfies

$$\mathcal{L}\{af(x, y) + bg(x, y)\} = a\mathcal{L}\{f(x, y)\} + b\mathcal{L}\{g(x, y)\} \qquad (4.57)$$

The 2D impulse signal $\delta(x, y)$ is defined in a way analogous to the 1D signal:

$$\iint \delta(0, 0) f(x, y) \, dx \, dy = f(0, 0) \qquad (4.58)$$

and is shown in Figure 4.28(a). Note that this is the product of two 1D delta functions:

$$\delta(x, y) = \delta(x)\delta(y) \qquad (4.59)$$

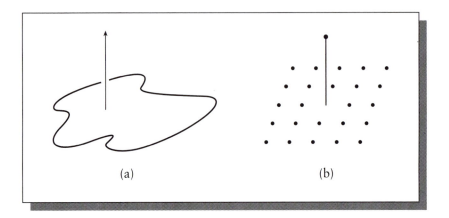

FIGURE 4.28

(a) $\delta(x, y)$. (b) $\delta[m, n]$.

The discrete 2D delta function $\delta[m, n]$ may be defined as follows:

$$\delta[m, n] = \begin{cases} 1 & m = 0 \text{ and } n = 0 \\ 0 & \text{otherwise} \end{cases} \tag{4.60}$$

and is shown in Figure 4.28(b).

4.6.2 Two-Dimensional Brakets

In two dimensions, the braket becomes a double integral or double sum. For continuous-time functions $f(x, y)$ and $g(x, y)$,

$$\langle f \, | \, g \rangle = \iint \overline{f(x, y)} g(x, y) \, dx \, dy \tag{4.61}$$

For discrete-time functions $f[m, n]$ and $g[m, n]$,

$$\langle f \, | \, g \rangle = \sum_m \sum_n \overline{f[m, n]} g[m, n] \tag{4.62}$$

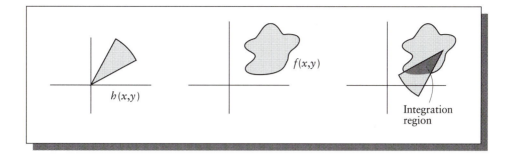

FIGURE 4.29
Two-dimensional convolution. The shaded area is the area integrated to find the convolution at (x, y).

4.6.3 Convolution

In general, the 2D convolution $g(x, y)$ of a pair of 2D continuous-time functions $f(x, y)$ and $h(x, y)$ is given by

$$g(x, y) = f * h = \iint f(x, y)g(x - \eta, y - \xi)\, d\eta\, d\xi$$

$$= h * f = \iint h(x, y)f(x - \eta, y - \xi)\, d\eta\, d\xi \tag{4.63}$$

For two discrete-time functions $f[m, n]$ and $h[m, n]$, the convolution is similar:

$$g[m, n] = f * h = \sum_{k_1} \sum_{k_2} f[m, n]g[x - k_1, y - k_2]$$

$$= h * f = \sum_{k_1} \sum_{k_2} h[m, n]f[x - k_1, y - k_2] \tag{4.64}$$

A graphical illustration of 2D convolution is shown in Figure 4.29. To find the convolution of $f(x, y)$ with $h(x, y)$ at any point (x_0, y_0), reflect h around the x and y axes, and then translate it so that its origin lines up with (x_0, y_0). Then multiply the two signals together at every point and sum the result. As k_1 and k_2 sweep out different values of (x_0, y_0), the entire input plane is swept and every point of f is convolved with h. Since convolution is commutative, we can swap the roles of f and h in this discussion and the results are the same.

4.6.4 Two-Dimensional Impulse Response

We can find the impulse response of a 2D LTI system as we did for the 1D case. We begin by using the sifting property of the 2D impulse function to select values of $f(x, y)$:

$$f(x, y) = \iint f(\eta, \xi)\delta(x - \eta, y - \xi)\, d\eta\, d\xi \tag{4.65}$$

Then we can find the response of a system $\mathcal{L}$ to this signal by

$$
\begin{aligned}
\mathcal{L}\{f(x, y)\} &= \mathcal{L}\left\{\iint f(\eta, \xi)\delta(x - \eta, y - \xi)\, d\eta\, d\xi\right\} \\
&= \iint f(\eta, \xi)\mathcal{L}\{\delta(x - \eta, y - \xi)\}\, d\eta\, d\xi \\
&= \iint f(\eta, \xi)h(x, y, \eta, \xi)\, d\eta\, d\xi
\end{aligned}
\tag{4.66}
$$

where $h(x, y; \eta, \xi) = \mathcal{L}\{\delta(x - \eta, y - \xi)\}$ is the *impulse response* of the 2D system. If the system is LTI, then as in the 1D case the impulse response is independent of the location of the impulse; so $h(x, y; \eta, \xi) = h(x - \eta, y - \xi)$. Thus

$$
\begin{aligned}
g(x, y) &= \mathcal{L}\{f(x, y)\} \\
&= \iint f(\eta, \xi)h(x - \eta, y - \xi)\, d\eta\, d\xi \\
&= f(x, y) * h(x, y)
\end{aligned}
\tag{4.67}
$$

4.6.5 Eigenfunctions and Frequency Response

The eigenfunctions of 2D systems are the 2D exponentials $e^{\omega(x+y)}$. The proof is similar to the 1D case. We find the output by writing the convolution of $f(x, y) = e^{\omega(x+y)}$ with an arbitrary system impulse response $h(x, y)$, and then apply linearity.

$$
\begin{aligned}
y(t) &= \iint h(\eta, \xi)f(x - \eta, y - \xi)\, d\eta\, d\xi \\
&= \iint h(\eta, \xi)e^{\omega((x-\eta)+(y-\xi))}\, d\eta\, d\xi \\
&= \iint h(\eta, \xi)e^{\omega(x+y)}e^{-\omega(\eta+\xi)}\, d\eta\, d\xi \\
&= e^{\omega(x+y)}\iint h(\eta, \xi)e^{-\omega(\eta+\xi)}\, d\eta\, d\xi \\
&= e^{\omega(x+y)}H(\omega)
\end{aligned}
\tag{4.68}
$$

So an input signal $e^{\omega(x+y)}$ emerges unchanged except for a complex scaling factor $H(\omega)$, defined by

$$H(\omega) = \iint h(\eta, \xi) e^{-\omega(\eta+\xi)} d\eta \, d\xi \qquad (4.69)$$

The function $H(\omega)$ is called the *frequency response* or *system transfer function* of the system with impulse response $h(x, y)$, as in the 1D case.

4.7 Further Reading

This chapter has provided only the basics of signals and systems. Digital signal processing has become sufficiently popular in recent years that a number of very readable and useful textbooks have appeared.

Good general texts on the basics of 1D digital signal processing include books by Oppenheim and Schafer [326], Gabel and Roberts [151], and Oppenheim and Willsky [327]. In particular, the 1983 book by Oppenheim and Willsky [327] is very accessible for study outside of a formal classroom setting. A different approach to the derivation of convolution is offered by Castleman [77], and Bracewell [61] offers additional discussion of many of the ideas only touched on here. Signal-processing code in C is available in the book by Reid and Passin [357].

Many signal-processing operations can be quite sensitive to issues of numerical stability and precision. Acton [3] provides a good introduction to this subject.

Multidimensional signal processing generalizes our ID descriptions and presents its own challenges. The book by Dudgeon and Merserau [130] reviews that field.

In this book we take the view that linear systems are easy to study and nonlinear systems are hard. This has been the attitude among most engineers and scientists for a long time, but it's beginning to change. A popular discussion of the emerging field of chaos theory has been written by Gleick [161]. An introduction to the qualitative behavior of dynamic systems may be found in the series by Abraham and Shaw, recently collected into a single volume [2]. This book will be particularly appealing to many people in computer graphics because of its rich visuals and predominantly geometric explanations of phase space. Another recent introduction to nonlinear dynamics is the two-volume set by Jackson [226, 227]. This also offers rich geometric pictures but requires rather more work to understand than Abraham and Shaw's book.

4.8 Exercises

Exercise 4.1

Characterize the following functions as linear or nonlinear, and as even, odd, or neither, and prove your characterization. In these functions, x is real and z is complex.

(a) $f(x) = 3x - 2$

(b) $f(x) = x^3 + x$

(c) $f(x) = e^{-x^2}$

(d) $f(z) = 3z - 2$

(e) $f(z) = z + \bar{z}$

(e) $f(z) = z - \mathrm{Re}(z)$

(f) $f(z) = z^2$

Exercise 4.2

Show that the following systems of functions are orthogonal:

(a) $\cos nx$, $n \in \mathcal{Z}$ and $n \geq 0$ on $[0, \pi]$

(b) $\cos nx$, $n \in \mathcal{Z}$ and $n \geq 1$ on $[0, \pi]$

(c) $\sin(2n + 1)x$, $n \in \mathcal{Z}$ and $n \geq 1$ on $[0, \pi/2]$

Exercise 4.3

Equation 4.70 provides the definition of the *Walsh functions*, an orthogonal family of functions. Write a program to plot any desired Walsh function, and plot functions 1, 2, 3, 4, 7, and 10. Do you think this could be a good set of basis functions for representing images? Why?

$$\phi_0(t) = 1 \quad 0 \leq t \leq 1$$

$$\phi_1(t) = \begin{cases} 1 & 0 \leq t < \frac{1}{2} \\ -1 & \frac{1}{2} < t \leq 1 \end{cases}$$

$$\phi_2^{(1)}(t) = \begin{cases} 1 & 0 \leq t < \frac{1}{4}, \frac{3}{4} < t \leq 1 \\ -1 & \frac{1}{4} < t \leq \frac{3}{4} \end{cases}$$

$$\phi_2^{(2)}(t) = \begin{cases} 1 & 0 \leq t < \frac{1}{4}, \frac{1}{2} < t \leq \frac{3}{4} \\ -1 & \frac{1}{4} < t \leq \frac{1}{2}, \frac{3}{4} < t \leq 1 \end{cases}$$

$$m = 1, 2, 3, \ldots$$

$$k = 1, 2, \ldots, 2^{m-1}$$

$$\phi_{m+1}^{(2k-1)}(t) = \begin{cases} \phi_m^{(k)}(2t) & 0 \le t < \frac{1}{2} \\ (-1)^{k+1}\phi_m^{(k)}(2t-1) & \frac{1}{2} < t \le 1 \end{cases}$$

$$\phi_{m+1}^{2k}(t) = \begin{cases} \phi_m^{(k)}(2t) & 0 \le t < \frac{1}{2} \\ (-1)^{k}\phi_m^{(k)}(2t-1) & \frac{1}{2} < t \le 1 \end{cases} \qquad (4.70)$$

Exercise 4.4

Draw the vectors $\phi_k[n] = e^{jk(2\pi/8)n}$ in the complex plane over one period ($n = 0, 1, \ldots, 7$) for each value of $k = 1, 2, \ldots, 8$. What happens when the frequency wraps (i.e., $n \ge 8$)?

Exercise 4.5

Prove that the convolution of two Gaussian bumps is another Gaussian bump.

Exercise 4.6

Derive properties E14 and E15.

Exercise 4.7

(a) Prove Equation 4.18.
(b) Prove Equation 4.19.
(c) Prove Equation 4.20.

Exercise 4.8

Prove Equation 4.50.

Exercise 4.9

What if the braket didn't conjugate its first argument? Work out the result of $\langle f | f \rangle$ under that condition. Is the result useful?

Exercise 4.10

Graphically convolve the signal $f(x)$ with the filter $g(x)$ as shown in Figure 4.30.

Exercise 4.11

Find the frequency response $H(\omega)$ for the following impulse responses.

(a) $h(t) = 5$
(b) $h(t) = 5t$
(c) $h(t) = 2t^2$

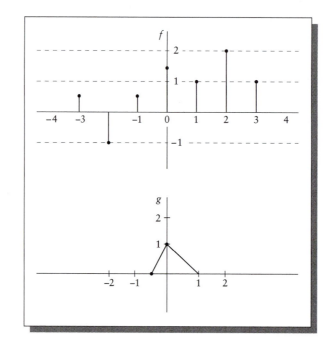

FIGURE 4.30

A signal $f(x)$ and a filter $g(x)$ for Exercise 4.10.

5

FOURIER TRANSFORMS

5.1 Introduction

An image displayed on a piece of paper or on a screen is made up of many small dots. Even photographic film has a built-in *grain size* that limits the spatial precision of the image. As we look ever closer at any stored image, we eventually hit the inherent *resolution limit* of the medium.

We often want to have as much spatial resolution as possible in our media, in order to show the crispest possible pictures. But in computer graphics, more resolution means more computation, and that also means more time. Often we don't have the resources to make images that have a resolution comparable to film grain, and instead we must satisfy ourselves with relatively coarse pictures, typically displayed on a 512×512 or 1024×1024 square grid. Usually the colors that may be represented are also limited. On a monitor, we usually have 2^8 or 2^{24} different color choices, each specified in RGB space to a precision of one part in 2^8 or 2^{10} [181].

How can such a coarse display possibly capture spiderwebs, the tiny glint on a hummingbird's feathers, or the streaks left by rain on a window? These phenomena may seem far too small, subtle, or both, to represent on such a coarse grid with a finite number of colors. We might expect to end up with a blocky image of almost uncorrelated colors as we strive to match these fine-scale structures with our rough displays.

The situation is of course not that bad, but the reasons why are not obvious. A very large part of the solution is the human visual system, which is why we studied it in such detail in the first unit. The HVS will fill in all sorts of detail from rough information. We just have to make sure that we're presenting it with all the information we can get our hands on.

One way to make sure our pictures are as good as they can be is to make sure that they contain nothing extraneous or wrong. This sounds fine in principle, but it turns out that the mere process of representing an inherently continuous color picture on a device with a finite number of spatial locations usually introduces errors of its own. These errors are known collectively as *aliasing*, and they lead to phenomena like jagged edges, thin objects that seem to be broken into pieces, and, in animations, objects that suddenly appear and disappear.

The source of this problem is that we are throwing away information when going from the high-resolution original to our relatively low-resolution image. We need to be very careful what information we lose: if we want to compress a Mozart piano concerto, we could simply leave out every occurrence of a flat or sharp note, but that would hardly capture the original in a compressed form. To complicate the problem, the human visual system will try to fill in for the information we lose. So we need to leave information out very carefully in such a way that the image we present to an observer is *interpreted* as a picture as well matched to the original as possible.

Of all the tools that have been developed for understanding and characterizing the quality of this match, in my opinion the most powerful is the *Fourier transform*. The Fourier transform takes a signal and represents it in *frequency space*. This alternate representation allows us to understand what happens when any continuous signal is turned into a set of samples. In our case, it will help us follow the transformation of a continuous visual image into dots on a screen or page.

The Fourier transform is a mathematical operator that decomposes a signal into a sum of weighted sines and cosines. The inverse transform runs the other way and combines those sines and cosines back into a time signal.

The advantage of the frequency-space representation is that it gives us a new vocabulary with which to discuss systems, and new tools for characterizing them. Our principal interest is in the processes of *sampling* and *reconstruction*. These operations are unavoidable in computer graphics, and are the source of aliasing in all its forms. They are best discussed in terms of the Fourier transform and the frequency-space representation of systems.

Because the frequency-space representation is central to understanding digital signal processing, we will develop that representation in detail in this chapter. We will use the ideas from the previous chapter to discuss continuous-time and discrete-time signals, and LTI and LSI systems in both signal and frequency space.

We will derive the Fourier transform in some detail because it is one of the most powerful analytic tools we have for analyzing systems. Developing a good intuitive understanding of the Fourier transform and its characteristics will serve you well when you consider any aliasing phenomena or develop any signal-processing programs. The best way to develop that intuition is to understand the reasoning behind the transform, rather than simply be able to execute the mechanics. The good news is that the principles involved are few in number and elegant in nature. I have attempted to phrase the development here so that it is relevant to computer graphics; I have omitted much interesting material that is not useful in the practice of computer graphics, or in the analysis of graphics systems as we typically consider them today. More complete treatments may be found in the references discussed at the end of the chapter.

This chapter will give us the concepts and vocabulary that we will need throughout this book for discussing the important problems of sampling and reconstruction, and many means of reducing or eliminating their effects.

5.2 Basis Functions

This section presents an argument that a sum of complex exponentials can match almost any real-valued function. We will get to this result in steps.

Our first goal is to show that functions may be represented as combinations of other, simpler *basis functions*. Our development will proceed by analogy to coordinate systems in Euclidean space.

5.2.1 Projections of Points in Space

Consider a typical 3D Euclidean space. To locate points, we create a reference *frame*, as in Figure 5.1(a), consisting of an origin and three (usually perpendicular) vectors, typically called $\mathbf{X}$, $\mathbf{Y}$, and $\mathbf{Z}$.

To represent any vector $\mathbf{V}$ in this space, we specify three coordinates. We can interpret those coordinates in at least two ways. One is that they are the components of a single 3D vector $\mathbf{V}$ from the origin. Another interpretation is that they specify the lengths of three *component vectors*, one for each coordinate axis. The lengths of these vectors correspond to the length of the projection of $\mathbf{V}$ on each axis; the lengths of these projections may be computed by the dot product of $\mathbf{V}$ on each axis.

A vector $\mathbf{V} = (x, y, z)$, in a space with axes represented by unit-length vectors $\mathbf{X}$, $\mathbf{Y}$, and $\mathbf{Z}$, may be written as the sum of the three component vectors $\mathbf{V}_x$, $\mathbf{V}_y$, and $\mathbf{V}_z$:

$$\begin{aligned} \mathbf{V} &= \mathbf{V}_x + \mathbf{V}_y + \mathbf{V}_z \\ &= (\mathbf{V} \cdot \mathbf{X})\mathbf{X} + (\mathbf{V} \cdot \mathbf{Y})\mathbf{Y} + (\mathbf{V} \cdot \mathbf{Z})\mathbf{Z} \end{aligned} \tag{5.1}$$

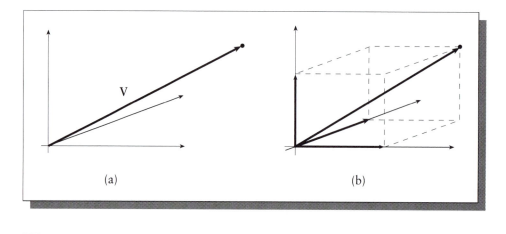

FIGURE 5.1

(a) A 3D reference frame made of three orthogonal vectors and an origin, and a vector **V**. (b) The point **V** specified by three vectors, one each for each axis of the frame.

Equation 5.1 is illustrated in Figure 5.1(b). Here we have represented a vector as the sum of three scaled *basis vectors* **X**, **Y**, and **Z**. The advantage of this representation is that we can now think of all the operations we might perform on any vector in terms of operations on just these three fixed vectors. This type of view is called a *basis representation*, and it is implicit in much of mathematics.

Basis representations for objects in a space have three properties we will find useful:

- Operation mapping: Any operations we may want to perform on the objects may be carried out by operations on the bases.

- Equivalence classes: We can compare any two objects easily, even if they do not immediately appear alike. If their basis representations are the same, then the two objects are the same (at least to within the characteristics represented by the basis functions).

- Completeness: A description of the bases and how they combine describes all possible objects in that space.

5.2.2 Projection of Functions

Let us now turn our attention from vectors to functions. Consider any 1D function $y = f(x)$. It is reasonable to ask if this function can be decomposed into a set of

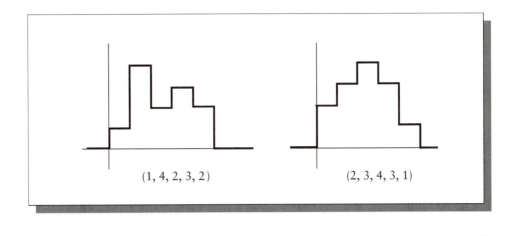

$(1, 4, 2, 3, 2)$ $(2, 3, 4, 3, 1)$

FIGURE 5.2

Two bar chart functions.

other, simpler functions, like the projection of a vector onto basis vectors. Such a projection would have the properties of a basis representation listed above.

By analogy to Euclidean space, we will combine our functions using simple addition. So we might write any function $f(t)$ as a sum of basis functions $\phi_i(t)$ and scalar weights c_i:

$$f(t) = c_1\phi_1(t) + c_2\phi_2(t) + c_3\phi_3(t) + \ldots + c_n\phi_n(t) \tag{5.2}$$

Consider an example class of functions we might like to capture, called the *five-sample unit-interval bar chart functions*, or more simply, the *bar chart functions*, illustrated in Figure 5.2. The bar chart functions are nonzero only between 0 and 5, and they have unit height within each interval of integers in that range.

We can define a set of five basis functions $\phi_1(t)$ to $\phi_5(t)$ to describe any bar chart function in the following way:

$$\phi_i(t) = \begin{cases} 0 & t < i - 1 \\ 1 & i - 1 \le t < i \quad i = 1, 2, 3, 4, 5 \\ 0 & t > i \end{cases} \tag{5.3}$$

These basis functions are illustrated in Figure 5.3. One way to look at this is to imagine that we have created a five-dimensional space (one for each basis function), so that each point in that space corresponds to some particular bar chart function.

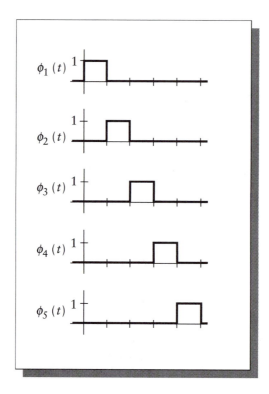

FIGURE   5.3

The five bar chart basis functions.

So a point $P = (p_1, p_2, p_3, p_4, p_5)$ corresponds to a bar chart function

$$b(t) = p_1\phi_1(t) + p_2\phi_2(t) + p_3\phi_3(t) + p_4\phi_4(t) + p_5\phi_5(t)$$

$$= \sum_{i=1}^{5} p_i\phi_i(t) \tag{5.4}$$

Figure 5.2 shows two examples of points in this space.

This simple example enabled us to answer by examination two important questions we must ask of all candidates for bases. We now ask those questions explicitly, because they are important when we generalize this procedure to more complicated situations.

- How many bases do we need? In 3D space, we need three basis vectors. For the bar charts, we needed five basis functions.

- Is this set of bases complete? In 3D space, the three vectors are mutually orthogonal, so linear algebra tells us that they *span* (and therefore describe) the entire space. For the bar charts, since each bar chart is completely characterized by its five heights, and each function specifies one of those heights, we have captured the entire class of bar chart functions.

Our answer to the second question for the bar charts was not rigorous; we would prefer a more satisfying answer that will generalize to more abstract spaces. Specifically, we need some tools to ensure that for any space we have enough basis functions, and that none of them are redundant. To satisfy the latter condition in 3D space, we need basis vectors that are *linearly independent*; so much the better if they are *orthogonal*, or all pairwise perpendicular. We can generalize the notion of orthogonality to functions.

5.2.3 Orthogonal Families of Functions

A useful definition of functional orthogonality is usually expressed with respect to each pair of functions in the set, within some interval $\Gamma = [t_1, t_2]$. Any two complex-valued functions $\phi_i(t)$ and $\phi_j(t)$ in the set are orthogonal if they satisfy the *orthogonality constraint*, presented here in braket form (in this section, all brakets use the integral form over the complex numbers):

$$\int_{t_1}^{t_2} \overline{\phi_i(t)}\phi_j(t)\, dt = \langle \phi_i | \phi_j \rangle_\Gamma = \begin{cases} 0 & i \neq j \\ \neq 0 & i = j \end{cases} \tag{5.5}$$

To interpret Equation 5.5 it may help to think of the braket as a sort of generalized dot product. This tells us that the projection of any function in the set onto any other function is 0, just as the projection of any two vectors in an orthogonal reference frame (such as X and Y axes in Euclidean space) is zero. When a set of functions is orthogonal, this tells us that we can combine them particularly easily to build up more complex functions in the space, in a way analogous to the representation of a vector in Euclidean 3D space by its projections onto the X, Y, and Z axes.

For example, suppose we had a function that was just a single scaled version of one of the basis functions; say $f(t) = r\phi_i(t)$ for $r \in \mathcal{R}$. If the family is orthogonal, then this is the simplest way to represent f; it can't be built from a combination of any of the other functions in the family because its projection onto any other basis (that is, $\langle f | \phi_k \rangle$ for $k \neq i$) is 0. If the family isn't orthogonal, then one more more of these projections might be nonzero, and we would have several ways of representing the same function f. There's nothing wrong with that, but it is often advantageous to know the simplest possible representation of something; when the simplest version can be used it reduces notational and conceptual clutter. Orthogonal families of functions also will make many manipulations easier, as we will see below.

We say that an orthogonal system is *normalized* over Γ if

$$\langle \phi_i | \phi_i \rangle_\Gamma = 1 \tag{5.6}$$

Any orthogonal system may be normalized by multiplying each function by the appropriate scaling factor μ_i:

$$\begin{aligned} 1 &= \langle \mu_i \phi_i | \mu_i \phi_i \rangle_\Gamma \\ &= \mu_i^2 \langle \phi_i | \phi_i \rangle_\Gamma \end{aligned} \tag{5.7}$$

so that

$$\mu_i = \frac{1}{\sqrt{\langle \phi_i | \phi_i \rangle_\Gamma}} \tag{5.8}$$

We define the *norm* of a function ϕ_i, written $\|\phi_i\|$, to be

$$\|\phi_i\| = \langle \phi_i | \phi_i \rangle \tag{5.9}$$

Thus, a system of equations is normalized if $\|\phi_i\| = 1$ for all i.

We want to find a *family* of orthogonal functions that is *complete* for some set of functions f, which means that each f in the set may be represented by a combination of those functions, just as any vector in 3D space may be represented by a combination of the three primary basis vectors. If no more orthogonal functions can be added to such a family, we say it is a complete *set*.

We will now see how to find the weights c_i for any given f and choice of ϕ_i. For simplicity, we will assume that the ϕ_i are real-valued functions, so $\langle \overline{\phi}_i | \phi_i \rangle = \langle \phi_i | \phi_i \rangle$. Suppose for now that we have found an orthogonal family of basis functions $\phi_i(t)$. Recall that Equation 5.2 expressed f as a weighted sum of each ϕ_i. If we know the bases, we only need to find the c_i to write out f in that basis representation.

Suppose that the summed basis functions ϕ_i approximate the original function, but are not an exact match. Rewriting Equation 5.2 to approximate $f(t)$,

$$f(t) \approx \sum_{i=1}^{n} c_i \phi_i(t) \tag{5.10}$$

we ask, What would be the best choice of the weights c_i to minimize the approximation error within some interval $\Gamma = [t_1, t_2]$?

We begin by defining the *mean squared error* (MSE) of this approximation over this interval. This name of the error term comes from its construction: at each point in the interval, we find the difference between the function and its approximation and square that difference. We then find the average (or *mean*) of this squared error over the interval. In symbols, the MSE is defined as

$$MSE = \frac{1}{t_2 - t_1} \int_{t_1}^{t_2} \left[f(t) - \sum_{i=1}^{n} c_i \phi_i(t) \right]^2 dt \tag{5.11}$$

Equation 5.11 contains everything we need to know to generate the weights c_i, but we would prefer a closed-form expression for each weight. To derive that expression, we begin by explicitly expanding the summation term and then squaring it:

$$
\begin{aligned}
MSE &= \frac{1}{t_2 - t_1} \int_{t_1}^{t_2} [f(t) - c_1 \phi_1(t) - c_2 \phi_2(t) - \cdots - c_n \phi_n(t)]^2 dt \\
&= \frac{1}{t_2 - t_1} \int_{t_1}^{t_2} [f^2(t) + c_1^2 \phi_1^2(t) + c_2^2 \phi_2^2(t) + \cdots + c_n^2 \phi_n^2(t) \\
&\qquad\qquad - 2c_1 f(t)\phi_1(t) - 2c_2 f(t)\phi_2(t) - \cdots - 2c_n f(t)\phi_n(t)] \, dt \\
&= \frac{1}{t_2 - t_1} \left\{ \left(\int_{t_1}^{t_2} f^2(t) \, dt \right) + c_1^2 k_1 + c_2^2 k_2 + \cdots + c_n^2 k_n \right. \\
&\qquad\qquad \left. - 2c_1 \gamma_1 - 2c_2 \gamma_2 - \cdots - 2c_n \gamma_n \right\}
\end{aligned}
\tag{5.12}
$$

The last expression uses the substitutions

$$
\begin{aligned}
k_i &= \langle \phi_i | \phi_i \rangle_\Gamma \\
\gamma_i &= \langle \overline{f} | \phi_i \rangle_\Gamma \\
\Gamma &= [t_1, t_2]
\end{aligned}
\tag{5.13}
$$

In the last expression in Equation 5.12, we have several terms of the form $(c_i^2 k_i - 2c_i \gamma_i)$. We can complete the square:

$$c_i^2 k_i - 2c_i \gamma_i = \left(c_i \sqrt{k_i} - \frac{\gamma_i}{\sqrt{k_i}} \right)^2 - \frac{\gamma_i^2}{k_i} \tag{5.14}$$

and rewrite the last expression in Equation 5.12 as

$$MSE = \frac{1}{t_2 - t_1} \left\{ \int_{t_1}^{t_2} f^2(t) \, dt + \sum_{i=1}^{n} \left(c_i \sqrt{k_i} - \frac{\gamma_i}{\sqrt{k_i}} \right)^2 - \sum_{i=1}^{n} \frac{\gamma_i^2}{k_i} \right\} \tag{5.15}$$

To minimize the MSE expressed in Equation 5.15, we drive the squared error term to zero by setting

$$c_i \sqrt{k_i} = \frac{\gamma_i}{\sqrt{k_i}} \tag{5.16}$$

for each i. Dividing both sides of Equation 5.16 by $\sqrt{k_i}$ gives us the closed-form expression we seek:

$$c_i = \frac{\gamma_i}{k_i} = \frac{\int_{t_1}^{t_2} f(t)\phi_i(t)\,dt}{\int_{t_1}^{t_2} \phi_i{}^2(t)\,dt} = \frac{\langle \overline{f} | \phi_i \rangle_\Gamma}{\langle \phi_i | \phi_i \rangle_\Gamma} \tag{5.17}$$

We have achieved our goal of finding the values of c_i that minimize the approximation error. Recall that Equation 5.10 expressed an approximation of any function f with a set n of mutually orthogonal, weighted, basis functions $\phi_1(t), \ldots, \phi_n(t)$, over an interval $[t_1, t_2]$. For any function f and set of basis functions, Equation 5.17 tells us how to compute the weight for each basis function.

One interpretation of Equation 5.10 is simply as a recipe for a change of coordinates from one space to another. The function f is "projected" onto each member of $\phi_i(t)$, much as a vector in 3D is projected onto each axis. The magnitude of each projection scales the associated base; the scaled bases are then summed together with those weights to represent the original function.

5.2.4 The Dual Basis

Sometimes we want to use a set of basis functions that are not orthogonal. In that case we can transform this "original" set of nonorthogonal bases into a new set that is orthogonal. This new set is called the *dual basis* [421] or *reciprocal basis* [54]. For a given family of basis functions $\{a(t)\}$, the dual basis is typically written as $\{\tilde{a}(t)\}$.

The characterizing feature of duals is that they form a basis that is orthogonal to the original basis. That is, for real functions a_i,

$$\langle a_i | \tilde{a}_k \rangle = \begin{cases} 1 & i = k \\ 0 & \text{otherwise} \end{cases} \tag{5.18}$$

Duals are useful because they give us the projection coefficients onto the original basis when that basis isn't orthogonal. Suppose we want to represent our function f as a sum of scaled basis functions $c_i a_i$:

$$f(t) = \sum_{i=1}^{\infty} c_i a_i \tag{5.19}$$

To find these c_i when the $\{a_i\}$ are not orthogonal, we find the projection of f onto the duals:

$$\langle f | \tilde{a}_k \rangle = \left\langle \sum_{i=1}^{\infty} c_i a_i \,\middle|\, \tilde{a}_k \right\rangle$$

$$= \sum_{i=1}^{\infty} c_i \langle a_i | \tilde{a}_k \rangle$$

$$= c_k \tag{5.20}$$

which gives us c_k, the coefficient on the kth basis function. So we use the dual functions to *analyze* a function and find its coefficients in some basis, and the original functions to *synthesize* the function back from its coefficients.

We can construct the dual basis corresponding to a given basis by a standard process called *Gram-Schmidt orthogonalization*, which we briefly review here [421]. We will discuss our functions as vectors because the operations have a strongly geometric flavor. But this procedure is perfectly applicable to functions; we only need to be able to compute the inner product to carry out the construction of the duals.

Suppose we have a trio of noncolinear vectors a, b, and c, and we want to make a new trio A, B, and C that are mutually orthogonal. We start by taking $A = a$, so this vector need not be changed at all. Now, to make a vector B out of b that will be orthogonal to A, we need to remove that component of b that is *not* perpendicular to A. That's easily found; it's just the projection of b onto A, as shown in Figure 5.4.

In other words, we can decompose b into two vectors, $b = b_{\|A} + b_{\perp A}$, one parallel to A and one perpendicular. The perpendicular part is the one we want:

$$B = b_{\perp A} = b - b_{\|A}$$

$$= b - \frac{b \cdot A}{A \cdot A} A \tag{5.21}$$

where we have found the parallel projection from the dot product of b on A. Now we have two mutually orthogonal vectors, A and B.

To make C, we repeat the process, removing those components of c that are parallel to either A or B:

$$C = c - c_{\|A} - c_{\|B}$$

$$= c - \frac{c \cdot A}{A \cdot A} A - \frac{c \cdot B}{B \cdot B} B \tag{5.22}$$

We can now normalize each vector simply by dividing by its magnitude.

Generalizing this procedure, any set of functions $\{a_i\}$ can be orthogonalized to a new family $\{v_i\}$ by the following algorithm:

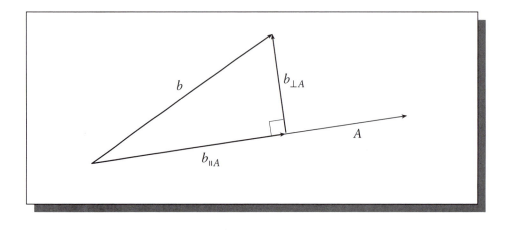

FIGURE 5.4

The projection of vector b onto A.

$$v_1 = a_1$$

$$v_i = a_i - \sum_{k=1}^{i-1} \frac{v_k \cdot a_i}{v_k \cdot v_k} v_k = a_i - \sum_{k=1}^{i-1} \frac{\langle v_k | a_i \rangle}{\langle v_k | a_k \rangle} v_k \tag{5.23}$$

This process is called *Gram-Schmidt orthogonalization*. Incidentally, we can write the process of Equation 5.23 concisely in matrix notation as $V = QR$, where the columns of Q are orthogonal, and R is an upper-triangular and invertible matrix; this is a convenient form for computation [421].

If a set of bases is orthogonal, then it is its own dual: $\{a_i\} = \{\tilde{a}_i\}$. We will exploit this property often in this book by restricting our attention to orthogonal functions.

5.2.5 The Complex Exponential Basis

In this section we will propose the complex exponentials as a basis for most real-valued functions. We will define the family and then show that they satisfy the complex orthogonality constraint.

Our candidate family for a set of n continuous-time basis functions is the set

$$\psi_n(t) = e^{jn\omega t}, \qquad n \in \mathcal{Z} \tag{5.24}$$

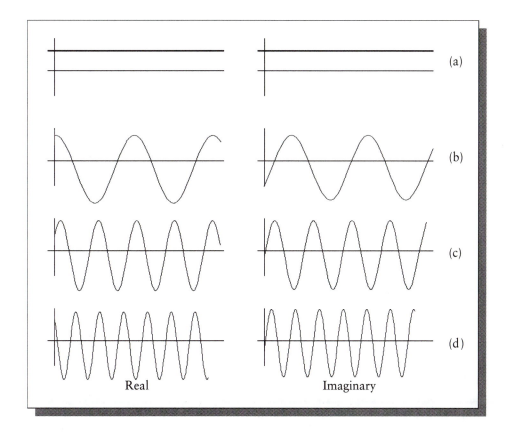

FIGURE 5.5

(a) $n = 0$: $\omega = 0$ and $T = \infty$. (b) $n = 1$: $\omega = 1$ and $T = 2\pi$. (c) $n = 2$: $\omega = 2$ and $T = 2\pi/2$. (d) $n = 3$: $\omega = 3$ and $T = 2\pi/3$.

These functions have a period $T = 2\pi/\omega$, and they are plotted for $n = 0, 1, 2, 3$ in Figure 5.5.

To test for orthogonality, we choose an interval of one period, starting at an arbitrary time t_0: $[T] = [t_0, t_0 + T]$. We then apply Equation 5.5 over this period to two functions $\psi_n(t)$ and $\psi_m(t)$:

$$\langle \psi_n | \psi_m \rangle_{[T]} = \int_{t_0}^{t_0 + 2\pi/\omega} e^{j\omega t(n-m)} dt \qquad (5.25)$$

If $n = m$, then $e^{j\omega t(n-m)} = e^0 = 1$, and the integral simplifies to

$$\int_{t_0}^{t_0+2\pi/\omega} dt = \frac{2\pi}{\omega} = T \tag{5.26}$$

If $n \neq m$, we recall from E11 (Table 4.1) that $\int e^{at}dt = e^{at}/a$, so

$$\frac{1}{j(n-m)\omega}e^{j(n-m)\omega t}\Big|_{t_0}^{t_0+2\pi/\omega} = \frac{1}{j(n-m)\omega}e^{j(n-m)\omega t_0}\left[e^{j2\pi(n-m)} - 1\right]$$
$$= 0 \tag{5.27}$$

The final reduction comes from noticing that the term in brackets is 0 because of E17. Summarizing the two results above:

$$\langle \psi_n | \psi_m \rangle_{[T]} = \begin{cases} 0 & n \neq m \\ T & n = m \end{cases} \tag{5.28}$$

Equation 5.28 was our goal in this section. It shows that the complex exponentials indeed form an orthogonal family. They are a complete set as well, but we will not prove that here. We will use this set as the basis for the Fourier series and Fourier transform below. To normalize this basis, we can divide each function ψ_i by its norm $\sqrt{T}$.

5.3   Representation in Bases of Lower Dimension

Suppose that we have a function f that takes two n-dimensional real vectors $\mathbf{a}$ and $\mathbf{b}$ and returns a scalar; that is, $f: \mathcal{R}^n \otimes \mathcal{R}^n \mapsto \mathcal{R}$. We have seen that if we have a set of basis functions that also map $\mathcal{R}^n \otimes \mathcal{R}^n$ to $\mathcal{R}$, we could find a set of coefficients that represent the projection of f onto this new basis.

What may be surprising is that we can represent our function f using bases that just map $\mathcal{R}^n$ to $\mathcal{R}$. We'll see how to do that in this section. Before we go through the math, however, we can draw a picture of the process in 2D that may help explain how it works. We'll map a 2D function $f: \mathcal{R} \otimes \mathcal{R} \mapsto \mathcal{R}$ onto 1D basis functions $\phi: \mathcal{R} \mapsto \mathcal{R}$.

Consider Figure 5.3. Here we have a function $f(x, y)$, and we have isolated the one-parameter function $g(y) = f_x(y)$; that's the curve parameterized by y at a given x. We ask how to find $g(y)$ in terms of a 1D family of orthonormal bases $\{b(t)\}$. We will assume for discussion that the function f is such that we can match $f_x(y)$ with just three bases, b_0, b_1, and b_2. We can then write

$$f_x(y) = \sum_{i=0}^{2} k_i b_i(y) \tag{5.29}$$

where the k_i describe how to combine the bases for this particular slice at x. We can find the k_i by evaluating three functions, $c_0(t)$, $c_1(t)$, and $c_2(t)$, at $t = x$; then $f_x(y)$ is

$$f_x(y) = \sum_{i=0}^{2} c_i(x)b_i(y) \tag{5.30}$$

These three functions c_i are just 1D, so there's no reason not to think of also projecting them onto the basis $\{b(t)\}$. The result will be three values for each function c_i describing how to combine the bases to get $c_i(t)$ at any t; these in turn give three values for combining the same bases to find the curve $f_y(x)$. You might try to convince yourself that these nine numbers correctly capture all the information in the original 2D function, given our guarantee that three bases were all that were needed. Then given the bases, we need only save the nine scalars, which may prove to be a very efficient way to store the function.

We'll now show how this works in general. Suppose we have a function $f: \mathcal{R}^n \otimes \mathcal{R}^n \mapsto \mathcal{R}$, and a set of orthonormal basis functions $\phi: \mathcal{R}^n \mapsto \mathcal{R}$, such that every slice of f is in the space spanned by $\{\phi\}$. Then for any two vectors $\mathbf{a}, \mathbf{b} \in \mathcal{R}^n$, we can write

$$f(\mathbf{a}, \mathbf{b}) = \sum_m c_m(\mathbf{a})\phi_m(\mathbf{b}) \tag{5.31}$$

where we have thought of f as a single curve given by the slice of f where $\mathbf{a}$ is held constant. We can project f onto the duals of the basis to get the coefficients c_m, and since the basis is orthonormal, it is its own dual; so

$$c_m(\mathbf{a}) = \int f(\mathbf{a}, \mathbf{b})\phi_m(\mathbf{b}) \, d\mathbf{b} \tag{5.32}$$

Now we can think of each $c_m(\mathbf{a})$ as a one-parameter curve in its own right, and project it too onto the basis:

$$c_m(\mathbf{a}) = \sum_n d_{m,n}\phi_m(\mathbf{a}) \tag{5.33}$$

where again we find the coefficients of the expansion from projection onto the basis functions:

$$d_{m,n} = \int c_m(\mathbf{a})\phi_n(\mathbf{a}) \, d\mathbf{a} \tag{5.34}$$

Now we can gather the pieces we have just found. Starting again from the original definition of f in Equation 5.31, and substituting Equation 5.33 for $c_m(\mathbf{a})$, Equation 5.34 for $d_{m,n}$, and Equation 5.32 for $c_m(\mathbf{a})$, we find

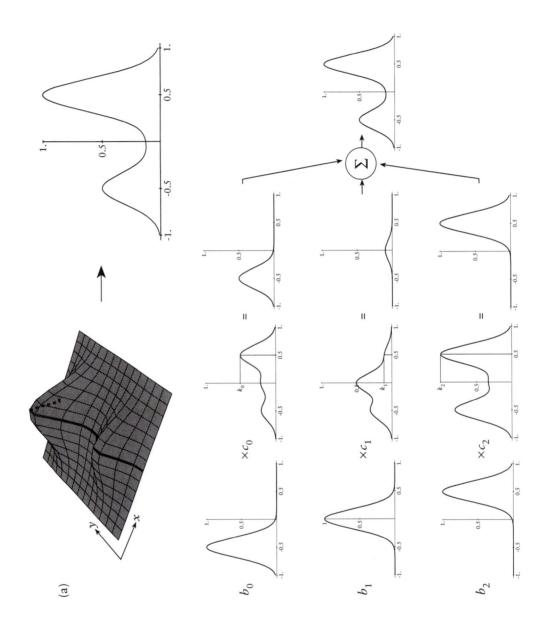

(a)

b_0 $\times c_0$ $=$

b_1 $\times c_1$ $=$

b_2 $\times c_2$ $=$

k_0 k_1 k_2

Σ

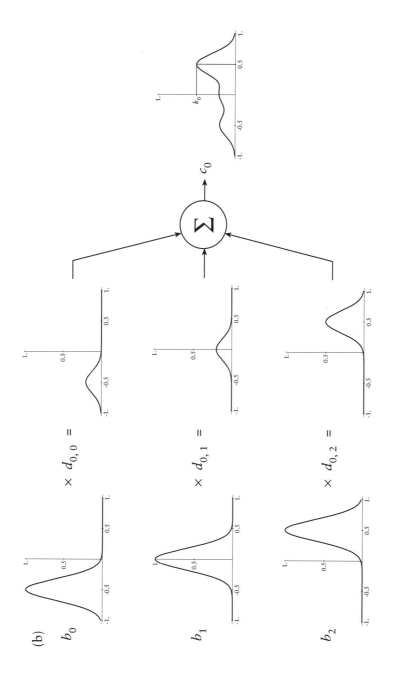

FIGURE 5.6

The projection of a 2D function onto 1D bases. (a) A slice of a 2D function is a 1D function, here made of two humps. The basis functions b_0, b_1, and b_2 are scaled and summed to match that slice. They are scaled by values of c_0, c_1, and c_2 evaluated at 0.5. (b) The functions c_0, c_1, and c_2 are themselves built from the bases, here scaled by d_0, d_1, and d_2.

$$f(\mathbf{a}, \mathbf{b}) = \sum_m c_m(\mathbf{a})\phi_m(\mathbf{b})$$

$$= \sum_m \sum_n d_{m,n}\phi_n(\mathbf{a})\phi_m(\mathbf{b})$$

$$= \sum_m \sum_n \left\{ \int c_m(\mathbf{a})\phi_n(\mathbf{a})\,d\mathbf{a} \right\} \phi_n(\mathbf{a})\phi_m(\mathbf{b})$$

$$= \sum_m \sum_n \left\{ \int \left[\int f(\mathbf{a}, \mathbf{b})\phi_m(\mathbf{b})\,d\mathbf{b} \right] \phi_n(\mathbf{a})\,d\mathbf{a} \right\} \phi_n(\mathbf{a})\phi_m(\mathbf{b}) \quad (5.35)$$

We can organize this as a matrix multiply by pulling one of the basis functions up front:

$$f(\mathbf{a}, \mathbf{b}) = \sum_m \sum_n \phi_m(\mathbf{b})k_{mn}\phi_n(\mathbf{a}) \quad (5.36)$$

where

$$k_{mn} = \iint f(\mathbf{a}, \mathbf{b})\phi_m(\mathbf{b})\phi_n(\mathbf{a})\,d\mathbf{b}\,d\mathbf{a} \quad (5.37)$$

In summary, gathering the basis functions into column vectors,

$$f(\mathbf{a}, \mathbf{b}) = \phi^t(\mathbf{b})K\phi(\mathbf{a}) \quad (5.38)$$

where $\phi^t(\mathbf{b})$ is a row vector (the transpose of the column vector) of basis functions evaluated at $\mathbf{b}$.

Although we have used a function of two parameters, all of this works for functions that map any number of parameters, as long as they are all the same size and the basis functions also take vectors of that size. The bookkeeping gets a bit more complicated with each level. For example, for three parameters $\mathbf{a}, \mathbf{b}, \mathbf{c}$ we get the equation sets (where we will temporarily use j as an integer index):

$$f(x, y, z) = \sum_i c_i(x, y)\phi_i(z)\,dz$$

$$c_i(x, y) = \int f(x, y, z)\phi_i(z)\,dz = \sum_j d_{ij}(x)\phi_i(y)\,dy$$

$$d_{ij}(x) = \int c_i(x, y)\phi_i(y)\,dy = \sum_k e_{ijk}(x)\phi_k(x)\,dy$$

$$e_{ijk} = \int d_{ij}(x)\phi_i(x)\,dx \quad (5.39)$$

yielding the equivalence

$$f(x, y, z) = \sum_i \sum_j \sum_k \int \phi_i(z) \int \phi_j(y) \int \phi_k(x) e_{ijk} \, dx \, dy \, dz \qquad (5.40)$$

We can write this in a more compact form using brackets; this shows the pattern behind the general formula at a glance, but would be a mystifying place to start because of all the suppressed subscripts and arguments:

$$f(x, y, z) = \left\langle \left\langle \left\langle m_{ijk} | \phi \right\rangle_{k \in \mathcal{Z}} \middle| \phi \right\rangle_{j \in \mathcal{Z}} \middle| \phi \right\rangle_{i \in \mathcal{Z}}$$

$$m_{ijk} = \left\langle \left\langle \left\langle e_{ijk} | \phi \right\rangle_{z \in \mathcal{R}} \middle| \phi \right\rangle_{y \in \mathcal{R}} \middle| \phi \right\rangle_{x \in \mathcal{R}} \qquad (5.41)$$

We can always build up a multidimensional transform like this from basis functions that map $\mathcal{R}^n \mapsto \mathcal{R}$. If we're taking the transform of an m-dimensional signal using n basis functions, we will end up with n^m coefficients. If the signal is discretized (say into an m-dimensional grid that is k units on a side), then the efficiency ϵ of the transformed representation may be written as $\epsilon = (k^m)/(n^m) = (k/n)^m$. If $k < n$, then the transformation represents a *compression* of the original data. Often this is a *lossy* compression, so that we can only recover an approximation of the original function from the projected form: for example, if we try to represent a cubic function from its projection onto linear bases. If $k > n$, we have an *expansion* of our storage requirements: for example, if we project a linear function onto cubic bases. By carefully choosing our bases, we may be able to find a lossy compression that saves computation and storage but retains some particular features of interest.

5.4 Continuous-Time Fourier Representations

The essence of the Fourier transform is that many real-valued signals may be represented by a combination of weighted complex sinusoids of different frequencies, amplitudes, and phases.

When this was first presented, it was not an obvious result, and was in fact resisted for many years. Interesting discussions of the history of the Fourier transform, and the surprisingly complex mathematical politics within which it was developed, are given in books by Oppenheim, Willsky, and Young [327] and Bracewell [61]. Briefly, the representation of functions as sums of harmonics began with Euler in 1748, who used trigonometric series to approximate functions, but abandoned them. The use of trigonometric series was disparaged from that point on by many influential mathematicians. When Fourier presented his now-famous paper in 1807, his ideas were ignored by much of the mathematical community, partly because he did not provide a formal basis for his arguments. Only when Dirichlet proved rigorous convergence conditions for the Fourier series in 1829 did the technique find acceptance. It is now an indispensable theoretical and practical tool.

In this section we will present the definitions for the Fourier series expansion and the Fourier transform. Specifically, we will define the Fourier series only for periodic signals, and the Fourier transform for aperiodic signals. The power of the Fourier transform is that it may be used for periodic signals as well.

5.5   The Fourier Series

The *Fourier series* allows us to represent a periodic, continuous signal as a sum of individual complex sinusoids. It is sometimes also called the *Fourier series expansion*.

Recall that Equation 5.28 demonstrated that the complex exponentials in Equation 5.24 are indeed a mutually orthogonal basis on the free interval $[T]$. The Fourier series takes any signal $x(t)$ and projects it onto the complex exponentials as a basis. The weight we get for each exponential is the proper scaling factor that allows us to sum the exponentials back together again to get the original signal.

Taking the period of a periodic signal $x(t)$ to be of width T, we may thus recover $x(t)$ in this interval using the complex exponential basis as

$$x(t) = \sum_k a_k \, e^{jk\omega t} = \langle \overline{a_k} | \psi_k \rangle \tag{5.42}$$

Note that we have used $\overline{a_k}$ in this equation since the braket conjugates its first argument. The coefficients a_k are given by Equation 5.17 using the family of Equation 5.24, and writing $\phi_i = \overline{\psi_k}$, finding

$$a_k = \frac{\langle \psi_k | x \rangle_{[T]}}{\langle \psi_k | \psi_k \rangle_{[T]}} = \frac{1}{T} \langle \psi_k | x \rangle_{[T]} \tag{5.43}$$

Recall that $[T]$ means any interval of width T.

Equations 5.42 and 5.43 show how to transform a signal with period T into a sum of complex sinusoids, and how to sum a set of sinusoids together again to recover the signal. They come naturally out of the orthogonality constraints over an interval (hence the restriction to periodic functions). The Fourier series expansion uses complex sinusoids as the basis functions, and finds the weights such that any approximation of n terms minimizes the mean squared error to the real function.

We will gather Equations 5.42 and 5.43 together with a small change to define the *Fourier series expansion* of a periodic signal $x(t)$ in the interval $[T]$, where $T = 2\pi/\omega$. We will distribute the normalizing factor $1/T$ by multiplying both equations by

$$\kappa_T = \frac{1}{\sqrt{T}} \tag{5.44}$$

Some authors choose not to distribute the normalizing factor, but to leave it on only one of the equations. I prefer it this way, because it emphasizes the symmetrical nature of the equations, and it simplifies the intuitive interpretation of an equal-power law we will discuss later. Making the normalization symmetrical will also make many of our later equations more symmetrical, and avoid messy scaling factors on one side of the transform or another.

Note that distributing this normalization factor does not change $x(t)$. It just means that the a_k are scaled by a factor $1/\kappa_T$, and we compensate for that change by multiplying by κ_T when we recompute $x(t)$ from the a_k.

The defining relations for the Fourier series expansion are

$$x(t) = \kappa_T \sum_k a_k \, e^{jk\omega t} \qquad = \kappa_T \left\langle \overline{a_k} \middle| \psi_k \right\rangle \qquad (5.45)$$

$$a_k = \kappa_T \int_T x(t) e^{-jk\omega t} dt = \kappa_T \left\langle \psi_k \middle| x \right\rangle_{[T]} \qquad (5.46)$$

Equation 5.45 is called the *synthesis* equation. Equation 5.46 is called the *analysis* equation. The coefficients a_k are called the *Fourier series coefficients* or *spectral coefficients* for $x(t)$.

These names come about because they tell us how to *analyze* a signal $x(t)$ and describe it in terms of scaled complex exponentials. The analysis equation represents the transformation of $x(t)$ from signal space into frequency space, where we can now speak of its various frequency components. To get $x(t)$ back again from this frequency space representation, we *synthesize* it from the coefficients a_k.

This is important news, because the frequency-space representation of a signal tells us all sorts of useful information about the signal. For example, suppose that there is no high-frequency information (that is, all the exponentials corresponding to $\omega > \omega_F$ for some ω_F are zero; that means $a_k = 0$ for $k > b$ for some integer b). Then we can *compress* the representation by simply throwing away the high-order coefficients; they're all zero, so there's no need to store them. This would also tell us that the signal is very smooth and slowly changing. If we want to represent the signal with samples, say pixels in a frame buffer, then there is some frequency ω_F that corresponds to the most quickly changing signals that we can represent for some particular spacing of pixels. This is very important, because it also means that if there are frequencies in the signal beyond that point, we will not be able to represent them directly. In fact, if we aren't careful these high frequencies will show up in our picture anyway, but in a distorted form we call *aliases*. The techniques of *anti-aliasing* for battling this phenomenon will occupy much of our attention in this and later chapters. The best way to understand aliasing is by looking at the frequency-space representation of a signal and considering how much energy it has at different frequencies. The analysis equation is our first tool for discovering that information, associating a large value of a_k with a large amount of energy at the frequency corresponding to $k\omega$.

Let's now look a bit more closely at Equation 5.46. We can only apply the series expansion to those signals for which this integral converges.

5.5.1 Convergence

So far we have no guarantee that the Fourier series for a given signal exists. We need a test that we can apply to a function that will guarantee that the expansions converge. Such a test is made up by the three conditions of the *Dirichlet criteria*.

The Dirichlet conditions require that a function be *absolutely integrable*. A function $f(t)$ is *absolutely integrable* if

$$\int_T |f(t)| < \infty \tag{5.47}$$

Two related measures we will find useful later on are *energy* and *square integrability*. The *energy* E in a function $f(t)$ in an interval $\Gamma = [a, b]$ is defined by

$$E(f)_\Gamma = \int_a^b |f(t)|^2 dt = \langle f | f \rangle_\Gamma \tag{5.48}$$

A function $f(t)$ is *square integrable* in an interval if $E(f)_\Gamma < \infty$.

The Dirichlet conditions that a function $f(t)$ must meet to have a Fourier series may be phrased in several ways. One useful formulation given by Oppenheim, Willsky, and Young [327] requires that

- $f(t)$ must be absolutely integrable.

- Within any period of the signal, there are only a finite number of minima and maxima.

- Within any period, there are only a finite number of discontinuities, each of which must itself be finite.

A *finite discontinuity* means that the interpolation of the function into the discontinuity must not be infinite from either the left or the right. This is illustrated in Figure 5.7.

Common engineering wisdom says that signals that fail these criteria are sufficiently rare in practice that they almost never crop up [151], and this seems to hold true in computer graphics as well. Notable exceptions are fractals [195], but they are indeed unusual.

Although it is true that physical signals usually satisfy these criteria, many useful abstract and idealized signals (such as the box and impulse) do not. It can be argued

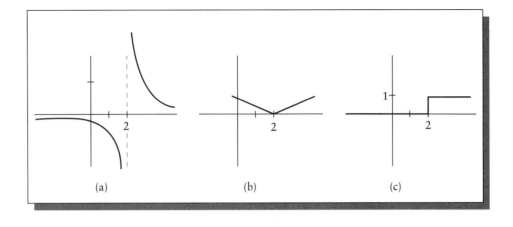

FIGURE 5.7

(a) The function $1/(x - 2)$ has an infinite discontinuity. (b) The function $|x - 2|$ has a finite discontinuity. (c) The step function that is 0 for $x < 2$ and 1 for $x \geq 2$ has a finite discontinuity.

that these signals represent other signals (which do satisfy the criteria) taken to some limit; for example, the impulse may be expressed as the limit of a Gaussian bump as the width goes to zero. These arguments can be complex and they are not particularly illuminating, so they are not presented here. We will simply assume from here on that all the signals in this book (unless otherwise stated), possess a Fourier series expansion (or transform), either directly or as the result of some limit argument. More discussion of this issue, and details of the limit arguments, may be found in the references mentioned in the Further Reading section.

Another implication of these conditions is the quality of the fit of the Fourier representation of a discontinuous signal. The Fourier series will converge even at points of discontinuity of the original signal; at these places the new signal is the average of the values on the left and right sides of the discontinuity (hence the requirement for finite discontinuities). Since the original and Fourier-synthesized signals differ only at discontinuities, they have the same energy.

The way the Fourier series represents a discontinuity in the input signal in its synthesized continuous signal is similar to how you would get from one trampoline to another slightly to the side and higher up. Standing on the trampoline, you would jump up and down higher and higher until at the critical moment you would shoot way up, and then fall on the other trampoline, slowly bouncing to a halt. Figure 5.8 shows this approximation to a step. As more terms are added to the series, the

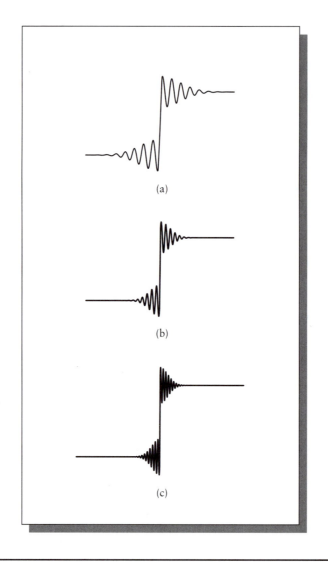

FIGURE 5.8

(a) The signals bounces into and out of a discontinuity. (b) Including more terms in the Fourier series. (c) Including even more terms compresses the ringing, but it doesn't change its amplitude.

bounces squeeze in more closely around the discontinuity, but they don't lose their height. This is known as the *Gibbs phenomenon*.

The source of the Gibbs phenomenon is that near a discontinuity, the signal recovered by the Fourier series synthesis equation looks like a compressed sinc function [61]. As more terms are included in the series, the sinc becomes horizontally compressed. This pushes more of its larger lobes (and thus the energy in the signal) toward its origin, and thus toward the discontinuity. Though the sinc may be made arbitrarily narrow, it can't be eliminated entirely; furthermore, its amplitude is not decreased by this compression. Thus, there will always be some amount of *ringing* near a discontinuity of a signal synthesized with the Fourier series.

5.6 The Continuous-Time Fourier Transform

The Fourier series was only defined for periodic functions. But we can extend the definition to handle aperiodic functions, which will result in the Fourier transform.

Our approach will be to enlarge the period of a periodic signal until one period fills the entire domain. This is similar to how Fourier generalized the series himself. He expressed his equations with respect to signals on a ring, so that they were by nature periodic. To find the expression for an aperiodic signal, he suggested enlarging the radius of the ring, essentially making the ring's circumference, and hence the signal's period, arbitrarily long. We will not phrase our discussion in these terms, but the essential limit argument remains the same.

We can approximate an aperiodic signal $x(t)$ in an interval $[a, b]$ with a periodic signal $\widetilde{x}(t)$, built so that $x(t) = \widetilde{x}(t)$ for $t \in [a, b]$. When $x(t)$ goes to zero, $\widetilde{x}(t)$ will repeat the active interval of $x(t)$ over and over. But we can define the active interval to include pieces of the zeros on the left and right. In other words, if $x(t)$ is nonzero only within an interval of support $[a, b]$, then we can choose for a single period of $\widetilde{x}(t)$ an interval $[a - d, b + d]$ for any real $d \geq 0$. In fact, the wider we define the interval, the better the match between the aperiodic input and the periodic representation.

Figure 5.9(a) shows an aperiodic signal $x(t)$ with an active interval $[-W/2, W/2]$. Figure 5.9(b) shows $\widetilde{x}(t)$, our periodic match to $x(t)$. The period is $[-T/2, T/2]$, where $T \geq W$, so the width of the flat zero region increases as T increases, as in Figure 5.9(c).

Let's derive the Fourier series coefficients for the periodic signal $\widetilde{x}(t)$. We begin by recalling the definition for the coefficients from Equation 5.46:

$$a_k = \kappa_T \left\langle \psi_k \middle| \widetilde{x} \right\rangle_{[-W/2, W/2]}$$
$$= \kappa_T \left\langle \psi_k \middle| \widetilde{x} \right\rangle_{[-T/2, T/2]}$$
$$= \kappa_T \left\langle \psi_k \middle| x \right\rangle_{[-T/2, T/2]}$$

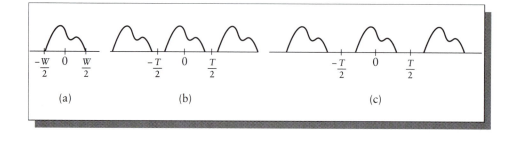

FIGURE 5.9

(a) An aperiodic signal $x(t)$, with an active interval from $-W$ to W. (b) The periodic signal $\widetilde{x}(t)$ matches $x(t)$ within the interval $-T/2$ to $T/2$, with $T = 3W/4$. (c) The periodic signal with $T = 2W$.

$$= \kappa_T \langle \psi_k | x \rangle$$
$$= \kappa_T \int x(t) e^{-jk\omega t} dt \tag{5.49}$$

where we chose $[-T/2, T/2]$ for the period of $\widetilde{x}(t)$, and then observed that $\widetilde{x}(t) = x(t)$ within that interval. The last step expresses our knowledge that $x(t) = 0$ outside the interval, so we can send the interval to $[-\infty, +\infty]$. Choosing T for the period implies the sampling frequency $\omega = 2\pi/T$.

We can write each scaled a_k as a sample from a continuous function $X_c(\omega)$, which we *define* as

$$X_c(\omega) \triangleq \int x(t) e^{-j\omega t} dt = \langle \psi | x \rangle \tag{5.50}$$

so that a_k is

$$a_k = \kappa_T \int X_c(t) e^{-j\omega t(k)} dt$$
$$= \kappa_T X_c(\omega k) \tag{5.51}$$

So the Fourier series coefficients are simply equally spaced samples of the continuous function $X_c(\omega)$, which only depend on the defining width T that encloses the active interval. Now that we've managed to define coefficients for our aperiodic signal, let's see what signal these coefficients synthesize; we'll call it $\hat{x}(t)$.

Recalling the synthesis equation for the Fourier series from Equation 5.45, plugging in the coefficients from Equation 5.51, and substituting $T = 2\pi/\omega$:

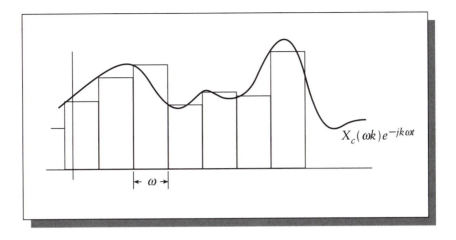

FIGURE 5.10

The Fourier series coefficients for an aperiodic signal may be represented as equally spaced samples of $X_c(\omega)$.

$$\hat{x}(t) = \kappa_T \langle \overline{a} | \psi \rangle$$
$$= \kappa_T \left\langle \kappa_T \overline{X_c(\omega k)} \middle| \psi \right\rangle$$
$$= \kappa_T^2 \left\langle \overline{X_c(\omega k)} \middle| \psi \right\rangle$$
$$= \frac{1}{T} \sum_k X_c(\omega k) e^{jk\omega t}$$
$$= \frac{1}{2\pi} \sum_k X_c(\omega k) e^{jk\omega t} \omega \qquad (5.52)$$

Look at the last line of Equation 5.52. We can consider this as an approximate integral, built from the sum of many small rectangles, each of height $X_c(\omega k)e^{jk\omega t}$ and width ω. Figure 5.10 shows this interpretation.

Recall that we want to push T to infinity, which will bring our approximate periodic signal $\tilde{g}(t)$ into closer agreement with an input periodic signal $g(t)$. As $T \to \infty$, $\omega \to 0$, and $\tilde{x}(t) \to x(t)$, so this summation approaches an integration. Thus we have recovered our original input signal: from aperiodic to aperiodic by way of periodicity! Passing the summation to an integral, we find

$$x(t) = \frac{1}{2\pi} \int X_c(\omega)e^{j\omega t}dt$$

$$= \frac{1}{2\pi} \left\langle \overline{X_c(\omega)} \middle| \psi \right\rangle \tag{5.53}$$

Together, Equations 5.50 and 5.53 make up the *continuous-time Fourier transform* (CTFT), our goal for this section. As with the series, we will normalize the two equations with a symmetric scaling factor κ, defined by

$$\kappa = 1/\sqrt{2\pi} \tag{5.54}$$

Here then is the definition of the Fourier transform:

$$X(\omega) = \frac{1}{\sqrt{2\pi}} \int x(t)e^{-j\omega t}dt = \kappa \left\langle \psi \middle| x \right\rangle \tag{5.55}$$

$$x(t) = \frac{1}{\sqrt{2\pi}} \int X(\omega)e^{j\omega t}d\omega = \kappa \left\langle \overline{X} \middle| \psi \right\rangle \tag{5.56}$$

Equation 5.55 is the *analysis* equation; Equation 5.56 is the *synthesis* equation. Sometimes the analysis equation is called the *forward Fourier transform* and the synthesis equation is called the *inverse Fourier transform*. Often the adjective "forward" is dropped, and we refer to taking "the Fourier transform" of some signal. The synthesis step is always qualified with the adjectives "reverse" or "inverse."

We call a signal $x(t)$ and its Fourier transform $X(\omega)$ a *Fourier pair*. When a lowercase roman letter is used for a signal, it is common to represent its Fourier transform with the corresponding capital. We can write the Fourier transform as an operator $\mathcal{F}$, so that $X(\omega) = \mathcal{F}\{x(t)\}$. We also use a two-headed arrow with a small $\mathcal{F}$ centered above to write Fourier pairs. Here is a summary of this notation:

$$\begin{aligned} X(\omega) &= \mathcal{F}\{x(t)\} \\ x(t) &= \mathcal{F}^{-1}\{X(\omega)\} \\ x(t) &\xleftrightarrow{\mathcal{F}} X(\omega) \end{aligned} \tag{5.57}$$

The function $X(\omega)$ is called the *spectrum* of $x(t)$. It gives the magnitude and phase of each complex exponential of frequency ω in $x(t)$. If $x(t)$ has any sharp corners, then high frequencies will be required to approximate those corners; smoother functions tend to have less high-frequency information.

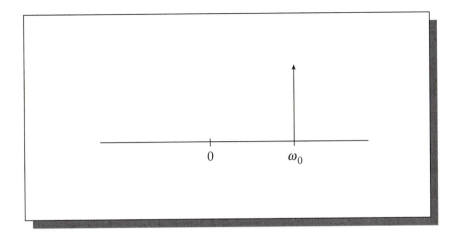

FIGURE 5.11

A plot of $X(\omega) = (1/\kappa)\delta(\omega - \omega_0)$.

5.6.1 Fourier Transform of Periodic Signals

Our derivation of the Fourier transform was based on an aperiodic input. The Fourier transform may also be used to analyze periodic signals; we will see that the transform in this case is closely related to the Fourier series.

Consider a periodic input signal $x(t)$ whose Fourier transform is a single impulse, located at ω_0 and with height $1/\kappa$:

$$X(\omega) = \frac{1}{\kappa}\delta(\omega - \omega_0) \tag{5.58}$$

This spectrum is shown in Figure 5.11.

We can find the signal $x(t)$ from the inverse Fourier transform of $X(\omega)$:

$$
\begin{aligned}
x(t) &= \kappa \int X(\omega)e^{j\omega t}dt \\
&= \kappa \int \frac{1}{\kappa}\delta(\omega - \omega_0)e^{j\omega t}dt \\
&= e^{j\omega_0 t}
\end{aligned}
\tag{5.59}
$$

So this spectrum represents the Fourier transform of a continuous-time, periodic function, namely a complex exponential with frequency ω_0.

We can generalize this result. Suppose that we have some periodic signal $x(t)$ with Fourier series coefficients a_k. We assert that the Fourier transform of this signal

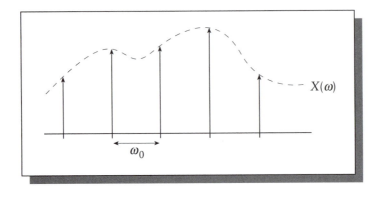

FIGURE 5.12

The scaled impulses of $X(\omega)$.

is a set of equally spaced impulses with spacing ω_0, each with height $a_k \kappa_T / \kappa$. To see that this is so, we write this spectrum $X(\omega)$, illustrated in Figure 5.12,

$$X(\omega) = \sum_k \frac{\kappa_T}{\kappa} a_k \delta(\omega - k\omega_0) \tag{5.60}$$

and take its inverse transform:

$$
\begin{aligned}
x(t) &= \kappa \left\langle \overline{X} \,\middle|\, \psi \right\rangle \\
&= \kappa \int \sum_k \frac{\kappa_T}{\kappa} a_k \delta(\omega - k\omega_0) e^{j\omega t} dt \\
&= \kappa_T \sum_k a_k \int \delta(\omega - k\omega_0) e^{j\omega t} dt \\
&= \kappa_T \sum_k a_k e^{j\omega_0 t} \\
&= \kappa_T \left\langle \overline{a} \,\middle|\, \psi \right\rangle
\end{aligned}
\tag{5.61}
$$

The last line of Equation 5.61 is the Fourier series synthesis equation for $x(t)$, which confirms our assertion.

So the Fourier transform of a periodic signal with frequency ω_0 (or period $T_0 = 2\pi/\omega_0$) is a set of impulses, spaced ω_0 apart, where the height of the impulse at $\omega - k\omega_0$ has height $a_k \kappa_T / \kappa$.

5.6.2 Parseval's Theorem

We mentioned earlier that we distributed the normalizing factors κ_T and κ to simplify a power relationship. That relationship states that a signal and its transform contain equal energy:

$$\frac{|F(\omega)|^2}{\text{energy density at } \omega} = \frac{|f(t)|^2}{\text{energy density at } t} \tag{5.62}$$

In braket notation, we may state:

$$\langle f | f \rangle = \langle F | F \rangle$$
$$E(f) = E(F) \tag{5.63}$$

This gives us some confidence that we have chosen a reasonable measure for energy. Since the Fourier transform is simply a change of basis, we would not expect the energy of the signal it represents to change, and this relationship says that indeed it does not. This property may be generalized for two functions f and g to a form known as *Parseval's theorem*:

$$\langle f | g \rangle = \langle F | G \rangle \tag{5.64}$$

Parseval's theorem tells us that the energy in a signal and its Fourier transform are the same. Thus if $x(t)$ gets narrower, $X(\omega)$ will become taller, wider, or both in order to maintain the energy relationship. The same situation holds in the opposite direction.

5.7 Examples

We now look at some examples of Fourier series and Fourier transforms.

5.7.1 The Box Signal

We begin by finding the Fourier series for the periodic function $b_{W,T}(t)$. This is the box function of width W repeating at an interval T, shown in Figure 5.13.

Recall that $\omega = 2\pi/T$ and our interval is $\Gamma = [-W/2, W/2]$. We start with the definition from Equation 5.46:

$$a_k = \kappa_T \langle \psi_k | x \rangle_{[T]} = \kappa_T \int_T x(t) e^{-jk\omega t} dt \tag{5.65}$$

Observe that for $k = 0$, $\psi_k = 1$, so we can immediately write a_0:

$$a_0 = \kappa_T \int_{-W/2}^{W/2} dt = \kappa_T W \tag{5.66}$$

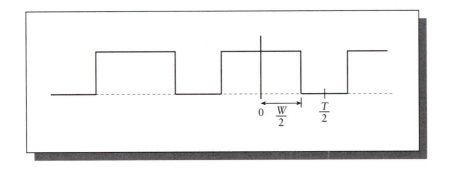

FIGURE 5.13

The box of width W and interval T.

For the other values of k, we can expand the fraction and simplify:

$$a_k = \kappa_T \langle \psi_k | x \rangle_{[T]}$$

$$= \kappa_T \int_{-W/2}^{W/2} e^{-jk\omega t} dt$$

$$= \kappa_T W \ \text{sinc} \left(\frac{Wk}{2\pi} \omega \right) \tag{5.67}$$

by property E21 (Table 4.1). Equations 5.66 and 5.67 specify the coefficients for $k = 0$ and $k \neq 0$, respectively. The values of a_k are plotted in Figure 5.14.

We can find the transform of the *aperiodic* function $b_W(t)$ with the Fourier transform. We begin with the analysis equation from Equation 5.55:

$$X(\omega) = \kappa \langle \psi | x \rangle$$

$$= \kappa \int_{-W/2}^{W/2} x(t) e^{-j\omega t} dt$$

$$= \kappa W \ \text{sinc} \left(\frac{W}{2\pi} \omega \right) \tag{5.68}$$

again using property E21. The spectrum of $b_W(t)$ is plotted in Figure 5.15.

We can observe a few similarities and differences between Figures 5.14 and 5.15. Notice that near the origin, they both look like sinc functions. The Fourier series representation of the periodic signal then turns around and starts to repeat, and it remains periodic. The Fourier transform of the aperiodic signal is a sinc that rings forever with decreasing amplitude. So the series expansion of the periodic box is

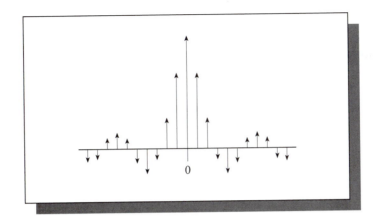

FIGURE 5.14

$\mathcal{F}\{b_{W,T}(t)\}$.

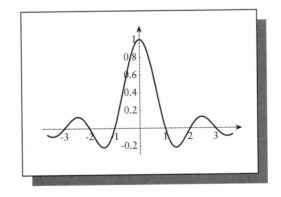

FIGURE 5.15

$\mathcal{F}\{b_W(t)\}$.

periodic, and the Fourier transform of the aperiodic box is aperiodic, though they have similar shapes near the origin.

To come full circle, let's now find the inverse transform of the spectrum in Equation 5.68. We expect something like the box signal $b_W(t)$ that we started with, but with the average value of the box at its discontinuities. We begin with the definition of the synthesis equation, Equation 5.56, and then substitute for $X(\omega)$:

$$
\begin{aligned}
x(t) &= \kappa \left\langle \overline{X(\omega)} \middle| \phi \right\rangle \\
&= \kappa \int \kappa W \operatorname{sinc}\left(\frac{W}{2\pi}\omega\right) \\
&= \kappa \int \frac{2\kappa}{\omega} \sin\left(\omega W/2\right) e^{j\omega t} d\omega \\
&= 2\kappa^2 \int \left[\cos(\omega t) + j\sin(\omega t)\right] \frac{\sin\left(\omega W/2\right)}{\omega} d\omega \\
&= \frac{1}{\pi} \int \cos(\omega t) \frac{\sin\left(\omega W/2\right)}{\omega} + j\sin(\omega t) \frac{\sin\left(\omega W/2\right)}{\omega} d\omega
\end{aligned}
\tag{5.69}
$$

Since $\sin(a)\sin(b) = \sin(-a)\sin(-b)$, the entire right-hand side of this last equation is odd. Note that for any odd function f, $\int f(\omega)\,d\omega = 0$, so this entire imaginary term goes to zero:

$$
x(t) = \frac{1}{\pi} \int \cos(\omega t) \frac{\sin\left(\omega W/2\right)}{\omega} d\omega
\tag{5.70}
$$

Thus we are left with a product of two trig functions. Substituting $a = t$ and $b = W/2$ lets us write this in a form that can be found in a table of standard integrals:

$$
\begin{aligned}
x(t) &= \frac{1}{\pi} \int \cos(a\omega) \frac{\sin(b\omega)}{\omega} d\omega \\
&= \begin{cases} 1 & |t| < W/2 \\ \frac{1}{2} & t = \pm W/2 \\ 0 & |t| > W/2 \end{cases}
\end{aligned}
\tag{5.71}
$$

So we have come full circle, from a box to its transform and back again to an almost-box. Equation 5.71 is equivalent to our box function except at the discontinuities $t = \pm W/2$, where it has the average value, as expected.

5.7.2 The Box Spectrum

Suppose that we now reinterpret our box to be a spectrum rather than a time signal. By taking the inverse transform of this spectrum, we can find what signal

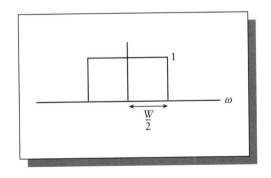

FIGURE 5.16

The box spectrum $b_W(\omega)$.

corresponds to a frequency-space box. We will redefine our box signal $b(t)$ to be a box spectrum $b_W(\omega)$:

$$b_W(\omega) = \begin{cases} 1 & |\omega| \le W/2 \\ 0 & |\omega| > W/2 \end{cases} \tag{5.72}$$

This is illustrated in Figure 5.16.

To find the Fourier transform for this aperiodic signal, we start with the synthesis equation:

$$
\begin{aligned}
x(t) &= \kappa \langle \overline{X} | \phi \rangle \\
&= \kappa \int X(\omega) e^{j\omega t} d\omega \\
&= \kappa \int_{-W/2}^{W/2} e^{j\omega t} d\omega \\
&= \kappa W \operatorname{sinc}\left(\frac{W}{2\pi} t\right)
\end{aligned}
\tag{5.73}
$$

by E21. Equation 5.73 is plotted in Figure 5.17.

Notice that for all the examples we have considered above, there is an inverse relationship between the width of the box and the frequency of the damped sinusoid. As the box gets narrower, the sinusoid spreads out (that is, it takes longer to reach its first zero crossing). As the box gets wider, the sinusoid contracts.

Intuitively, we can think of the limit of this process as a box of no width, and a sinusoid whose first zero is at infinity and is therefore flat. We will confirm this intuition when we look at impulse signals.

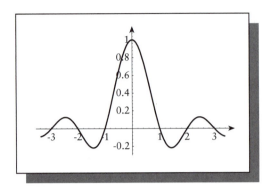

FIGURE 5.17

$\mathcal{F}^{-1}\{b_W(\omega)\}$.

To get a feeling for this trade-off, think of the box spectrum as telling us that to create a new time signal, we add up complex exponentials with frequency from 0 to some upper limit. With a low cutoff frequency, the synthesized signal will be gentle and smooth. As we add higher and higher frequencies, we can begin to include sharper corners in our signal. So the wider the box is in frequency space, the higher the frequency of the exponentials that we sum, and the more angular the synthesized function can be.

5.7.3 The Gaussian

The unnormalized *Gaussian function* is a smooth bump, which may be given by

$$g(t) = e^{-t^2/\sigma^2} \tag{5.74}$$

The area under the Gaussian is

$$\int e^{-t^2/\sigma^2} = \frac{1}{\sqrt{2\pi\sigma^2}} = \frac{\kappa}{\sigma} \tag{5.75}$$

The factor σ^2 is the *variance*, and its square root σ is the *standard deviation*.

The Gaussian is particularly attractive for several reasons. Consider the Fourier transform of a Gaussian $f(t) = e^{-\pi t^2}$, where we set $\kappa/\sigma = \pi$.

$$F(\omega) = \kappa \langle \psi | f \rangle$$
$$= \kappa \int e^{-\pi t^2 - j\omega t} dt$$

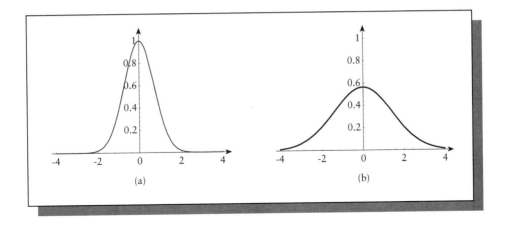

FIGURE 5.18

(a) A Gaussian bump. (b) Its Fourier transform.

$$= \kappa \int e^{a} e^{-\pi[t+(j\omega/2\pi)]^{2}} \, dt \tag{5.76}$$

We can complete the square and solve for $a = (-\omega^{2}/4\pi)$ in the last equation. Since this is independent of t, we can pull it out front. Then by substituting $u = t+(j\omega/2\pi)$, and $du = dt$, we can write

$$\begin{aligned}
F(\omega) &= \kappa e^{-\omega^{2}/4\pi} \int e^{-\pi[t+(j\omega/2\pi)]^{2}} \, dt \\
&= \kappa e^{-\omega^{2}/2\pi} \int e^{-\pi u^{2}} \, du \\
&= \kappa e^{-\omega^{2}/2\pi} \\
&= \kappa e^{-\omega^{2}} \kappa^{2}
\end{aligned} \tag{5.77}$$

where we have used property E20. So the Fourier transform of a Gaussian bump is another Gaussian bump, as shown in Figure 5.18.

The Gaussian is closely related to the complex exponentials, which as we have seen are eigenfunctions of LTI systems. It is because of this connection that Gaussians pass through the Fourier transform unchanged in form: the Fourier transform of a Gaussian is another Gaussian.

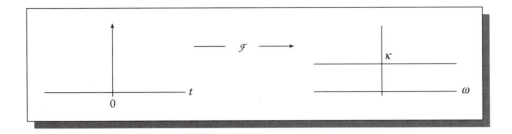

FIGURE   5.19

$\mathcal{F}\{\delta(t)\} = \kappa.$

5.7.4 The Impulse Signal

Taking the Fourier transform of the impulse $x(t) = \delta(t)$ is easy:

$$
\begin{aligned}
X(\omega) &= \kappa \left\langle \psi \middle| \delta \right\rangle \\
&= \kappa \int \delta(t) e^{-j\omega t} dt \\
&= \kappa e^{0} \\
&= \kappa
\end{aligned}
\tag{5.78}
$$

Thus the Fourier transform of an impulse is a flat spectrum, with equal energy at every frequency, as shown in Figure 5.19. The opposite interpretation is also true. Starting with an impulse $X(\omega) = \delta(\omega)$ in the frequency domain, we can take its inverse Fourier transform:

$$
\begin{aligned}
x(t) &= \kappa \left\langle \overline{\delta(\omega)} \middle| \psi \right\rangle \\
&= \kappa \psi(0) = \kappa e^{0} \\
&= \kappa
\end{aligned}
\tag{5.79}
$$

So the inverse transform of an impulse is a flat signal with equal height over all time, as shown in Figure 5.20.

We sometimes say that such a flat signal is a *DC* signal, by analogy to the voltage-time plot of *direct current* transmission of electrical power. The amplitude of the Fourier transform of a signal at $\omega = 0$ is sometimes called that signal's *DC component*. Thus a flat signal is *pure DC*, since its transform only has energy at $\omega = 0$. An impulse in time corresponds to a spectrum with equal energy at all frequencies.

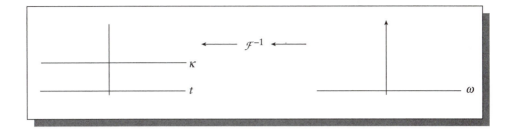

FIGURE 5.20

$\mathcal{F}^{-1}\{\delta(\omega)\} = \kappa.$

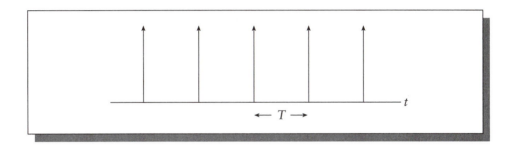

FIGURE 5.21

The impulse train.

5.7.5 The Impulse Train

Recall the shah function, or impulse train, from Equation 4.39 where the impulses appear at equal intervals of width T:

$$\text{III}_T(t) = \sum_k \delta(t - kT) \tag{5.80}$$

This function is plotted in Figure 5.21.

Let's find the Fourier transform for this signal. We begin by recalling from Equations 5.60 and 5.61 that for any periodic signal $x(t)$ with frequency ω_0 (recall $\omega_0 = 2\pi/T$), and Fourier series coefficients a_k, the strength of the signal at each harmonic $k\omega_0$ of the signal's frequency is $\kappa_T a_k$.

We can apply this observation directly to finding the transform of the periodic shah signal. So we begin by finding the Fourier series coefficients over a period

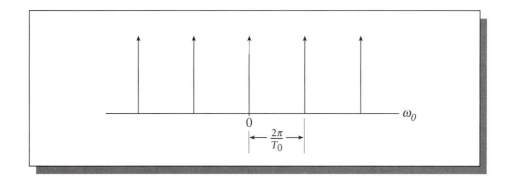

FIGURE 5.22
$\mathcal{F}\{\mathrm{III}_{T_0}(t)\}$.

centered at the origin:

$$
\begin{aligned}
a_k &= \kappa_T \left\langle \psi \mid x \right\rangle_{[T]} \\
&= \kappa_T \left\langle \psi \mid \delta \right\rangle_{[-T_0/2, T_0/2]} \\
&= \kappa_T \psi(0) \\
&= \kappa_T
\end{aligned}
\tag{5.81}
$$

So all the coefficients are the same. We now plug these into the Fourier transform for periodic signals from Equation 5.60:

$$
\begin{aligned}
X(\omega) &= \sum_k \frac{\kappa_T}{\kappa} a_k \delta(\omega - k\omega_0) \\
&= \sum_k \frac{\kappa_T^2}{\kappa} \delta(\omega - k\omega_0) \\
&= \frac{1}{\kappa T} \sum_k \delta\left(\omega - k\frac{2\pi}{T_0}\right)
\end{aligned}
\tag{5.82}
$$

Equation 5.82 is plotted in Figure 5.22. The essential point to notice is that a sequence of equally spaced impulses is turned into another sequence of equally spaced impulses, though their heights and intervals are different in the two spaces. In symbols,

$$
\mathrm{III}_{T_0}(t) \overset{\mathcal{F}}{\longleftrightarrow} \frac{1}{\kappa T} \mathrm{III}_{\omega_0}(\omega)
\tag{5.83}
$$

Notice that as the interval T_0 in signal space decreases and the pulses start to arrive closer together, the interval $2\pi/T_0$ in frequency space gets larger and there is more room between impulses in the spectrum. We will see in the next chapter that this inverse relationship between impulse intervals is the reason we can sometimes reduce aliasing by sampling more often.

5.8 Duality

The Fourier transform possesses a very useful property known as *duality*. The intuitive interpretation is that if you have a picture of two functions that you know are a Fourier transform pair, then it doesn't matter which one you label "signal" and which one "spectrum"; both labeling schemes are correct! Note that we are speaking here only of the Fourier transform and not the series representation; the latter does not share this property. This form of duality is only strictly true for the symmetrical definition used in this book; if one puts the normalizing factors on just the analysis or synthesis equations, a squared normalizing factor or its inverse will have to be inserted on one side or the other of the duality relation.

We have intimated duality with the box and impulse transform examples in the previous section. Consider the following Fourier transform pairs:

$$\delta(t) \overset{\mathcal{F}}{\longleftrightarrow} \kappa$$
$$\kappa \overset{\mathcal{F}}{\longleftrightarrow} \delta(\omega) \tag{5.84}$$

and

$$b_W(t) \overset{\mathcal{F}}{\longleftrightarrow} \kappa W \operatorname{sinc}\left(\omega \frac{W}{2\pi}\right)$$
$$\kappa W \operatorname{sinc}\left(t \frac{W}{2\pi}\right) \overset{\mathcal{F}}{\longleftrightarrow} b_W(\omega) \tag{5.85}$$

These rather remarkable pairs of transformations are not unique, but are representative of the general principle of duality.

To be a bit more general, suppose you have a function $f(t)$ with an associated Fourier transform $g(\omega) = \mathcal{F}\{f(t)\}$. Now think of $g(\omega)$ as a *time* signal; that is, simply replace ω with t in the definition of g, resulting in $g(t)$. What is the transform of this signal, $h(\omega) = \mathcal{F}\{g(t)\}$? The principle of duality tells us that $h(\omega) = f(-\omega)$.

We will first show this principle using integral notation. Write two functions f and g in terms of two variables u and v:

$$f(u) = \kappa \int g(v)e^{-juv}dv \tag{5.86}$$

Then with $u = t$ and $v = -\omega$,

$$f(t) = \kappa \int g(-\omega)e^{jt\omega}d\omega \tag{5.87}$$

which is the synthesis equation for the signal $f(t)$ with Fourier transform $g(-\omega)$. Now substitute $u = \omega$ and $v = t$ to get

$$f(\omega) = \kappa \int g(t)e^{-j\omega t}dt \tag{5.88}$$

This is the analysis equation for signal $g(t)$ with spectrum $f(\omega)$.

Thus we have the two related Fourier pairs

$$g(t) \overset{\mathcal{F}}{\longleftrightarrow} f(\omega)$$
$$f(t) \overset{\mathcal{F}}{\longleftrightarrow} g(-\omega) \tag{5.89}$$

We can write the same thing in braket notation. Here we will include the domain of the functions explicitly, since the very nature of duality makes it unclear from context:

$$g(\omega) = \kappa \langle \psi(t)| f(t) \rangle$$
$$g(t) = \kappa \left\langle \overline{f(\omega)} \middle| \psi(\omega) \right\rangle \tag{5.90}$$

Duality is important primarily for its conceptual power, relating the two domains in such a symmetrical way. Duality also immediately doubles our repertoire of Fourier transform pairs, since anything calculated in one domain can be immediately applied to the other.

Figure 5.23(a) shows a signal $f(t)$ and its transform $F(\omega)$ from a table. We can immediately write a new transform pair $\mathcal{F}\{f(\omega)\} = F(-\omega)$, as in Figure 5.23(b).

5.9   Filtering and Convolution

Recall the definition of a system's frequency response in Equation 4.54:

$$H(\omega) = \int h(\tau)e^{\omega\tau}d\tau \tag{5.91}$$

This definition is of the same form as the Fourier transform analysis equation. This relates the two methods we have seen for characterizing a system, using either the impulse response or the frequency response. Thus we have the very useful fact that the system response $H(\omega)$ and the impulse response $h(t)$ form a Fourier pair:

$$h(t) \overset{\mathcal{F}}{\longleftrightarrow} H(\omega) \tag{5.92}$$

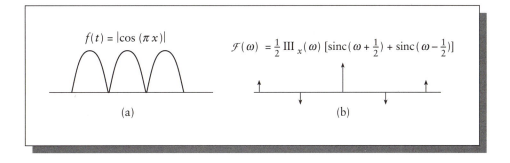

FIGURE 5.23

(a) A signal $f(t)$ and its transform. (b) The signal of (a) interpreted as a spectrum and its inverse transform, given by the duality property.

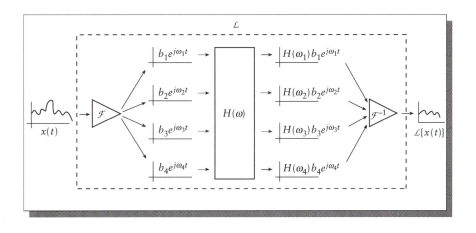

FIGURE 5.24

A linear filter modulates a signal by attenuating or magnifying each exponential component individually.

The frequency response of an LTI system is a powerful way to characterize a system completely. This is because we can break down any input into a sum of complex exponentials, compute the response of the system by simply applying the complex scaling factor to each exponential, then again summing together the weighted exponentials. This process is diagrammed in Figure 5.24.

This is the process of *filtering*. As an example, filters are often provided explicitly in audio electronics equipment. The bass and treble controls on a stereo are filters for the low and high frequencies: increasing the bass response means boosting the lower frequencies as they pass through the amplifier. In other words, $H(\omega)$ is increased for values of ω in the range called "bass." A *graphic equalizer* is a similar device, but it has multiple controls, each controlling its own interval of frequencies. Everyday filters also appear in lighting equipment; a tinted lamp shade reduces the amplitude of some frequencies of light.

Because of the importance of filters, we will now look more closely at filtering in both signal and frequency space. We will see that we can choose to apply a filter in frequency space or in signal space, depending on which is more intuitive or computationally practical.

We have seen that the response $y(t)$ of any LTI system may be found from the convolution of the input signal $x(t)$ with the system's impulse response $h(t)$. So we begin our study of filtering by looking at the Fourier transform of a convolution. We want to find $Y(\omega)$, the Fourier transform of $f(t) * h(t)$.

$$
\begin{aligned}
Y(\omega) &= \kappa \left\langle \psi \mid f * h \right\rangle \\
&= \kappa \int \left(f(t) * h(t) \right) e^{j\omega t} dt \\
&= \kappa \int \left(\int f(t) h(t - \tau) \, d\tau \right) e^{j\omega t} dt
\end{aligned}
\tag{5.93}
$$

We can switch the order of integration, writing

$$
\begin{aligned}
Y(\omega) &= \kappa \int f(t) \int h(t - \tau) \, dt \, e^{j\omega t} d\tau \\
&= \kappa \int f(t) e^{-j\omega \tau} \frac{1}{\kappa} H(\omega) \, d\tau \\
&= H(\omega) \int f(t) e^{-j\omega \tau} d\tau \\
&= H(\omega) F(\omega)
\end{aligned}
\tag{5.94}
$$

so

$$
\mathcal{F}\{f(t) * h(t)\} = F(\omega) H(\omega)
\tag{5.95}
$$

where in the second step we applied the delay property from Table 5.1, which states that

$$
\begin{aligned}
\mathcal{F}\{g(t - t_0)\} &= e^{-j\omega t_0} \mathcal{F}\{g(t)\} \\
&= e^{-j\omega t_0} G(\omega)
\end{aligned}
\tag{5.96}
$$

Property name	Transform pair
Transformation	$f(t) \xleftrightarrow{\mathcal{F}} F(\omega)$
Linearity	$af(t) + bg(t) \xleftrightarrow{\mathcal{F}} aF(\omega) + bG(\omega)$
Duality	$F(t) \xleftrightarrow{\mathcal{F}} f(-\omega)$
Scaling	$f(at) \xleftrightarrow{\mathcal{F}} \frac{1}{a} F\left(\frac{\omega}{a}\right)$
Delay	$f(t - t_0) \xleftrightarrow{\mathcal{F}} e^{-j\omega t_0} F(\omega)$
Modulation	$e^{j\omega_0 t} f(t) \xleftrightarrow{\mathcal{F}} F(\omega - \omega_0)$
Convolution	$f(t) * g(t) \xleftrightarrow{\mathcal{F}} F(\omega)G(\omega)$
Multiplication	$f(t)g(t) \xleftrightarrow{\mathcal{F}} F(\omega) * G(\omega)$
Time differentiation	$\frac{d^n}{dt^n} f(t) \xleftrightarrow{\mathcal{F}} (j\omega)^n F(\omega)$
Time integration	$\int_{-\infty}^{t} f(\tau)\, d\tau \xleftrightarrow{\mathcal{F}} \frac{F(\omega)}{j\omega} + \pi F(0)\delta(\omega)$
Frequency differentiation	$-jtf(t) \xleftrightarrow{\mathcal{F}} \frac{dF(\omega)}{d\omega}$
Frequency integration	$\frac{f(t)}{-jt} \xleftrightarrow{\mathcal{F}} \int F(\omega')\, d\omega'$
Reversal	$f(-t) \xleftrightarrow{\mathcal{F}} F(-\omega)$

TABLE 5.1
Fourier transform properties.

The principle of duality tells us that there is also a symmetrical relationship to Equation 5.95, specifically that two spectra may be convolved by multiplying their associated time signals. This is known as the *multiplication property*:

$$X(\omega) * H(\omega) = f(t)h(t) \tag{5.97}$$

The central point of this section may be summarized in the following way. Convolving two signals is identical to multiplying their spectra. Convolving two spectra is identical to multiplying their signals. In symbols,

$$F(\omega)H(\omega) = \mathcal{F}\{f(t) * h(t)\}$$
$$f(t)h(t) = \mathcal{F}\{F(\omega) * H(\omega)\} \tag{5.98}$$

Equation 5.98 is important both theoretically and practically. Recall from our discussion of convolution that a direct implementation of convolution can be very expensive. When signals become sufficiently large, it may be cheaper to take the Fourier transform of both signals, multiply their spectra, and then take the inverse transform back into signal space. This is even more attractive if the frequency response $H(\omega)$ can be precomputed and saved.

To find the impulse response $h(t)$ from an input $x(t)$ and an output $y(t)$, we observe that $y(t) = x(t) * h(t)$, or equivalently, $Y(\omega) = X(\omega)H(\omega)$. Thus

$$H(\omega) = \frac{Y(\omega)}{X(\omega)}, \qquad X(\omega) \neq 0 \qquad (5.99)$$

so the impulse response $h(t)$ may be found from

$$\begin{aligned} h(t) &= \mathcal{F}^{-1}\{H(\omega)\} \\ &= \mathcal{F}^{-1}\left\{ \frac{Y(\omega)}{X(\omega)} \right\} \\ &= \mathcal{F}^{-1}\left\{ \frac{\mathcal{F}\{y(t)\}}{\mathcal{F}\{x(t)\}} \right\} \end{aligned} \qquad (5.100)$$

If we measure the output $y(t)$ for a known input, we can find the impulse response numerically. If we know the output analytically and we can find the appropriate Fourier transforms, we can find an analytic expression for the impulse response $h(t)$ to characterize the system.

In general, almost all filtering tasks can be usefully examined in frequency space, where we ask what happens to the spectrum of a signal as it passes through some system. Typically an important part of the analysis involves considering how the spectrum of the signal is scaled by the frequency response of the system, which for a linear, time-invariant system is the Fourier representation of its impulse response. Thus such a filtering task may be viewed either as multiplication of two spectra or convolution of the signals. In practice, both approaches have advantages in different hardware and software settings.

Convolution has an intuitive interpretation when one of the signals consists only of impulses. For example, suppose a system with frequency response $H(\omega)$ is given as input a signal $x(t)$ that is a string of impulses:

$$x(t) = \sum_n \delta(t - nT) \qquad (5.101)$$

Then as we have seen, $X(\omega)$ is also a string of impulses, so $\mathcal{F}\{x(t) * h(t)\} = X(\omega)H(\omega)$ with $X(\omega)$ from Equation 5.83 will yield

$$\begin{aligned} Y(\omega) &= X(\omega)H(\omega) \\ Y(\omega) &= \frac{\kappa_T}{\kappa} \sum_k \delta\left(\omega - k2\pi/T\right) H(\omega) \end{aligned} \qquad (5.102)$$

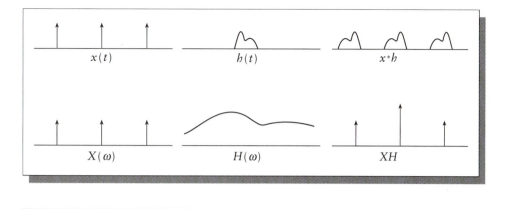

FIGURE 5.25

The frequency-space equivalent of convolution with the shah function.

Equation 5.102 shows us that when a series of pulses is convolved with a signal, the resulting spectrum is built by taking samples of the system's frequency response. This is shown in Figure 5.25.

5.9.1 Some Common Filters

Of the many common types of filters, three in particular will be useful to us. We will first review these filters in their ideal (or perfect) forms; they are illustrated in Figure 5.26.

An ideal (or perfect) *low-pass filter* allows frequencies below some threshold ω_T to pass unchanged, while those above the threshold are removed; in other words, an ideal low-pass filter $L(\omega)$ has frequency response

$$L(\omega) = \begin{cases} 1 & \omega \leq \omega_T \\ 0 & \omega > \omega_T \end{cases} \tag{5.103}$$

An ideal *high-pass filter* $H(\omega)$ has the opposite characteristic:

$$H(\omega) = \begin{cases} 0 & \omega \leq \omega_T \\ 1 & \omega > \omega_T \end{cases} \tag{5.104}$$

An ideal *band-pass filter* $B(\omega)$ combines the previous two, passing only those fre-

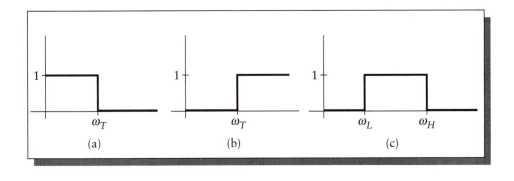

FIGURE 5.26

(a) An ideal low-pass filter. (b) An ideal high-pass filter. (c) An ideal band-pass filter.

quencies with a given band (ω_L, ω_H):

$$B(\omega) = \begin{cases} 0 & \omega < \omega_L \\ 1 & \omega_L \leq \omega \leq \omega_H \\ 0 & \omega > \omega_H \end{cases} \tag{5.105}$$

Because each of these filters has a finite width in frequency space, they have infinite width in signal space; such filters are called *infinite impulse response* (IIR) filters. By comparison, a filter with finite support in signal space is called a *finite impulse response* (FIR) filter.

Consider trying to implement an ideal low-pass filter in signal space. Since the impulse response is infinite, its implementation requires convolving with the signal over all time, from before the big bang to after eternity. This is impossible, so somehow we need to convert our ideal IIR filters into realizable FIR filters. The typical approach is to *window* the filter, by multiplying the impulse response with some function that has finite support. Of course, this changes the impulse response, which changes the filter characteristics in frequency space. Some standard windowing functions include the box, the Gaussian bump, and the sinc function. The trade-offs involved in windowing a filter appropriately are complicated; pointers to the literature appear in the Further Reading section.

When a filter is windowed to make it physically possible, the perfect behavior shown in Figure 5.26 is degraded. In general, each of the sharp discontinuities is smeared into a range of frequencies, and the filter response rings near the transitions. Figure 5.27 shows a close-up near the discontinuity in a low-pass filter. The ideal threshold frequency ω_T is spread out into a *transition band* (ω_p, ω_s), within which the filter's response drops off. The region below ω_p is called the *pass band*, and the

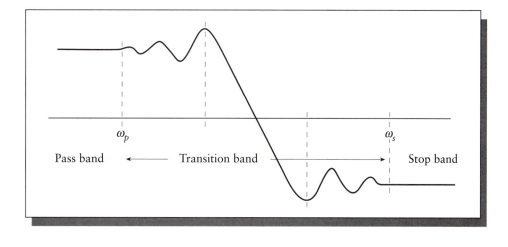

FIGURE 5.27

A realizable filter has no sharp discontinuities.

region above ω_s is called the *stop band*. The locations of ω_p and ω_s are generally determined by the application; they are typically placed as near the discontinuity as possible, without allowing the response in the pass- or stop-bands to stray "too far" from flatness. Notice that the filter ripples, or *rings*, near the transition band. As a filter approaches the ideal, it rings less, the response in the stop and pass bands flattens, and the transition band narrows; this causes an unavoidable widening of the impulse response in the signal domain.

We will often use the ideal filters in our theoretical material, though we will always need to deal with realizable filters when discussing implementations.

5.10 The Fourier Transform Table

Table 5.1 lists a number of properties of the Fourier transform, with their common names. We will not prove these properties, since we will only be using them occasionally. Detailed proofs may be found in most signal-processing texts. Because of duality, we can reverse the meanings of the variables t and ω, as in the case of multiplication and convolution.

5.11   Discrete-Time Fourier Representations

Most computer graphics are concerned with sampled signals. The basic ideas of Fourier transforms can be applied to such signals, but there are a few subtle, significant changes that make the results quite different.

In this section we will derive expressions for the discrete-time versions of the Fourier series and Fourier transform. Remember that as with the term "continuous-time," the phrase "discrete-time" actually refers to any discrete parameter.

5.11.1   The Discrete-Time Fourier Series

We begin by deriving the expressions for the *discrete-time Fourier series*. We will base our discussion on finding the transform for a periodic signal $x[n]$, which is defined over the interval $[0, N) = [N]$. Since $x[n]$ is periodic, $x[n + N] = x[n]$.

We begin with the basis functions. By analogy with the Fourier transform, we will use sampled complex exponentials with period N. The *complete set* of these is given by

$$\psi'_k[n] = e^{jk(2\pi/N)n}, \qquad k \in [N] \tag{5.106}$$

When the index k is part of a summation, or is otherwise understood in context, we will usually omit it and write simply $\psi'[n]$.

In contrast to the continuous case, there are only N discrete complex exponentials of period N. To see this, write the value of $\psi'_{k+N}[N]$ for any integer k:

$$\begin{aligned}
\psi'_k + N[n] &= e^{j(k+N)(2\pi/N)n} \\
&= e^{jk(2\pi/N)n} e^{jN(2\pi/N)n} \\
&= \psi'_k[n] e^{j2\pi n} \\
&= \psi'_k[n] \tag{5.107}
\end{aligned}$$

where the last line used E17. So after we have created the first N sampled complex exponentials of period N, we start repeating them, beginning with $\psi'_N[n] = \psi'_0[n]$. This observation has several important ramifications; we will see that this property is one of the factors leading to aliasing in digital systems.

It will be useful to us to know that the sum of any $\psi'_k[n]$ over any period (that is, any set of N contiguous samples) is 0, unless the function is constant. That is,

$$\sum_{n=0}^{N-1} e^{jk(2\pi/N)n} = \sum_{n\in[N]} e^{jk(2\pi/N)n} = \begin{cases} N & k = 0, \pm N, \pm 2N, \ldots \\ 0 & \text{otherwise} \end{cases} \tag{5.108}$$

Equation 5.108 comes directly from the finite sum of a geometric series.

We now turn to representation of a discrete signal $x[n]$ by these basis functions. Again by analogy to the Fourier transform, we write the signal as a linear combination of the (now discrete) basis functions:

$$x[n] = \sum_{k \in [N]} a_k \psi'[n] = \sum_{k \in [N]} a_k e^{jk(2\pi/N)n} = \langle \overline{a} | \psi' \rangle_{[N]} \tag{5.109}$$

Notice that the summation only includes N distinct terms; this is because there are only N distinct complex sinusoids, as we discovered above. We can expand Equation 5.109 into a matrix equation, expressing the N unknown scalars a_k in terms of the N known $x[n]$ values and the $N \times N$ matrix of exponentials.

$$\begin{bmatrix} x_0 \\ x_1 \\ \vdots \\ x_{N-1} \end{bmatrix} = \begin{bmatrix} a_0 \\ a_1 \\ \vdots \\ a_{N-1} \end{bmatrix} \begin{bmatrix} 1 & 1 & 1 & 1 & \cdots & 1 \\ 1 & e^{\gamma} & e^{2\gamma} & e^{3\gamma} & \cdots & e^{(N-1)\gamma} \\ 1 & e^{\gamma 2} & e^{2\gamma 2} & e^{3\gamma 2} & \cdots & e^{(N-1)\gamma 2} \\ \vdots & \vdots & \vdots & \vdots & & \vdots \\ 1 & e^{\gamma(N-2)} & e^{2\gamma(N-2)} & e^{3\gamma(N-2)} & \cdots & e^{(N-1)\gamma(N-2)} \\ 1 & e^{\gamma(N-1)} & e^{2\gamma(N-1)} & e^{3\gamma(N-1)} & \cdots & e^{(N-1)\gamma(N-1)} \end{bmatrix} \tag{5.110}$$

where for compactness we have substituted

$$\gamma = \frac{j2\pi}{N} \tag{5.111}$$

If we write Equation 5.110 in matrix form as $X = AF$, then we could solve for the coefficients by inverting F, yielding $A = XF^{-1}$. This inversion is only possible if F is nonsingular. We know this condition is met because it is built from the $\psi'[n]$ functions, which are orthogonal; thus, the columns are linearly independent, and the matrix may be inverted.

But matrix inversion is a costly process, particularly for large matrices. We would prefer a simple, closed-form solution for the coefficients a_k in Equation 5.109 in terms of the $x[n]$.

To find this expression, multiply Equation 5.109 on both sides by $e^{-jr(2\pi/N)n}$ and sum over N terms:

$$\sum_{n \in [N]} x[n] e^{-jr(2\pi/N)n} = \sum_{n \in [N]} \sum_{k \in [N]} a_k e^{j(k-r)(2\pi/N)n} \tag{5.112}$$

Since summation is commutative, we can reverse the summation of the right-hand term, and pull out the now-constant a_k:

$$\sum_{n \in [N]} x[n] e^{-jr(2\pi/N)n} = \sum_{k \in [N]} a_k \sum_{n \in [N]} e^{j(k-r)(2\pi/N)n} \tag{5.113}$$

Consider the rightmost summation in Equation 5.113. Equation 5.108 says that when $k = r$, it will have the value N, and it will be 0 otherwise. Thus, the terms on the right-hand side will be of the form $a_k 0$ or $a_k N$, the latter being the only nonzero term, and only appearing at $r = k$. So the entire right-hand side is simply $a_r N$. This is the closed-form expression for the coefficients we sought:

$$a_r = \frac{1}{N} \sum_{n \in [N]} x[n] e^{-jr(2\pi/N)n} = \frac{1}{N} \langle \psi' | x \rangle_{[N]} \tag{5.114}$$

Together, Equations 5.109 and 5.114 show how to transform a sampled function $x[n]$ with period N into and out of frequency space. We distribute the normalizing term $1/N$ symmetrically as before, writing $\kappa_N = 1/\sqrt{N}$. We define the *discrete-time Fourier series* pair below:

$$x[n] = \kappa_N \sum_{k \in [N]} a_k e^{jk(2\pi/N)n} = \kappa_N \langle \overline{a} | \psi' \rangle_{[N]} \tag{5.115}$$

$$a_k = \kappa_N \sum_{n \in [N]} x[n] e^{-jk(2\pi/N)n} = \kappa_N \langle \psi' | x \rangle_{[N]} \tag{5.116}$$

As before, the expression for $x[n]$ is called the *synthesis* equation, and that for a_k is called the *analysis* equation.

Recall from the definition that the summation range represented by $[N]$ may be satisfied by any N contiguous values from $m \bmod N$ to $(m + N) \bmod N$. Suppose we write out the expansion explicitly for both $m = 0$ and $m = 1$:

$$\begin{aligned} x_{m=0}[n] &= a_0 \psi'_0[n] + a_1 \psi'_1[n] + \cdots + a_{N-1} \psi'_{N-1}[n] \\ x_{m=1}[n] &= \qquad\qquad a_1 \psi'_1[n] + \cdots + a_{N-1} \psi'_{N-1}[n] + a_N \psi'_N[n] \end{aligned} \tag{5.117}$$

Since $x_{m=0}[n] = x_{m=1}[n]$, and recalling from Equation 5.107 that $\psi'_0[n] = \psi'_N[n]$, we find

$$\begin{aligned} x_{m=0}[n] - x_{m=1}[n] &= 0 = a_0 \psi'_0[n] - a_N \psi'_N[n] \\ a_0 &= a_n \end{aligned} \tag{5.118}$$

Since this hold true for all choices of m, we find that

$$a_k = a_{k+N} \tag{5.119}$$

Equation 5.119 is very important; it is one of the essential characteristics of the discrete Fourier series for discrete signals. It comes about because there are only N

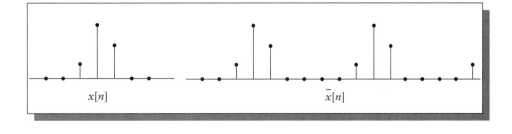

FIGURE 5.28

Building a periodic signal $\widetilde{x}[n]$ from an aperiodic signal $x[n]$.

distinct complex exponentials with period N; thus, the discrete-time Fourier series contains only N unique terms. The coefficient a_0 represents the amplitude of the constant part of the signal, and larger values of k refer to coefficients on higher frequencies of the signal.

5.11.2 The Discrete-Time Fourier Transform

We now turn to the *discrete-time Fourier transform* (DTFT). This is appropriate for aperiodic signals. As with the continuous-time Fourier transform, the basic idea is to approximate an aperiodic signal $x[n]$ with a periodic signal $\widetilde{x}[n]$ that matches x within one period. When $x[n]$ goes to zero, $\widetilde{x}[n]$ repeats the signal $x[n]$ over and over. As the period tends to infinity, the match covers more of the input range and is thus more accurate.

We begin with a finite-width signal $x[n]$. Without loss of generality, we assume that this signal is centered around 0, and $x[n] = 0$ if $|n| > W/2$. We construct an approximation $\widetilde{x}[n]$ by

$$\widetilde{x}[n] = \begin{cases} x[n] & |n| \le N/2 \\ x[n \bmod N/2] & |n| > N/2 \end{cases} \tag{5.120}$$

as shown in Figure 5.28.

We can write the discrete Fourier series approximation for $\widetilde{x}[n]$ from Equation 5.116:

$$\widetilde{x}[n] = \kappa_N \left\langle \overline{a} \middle| \psi' \right\rangle_{[N]} \tag{5.121}$$

So we start by finding the coefficients a_k:

$$
\begin{aligned}
a_k &= \kappa_N \left\langle \psi' \,\middle|\, \widetilde{x} \right\rangle_{[-W/2,\,W/2]} \\
&= \kappa_N \left\langle \psi' \,\middle|\, x \right\rangle \\
&= \kappa_N \sum_n e^{-jk(2\pi/N)n} x[n]
\end{aligned}
\tag{5.122}
$$

The infinite limits on the last line come from the fact that $x[n]$ is 0 outside of $W/2$, by definition. As in the continuous case, we write the coefficients as samples of a continuous function $X(\Omega)$:

$$
a_k = \kappa_N X(k\Omega)
\tag{5.123}
$$

where $X(\Omega)$ is defined by

$$
\begin{aligned}
X(\Omega) &= \sum_{n=-\infty}^{+\infty} x[n] e^{-j\Omega n} = \left\langle \psi' \,\middle|\, x \right\rangle \\
\Omega &= 2\pi/N
\end{aligned}
\tag{5.124}
$$

Note that we are using Ω to represent frequency for discrete signals; the time-frequency pairs are usually x and ω for continuous time and n and Ω for discrete time. Thus each a_k is one of a set of equally spaced samples of the "envelope" formed by $X(\Omega)$. We can now plug these coefficients into the synthesis formula:

$$
\begin{aligned}
\widetilde{x}[n] &= \kappa_N \left\langle \overline{a} \,\middle|\, \psi' \right\rangle_{[N]} \\
&= \kappa_N \sum_{k \in [N]} \kappa_N X(k\Omega) e^{jk\Omega n} \\
&= \frac{1}{2\pi} \sum_{k \in [N]} X(k\Omega) e^{j\Omega n} \Omega
\end{aligned}
\tag{5.125}
$$

The last step comes from noting that $\kappa^2 = 1/N = \Omega/2\pi$. This equation represents a discrete approximation to an integral, where each rectangle has height $X(k\Omega)e^{j\Omega n}$ and width Ω, as shown in Figure 5.29.

As $N \to \infty$, $\widetilde{x}[n] \to x[n]$, and $\Omega \to 0$. So the summation in Equation 5.125 passes to integration and becomes

$$
x[n] = \frac{1}{2\pi} \int_{2\pi} X(\Omega) e^{j\Omega n} d\Omega = \kappa \left\langle \overline{X} \,\middle|\, \psi' \right\rangle_{[2\pi]}
\tag{5.126}
$$

Since $X(\Omega)e^{j\Omega n}$ is periodic with period 2π, any region of integration with width 2π will work. We have now found the defining equations for the discrete-time Fourier transform, which are summarized below.

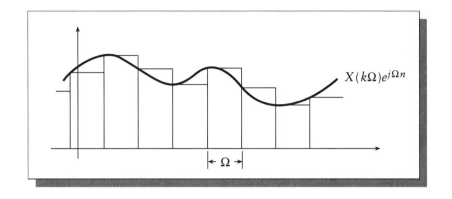

FIGURE 5.29

The expression $\sum\limits_{k \in [N]} X(k\Omega)e^{j\Omega n}\Omega$ approximates an integral.

$$x[n] = \frac{1}{\sqrt{2\pi}} \int_{2\pi} X(\Omega)e^{j\Omega n} d\Omega = \kappa \langle \overline{x} | \psi' \rangle_{[2\pi]} \qquad (5.127)$$

$$X(\Omega) = \frac{1}{\sqrt{2\pi}} \sum_n x[n]e^{-j\Omega n} \quad = \kappa \langle \psi' | x \rangle \qquad (5.128)$$

We will extend the notation of Equation 5.57 to discrete signals as follows:

$$\begin{aligned}
X(\Omega) &= \mathcal{F}\{x[n]\} \\
x[n] &= \mathcal{F}^{-1}\{X(\Omega)\} \\
x[n] &\overset{\mathcal{F}}{\longleftrightarrow} X(\Omega)
\end{aligned} \qquad (5.129)$$

Table 5.4 gives the properties of the discrete Fourier transform. These properties are similar to those listed in Table 5.1 for the continuous case.

The Dirichlet conditions that specified convergence of the Fourier transform integral have counterparts in the digital domain. One way to state these conditions is to require the discrete function $x[n]$ be *absolutely summable* [326], which means it satisfies

$$\sum_n |x[n]| < \infty \qquad (5.130)$$

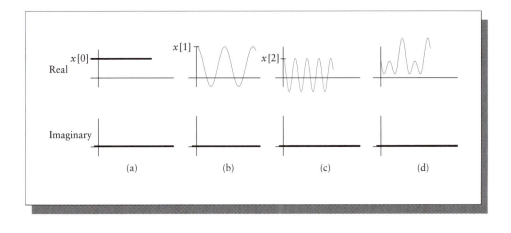

FIGURE 5.30

(a) $x[0]$. (b) $x[1]e^{-j\Omega}$. (c) $x[2]e^{-2j\Omega}$. (d) Parts (a), (b), and (c) added together.

An alternative, weaker condition requires the signal to have finite energy (this is weaker because some signals that are not absolutely summable can have finite energy). The energy $E(x)$ of a discrete function $x[n]$ is defined as

$$E(x) \triangleq \sum_n x^2[n] = \langle x\,|\,x \rangle \tag{5.131}$$

If $E(x) < \infty$, the summation will converge.

Example of the DTFT

As an example of the discrete-time Fourier transform, let's suppose we have an input signal $x[n]$ that is nonzero for only $n = 0, 1, 2$. Let's take the Fourier transform of this signal:

$$\begin{aligned} X(\Omega) &= \kappa \langle \psi'\,|\,x \rangle \\ &= \kappa \sum_n x[n]e^{-j\Omega n} \\ &= \kappa \left(x[0] + x[1]e^{-j\Omega} + x[2]e^{-2j\Omega} \right) \end{aligned} \tag{5.132}$$

So $X(\Omega)$ is built from just the first three complex exponentials. These are graphed in Figure 5.30. Note that although $x[n]$ was aperiodic, $X(\Omega)$ is periodic.

We'll now confirm that we get back what we started with. Before we start, we can use property E21 to find the identity

$$\int_{2\pi} e^{j\alpha t} dt = 2\pi e^{j\alpha\pi} \operatorname{sinc}(\alpha) \tag{5.133}$$

We also recall that $\operatorname{sinc}(k) = 0$ for any integer k. Let's now take the inverse transform of the spectrum in Equation 5.132:

$$
\begin{aligned}
x[n] &= \kappa \langle \overline{x} | \psi' \rangle_{[2\pi]} \\
&= \kappa \int_{2\pi} X(\Omega) e^{j\Omega n} d\Omega \\
&= \kappa \int_{2\pi} \kappa \left(x[0] + x[1] e^{-j\Omega} + x[2] e^{-2j\Omega} \right) e^{j\Omega n} d\Omega \\
&= \kappa^2 \left\{ \left(x[0] \int_{2\pi} e^{j\Omega n} d\Omega \right) + \left(x[1] \int_{2\pi} e^{j\Omega(n-1)} d\Omega \right) + \left(x[2] \int_{2\pi} e^{j\Omega(n-2)} d\Omega \right) \right\}
\end{aligned}
\tag{5.134}
$$

Using the identity from Equation 5.133, we write the particular value of this expression for $n = 0$:

$$
\begin{aligned}
x[0] &= \frac{1}{2\pi} \left\{ \left(x[0] \int_{2\pi} 1 \, d\Omega \right) + \left(x[1] \int_{2\pi} e^{-j\Omega} d\Omega \right) + \left(x[2] \int_{2\pi} e^{-2j\Omega} d\Omega \right) \right\} \\
&= \frac{1}{2\pi} \left\{ (x[0] 2\pi) + \left(4\pi^2 e^{j\pi} \operatorname{sinc}(1) \right) + \left(4\pi^2 e^{2j\pi} \operatorname{sinc}(2) \right) \right\} \\
&= x[0]
\end{aligned}
\tag{5.135}
$$

because $\operatorname{sinc}(1) = \operatorname{sinc}(2) = 0$. Similar expressions for $x[1]$ and $x[2]$ yield the same results, so we have successfully transformed our signal $x[n]$ into the frequency domain to get $X(\Omega)$, and then transformed that spectrum back into the signal domain to recover $x[n]$.

5.12 Fourier Series and Transforms Summary

We have covered four types of Fourier representations. In the continuous domain, we had a series and a transform definition for periodic and aperiodic signals, respectively. We had the same pair in the discrete domain. Table 5.2 presents a summary of these results in both integral and braket forms.

$$
\begin{aligned}
\psi &= e^{j\omega t} & \kappa &= 1/\sqrt{2\pi} \\
\psi_k &= e^{jk\omega t} & \kappa_T &= 1/\sqrt{T} \\
\psi' &= e^{jk(2\pi/N)n} & \kappa_N &= 1/\sqrt{N}
\end{aligned}
\tag{5.136}
$$

		Fourier series	Fourier transform
Continuous time	Synthesis	$x(t) = \dfrac{1}{\sqrt{T}} \displaystyle\sum_{k=-\infty}^{+\infty} a_k e^{jk\omega t}$ $x = \kappa_T \left\langle \overline{a} \middle| \psi \right\rangle$	$x(t) = \dfrac{1}{\sqrt{2\pi}} \displaystyle\int_{-\infty}^{+\infty} X(\omega) e^{j\omega t}\, d\omega$ $x = \kappa \left\langle \overline{X} \middle| \psi \right\rangle$
	Analysis	$a_k = \dfrac{1}{\sqrt{T}} \displaystyle\int_{T} x(t) e^{-jk\omega t}\, dt$ $a_k = \kappa_T \left\langle \psi \middle| x \right\rangle_{[T]}$	$X(\omega) = \dfrac{1}{\sqrt{2\pi}} \displaystyle\int_{-\infty}^{+\infty} x(t) e^{-j\omega t}\, dt$ $X = \kappa \left\langle \psi \middle| x \right\rangle$
Discrete time	Synthesis	$x[n] = \dfrac{1}{\sqrt{N}} \displaystyle\sum_{k\in[N]} a_k e^{jk(2\pi/N)n}$ $x = \kappa_N \left\langle \overline{a} \middle| \psi' \right\rangle_{[N]}$	$x[n] = \dfrac{1}{\sqrt{2\pi}} \displaystyle\int_{2\pi} X(\Omega) e^{j\Omega n}\, d\Omega$ $x = \kappa \left\langle \overline{X} \middle| \psi' \right\rangle_{[2\pi]}$
	Analysis	$a_k = \dfrac{1}{\sqrt{N}} \displaystyle\sum_{k\in[N]} x[n] e^{-jk(2\pi/N)n}$ $a_k = \kappa_N \left\langle \psi' \middle| x \right\rangle_{[N]}$	$X(\Omega) = \dfrac{1}{\sqrt{2\pi}} \displaystyle\sum_{n=-\infty}^{+\infty} x[n] e^{-j\Omega n}$ $X = \kappa \left\langle \psi' \middle| x \right\rangle$

TABLE 5.2
Fourier transform summary.

Notice how similar all the braket forms appear. This is one reason we use the braket in this book; it clearly shows that in all domains, the Fourier transformation is simply the projection of a signal onto a new basis made of complex exponentials. The interpretation of the braket as a sum or integral, and the appropriate range of the operator, are the only distinguishing factors between the various forms.

A list of some useful transform pairs for the CT Fourier transform is shown in Table 5.3.

Many more Fourier transform pairs may be found in the references listed under Further Reading. Always be sure that you know what normalization convention is used by each author. We are using the symmetrical convention in this book, but the 2π normalization factor might appear on only one equation or the other, or in the exponent of the basis functions. You can generally tell the convention by looking at one of the simple pairs, such as the transform of a constant or an impulse function.

If you use symbolic or numerical mathematics software to compute Fourier transforms, you'll again need to know how that package treats the normalization constants. Try a couple of simple transforms to see what convention is used by that software. Note that different packages within the same system may use different conventions.

5.13 Convolution Revisited

Let's find the DTFT of a convolution sum. From Equation 5.128 we can write the Fourier series for $y[n]$:

$$
\begin{aligned}
Y(\Omega) &= \mathcal{F}\{y[n]\} \\
&= \kappa \langle \psi' \,|\, x \rangle \\
&= \kappa \sum_n y[n] e^{-j\Omega n} \\
&= \kappa \sum_n \sum_k x[k] h[n-k] e^{-j\Omega n}
\end{aligned}
\tag{5.137}
$$

We can switch the order of the summations, and noticing that $x[k]$ is independent of n, bring it out front:

$$
\begin{aligned}
Y(\Omega) &= \kappa \sum_k x[k] \sum_n h[n-k] e^{-j\Omega n} \\
&= \kappa \sum_k x[k] e^{-j\Omega n} H(\Omega)
\end{aligned}
\tag{5.138}
$$

The last transformation comes from the time-shifting property of the Fourier series, which expresses the transform pair $x[n-n_0] \overset{\mathcal{F}}{\longleftrightarrow} e^{-j\Omega n_0} X(\Omega)$, as in Table 5.4.

Time signal	Spectrum
$\delta(t)$	κ
a	$\dfrac{a\delta(\omega)}{\kappa}$
$\cos(at)$	$\dfrac{\kappa}{2}\left[\delta(\omega+a)+\delta(\omega-a)\right]$
$\sin(at)$	$\dfrac{j\kappa}{2}\left[\delta(\omega+a)-\delta(\omega-a)\right]$
e^{jat}	$\dfrac{\delta(\omega-a)}{\kappa}$
$e^{-a|t|}$	$\dfrac{2a\kappa}{a^2+w^2}$
e^{-at^2}	$\kappa\sqrt{\dfrac{\pi}{a}}e^{-\omega^2/4a}$
$\delta(t-a)$	κe^{-jwa}
$\mathrm{III}_a(t)$	$\dfrac{\kappa_T}{\kappa}\,\mathrm{III}_{2\pi/a}(\omega)$
$b_W(t)$	$\kappa W\,\mathrm{sinc}\left(\omega\dfrac{W}{w\pi}\right)$
$\displaystyle\sum_n b_W(t-nT)$	$\dfrac{W\kappa_T^2}{\kappa}\displaystyle\sum_n \mathrm{sinc}\left(\omega\dfrac{nW}{\pi}\right)\delta\left(\omega-n\dfrac{2\pi}{T}\right)$

TABLE 5.3
Some CT Fourier transform pairs.

Property name	Transform pair
Transformation	$f[n] \overset{\mathcal{F}}{\longleftrightarrow} F(\Omega)$
Linearity	$af[n] + bg[t] \overset{\mathcal{F}}{\longleftrightarrow} aF(\Omega) + bG(\Omega)$
Duality	$f[n] \overset{\mathcal{F}}{\longleftrightarrow} f(\Omega)$
Scaling	$f[an] \overset{\mathcal{F}}{\longleftrightarrow} \dfrac{1}{a} F\left(\dfrac{\Omega}{a}\right)$
Delay	$f[n - n_0] \overset{\mathcal{F}}{\longleftrightarrow} e^{-j\Omega n_0} F(\Omega)$
Modulation	$e^{j\Omega_0 n} f[n] \overset{\mathcal{F}}{\longleftrightarrow} F(\Omega - \Omega_0)$
Convolution	$f[n] * g[n] \overset{\mathcal{F}}{\longleftrightarrow} F(\Omega)G(\Omega)$
Multiplication	$f[n]g[n] \overset{\mathcal{F}}{\longleftrightarrow} F(\Omega) * G(\Omega)$
Time differentiation	$\dfrac{d^a}{dn^a} f[n] \overset{\mathcal{F}}{\longleftrightarrow} (j\Omega)^a F(\Omega)$
Time integration	$\displaystyle\int_{-\infty}^{n} f[\tau]\, d\tau \overset{\mathcal{F}}{\longleftrightarrow} \dfrac{F(\Omega)}{j\Omega} + \pi F(0)\delta(\Omega)$
Frequency differentiation	$-jnf[n] \overset{\mathcal{F}}{\longleftrightarrow} \dfrac{dF(\Omega)}{d\Omega}$
Frequency integration	$\dfrac{f[n]}{-jn} \overset{\mathcal{F}}{\longleftrightarrow} \displaystyle\int F(\Omega')\, d\Omega'$
Reversal	$f[-n] \overset{\mathcal{F}}{\longleftrightarrow} F(-\Omega)$

TABLE 5.4
Discrete Fourier transform properties.

Since $H(\Omega)$ is independent of k, we can move it out of the summation, and then notice that what's left is the Fourier series for $x[n]$:

$$Y(\Omega) = H(\Omega) \sum_k x[k]e^{-j\Omega n}$$
$$= H(\Omega)X(\Omega) \tag{5.139}$$

Thus we have arrived at the *convolution transform pair*, which by duality extends to the *multiplication transform pair*, summarized as

$$X(\Omega)H(\Omega) = \mathcal{F}\{x[n] * h[n]\}$$
$$x[n]h[n] = \mathcal{F}^{-1}\{X(\Omega) * H(\Omega)\} \tag{5.140}$$

5.14 Two-Dimensional Fourier Transforms

The Fourier transform, in both continuous-time and discrete-time cases, can be directly generalized to two dimensions. The only conceptual change is that we now project a 2D signal onto a set of 2D basis functions. The practical result is that our summations and integrals become double summations and integrals, the kernels of the transformation become 2D, and the overall normalizing terms are squares of the 1D terms.

In this section we will skip over the derivation of the 2D Fourier series and head directly to the transform.

Just as we chose (x, y) and $[m, n]$ arbitrarily for the input spaces of generic 2D signals, we represent the frequency domain of a continuous-time signal by the Greek letters (μ, ν), and the frequency domain of a discrete-time signal by the Greek letters (η, ξ).

5.14.1 Continuous-Time 2D Fourier Transforms

Our new basis functions will be denoted ψ_2 for the continuous-time case, and are given by

$$\psi_2 = e^{j(\mu x + \nu y)} \tag{5.141}$$

This family of functions has the associated normalization constants

$$\kappa^2 = \frac{1}{2\pi} \tag{5.142}$$

The *2D continuous-time Fourier transform* (2D CTFT) is given by the projection of a 2D signal onto these 2D basis functions. Generalizing the 1D case, we have

$$F(\mu, \nu) = \frac{1}{2\pi} \iint f(x, y) e^{-j(\mu x + \nu y)} \, dx \, dy = \kappa^2 \left\langle \psi_2 \middle| f \right\rangle$$

$$f(x, y) = \frac{1}{2\pi} \iint F(\mu, \nu) e^{-j(\mu x + \nu y)} \, d\mu \, d\nu = \kappa^2 \left\langle \overline{F} \middle| \psi_2 \right\rangle \tag{5.143}$$

The new kernel ψ_2 is *separable*. A function $f(x, y)$ is separable if it is the product of two functions, each dependent on only x and y:

$$f(x, y) = f_1(x) f_2(y) \tag{5.144}$$

The basis ψ_2 is separable since

$$\psi_2 = e^{j(\mu x + \nu y)} = e^{j\mu x} e^{j\nu y} \tag{5.145}$$

This observation can be a great help in practice. It means that we may write the analysis equation as the cascade of two 1D transformations:

$$F_y(\mu, y) = \kappa \int f(x, y) e^{-j\mu x} \, dx$$

$$F(\mu, \nu) = \kappa \int F_y(\mu, y) e^{-j\nu y} \, dy \tag{5.146}$$

Equation 5.146 has important practical ramifications. It tells us that we can take the 2D Fourier transform of a signal by taking two successive 1D passes, either transforming all the rows and then all the columns, or vice versa. The synthesis formula shares this property.

Because of this property, the 2D Fourier transform inherits all of the properties of the 1D transform, such as scaling, convolution, modulation, and so forth.

The 2D complex Fourier transform is often illustrated by a pair of images. Typically these images display the magnitude and phase of the transform, although some authors present the real and imaginary parts instead. The dynamic range of the transform is often much larger than that of photographic film and most printing technologies, so it is usually altered before display. Because a linear compression tends to lose much of the signal, most pictures of Fourier transforms instead present the logarithms of the magnitude and phase. A typical presentation is shown in Figure 5.31.

It is not unusual to also see the transform displayed in *decibels* (dB). The definition of the decibel transformation is

$$\mathrm{dB}\,(x) = x_{dB} = -20 \log_{10}(x) \tag{5.147}$$

To get a feeling for decibels, observe that

$$\mathrm{dB}\,(2x) \approx 6 + \mathrm{dB}\,(x) \tag{5.148}$$

so doubling of the input corresponds to an increase of about 6 decibels.

To see the 2D Fourier transform in action, look at Figures C and D in the introduction to this unit. They show the processing of a 2D signal, and its Fourier transform, through an idealized rendering system.

E x a m p l e :   T h e   2 D   C o n t i n u o u s   B o x

Consider the 2D aperiodic box signal $b_{W,H}(x, y)$ shown in Figure 5.32. This signal is defined by

$$b_{W,H}(x, y) = \begin{cases} 1 & |x| \leq W/2 \text{ and } |y| \leq H/2 \\ 0 & \text{otherwise} \end{cases} \tag{5.149}$$

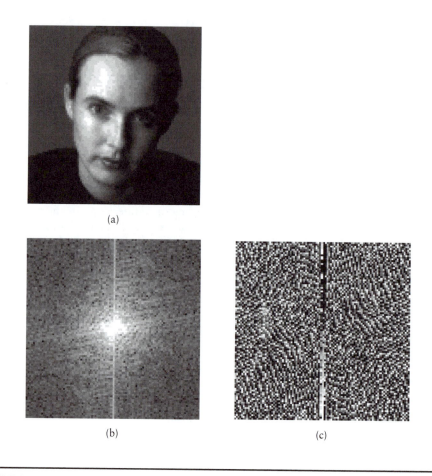

(a)

(b)   (c)

FIGURE 5.31

The 2D Fourier transform. (a) An image $f(x, y)$. (b) The magnitude of the transform: $|F(\mu, \nu)|$. (c) The phase of the transform: $\mathrm{Re}\{F(\mu, \nu)\} / \mathrm{Im}\{F(\mu, \nu)\}$.

Before we take the transform we will pause for a moment to consider what to expect. The input signal $b_{W,H}(x, y)$ is a separable function, built from the product of two 1D boxes. We know that the Fourier transform of a box is a sinc, and we saw above that a 2D transform may be taken as a sequence of two 1D transforms. Intuitively, we would expect the horizontal pass to spread out the horizontal box into a sinc, and the vertical pass to do the same. Thus we would expect the Fourier

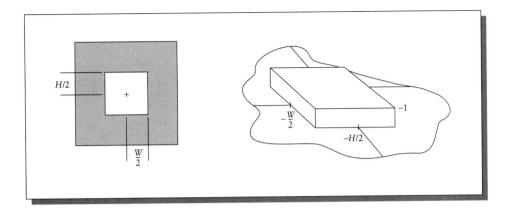

FIGURE 5.32

The 2D box $b_{W,H}(x,y)$ of half-width W and half-height H.

transform of the 2D box to be the product of two 1D sinc functions, one along each axis.

To confirm this analysis, we find the transform directly, starting with the definition by E21.

$$
\begin{aligned}
B(\mu,\nu) &= \kappa^2 \left\langle \psi_2 \middle| b_{W,H} \right\rangle \\
&= \frac{1}{2\pi} \iint b_{W,H}(x,y) e^{-j(\mu x + \nu y)} \, dx \, dy \\
&= \frac{1}{2\pi} \int_{-H/2}^{H/2} \int_{-W/2}^{W/2} e^{-j\mu x} e^{-j\nu y} \, dx \, dy \\
&= \frac{1}{2\pi} \left[\int_{-H/2}^{H/2} e^{-j\nu y} \, dy \right] \left[\int_{-W/2}^{W/2} e^{-j\mu x} \, dx \right] \\
&= \frac{1}{2\pi} \left[2\frac{H}{2} \operatorname{sinc}\left(\nu \frac{H}{2\pi} \right) \right] \left[2\frac{W}{2} \operatorname{sinc}\left(\mu \frac{W}{2\pi} \right) \right] \\
&= \frac{WH}{2\pi} \operatorname{sinc}\left(\frac{\nu H}{2\pi} \right) \operatorname{sinc}\left(\frac{\mu W}{2\pi} \right)
\end{aligned}
\tag{5.150}
$$

A plot of $B(\mu,\nu)$ is shown in Figure 5.33. This product of two sinc functions confirms our discussion above; note that it is not radially symmetrical.

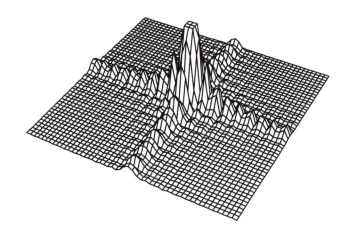

FIGURE 5.33

$\mathcal{F}\{b_{W,N}(x, y)\}$.

5.14.2 Discrete-Time 2D Fourier Transforms

As with the 1D case, we can define discrete basis functions ψ_2':

$$\psi_2' = e^{j(2\pi/N)(\eta x + \xi y)} \tag{5.151}$$

with the associated normalization constant

$$\kappa_N^2 = \frac{1}{N} \tag{5.152}$$

The *2D discrete-time Fourier transform* (2D DTFT) is given by the projection of a discrete signal onto the sampled exponentials:

$$F(\eta, \xi) = \frac{1}{2\pi} \sum_m \sum_n f[m,n] e^{-j(2\pi/N)(\eta m + \xi n)} \qquad = \kappa^2 \langle \psi_2' | f \rangle$$

$$f[m,n] = \frac{1}{2\pi} \int_{2\pi} \int_{2\pi} F(\eta, \xi) e^{-j(2\pi/N)(\eta m + \xi n)} \, d\eta \, d\xi = \kappa^2 \langle \overline{F} | \psi_2' \rangle \quad (5.153)$$

The properties of the continuous-time transform discussed above mostly carry over into the discrete domain.

Example: The 2D Discrete Box

In considering the 2D DTFT, we might want to look at the transform of the discrete 2D box $b_{W,H}[m, n]$.

$$b_{W,H}[m, n] = \begin{cases} 1 & |m| \leq W/2 \text{ and } |n| \leq H/2 \\ 0 & \text{otherwise} \end{cases} \tag{5.154}$$

We expect a result similar to the 1D DTFT for a box, but again it will be the product of two such transforms. To confirm this, we again calculate the transform directly by E16.

$$\begin{aligned} B[\eta, \xi] &= \kappa^2 \langle \psi_2' | b_{W,H} \rangle \\ &= \frac{1}{2\pi} \sum_m \sum_n b_{W,H}[m, n] e^{-j(2\pi/N)(\eta m + \xi n)} \\ &= \frac{1}{2\pi} \left[\sum_{m=-W/2}^{W/2} e^{-jm\eta} \right] \left[\sum_{n=-H/2}^{H/2} e^{-jn\xi} \right] \\ &= \frac{1}{2\pi} \frac{\sin\left[(\eta/2)(W+1)\right]}{\sin(\eta/2)} \frac{\sin\left[(\xi/2)(H+1)\right]}{\sin(\xi/2)} \end{aligned} \tag{5.155}$$

Notice again the result $B[\eta, \xi]$ is not radially symmetric, but it is the product of two 1D box transforms.

5.15 Higher-Order Transforms

The discussions of the previous sections can be generalized beyond one and two dimensions. For example, the Fourier transform in N dimensions may be defined in terms of the spatial vector $x = (x_0, x_1, x_2, \ldots, x_{N-1})$ and the frequency vector $v = (\omega_0, \omega_1, \omega_2, \ldots, \omega_{N-1})$. The continuous-time N-dimensional Fourier transform is then given by

$$F(v) = (2\pi)^{-N/2} \int f(x) e^{-jv \cdot x} \, dx = \kappa^N \langle e^{-jv \cdot x} | f \rangle$$
$$f(x) = (2\pi)^{-N/2} \int F(v) e^{-jv \cdot x} \, dv = \kappa^N \langle \overline{F} | e^{jv \cdot x} \rangle \tag{5.156}$$

Because the N-dimensional kernels are separable in N dimensions, the properties we have discussed for 1D transforms all carry through into the N-dimensional case.

We can also define the N-dimensional discrete-time Fourier transform in a similar way.

5.16 The Fast Fourier Transform

The Fourier transform can be expensive to implement. In 1965 the world of signal processing and many disciplines based upon it experienced a revolution when the *fast Fourier transform* (FFT) algorithm was published in a classic paper by Cooley and Tukey [104]. This paper presented an ingenious way to structure the problem that made its computation for large problems efficient and practical.

Since then, the FFT has become a staple algorithm in many signal-processing packages, and has been implemented in special-purpose hardware from boards to custom chips. An introduction to the algorithm and its implementation may be found in an article by Bergland [40].

We will not discuss the implementation of the FFT in this book. To do justice to the technique, and address the appropriate issues of machine precision, register size, and so forth, would require many details that are well handled elsewhere. These issues are very important and require bit-level attention to insure speed, stability, and accuracy. The reader who wishes more information on the FFT may find additional pointers to the literature in the Further Reading section.

5.17 Further Reading

The classic text on the Fourier series and the Fourier transform is Bracewell's book [61]. The book by Tolstov [438] covers much of the same material and offers a good place to find alternative explanations. The Fourier transform in the context of signal processing is discussed by Gabel and Roberts [151], as well as by Oppenheim et al. [326, 327].

The fast Fourier transform developed by Cooley and Tukey is described in a classic paper [104]. The FFT is summarized and surveyed in Bergland's paper [40]. A more up-to-date description of the FFT may be found in the book by Reid and Passin [357], which includes explicit source code in the C language.

A good general book on 2D digital signal processing is Pratt [345]. An older but still valuable text is Castleman's book [77]. Digital signal processing in one, two, or more dimensions is covered in detail by Dudgeon and Merserau [130]. An excellent introduction to the design and use of digital filters is given by Hamming [185].

5.18 Exercises

Exercise 5.1

Prove the modulation property using duality, convolution, and the continuous-time Fourier transform.

Exercise 5.2

Consider the signal $f(t) = \sin[(w + 0.5)t] / \sin[0.5t]$, which (except for a scaling factor) is the DFT of a box with width w. The signal blows up to infinity when the denominator is zero but the numerator is not.

(a) For what values of t is the denominator zero?

(b) What values of w will cause the numerator to be zero at all of those values of t?

(c) What can you say about the period of f based on the values for w you just derived?

Exercise 5.3

Suppose you had the signal

$$f(t) = \begin{cases} 0 & t < 0 \\ 2 & 0 \leq t < 1 \\ 4 & 1 \leq t < 2 \\ 3 & 2 \leq t < 3 \\ 0 & 3 \leq t \end{cases}$$

Find the analytic Fourier transform $F(\omega)$ for this signal $f(t)$.

(a) Derive the inverse transform of this spectrum, $f'(t) = \mathcal{F}^{-1}\{F(\omega)\}$.

(b) Compare the signals $f(t)$ and $f'(t)$. Are they identical? If not, summarize their differences.

(c) Use a symbolic mathematics program to compute the Fourier transform $F_M(\omega)$ and the reconstructed signal $f'_M(t)$. Make sure you determine what conventions are used by the program (e.g., the normalization constants may not be symmetrical).

(d) Summarize any differences between the program's definition of Fourier transforms and those in this chapter. If there are differences, suggest their motivation.

(e) Compare $f(t)$ and $f'_M(t)$ and summarize any differences.

(f) Compare $f'(t)$ and $f'_M(t)$ and summarize any differences.

Exercise 5.4

Consider the N-dimensional continuous-time Fourier transform given in Equation 5.156.

(a) Write out the equations for the 3D CTFT in explicit form (i.e., expand out the vectors with explicit values).

(b) Write the equations for the 3D DTFT in vector form.

(c) Write out the form of a 3D convolution.

(d) Could you theoretically implement a 3D DTFT using a 1D DTFT as a sub-routine?

Exercise 5.5

(a) Write the band-pass filter of Equation 5.105 as a product of shifted low-pass and high-pass filters given in Equations 5.103 and 5.104.

(b) Take the inverse Fourier transform of the filter expression from (a).

Exercise 5.6

Compare the coefficient definition in Equation 5.23 with the Gram-Schmidt orthogonalized coefficient in Equation 5.17. What does this tell you about the Fourier coefficients?

Exercise 5.7

Prove the duality of multiplication and convolution expressed by Equation 5.97.

6

WAVELET TRANSFORMS

6.1 Introduction

This chapter is devoted to *wavelets*. The *wavelet transform* is a projection of a signal onto a series of basis functions called the *wavelet basis*.

Our motivation for studying wavelets is that for some signal analysis questions, they are more convenient than Fourier transforms. Many of the signals that we deal with in computer graphics are *nonstationary*. That is, they are not statistically the same everywhere. In our case, they possess a lot of high-frequency information in some places, and very little of it in others. This is the reason why the techniques of *adaptive supersampling* (discussed in Chapter 9) have been developed and work so well. In regions of an image with a lot of edges, textures, and shadows, we need to sample densely in order to account for the high frequencies in that region. If the image has a single flat color for a background, then we can sample very sparsely.

The only analytic tool we have so far for analyzing the frequency content of a signal is the Fourier transform, in its different varieties. The Fourier basis functions have *infinite support*; they exist everywhere in the signal domain. If our signal has finite support, then we need to get the basis functions to cancel each other out beyond our region of interest.

The Fourier transform doesn't allow us to look at the frequency content of just one piece of a signal independently of what's happening elsewhere; we always integrate over the *entire* signal, and get back the frequency content over its entire duration. If there's a high-frequency burst somewhere in the midst of a predominantly low-frequency signal, we will only find out that the signal contains some high-frequency information; the Fourier transform doesn't tell us anything about the location or extent of that burst, or even that it was a burst at all and not a diffuse smattering of high frequencies.

This is often undesirable. For example, consider a piece of music, particularly "classical" music of the Western hemisphere in the last few centuries. We know that over time, different pitches (or notes) are played for different durations. At a given time, some notes are sounding and others are not; suppose a particular note rings for only a second or so at two minutes into a ten-minute piece. The Fourier transform of the complete piece will reveal that there is some component of that note in the piece, but we have no idea if it occurred once, many times, or was playing continuously throughout.

The desire to describe the frequency content in a short segment of the signal led to the development of a variety of techniques aimed at providing local descriptions of signals, as surveyed by Meyer [302].

We will see that the *short-term Fourier transform* provides a set of tools for isolating pieces of a signal and examining ranges of frequencies. But unfortunately, these tools are rather blunt; they use finite basis functions that are built out of infinite bases, and that tends to introduce some artifacts into the analysis.

Wavelets were developed to address just these problems. The *wavelet transform* takes an input signal and projects it onto a new set of basis functions, which are called *wavelets*. The remarkable thing is that the wavelets can have compact support. Therefore to match a finite signal, we can put together a finite number of finite wavelets. The wavelets are then combined with the appropriate parameters to reconstruct the input signal.

The sorts of questions we posed above, dealing with local bursts of information and localized frequency ranges, are easily and naturally addressed by wavelets. They form a hierarchy of signals from the input. The analysis property of wavelets allows us to look at signals from different *resolutions*, as well as different frequency ranges. We use the word *resolution* to refer to the number of samples in a signal; this also describes the *level of detail* in the signal.

Wavelets form a 2D family of functions that are derived from an original function, v, called the *scaling function*. From the scaling function we create one *mother wavelet*, and all the other wavelets spring from scaled, dilated, and shifted versions of that mother wavelet. Wavelets can form an orthonormal basis and can be implemented quickly using a fast wavelet transform analogous to the fast Fourier transform.

One principal reason for studying wavelets is that they lead to a natural technique for building a compressed representation of a signal, where the smooth parts are represented by just a little bit of information, and the more complex (high-frequency) parts are given only as much additional bandwidth as they require.

As an example, suppose that we want to compute the discrete inner product of two n-element vectors $\mathbf{v}_1$ and $\mathbf{v}_2$. The straightforward approach requires n multiplies and $n-1$ additions. By analogy with the Fourier transform, let's write the wavelet transform of a vector as $\mathcal{W}(\mathbf{v})$. Because the transform is linear,

$$\mathcal{W}(\mathbf{v}_1 \cdot \mathbf{v}_2) = \mathcal{W}(\mathbf{v}_1) \cdot \mathcal{W}(\mathbf{v}_2) \tag{6.1}$$

Suppose that the wavelet-transformed vectors only have $k < n$ nonzero elements. Then we only need k multiplies and $k-1$ additions to compute the same result (plus the cost of inverting the result). In some special cases, we can actually get these kinds of savings. More generally, the wavelet-transformed vector has many elements that are *nearly* zero. By ignoring these elements (that is, setting them to zero), we get the speedup described above, though we have now introduced some error. One of the beauties of wavelets is that they are structured in such a way that this error can be made quite small. These savings become substantial when we move from vector multiplication to matrix multiplication, where the number of multiplies grows proportionally to n^2 where n is the number of elements on one side of the matrix.

Wavelets are proving to have great value in computer graphics, where we often encounter signals that are mostly smooth, but contain important regions of high-frequency content. For example, consider an illumination function describing light falling on a point in space. If there is a strong light source nearby that is partly blocked by an opaque object, then the illumination seen from that point will fall from bright to dark as we sweep over the boundary from illumination to shadow. On both sides of this shadow edge the illumination is fairly smooth. So we can represent this illumination signal by just a little bit of information in the smooth regions, and concentrate more resources on getting a good description of the discontinuity. This has the same sort of appeal as adaptive sampling, where we put our resources only where they're needed. This leads to more efficient rendering algorithms, because we can represent complicated illumination and shading functions with efficient wavelet representations that allow us to save on work where the signals are smooth. We will see examples of such algorithms in Unit III.

The field of wavelets is new and fast-growing. This chapter summarizes the basic principles behind wavelets by studying one example family of wavelets called the *Haar basis* in detail. The Haar basis is particularly easy to work with because the basis functions are their own duals (as discussed in Section 5.2.4). In general, most wavelets are not orthogonal and thus not their own duals.

This chapter is not meant to be a thorough development of the theory of wavelets or the wavelet transform. The intention here is to develop intuition and a general understanding of the principles, rather than fluency with the mechanics. Therefore we will approach the same material in a number of different ways, showing the general outlines behind several interpretations of the theory. We will try to demonstrate the general ideas through discussion and intuition rather than formality and rigor.

6.2   Short-Time Fourier Transform

The Fourier transform is a powerful analysis tool for computing and interpreting the frequency representation of a signal. But the transform is defined over *all time* (or for an image, the entire image plane, not just the finite region where we may have pixel values). We repeat the definition of the continuous-time Fourier transform from Equation 5.55:

$$X(\omega) = \kappa \langle \psi | x \rangle$$
$$= \kappa \int x(t) e^{-j\omega t} dt \qquad (6.2)$$

Recall our convention that the limits on an integral without indices, such as this one, are infinity in both directions. So this formulation tells us about the frequency content of the *entire* signal.

The complex exponentials used as the basis functions for the Fourier transform present a problem if we're only interested in part of the signal. These basis functions have infinite extent; if a signal has a finite support in the time domain (i.e., it's zero outside of some region), then we will require many terms in the transform to get the functions to cancel out beyond the finite interval. The coefficients on these terms are often very small, and they're all important. If we decide to save storage and effort by truncating the Fourier series and ignoring high-order terms, we affect the quality of our signal description *everywhere*, not just in the high-frequency regions.

There are many signals that have different frequency content in different places. For example, suppose you were about to embark on a 1,000-mile journey by automobile, and someone mentioned to you that somewhere along the road there are some sharp turns and you should go slowly. You could be very conservative and drive slowly the whole way, but this information would be much more useful if you knew *where* the sharp turns were located; then you could slow down only where necessary.

We can think of an image in the same way; the high-frequency content of a smooth background is rather small, but if there's an object with a complex texture in the foreground, we'd expect the high-frequency content in that region to be larger.

It's natural to think about addressing these questions by isolating sections of the signal and taking independent Fourier transforms of those pieces. This approach is called the *short-term Fourier transform* (or STFT).

To take the STFT of a signal, we multiply the signal with a *window function* that is typically nonzero only in the region in which we're interested. This window function (also called the *analysis filter* or *analysis window*) is central to the STFT method. We want it to be zero outside the region of interest and unity within. If we use a simple box function, effectively just clamping the signal to zero outside the region of interest, then we will almost certainly introduce high frequencies at the edges of the window, where the signal will need to suddenly jump to zero; this is illustrated in Figure 6.2.

The art to getting a meaningful STFT is finding a window function that simultaneously isolates just the part of the signal we're interested in (leaving that signal untouched), eliminates the rest of the signal, and introduces no artifacts (this usually means a smooth transition at the edges). These goals are mutually antagonistic. A common compromise is to use a Gaussian for the window function; in this case the STFT is called a *Gabor transform*. Figure 6.2 shows the result of using this window shape.

Let's look at the implications of windowing a signal. Suppose the windowed signal is centered at time t_g. We can then write the windowed signal simply as the product of the signal x and the window g; the Fourier transform of this product will be written X_g:

$$X_g(t_g, \omega) = \kappa \int x(t) g(t - t_g) e^{-j\omega t} dt \tag{6.3}$$

We can see that this windowing operation introduces high frequencies into the result. Recall that multiplying with a box in the time domain is equivalent to convolving with a sinc in the frequency domain; this will diffuse the spectrum because of the infinite support of the sinc function.

We can interpret Equation 6.3 as the signal x projected onto new basis functions that are windowed exponentials:

$$X_g(t_g, \omega) = \kappa \int x(t) \left[g(t - t_g) e^{-j\omega t} \right] dt \tag{6.4}$$

So these new functions, $g(t - t_g) e^{-j\omega t}$, form the new basis for the transform.

Let's pause for a moment and see how this translates to discrete signals. Recalling the definition for the discrete Fourier transform from Equation 5.128:

$$\begin{aligned} X(\Omega) &= \kappa \langle \psi' | x \rangle \\ &= \kappa \sum_n x[n] e^{-j\Omega n} \end{aligned} \tag{6.5}$$

We can apply a filter g centered at sample n_g:

$$X_g(n_g, \Omega) = \kappa \sum_n x[n] g[n - n_g] e^{-j\Omega n} \tag{6.6}$$

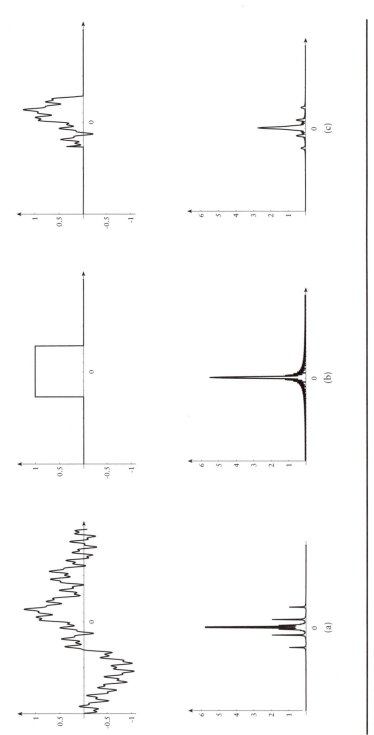

FIGURE 6.1

Using a box window to isolate a piece of signal. (a) The original signal and its Fourier transform. (b) The box window and its Fourier transform. (c) The resulting windowed signal and its Fourier transform.

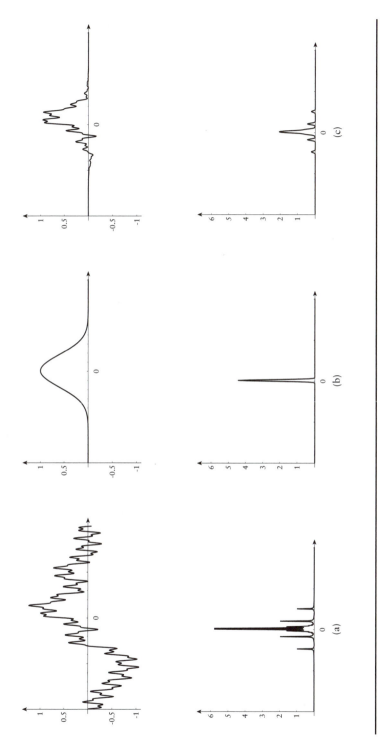

FIGURE 6.2

Using a Gaussian window to isolate a piece of signal. (a) The original signal and its Fourier transform. (b) The Gaussian window and its Fourier transform. (c) The resulting windowed signal and its Fourier transform.

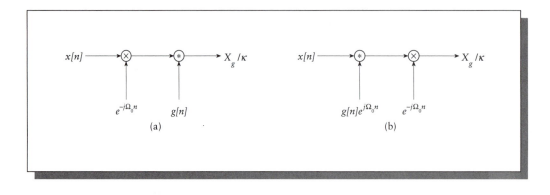

FIGURE 6.3

Two views of $X_g(n_g, \Omega_0)$. (a) Modulating x and then convolving with g. (b) Convolving x with a modulated window and then modulating the result.

At a particular frequency Ω_0, we get

$$
X_g(n_g, \Omega_0) = \kappa \sum_n \left(x[n] e^{-j\Omega_0 n} \right) g[n - n_g]
$$

$$
= \kappa \left(x[n] e^{-j\Omega_0 n} \right) * g[n] \tag{6.7}
$$

where we've written the filtering operation as a convolution. We can think of this form of X_g as taking a signal, modulating it up to Ω_0, and then convolving it with the window filter g; this interpretation is shown in Figure 6.3(a).

Alternatively, we can convolve the signal with the filter first, as in Equation 6.4, writing

$$
X_g(n_g, \Omega_0) = \kappa e^{-j\Omega_0 n} \left(x[n] * g[n] e^{j\Omega_0 n} \right) \tag{6.8}
$$

This interpretation is shown in Figure 6.3(b). These two views lead us to quite different strategies for implementations.

Returning to the continuous domain, consider that we will typically move the filter window in equal steps across the signal, and likewise analyze equal increments in frequency. Taking $t = nt_0$, where t_0 is the filter step size, and $\omega = m\omega_0$, where ω_0 is the frequency step size, then for all $m, n \in \mathcal{Z}$,

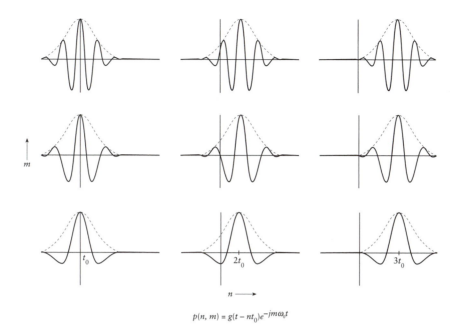

$$p(n, m) = g(t - nt_0)e^{-jm\omega_0 t}$$

FIGURE 6.4

The two-parameter family of basis functions, $g(t - nt_0)e^{-jm\omega_0 t}$, dependent on t_0 and ω_0 and parameterized by n and m. These form the basis for the STFT.

$$X_g(n, m) = \kappa \int x(t)g(t - nt_0)e^{-jm\omega_0 t}dt$$

$$= \kappa \int x(t)\left[g(t - nt_0)e^{-jm\omega_0 t}\right] dt \qquad (6.9)$$

The last line of Equation 6.9 is an important link to wavelets. It shows that we can consider $X_g(n, m)$ to be based on a two-parameter family of basis functions, $g(t - nt_0)e^{-jm\omega_0 t}$, dependent on t_0 and ω_0 and parameterized by n and m. This family of functions is shown in Figure 6.4. So the STFT projects the input function onto these basis functions.

We say that the STFT basis functions have "compressed" support, because most of their energy is near the center, although they never go completely to zero (since the windowing Gaussian never drops completely to zero). They're something of a compromise between the convenient (but infinite) exponentials and the desire for finite support.

6.3   Scale and Resolution

The Fourier transform is principally concerned with the *frequency* and *phase* information in a signal. The wavelet transform is similar in some ways and allows us to look at the signal from different *scales* and different *resolutions*.

These terms already have meanings in signal processing and they mean something different here. It will be helpful to have an idea of what these terms mean in this context before we go more closely into wavelets.

We will consider *scale* first. Imagine a map of a city, where 1 centimeter is equal to 1 kilometer. If we photoreduce the map to half its original size, then 1 centimeter will now correspond to 2 kilometers; the scale has doubled. Similarly, if we enlarge the original map by a factor of two, then we say the scale has halved. So the scale describes how much of the original signal corresponds to one unit (which is often the value associated with one equally spaced sample) of a representation of that signal.

When applied to wavelets, *resolution* refers to the amount of information in a signal; this is related to its frequency content. If we low-pass filter a signal, we don't change its scale but we alter its resolution.

In terms of signals, suppose we have a four-element discrete signal, $s_0 = [0, 0, 2, 2]$. We can create a new version of this signal by averaging together successive pairs of values, creating $s_1 = [0, 2]$. Like the map that has been shrunk down, each element of s_1 now covers twice the territory in the original signal as each element in s_0, so the scale has doubled. If we repeat this operation, we get $s_2 = [1]$; the scale of s_2 is four times the scale of s_0 and the resolution has changed. Suppose we return to the original signal s_0, and now low-pass filter it with a simple filter, creating $s_f = [0.25, 0.75, 1.25, 1.75]$. The scale of s_f is the same as s_0, but the resolution of the signal has changed.

These two ideas crop up all the time in wavelets, because the basic idea is to create a number of signals from the original, each at a different scale. Wavelets allow us to perform the equivalent of photoreducing a map, by building smaller signals that contain the same general information as the larger ones.

6.4   The Dilation Equation and the Haar Transform

We will explore wavelets by discussing a single example. The canonical example for a wavelet basis, and the one we will use, is the *Haar wavelet*, named for a set of functions introduced by A. Haar in 1910 [302].

The heart of the wavelet method is the *dilation equation*. The dilation equation tells us how to create a function from dilated, scaled, and shifted versions of some original, canonical function. Note that for a given function $v(x)$, we can *dilate* (i.e., compress or widen) that function by some amount a by computing $v(ax)$, we can *scale* the function by s by computing $sv(x)$, and we can *shift* the function by an amount b by computing $v(x + b)$. Combining these, we would have $sv(ax + b)$. For some functions v, we can combine dilated, scaled, and shifted versions of themselves to duplicate the original. For a dilation factor of 2, the dilation equation reads

$$v(x) = \sum_{k=0}^{N} c_k v(2x - k) \tag{6.10}$$

The coefficients c_k are usually real for a real-valued v. We often apply the dilation equation recursively; to keep the generations straight, we can index the functions:

$$v_i(x) = \sum_{k=0}^{N} c_k v_{i-1}(2x - k) \tag{6.11}$$

Before looking at how the dilation equation applies to functions, we pause to note that (with a little generalization) it also describes a class of objects called *2D reptiles* [174]. A reptile is a 2D figure that can be assembled from several smaller copies of itself. A familiar reptile is the square: a square may be built by combining four smaller, shifted squares (in this case we leave the top and right sides, and right-side corners, open). Begin with a square function $S(x, y)$ defined by

$$S(x, y, lx, ly, s) = \begin{cases} 1 & lx \leq x < lx + s \text{ and } ly \leq y < ly + s \\ 0 & \text{otherwise} \end{cases} \tag{6.12}$$

We can assemble S from four smaller copies:

$$S(x, y, lx, ly, s) = \begin{array}{l} S(x, y, x, \quad\quad y, \quad\quad s/2) \\ + \quad S(x, y, x + s/2, \quad y, \quad\quad s/2) \\ + \quad S(x, y, x, \quad\quad y + s/2, \quad s/2) \\ + \quad S(x, y, x + s/2, \quad y + s/2, \quad s/2) \end{array} \tag{6.13}$$

as illustrated in Figure 6.5(a).

In this example, we took the original square S and produced four new copies, each of which was dilated and shifted before being combined to make the original square. Note that the result is not a set of functions similar to the input; these scaled copies, added together, are *equal* to the input. If we generalize the scaling coefficients c_k in 2D to more general transformations that include rotation and reflection, then we can make the other three examples in Figure 6.5.

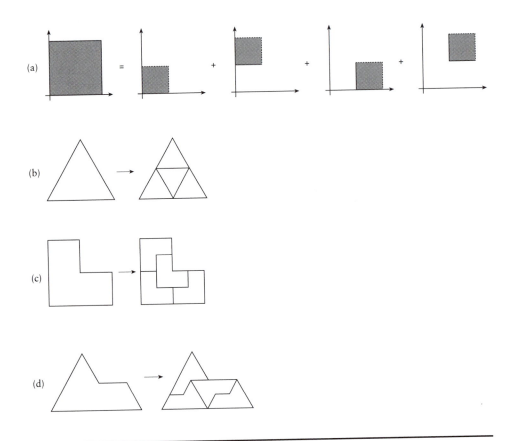

FIGURE 6.5

Reptiles are 2D figures that can be combined to make copies of themselves. (a) Four squares make a square. (b) Equilateral triangle. (c) The L-box. (d) The sphinx.

Let's now return to functions. One common example of a function that satisfies the dilation equation is a simple box $y(t)$ of unit height over the interval $[0, 1]$ illustrated in Figure 6.6(a). We will label this $y_0(t)$ to distinguish it from the descendants we will generate below.

$$y_0(t) = \begin{cases} 1 & 0 \leq t \leq 1 \\ 0 & \text{otherwise} \end{cases} \tag{6.14}$$

In the dilation equation we will set all the coefficients to 0 except $c_0 = c_1 = 1$. Then we find

$$y_1(t) = y_0(2t) + y_0(2t - 1) \tag{6.15}$$

So $y_1(t)$ is made up of two half-width boxes, as shown in Figure 6.6(b). Taking another step, we find that y_2 is made up of two copies of y_1, which is equivalent to four copies of y_0:

$$
\begin{aligned}
y_2(t) &= y_1(2t) + y_1(2t - 1) \\
&= y_0(2t) + y_0(2t - 1) + y_0(2t - 2) + y_0(2t - 3)
\end{aligned}
\tag{6.16}
$$

This is shown in Figure 6.6(c) and (d). We can continue the recursion indefinitely.

The dilation equation is the key to wavelets. Much work has been expended on finding functions (and their coefficients) that satisfy it; we will stick with the box, and $c_0 = c_1 = 1$ for now.

The dilation equation tells us how to find a function v that can be built from a sum of copies of itself (after dilation, translation, and scaling). A function satisfying this criterion is called a *scaling function*. From each scaling function v we can then create a corresponding set of *wavelets*, which are the basis functions for the wavelet transform. The Greek letter ψ is often used in the wavelet literature to denote the wavelet basis functions, just as it's used in some signal-processing literature to denote the Fourier basis functions. The wavelet literature also sometimes uses the letter w to represent a wavelet; we will adopt this notation to avoid confusion. The Fourier transform of a wavelet will thus use the symbol W.

The recipe for constructing a wavelet from the scaling function looks very similar to the dilation equation. In fact, it uses the same coefficients, only in opposite order and with alternating signs. To construct the first wavelet (which we will call w^0) from the basis function, we apply

$$
w^0(t) = \sum_{k \in \mathcal{Z}} (-1)^k c_{1-k} v(2t - k)
\tag{6.17}
$$

So in our example, when $v(t)$ is the unit box and all $c_i = 0$ except $c_0 = c_1 = 1$, we find

$$
w^0(t) = v(2t) - v(2t - 1)
\tag{6.18}
$$

which is shown in Figure 6.7(a). We will see in a moment how to generate higher-order wavelets directly from w^0. To set the stage, consider what happens when we apply the dilation equation to w^0:

$$
w^i(t) = \sum_{k=0}^{N} c_k w^{i-1}(2t - k)
\tag{6.19}
$$

This is actually a number of individual wavelets w^0, shifted, scaled, dilated, and combined to form the complete set $w^i(t)$.

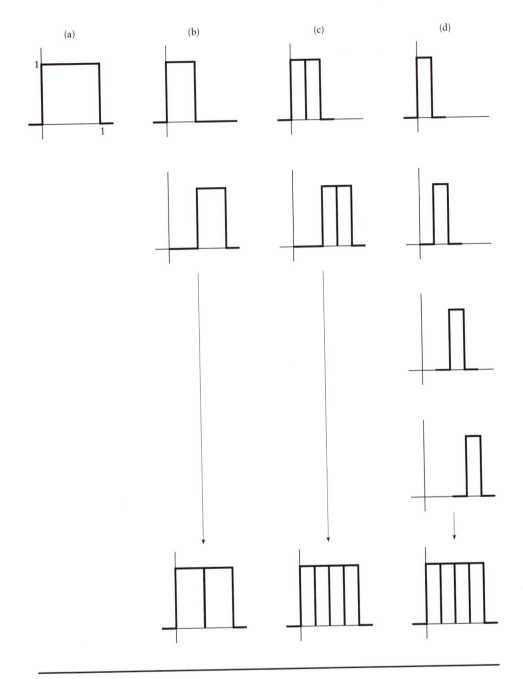

FIGURE 6.6

The dilation equation applied to the box. (a) The box function y_0. (b) First generation: two copies of y_0. (c) Second generation: two copies of y_1. (d) Another look at the second generation: four copies of y_0.

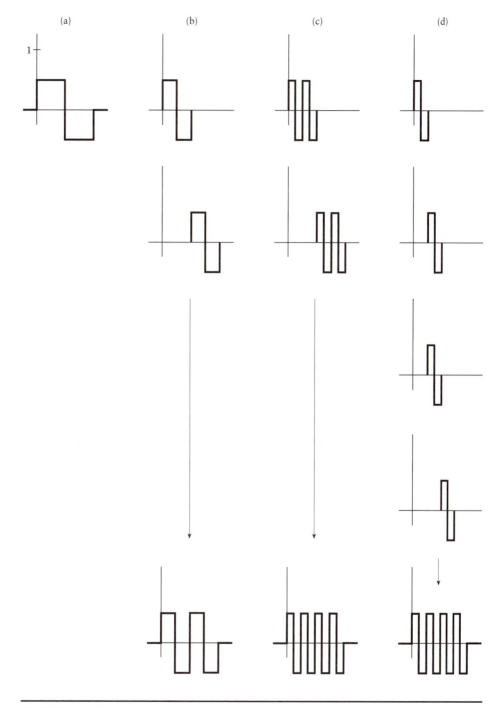

FIGURE 6.7

Building up the Haar wavelets. (a) $w^0(t) = v(2t) - v(2t - 1)$. (b) $w^1(t) = w^0(2t) + w^0(2t - 1)$. (c) $w^2(t) = w^1(2t) + w^1(2t - 1)$. (d) $w^2(t) = w^0(2t) + w^0(2t - 1) + w^0(2t - 2) + w^0(2t - 3)$.

Continuing the recursion, w^1 and w^2 are given by

$$w^1(t) = w^0(2t) + w^0(2t - 1) \tag{6.20}$$
$$w^2(t) = w^1(2t) + w^1(2t - 1)$$
$$= w^0(2t) + w^0(2t - 1) + w^0(2t - 2) + w^0(2t - 3) \tag{6.21}$$

and are shown in Figure 6.7(b)–(d). The individual functions that we have been combining are shifted, scaled, and dilated versions of w^0; these particular functions are called the *Haar wavelets*.

Another set of wavelets is built from what are colloquially called the *hat functions*. These are shown in Figure 6.8. Once again, an original function, here $\triangle(t)$, is dilated and shifted. The original function is given by

$$\triangle(x) = \begin{cases} 2t & 0 \le t \le 1/2 \\ 2(1 - t) & 1/2 \le t \le 1 \\ 0 & \text{otherwise} \end{cases} \tag{6.22}$$

The shifted and dilated functions are referred to as $\triangle_n(t)$, where

$$\triangle_n(t) = \triangle(2^j t - k), \quad n = 2^j + k \quad j \ge 0, \quad 0 \le k < 2^j \tag{6.23}$$

The nonzero *support* of $\triangle_n(t)$ is $I_n = [k2^{-j}, (k + 1)2^{-j}]$.

The hat functions (together with the constant function 1 and the linear function $\triangle_0 = x$) form the *Schauder basis* [302]. This set of bases is able to capture linear functions more efficiently than the Haar bases because it has two *vanishing moments* and no discontinuities in the function, discussed in more detail below.

Wavelets may be written individually as $w^{a,b}$, which are a two-parameter family of functions based on the original wavelet w^0 (this is sometimes called the *generating* or *mother wavelet*). The parameters a and b give rise to a wavelet $w^{a,b}$ by the following formula:

$$w^{a,b}(t) = \frac{1}{\sqrt{a}} w^0 \left(\frac{t - b}{a} \right) \tag{6.24}$$

To see how the wavelets act as a basis, let's begin by writing down the *wavelet transform*, the wavelet analog to the Fourier transform:

$$X(a, b) = \frac{1}{\sqrt{a}} \int x(t) w^0 \left(\frac{t - b}{a} \right) dt \tag{6.25}$$

Here a is the dilation parameter and b is the translation parameter.

By analogy to the STFT, we can parameterize a and b in terms of constants a_0 and b_0. The mechanism is slightly different, however. Recall that when we scale a map or image, we usually want to do so in equal jumps; that is, we want each successive

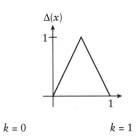

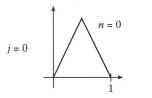

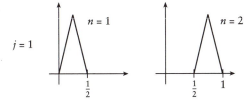

$k = 0$ $k = 1$ $k = 2$ $k = 3$

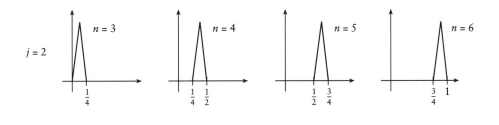

FIGURE 6.8

The hat basis functions $\triangle_n(t)$.

magnification to be an equal *percentage* increase over the previous magnification. This is a geometric rather than arithmetic progression in the magnification, so the dilation parameter a goes up as $a_0{}^m$. To ensure that the adjacent translations still abut at each scale, the translation parameter needs to be tied to the dilation parameter; when the wavelet shrinks, we need to move copies by smaller amounts. We therefore set $b = nb_0a_0{}^m$. Then for $a_0 > 1$, $b_0 > 0$, and $m, n \in \mathcal{Z}$, we find:

$$X(a_0, b_0, m, n) = a_0{}^{-m/2} \int x(t)w^0 \left(\frac{t}{a_0{}^m} - nb_0 \right) \qquad (6.26)$$

As the value of a increases, the wavelet $w^{a,0}(t) = |a|^{-1/2}w(t/a)$ compresses together, so it is capable of representing a signal that changes quickly. As a decreases, the wavelet widens, reducing its ability to capture quickly changing signals and covering more of the domain. The translation parameter b controls the center of the wavelet. The way these parameters influence the wavelet is shown in Figure 6.9; their Fourier transforms appear in Figure 6.10.

It's easy to see that the Haar wavelets are orthogonal. Because the wavelets have compact support, we can see that any two wavelets at the same scale, $w^{a,b}$ and $w^{a,b+k}$ for any $k \neq 0$, are disjoint, as shown in Figure 6.11(a), and therefore orthogonal. Wavelets at different scales are also orthogonal: for any two wavelets $w^{a,b}$ and $w^{a+k,b}$ for any $k \neq 0$, if $k > 0$, then $w^{a+k,b}$ will sit completely within a constant-valued piece of $w^{a,b}$, as shown in Figure 6.11(b).

The Haar basis is most *efficient* at representing signals that are piecewise-constant. By efficient in this context we mean that many of the wavelet coefficients in this basis will be zero for such a signal. To see this, consider first of all that the inner product $\langle w^{0,0}(t) | \alpha \rangle$ of the Haar mother wavelet $w^{0,0}(t)$ and a constant function α is zero. This is easy to see from the shape of the Haar wavelet; it is made up of two equal-sized boxes, one above and one below the axis. So if we have a constant signal, the DC coefficient b^v (discussed below) will capture the amplitude of the signal, and every one of the Haar wavelets $w^{i,j}$ will have a coefficient of zero.

Now suppose we have a signal f that is made up of small constant segments. For simplicity, we will assume that the segments are constant between *dyadic points*; that is, multiples of some power of two. For example, a segment might extend over $[a2^{-i}, (a + 1)2^{-i}]$ for some integer a. As the Haar basis functions are dilated (and thus cover less of the signal), eventually there will come a point where one wavelet will exactly cover this interval. Now we just have a magnified version of what we saw earlier; the projection of this constant segment on this shrunk-down wavelet will be zero. By the same argument, all the smaller wavelets in this interval will also have a coefficient of zero. Because the coefficients drop to zero after some point, we can ignore them: this leads to less storage and faster transformations, hence improved efficiency.

We generalize this notion by computing the *moments* of the wavelet functions with respect to the monomials. We say that *moment i* of a function is the projection

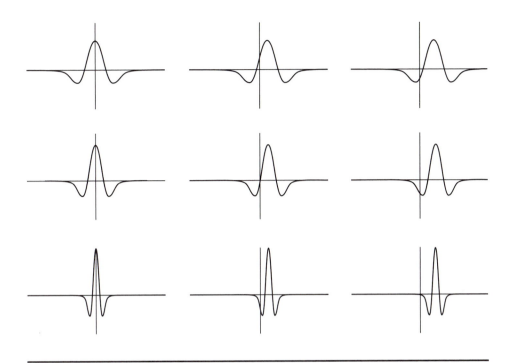

FIGURE 6.9

The two-parameter family of wavelet basis functions, $|a|^{-1/2}w(t - b/a)$ for $a = a_0{}^m$ and $b = nb_0a_0{}^m$ for a range of values of n and m. The particular wavelet used in this figure is the twice-differentiated Gaussian, $w(t) = (1 - t^2)e^{-t^2/2}$.

of that function against the monomial x^i:

$$m_i = \langle f \,|\, x^i \rangle = \int_a^b f(x)x^i \, dx \qquad (6.27)$$

If all of the moments $i = 0, 1, \ldots, M - 1$ are zero for some function, we say that function has M *vanishing moments*. If a function has M vanishing moments, then when the wavelets shrink down to the point where they cover a piece of signal that is a polynomial of degree $M - 1$ or less, the coefficient on that wavelet and all smaller wavelets will be zero.

We will see how to use Haar wavelets to represent signals in the next section.

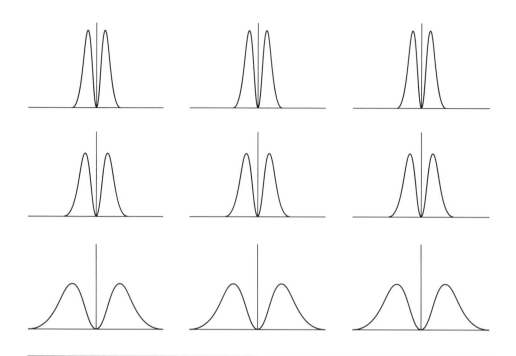

FIGURE 6.10

The Fourier transforms of the functions in Figure 6.9.

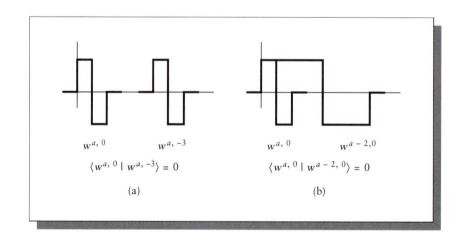

$w^{a,\,0}$ $w^{a,\,-3}$

$\langle w^{a,\,0} \mid w^{a,\,-3} \rangle = 0$

(a)

$w^{a,\,0}$ $w^{a-2,0}$

$\langle w^{a,\,0} \mid w^{a-2,\,0} \rangle = 0$

(b)

FIGURE 6.11

(a) Two wavelets at the same scale are orthogonal. (b) Two wavelets at different scales are orthogonal.

6.5 Decomposition and Reconstruction

A wavelet transformation is built from the scaling function $v(t)$, the wavelet coefficients $b^{a,b}$, and the wavelets $w^{a,b}(t)$.

To see how this works, consider the simple function shown in Figure 6.12. This function $x(t)$ is piecewise-constant on 1/4-sized pieces of the unit interval. The scaling function $v(t)$ and the first two generations of wavelets, $w^{0,0}$ to $w^{1,1}$, are shown in Figure 6.12. Suppose we have a four-valued column input vector $x(t) = [5, -3, 2, 8]^t$; then we can write the wavelet transform of x as

$$x(t) = 3v(t) + -2w^{0,0}(t) + 4w^{1,0}(t) + -3w^{1,1}(t) \qquad (6.28)$$

If we expand the wavelet basis functions, we can see how they contribute to the total:

$$
\begin{array}{rrrr|r}
 & 3 & 3 & 3 & 3 & 3v(t) \\
+ & -2 & -2 & 2 & 2 & -2w^{0,0}(t) \\
+ & 4 & -4 & 0 & 0 & 4w^{1,0}(t) \\
+ & 0 & 0 & -3 & 3 & -3w^{1,1}(t) \\
\hline
= & 5 & -3 & 2 & 8 & x(t)
\end{array}
\qquad (6.29)
$$

This is shown graphically in Figure 6.12(b).

The numbers $(3, -2, 4, -3)$ in Equation 6.28 are the coefficients on the wavelet functions that match the input function; they are the *wavelet coefficients* and are often denoted as $b^{a,b}$. The coefficient on v is written b^v.

The indices a and b on the coefficients refer to the *level* of the wavelet and its *position*. The first index, a, tells us how much the wavelet is dilated. Higher values of a indicate wavelets with narrower bases of support, and thus are able to capture relatively quickly changing information. The different values of b tell us where in the signal this wavelet is located. Since each time we increase the resolution we double the number of wavelets, in general for any value of a the value of b will run from 0 to $2^a - 1$. For simplicity, we will sometimes write $w^0(t)$ as $w^{0,0}(t)$.

The wavelet transform is not expensive to compute. It has a lot in common with the fast Fourier transform and may be very efficiently programmed; details may be found in Strang [423]. The principles behind the wavelet transform are straightforward and easy to follow for a simple wavelet.

The basic idea is to low-pass filter the original signal to get a "smoothed" version, and then find the difference between the smoothed signal and the original. Then we smooth again, find the difference between the once- and twice-smoothed versions, and so on until the signal has been smoothed into a single number. All of our examples in this section will take place in the discrete domain using the signal $x = [5, -3, 2, 8]^t$.

Let's look at the process from a high level before writing the math. In the Haar wavelet transform, the amplitude of the scaling function v, denoted b^v, will represent

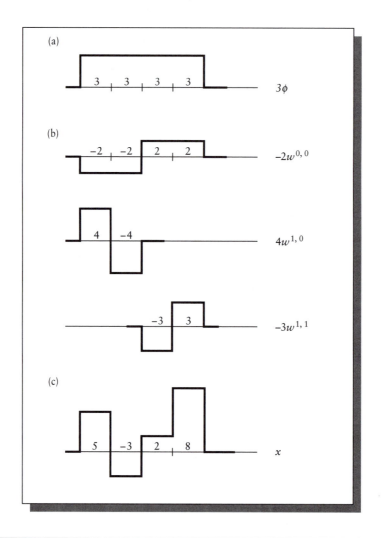

FIGURE 6.12

(a) A simple piecewise-constant function $x(t)$ on the unit interval. (b) The first two generations of wavelets. (c) Matching $x(t)$ with the wavelet transform $[3, -2, 4, -3]$.

the DC (or average) value of the signal, as shown at the bottom of Figure 6.13. Moving upward in the figure, to build up the signal from that flat function, we first add in a version of the biggest wavelet $w^{0,0}$, scaled by $b^{0,0}$, which will split the signal into two constant pieces. The next wavelets are each a half-interval wide, so we can think of adding to our growing stack a pair of side-by-side wavelets, independently scaled by $b^{1,0}$ and $b^{1,1}$. Our goal is to find the $b^{a,b}$. We will compute these wavelet coefficients one at a time, transforming the signal as we go. We built up the signal from bottom to top in the figure, but we compute the coefficients in the other direction. We will start with the finest detail first, and work our way out to the DC component. In effect we will be smoothing out the signal at each step by running a very simple low-pass filter over it.

The Haar transform repeats a very simple step many times. The step takes two adjacent values in the signal and replaces them with two new numbers: their average value, and the amplitude of the wavelet that will add to the average to recreate the original values. In effect we low-pass filter a section of the signal, and record how to displace the local average (or DC) value to recover it. If the signal has more than two entries, we apply this process to all adjacent pairs in parallel. This requires that the input signal have a length that is exactly a power of two. In other words, we are *subsampling* the signal because we are stepping along the signal in units of two and ignoring every other one.

At each step, we replace a pair of values p and q by their *mean* m and *wavelet amplitude* w. Given a pair of adjacent signal values p and q, it's easy to find m and w:

$$m = \frac{p+q}{2}, \qquad w = \frac{p-q}{2} \tag{6.30}$$

To recover p and q,

$$p = m + w, \qquad q = m - w \tag{6.31}$$

The values of w are the wavelet coefficients for that section of the signal. The array of means m are the pairwise-average values of the signal; this is then a smoothed version of the original. We can then repeat exactly the same process on this new, smoothed signal.

We can conveniently compute m and w for all adjacent pairs simultaneously, at every level of the transform, with a single matrix multiplication.

We repeat the process, generating wavelet coefficients and a smoother signal at each step, until we end up with a signal of length 1; that's the constant-amplitude scaling function v.

To make this verbal description precise, we'll now give a symbolic representation. We will use an *operator* notation to keep the expressions simple. We will discuss operators in more detail in Chapter 16; for now, we can simply think of them as another way to write a function applied to a signal.

We will encounter four operators in the following discussion, one for each step of the process. The operator $\mathcal{L}$ performs the smoothing $m = (p+q)/2$, resulting

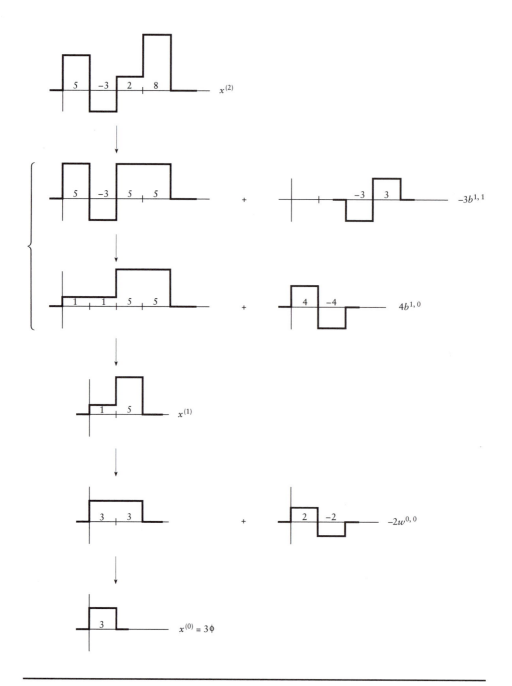

FIGURE 6.13

The input signal $x = [5, -3, 2, 8]^t$. Below that, the series of wavelets that stack together to form the signal.

in a half-sized, smoothed signal. The operator $\mathcal{H}$ computes the wavelet amplitude $w = (p - q)/2$, giving us the wavelet coefficients at that level. To rebuild the signal from these values, the operator $\mathcal{L}^*$ stretches out a signal of length n to $2n$ by doubling each entry; this turns each average-value m into two adjacent m's. The operator $\mathcal{H}^*$ takes each wavelet amplitude w and doubles it just like $\mathcal{L}^*$, but it negates the second value, turning it into a $[w, -w]$ pair that is ready to be added to the $[m, m]$ pair created by $\mathcal{L}$. The $\mathcal{L}$ operator acts as a *low-pass* filter; the $\mathcal{L}^*$ operator is a simple zooming operator. The $\mathcal{H}$ operator is a *high-pass* filter; $\mathcal{H}^*$ also zooms, but it negates the second value. In symbols,

$$\mathcal{L}(a, b, c, d) = (a + b, c + d)$$
$$\mathcal{L}^*(a, b) = (a, a, b, b)$$
$$\mathcal{H}(a, b) = \left(\frac{a - b}{2}, \frac{c - d}{2} \right)$$
$$\mathcal{H}^*(a, b) = (a, -b) \tag{6.32}$$

Armed with this interpretation, we can describe the operators in somewhat more general terms. We will see that each one can be represented in practice by a straightforward matrix construction.

6.5.1 Building the Operators

We begin by defining the low-pass filter $\mathcal{L}$ (also called the *fine-to-coarse filter*, the *decomposition filter*, and the *restriction operator*). One way we will stress the intuitive interpretation of these operators is to use a nonsymmetric normalization term. Recall from Chapter 5 that the Fourier transform can be normalized a number of different ways, and we chose to use a symmetric scale factor κ in front of both the analysis and synthesis equations, rather than κ^2 (or $1/\kappa^2$) in front of just one of them. Similarly, wavelets require a normalization term, which for our examples would be $1/\sqrt{2}$ on both equations, or $1/2$ on just one of them. We'll use the latter here because it emphasizes the averaging nature of the operator $\mathcal{L}$, even though it's asymmetrical.

Suppose we have an input signal x containing 2^n entries; we will call this signal $x^{(n)}$ (the parentheses are intended to remind us that this index is not an exponent). The filter may be written as an operator on a signal $x^{(n)}$ with 2^n entries, producing a new signal $x^{(n-1)}$ with only 2^{n-1} entries. Each of these new i entries is given by evaluating $\mathcal{L}f$ for a particular value of i. $\mathcal{L}$ is made up of the coefficients from the wavelet's dilation equation:

$$\mathcal{L}_{ik} = c_{2i-k} \tag{6.33}$$

The whole matrix is then scaled by $1/2$. Using this formula, we can find the result of applying $\mathcal{L}$ to $x^{(k)}$ to find entry i of $x^{(k-1)}$:

$$(\mathcal{L}x)(i) = \frac{1}{2}\sum_{k \in \mathcal{Z}} c_{2i-k}x(k) \quad i = 1, \ldots, \frac{n}{2} \tag{6.34}$$

Using the example $x^{(2)} = [5, -3, 2, 8]^t$ (so $n = 2$), and for a wavelet where all the coefficients $c_i = 0$ for $i \neq 0, 1$, we apply Equation 6.34 and find

$$
\begin{aligned}
i = 1: & \quad (1/2)[\cdots + c_2x(0) + \boldsymbol{c_1 x(1)} + \boldsymbol{c_0 x(2)} + c_{-1}x(3) + c_{-2}x(4) + c_{-3}x(5) + \cdots] \\
i = 2: & \quad (1/2)[\cdots + c_4x(0) + c_3x(1) + c_2x(2) + \boldsymbol{c_1 x(3)} + \boldsymbol{c_0 x(4)} + c_{-1}x(5) + \cdots]
\end{aligned}
\tag{6.35}
$$

where the four nonzero entries have been highlighted in bold. Eliminating the zero entries, we end up with a fairly simple matrix equation:

$$\mathcal{L}x = \frac{1}{2}\begin{bmatrix} c_1 & c_0 & 0 & 0 \\ 0 & 0 & c_1 & c_0 \end{bmatrix}\begin{bmatrix} x(1) \\ x(2) \\ x(3) \\ x(4) \end{bmatrix} \tag{6.36}$$

For the Haar wavelet, $c_0 = c_1 = 1$, so the new, smoothed signal $x^{(1)}$ is simply

$$x^{(1)} = \mathcal{L}x^{(2)} = \begin{bmatrix} \frac{1}{2} & \frac{1}{2} & 0 & 0 \\ 0 & 0 & \frac{1}{2} & \frac{1}{2} \end{bmatrix}\begin{bmatrix} 5 \\ -3 \\ 2 \\ 8 \end{bmatrix} = \begin{bmatrix} 1 \\ 5 \end{bmatrix} \tag{6.37}$$

Notice that this matrix averages together adjacent pairs of values, computing $a/2 + b/2$, which is the value of m in Equation 6.30. This new signal now contains only half as many entries as the original; we have low-pass filtered the input signal (with a box filter) and resampled the result at half the prior sampling rate.

We can now repeat the process, smoothing the new signal again:

$$x^{(0)} = \mathcal{L}x^{(1)} = \begin{bmatrix} \frac{1}{2} & 0 \\ 0 & \frac{1}{2} \end{bmatrix}\begin{bmatrix} 1 \\ 5 \end{bmatrix} = \begin{bmatrix} 3 \end{bmatrix} \tag{6.38}$$

This sequence of signals is shown in Figure 6.14(a).

Now we want to find a description of what changes when each signal $x^{(n)}$ is smoothed to form $x^{(n-1)}$. In other words, if the smoother signal were "expanded" to twice its length (similar to pixel replication for fast zooming of an image), then we could subtract the lower-resolution, smoother signal from the higher-resolution one, and get a "difference signal."

In Section 6.8 we will see a formalism for describing the spaces spanned by the signal at different resolutions. For now, we notice that the signals $x^{(n)}$ and

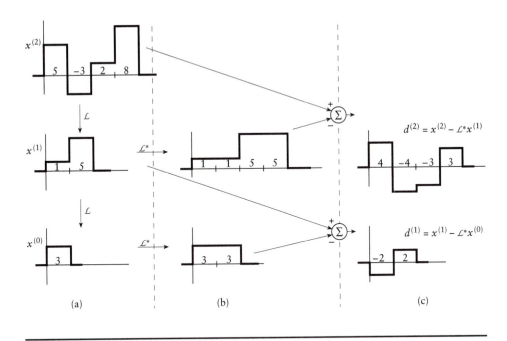

FIGURE 6.14

The original signal $x^{(2)} = [5, -3, 2, 8]^t$. (a) The smoothed signals $x^{(1)}$ and $x^{(0)}$, each half as long as the previous one. (b) Each $x^{(k)}$ enlarged using the $\mathcal{L}^*$ operator. (c) The difference signal lost at each level of smoothing.

$x^{(n-1)}$ may be considered to inhabit two different spaces A^n and A^{n-1}. To find the difference between two signals, we would like to find a set of functions that spans the difference space $A^{n-1} - A^n$. This isn't always easy [90].

For our example, the *coarse-to-fine* operator $\mathcal{L}^*$ subtracts the low-resolution signal from the higher-resolution version directly. It is defined similarly to $\mathcal{L}$, but the coefficients in the equation have switched position:

$$(\mathcal{L}^*x)_k = \sum_{i \in \mathcal{Z}} c_{2i-k}x(k) \quad k = 1, \ldots, n \tag{6.39}$$

All that this operator really does is make sure that we pick up each index of the lower-resolution signal twice before we move on to the next. Let's use this equation to form $(\mathcal{L}^*x^{(1)})$, the four-element signal that blows up the two-element signal $x^{(1)}$:

$$
\begin{aligned}
j = 1 : & \quad \cdots + c_{-1}x(0) + \boldsymbol{c_1 x(1)} + c_3 x(2) + c_5 x(3) + \cdots \\
j = 2 : & \quad \cdots + c_{-2}x(0) + \boldsymbol{c_0 x(1)} + c_2 x(2) + c_4 x(3) + \cdots \\
j = 3 : & \quad \cdots + c_{-3}x(0) + c_{-1}x(1) + \boldsymbol{c_1 x(2)} + c_3 x(3) + \cdots \\
j = 4 : & \quad \cdots + c_{-4}x(0) + c_{-2}x(1) + \boldsymbol{c_0 x(2)} + c_2 x(3) + \cdots
\end{aligned}
\tag{6.40}
$$

which again turns into the simple equation

$$
\mathcal{L}^*g =
\begin{bmatrix}
c1 & 0 \\
c0 & 0 \\
0 & c1 \\
0 & c0
\end{bmatrix}
\begin{bmatrix}
x(1) \\
x(2)
\end{bmatrix}
\tag{6.41}
$$

Each of these "enlargements" is illustrated in our test case in Figure 6.14(b).

Now we can find the difference we wanted. The difference signal $d^{(n)}$ corresponding to the detail lost when signal $x^{(n)}$ is smoothed to signal $x^{(n-1)}$ is given by

$$
d^{(n)} = x^{(n)} - \mathcal{L}^*x^{(n-1)} = (\mathcal{I} - \mathcal{L}^*\mathcal{L})x^{(n)}, \quad n = N, \dots, 1
\tag{6.42}
$$

where $\mathcal{I}$ is the *identity* operator: $\mathcal{I}x = x$. These difference signals are shown in Figure 6.14(c).

It's now easy to recover the original function $x^{(N)}$ from the smoothest version $x^{(0)}$ and the difference signals $d^{(0)}$ through $d^{(N-1)}$; the formula is simply

$$
x^{(n)} = d^{(n)} + \mathcal{L}^*x^{(n-1)} \quad n = 1, \dots, N
\tag{6.43}
$$

This decomposition provides a nice way of looking at the signal over multiple resolutions, but it doesn't explicitly provide us with the wavelet transform; that is, we don't have the coefficients b_i that describe the amplitudes of the basis wavelets. Clearly these coefficients are stored in the $d^{(k)}$, but they are also easily obtained from the $x^{(n)}$ themselves.

To find the wavelet coefficients, we need only build a new high-pass filter $\mathcal{H}$, such that $\mathcal{H}\mathcal{L}^* = \mathcal{I}$. Like $\mathcal{L}$, this filter also has a $1/2$ in front. The coefficients of this filter are given by

$$
\mathcal{H}_{ik} = (-1)^{k+1}c_{k+1-2i}
\tag{6.44}
$$

For example, for the two-coefficient case we find

$$
\mathcal{H} = \frac{1}{2}
\begin{bmatrix}
c_0 & -c_1 & 0 & 0 \\
0 & 0 & c_0 & -c_1
\end{bmatrix}
\tag{6.45}
$$

This filter gives the coefficients on $d^{(n)}$ when passing from step $n+1$ to n.

For the Haar wavelets, this matrix becomes

$$\mathcal{H} = \begin{bmatrix} \frac{1}{2} & -\frac{1}{2} & 0 & 0 \\ 0 & 0 & \frac{1}{2} & -\frac{1}{2} \end{bmatrix} \tag{6.46}$$

Notice that these are just the values needed to find the coefficient w in Equation 6.30. We can now state the complete algorithm for finding the wavelet coefficients.

Decomposition: Given a signal $x^{(N)}$ containing 2^N components, for $n = N, \cdots, 1$ compute

$$\begin{aligned} x^{(n-1)} &= \mathcal{L}x^{(n)} \\ b^{(n-1)} &= \mathcal{H}x^{(n)} \end{aligned} \tag{6.47}$$

Reconstruction: Given $x^{(0)}$ and $b^{(0)} \ldots b^{(N-1)}$, for $n = 1, \ldots, N$ compute

$$x^{(n)} = \mathcal{L}^* x^{(n-1)} + \mathcal{H}^* b^{(n-1)} \tag{6.48}$$

You may notice that the matrices $\mathcal{L}$ and $\mathcal{H}$ have a premultiplied value of $1/2$, while the "reverse" matrices $\mathcal{L}^*$ and $\mathcal{H}^*$ don't. As I mentioned before, this is a normalizing factor, just like the $1/\sqrt{2\pi}$ factor in the Fourier transform. We can distribute the $1/2$ by using a factor of $1/\sqrt{2}$ on all four matrices. I chose to leave the equations asymmetrical because it makes it easier to see how the Haar coefficients appear in the matrices.

This algorithm can be thought of as a tree or pyramid, as diagrammed in Figure 6.15.

A more conventional signal-processing view of the algorithm is given in Figure 6.16. Here the notation $\uparrow 2$ means that a signal is *upsampled* by a factor of 2 by inserting zeros; for example, $[a, b]$ turns into $[a, 0, b, 0]$. Similarly, $\downarrow 2$ means that a signal is *downsampled* by a factor of 2 by ignoring every other sample; for example, $[a, a, b, b]$ turns into $[a, b]$. This form of the wavelet transform makes use of three operators in addition to the upsampling and downsampling operators. For the Haar wavelets, the operator $\mathcal{A}$ averages its input:

$$\mathcal{A} : y[k] = \begin{cases} (x[k] + x[k-1])/2 & k \text{ is odd} \\ (x[k+1] + x[k-1])/2 & k \text{ is even} \end{cases} \tag{6.49}$$

the operator $\mathcal{C}$ copies:

$$\mathcal{C} : y[k] = \begin{cases} x[k] & k \text{ is odd} \\ x[k-1] & k \text{ is even} \end{cases} \tag{6.50}$$

and the operator $\mathcal{R}$ replicates with alternating sign:

$$\mathcal{R} : y[k] = \begin{cases} x[k] & k \text{ is odd} \\ -x[k-1] & k \text{ is even} \end{cases} \tag{6.51}$$

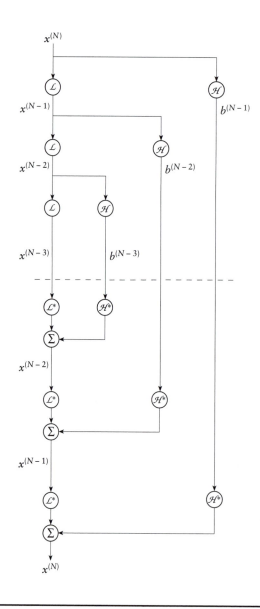

FIGURE 6.15

The decomposition of a signal into wavelet coefficients and smoothed versions (top half). The reconstruction of a signal from smooth versions and wavelet coefficients (bottom half).

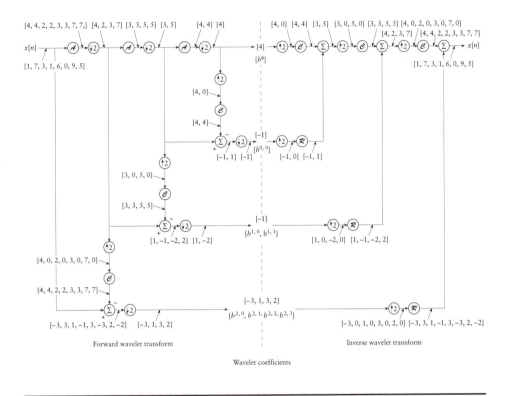

FIGURE 6.16

The pyramid algorithm in signal-processing terms.

Notice that in Figure 6.16 the input signal $x_0[n]$ with m samples is split into two new signals, with m and $m/2$ samples, respectively. The new, half-length signal $x_1[n]$ is then operated on by the next step. If it requires U units of work to calculate one stage of the transform on x_0, then it takes $U/2$ units to transform x_1, and $U/4$ units to transform x_2. In the limit,

$$U + \frac{U}{2} + \frac{U}{4} + \cdots < 2U \tag{6.52}$$

so the total amount of work required is (asymptotically) linear in the size of the input array. No invertible transform can be any less expensive than this (though in practice the cost of each step can vary among transforms).

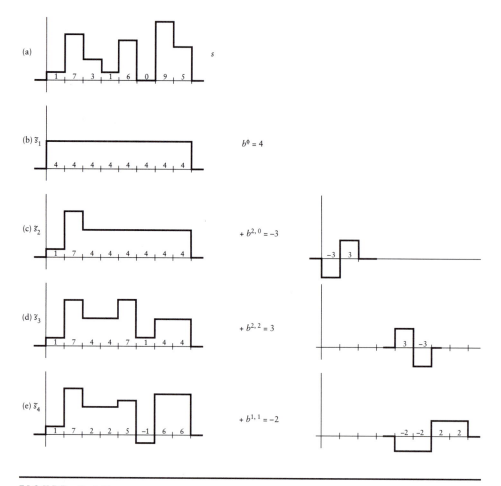

FIGURE 6.17

Wavelet compression, demonstrated by successively adding in terms of increasing magnitude. (a) The original signal. (b)–(i) Increasingly close fits to (a) using more wavelets. (*Continued on next page.*)

6.6 Compression

The wavelet decomposition in Figure 6.16 is a good example of how wavelets are useful for compression. The eight-element input signal in Figure 6.17(a) is turned into eight wavelet coefficients:

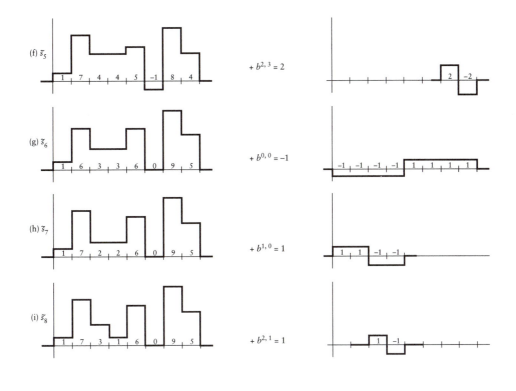

FIGURE 6.17 (continued)

Wavelet compression, demonstrated by successively adding in terms of increasing magnitude. (a) The original signal. (b)–(i) Increasingly close fits to (a) using more wavelets.

$$[1, 7, 3, 1, 6, 0, 9, 5] \rightarrow \left[b^v, b^{0,0}, b^{1,0}, b^{1,1}, b^{2,0}, b^{2,1}, b^{2,2}, b^{2,3}\right]$$
$$= [4, -1, 1, -2, -3, 1, 3, 2] \qquad (6.53)$$

The technique of *compression* is used to create an approximation of the signal with fewer values (say m) than the original (say for transmitting a rough idea of the signal over a channel where sending the full signal is too expensive). One way to compress is to take the Fourier transform of the signal and then retain only the first m Fourier coefficients. That makes sense because the first few Fourier terms represent the low-frequency information in the signal, and higher terms add in higher frequencies, although as I mentioned earlier, loss of the high-frequency information will affect the entire signal.

In the wavelet transform, we don't want to keep simply the lowest-order terms, but rather those with the largest magnitude, wherever they may be. For example, if we could only save one of the eight terms in Equation 6.53, which would it be? If we estimate the error E in any m-term approximation $\tilde{s}_m$ of s by the sum of the element-by-element errors, then all our error terms will be integers (this will make it easy to compare various error figures; other error metrics are addressed in the exercises). The error E is then given by

$$E = \sum_k |s[k] - \tilde{s}_m[k]| \qquad (6.54)$$

If we compute this error for each of the eight coefficients in Equation 6.53, then we find these measures (using the same order):

$$E_1 = [22, 34, 32, 32, 32, 32, 32, 32] \qquad (6.55)$$

So the best one-coefficient approximation $\tilde{s}_1$ to s has an error of only 24. This is given by $b^v v$, as shown in Figure 6.17(b). Notice that this is also the coefficient with the greatest magnitude.

Our signal $\tilde{s}_1 = b^v v$ is now an eight-element vector with a constant value of four. What's the next best term to add in? We can compute the error between s and $\tilde{s}_1$, plus each of the remaining wavelets to find:

$$E_2 = [\bullet, 34, 18, 20, 20, 16, 22, 18, 22] \qquad (6.56)$$

So $\tilde{s}_2 = \tilde{s}_1 + b^{2,0} w^{2,0}$ represents the best two-coefficient approximation to s, as shown in Figure 6.17(c). Observe that the largest coefficient magnitude available at this step was 3, and only $b^{2,0}$ and $b^{2,2}$ are of this size. We might then expect that $b^{2,2}$ is going to be our next best choice, and indeed we can write out the new errors to confirm this:

$$E_3 = [\bullet, 14, 16, 14, \bullet, 16, 12, 16] \qquad (6.57)$$

The rest of the development is shown in Figure 6.17(d)–(i).

Note that it is important to keep track of which wavelet is saved at each step. We might keep a list of pairs, the first element representing the wavelet index for that coefficient, and the second representing that coefficient's value. Our example would be

$$\{ (4, 1), (-3, 5), (3, 7), (-2, 4), (2, 8), (-1, 2), (1, 3), (1, 6) \} \qquad (6.58)$$

where wavelet index 1 stands for v, index 2 is $w^{0,0}$, and so on, so index 8 stands for $w^{2,3}$. Of course, if we save all these pairs we've expanded our storage rather than compressed it, so typically only the first few pairs are retained; wavelet coefficients for real-world signals seem to often decrease in magnitude very quickly, making this form of compression attractive.

6.7 Coefficient Conditions

We can roll together the matrix operations from the previous sections into a single interleaved calculation. When we look to invert this matrix equation, we will find that it requires some conditions on the coefficients, which in turn influence the types of functions that can be used to satisfy the dilation equation, which then influence the types of wavelets we can build.

Notice that both the $\mathcal{L}$ and $\mathcal{H}$ operators downsample their inputs by a factor of 2; that is, their outputs are half as big as their inputs. Therefore the matrix forms of these operators have dimensions $n \times 2n$. We can put them together, interleaved, to create a single composite matrix A. For a wavelet with four nonzero coefficients c_0, c_1, c_2, c_3, this becomes

$$
A = \begin{bmatrix}
c_0 & c_1 & c_2 & c_3 & & & & & & \\
c_3 & -c_2 & c_1 & -c_0 & & & & & & \\
 & & c_0 & c_1 & c_2 & c_3 & & & & \\
 & & c_3 & -c_2 & c_1 & -c_0 & & & & \\
 & & & & & \ddots & & & & \\
 & & & & & & c_0 & c_1 & c_2 & c_3 \\
 & & & & & & c_3 & -c_2 & c_1 & -c_0 \\
c_2 & c_3 & & & & & & & c_0 & c_1 \\
c_1 & -c_0 & & & & & & & c_3 & -c_2
\end{bmatrix}
\tag{6.59}
$$

To invert the transform, we need to find A^{-1}. Recall that the inverse of an orthogonal matrix is equal to its transpose [420]. We have seen that the wavelet basis is orthogonal, so it is reasonable to consider A^t as a candidate for A^{-1}:

$$
A^t = \begin{bmatrix}
c_0 & c_3 & & & & & & c_2 & c_1 \\
c_1 & -c_2 & & & & & & c_3 & -c_0 \\
c_2 & c_1 & c_0 & c_3 & & & & & \\
c_3 & -c_0 & c_1 & -c_2 & & & & & \\
 & & c_2 & c_1 & c_0 & c_3 & & & \\
 & & c_3 & -c_0 & c_1 & -c_2 & & & \\
 & & & & & & \ddots & & \\
 & & & & & c_2 & c_1 & c_0 & c_3 \\
 & & & & & c_3 & -c_0 & c_1 & -c_2
\end{bmatrix}
\tag{6.60}
$$

Notice how the wrapped-around tail ends of the coefficients show up in the upper-right corner rather than the lower-left. Multiplying these two together, we find

$$AA^t = \begin{bmatrix} \alpha & 0 & \beta & 0 & \dots & 0 & 0 & \beta & 0 \\ 0 & \alpha & 0 & \beta & \dots & 0 & 0 & 0 & \beta \\ \beta & 0 & \alpha & 0 & \dots & 0 & 0 & 0 & 0 \\ 0 & \beta & 0 & \alpha & \dots & 0 & 0 & 0 & 0 \\ \vdots & & & & \ddots & & & & \vdots \\ 0 & 0 & 0 & 0 & \dots & \alpha & 0 & \beta & 0 \\ 0 & 0 & 0 & 0 & \dots & 0 & \alpha & 0 & \beta \\ \beta & 0 & 0 & 0 & \dots & \beta & 0 & \alpha & 0 \\ 0 & \beta & 0 & 0 & \dots & 0 & \beta & 0 & \alpha \end{bmatrix} \tag{6.61}$$

where

$$\alpha = c_0{}^2 + c_1{}^2 + c_2{}^2 + c_3{}^2$$
$$\beta = c_0 c_2 + c_1 c_3$$

In words, we have a main diagonal of α, with diagonals of β one column to the left and one to the right (or, equivalently, one row above and below) of the main diagonal, with appropriate wraparound effects.

The product AA^t will be the identity (and thus A^t will be confirmed as A^{-1}) if $\alpha = 1$ and $\beta = 0$ in Equation 6.61. These are the first two conditions we will demand from our dilation equation coefficients:

1 $c_0{}^2 + c_1{}^2 + c_2{}^2 + c_3{}^2 = 1$

2 $c_0 c_2 + c_1 c_3 = 0$

Notice that the Haar matrices used in the previous section don't satisfy these conditions. As noted earlier, they could be adjusted by a scale factor of $1/\sqrt{2}$. Then we'd have $c_0 = c_1 = 1/\sqrt{2}$, so $\alpha = c_0{}^2 + c_1{}^2 = 1$, as desired. And since $c_2 = c_3 = 0$, we have $\beta = 0$ as well.

The Haar wavelets have only *zero-order* matching properties; that is, they can only match functions that are piecewise-constant. When building up to the integral in calculus, we start with the zero-order rectangles to approximate an area under a curve, but we then move on to trapezoids, which have *first-order* matching; that is, they can exactly match any piecewise linear function. Higher-order curves (e.g., quadratics and cubics) give us even better continuity.

When discussing matching, it is important to note that it is combinations of the scaling functions that actually match (or duplicate) the function. The wavelets that are derived from the scaling function may individually have very strange shapes (such as that in Figure 6.18), but they combine in just the right way to make something much less bizarre and more regular.

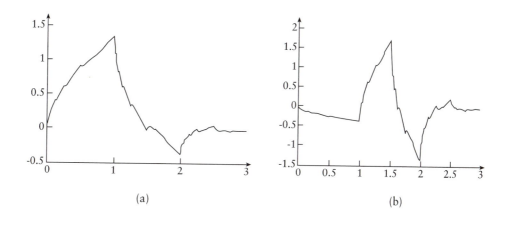

FIGURE 6.18

(a) The scaling function v generated by D_4. (b) The first wavelet $w^{0,0}$ generated by D_4.

We say that the *order* of the wavelet is the type of signal that can be matched by the scaling function. The *regularity* of each function is the number of times the function is continuously differentiable.

We can move from the zero-order continuity offered by the Haar wavelets to first-order continuity by imposing two additional conditions. For a four-coefficient wavelet:

3 $c_3 - c_2 + c_1 - c_0 = 0$

4 $0c_3 - 1c_2 + 2c_1 - 3c_0 = 0$

These two conditions respectively enforce the first two vanishing moments. When these two conditions are joined to the two others above, we get a set of four coefficients that generate wavelets that can match any linear function [302]. These are called the *Daubechies first-order wavelets*, sometimes written D_4, and are given by

$$c_0 = \frac{1}{4}\left(1 + \sqrt{3}\right) \approx 0.68301$$

$$c_1 = \frac{1}{4}\left(3 - \sqrt{3}\right) \approx 1.18301$$

$$c_2 = \frac{1}{4}\left(3 + \sqrt{3}\right) \approx 0.31400$$

$$c_3 = \frac{1}{4}\left(1 - \sqrt{3}\right) \approx -0.18301 \tag{6.62}$$

The scaling function v and first-order wavelet $w^{0,0}$ based on these coefficients are shown in Figure 6.18. The coefficients for higher-order wavelets may be found in Daubechies' book [115]. Note that the coefficient values in the literature often include the $1/\sqrt{2}$ normalization factor.

In general, the *order* of the wavelet describes its ability to match a polynomial. As we saw earlier, we can define the order of a wavelet in terms of its projection onto the monomials (that is, its vanishing moments); a wavelet $w^{a,b}(x)$ of order p satisfies

$$\int x^m w^{a,b}(x)\, dx = 0, \quad 0 \le m \le p - 1 \tag{6.63}$$

We can summarize the coefficient conditions for a wavelet of order p generated by this type of construction, as discussed in Xu and Shann [493]:

$$c_k = 0 \qquad\qquad \text{for } k \notin \{0, 1, \ldots, 2p - 1\}$$

$$\sum_k c_k = 2$$

$$\sum_k (-1)^k k^m c_k = 0 \qquad\qquad \text{for } 0 \le m \le p - 1$$

$$\sum_k c_k c_{2k-m} = 2\delta(m) \qquad\qquad \text{for } 1 - p \le m \le p - 1 \tag{6.64}$$

The coefficients $c_0 = c_1 = 1$ for the Haar wavelets correspond to $p = 1$, and the Daubechies coefficients in Equation 6.62 correspond to $p = 2$.

Although the first wavelet from D_4 appears in Figure 6.18, we haven't seen yet how to actually compute the values of the wavelet function. It is remarkable that we don't actually ever need to find the wavelets at all! As long as we have the coefficients, then we can carry out the wavelet transforms described above, and decompose and reconstruct our signals.

The reason we don't need the wavelets explicitly is because we really only need to find the projection (that is, the inner product) of the signal with the various wavelet functions. It may be surprising, but we can compute those inner products without actually generating the wavelet function itself [429]. The idea is to create an integration rule from just the coefficients. The integration rule is based on sampling the function at a number of points and weighting those samples (we will have much more to say about integration methods in Chapter 16). If the rule is not very good, then we will get a result that matches the signal at the sample points but might be a very poor approximation between them. More sophisticated rules are better able to estimate the signal, and thereby compute the inner product of the signal with a weighting function. Sweldens and Piessens have shown how to compute high-quality inner products with just the wavelet coefficients [429].

It is interesting to think about the wavelet functions themselves; Figure 6.18 has an intriguing shape. When evaluating wavelet functions, we need to be careful, since we have almost no guarantees on the shape, range, or continuity of the functions generated by a particular set of coefficients.

We can make the job easier by limiting our attention to values of the wavelet function at *dyadic* points; those are given by $n2^{-m}$, for $n, m \in \mathcal{Z}$. We can find these points by recursive midpoint subdivision. If we know the value of the scaling function v at the integers, then we can use the dilation equation to find the values at the half-integers. From those values, we find the values at the quarter-integers, and so on, recursing to any dyadic point of interest. So the only remaining trick is to find the starting points.

To find the starting values, we can look for *fixed points* of the recursion [90]; that is, points that don't change in value as the dilation equation is applied. We find these by writing the dilation equation as a recursive matrix equation and finding the eigenvectors of the matrix. These eigenvectors are the values of the points that are passed through by the matrix unchanged except for scale.

Let's find the endpoint values for D_4. We begin by writing the dilation equation from Equation 6.10 for v_1 and v_2:

$$v(1) = \mathbf{c_0 v(2)} + \mathbf{c_1 v(1)} + c_2 v(0) + c_3 v(-1)$$
$$v(2) = c_0 v(4) + c_1 v(3) + \mathbf{c_2 v(2)} + \mathbf{c_3 v(1)} \tag{6.65}$$

We only wrote the values for the nonzero coefficients $c_0 \ldots c_3$. We've marked in bold the nonzero products; the scaling function v is zero outside the interval $[1, 2]$. The result is that we can write a small recurrence equation:

$$\left[\begin{array}{c} v(1) \\ v(2) \end{array} \right] = \left[\begin{array}{cc} c_1 & c_0 \\ c_3 & c_2 \end{array} \right] \left[\begin{array}{c} v(1) \\ v(2) \end{array} \right] \tag{6.66}$$

which we can write as $\mathbf{v} = M\mathbf{v}$. We'll now find the eigenvalues λ_1, λ_2 of M. Recall that these are the solutions to $\det(M - \lambda \mathcal{I}) = 0$ [420]. We write

$$\det \left[\begin{array}{cc} c_1 - \lambda & c_0 \\ c_3 & c_2 - \lambda \end{array} \right] = 0 \tag{6.67}$$

For the coefficients of D_4 in Equation 6.62, there are two eigenvalues associated with this matrix: $\lambda_1 = 1$ and $\lambda_2 = 1/2$. The corresponding eigenvectors are

$$v_1 = \left[-\frac{1 + \sqrt{3}}{-1 + \sqrt{3}}, 1 \right] = [4c_0, 4c_3], \qquad v_2 = [-1, 1] \tag{6.68}$$

These vectors give us the two values that allow us to find all the others. In other words, we have found that $[v(0), v(1)] = [4c_0, 4c_3]$. From these two values we can use Equation 6.11 to find the value of v at all other dyadic points.

For example, to find $v(3/2)$, we write

$$
\begin{aligned}
v(3/2) &= c_0 v(3) + c_1 v(2) + c_2 v(1) + c_3 v(0) \\
&= c_1 v(2) + c_2 v(1) \\
&= c_1 4 c_3 + c_2 4 c_0 \\
&= 0
\end{aligned}
\tag{6.69}
$$

6.8 Multiresolution Analysis

Each application of the low-pass filter $\mathcal{L}$ in the previous section halves the number of samples representing our signal. We can think of this series of signals as representing the original signal at a variety of *resolutions*.

The technique of *multiresolution analysis* provides a formalism for discussing this property of wavelets. We can think of the input signal as belonging to a space of signals, and then we construct a nested chain of such spaces, each one containing the signal at a lesser resolution.

The scaling function $v(t)$ implies a space V_0, which is the space of all functions $cv(t)$ for some constant c. Similarly, the first wavelet, $w^0(t) = w^{0,0}(t)$, implies a space W_0, which is the space of all functions $cw^0(t)$. By construction, these two spaces are orthogonal:

$$
\int [av(t)] \, [bw^0(t)] = 0
\tag{6.70}
$$

If we combine the two spaces by a Cartesian sum, we generate a third, new space, V_1:

$$
V_1 = V_0 \oplus W_0
\tag{6.71}
$$

This new space contains the functions that are combinations from the two subspaces:

$$
V_1 : f(t) = av(t) + bw^0(t)
\tag{6.72}
$$

These are illustrated in Figure 6.19 for the Haar wavelets. So V_1 contains all functions built from two individually scaled, dilated, and translated copies of the original scaling function.

There are two essential points to notice about our new space of functions, V_1. The first is that it was built by combining one space with a second, orthogonal space. For example, consider the space P_0, which contains all polynomials of order 0; that is, all constant functions $f_0(x) = c_0$ for some $c_0 \in \mathcal{R}$. We might have another space P_1, which contains all first-order polynomials, or linear functions $f_1(x) = c_1 x + c_0$ for $c_1, c_0 \in \mathcal{R}$, and a space P_2 for quadratics $f_2(x) = c_2 x^2 + c_1 x + c_0$, and so on. We can build up as many spaces as we like, where each P_k contains the polynomials $f_k(x) = \sum_{i=0}^{k} c_i x^i$.

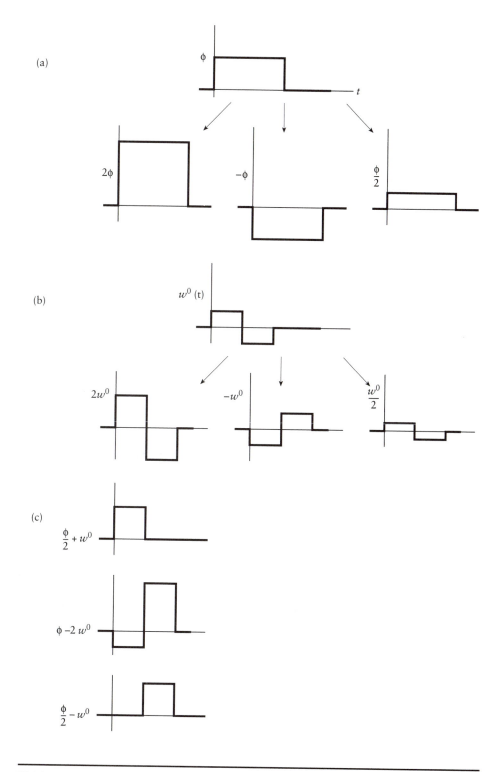

FIGURE 6.19

(a) The space $V_0 = av(t)$. (b) The space $W_0 = bw^0(t)$. (c) The space $V_1 = V_0 \oplus W_0 = av(t) + bw^0(t)$.

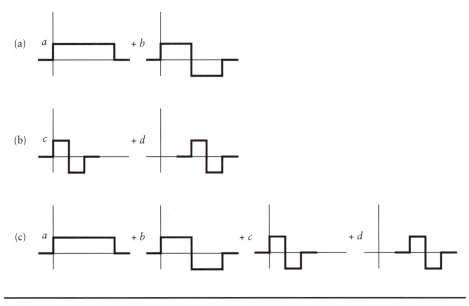

FIGURE 6.20

(a) The space V_1. (b) The space W_1. (c) The space $V_2 = V_1 \oplus W_1$.

The second important point about this construction is that the spaces are *nested*. All the functions $f_k(x)$ in the space P_k are contained in the larger space P_{k+n}, for all $n > 0$. We write this sequence of nested spaces as $P_0 \subset P_1 \subset P_2$. In terms of our construction of V_1, we find $V_0 \subset V_1$, since all functions $av(t)$ are in the space of the functions $av(t) + bw^0(t)$. In general, we can build a sequence of closed, nested subspaces V_i, such that

$$\cdots \subset V_{-2} \subset V_{-1} \subset V_0 \subset V_1 \subset V_2 \subset \cdots \tag{6.73}$$

We are now ready to describe the multiresolution framework for wavelets. Each space V_m is made up of all linear combinations of the functions $v(2^m t - k)$, and each space W_m is made up of all linear combinations of the functions $w^0(2^m t - k)$. For example, the space V_2 contains four copies of the scaling function, each quarter-width and individually scaled. We get this by combining V_1 with W_1, which is the set of quarter-wavelets, as shown in Figure 6.20. We can write this as

$$V_2 = V_1 \oplus W_1$$
$$= V_0 \oplus W_0 \oplus W_1 \tag{6.74}$$

In general, we build each space V_{m+1} by combining the space V_m with an orthogonal space W_m, recursively working our way back to V_0:

$$V_{m+1} = V_m \oplus W_m$$
$$= V_0 \oplus W_0 \oplus W_1 \oplus \cdots \oplus W_m \quad (6.75)$$

We will summarize these properties with respect to all functions in the class $f \in L^2(R)$, that is, all functions that satisfy $\int [f(t)]^2 < \infty$. In general, a *multiresolution analysis* is a set of closed subspaces V_m, $m \in \mathcal{Z}$, with the following properties:

1 Containment: $V_m \subset V_{m+1}$.

2 Distinctness: $\bigcap_m V_m = \emptyset$.

3 Completeness: $\bigcup_m V_m = L^2(R)$.

4 Shifting: if $f(t) \in V_m$, then $f(t - k) \in V_m$ for all $k \in \mathcal{Z}$.

5 Scaling: if $f(t) \in V_m$, then $f(2t) \in V_{m+1}$, for all $f \in L^2(R)$.

6 Basis: There exists a scaling function $v(t) \in V_0$, such that for all m, the set of functions

$$\{v_{mn}(t) = 2^{-m/2} v(2^{-m} t - n)\}$$

forms an orthonormal basis for V_m; that is,

$$\int v_{mp}(t) v_{mq}(t)\, dt = \begin{cases} 1 & p = q \\ 0 & \text{otherwise} \end{cases}$$

Wavelets work out so well because these properties are inherently satisfied by design. In particular, the dilation equation implies containment and scaling.

6.9 Wavelets in the Fourier Domain

Let's look at the dilation equation in the Fourier domain. Taking $v(t)$ from Equation 6.11 and plugging it into the Fourier transform from Equation 5.55 to find its transform $\Phi(\omega)$, we find

$$\Phi(\omega) = \kappa \int v(t) e^{-j\omega t} dt$$
$$= \kappa \int \sum_k c_k v(2t - k) e^{-j\omega t} dt$$
$$= \kappa \sum_k c_k \int v(2t - k) e^{-j\omega t} dt \quad (6.76)$$

Setting $y = 2t - k$, we find

$$
\begin{aligned}
\Phi(\omega) &= \kappa \sum_k c_k \int v(y) e^{-j\omega k/2} e^{-j\omega y/2} dy \\
&= \kappa \sum_k c_k e^{-jk\omega/2} \int v(y) e^{-jy\omega/2} dy \\
&= \left(\sum_k c_k e^{-jk\omega/2} \right) \left(\kappa \int v(y) e^{-jy\omega/2} dy \right) \\
&= P(\omega/2)\Phi(\omega/2)
\end{aligned} \tag{6.77}
$$

where we have set the symbol $P(\omega) = \sum_k c_k e^{-jk\omega}$. There is a natural recursion in Equation 6.77, inherited from the dilation equation. Following this recursion, we see that if $\Phi(\omega) = P(\omega/2)\Phi(\omega/2)$, then $\Phi(\omega/4) = P(\omega/2)[P(\omega/4)\Phi(\omega/4)]$, and so on, leading us to conclude

$$
\Phi(\omega) = \prod_{k=1}^{\infty} P\left(\frac{\omega}{2^k}\right) \tag{6.78}
$$

The conditions on the coefficients we mentioned earlier have counterparts in the frequency domain. For example, the condition in Equation 6.64 can be specified in the frequency domain by requiring that $P(\omega)$ has a zero of order p at $\omega = \pi$; that is, $P(\omega)$ contains a term $1/(w - \pi)^p$ [90].

Consider now what happens to the Fourier transform $W(\omega)$ as a wavelet $w(t)$ is dilated. We know from the delay property of Table 5.1 that when $w(t)$ and $W(\omega)$ form a Fourier pair, then

$$
w^{ab}(t) = \frac{1}{\sqrt{a}} w\left(\frac{t-b}{a}\right) \overset{\mathcal{F}}{\longleftrightarrow} W^{ab}(\omega) = \sqrt{a}\, W(a\omega)\, e^{-jb\omega} \tag{6.79}
$$

This is as expected; as the wavelet is stretched in time ($a < 1$), its Fourier transform compresses, and vice versa.

We can state the Parseval relation for the wavelet transform that mirrors the relation for the Fourier transform in Equation 5.64. The relation involves a constant C_w, which is central to a formula called the *resolution of identity*. This is basically a compact statement that we can reconstruct a function from its wavelet coefficients, the wavelet functions, and the constant C_w. The resolution of identity is

$$
x(t) = \frac{1}{C_w} \int_{-\infty}^{\infty} \int_{0}^{\infty} \frac{1}{a^2} b^{a,b} w^{a,b}(t)\, da\, db \tag{6.80}
$$

The equation says we can find $x(t)$ by scaling each wavelet $w^{a,b}(t)$ by its corresponding coefficient $b^{a,b}$, and scaling that product by the inverse-square of the dilation coefficient a. The result is equal to $x(t)$ except for a constant, called C_w and given by

$$C_w = \int_0^\infty \frac{\Phi(\omega)^2}{\omega} \, d\omega \tag{6.81}$$

The Parseval relation may now be written as

$$C_w \int |x(t)|^2 dt = \iint \frac{1}{a^2} |b^{a,b}|^2 \, da \, db \tag{6.82}$$

It is instructive to compare the time-frequency localization of the wavelet transform and the short-time Fourier transform, as in Figure 6.21. In this figure, we put a dot at the center of each transform; the horizontal position is the time at the transform's center, the vertical position is its frequency. Notice that in the STFT, the dots are regularly spaced. We position the window at a time nt_0; integer values of n yield equal horizontal spacing. We take the transform at frequency $m\omega_0$, yielding equal vertical spacing. So once we've picked our values of t_0 and ω_0, we generate a whole family of transforms at equal increments. The reason that the pattern is so regular is because we have a constant window for all times and all frequency ranges.

The figure also contains the pattern for the wavelet transform. Notice first how the horizontal spacing adjusts to the frequency; as the frequency goes up and the time-domain support of the wavelet decreases, copies of the wavelet need to be located closer together in order to cover the domain. Also notice that the spacing in frequency space moves geometrically. This implies that the ratio of the bandwidth of the wavelet to its center frequency is constant. In other words, if we plot frequency on a logarithmic scale, the frequency response of each wavelet has an equal shape. In electrical engineering, this is called a *constant-Q resonant filter*.

We can compare wavelets and short-time Fourier transforms in another way as well. A common method for displaying the frequency content of 1D signals is to use the STFT to compute a *spectrogram*. Here we plot the magnitude of the signal's STFT along a line representing the signal. This is a common technique for displaying the spectral content of time-varying signals such as speech and musical sounds, where the signal is swept over time. An example is shown in Figure 6.22(a). The vertical columns are generated by the different temporal windows as they are positioned in equal time increments. An alternative view of the same information is to look at the frequency information of the signal over all times, as shown in Figure 6.22(b). This represents the *filter bank* approach to displaying the frequency content of a changing signal.

The corresponding diagram for wavelets is called the *wavelet spectrogram*, or the *scalogram* [358]. Here we plot the magnitude of the wavelet response at different scales. Figure 6.23(a) shows the scalogram corresponding to an impulse function $\delta(t - t_0)$. In the scalogram, we see a high response at very fine scales, isolating the impulse accurately. As the scale becomes larger, the impulse diffuses, resulting in

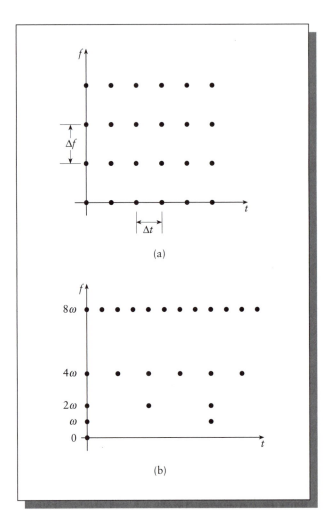

FIGURE 6.21

(a) The STFT lattice. The horizontal axis is time, the vertical axis is frequency. Each increment of m, n causes equal steps on both axes. (b) The wavelet lattice.

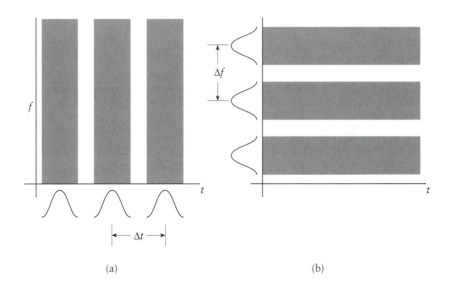

(a)   (b)

FIGURE 6.22

(a) Spectrograms. The signal is plotted horizontally, and the magnitude of the transform is indicated by color (black is a small value, white is large). The STFT gives the frequency content of the signal within different time windows. (b) Filter banks. Here we see the amount of spectral energy in the entire signal for different frequency ranges, as represented by different filters.

a cone-shaped region. Figure 6.23(b) shows the STFT spectrogram for the same impulse; notice that the time localization is limited to the Δt width of the analysis window. Another scalogram/spectrogram pair is shown in Figure 6.23(c) and (d). Here the response is to a set of three sine waves, at f_0, $2f_0$, and $4f_0$. Notice that the frequency resolution in the spectrogram is a constant Δf resulting from the fixed window, while the scalogram's response enlarges with increasing scale.

So wavelets *adapt* to the frequency at which they are applied. At low frequencies, they include large sections of the signal, and they are spaced far apart. At higher frequencies, the wavelets are packed more closely together and include smaller pieces of the signal.

This behavior is just what we specified at the start of the chapter. When we're interested in the low-frequency content of a signal, we use a wide window and include a lot of the signal; then we move the window a far distance and repeat. When we want to analyze the high-frequency content, we shrink the window to include just a

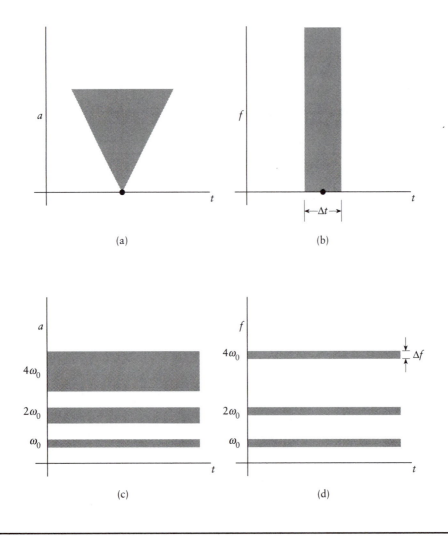

(a)   (b)

(c)   (d)

FIGURE   6.23

(a) The scalogram for an impulse function. (b) The spectrogram corresponding to (a). (c) The scalogram for a sum of three sines. (d) The spectrogram corresponding to (c). Redrawn from Rioul and Vetterli in *IEEE SP Magazine*.

bit of the signal, and move the window in much smaller steps. This is difficult to do with an STFT, but wavelets have this behavior built in; that is their main strength.

6.10 Two-Dimensional Wavelets

Just as we built Fourier transforms for 2D signals, we can also build 2D wavelet transforms. These are immediately useful for image storage and compression, but we will see in Chapter 16 that 2D wavelets are also very useful for representing matrices, in particular the matrices that are part of the basic equations describing how light moves throughout a scene.

There are a variety of methods for constructing multidimensional wavelets; pointers to some of these may be found in the work of Jawerth and Sweldens [229]. In this section we will focus on two of the most popular methods, called the *rectangular* and *square* deconstructions (though the less descriptive names *standard* and *nonstandard* have also been used [42]). We will discuss them in turn below.

Both sets of methods rely on forming the *tensor product* of two one-parameter functions $a(t)$ and $b(t)$. Let's call the 2D coordinates x and y. The idea is that one of these functions is passed the x parameter, and the other the y parameter, and the value of the 2D function is the product of these two independent function evaluations; for example, the value at (x, y) is $a(x)b(y)$. We write this new two-parameter function as $(a \otimes b)(x, y)$.

In all of our discussions below, we will assume that we have been given an input signal at a resolution of $2^N \times 2^N$. This signal may be a sampled 2D function, a matrix, an image, or any other real-valued 2D data.

6.10.1 The Rectangular Wavelet Decomposition

Perhaps the most straightforward multidimensional wavelet is given by the *rectangular* (or *standard*) form. The idea is to make tensor products of all the various functions involved in a 1D wavelet transform, and then use those functions for the 2D signal.

In other words, suppose we were given a four-element input vector $x[n]$. To match this with the Haar basis, we would have coefficients on the scaling function $v = (1, 1, 1, 1)$, the four-element wavelet $w^{0,0} = (1, 1, -1, -1)$, and the two two-element wavelets $w^{1,0} = (1, -1, 0, 0)$ and $w^{1,1} = (0, 0, 1, -1)$. To make the 2D basis set, we build the sixteen tensor products that come from the combination of these four functions. Since each input function is four elements large, the resulting basis functions are 4×4 matrices. Figure 6.24 summarizes these sixteen functions.

Notice that these functions have forms that are very similar to the 1D situation. We have a single function that takes an average $(v \otimes v)$, and fifteen other functions

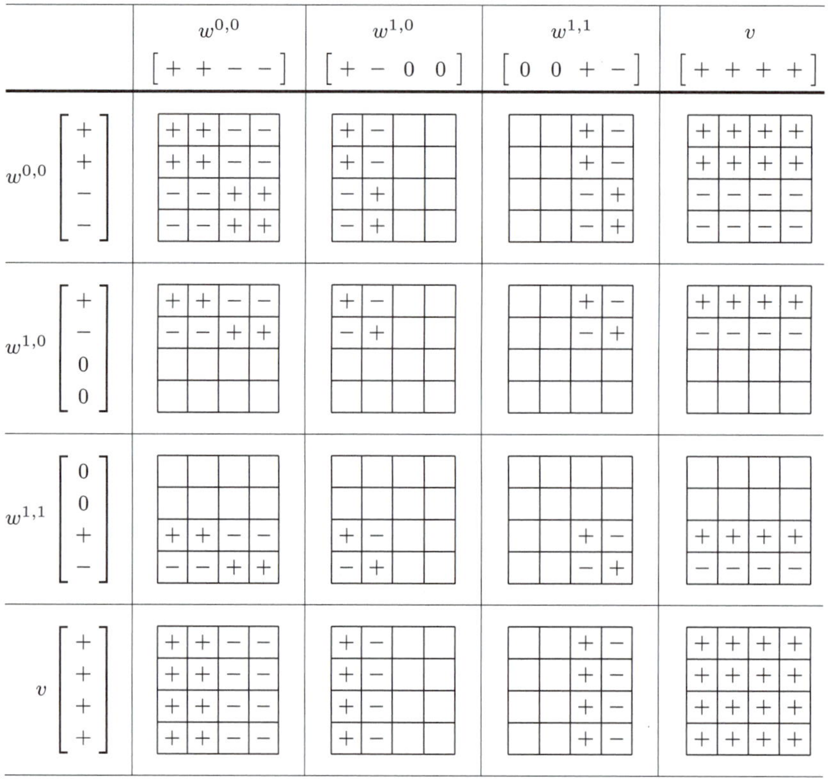

	$w^{0,0}$ $[\,+\ +\ -\ -\,]$	$w^{1,0}$ $[\,+\ -\ \ 0\ \ 0\,]$	$w^{1,1}$ $[\,0\ \ 0\ \ +\ -\,]$	v $[\,+\ +\ +\ +\,]$
$w^{0,0}$ $\begin{bmatrix}+\\+\\-\\-\end{bmatrix}$	+ + − − + + − − − − + + − − + +	+ − + − − + − +	\ \ + − \ \ + − \ \ − + \ \ − +	+ + + + + + + + − − − − − − − −
$w^{1,0}$ $\begin{bmatrix}+\\-\\0\\0\end{bmatrix}$	+ + − − − − + +	+ − − +	\ \ + − \ \ − +	+ + + + − − − −
$w^{1,1}$ $\begin{bmatrix}0\\0\\+\\-\end{bmatrix}$	+ + − − − − + +	+ − − +	\ \ + − \ \ − +	+ + + + − − − −
v $\begin{bmatrix}+\\+\\+\\+\end{bmatrix}$	+ + − − + + − − + + − − + + − −	+ − + − + − + −	\ \ + − \ \ + − \ \ + − \ \ + −	+ + + + + + + + + + + + + + + +

FIGURE 6.24

The sixteen basis functions for the rectangular wavelet decomposition of a 4×4 matrix. Each function is made by the tensor product of the function in the top row with the function on the left; for example, the third function on the top row is given by $w^{1,1} \otimes w^{0,0}$.

that sum to zero but encode local differences (or high-frequency information) in the signal at different scales. By design, the term-by-term sum of each basis function (except $v \otimes v$) is zero, and the sum of the term-by-term products of any two different bases is zero; that is, the bases form an orthogonal set.

The new wrinkle in 2D is that we compute the difference information in several directions. In particular, scanning the table shows that we compute high-frequency information distributed in three different directions: left to right (e.g., $w^{1,0} \otimes v$), up to down (e.g., $v \otimes w^{1,0}$), and diagonally (e.g., $w^{1,0} \otimes w^{1,1}$).

$$\begin{bmatrix} 1 & 2 & 4 & 5 \\ 2 & 1 & 4 & 5 \\ 2 & 1 & 3 & 3 \\ 3 & 6 & 3 & 3 \end{bmatrix} \rightarrow \frac{1}{4} \begin{bmatrix} -3 & 1 & -1 & 0 \\ 0 & -2 & 0 & 0 \\ -3 & 4 & 0 & -3 \\ -3 & -1 & -1 & 12 \end{bmatrix}$$

FIGURE 6.25

An example decomposition in the rectangular wavelet basis.

To transform a 2D signal into this basis, for each basis we simply multiply the signal term by term, sum the result, and divide by a normalizing factor (here equal to the number of nonzero terms in the basis function). Note that this all works only if the wavelets are their own duals, as in the case of the Haar bases.

Figure 6.25 shows an example transformation under this basis. The matrix M has been designed to demonstrate the various types of directional information that this basis picks up most efficiently; note that five of the sixteen wavelet coefficients are zero. To illustrate the procedure, for the upper-left coefficient we find

$$\frac{(1+2+2+1)-(4+5+4+5)-(2+1+3+6)+(3+3+3+3)}{16} = -\frac{3}{4}$$

6.10.2 The Square Wavelet Decomposition

The basis functions in the last section had both square and rectangular regions of nonzero elements. This is useful when we want to construct a decomposition that is anisotropic; that is, we are concerned with different scale ranges along different dimensions. If we treat all dimensions the same way, we can construct a decomposition that has only square terms; it's called the *square* (or *nonstandard*) decomposition.

Once again we will build the basis functions from tensor products of the scaling function v and the wavelets $w^{a,b}$. This time, though, we will be guided by an analogy to the multiresolution analysis discussed in Section 6.8.

We begin with the simplest 2D basis function formed by $v \otimes v$; that is, a box. Recall that translates of v span a piecewise-constant space of one dimension, which we will write $V_0^{(1)}$. By analogy, if v is one unit on a side, then integer translates of $v \otimes v$ span a 2D space $V_0^{(2)}$ made up of all the functions that are piecewise-constant over integer-sized squares, as shown in Figure 6.26(a).

As in the 1D case, we would like to move to a space $V_1^{(2)}$, which is piecewise-constant over *half*-integer-sized boxes, as shown in Figure 6.26(b). To move from the lower-resolution to the higher-resolution space, we make the Cartesian product

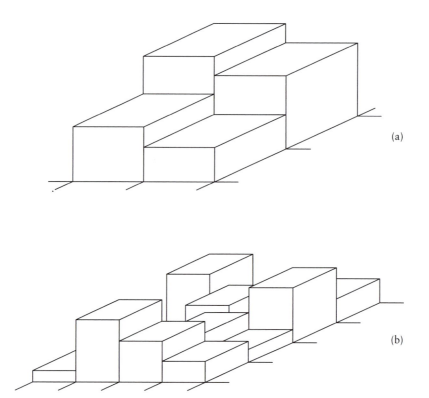

FIGURE 6.26
(a) The space $V_0^{(2)}$. (b) The space $V_1^{(2)}$.

of $V_0^{(2)}$ with the "detail" space $W_0^{(2)}$, such that

$$V_0^{(2)} \oplus W_0^{(2)} = V_1^{(2)}, \qquad W_0^{(2)} \perp V_0^{(2)} \tag{6.83}$$

That is, the detail space is orthogonal to the low-resolution space, and adds just the information we need to get to a better resolution. Eventually, $V_\infty^{(2)}$ will be able to match all 2D functions $f(x, y)$.

To find $W_0^{(2)}$, we again take a cue from the 1D case and make the four tensor-product functions that come from the four combinations of the scaling function v and the first wavelet $w^{0,0}$. That is, we build $v \otimes v$, $v \otimes w^{0,0}$, $w^{0,0} \otimes v$, and $w^{0,0} \otimes w^{0,0}$. These four basis functions are shown in Figure 6.27. We have given them the labels A, H, V, and D, respectively.

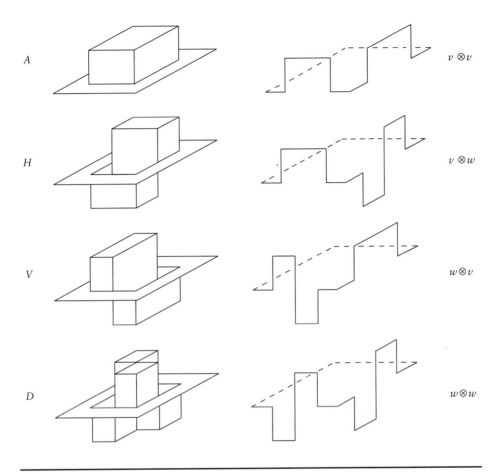

FIGURE 6.27

The four basic functions in the square basis.

These four functions can match any 2×2 signal. The decomposition can be written simply by observing that

$$\begin{bmatrix} a & b \\ c & d \end{bmatrix} = g_A A + g_H H + g_V V + g_D D \qquad (6.84)$$

That is, an input matrix with elements (a, b, c, d) is the sum of the four basis functions weighted by the coefficients (g_A, g_H, g_V, g_D). To find these coefficients, we can write

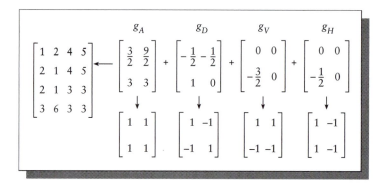

FIGURE 6.28

Decomposition of the example matrix into the square basis.

out Equation 6.84 as four linear equations:

$$a = g_A + g_H + g_V + g_D$$
$$b = g_A - g_H + g_V - g_D$$
$$c = g_A + g_H - g_V - g_D$$
$$d = g_A - g_H - g_V + g_D \qquad (6.85)$$

So we now have four equations in four unknowns. Some straightforward algebra reveals the expressions for the unknowns:

$$g_A = (a + b + c + d)/2$$
$$g_D = (2g_A - b - c)/2$$
$$g_V = (a + b - 2g_A)/2$$
$$g_H = a - g_V - g_D - g_A \qquad (6.86)$$

The transformation of the matrix in Figure 6.25 is shown in Figure 6.28. Note that seven of the sixteen coefficients are zero. In this figure, the two-by-two matrix associated with g_A represents the g_A coefficients for the four corners of the original matrix. That is, to reconstruct the upper-left two-by-two corner of the matrix, select the upper-left coefficient from each of the four coefficient matrices, scale its associated two-by-two pattern of positive and negative ones, and add these four scaled patterns together. Arranging the coefficients into these little matrices is just meant as a notational aid; they could be organized in other ways.

6.11   Further Reading

Gilbert Strang has written two fine introductions to wavelets; much of this chapter was based on the information they present [422, 423]. Another recent introductory article is the one by Jawerth [229]. An excellent survey book with both historical and future perspectives has been written by Meyer [302]; this short book serves as a fine introduction to the subject. A more complete survey of theory and applications may be found in the book edited by Chui [90]. A good overview of wavelets and their application to signal processing may be found in Rioul and Vetterli [359]. We only touched on the short-term Fourier transform; a detailed discussion is given in Nawab's essay [316].

The methods of multiresolution signal decomposition are discussed in more detail in the book by Akansu and Haddad [5], where wavelets are integrated into a general framework. Extensive, detailed discussions of wavelets may be found in the lectures by Daubechies [115]. Both this book and the article by Rioul and Vetterli [359] contain rich, recent bibliographies.

Explicit source code for computing various wavelet transformations (including D_4) in different computer languages is available in the various second editions of *Numerical Recipes* by Press et al. [348]. C code is also available in the introductory article by Cody [94].

Applications of wavelets to computer graphics are only beginning to appear, but they have already been applied to the solution of integral equations (discussed in Chapter 16) for rendering. Some good references relevant to this subject include a discussion of Galerkin integration by Xu and Shann [493] and the quadrature analysis by Sweldens and Piessens [429]. The use of wavelets to compress the matrices involved in solving integral equation problems is addressed by Alpert [8], and other methods are covered by Beylkin et al. [42] and Alpert et al. [7]. The application of wavelets to nonuniform sampling is discussed by Feichtenger and Gröchenig [142, 143].

6.12   Exercises

Exercise 6.1
Show that the "Mexican hat" wavelet

$$w(x) = (1 - 2x^2)e^{-x^2}$$

has two vanishing moments.

Exercise 6.2

Carry out the error computation at the start of Section 6.6 using the same signal, but use the RMS error metric

$$E = \left[\sum_k |s[k] - \tilde{s}_m[k]|^2 \right]^{1/2}$$

Do you get the same order of wavelet inclusion?

Exercise 6.3

Using the Haar bases, find the wavelet transform for the signal $\{9, 11, 13, -1, -2, 8, -1, -9\}$. Plot the scaled basis functions.

Exercise 6.4

Implement the Haar transform, and either implement or find an implementation of the Fourier transform.

(a) Create a 256-sample of a single period of a sine wave, $f[n] = \sin(x_n)$, $n \in [0, 255]$, $x_n = 2n\pi/255$. Find the Haar and Fourier transforms of this signal. Using the compression method of Section 6.6 with an RMS error metric (see Exercise 2), plot the RMS error as a function of the number of wavelet coefficients used. Plot the RMS error as a function of the number of Fourier coefficients, taking them in order of increasing frequency starting with DC.

(b) Repeat (a) with the signal $f[n] = |\sin(x_n)|$.

(c) Repeat (a) with the signal $f[n] = \sin(x_n) + \exp[-(x_n - (\pi/3))^3]$.

7

MONTE CARLO INTEGRATION

7.1 Introduction

In previous chapters we have looked at the Fourier and wavelet transformations
of signals. These powerful transformations give us the means for discussing what
happens when we sample and reconstruct a signal.

Another useful set of tools may be developed by reconsidering the formulation
of a particular piece of the rendering problem. Consider for the moment creating a
picture by sampling the image plane, where we ultimately want to find color values
for each pixel. The theory of signal processing tells us how to design a filter $h(x, y)$
to be placed over each pixel, which will determine the contribution of the underlying
image signal $s(x, y)$ at that location. So the final value p of the sample at some
particular (x, y) may be written as

$$p(x, y) = \iint_P s(x, y)h(x - \mu, y - \nu)\, d\mu\, d\nu \qquad (7.1)$$

where P is the pixel area.

Once we have used signal processing to design the filter h and set up this integral, we are free to evaluate it any way we like. The signal-processing approach uses Fourier theory to guide us in taking a number of samples of s and combining them with h to reconstruct the continuous-time function p. Given that description of the signal, we can filter it to get the final value. But perhaps this is more effort than we really need. After all, we only want a final value at the pixel; perhaps reconstructing the complete signal is overkill. There may be a better way to evaluate the integral.

The problem of efficient numerical integration is not new, but it is not nearly as old as analytic integration. The techniques collectively called *Monte Carlo* were developed in the 1940s to solve complex integrals with the newly developed electronic computers. The name comes from the essential role played by random numbers in choosing samples of the function used to estimate its integral. A short but interesting history of Monte Carlo methods appears in Chapter 1 of Hammersley and Handscomb's book [183].

This chapter will focus on the ideas behind the Monte Carlo method and its applications to computer graphics. Monte Carlo methods use many results from basic statistics and probability; you should be comfortable with these ideas, which are briefly reviewed in Appendix B.

7.2 Basic Monte Carlo Ideas

Monte Carlo methods are designed to find the parameters of a distribution that specifies a *random variable*. So we begin with some observations (or values) of the random variable, and a guess at the form of its distribution. We then try to find the parameters of that distribution that match observed values of the random variable.

As an analogy, suppose that we want to estimate the amplitude of thunderclaps during a particular rainstorm. We guess that the volume v of the claps is described by a random variable whose values follow an exponential distribution $\exp[-\lambda v^2]$. Then, by finding the amplitude of several thunderclaps, we try to find the parameter λ that characterizes that distribution. Notice that each thunderclap is an independent random variable η_i distributed according to the exponential distribution $F_e(y)$ (all of these terms are discussed in Appendix B).

The point of this procedure is that if we can characterize the distribution from which a random variable is drawn, then we can evaluate a variety of useful measures based on that distribution. The integral of the random variable over some domain is not the only such measure of interest in rendering, but it will be our driving problem in this chapter.

A parameter estimated by Monte Carlo methods is called an *estimand*. We find a value for the estimand (called an *estimate*) by working with a number of observed random variables, called the *sample* (or *sample set*); the number of observations is called the *sample size*. Since we have already encountered these words with different meanings in signal processing, we will use the term *observation* rather than sample, and *observation set* to mean the collection of observations. So the *observation set size* refers to the number of observations we are going to work with to find our estimand.

In graphics we are often concerned with finding the mean μ of a random variable. If we have n observations η_i, we might simply *average* them together to form a first guess for the mean $\bar{\eta}$:

$$\bar{\eta} = \sum_{i=1}^{n} \eta_i / n \tag{7.2}$$

In fact this approach is provably correct; the mean will eventually approach the average [183].

We will say that a random variable η is *normal (μ, σ)*, for mean μ and standard deviation σ, if it fits the normal distribution $F_n((t - \mu)/\sigma)$. Suppose that $\eta_1, \eta_2, \ldots$ is a sequence of n independent, identically distributed random variables with mean μ and standard deviation σ. Their average

$$\bar{\eta} = \frac{1}{n} \sum_{i=1}^{n} \eta_i \tag{7.3}$$

is asymptotically normal $(\mu, \sigma/\sqrt{n})$. That is, values for the average fit a normal distribution with mean μ and standard deviation $\sigma/\sqrt{n}$. This is important. In other words, as we take more samples and produce new values for the estimand, the estimated values themselves will tend to be normally distributed. This is true even if the random variable itself is not normally distributed! The reason that this is useful is because it shows us that the mean of the estimates is the same as the mean of the random variable, which is what we are seeking. Thus the estimates themselves lead to a value for the mean.

A slightly more sophisticated approach would form a *weighted average* by applying a different weight w_i to each observation and then normalizing the result by the sum of the weights:

$$\bar{\eta} \approx \frac{\displaystyle\sum_{i=1}^{n} w_i \eta_i}{\displaystyle\sum_{i=1}^{n} w_i} \tag{7.4}$$

This process leads us to ask if there is some set of weights w_i that results in a more accurate value for $\bar{\eta}$ in Equation 7.4 than Equation 7.2 (where, implicitly, each $w_i = 1$). Even more broadly, are there other functions of the η_i that are even better than Equation 7.4? In this context, "better" means a more accurate estimate of the true mean with the same number of samples. Most of the Monte Carlo literature is involved in exploring answers to these questions.

Some terminology will help the following discussion. Equations 7.2 and 7.4 are two instances of a function $t(\eta_i)$ that takes as input our observations and returns a value for the estimand. We call such a function an *estimator*. In the literature, we see phrases like "the estimator t" and "the estimate t" used to distinguish the function t from a particular result returned by that function.

We call the distribution of the random variable we seek the *parent distribution*. In the example given earlier, the parent distribution is the true distribution of amplitudes of thunderclaps. Since the underlying value of η is a random variable, the values returned by the estimator t are also random variables. This is because the values of η are simply mapped through t; the differences between different observations will be propagated by t, so it is a random variable as well. If t collapses the observation in some dimension (e.g., the function $t(\eta_i) = 0$ for all η_i), then it may be a constant, but we will still consider that to be a random variable in this context. In the Monte Carlo literature, the set of estimands produced by $t(\eta_i)$ is called the *sampling distribution*; as before, to avoid conflict with the signal-processing terminology of sampling, we call this the *estimand distribution*.

Our goal, then, is to find an estimator that will take observations of the random variable η and produce an estimate of the parameters of the parent distribution, such that the estimand distribution (that is, the collection of estimands) is located near the true value of the estimand and is concentrated in a narrow band.

It turns out that we can find the estimand distribution $T(u)$ in terms of the estimator $t(y)$ and the parent distribution $F(y)$; this distribution is given by

$$T(u) = P(t(\eta) \le u) = \int_{t(y) \le u} dF(y) \tag{7.5}$$

Given an F and a t, we are interested in the difference between the result of the estimator $t(\eta)$ and the true value of the parameter we seek (traditionally called θ). This difference may be expressed by the expected value of the difference between the estimate and θ:

$$\beta = E[t(\eta) - \theta] = \int (t(y) - \theta)\, dF(y) \tag{7.6}$$

where $E[a]$ is the *expected value* of a. The value β is called the *bias* of the estimator t; it indicates the extent to which the estimate misses the true value of θ. In other words, $\theta + \beta$ is the mean of the estimand distribution, rather than the desired value θ. We can measure the variance of t as

$$\sigma_t{}^2 = E[(t(\eta) - E[t(\eta)])^2] = E[(t - \theta - \beta)^2]$$
$$= \int (t(y) - \theta - \beta)^2\, dF(y) \tag{7.7}$$

The value $\sigma_t{}^2$ is called the *sampling variance* of t; in our case we call it the *estimand variance*. The square root of $\sigma_t{}^2$ is the standard deviation of the estimand distribution; for specificity it is usually called the *standard error*, or in our case the *estimand error*.

We can use this terminology to make our discussion of estimators more precise. We say that $t(y)$ is a "good" estimator if β and σ_t^2 are both small. This is just a restatement of our condition that the estimands be located near θ and be contained in a narrow band. If $\beta = 0$, we say that the estimator is *unbiased*. There is nothing inherently bad or undesirable about a biased estimator, as long as we understand the bias and can correct for it. If σ_t^2 is smaller than for any other estimator, then we say that t is a *minimum-variance estimator*.

There are many types of estimators. When you are searching for an estimator, sometimes it helps to narrow the field of candidates. A classic approximation is to limit the search to *linear estimators*, that is, linear functions of the observations, as in Equation 7.4. The best estimator from this class for a given problem is called the *minimum-variance linear estimator*.

Classic Monte Carlo methods create an estimand G by combining n identically distributed, independent random variables η_i. If each random variable η_i is evaluated by a function g_i and scaled by a weight λ_i, then the estimand G may be formed as the sum of these weighted functions:

$$G = \sum_{i=1}^{n} \lambda_i g_i(\eta_i) \tag{7.8}$$

Since the values η_i are random variables, the function values $g_i(\eta_i)$ are as well. Thus we can find their mean, or expected value $E[G]$, as

$$\begin{aligned} E[G] &= E\left[\sum_{i=1}^{n} \lambda_i g_i(\eta_i)\right] \\ &= \sum_{i=1}^{n} \lambda_i E\left[g_i(\eta_i)\right] \end{aligned} \tag{7.9}$$

since the expected value operator E is linear, and therefore can be passed through the summation. Suppose that all the $g_i(x)$ are the same function $g(x)$, and all $\lambda_i = 1/n$. Then the expected value simplifies to

$$\begin{aligned} E[G] &= E\left[\frac{1}{n}\sum_{i=1}^{n} g(\eta_i)\right] \\ &= \frac{1}{n}\sum_{i=1}^{n} E\left[g(\eta_i)\right] \\ &= E[g(x)] \end{aligned} \tag{7.10}$$

Equation 7.10 is a crucial result. It tells us that G, the weighted average of our n values of g, has the same expected value, or mean, as g itself. So to find the mean of the function g, we can find the mean of its weighted samples; with enough samples the latter will eventually become the former.

Given that Equation 7.10 approximates $E[g]$, we would like to know how quickly it arrives at the correct answer. To find this speed of convergence, we find the variance of the estimator:

$$
\begin{aligned}
\mathrm{var}(G) &= \mathrm{var}\left(\frac{1}{n}\sum_{i=1}^{n} g(\eta_i)\right)\\
&= \sum_{i=1}^{n}\frac{1}{n^2}\,\mathrm{var}\left(g(\eta_i)\right)\\
&= \frac{1}{n}\,\mathrm{var}\left(g(x)\right)\\
&= \frac{1}{n}\sigma_p{}^2
\end{aligned}
\tag{7.11}
$$

where σ_p is the standard deviation of the parent distribution. Thus the standard deviation σ_G of G is

$$
\sigma_G = \frac{1}{\sqrt{n}}\sigma_p
\tag{7.12}
$$

So the deviation in our estimate is related to the deviation of the parent distribution, and decreases with the *square root* of the number of samples n. This is a fundamental result of classical Monte Carlo.

Sometimes we wish to find the variance of the parent distribution, rather than its mean. An unbiased estimator of the variance of the parent distribution is given by

$$
s^2 = \frac{\eta_1{}^2 + \cdots + \eta_n{}^2 - n\bar{\eta}^2}{n-1}
\tag{7.13}
$$

which has a standard deviation of about

$$
\sigma_{s^2} \approx \sigma_p^2 / \sqrt{n/2}
\tag{7.14}
$$

The estimand error given by Equation 7.12 is exact, but the estimand error of Equation 7.14 is only an estimate and depends on the fourth moment of the parent distribution (though it is exact when the parent distribution is a normal distribution) [183]. Another estimate of the error is given by

$$
\sigma_s \approx \sigma_p / \sqrt{2n}
\tag{7.15}
$$

This formula for the estimand error is common, but biased.

When these formulas are used for actual computation, we usually replace the parameter by its value. Thus in Equation 7.12 the value of σ would use s calculated by Equation 7.13.

The biggest problem with Monte Carlo methods in general is the extremely slow convergence of the estimand. Equation 7.12 shows that the estimand error is inversely proportional to the square of the size of the observation set; in other words, the algorithm has convergence $O(1/\sqrt{n})$. Thus to halve the error, we must quadruple the number of samples. In general, to reduce the error in n samples by a factor α, we must take $\alpha^2(n-1)$ more samples. When the desired error is small, n is typically very large. In computer graphics each sample is very expensive to evaluate. This form of estimator effectively tells us that each successive sample helps us out less and less, even though typically they all come at the same enormous cost. Much of the research in Monte Carlo methods has been directed at increasing the convergence of the estimator, or getting better results from fewer samples.

7.3 Confidence

It is often important that we have some measure of the *confidence* in a Monte Carlo estimate. That is, when we have generated a particular estimate based on some number of samples, can we express quantitatively how certain we are that our estimate is correct? Such a measure would allow us to make statements of the form, "We are 85% confident that the average value is within 5% of the estimate." Sometimes confidence is straightforward to determine, but more often it is very difficult. It usually requires that we make some a priori determination of the form of the parent distribution.

For example, let us *suppose* that the parent distribution is normal. We will now develop a tool that allows us to make meaningful statements about the quality of our estimate of the mean μ of the parent distribution. The interesting thing about this result will be that it does not involve estimating σ_p, so our confidence for one parameter is not based on a good estimate for another, which would be a troubling situation.

We begin by defining the *alpha measures* on a set of observations of a random variable. We define these for a fixed observation set size n and for each nonnegative integer k:

$$\alpha_k = \frac{1}{n}\sum_{i=1}^{n}\eta_i{}^k \tag{7.16}$$

In particular, the first alpha measure is the mean: $\alpha_1 = \bar{\eta}$. Using these quantities, we can define *Student's t distribution*. Consider the two mutually independent random variables

$$\eta_{t1} = (\alpha_1 - m)\sqrt{n}$$
$$\eta_{t2} = \frac{n}{n-1}(\alpha_2 - \alpha_1{}^2) \tag{7.17}$$

We can form a ratio t called *Student's ratio* as

$$t = \frac{\eta_{t1}}{\sqrt{\eta_{t2}}} = \sqrt{n-1}\frac{\alpha_1 - m}{\sqrt{\alpha_2 - \alpha_1{}^2}} \tag{7.18}$$

Since it is a function of random variables, t itself is also a random variable. It has a density function $S_{n-1}(x)$ given by the somewhat awkward formula

$$S_{n-1}(x) = \frac{1}{\sqrt{(n-1)\pi}} \frac{\Gamma\left(\frac{n}{2}\right)}{\Gamma\left(\frac{n-1}{2}\right)} \left(1 + \frac{x^2}{n-1}\right)^{-n/2} \tag{7.19}$$

where the Gamma function $\Gamma(t)$ is defined by

$$\Gamma(t) = \int_0^\infty x^{t-1}e^{-x}\,dx \tag{7.20}$$

The distribution $S_{n-1}(x)$ is called *Student's t distribution with* $(n-1)$ *degrees of freedom*. We can write the variance of the observation set s^2 as

$$s^2 = \frac{1}{n}\sum_{i=1}^n \eta_i{}^2 - \left(\frac{1}{n}\sum_{i=1}^n \eta_i\right)^2 \tag{7.21}$$

We are now ready to create the confidence test. In the last paragraph we defined the random variable t to have a distribution given by $S_{n-1}(x)$. Since the distribution tells us the cumulative likelihood that a random variable will take on a value less than or equal to a given value, we can find the chance that the variable will land in some range as an integral of the distribution function throughout that range. So the likelihood that t is between two reals a and b may be found from

$$P(a < t \leq b) = \int_a^b S_{n-1}(x)\,dx \tag{7.22}$$

Some algebra allows us to rewrite this as

$$P\left(\alpha_1 - \frac{b\sqrt{s^2}}{\sqrt{n-1}} \leq m < \alpha_1 - \frac{a\sqrt{s^2}}{\sqrt{n-1}}\right) = \int_a^b S_{n-1}(x)\,dx \tag{7.23}$$

Equation 7.23 is the tool I promised earlier. Given n samples and two limits a and b, the probability that the true mean is within the interval $[a, b]$ may be found explicitly as the integral over a piece of $S_{n-1}(x)$, which does not require estimating σ_p. Typically these integrals are precomputed and stored in a look-up table, indexed by a, b, n, and $\alpha_1 = \overline{\eta}$.

This analysis breaks down if the parent distribution is not normal; the less normal the distribution, the less accurate our estimate will be. It is difficult to find a completely accurate test for normality of a distribution, though several partial tests such as Shapiro and Silverman's [394] have been developed; they are surveyed in Spanier and Gelbard's book [415].

7.4 Blind Monte Carlo

We may distinguish two approaches to improving our estimate: those that do not require any a priori information about the signal (which I call *blind* Monte Carlo), and those that use some knowledge of the function being integrated (which I call *informed* Monte Carlo). We begin with blind techniques in this chapter.

We will summarize five types of blind Monte Carlo methods:

- crude Monte Carlo

- rejection Monte Carlo

- blind stratified sampling

- quasi Monte Carlo

- weighted Monte Carlo

7.4.1 Crude Monte Carlo

Crude Monte Carlo (or basic Monte Carlo) is the approach that we discussed in detail in the previous section. For completeness, we briefly repeat the estimator and its error values here. In computer graphics, we are usually interested in the mean (or average) value θ of a signal $f(x)$ over some domain, which without loss of generality we take as $[0, 1]$:

$$\theta = \int_0^1 f(x)\, dx \tag{7.24}$$

If we generate n independent, uniformly distributed random variables $\xi_i \in [0, 1]$, then from the quantities $f_i = f(\xi_i)$ we can find an unbiased estimator $\overline{f}$

$$\overline{f} = \frac{1}{n} \sum_{i=1}^{n} f_i \tag{7.25}$$

As shown in the previous section, this estimator has a variance

$$\sigma_{\bar{f}}^2 = \frac{1}{n} \int_0^1 (f(x) - \theta)^2 dx = \sigma^2/n \tag{7.26}$$

where σ^2 is the variance of f, the parent distribution. Its estimand error is given by

$$\sigma_{\bar{f}} = \sigma_p/\sqrt{n} \tag{7.27}$$

Equation 7.25 is usually referred to as the *crude Monte Carlo* estimator of θ.

Although the $O(1/\sqrt{n})$ convergence of crude Monte Carlo is slow with respect to the number of samples, it isn't as bad as *rejection* Monte Carlo.

7.4.2 Rejection Monte Carlo

The *rejection* (or *hit-or-miss*) technique is worth discussing because it used to be the one that was most strongly recommended for Monte Carlo problems [414]. In fact, it should be avoided whenever possible, as we will see.

The idea is known as rejection because it is based on creating a number of samples and rejecting those that don't meet a certain condition. Crude Monte Carlo evaluates all the samples it generates, but rejection Monte Carlo requires us to create a sample, test it to see if we really do want to evaluate it, and then proceed only if the test succeeds. This can become very expensive if the cost of either generating or testing samples is high, or if there is a very low likelihood of success. In the latter case we end up spending most of our time generating and disposing of samples, rather than evaluating samples and building up an estimate of the integral.

Suppose that we have a function $f(x)$ that is bounded by $[0, 1]$ when $0 \le x \le 1$. If we look at $y = f(x)$, then in the interval $[0, 1]$ the curve is entirely bounded by the unit square. We seek the mean θ, which is simply the percentage of the square's area lying under the curve. We can write this as

$$f(x) = \int_0^1 g(x, y)\, dy \tag{7.28}$$

where

$$g(x, y) = \begin{cases} 0 & \text{if } f(x) < y \\ 1 & \text{if } f(x) \ge y \end{cases} \tag{7.29}$$

Then θ is the area under the curve, given by a double integral:

$$\theta = \int_0^1 \int_0^1 g(x, y)\, dx\, dy \tag{7.30}$$

We can imagine finding an estimate for θ with a thought experiment. Imagine throwing n darts at random into the unit square, and then counting the number that land below $y = f(x)$. Recall that the binomial distribution $F_e(y)$ gives us the number of successful events out of n trials, when the probability of success of each one is $0 \leq p \leq 1$. Thus this dart-throwing approach is sampling from the binomial distribution with $p = \theta$ (the chance of success on each throw is the ratio of the area under the curve to the total area of the square). The binomial distribution's variance can be shown, according to Hammersley and Handscomb [183], to be

$$\sigma_b{}^2 = \theta(1 - \theta)/n \qquad (7.31)$$

From above, we have the variance $\sigma_{\bar{f}}{}^2$ for crude Monte Carlo:

$$\sigma_{\bar{f}}{}^2 = \frac{1}{n} \int_0^1 (f(x) - \theta)^2 dx = \frac{1}{n} \int_0^1 f^2\, dx - \theta^2/n \qquad (7.32)$$

Comparing the two, we find the amount of error due to rejection *beyond* that due to crude Monte Carlo:

$$\sigma_b{}^2 - \sigma_{\bar{f}}{}^2 = \frac{\theta}{n} - \frac{1}{n} \int_0^1 f^2 dx$$

$$= \frac{1}{n} \int_0^1 f(1 - f)\, dx > 0 \qquad (7.33)$$

Thus the error due to rejection methods is *always* worse than that of crude Monte Carlo. The use of rejection instead of crude Monte Carlo gave the entire field of Monte Carlo a bad reputation for many years; the convergence is so poor that the technique is often excruciatingly slow. The improvement in crude Monte Carlo is the avoidance of an unnecessary step in the calculation: it replaces the 2D function $g(x, y)$ by its 1D expectation $f(x)$. This makes a significant change to the convergence properties of the method.

This comparison points out an important rule of thumb that is worth keeping in mind for all Monte Carlo work. Hammersley and Handscomb [183] phrase this principle simply and directly in their book: "If, at any point of a Monte Carlo calculation, we can replace an estimate by an exact value, we shall reduce the sampling error in the final result."

This is a basic principle that we should apply whenever possible to improve Monte Carlo sampling of all types.

7.4.3 Blind Stratified Sampling

Suppose that we are executing a Monte Carlo algorithm and picking random positions to generate observations. We know that eventually the samples will follow a particular distribution due to the process used to generate them, but there's no guarantee that any specific group of sequentially generated samples will have that distribution. For example, the first n samples generated might all land in almost the same spot in the domain. We would like very much to avoid such *clumping*. Our signal inhabits the entire domain, so our samples should as well. When samples are precious, as they are in computer graphics, we would usually like them to sample the domain as efficiently as possible right from the start.

One way to accomplish this is called *stratified sampling*. The basic idea is to break up the domain of the integrand into regions, or *strata* (singular *stratum*), where each region represents an equal amount of information. When we know nothing of the underlying function, we call this approach *blind stratified sampling* because we have to guess at the best subdivision of the domain without knowing anything about the function. For example, suppose we divide the 1D domain $[0, 1]$ into k equal regions with intervals (α_{k-1}, α_k), where $\alpha_0 = 0$ and $\alpha_1 = 1$. If we decide beforehand to take n_j samples in domain j, then we can write an unbiased estimator

$$t = \sum_{j=1}^{k} \sum_{i=1}^{n_j} \frac{\alpha_j - \alpha_{j-1}}{n_j} f(\alpha_{j-1} + (\alpha_j - \alpha_{j-1})\xi_i) \tag{7.34}$$

with variance

$$\sigma_t{}^2 = \sum_{j=1}^{k} \frac{\alpha_j - \alpha_{j-1}}{n_j} \int_{\alpha_{j-1}}^{\alpha_j} f(x)^2 \, dx - \sum_{j=1}^{k} \frac{1}{n_j} \left\{ \int_{\alpha_{j-1}}^{\alpha_j} f(x) \, dx \right\}^2 \tag{7.35}$$

This variance can often be better than for crude Monte Carlo.

The efficiency of stratified sampling increases proportionally to the square of the number of strata [183]. This means a small increase in the number of strata can have a large effect on the quality of our sampling.

One problem with this approach is that different domains have different distributions of information; a region that is important to one function might be irrelevant to another. Thus we would like to subdivide our domains using as much knowledge as possible about the underlying function. Therefore we will discuss a variation on this technique under the section on *informed* Monte Carlo.

7.4.4 Quasi Monte Carlo

In blind stratified sampling, we tried to distribute our samples in such a way that they hit all the important parts of the domain in a roughly uniform but nonperiodic way. We did this by breaking up the domain into pieces, and then randomly sampling each piece. An alternative is to directly generate a sequence of samples that have the same characteristics.

This is the approach taken by *quasi Monte Carlo*, which is also known as *number-theoretic Monte Carlo* [502]. This approach uses no random numbers, but instead employs techniques from number theory to generate a set of sample points that are roughly uniform but aperiodic throughout the domain.

Several sequences based on number theory are summarized by Warnock [471]. The *Halton sequence* is defined for N-dimensional points x_i. Suppose that we are generating an N-dimensional point x_m; it is defined by

$$x_m = (\phi_2(m), \phi_3(m), \ldots, \phi_{p_{N-1}}(m), \phi_{p_N}(m)) \tag{7.36}$$

where p_i refers to the ith prime number ($p_1 = 2, p_2 = 3, p_3 = 5, \ldots$) and the function $\phi_r(m)$ is the *radical-inverse* function of m to the base r. The value of $\phi_r(m)$ is obtained by writing m in base r and then reflecting the digits around the decimal point. For example, using the subscript to indicate base, 26_{10} is 11010_2, and reflecting that gives $0.01011_2 = 11/32$. In base 3, $19_{10} = 201_3$, and reflecting that gives $0.102_3 = 11/27$. Writing $\phi_r(m)$ symbolically for a number m:

$$m = a_0 r^0 + a_1 r^1 + \cdots + a_i r^i + \cdots$$
$$\phi_r(m) = a_0 r^{-1} + a_1 r^{-2} + \cdots + a_i r^{-(i+1)} + \cdots \tag{7.37}$$

We might ask how well this pattern distributes samples over the image plane. One method for characterizing patterns is to measure their *discrepancy* [471], which is a single number. Small discrepancies correspond to evenly distributed (or *equidistributed*) patterns, and large discrepancies correspond to patterns that are unevenly distributed (which causes visible effects like clumping and large sparse regions). Warnock notes that if this first point, x_0, is placed at $(1, 1, \ldots, 1)$ then the discrepancy is usually lower than if this point is placed at the origin.

The *Hammersley sequence* is very similar to the Halton sequence; it is defined by

$$x_m = (m/N, \phi_2(m), \phi_3(m), \ldots, \phi_{p_{N-2}}(m), \phi_{p_{N-1}}(m)) \tag{7.38}$$

where p_n is the nth prime number, starting with $p_1 = 1$ (so $p_7 = 13$).

The *Zaremba sequence* builds on these ideas. It is defined in terms of a *folded radical-inverse* function $\psi_r(m)$, similar to $\phi_r(m)$. Again writing m in its expansion base r, as in Equation 7.37, we define

$$\psi_r(m) = (a_0 + 0)_{\bmod r} r^{-1} + (a_1 + 1)_{\bmod r} r^{-2} + \cdots + (a_i + i)_{\bmod r} r^{-(i+1)} + \cdots \tag{7.39}$$

The difference between $\psi_r(m)$ and $\phi_r(m)$ is the addition of the positional index of the digit to its value, and then taking the result mod r at each location. For example, when $m = 26_{10}$ and $r = 2$, the reversed form of m (from above) is 0.01011_2, so we add the index and take the sum modulo 2 at each digit:

$$
\begin{array}{r|ccccccccccc}
 & . & 0 & 1 & 0 & 1 & 1 & 0 & 0 & 0 & 0 & 0 \\
+ & & 0 & 1 & 2 & 3 & 4 & 5 & 6 & 7 & 8 & 9 \\
= & & 0 & 2 & 2 & 4 & 5 & 5 & 6 & 7 & 8 & 9 \\
\mathrm{mod}2 & & 0 & 0 & 0 & 0 & 1 & 1 & 0 & 1 & 0 & 1 \\
\end{array}
\tag{7.40}
$$

which we may write as $\psi_2(26) = 0.0000110\overline{1}_2$, where the overline indicates an infinitely repeated sequence of digits. Our other example, $m = 19$ and $r = 3$, is similar; the reflected digits are 0.102_3, and the addition and modulo operations are

$$
\begin{array}{rccccccccccc}
 & . & 1 & 0 & 2 & 0 & 0 & 0 & 0 & 0 & 0 & 0 \\
+ & & 0 & 1 & 2 & 3 & 4 & 5 & 6 & 7 & 8 & 9 \\
= & & 1 & 1 & 4 & 3 & 4 & 5 & 6 & 7 & 8 & 9 \\
\mathrm{mod}\,3 & & 1 & 1 & 1 & 0 & 1 & 2 & 0 & 1 & 2 & 0 \\
\end{array}
\tag{7.41}
$$

so $\psi_3(19) = 0.111\overline{012}_3$.

Each N-dimensional point x_m generated by the Zaremba sequence is given by

$$
x_m = (\psi_2(m), \psi_3(m), \ldots, \psi_{p_{N-1}}(m), \psi_{p_N}(m))
\tag{7.42}
$$

Warnock also gives some advice on how to compute the discrepancy in practice, and provides explicit algorithms that are tuned for efficiency for calculating the discrepancy of various sequences. The estimand error for quasi Monte Carlo is, for constants b and k,

$$
\sigma_q = k\sqrt{(\log n)^b / n}
\tag{7.43}
$$

7.4.5 Weighted Monte Carlo

Recall the nonuniform weighting method of Equation 7.4:

$$
\theta = \frac{\displaystyle\sum_{i=1}^{n} w_i \eta_i}{\displaystyle\sum_{i=1}^{n} w_i}
\tag{7.44}
$$

In crude Monte Carlo, all $w_i = 1$. In this section we describe *weighted Monte Carlo*, which is a method for selecting the w_i to improve the convergence of the estimator.

Weighted Monte Carlo is based on using a reconstruction rule of higher order than the simple average of crude Monte Carlo. The method of weighted Monte Carlo was first described by Yakowitz et al. [494]. The basic idea parallels the development of integration in most calculus texts.

Integration is usually introduced by the use of an increasingly dense set of rectangles to estimate the area under a curve. The total area of these rectangles is known as a Riemann sum approximation to the integral. Crude Monte Carlo in 1D effectively makes that approximation, assuming that each rectangle has equal width: the area is approximated by n rectangles with height $f(x_i)$ and uniform width $1/n$. If the samples are not uniformly spaced, then this assumption doesn't match the reality, as Figure 7.1(a) illustrates.

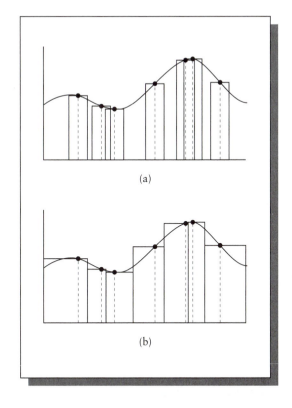

FIGURE 7.1

(a) Crude Monte Carlo assumes all boxes have equal width. (b) A better estimate is to use the correct width for each box.

In fact, each box has a width that is determined by the locations of its nearest neighbors (or the limits of the domain for samples on the end). A better approximation would weight each sample value by the area of this rectangle, as shown in Figure 7.1(b). We can continue following our analogy and move from rectangles to trapezoids. The associated estimator for the domain $[0, 1]$ then becomes

$$\theta_n = \frac{1}{2}\left[x_1 f(x_0) + \sum_{i=1}^{n}(x_{i+1} - x_{i-1})f(x_i) + (1 - x_n)f(x_{n+1})\right]$$

$$= \frac{1}{2}\left[\sum_{i=0}^{n}(x_{i+1} - x_i)(f(x_i) + f(x_{i+1}))\right] \tag{7.45}$$

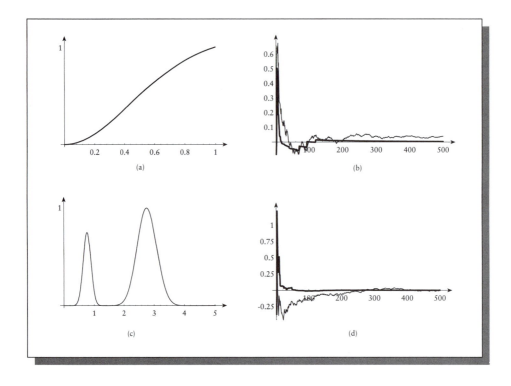

FIGURE 7.2

(a) $f(x) = x^2/(x^2+1)^{3/2}$. (b) Error in $f(x)$ as a function of number of samples n. Crude Monte Carlo is the thin line, weighted is heavy. (c) $g(x) = e^{-5(x-2.75)^2} + e^{-30(x-0.75)^2}$. (d) Error in $g(x)$ as a function of number of samples n.

Yakowitz et al. [494] have shown that if f has a continuous second derivative, then for some constant M, this estimator has an estimand error given by

$$\sigma_w < M/n^2 \tag{7.46}$$

This is far better than the $\sigma_p/\sqrt{n}$ estimand error of crude Monte Carlo. To illustrate the convergence properties of crude and weighted Monte Carlo, Figure 7.2 shows the error from each method for two functions. One is a polynomial, the other a sum of two Gaussians, intended to approximate a pair of finite light sources illuminating a point on a surface.

So far we have discussed only 1D integration. Everything we have said in fact holds for one, two, and three dimensions, though the quality of improvement diminishes with increasing dimensionality [493].

7.4.6 Multidimensional Weighted Monte Carlo

In dimensions greater than 1, there are two general approaches for weighted Monte Carlo estimation [494].

The first is a *nearest-neighbor* approach, which generalizes the idea of the rectangular rule. The idea is to partition the domain into as many cells as there are samples. The cells tile the domain without gaps or overlaps, and each point in each cell is closer to the sample point associated with that cell than with any other sample point. In two dimensions, this is the *Voronoi diagram* induced by the sample points, illustrated in Figure 7.3(a). If we assume that each cell has a constant height given by the value of its associated sample, then we get a signal such as the one in Figure 7.3(b).

If we have n sample points x_i, then we also have n cells c_i, each with volume $V(c_i)$ (in 2D, this is the area of the cell). Then we can find the mean by weighting each sample by the volume of its associated cell:

$$\mu = \sum_{i=0}^{n} V(c_i) f(x_i) \tag{7.47}$$

The estimand error in this estimator for n samples in a d-dimensional space can be shown to be

$$\sigma_t = O\left(1/n^{2/d}\right) \tag{7.48}$$

When $d = 2$, this convergence is

$$\sigma_t = O\left(1/n\right) \tag{7.49}$$

which is far better than the $O(1/\sqrt{n})$ convergence of crude Monte Carlo. Surprisingly, in four dimensions, when $d = 4$, this estimand is no better than crude Monte Carlo, and for dimensions $d > 4$, the convergence for the nearest-neighbor rule is slower than crude Monte Carlo [493].

The other approach is the *trapezoid* approach, which generalizes the 1D trapezoid algorithm used for integration. This is a rather different method than the nearest-neighbor algorithm just discussed, since it requires taking additional samples of the function in order to evaluate the estimator.

We will first look at the algorithm in 2D. Suppose there are three samples in the unit square, as shown in Figure 7.4(a). If we draw a vertical and horizontal line through each sample point, then we induce a set of sixteen rectangles, as shown in Figure 7.4(b).

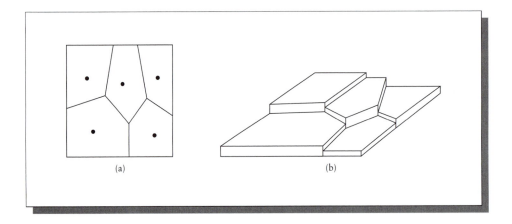

FIGURE 7.3

(a) The Voronoi diagram for a few sample points in the unit square. (b) The piecewise-constant signal based on (a).

Suppose that in addition to the three samples we know, we evaluate the function at the other twenty-two grid intersections. This gives us a value at each intersection, as shown in Figure 7.5(a). Recall that the area of a trapezoid is its width times the average of its heights. In 2D, the volume of the cell is approximated as the area of its base times the average of its heights. Note that this isn't the same as passing a plane over the four corners of the cell, since in general no plane can interpolate four arbitrary heights. The approximation instead places a horizontal plane at the average height, as shown in Figure 7.5(b). So, although the trapezoid rule is continuous in one dimension, in general it will not be so in higher dimensions.

The estimate of the mean is found by summing the volumes of each of these rectangular prisms.

In general, suppose that we are interested in the mean value θ of a function

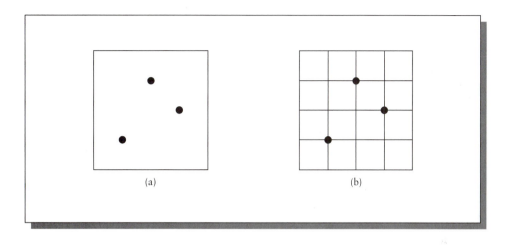

FIGURE 7.4

(a) Three samples in the unit square. (b) The rectangles they induce.

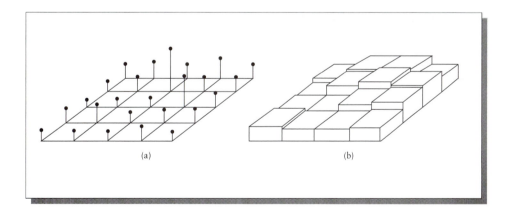

FIGURE 7.5

(a) Function values at grid intersections. (b) Constant approximations in each rectangle.

f in a d-dimensional hypercube Ω, which has limits $[0, 1]$ in each dimension. We begin with a set of n sample points $\mathbf{x}_i$, where each $\mathbf{x}_i$ is a d-dimensional vector; we write $\mathbf{x}_i = \{\mathbf{x}_{i,1}, \ldots, \mathbf{x}_{i,d}\}$. To set up the indexing, we will gather together the bth component of each $\mathbf{x}_i$, sort the result, and call it $\mathbf{a}_b$. We use these values to create a new list of n vectors $\mathbf{y}_i$. $\mathbf{y}_{1,d}$ contains the first element of $\mathbf{a}_d$; that is, it is the vector of the smallest values of the $\mathbf{x}_i$ vectors in each dimension. $\mathbf{y}_2$ is the vector of second-smallest values, and so on. Formally, we write

$$\mathbf{a}_d = \text{sort}\left\{ \bigcup_i \mathbf{x}_{i,d} \right\}$$

$$\mathbf{y}_i = \{\mathbf{a}_{1,i}, \ldots, \mathbf{a}_{n,i}\} \tag{7.50}$$

We also create two bounding vectors, $\mathbf{y}_0 = \mathbf{0}$ and $\mathbf{y}_{n+1} = \mathbf{1}$. To build up the sum, we walk through the list by visiting each point in $[0, 1]$ and finding the area of the parallelepiped for which that point is the corner closest to the origin. The volume of the cell is found by multiplying together the lengths of each of its sides. We then scale that volume by the average value of the function evaluated at each corner.

We enumerate the corners by creating a list S of the coordinates of each corner. This is found by taking the corner under consideration, and finding the coordinates when that point is pushed one step in each combination of directions. We then evaluate the function at all these points and divide the result by the number of points involved.

Formally, for d dimensions and n starting samples,

$$\theta = \sum_{k_1=1}^{n} \cdots \sum_{k_d=1}^{n} \left\{ \prod_{j=1}^{d} (\mathbf{y}_{k_j+1,j} - \mathbf{y}_{k_j,j}) \times \frac{1}{2^d} \sum_{V \in S(k_1, \ldots, k_d)} f(V) \right\} \tag{7.51}$$

where S is the set of points given by

$$S(k_1, \ldots, k_d) = \bigcup_{s_1=0,1} \cdots \bigcup_{s_d=0,1} (\mathbf{y}_{k_1+s_1,1}, \ldots, \mathbf{y}_{k_d+s_d,d}) \tag{7.52}$$

To illustrate in 2D (so $d = 2$), we write down the $\mathbf{x}_i$ for the $n = 3$ points in Figure 7.3(a), and derive the corresponding $\mathbf{y}_i$ vectors. We then show the points involved in evaluating a sample rectangle.

$$\mathbf{x}_1 = (.3, .7), \qquad \mathbf{x}_2 = (.8, .9), \qquad \mathbf{x}_3 = (.6, .4) \tag{7.53}$$

so

$$\mathbf{y}_1 = (.3, .4), \qquad \mathbf{y}_2 = (.6, .7), \qquad \mathbf{y}_3 = (.8, .9) \tag{7.54}$$

After six rectangles have been evaluated, $k_1 = 2$ and $k_n = 3$. Then the function S gives the set of points

$$S(2, 3) = \{(\mathbf{y}_{2,1}, \mathbf{y}_{1,2}), (\mathbf{y}_{2,1}, \mathbf{y}_{2,2}), (\mathbf{y}_{3,1}, \mathbf{y}_{1,2}), (\mathbf{y}_{3,1}, \mathbf{y}_{2,2})\}$$
$$= \{(.6, .4), (.6, .7), (.8, .4), (.8, .7)\} \tag{7.55}$$

The expression for the convergence of this approach is the same as that of the nearest-neighbor method given in Equation 7.48, except that now n refers to the total number of samples taken, rather than just the starting set. If there are n samples in the original set of d-dimensional samples $\mathbf{x}_i$, then we need a total of $N = (n + 2)^d$ samples, requiring $(n + 2)^d - n$ new samples to be evaluated. When $n \gg d$, this cost is significant. For example, in $d = 2$ dimensions, if we start with $n = 12$ samples, we need to take 132 more to evaluate the trapezoidal estimator.

When samples are expensive, as in computer graphics, the increased speed of convergence may be more than offset by the increased cost of estimating each sample. In other words, this technique may produce a much better result for 144 samples than some other method, but that result may be far more precise than we require; a cruder technique that gives an acceptable answer after a smaller number of samples may be preferable. The basic problem is that the number of samples required by this method does not increase in small increments but in huge jumps, so we don't have the option to stop as soon as our estimate has enough precision.

7.5 Informed Monte Carlo

Blind Monte Carlo techniques are based on trying to find good estimates for signals about which we know nothing. If we do know something about the signal, then we should exploit that information to the fullest in order to save time and computational expense. We call methods that use knowledge about the signal to guide the sampling *informed Monte Carlo*.

Each informed Monte Carlo method exploits some knowledge or estimate of the underlying integrand $f(x)$ to direct the placement of sample points.

We will summarize four important informed Monte Carlo methods:

- informed stratified sampling

- importance sampling

- control variates

- antithetic variates

7.5.1 Informed Stratified Sampling

We saw earlier that blind stratified sampling was a technique for subdividing the domain so that even a small number of samples would be roughly uniformly scattered over the domain.

This is an advantage over simpler methods that might produce clumps of samples, but with knowledge of the function we can do even better. Suppose we stratify the

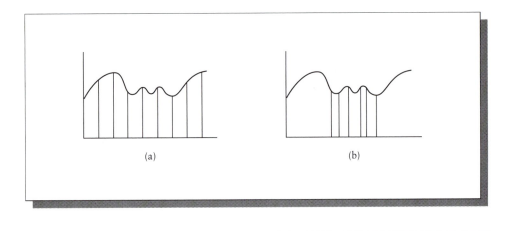

FIGURE 7.6

(a) A function and a set of uniformly sized strata. (b) The same function and a set of nonuniformly sized strata.

domain of a function as in Figure 7.6(a). This isn't the best stratification: some very simple pieces of the function are represented by many strata, while complex regions of the domain get only one stratum. A better subdivision is shown in Figure 7.6(b), where each sample has a chance to report about the same amount of useful information.

There are two general approaches to building the stratification. Suppose that each stratum i has variance V_i and mean μ_i. Then one good strategy is to subdivide so that each V_i is less than $\max(\mu_i - \mu_k), i \neq k$. A better approach is to choose the α_k so that the V_i are as uniform as possible [183].

When we have access to the underlying function f, then the sample points should be chosen so that the relative proportions of the n_k, the number of samples in domain k, is proportional to the difference [183]:

$$n_k \propto (\alpha_k - \alpha_{k-1}) \int_{\alpha_{k-1}}^{\alpha_k} f^2(x)\, dx - \left[\int_{\alpha_{k-1}}^{\alpha_k} f(x)\, dx \right]^2 \qquad (7.56)$$

7.5.2 Importance Sampling

Importance sampling is a powerful general method for reducing the variance in many Monte Carlo calculations [239]. In the ideal situation, importance sampling can eliminate variance altogether through the use of *zero-variance estimation*.

Zero-variance methods are Monte Carlo techniques, but they are designed to yield provably consistent and *exact* estimates with no statistical variation.

At the heart of importance sampling is the following somewhat specialized observation. Suppose we want the definite integral of a product of real functions over some interval, and we know one of the functions analytically or numerically. Then we can use that information to guide our sampling of the product, and get a good answer more quickly than if we did not know one of the functions. In symbols, we have two real-valued functions $f: \mathcal{R}^n \mapsto \mathcal{R}$ and $g: \mathcal{R}^n \mapsto \mathcal{R}$, and we want to find the integral of their product over some n-dimensional domain Ω:

$$I = \int_\Omega f(\mathbf{x}) g(\mathbf{x}) \, d\mathbf{x} \qquad (7.57)$$

Some important problems in rendering may be expressed as finding integrals of this form (for example, f could be a filter over a pixel and g an image function, so that I is the color value of a pixel).

We will see that the idea of importance sampling is that some regions of the function will contribute more to the final estimate than other regions. These are typically places where the function has a large value, or varies in value significantly and quickly. We say that these regions have more "importance" than others. The goal will be to sample these regions more densely to get a better idea of what's happening. But we need to compensate for the nonuniform sampling so that we don't bias our final answer.

We can develop importance sampling from some basic ideas. Suppose that we want to find the integral of a 1D function $g(x)$ over some interval Γ:

$$G = \int_\Gamma g(x) \, dx \qquad (7.58)$$

We can draw uniformly distributed samples η_i from the interval Γ and compute an estimate of the integral by summing the values:

$$G = \sum_i^n g(x_i) \qquad (7.59)$$

We can write this operation in another way that will open up some new possibilities. We write the integral as the product of g with another function f, which we call the *importance function*. The function f is the probability density function for the samples. We can write the integral above as

$$G = \int g(x) f_u(x) \, dx \qquad (7.60)$$

where $f_u(x) = 1$. To estimate Equation 7.60, we draw random variables η_i from the density function defined by f (that is, $\eta \sim f$), and evaluate $g(\eta_i)$, summing them as in Equation 7.59.

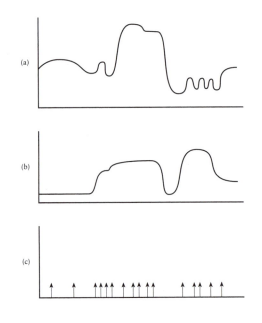

FIGURE 7.7

(a) A function $g(x)$. (b) An importance function $f(x)$ for g. (c) Samples chosen from the density function f.

Suppose we choose a function f that is large where g is "interesting" (as defined above), and small otherwise, as in Figure 7.7. Then when we draw our samples from f, we will get more samples in the important regions of g, and fewer in the less interesting regions, as shown in Figure 7.7(c).

This is a good idea, but now we're no longer integrating g alone; we're getting the product of g and f. Another way to think of this is that as we draw samples from g, the weight we attach to those samples is given by the corresponding value of f. Where f is large, we weight the sample by a large value, since we consider it important. So rather than integrating $g(x)$, we're integrating the product $g(x)f(x)$. Since our interest is in integrating g to find G, we can compensate by dividing through by f:

$$G = \int \frac{g(x)f(x)}{f(x)} \, dx$$
$$= \int \left[\frac{g(x)}{f(x)} \right] f(x) \, dx \qquad (7.61)$$

Nasal   Temporal

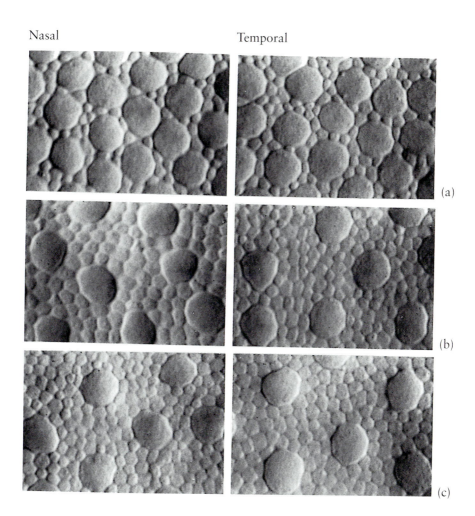

(a)

(b)

(c)

FIGURE 1.5

Photomicrographs of the human retina at different distances from the center. The large cells are cones and the small ones are rods. The photos are each about 44 μm in width. (a) 1.35 mm from the center of the retina. (b) 5 mm from the center of the retina. (c) 8 mm from the center of the retina. *(Courtesy of Christine Curcio.)*

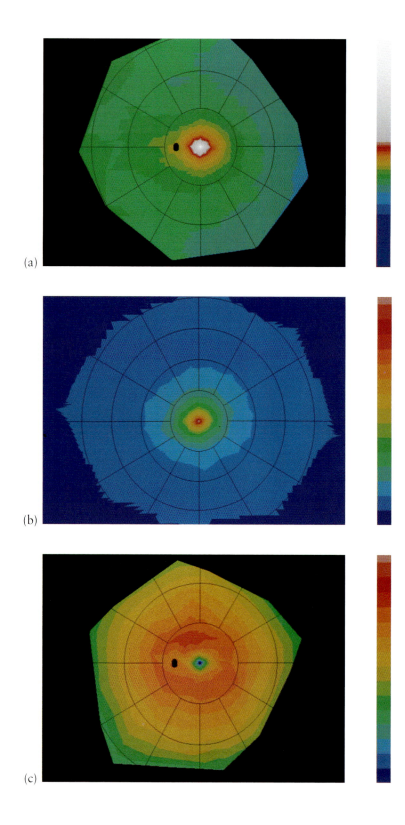

(a)

(b)

(c)

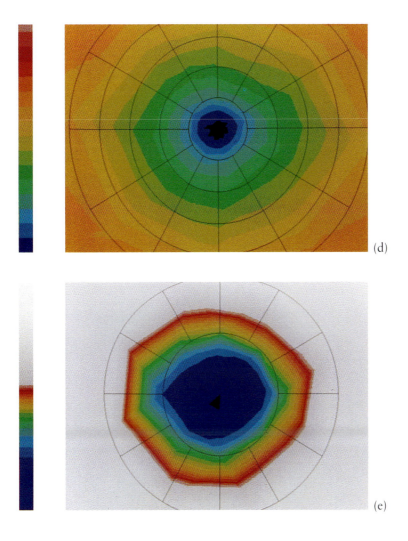

(d)

(e)

FIGURE 1.6

Photoreceptor density in the human retina. (a) Cones in the entire retina; circles are 5.94 mm apart. The black oval is the optic disk. (b) Cones in the fovea; circles are 0.4 mm apart. (c) Rods for the entire retina; circle spacing as in (a). (d) Rods near the fovea; circle spacing as in (b). (e) Rods immediately around the fovea; circles are 0.2 mm apart. *(Courtesy of Christine Curcio.)*

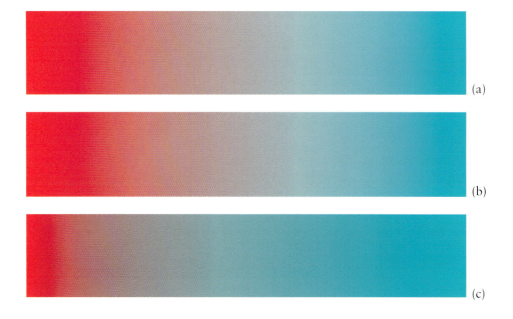

(a)

(b)

(c)

FIGURE 2.6
(a) Color interpolation in RGB space. (b) The same colors in XYZ space.
(c) The same colors in $L^*u^*v^*$ space.

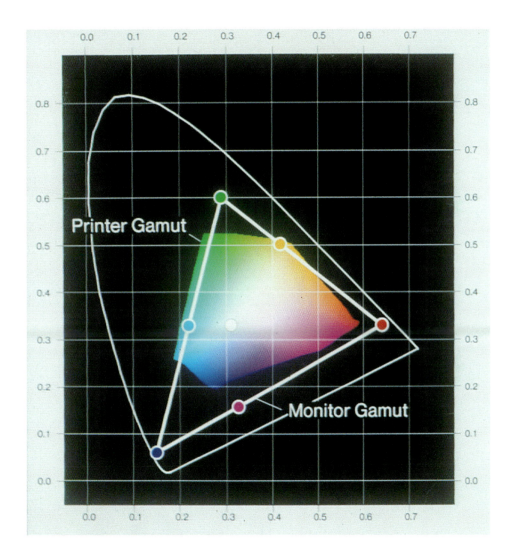

FIGURE 3.32
A printer gamut and a monitor gamut on a chromaticity diagram. Reprinted, by permission, from Stone et al. in *ACM Transactions on Graphics*, fig. 8, p. 265.

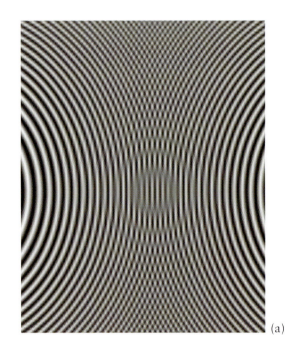

(a)

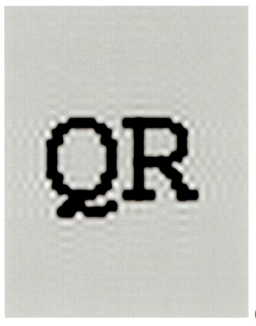

FIGURE 10.90
Reconstruction filter phenomena.
(a) Ringing. (b) Sample-frequency ripple.
(c) Anisotropy. (d) Filter blurring.
(e) Reconstruction error. Reprinted, by permission, from Mitchell and Netravali in *Computer Graphics (Proc. Siggraph '88)*, figs. 4, 6, 8, 9, 11, pp. 226–228.

(b)

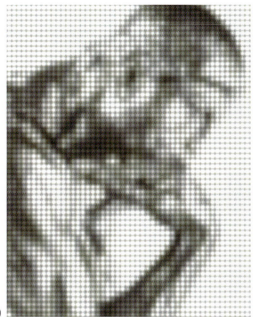

(c)

(d)

(e)

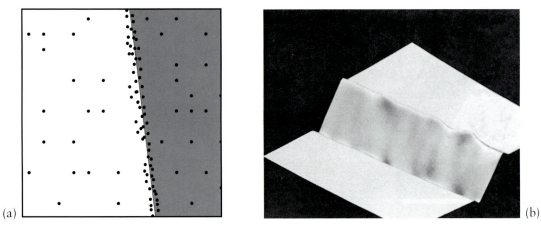

(a)

(b)

FIGURE 10.101

(a) The test situation: a straight edge between black and white regions. (b) A failure of weighted-average reconstruction. Reprinted, by permission, from Mitchell in *Computer Graphics (Proc. Siggraph '87)*, fig. 11, p. 72.

FIGURE 10.103

Reconstruction with the Mitchell multistage filter. Reprinted, by permission, from Mitchell in *Computer Graphics (Proc. Siggraph '87)*, fig. 14, p. 72.

There are three conditions we need to satisfy to apply Equation 7.61 [239]:

1 $f(x) \geq 0$

2 $\int f(x)\,dx = 1$

3 $\dfrac{g(x)}{f(x)} < \infty$ except at a countable number of points

The variance of Equation 7.61, as described in Kalos and Whitlock [239], is

$$\sigma_{g/f}{}^2 = \int \left(\frac{g^2(x)}{f^2(x)} \right) f(x)\,dx - G^2 \tag{7.62}$$

Since G^2 is the variance of the original signal, we would like the integral to be as small as possible. If we could get the integral down to zero, then we would be introducing no new variance into the estimate at all, which would be the best situation. We would like to find the best f to minimize this integral. It may be tempting to choose an f that is large, causing the denominator to drive the fraction to zero, but the three conditions mentioned above must still be satisfied.

An alternative is to use Lagrange multipliers [239]. Here we try to pick a scalar λ to minimize

$$L(f) = \int \frac{g^2(x)}{f(x)}\,dx + \lambda \int f(x)\,dx \tag{7.63}$$

To find the minimum of this function, we differentiate and set the result to zero:

$$0 = \frac{\partial}{\partial f}\left[\int \frac{g^2(x)}{f(x)}\,dx + \lambda \int f(x)\,dx \right]$$

$$= -\frac{g^2(x)}{f^2(x)} + \lambda \tag{7.64}$$

Solving for $f(x)$, we find

$$f(x) = \lambda|g(x)| \tag{7.65}$$

So the ideal $f(x)$ is some multiple of the absolute value of $g(x)$. An example is shown in Figure 7.8.

We now need to find the value of λ. Recall condition 2 above on f, which stated that $\int f(x)\,dx = 1$. If $g(x) \geq 0$, then $f(x) = \lambda g(x)$, so

$$1 = \int \lambda g(x)\,dx$$

$$= \lambda \int g(x)\,dx$$

$$= \lambda G \tag{7.66}$$

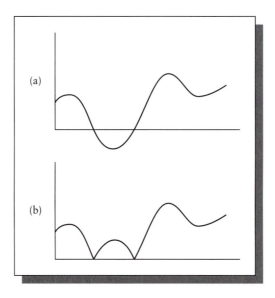

FIGURE 7.8
(a) $g(x)$. (b) $f(x) = |g(x)|$.

where the last step used the definition of G from Equation 7.58. We find then that $\lambda = 1/G$. So we can construct $f(x)$ from

$$f(x) = \frac{g(x)}{G} \tag{7.67}$$

Now that we have defined $f(x)$, we would like to know how good it is as a function to direct our sampling strategy. Let's proceed by drawing samples from $g(x)/f(x)$ using the density function $f(x)$, and forming the integral G_n after the first n samples:

$$G_n = \frac{1}{N} \sum_{i=1}^{N} \frac{g(x_i)}{f(x_i)}$$

$$= \frac{1}{N} \sum_{i=1}^{N} \frac{g(x_i)}{g(x_i)/G}$$

$$= \frac{1}{N} \sum_{i=1}^{N} G$$
$$= G \qquad\qquad (7.68)$$

This derivation shows us that this choice of $f(x)$ gives us a *perfect* density function for use with this $g(x)$; after any n samples, the estimated integral is identical to the true result.

There is a drawback to this scheme, and that is that in order to build $f(x)$, we need to already know G, which is precisely what we are seeking. Of course, if we already knew G, then we wouldn't bother with Monte Carlo at all, so it may appear that this approach is useless. But we don't need to use exactly the right $f(x)$; any function $\widetilde{f}(x)$ "close" to $f(x)$ will reduce the variance because it will cluster samples more densely where they will matter most in the final result.

The correct use of "close" in this regard is difficult to quantify. Shirley has presented some results [402] that show that when $\widetilde{f}(x)$ departs too far from the ideal $f(x)$, the variance of the estimate can actually *increase* dramatically, giving us much more work to do than if we simply drew samples uniformly. However, when the function is chosen carefully, the variance can also be decreased by a dramatic amount [239].

It's important when choosing $\widetilde{f}(x)$ that it satisfy the three constraints listed earlier. An analytic compliance with these constraints is best, but a numerical integration of sufficient accuracy, followed by a normalization phase, will allow any bounded function to be used for $\widetilde{f}(x)$.

7.5.3 Control Variates

The method of *control variates* is similar to importance sampling [183].

The basic idea of control variates is to break the integral into the sum of two new integrals, one of which can be handled theoretically. If the new function is positively correlated with the function we started with, then it will tend to produce values that correspond with those we evaluate numerically.

So we take our unknown function f and combine it with a known, analytically integrable function ϕ. In symbols,

$$\theta = \int_0^1 f(x)\,dx$$
$$= \int_0^1 \phi(x)\,dx + \int_0^1 [f(x) - \phi(x)]\,dx \qquad (7.69)$$

The function $\phi(x)$ is called the *control variate* for f. We have broken the integral into two parts, one analytic and free from error, the other numerical with an associated error. Since the total contribution of the numerical integral to the final estimate is reduced, the amount of error contributed by that integral is also reduced. The more substantial we can make the contribution of $\phi(x)$, the less error we will have in the result.

Thus we have contradicting demands on ϕ: it must be simple enough to integrate analytically, yet complicated enough to do a good job of matching f. Each new application requires a new weighing of these conflicting demands, and the associated search for ϕ.

The variance for this method [183] may be shown to be

$$\text{var}(t) + \text{var}(t') - 2\,\text{cov}(t, t') \tag{7.70}$$

The method of control variates is a good demonstration of the power we get from the principle of replacing approximate operations with exact ones.

7.5.4 Antithetic Variates

The method of *antithetic variates* takes an approach opposite to that of control variates. Rather than augment our samples with values from a positively correlated function, we combine our estimator t with a second, *negatively* correlated estimator t'. We choose this estimator so that it has the same expectation as t, though we don't know the actual expected value for either function. Then both estimators are unbiased, and because they are negatively correlated, their average

$$\theta_a = (t + t')/2 \tag{7.71}$$

will be an unbiased estimator for θ, with variance, according to Hammersley and Handscomb [183],

$$\sigma_a{}^2 = \frac{1}{4}\,\text{var}(t) + \frac{1}{4}\,\text{var}(t') + \frac{1}{2}\,\text{cov}(t, t') \tag{7.72}$$

where $\text{cov}(t, t')$ is negative. This variance can sometimes be made smaller than that for crude Monte Carlo for an appropriate estimator t'.

For example, suppose that ξ is a uniformly distributed random variable. Then $1 - \xi$ is also uniformly distributed. Thus $f(\xi)$ and $f(1 - \xi)$ are both unbiased estimators of θ. If f is monotonically increasing or decreasing in an interval Γ, then $t = f(\xi)$ and $t' = f(1 - \xi)$ will be negatively correlated within Γ, so we can find θ_a from

$$\theta_a = \frac{1}{2}(t + t') = \frac{1}{2}f(\xi) + \frac{1}{2}f(1 - \xi) \tag{7.73}$$

Antithetic variates are usually easier to find than control variates, so they are more common in practice [183].

7.6 Adaptive Sampling

Adaptive sampling attempts to bridge the gap between informed and blind Monte Carlo methods. It begins with a blind sampling of the domain, and from that information tries to guess something about the nature of the function being sampled. That guess is used to create a function that is then used to guide one of the informed sampling techniques above.

One of the most common applications of adaptive sampling in computer graphics begins with a generic stratification of the domain, which is used to drive a blind Monte Carlo algorithm. This sampling typically continues until a predetermined number of samples have been drawn. Those samples are then examined and a guess g is constructed to match the underlying function f. This g is then used to drive an importance sampling routine, which may update g periodically to improve the estimate and speed of convergence.

We will revisit this idea in much more detail in the following chapters.

7.7 Other Approaches

As we have seen above, there are two main approaches to improving the efficiency of Monte Carlo: finding a better estimator, and more carefully selecting where to place our samples. These different strategies may be applied in a variety of ways, depending on whether or not we know something about the underlying function.

We have not listed all the efficiency methods developed since Monte Carlo was introduced in the 1940s. Further information on other approaches may be found in the references in the Further Reading section, particularly in the work of Hammersley and Handscomb [183] and Spanier and Gelbard [415].

7.8 Summary

Figure 7.9 gives a summary of the nine methods for Monte Carlo estimation discussed in this chapter.

The efficiency of these techniques varies widely, depending on the functions involved. For informed strategies, the quality of the auxiliary function can make a great difference in accelerating convergence. Hammersley and Handscomb [183] have evaluated a single test function consistently with a variety of methods. In rough terms, they found what we would expect: informed techniques were superior to blind methods, and the more knowledge that could be applied in the form of a good auxiliary function, the faster the technique converged.

Reasonable arguments may be found in Kalos and Whitlock [239] advocating importance sampling over stratified sampling, and vice versa in Shirley [402]. These

Name	Estimator	Estimand error
Crude MC	$\dfrac{1}{n}\sum_{i=1}^{n}\eta_i$	$\dfrac{\sigma_p}{\sqrt{n}}$
Rejection	Rejection	$\dfrac{\sqrt{\mu(1-\mu)}}{\sqrt{n}}$
Blind stratification	$\sum_{j=1}^{k}\sum_{i=1}^{n_j}\dfrac{\alpha_j-\alpha_{j-1}}{n_j}$ $\times f(\alpha_{j-1}+(\alpha_j-\alpha_{j-1})\xi_i)$	$\left[\sum_{j=1}^{k}\dfrac{\alpha_j-\alpha_{j-1}}{n_j}\int_{\alpha_{j-1}}^{\alpha_j}f(x)^2\,dx\right.$ $\left.-\sum_{j=1}^{k}\dfrac{1}{n_j}\left(\int_{\alpha_{j-1}}^{\alpha_j}f(x)\,dx\right)^2\right]^{1/2}$
Quasi MC	$\dfrac{1}{n}\sum_{i=1}^{n}\eta_i$	$\dfrac{k\sqrt{(\log n)^b}}{n}$
Weighted MC	$\dfrac{1}{2}\left[\sum_{i=0}^{n}(y_{i+1}-y_i)(f(y_i)+f(y_{i+1}))\right]$	M/n^2
Informed stratification	Same as for blind stratification	Same as for blind stratification
Importance sampling	$\displaystyle\int_0^1\dfrac{f(x)}{g(x)}\,dG(x)$	$\displaystyle\int_0^1\left(\dfrac{f(x)}{g(x)}-\mu\right)^2 dG(x)$
Control variates	$\displaystyle\int_0^1\phi(x)\,dx+\int_0^1[f(x)-\phi(x)]\,dx$	$\sqrt{\operatorname{var}(t)+\operatorname{var}(t')-2\operatorname{cov}(t,t')}$
Antithetic variates	$(t+t')/2$	$\sqrt{\dfrac{1}{4}\operatorname{var}(t)+\dfrac{1}{4}\operatorname{var}(t')+\dfrac{1}{2}\operatorname{cov}(t,t')}$

FIGURE 7.9

A summary of Monte Carlo methods.

are both true depending on the function being integrated, the quality of the importance function, and the quality of the stratification. It's probably true that if we have a good idea of the function's shape, importance sampling will lead to a faster solution than informed stratification, but when nothing is known about the integrand, blind stratification will usually be superior to importance sampling with an arbitrarily guessed importance function. This is an area where experience with the particular function being sampled is of great value. Many of the techniques in Chapter 10 are the result of different practitioners' approaches to this challenging engineering problem.

7.9 Further Reading

A very early and explicit discussion of Monte Carlo methods in practice may be found in Cashwell and Everett [76].

Much of this chapter is based on the excellent book by Hammersley and Handscomb [183]. This is an ideal starting point for further reading on both theoretical and practical issues. Another good book for study and reference is the volume by Kalos and Whitlock [239]. The book by Spanier and Gelbard [415] is much more advanced in some areas and offers more detail.

The classic paper by Halton [182] is a difficult but complete survey of work up to 1970. Different quasi-Monte Carlo patterns were studied extensively and compared by Warnock, who has provided a wealth of comparative data [471]. An extensive and detailed (but difficult) discussion of quasi-Monte Carlo and pseudorandom numbers has been presented by Niederreiter [319].

There are many reports on Monte Carlo work in the physics and nuclear engineering literature, where accurate simulation of complex phenomena like those in computer graphics has received a lot of careful scrutiny. Pointers to these reports may be found in the books above.

7.10 Exercises

Exercise 7.1

Using a standard random-number generator, take random samples of the function x^2 over the interval $[0, 3]$. What is the true mean of this function? Plot the estimated mean as a function of the number of samples.

Exercise 7.2

Using a standard uniformly distributed random-number generator, plot the absolute error in the estimate of the integral of $f(x) = x^2$ in the interval $[0, 3]$ as a function of the number of samples taken, using the estimators below. Plot the error for 1 to 100 samples for each estimator.

  (a) Averaged random samples.
  (b) An importance function $g(x) = x$.
  (c) An importance function $g(x) = x^2$.
  (d) An importance function $g(x) = x^3$.
  (e) An importance function $g(x) = 3x^3$.
  (f) Five uniform strata.
  (g) Ten uniform strata.
  (h) Twenty uniform strata.

Exercise 7.3

Describe how you would apply the method of control variates to finding the integral

$$\int_0^1 \sin(t) \left[1 + \cos(e^{-t^2} \sin t)\right] \tag{7.74}$$

Many of the sleights in this book are presented in two segments. For example, you begin a vanish called the French Drop by showing a small object in your left hand and removing it with your right .... After you have learned to do that smoothly and well, you are ready to add the secret move which will make the coin vanish. This time you do the same moves in the same natural manner, but at the right moment you secretly allow the coin to drop into your left palm while your right continues on as though still holding it.

Bill Tarr
("Now You See It, Now You Don't!," 1976)

8

UNIFORM SAMPLING AND RECONSTRUCTION

8.1 Introduction

In the introduction to Unit II, I presented aliasing as a motivating reason for the study of signal processing in computer graphics. The best way to discuss aliasing is to look at what happens in the frequency domain when a continuous signal is *sampled* (turned into a discrete signal) and *reconstructed* (turned back into a continuous signal). Our discussion of the Fourier transform in both continuous and discrete time has given us the tools to look at frequency space and the effect of different signal-processing operations in that space.

Many of our input signals in computer graphics are conceptually continuous. We can argue that all physical signals are ultimately quantized to the Planck constant of the universe, but at least some of the signals used in computer graphics are *mathematically* continuous, such as the surface of a sphere or polygon.

Most of computer graphics works with discrete versions of these aperiodic, continuous signals. This is because most of the operations we want to perform on these signals become complex if we try to perform them analytically. The transition from

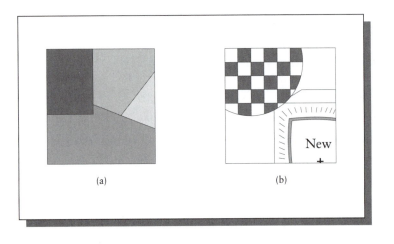

FIGURE 8.1

(a) The average color in this pixel is the sum of the colors of each fragment, weighted by its area.
(b) A pixel containing curved objects and textures.

continuous to discrete involves taking a series of sample values of the signal. If these values are taken at equal intervals, we say that the sampling is *uniform*.

We will focus exclusively on uniform sampling in this chapter. We begin with two examples showing how sampling and reconstruction problems occur in computer graphics.

8.1.1 Sampling: Anti-Aliasing in a Pixel

Consider a simple scheme for anti-aliasing polygonal scenes, in which we want to find a single color to represent each square pixel. One common approach is to average together the colors of all the polygon fragments visible in the pixel, weighted by their individual areas. Anything not covered by a polygon fragment is assumed to be part of the background, with its own color. An example of this approach is shown in Figure 8.1(a).

If there are n fragments (including the background), each with color $\mathbf{C}_i$ and area A_i, then we write the average $\overline{\mathbf{C}}$ color as

$$\overline{\mathbf{C}} = \sum_{i=0}^{n-1} \mathbf{C}_i A_i \tag{8.1}$$

Evaluation of this equation requires only knowing the area and color of each fragment, so it is equally valid for any kinds of objects in our pixel. Let's suppose we also support arbitrary curved surfaces.

To evaluate Equation 8.1, we need values for both the color and area of each fragment. Both of these values can be difficult to evaluate. Suppose that each surface has an irregular shape, and contains a complex texture, as in Figure 8.1(b); finding the average color requires integrating over the visible fragment of each surface. Obtaining an analytic expression for the visible area of the fragment may be difficult, and then analytically integrating the texture over that area can also be difficult, even assuming that an analytic expression for the texture is available. The problem gets even harder if the objects are moving, requiring our averages of area and color to also include a temporal component.

This type of analytic anti-aliasing can work in simple rendering systems where the geometry and color components are simple, such as a smooth-shaded polygon renderer, but as we have seen, it quickly becomes intractable when the objects move and their surface colors become complex.

Therefore, the analytic approach is useful in situations where the signal being imaged is relatively simple and well understood, such as flat polygons and text, but it is rarely used in general-purpose rendering systems because of the difficulty (or impossibility) in finding the necessary analytic expressions.

A popular alternative to this analytic approach is to approximate the various values in Equation 8.1 numerically. We take a number of point samples within the pixel, and try to guess the values of n, $\mathbf{C}_i$, and A_i from those samples, as shown in Figure 8.2. Here we have nine points $\mathbf{C}_i$, each representing an area $A_i = 1/9$, so we can approximate $\overline{\mathbf{C}}$ as

$$\overline{\mathbf{C}} \approx \sum_{i=1}^{9} \frac{\mathbf{C}_i}{9} \tag{8.2}$$

The number of samples we need to get good estimates depends on the spatial distribution of the samples in the pixel, the quality of our approximation method, and the complexity of the scene within the pixel. When we have taken a sufficient number of point samples, we can use them to synthesize a new, continuous-time signal.

The advantage of the point-sampling approach is that in many situations, point samples may be taken from signals that are too complex to represent analytically. If we relied on the analytic technique alone, when the complexity passed a certain limit we would have to give up and tell our users that we simply cannot render certain types of scenes, or start making approximations that may be unacceptable. Using a discrete version of the signal, even if each sample is very expensive to compute, we can still evaluate the signal and process it.

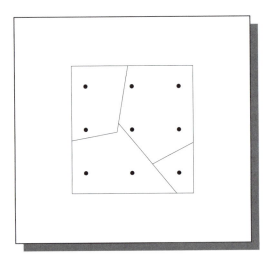

FIGURE 8.2

Taking point samples within the pixel to evaluate its contents.

8.1.2 Reconstruction: Evaluating Incident Light at a Point

To illustrate the need to synthesize a new, continuous-time signal from a set of samples, suppose we want to find the light incident upon a point on an opaque surface. The light may be considered a continuous-time 2D signal $f(\theta, \phi)$ defined everywhere on the hemisphere centered at the point and covering it and the surface, as in Figure 8.3.

The description of the incident light can depend on every object in the scene, and the complex interactions of light between those objects before they reach this point. Finding an analytic expression for this signal may be impossible; if possible, it would probably be horribly complex. So we approximate $f(\theta, \phi)$ by taking a number of point samples as we did for the scene under a pixel, creating a sampled signal $\tilde{g}[n]$, defined only for n different points (θ_n, ϕ_n).

We now want to find how this light interacts with the surface. We will assume for the moment a common model that describes the reflection properties of a surface with a function $r(\theta, \phi)$ that provides the intensity of the light reflected from the surface for each direction (θ, ϕ) on the hemisphere, into some particular direction of interest, as in Figure 8.4. (We'll ignore color right now for the sake of simplicity.)

The reflection function $r(\theta, \phi)$ is a continuous-time function in two parameters. If we simply apply r to each of our samples and sum, we will be ignoring all the

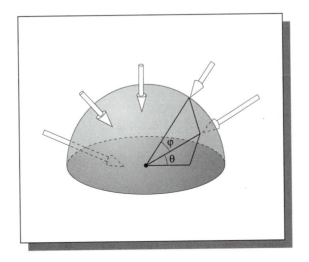

FIGURE 8.3

The light $g(\theta, \phi)$ striking a point comes from its enclosing hemisphere.

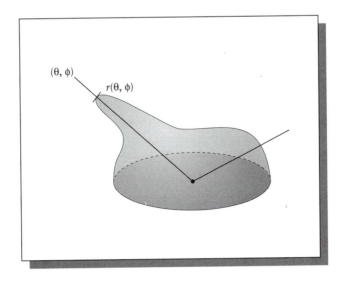

FIGURE 8.4

The light from each incident direction (θ, ϕ) is reflected with intensity $r(\theta, \phi)$.

light information between the samples. Our samples of the incident light are just representatives of the complete description; if we are lucky, they approximate the average light in their general area. To find the total description of the incident light, we need to *reconstruct* the continuous-time signal $g(\theta, \phi)$ from its discrete version $\tilde{g}[n]$. We can then multiply the incident light and the reflection together, finding the total light v reflected from the surface in some direction:

$$v = \int_0^{2\pi} \int_0^{\pi} g(\theta, \phi) r(\theta, \phi) \, d\theta \, d\phi \tag{8.3}$$

8.1.3 Outline of this Chapter

We will have much more to say about practical techniques for anti-aliasing later. Our purpose behind this discussion was to demonstrate that in computer graphics we need to both *sample* and *reconstruct* signals to do our work, and to get into the mood for discussing anti-aliasing.

Aliasing can creep into our system during both the sampling and reconstruction steps. Our goal will be to find those conditions under which we can take a signal, sample it, and then reconstruct exactly the same signal by combining just the samples.

We will first look closely at sampling, detailing what happens when we take a continuous, aperiodic signal and sample it at equally spaced intervals, creating a new, discrete signal. It turns out that the Fourier transform of this discrete signal is always periodic; this forces us to interpret the sampled signal as just one period of a continuous, periodic discrete signal.

If we want to reconstruct our original aperiodic signal, then we need to somehow first make the sampled signal periodic; this is the problem of reconstruction. We will see that there is a precise theoretical condition called the *sampling theorem* that tells us when this necessary periodic-to-aperiodic transformation may be made without error; when this condition is not met during either sampling or reconstruction, the reconstructed continuous signal contains unwanted energy that shows up as aliasing artifacts.

8.1.4 Uniform Sampling and Reconstruction of a 1D Continuous Signal

We mentioned above that the Fourier transform of a uniformly sampled signal is periodic in frequency space. This is a very important result, and it is straightforward to prove.

To *sample* or *digitize* a signal is to evaluate it at a series of values of its parameter. To sample a signal *uniformly* or *periodically* means that the parameters of the sample values are themselves taken from a periodic function.

In one dimension, we uniformly sample a continuous signal $f(t)$ with a shah function $s(t) = \text{III}_{T_0}(t)$ of period T_0 to create a sampled signal $g(nT_0)$:

$$g(nT_0) = f(t)s(t) \tag{8.4}$$

This may be drawn in a system diagram, as in Figure 8.5. The output of the system, $g(t)$, is defined as 0 at all values of t except nT_0, where it is the value of $f(t)$, as in Figure 8.6.

We would like to find the Fourier transform of $g(t)$. The convolution property of Fourier transforms tells us that multiplication in the signal domain is equivalent to convolution in the frequency domain, so

$$\begin{aligned}
G(\omega) &= F(\omega) * S(\omega) \\
&= F(\omega) * \frac{\kappa_T}{\kappa} \text{III}_{\omega_0}(\omega) \\
&= F(\omega) * \frac{\kappa_T}{\kappa} \sum_k \delta(\omega - k\omega_0) \\
&= \frac{\kappa_T}{\kappa} \sum_k F(\omega - k\omega_0)
\end{aligned} \tag{8.5}$$

where on the second line we substituted the Fourier transform of the shah function from Equation 5.83.

This is the result promised at the start of this section. Equation 8.5 tells us that the Fourier transform of $g(t)$ is a periodic repetition of the transform of $f(t)$, repeated with a period of ω_0. This is illustrated in Figure 8.7.

In Figure 8.7, the spectrum of $F(\omega)$ is *bandlimited*, which means that the spectrum has finite support. In other words, for all $|\omega| > \omega_F$, $F(\omega) = 0$. The frequency ω_F is called the *cutoff frequency* for the signal $f(t)$.

Equation 8.5 says that copies of $F(\omega)$ are placed at intervals of ω_0, which is derived from the period T_0 of the sampling shah function $s(t)$ by $\omega_0 = 2\pi/T_0$. When $|\omega_0| > 2\omega_F$, there is sufficient space between copies of $F(\omega)$ that they do not overlap, as shown in Figure 8.8(a). When $|\omega_0| < 2\omega_F$, then the copies of $F(\omega)$ overlap with one another and sum together, as shown in Figure 8.8(c).

Recall that we often want to reconstruct our original signal $f(t)$ from its sampled version $g(t)$. Stated another way, we want to reconstruct $f(t)$ from its samples $f(nT)$. In practice we will often modify the samples in some way before reconstruction, but recovery of the input signal from its samples is the simplest form of the problem and includes all the relevant issues.

If we can somehow find $F(\omega)$ knowing only $g(t)$, then we can recover $f(t)$ using the inverse Fourier transform $f(t) = \mathcal{F}^{-1}\{F(\omega)\}$. Consider again Figure 8.8. When $\omega_0 \leq 2\omega_F$, the spectrum $G(\omega)$ contains multiple, identical copies of $F(\omega)$ at periodic intervals. But this is not the same as $F(\omega)$. The inverse transform for $G(\omega)$ gives

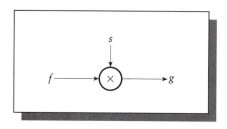

FIGURE 8.5

A sampling system.

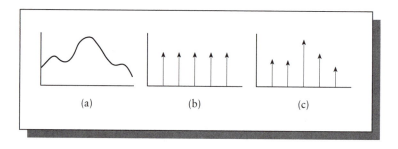

FIGURE 8.6

(a) $f(t)$. (b) $s(t)$. (c) $g(t) = f(t)s(t)$.

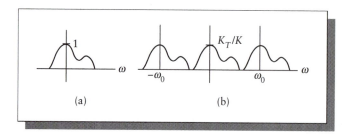

FIGURE 8.7

(a) $F(\omega)$. (b) $G(\omega) = \frac{\kappa_T}{\kappa} \sum_k F(\omega - k\omega_0)$.

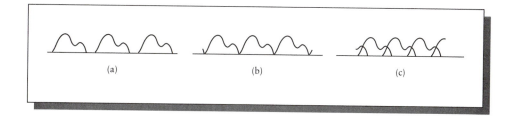

FIGURE 8.8

(a) Because $\omega_0 > 2\omega_F$, the copies of $F(\omega)$ do not overlap. (b) At exactly $\omega_0 = 2\omega_F$, the copies of $F(\omega)$ just touch each other. (c) When $\omega_0 < 2\omega_F$, the copies of $F(\omega)$ overlap and sum together.

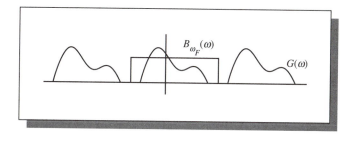

FIGURE 8.9

$F(\omega) = G(\omega)B_{\omega_F}(\omega)$.

the signal $g(t)$, which is zero everywhere but $t = nT_0$; the extra copies of $F(\omega)$ serve to suppress the information between samples of $g(t)$. To get back $f(t)$, we need to isolate just the center copy of $F(\omega)$. One way to do this is to multiply $G(\omega)$ with a box spectrum $B_{\omega_F}(\omega)$, as shown in Figure 8.9:

$$F(\omega) = G(\omega)B_{\omega_F}(\omega) \tag{8.6}$$

and then we can recover $f(t)$ from the inverse transform. The critical point here is that the central copy of $F(\omega)$ needs to be isolated; that means no other copies can overlap with it.

The copies of $F(\omega)$ are distinct only when $\omega_0 \geq 2\omega_F$. When this condition is not fulfilled, copies of $F(\omega)$ overlap and sum together. For example, when the sampling frequency is too low, and we then filter with the box, the value of $G(\omega)$ for some $\omega < \omega_F$ is not $F(\omega)$ but rather $F(\omega) + F(\omega')$ for some $\omega' \neq \omega_F$, as illustrated in Figure 8.10.

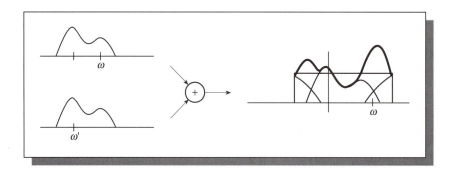

FIGURE 8.10

When $\omega_0 < 2\omega_F$, some energy at $\omega' \neq \omega_F$ adds itself to the energy at ω.

Because the energy at ω' adds to the energy at ω, we say that ω' is an *alias* for ω. When $\omega_0 < 2\omega_F$, the sampled spectrum $G(\omega)$ is said to contain *aliases*, or is *aliased*, and we will be unable to recover our original signal $f(t)$ from its samples. When $\omega_0 \geq 2\omega_F$, then an isolated copy of $F(\omega)$ exists and we can extract it.

This observation is the celebrated sampling theorem for 1D signals and uniform sampling. We state it here as

> **The 1D Uniform Sampling Theorem** (first half):
> A bandlimited signal $f(t)$ with cutoff frequency ω_F may be perfectly reconstructed from its samples $f(nT_0)$ if $2\pi/T_0 \geq 2\omega_F$.

The frequency ω_F is called the *Nyquist frequency* for the signal; the sampling rate T_0 is called the *Nyquist rate*. If a signal is sampled less often than required by the sampling theorem, we say that the signal is *undersampled*. Similarly, if a signal is sampled more often than necessary, it is *oversampled*.

The only requirements imposed by the sampling theorem are that $f(t)$ be band-limited, and that we sample with a frequency at least twice as fast as the highest frequency in $f(t)$.

8.1.5 What Signals Are Bandlimited?

As we mentioned earlier, the types of signals typically encountered in computer graphics have compact support. For example, the image of a polygon has definite, sharp borders. What does this mean in terms of the sampling theorem? A strict interpretation says that any signal with compact support cannot be correctly sampled and then reconstructed because a signal cannot simultaneously have finite width (i.e., have compact support in signal space) and be bandlimited (i.e., have compact support in frequency space). The rule of thumb is that increasingly sharp edges in a signal require increasingly high frequencies.

To see this, consider any signal $x(t)$ such that $x(t) = 0$ for all $|t| > W/2$. We can write $x(t)$ as the product of itself and a box that just encloses it, since the box is unity where $x(t)$ is defined, and zero elsewhere:

$$x(t) = b_W(t)x(t) \tag{8.7}$$

The Fourier transform of $b_W(t)$ is given by Equation 5.15. Thus the Fourier transform of Equation 8.7 is

$$X_B(\omega) = \kappa W \operatorname{sinc}\left(\frac{W}{2\pi}\omega\right) * X(\omega) \tag{8.8}$$

Since the sinc function has infinite width, when we convolve $X(\omega)$ with the sinc in frequency space, as long as $X(\omega)$ has at least one nonzero value, the left-hand side of Equation 8.8 has infinite extent. Our only assumption was that $x(t)$ had finite width. Thus if $x(t)$ has finite width, its Fourier transform has infinite width.

This is another reason why aliasing problems are so prevalent in computer graphics. Our signals typically have finite width: for example, a sphere of some finite radius, a pixel of some size, or a texture of some given width and height. Even if we deal with continuous representations of these objects, when we sample them we are giving up any hope of recreating them without error; the very fact that they have finite extent means that no finite number of samples will ever perfectly capture their edges, which require arbitrarily high frequencies.

We can ameliorate this problem somewhat by treating each finite signal as one period of an infinite, periodic signal. Since the signal is now considered infinite, we can hope to capture the signal with a finite number of samples. This will be our approach in later chapters.

8.2 Reconstruction

We now turn to the problem of recovering $f(t)$ from its samples $f(nT)$.

The sampling theorem for uniformly spaced samples says that as long as the sampling rate is at least twice the highest frequency in the signal, the signal can be recovered from its samples. This recovery process is called *reconstruction*.

If the sampling theorem is met for some signal $f(t)$, then we can reconstruct it by applying a perfect low-pass filter with width ω_F to $G(\omega)$, as in Equation 8.6. An important practical observation is that multiplication in the frequency domain is equivalent to convolution in the signal domain. So the recovered signal with spectrum

$$F(\omega) = G(\omega)R(\omega) \tag{8.9}$$

may be computed in the time domain by Equation 8.6 as

$$f(t) = g(t) * r(t)$$
$$= \sum_n g(t)r(t - nT) \tag{8.10}$$

for some *reconstruction filter* $r(t)$.

Equation 8.10 is an *interpolation formula* that tells us how to derive new values for $f(t)$ between sample points $f(nT)$, using the filter $r(t)$. In Equation 8.6 we multiplied in frequency space with a box with cutoff frequency ω_F. We repeat here the inverse Fourier transform for a box spectrum from Equation 5.73:

$$b(t) = \mathcal{F}^{-1}\left\{B_{\omega_F}(\omega)\right\} = \kappa \omega_F \operatorname{sinc}\left(\frac{\omega_F}{2\pi}t\right) \tag{8.11}$$

If we use the box for filtering in frequency space, then our reconstruction filter $r(t) = b(t)$, so

$$f(t) = \sum_n f(nT)\kappa\omega_F \operatorname{sinc}\left(\frac{\omega_F}{2\pi}(t - nT)\right)$$
$$= (\kappa\omega_F)\sum_n f(nT)\operatorname{sinc}\left(\frac{\omega_F}{2\pi}(t - nT)\right) \tag{8.12}$$

Equation 8.12 is called the *bandlimited reconstruction formula*, because it tells us how to reconstruct any correctly sampled bandlimited signal from its Fourier transform, using the canonical reconstruction filter $\operatorname{sinc}((\omega_F/2\pi)(t - nT))$.

Recall that when a signal is bandlimited, the signal itself has infinite extent. This condition is satisfied by periodic signals.

We can now state the full Uniform Sampling Theorem:

> **The 1D Uniform Sampling Theorem:** A bandlimited signal $f(t)$ with cutoff frequency ω_F, sampled with frequency T_0 such that $2\pi/T_0 \geq 2\omega_F$, may be perfectly reconstructed from its samples $f(nT_0)$ by convolution with the reconstruction filter
>
> $$r(t) = \operatorname{sinc}\left(\frac{\omega_F}{2\pi}(t - nT_0)\right) \tag{8.13}$$

Equation 8.12 tells us that we can reconstruct the signal $f(t)$ by working entirely in the spatial domain. We place a copy of the sinc function at each sample location nT, and scale it by the sample height $f(nT)$ at that point. The sum of all these scaled sinc functions is the original signal $f(t)$. An illustration of this technique is shown in

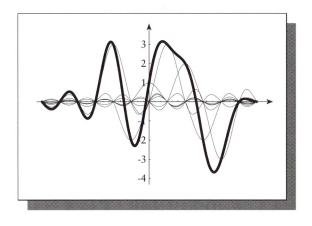

FIGURE 8.11

Reconstructing a signal from a sum of sinc functions.

Figure 8.11. Note that the sincs go through zero at every sample point but the one they are centered over.

So to reconstruct a signal f from its sampled version g, we have two options, one in each domain. In the frequency domain, we may find $F = GB$; the Fourier transform of the signal is equal to the periodic spectrum of G times a box filter B, which isolates just the center copy. In the spatial domain, we may compute $f = g * b$, where we convolve the sampled signal g with the inverse transform of the box function b (which is a sinc). Both of these approaches are useful conceptually. One will usually be computationally cheaper than the other in most practical situations; the choice usually depends on which representation of the signals is most easily computed (or already available), and whether the output needs to be in signal or frequency space.

We said earlier that when the sampling rate is too low, copies of $F(\omega)$ will overlap each other, so some energy from above the cutoff frequency will leak into the central copy (or *alias*), disrupting our attempts at reconstruction. Aliasing can also occur if we reconstruct improperly. For example, the spectrum $F(\omega)$ of some signal and the spectrum of its sampled version $G(\omega)$ are shown in Figure 8.12(a) and (b). If we make a poor choice for the reconstruction filter $B(\omega)$, say a box with width $2\omega_F$ as in Figure 8.12(c), then the reconstructed signal will not match the input, since $G(\omega)B(\omega) \neq F(\omega)$.

In this case the problem is not *aliasing* in the strict sense, since we do not have energy from above the Nyquist limit leaking into the central copy. In fact, the sampling

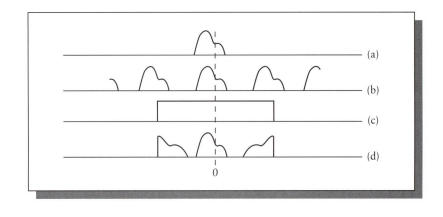

FIGURE 8.12

(a) The spectrum $F(\omega)$ of an input signal. (b) The spectrum of $G(\omega)$ when the sampling theorem is met. (c) A poor choice of filter $B(\omega)$. (d) The resulting spectrum $G(\omega)B(\omega) \neq F(\omega)$.

theorem is met by Figure 8.12(b); it's the reconstruction step that is introducing error. Unfortunately, sometimes in the graphics literature this effect is also referred to as aliasing. It is better to reserve the term *aliasing* for the effects due to undersampling, and refer to the effects of poor reconstruction as *reconstruction errors*.

To show the effect of sampling rate on a signal, Figure 8.13(a) shows a signal $f(t)$ made up of a fixed number of cycles of a sine wave (here we use $f(t) = (\sin(x)+1)/2$ so that $0 \le f(t) \le 1$). Figure 8.13(b) shows the result of sampling that signal with shah functions of gradually decreasing period, and thus increasing frequency. As the period goes down, we have more samples within the finite interval within which the signal is defined. When the sampling frequency reaches the Nyquist limit, our samples are sufficiently close to capture $f(t)$, and further numbers of samples don't improve our estimate; above that rate we are oversampling. We used a sinc function to reconstruct each row of Figure 8.13(b).

8.2.1 Zero-Order Hold Reconstruction

A common hardware setup for displaying computer-generated images is the combination of a frame buffer and a rectangular-grid-based display device. For the current discussion, we will assume that such devices display a constant-intensity signal between samples; an LED display with a diffuser or a high-resolution print image may match this assumption well. A CRT probably would not, because the color at each

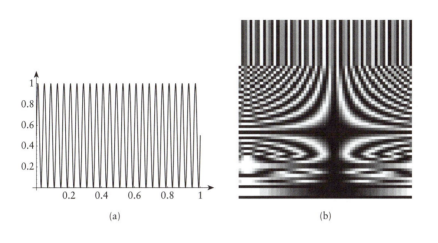

(a)   (b)

FIGURE 8.13

(a) $f(t) = (\sin(x) + 1)/2$. (b) Reconstruction of $f(t)$ after sampling with different shah functions. The frequency of the sampling function increases along the vertical axis.

point is ideally represented by a Gaussian bump and not a flat field of color, as discussed in Chapter 3. However, the assumption that the signal is constant between display centers is much easier to work with, which is why we use it here. We will focus our discussion on a single scan line of pixels, though in two dimensions there can be interactions between adjacent scan lines.

If we only store color values at the centers of pixels, then we are essentially letting the display device fill in the signal between pixels with whatever intensity is generated between one pixel center and the next. Under our assumption, the reconstructed signal $r(t)$ between two samples $r(nT)$ and $r(n(T+1))$ is just $r(nT)$. This is called a *zero-order reconstruction*, or *zero-order hold*, and is illustrated in Figure 8.14 [282].

We can describe the system with a system diagram like Figure 8.15. When our rendering is complete, we have built an estimate of the image $f(t)$ that we would like to display. We know that we will show this on a device with interpixel spacing p, so we make sure that $f(t)$ is bandlimited to $\omega_F \leq \pi/p$. We then sample the signal with a shah function $s(t)$, which has an impulse at the center of each pixel, resulting in a sampled signal $g(t) = f(t)s(t)$.

The zero-order hold may be modeled by a filter with an impulse response $h_p(t)$

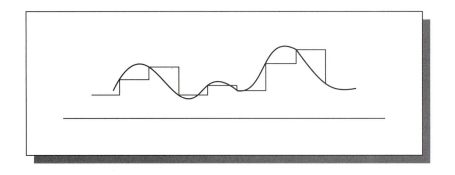

FIGURE 8.14

A zero-order hold simply holds one sample until the next arrives.

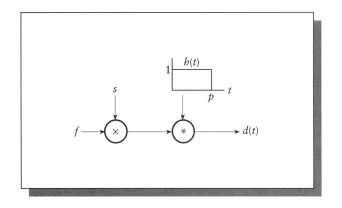

FIGURE 8.15

A model of zero-order hold.

such that

$$h_p(t) = \begin{cases} 0 & t < 0 \\ 1 & 0 \le t \le p \\ 0 & p < t \end{cases} \tag{8.14}$$

When we apply this to $g(t)$, we get the display signal $d(t)$:

$$d(t) = g(t) * h_p(t) \tag{8.15}$$

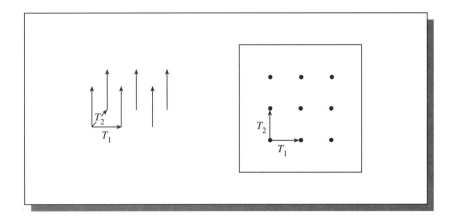

FIGURE 8.16
A 2D shah function with periods T_1 and T_2.

8.3 Sampling in Two Dimensions

We now turn our attention to sampling in two dimensions. The 2D sampling theory is very similar to the 1D case. The difference is simply in the complexity of the notation. Each equation gets a bit more than twice as complicated, because many symbols now appear with two different names (one for each axis) and they must be kept distinct. The *ideas* in this section parallel those in previous sections, though the equations are much busier.

Let's suppose that we are given a continuous-time 2D function $f(x, y)$, sampled on a rectangular grid with periods (T_1, T_2), as in Figure 8.16. This forms the sampled signal $f(mT_1, nT_2) = g[m, n]$. Under what conditions can we recover f from g?

To express g, we start with a sampling signal $s[m, n]$ with periods T_1 and T_2,

$$s[m, n] = \sum_m \sum_n \delta(x - mT_1, y - nT_2) \tag{8.16}$$

and then multiply s with f to form g.

$$\begin{aligned} g[m, n] &= f(x, y)g[m, n] \\ &= \sum_m \sum_n f(x, y)\delta(x - mT_1, y - nT_2) \\ &= f(mT_1, nT_2) \end{aligned} \tag{8.17}$$

We want to find $\mathcal{F}\{g\}$. Since $g[m, n] = \mathcal{F}^{-1}\{G(\mu, \nu)\} = f(mT_1, nT_2)$, we can

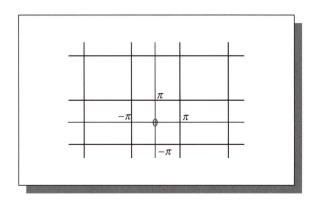

FIGURE 8.17

Tiling the infinite plane with squares 2π on a side.

simply find the 2D CTFT transform of f and then sample it appropriately. We begin with the 2D CTFT of f:

$$
\begin{aligned}
g[m, n] &= f(mT_1, nT_2) \\
&= \mathcal{F}^{-1}\left\{\mathcal{F}\left\{f(x, y)\right\}\right\} \\
&= \frac{1}{2\pi} \iint F(\mu, \nu) e^{j(mT_1\mu + nT_2\nu)} \, d\mu \, d\nu \\
&= \frac{1}{2\pi} \iint \frac{1}{T_1 T_2} F(\lambda_1/T_1, \lambda_2/T_2) e^{j(m\lambda_1 + n\lambda_2)} \, d\lambda_1 \, d\lambda_2
\end{aligned}
\tag{8.18}
$$

using the substitutions

$$
\lambda_1 = \mu T_1 \quad \text{and} \quad \lambda_2 = \nu T_2
\tag{8.19}
$$

The double integration covers the entire plane. We will break up the plane into an infinite collection of squares, each 2π on a side, as shown in Figure 8.17. These squares cover the plane with no gaps or overlap, so finding the integral over each square and summing the result will give us the same value as integrating over the plane. We will place one square centered at the origin, and simply abut the rest in rows and columns.

We write $SQ(k_1, k_2)$ to indicate the square with origin at (k_1, k_2). Breaking down the integral above into these squares gives

$$
g[m, n] = \frac{1}{2\pi} \sum_{k_1} \sum_{k_2} \iint_{SQ(k_1, k_2)} \frac{1}{T_1 T_2} F(\lambda_1/T_1, \lambda_2/T_2) e^{j(m\lambda_1 + n\lambda_2)} \, d\lambda_1 \, d\lambda_2
\tag{8.20}
$$

We now make another set of substitutions to remove the awkward integral. We can set the integrals to cover just one square and choose the limits of the square with the arguments in the function by substituting

$$\eta = \lambda_1 + 2\pi k_1 \quad \text{and} \quad \xi = \lambda_2 + 2\pi k_2 \tag{8.21}$$

Plugging these in for λ_1 and λ_2, expanding the exponentials and then collecting them again, yields

$$g[m,n] = \sum_{k_1} \sum_{k_2} \frac{1}{2\pi} \int_{-\pi}^{\pi} \int_{-\pi}^{\pi} \frac{1}{T_1 T_2} F\left(\frac{\eta 2\pi k_1}{T_1}, \frac{\xi 2\pi k_2}{T_2}\right) e^{j(m\eta + n\xi)} e^{-j(2\pi k_1 m + 2\pi k_2 n)} \, d\eta \, d\xi$$

$$\tag{8.22}$$

This equation is certainly a monster, but it can be tamed. The last exponential is identically 1 for all integer values of k_1, k_2, m, and n, giving us

$$
\begin{aligned}
g[m,n] &= \sum_{k_1} \sum_{k_2} \frac{1}{2\pi} \int_{-\pi}^{\pi} \int_{-\pi}^{\pi} \frac{1}{T_1 T_2} F\left(\frac{\eta 2\pi k_1}{T_1}, \frac{\xi 2\pi k_2}{T_2}\right) e^{j(m\eta + n\xi)} \, d\eta \, d\xi \\
&= \int_{-\pi}^{\pi} \int_{-\pi}^{\pi} G[\eta, \xi] e^{j(m\eta + n\xi)} \, d\eta \, d\xi \\
&= \mathcal{F}^{-1}\{G[\eta, \xi]\}
\end{aligned}
\tag{8.23}
$$

We have now found the Fourier transform of the discrete signal $g[m,n]$, derived from sampling the continuous-time signal $f(x,y)$. Remember that our goal is to recover f from g. We will find this is only possible under certain conditions. To find those conditions, it will be very useful to consider just what $G[\eta, \xi]$ represents in terms of $F(\mu, \nu)$.

From the derivation above, we write $G[\eta, \xi]$ as

$$G[\eta, \xi] = \frac{1}{2\pi} \sum_{k_1} \sum_{k_2} \frac{1}{T_1 T_2} F\left(\frac{\eta 2\pi k_1}{T_1}, \frac{\xi 2\pi k_2}{T_2}\right) \tag{8.24}$$

This shows us that G contains an infinite number of periodic replications of F at intervals of $(2\pi/T_1, 2\pi/T_2)$, as illustrated in Figure 8.18. The centers of the replicants lie on a square grid with one point at the origin and the others at vectors $(k_1 2\pi/T_1, k_2 2\pi/T_2)$.

So G contains F at the center, plus many copies at regular intervals in both directions. If we can isolate the one copy of F lying at the origin, then we can take its inverse transform and achieve our goal of recovering f from g (here, via G).

Under what conditions can we isolate the center copy of F from within G? Figure 8.19 shows that we can draw a square grid around the replicant centers. Each square has width $2\pi/T_1$ and height $2\pi/T_2$, with one square at the origin and others surrounding it.

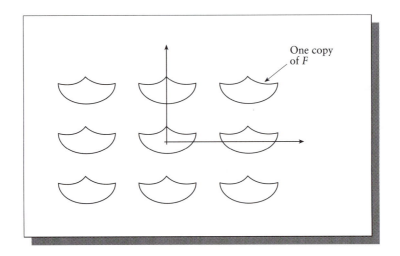

FIGURE 8.18

The spectrum of G contains an infinite grid of replications of F.

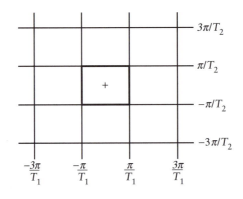

FIGURE 8.19

The squares of isolation in G.

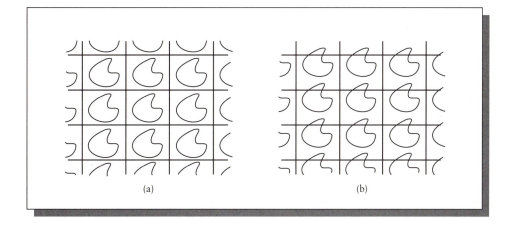

(a) (b)

FIGURE 8.20

(a) The spectrum F fits within the limiting square in G. (b) The spectrum F does not fit within the limiting square, so copies of F in G overlap and sum.

If the spectrum of f fits within one of these squares, then the various replicants will not overlap, as in Figure 8.20(a). But if the spectrum of f exceeds the limits of the square, then the replicants will overlap and sum together. This will happen at every location, including the center one, which will ruin our chances of recovering a pure copy of F. This overlap is shown in Figure 8.20(b).

This overlap is 2D *aliasing*. If the spectrum of f is outside of this box, then we will be unable to sample f on this grid and then get f back later. Of course, we can change the grid, making the boxes larger by placing the samples more closely together. Since the box sides are $(2\pi/T_1, 2\pi/T_2)$, we can enlarge the boxes by shrinking the sampling interval of the sampling array of impulses s, and thus the density of g. But for any regular grid there will always be a box and F will have to fit within it.

We say that f is *bandlimited* if its spectrum is zero beyond some finite range. We can formalize this in the 2D sampling theorem for uniform samples, which specifies the Nyquist limits in the x and y directions for the 2D spectrum $F(\mu, \nu)$:

> **The 2D Uniform Sampling Theorem** (first half): A bandlimited signal $f(x, y)$ with cutoff frequencies μ_F and ν_F may be perfectly reconstructed from its samples $f(mT_1, nT_2)$ if $2\pi/T_1 \geq 2\mu_F$ and $2\pi/T_2 \geq 2\nu_F$.

If F satisfies the conditions of the 2D sampling theorem, then it is sufficiently bandlimited that we may write G within the center square as

$$G[\mu T_1, \nu T_2] = \frac{1}{2\pi} \frac{1}{T_1 T_2} F(\mu, \nu) \qquad \text{for } |\mu| \leq \pi/T_1 \text{ and } |\nu| \leq \pi/T_2 \qquad (8.25)$$

We may simply invert Equation 8.25 to recover F from G:

$$F(\mu, \nu) = \begin{cases} 2\pi T_1 T_2 G[\mu T_1, \nu T_2] & |\mu| < \pi/T_1 \text{ and } |\nu| < \pi/T_2 \\ 0 & \text{otherwise} \end{cases} \qquad (8.26)$$

8.4 Two-Dimensional Reconstruction

The 2D sampling theorem tells us that when F is appropriately bandlimited, we can recover $f(x, y)$ from a sampled version $f(mT_1, nT_2)$. In this section we present the mechanics of this *reconstruction*. We will see that it again closely parallels the 1D case.

We apply the inverse Fourier transform to the central square of $G[\eta, \xi]$. The expressions will quickly get very busy again because almost everything appears twice, but as in the last section the ideas are almost the same as in the 1D case. To make the notation a trifle simpler, we will use the substitutions

$$W_1 = \pi/T_1 \quad \text{and} \quad W_2 = \pi/T_2 \qquad (8.27)$$

We start with the definition of the inverse transform, narrow the range of integration to the center square, and substitute the value for G from Equation 8.25:

$$\begin{aligned} f(x, y) &= \frac{1}{2\pi} \iint F(\mu, \nu) e^{j(\mu x + \nu y)} d\mu \, d\nu \\ &= \frac{1}{2\pi} \int_{-W_1}^{W_1} \int_{-W_2}^{W_2} 2\pi T_1 T_2 G[\mu T_1, \nu T_2] e^{j(\mu x + \nu y)} \, d\mu \, d\nu \\ &= \frac{1}{2\pi} \int_{-W_1}^{W_1} \int_{-W_2}^{W_2} 2\pi T_1 T_2 \mathcal{F}\{g[n, m]\} \, e^{j(\mu x + \nu y)} \, d\mu \, d\nu \end{aligned} \qquad (8.28)$$

Now we can expand the Fourier transform of g explicitly to find:

$$\begin{aligned} f(x, y) &= \frac{1}{2\pi} \int_{-W_1}^{W_1} \int_{-W_2}^{W_2} 2\pi T_1 T_2 \left[\frac{1}{2\pi} \sum_m \sum_n g[m, n] e^{j(\mu T_1 n + \nu T_2 n)} \right] e^{j(\mu x + \nu y)} \, d\mu \, d\nu \\ &= T_1 T_2 \frac{1}{2\pi} \sum_m \sum_n g[m, n] \int_{-W_1}^{W_1} \int_{-W_2}^{W_2} e^{j[\mu(T_1 m - x) + \nu(T_2 n - y)]} \, d\mu \, d\nu \\ &= T_1 T_2 \frac{1}{2\pi} \sum_m \sum_n g[m, n] \int_{-W_1}^{W_1} e^{j[\mu(T_1 m - x)]} \, d\mu \int_{-W_2}^{W_2} e^{j[\nu(T_2 n - y)]} \, d\nu \end{aligned}$$

$$(8.29)$$

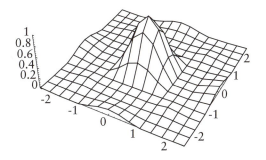

FIGURE 8.21

The 2D reconstruction filter $r(x, y; m, n) = \text{sinc}\left[\frac{W_1}{\pi}(x - T_1 m)\right] \text{sinc}\left[\frac{W_2}{\pi}(y - T_2 n)\right]$.

There is no question that Equation 8.29 is another monster. But notice the integrals on the right are in the form of property E19, so we may rewrite them:

$$f(x, y) = T_1 T_2 \frac{1}{2\pi} \sum_m \sum_n g[m, n] \frac{2 \sin\left[(x - T_1 m)W_1\right]}{(x - T_1 m)} \frac{2 \sin\left[(y - T_2 n)W_2\right]}{(y - T_2 n)}$$

$$= \frac{4\pi^2}{W_1 W_2} \frac{1}{2\pi} \sum_m \sum_n g[m, n] \frac{\sin\left[(x - T_1 m)W_1\right]}{(x - T_1 m)} \frac{\sin\left[(y - T_2 n)W_2\right]}{(y - T_2 n)}$$

$$= 2\pi \sum_m \sum_n g[m, n] \frac{\sin\left[(x - T_1 m)W_1\right]}{W_1(x - T_1 m)} \frac{\sin\left[(y - T_2 n)W_2\right]}{W_2(y - T_2 n)}$$

$$= 2\pi \sum_m \sum_n g[m, n] \, \text{sinc}\left[\frac{W_1}{\pi}(x - T_1 m)\right] \text{sinc}\left[\frac{W_2}{\pi}(y - T_2 n)\right] \quad (8.30)$$

This completes our reconstruction of $f(x, y)$. The reconstruction filter $r(x, y; m, n)$ is given by

$$r(x, y; m, n) = \text{sinc}\left[\frac{W_1}{\pi}(x - T_1 m)\right] \text{sinc}\left[\frac{W_2}{\pi}(y - T_2 n)\right] \quad (8.31)$$

and is plotted in Figure 8.21. Notice that r is not radially symmetric; it is the product of two orthogonal sinc functions.

We can now state the full 2D Uniform Sampling Theorem:

> **The 2D Uniform Sampling Theorem:** A bandlimited signal $f(x, y)$ with cutoff frequencies μ_F and ν_F sampled with frequency T_1 and T_2 such that $2\pi/T_1 \geq 2\mu_F$ and $2\pi/T_2 \geq 2\nu_F$ may be perfectly reconstructed from its samples $f(mT_1, nT_2)$ by convolution with the reconstruction filter
>
> $$r(x, y; m, n) = \mathrm{sinc}\left[\frac{W_1}{\pi}(x - T_1 m)\right] \mathrm{sinc}\left[\frac{W_2}{\pi}(y - T_2 n)\right] \qquad (8.32)$$

So to find the value of $f(x_0, y_0)$, conceptually move the reconstruction filter so its center is at (x_0, y_0), and multiply it with the sampled signal g. The sum of the point-by-point product of these two functions times 2π yields the value of $f(x_0, y_0)$. This procedure isn't practical, however, because the sinc function has infinite support, and g is infinitely periodic in both dimensions. Thus, we would need to carry out the products and summations to infinity in two directions to find the correct result.

Notice that Equation 8.30 has the form of a double convolution sum. This confirms the general approach. As we discussed for 1D reconstruction, filtering a spectrum with a box is equivalent to convolving the signal with a sinc.

8.5   Reconstruction in Image Space

As an example of the importance of proper reconstruction, we will return to our discussion of pixel colors from the start of the chapter. We will show that simply averaging the sample values is a poor idea, and suggest a better route.

8.5.1   The Box Reconstruction Filter

Recall Equation 8.2. To derive that equation, we reasoned that there were nine uniformly distributed samples in the pixel, each representing an equal amount of area. So we simply weighted each one by 1/9 and added them together.

Consider this now in terms of reconstruction; this simple averaging is not equivalent to convolving each of the nine samples with the necessary sinc function. Since we're not satisfying the requirements of the sampling theorem, this process cannot recover the signal correctly. Let's look at what signal this process of approximate reconstruction actually does synthesize.

To make the presentation simpler, we will rephrase the discussion in one dimension. We assume some underlying signal $f(t)$, which we sample with a shah function

$s_{T_0}(t)$, as in Figure 8.22(a) and (b); their product $g(t) = f(t)s_{T_0}(t)$ is equivalent to our point samples in a pixel. We will say that our 1D "pixel" spans the interval $\Gamma = [-2T_0, 2T_0]$. To make sure we have no aliasing, we'll pick $f(t) = \cos(\alpha t)$, with $\alpha = (2\pi)/(3T_0)$ (any value of $\alpha < \pi/T_0$ will guarantee accurate sampling).

Our simple reconstruction scheme adds up all the values in the pixel and averages them; this is equivalent to multiplying $g(t)$ with a box whose width covers one pixel, $h(t) = b_{4T_0}(t)$, as shown in Figure 8.22(d). Note that each box will contain either one or two samples, depending on where the pixel boundaries are, because we're sampling at 2/3 of the Nyquist rate.

To find the reconstructed signal, we shift the box to each sample and scale it, resulting in the reconstructed signal $h * fs$ in Figure 8.22(e). Resampling by the pixel samples in Figure 8.22(f) gives

$$r(t) = p(t)\left[h(t) * g(t)\right] \tag{8.33}$$

as shown in Figure 8.22(g). Finally, we convolve again with the device's characteristic display function $m(t)$ in Figure 8.22(h), giving us $d = m * \{p[h * (fs)]\}$, as shown in Figure 8.22(i).

The new signal $d(t)$ certainly has a value at each pixel center, but it seems unlikely that we have reconstructed correctly, since we have not followed the sampling theorem and convolved with a sinc. In fact, we convolved with the inverse transform of a sinc instead. To see what $d(t)$ represents, let's find its Fourier transform $D(\omega)$.

Figure 8.23 shows the Fourier space representation of the signals in Figure 8.22. We know that the transform of a shah is another shah:

$$S(\omega) = \frac{\kappa_T}{\kappa}\,\text{III}_{\omega_0}(\omega) \tag{8.34}$$

The Fourier transform of a cosine is easily found. Since $\cos(\alpha t) = (e^{j\alpha t} + e^{-j\alpha t})/2$, then by linearity its transform is

$$\begin{aligned}
\mathcal{F}\{\cos(\alpha t)\} &= \mathcal{F}\left\{\frac{e^{j\alpha t} + e^{-j\alpha t}}{2}\right\} \\
&= \mathcal{F}\left\{\frac{e^{j\alpha t}}{2}\right\} + \mathcal{F}\left\{\frac{e^{-j\alpha t}}{2}\right\} \\
&= \frac{\kappa}{2}\left(\delta(\omega - \alpha) + \delta(\omega + \alpha)\right)
\end{aligned} \tag{8.35}$$

This seems reasonable; to make a signal $\cos(\alpha t)$, we need only add the two complex exponentials $e^{j\alpha t} + e^{-j\alpha t}$; the imaginary parts cancel each other out and we're left with the real cosine term.

Since multiplication in one domain matches convolution in the other, we know that $g(t) = f(t)s(t)$ is equivalent to $G(\omega) = F(\omega) * S(\omega)$.

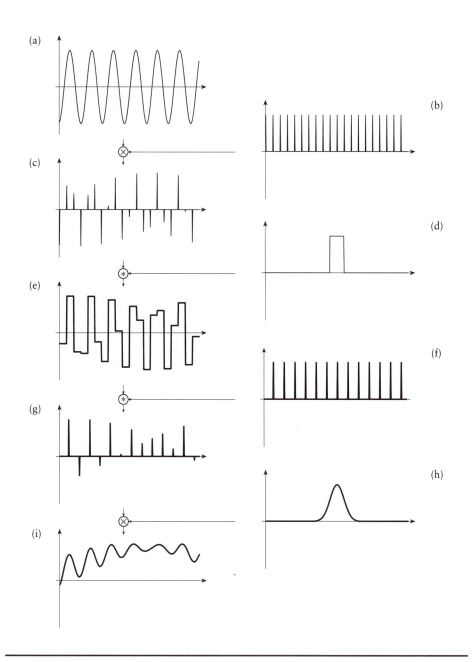

FIGURE 8.22

One-dimensional box filtering in signal space. (a) The original signal $f(t)$. (b) A sampling impulse train $s_{r_0}(t)$. (c) The sampled signal $f(t)s_{r_0}(t)$. (d) A box reconstruction filter. (e) The reconstructed signal. (f) A resampling impulse train. (g) The resampled signal. (h) The device display function. (i) The displayed signal.

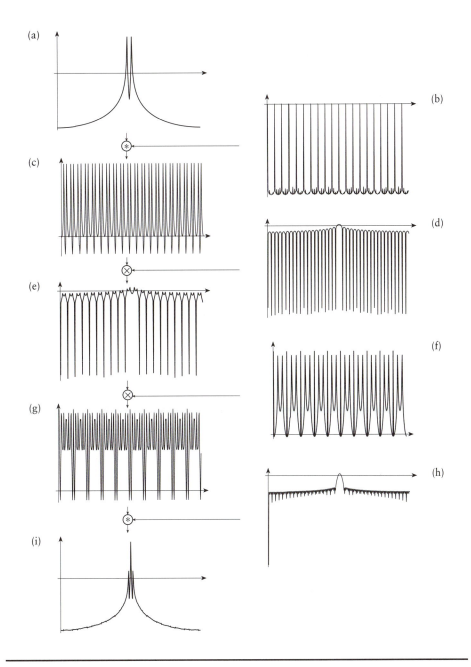

FIGURE 8.23

One-dimensional box filtering in frequency space. (a)–(i) The Fourier transforms of the signals in Figure 8.22(a)–(i), respectively.

Similarly, we know from before that the transform of a box is a sinc, so we can find $H(\omega)$ from $h(t)$ as

$$H(\omega) = 4T_0\kappa \operatorname{sinc}\left(\frac{2T_0}{\pi}\omega\right) \tag{8.36}$$

as shown in Figure 8.23(d). The convolution in space is then multiplication in frequency; our reconstructed signal HG is in Figure 8.23(e). Then resampling with the pixels P shown in Figure 8.23(f) leads to the resulting

$$B(\omega) = P(\omega) * [H(\omega)G(\omega)] \tag{8.37}$$

shown in Figure 8.23(g). Finally we multiply this with the display's own built-in reconstruction filter to get

$$D = M\{P * [H(F * S)]\} \tag{8.38}$$

Compare the original spectrum $F(\omega)$ in Figure 8.23(a) with the reconstructed spectrum in Figure 8.23(i). They are clearly not the same. There are many new high frequencies in our reconstructed signal that don't belong. They die off in amplitude following a sinc wave, but they never disappear. So even though our sampling was perfect, our reconstruction was not and we did not recover our original signal.

This type of reconstruction is usually referred to by the unfortunate name of "box filtering" in computer graphics. This is somewhat misleading, since a box filter is exactly appropriate for multiplication in frequency space, but very poor for convolution in signal space. A more meaningful term for this approach would be "image-box filtering," since that indicates that we are reconstructing with a box in image (or signal) space.

Image-box filtering is not a total loss. The sinc function in frequency space meets our basic qualitative criteria: the central copy of $F(\omega)$ isn't attenuated too much, and higher copies are suppressed (scaled down in amplitude). It would be nice if the central copy was untouched and the higher harmonics completely damped, but the sinc at least does part of the job.

A box is probably the easiest reconstruction filter to program, but it is far from ideal; its finite support and sharp edges guarantee a wide Fourier transform, and thus leakage of high frequencies in the output.

8.5.2 Other Reconstruction Filters

Given that the box is a poor choice for a reconstruction filter, and a full sinc is impossible to implement, what other shape might perform better? This question immediately plunges us into the world of filter design. We will discuss filter approximation in more detail in Chapter 10. Right now we will just make some general observations about the implications of different filter shapes and their effects on reconstruction.

As we saw in the previous chapter, filters are often classified as having a finite impulse response (FIR) or an infinite impulse response (IIR). We have seen that the ideal 1D reconstruction filter in frequency space is the box, but that the inverse transform of this finite-support spectrum is an IIR sinc function. We cannot convolve a signal with this function in a practical system because it requires us to have access to the signal from negative to positive infinity. What we would prefer is a filter that comes close to the box in frequency space, but still has a finite, reasonable width in signal space. The basic difficulty is that, as we have seen, there is a natural inverse relationship between the width of a signal and its Fourier transform; the narrower one becomes, the wider the other spreads. We cannot really hope to find a very boxlike filter with a small and finite impulse response.

Much of the field of filter design is aimed toward resolving this tension by producing FIR filters with good frequency selectivity. Because the process is inherently a trade-off, for each set of different desired characteristics there is a different approach and set of filters. There is no one filter design technique that is superior to all others in all applications.

One practical method for making a good equivalent to a spectral box is to design a filter that drops off to a very small value outside of some interval in both spaces. A popular choice is the Gaussian bump. We can easily find the signal that corresponds to a Gaussian filter of any particular width. If we think of the Gaussian as dropping off "almost to zero" at some distance from the center, then we might simply assert that it is zero beyond some distance in both spaces, thereby approximating a signal with finite support in both spaces. This is illustrated in Figure 8.24. This is analogous to *windowing* the Gaussians with a box in each domain. The resulting signal and spectrum no longer form a Fourier pair, but if we choose the cutoffs carefully, they can be close.

We will look more closely at reconstruction techniques when we survey practical signal-processing methods for computer graphics in Chapter 10.

8.6 Supersampling

It is common wisdom in computer graphics that you can reduce the aliasing artifacts in a picture by *supersampling*. Supersampling mean taking samples at a higher frequency then you expect to eventually resample at. For pictures, this means sampling more finely than once per pixel.

A common supersampling method is to place an $n \times n$ grid of *supersamples* within each pixel, and then filter them into one value for that pixel. An example for $n = 2$ is shown in Figure 8.25.

This approach has a lot to offer: it's conceptually simple and easy to implement.

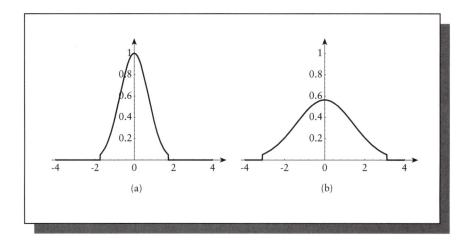

FIGURE 8.24

A Fourier pair of Gaussians and their cutoff points. (a) The time signal. (b) Its Fourier transform.

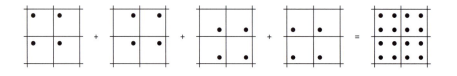

FIGURE 8.25

Four different pixel centers for four separate images.

The downside is that it can be very slow; for the $n \times n$ grid, the rendering time goes up quadratically with n. Many rendering systems use values of 2, 3, or 4 for n, and values of 8 and more are not uncommon. Therefore it is important that we understand just what happens as n increases, so we can use the smallest value required for a desired amount of aliasing reduction.

For simplicity, we will consider the monochromatic 1D case, where the image corresponds to the intensity along a scan line, and the basic sampling function corresponds to pixel centers.

Suppose that the scan line image is modeled by a CT signal $c(t)$. Almost certainly, $c(t)$ will not be bandlimited, since it is defined by the models and the lights in the scene. There are a special few classes of signals for which we can create $c(t)$ so that

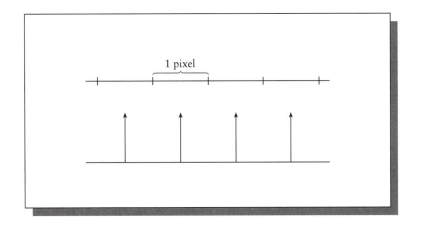

FIGURE 8.26

A pixel grid and the sampling function that models it.

we are guaranteed it is bandlimited [325], but such models are rare, and for most 3D models, $c(t)$ will not be guaranteed to be bandlimited. We will assume, however, that the energy in $C(\omega)$ tends to diminish as ω increases; that is, the higher the frequency, in general, the less of a contribution it makes. This condition seems to be fulfilled by most realistic images.

To model the rendering system we create a sampling function $s_p(t)$, which is made of impulses spaced p units apart, equal to the distance between pixel centers:

$$s_p(t) = \text{III}_p(t) \tag{8.39}$$

This is diagrammed in Figure 8.26.

The result of sampling the signal $c(t)$ is a DT signal $d[n] = c[pn]$, which we can display directly by assigning the value of $d[n]$ to pixel n.

We know that

$$\text{III}_p(t) \stackrel{\mathcal{F}}{\longleftrightarrow} \text{III}_{2\pi/p}(\omega) \tag{8.40}$$

so our sampling frequency $\omega_s = 2\pi/p$. The sampling theorem tells us that the Nyquist frequency ω_N for this sampling density is given by $\omega_s = 2\omega_N$, so $\omega_N = \pi/p$. This is the cutoff frequency for our pixel sampling; any energy above this frequency will not get sampled properly, and will show up as some sort of aliasing effect.

Let's supersample this signal and see what happens. Our model of supersampling is shown in Figure 8.27. We first sample the image function with an impulse train that takes several samples per pixel. This result is then reconstructed and filtered, and the new signal is resampled at the pixel rate.

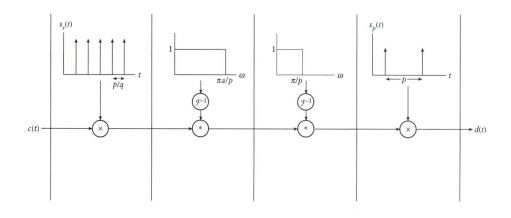

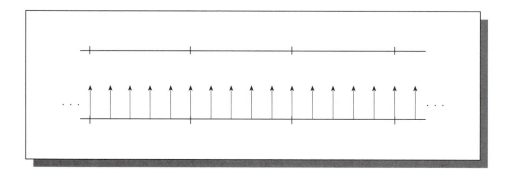

FIGURE 8.27

A model of supersampling.

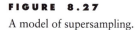

FIGURE 8.28

A pixel grid and a supersampling impulse train.

The supersampling impulse train $s_s(t)$, which takes a samples in each pixel, is given by

$$s_s(t) = \text{III}_{p/a}(t) \tag{8.41}$$

and is diagrammed in Figure 8.28.

As in the pixel-rate case, the result of rendering is a discrete signal $g[n] = c[np/a]$. The new sampling frequency is $\omega_s = 2\pi a/p$, so the new Nyquist frequency is $\omega_N =$

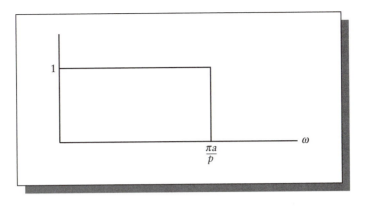

FIGURE 8.29
The reconstruction filter $R(\omega)$.

$a\pi/p$; the limit of useful information is a factor of a higher than for pixel-level sampling.

We cannot display $g[n]$, though, since it is not matched to our pixel display function; we cannot assign all a values to any one pixel. To display $g[n]$, we first reconstruct it as a continuous-time signal and then resample that signal at the pixel rate. We will take the opportunity to filter the signal between these two steps to reduce aliasing.

First we reconstruct the continuous-time function $g(t)$ from the discrete-time function $g[n]$ by low-pass filtering the latter. For now, we will assume perfect filtering, and use a low-pass reconstruction filter $R(\omega)$ with cutoff frequency $\omega = a\pi/p$,

$$R(\omega) = b_{a\pi/p}(\omega) \tag{8.42}$$

as in Figure 8.29, and multiply it with the spectrum of $g[n]$:

$$N(\omega) = G(\Omega)R(\omega) \tag{8.43}$$

The next step is to low-pass filter $N(\omega)$, so that when we sample it with the pixel-rate impulse train $s_p(t)$, we won't introduce any new aliasing. We saw above that the cutoff frequency for $s_p(t)$ is $\omega_N = \pi/p$, so we can build a low-pass filter $F(\omega)$ from a box with this half-width:

$$F(\omega) = b_{\pi/p}(\omega) \tag{8.44}$$

This filter is shown in Figure 8.30.

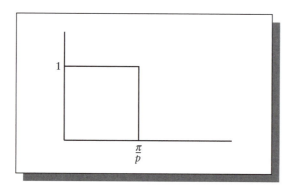

FIGURE 8.30

The low-pass filter $F(\omega)$.

We now have a new bandlimited signal $B(\omega)$:

$$B(\omega) = F(\omega)G(\omega) \tag{8.45}$$

Since $B(\omega)$ is correctly bandlimited, we can sample it with $s_p(t)$ with confidence that we won't introduce any new aliasing errors. The result is a new display signal $d_s[n]$, which is now matched to our display pixel rate. In signal and frequency space, the expressions for $d_s[n]$ are

$$d_s[n] = s_p(t)\,(f(t) * (r(t) * (s_s(t)c(t))))$$
$$D_s[n] = S_p(\omega) * (F(\omega)R(\omega)\,(S_s(\omega) * C(\omega))) \tag{8.46}$$

corresponding to Figure 8.27.

What have we gained by supersampling? When we sampled at the pixel rate to create $d_p[n]$, any information above π/p turned into alias artifacts. When we supersampled to create $d_s[n]$, we initially sampled at $a\pi/p$. By reconstructing and filtering, we eliminated the chance that any information below $a\pi/p$ would turn into aliases.

Thus any energy in the band $\pi/p < \omega < a\pi/p$ that turned into artifacts in the pixel-sampled image has been correctly accounted for in the supersampled image. If the image $c(t)$ indeed has generally less energy with increasing frequency, as we assumed above, then we have eliminated aliasing information where it mattered the most. As we increase the value of a, we remove more and more aliases from the image.

It is important to note that by construction,

$$F(\omega)R(\omega) = F(\omega) \tag{8.47}$$

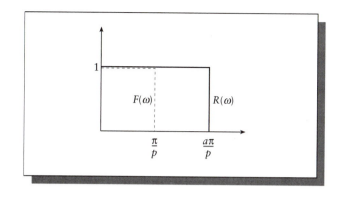

FIGURE 8.31

By construction, $F(\omega)R(\omega) = F(\omega)$.

since $F(\omega)$ is a box function that is completely contained within $R(\omega)$, as shown in Figure 8.31.

This is the reason we don't usually explicitly reconstruct when implementing this technique; the perfect low-pass filter contains the perfect reconstruction filter for this operation. On the other hand, as we mentioned earlier, nobody implements perfect filters because they require infinite information. So the reconstruction, if performed explicitly, is not usually exact, and the low-pass filter also is not.

As we discussed above, there is no one choice in signal space for an approximation to the impulse response of a perfect filter. We will discuss this in more detail later, but we note now that common choices include boxes, Gaussians, and clipped sinc functions. Strictly, one should be sure that whatever choice is made for reconstruction and low-pass filters, the reconstruction step is only ignored if the two filters nest.

If the low-pass filter is not completely (or at least substantially) within the reconstruction filter, the two stages should be implemented separately. Otherwise the filtering will be imperfect, and aliases will show up in the reconstructed signal.

8.7 Further Reading

Bracewell's book on Fourier theory [61] and the book by Oppenheim et al. [327] contain discussions of 1D sampling and reconstruction that will be useful as an expanded introduction. Additional details may be found in the books by Oppenheim and Schafer [326] and Gabel and Roberts [151].

For extensive discussions of multidimensional sampling and reconstruction, see the book by Dudgeon and Merserau [130]. They also discuss hexagonal sampling lattices in some detail. An extensive discussion of sampling and filtering issues in computer graphics is offered by Wolberg [485], who also provides a wealth of implementation information. A thorough discussion of the sampling theorem and various extensions to it is presented by Jerri [231].

8.8 Exercises

Exercise 8.1

Consider the image $d(t)$ shown across one scan line of a display device after a band-limited signal $f(t)$ has been sampled with a shah function $s(t)$ and then reconstructed with a zero-order sample-and-hold impulse response $h_p(t)$. Writing $g(t) = f(t)s(t)$, we can write this equation in both signal and Fourier spaces:

$$d(t) = g(t) * h_p(t)$$
$$D(\omega) = G(\omega)H(\omega) \tag{8.48}$$

A plot of $d(t)$ for a given $f(t)$ and an interpixel spacing W is shown in Figure 8.32.

As Figure 8.32 shows, $d(t) \neq f(t)$. We recall that when the reconstruction filter $r(t)$ is a sinc function of the appropriate frequency, then we can reconstruct $f(t)$ exactly.

To make our display match our function, we can insert a hypothetical filter with impulse response $m(t)$ into the system just before the sample-and-hold, so that the series of filters $m(t) * h_p(t) = r(t)$. In symbols,

$$f(t) = g(t) * m(t) * h_p(t)$$
$$= g(t) * r(t) \tag{8.49}$$

We know that when $m(t) * h_p(t) = r(t)$, then reconstruction will be perfect. We can find $m(t)$ by writing the system in the frequency domain, since we know both $R(\omega)$ and $H_p(\omega)$:

$$F(\omega) = G(\omega)R(\omega)$$
$$= G(\omega)M(\omega)H_p(\omega) \tag{8.50}$$

so we can solve for $M(\omega)$:

$$M(\omega) = R(\omega)/H_p(\omega) \tag{8.51}$$

(a) We might expect to see the filter $M(\omega)$ in every output device, so that the displayed signal $d(t)$ would match the original input $f(t)$. Is such a filter inside every CRT? If not, why not?

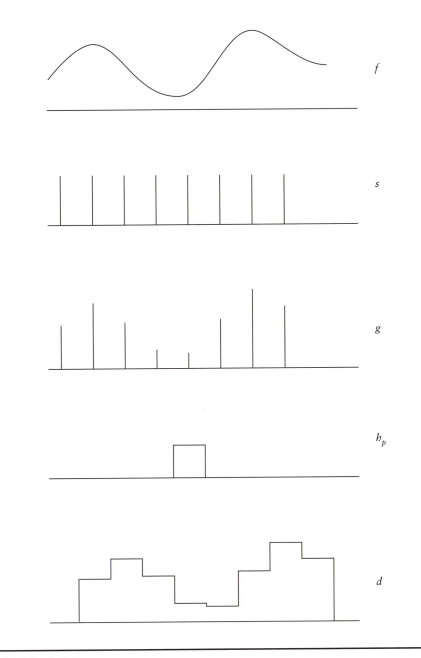

FIGURE 8.32

A simplified system diagram for device display for Exercise 8.1.

(b) If you answered no to (a), then you could still consider implementing $M(\omega)$ (or its equivalent impulse response $m(t)$) in software in a rendering program. Do you know of any software incorporating this filter? Would you advocate its inclusion in software rendering systems? If so, carefully describe where and how you would implement it. If not, explain your reasoning.

Exercise 8.2

Suppose we have a Gaussian spectrum $F(\omega) = e^{-\alpha\omega^2}$, and we assert that $F(\omega) = 0$ for all values of ω above some cutoff ω_c, so that you had a new spectrum $F'(\omega)$ such that $F'(|\omega| > \omega_c) = 0$.

(a) Write an expression for $F'(\omega)$ as the product of a Gaussian and a box.

(b) Find the inverse transform of $F'(\omega)$.

(c) Compare your answer to (b) with the inverse transform of $F(\omega)$. What can you say about the effect in the signal domain of windowing the filter in frequency space? What happens qualitatively to the spectrum as the cutoff frequency moves in toward the center of the hump? What does this require of the time signal?

(d) Answer parts (a) through (c), but reverse the domains. That is, consider a time signal $f(t) = e^{-\alpha t^2}$, clipped to zero for all $t > t_c$, so you had a new signal $f'(t)$ such that $f'(|t| > t_c) = 0$. Find the Fourier transform of $f(t)$, $f'(t)$, and compare them as in (c).

(e) Compare your answers to parts (c) and (d). Where would you window the Gaussian: frequency space, signal space, or both?

(f) How would you apply a clipped Gaussian in signal space?

Once is an instance. Twice may be an accident.
But three times or more makes a pattern.

Diane Ackerman
(Preface, in "By Nature's Design," Pat Murphy
and William Neill, 1993)

9

NONUNIFORM SAMPLING AND RECONSTRUCTION

9.1 Introduction

This chapter discusses the signal processing theory behind *nonuniform sampling*, which is the label we give to any sampling pattern that cannot be described as a regular lattice. Nonuniform signal processing has become important in computer graphics in recent years for two principal reasons: it offers us the chance to use *variable sampling density*, and it allows us to *trade structured aliasing for noise*. We will discuss these ideas in turn.

9.1.1 Variable Sampling Density

Consider the typical modern image-synthesis system. To generate an image, we need to estimate the image-plane signal. From a signal-processing point of view, this requires sampling the underlying continuous image signal at a rate above the Nyquist frequency. There is a tremendous range of image types and image complexities, and

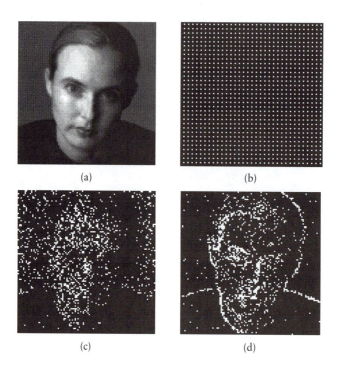

(a) (b)

(c) (d)

FIGURE 9.1

(a) An image we would like to sample. (b) The high sampling density required for the face induces a
high-density pattern everywhere. (c) An adaptive pattern where density is proportional to intensity.
(d) An adaptive pattern where density is proportional to local contrast.

we don't yet have a good measure to describe a "typical" image, or even to categorize
the types of images. But most images made today, whether intended for use as stills
or frames of animation, are typically not of uniform complexity. There are regions
of great complexity (typically in the foreground, where there can be many objects
and textures) and regions of relative uniformity (typically in the background or
in shadows, where the image function is constant or only slowly changing). In
computer graphics every sample is sufficiently expensive that we don't want to waste
even a single sample of the image function; each sample is very expensive to compute.
Where should our samples be placed so they will do us the most good?

Uniform sampling establishes a single, constant sampling density across the image.
For example, consider Figure 9.1(a). If we want to capture the high-frequency
information in the foreground of the scene, then we need a sampling rate that will

satisfy the Nyquist limit in that region. Because uniform sampling applies the same sampling pattern everywhere in the scene, the entire image plane will be covered with the pattern generated in response to that one region, as shown in Figure 9.1(b). This image has a smooth, flat background, so we will take many identical samples of this background, even though the frequency information in this part of the scene is very low.

This seems wasteful, but the only technique we have discussed so far for increasing the sampling density anywhere is to increase the sampling density everywhere. Our intuition may say that in smooth regions, such as the background of Figure 9.1(a), we only need a few samples, widely spaced, in contrast to the dense distribution needed in the foreground. Such sampling distributions are shown in Figure 9.1(c) and (d). Although we have been discussing a concrete example, these issues apply to any signal.

Note that there is no theoretical principle stopping us from placing and evaluating samples anywhere we want. But completely unstructured sampling raises two problems: the first is to figure out how many samples we need in each region of the signal, and the second is what to do with the samples once we've evaluated them. These are the *refinement* and *reconstruction* problems, discussed next.

We solved the refinement problem in the example by observation, but in general we would like an automatic method that will determine where a high sampling density is required, and where a lower-density distribution will do. This is called *adaptive sampling*. We will discuss some approaches to adaptive sampling below and in the next chapter.

The second problem mentioned above is *reconstruction*: what we should do with the samples once they have been evaluated. When the samples aren't on a regular lattice, we are faced with *nonuniform reconstruction*. Typically we will want to take our high-density samples and somehow reduce them to a single value representative of the region. In previous chapters we saw that to accomplish this with uniform samples, we could reconstruct a continuous-time signal from the samples, low-pass filter that signal to the Nyquist limit of the resampling grid, and then resample the filtered signal. This basic idea still holds, but the reconstruction part is harder. All of our sampling and reconstruction formulas in Chapter 8 were based on samples taken in equal increments of T, the sampling rate. If we sample adaptively as discussed above, then we may have holes in our string of regularly spaced samples, or they may not even be spaced on a regular grid at all. We will need new methods to reconstruct from nonuniform samples; these are discussed in this chapter and the next.

9.1.2 Trading Aliasing for Noise

All of the signal processing theory in the preceding chapters has been built on the assumption that our samples are regularly spaced by an equal amount. In 1D, each sample was separated from the next by the sampling interval T. In 2D, each sample was T_x units from its left and right neighbors, and T_y units from its neighbors above and below; for a square grid, $T_x = T_y$. We saw that corresponding to this sampling rate is a maximum frequency that can be captured from the signal. Any energy belonging to frequencies above the Nyquist rate belonging to that sampling pattern will alias and become an inseparable part of our estimated signal.

This is a pretty bad situation, since it is common for the signals used in computer graphics to include arbitrarily high frequencies. For example, an image or illumination signal with a single sharp border, such as the silhouette of a sphere, the edge of a polygon, or the line between two squares on a black-white checkerboard, will contain infinitely high frequencies. The amount of energy drops off as the frequency goes up, but in general we don't know where the frequency cutoff point should be. Much of the time we simply sample at higher and higher rates, with increasingly dense sets of samples, until we either meet a threshold or simply give up and stop sampling.

Let's look more closely at our theory and see what we might change in an attempt to make problems such as sampling the image in Figure 9.1 more tractable. We have assumed that our samples are instantaneous values of the signal; that is, when sampling a function f with a sample at x_i, the value of the sample is $f(x_i)$. We can imagine changing this so that the value of the sample is something else, say

$$\int_{x_i-\epsilon_i}^{x_i+\epsilon_i} f(x) \tag{9.1}$$

for some choice of ϵ_i. This approach has been explored in various ways, most notably with cone tracing by Amanatides [9] and beam tracing by Heckbert and Hanrahan [211]. Those methods have merit, but they lose the simplicity of the point-sampling approach. Evaluating a signal at a single point is in general a much easier and better-understood problem than integrating over a small region; indeed, many point samples can be used to evaluate an integral, as we saw in our discussion of Monte Carlo integration in Chapter 7. Another advantage of point sampling is its computational efficiency; ray tracing is a sophisticated and efficient tool for evaluating point samples of many signals encountered in image synthesis.

A different generalization of the sampling theory we have seen so far is to change the quantization of the sample. Rather than assign a single number to the sample value, we could instead attach to it an interval, perhaps with an associated confidence function expressing our expectation of the likelihood of the various values in the interval. This approach has not been developed very much in computer graphics. The potential is interesting; perhaps we could find a way to compute rough estimates of the value of signals much more cheaply than high-accuracy values. Then many rough samples might combine to give an equally useful representation of the signal as a smaller number of accurate samples, at less cost. Although interval analysis has

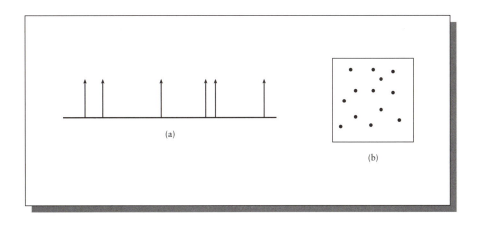

FIGURE 9.2

(a) Stochastic sampling in 1D. (b) Stochastic sampling in 2D.

appeared in computer graphics, I do not know of any reported work that explores this particular approach for rendering problems.

Another alternative is to move the samples off the regular, uniform pattern. So rather than sample a 1D signal at equal increments of T, evaluating $f(t_n) = f(nT)$, we allow the samples to fall anywhere "at random," as in Figure 9.2(a). In computer graphics, this approach is called *stochastic sampling*. The precise meaning of random in this application is important, and we will return to the subject below. Stochastic sampling may be applied in 2D, so rather than placing samples on a rectangular or hexagonal grid, we allow them to fall anywhere in the domain "at random," as in Figure 9.2(b).

Stochastic sampling is thus a special form of nonuniform sampling where the samples are *aperiodic*, meaning that there is no single structure that is repeated by translation at equal intervals across the domain. Since there is no repeated unit, there is no "pattern" associated with aperiodic sampling, but rather just a single arrangement of samples.

We will analyze some different aperiodic sampling distributions below, for different interpretations of "random" when the samples are placed. The major result of that section will be that if the samples are placed randomly in the domain, the highly structured aliasing artifacts that intrude in uniformly sampled signals turn into high-frequency *noise*. The resulting reconstructed signal is still wrong, in the sense that we have not captured all the high-frequency information contained in the original signal, but the nature of the resulting problem has changed. Figure 9.3

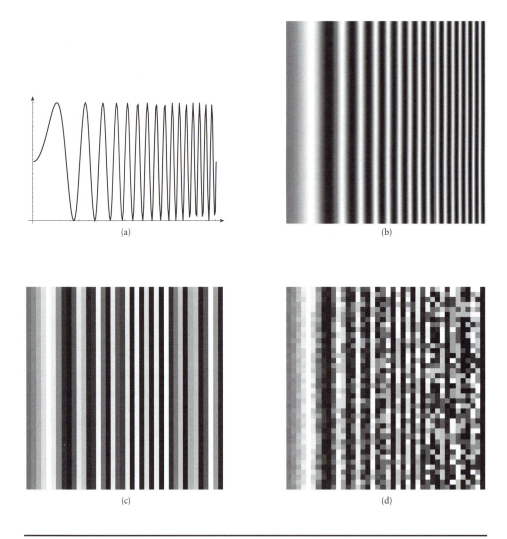

FIGURE 9.3

(a) The function $f(x) = \sin(2\pi(4x)^2)$ over the interval $[0, 1]$. (b) $f(x)$ sampled on a 200×200 grid. (c) $f(x)$ sampled on a uniform 40×40 grid; notice the aliasing on the right side. (d) $f(x)$ sampled on a jittered 40×40 grid; the regular aliasing artifacts have been turned into noise artifacts.

shows a comparison of the same image sampled uniformly and stochastically, with the same number of samples. The regular structures that come from the sampling have been turned into high-frequency noise.

Whether this is an advantage or not depends on the intended use of the sampled signal. If it is an image to be shown to a person, the noisy version is often superior because the human visual system is able to ignore a surprising amount of noise of different characteristics, while it spots structured aliasing artifacts quite easily. Thus a noisy picture can "look better" than one that is aliased, though neither is more accurate than the other in terms of the numerical quality of match to the underlying image signal. If you are creating an image for the purpose of analysis, either manually or by machine, then the noise may prove to be a greater impediment than organized aliasing errors. For these signals and others, such as illumination functions, you must consider what information is desired from the signal and how it will be used. But for many applications, stochastic sampling represents a powerful way to sample a signal that contains arbitrarily high frequencies without incurring the risk of introducing new structures that appear to be part of the signal. We will return to this subject in more detail later on.

9.1.3 Summary

This introduction has presented two main points. First, adaptive sampling is intuitively appealing, because it allows us to put more samples where they are needed, and fewer samples in smooth areas of the signal. Second, though we have not yet proven it, stochastic sampling allows us to trade regular aliasing artifacts for high-frequency noise, which is sometimes more acceptable to the human visual system when looking at images.

We need to be careful when creating noisy pictures. If the noise is of low frequency, then it can create ugly artifacts that are just as objectionable as aliasing. As a general rule of thumb for images, if the noise is beyond the Nyquist frequency, then it will look better than aliases from those frequencies.

The sections below will examine nonuniform sampling and reconstruction in more detail.

9.2 Nonuniform Sampling

There are many types of nonuniform sampling methods. Some are based on a prototype *tile*, which is a small precomputed pattern that is replicated (with transformations) over the domain. Others are based on generating sample locations on demand as the sampling proceeds.

We will explore these in turn.

9.2.1 Adaptive Sampling

As discussed above, many of the signals used in computer graphics have some regions of high complexity and detail, and other regions that are simple, in the sense that the signal is smooth or even constant within the region. Adaptive sampling methods attempt to put samples where they will do the most good by concentrating them in complex regions and leaving them sparse in simple regions.

We are rather lucky in computer graphics to have the freedom to take samples anywhere we want, and then go back and revisit the signal to gather more samples. Many other disciplines that use signal-processing techniques do not have this freedom. For example, the telephone company needs to sample and reconstruct audio signals in real time from an audio stream that only comes by once. A similar situation holds true for television transmission and reception; in a TV receiver, the video signals comes off the antenna and into the set, and there is no chance to go back and pick up missed pieces of the signal.

In signal-processing terms, the idea is to adapt the *local sampling rate* to the *local bandwidth* in a given part of the image. Although we have been discussing an image as a concrete example, these issues apply to any signal where the local bandwidth varies more than a little. We can think of the local bandwidth as the result of taking a short-term Fourier transform of the signal in some narrow region, as discussed in Chapter 6. Recall that in that chapter we pointed out some problems with the STFT. But we will use this idea mostly as a conceptual tool in this chapter and not for actual computation. We will see various practical means for estimating local bandwidth in the section on reconstruction below and in Chapter 10.

Adaptive sampling is often implemented by first sampling with a *base pattern* of some predetermined density. This creates a set of *base samples*, which form our first estimate of the image. Typically, we examine these samples to determine if we need to take more samples to refine our estimate. We evaluate the samples with respect to some *refinement criteria*. If we decide more samples are required, then we invoke a *refinement strategy* that creates and evaluates additional samples in the region. This step may only be applied once, resulting in a *two-stage refinement strategy*. More generally, the refinement step may be applied iteratively until the criteria are met or some upper limit on the number of iterations is exceeded, in effect refining our sampling of the signal. This sampling technique is called *adaptive refinement*.

The central issues in adaptive refinement are how to estimate the local bandwidth of the signal, where to place new samples, and what criteria to use to terminate the refinement process.

Kirk and Arvo have pointed out [246] that the most straightforward form of refinement procedure tends to introduce a bias into the final result. The problem is that there is a subtle connection between the values of the base samples, the refinement test, and the value of the final set of samples.

They demonstrate this with an elegant argument presented below. The departure

```
EstimateMean(S,T)                    Draw n samples from signal X.
    S ← {X₁, X₂, ..., Xₙ}
    if quality(Sₙ) > T               Do the initial samples meet our criteria?
    then
        μ ← S̄                       Yes, the easy case. Use the sample mean.
    else
        μ ← TrueMean(S)              No, the hard case. Invoke the oracle.
    endif
    return(μ)
end
```

FIGURE 9.4

Simple but biased adaptive refinement.

point is the pseudocode shown in Figure 9.4 that shows a simple form of adaptive sampling. We will assume that our goal is to find the mean value of a signal within some region; this is often what we are after in image synthesis.

The refinement function is called with an initial set of n base samples S_i, and some quality condition T. If the samples meet the quality condition, then we use the mean of those samples as our estimate of the true mean. Otherwise, we invoke some more costly procedure to get a better estimate of the mean. Kirk and Arvo refer to this step as "invoking an oracle," which is meant to imply that the second procedure is expensive but perfectly accurate and always returns the true mean. This oracle is typically approximated by taking many additional samples and averaging them, though other implementations are possible.

The procedure of Figure 9.4 is *biased*, meaning that we can expect the presence of some consistent, repeatable error from any input. To isolate the bias in the technique, we will construct a simple test case. Imagine that we are sampling a square domain with area 1 made up of k vertical stripes of different widths, as in Figure 9.5. Each stripe i has area w_i and constant intensity value I_i. The true mean value $\bar{I}$ of this signal is then

$$\bar{I} = \sum_{i=1}^{k} I_k w_k \qquad (9.2)$$

(because the square has unit area and the stripes tile the square, the weights are normalized; that is, $\sum_{i=1}^{k} w_i = 1$).

Let's now find the value returned by the algorithm in Figure 9.4. We will assign probabilities $P[\text{easy}]$ and $P[\text{hard}]$ to our chances of getting an easy or hard set of

FIGURE 9.5

The geometry for analyzing bias.

samples, and expected values $E[\mu_{\text{easy}}]$ and $E[\mu_{\text{hard}}]$ to the value of the mean computed for the two cases. Note that $P[\text{hard}] = 1 - P[\text{easy}]$. The expected value of the algorithm is then the two expected values weighted by their respective probabilities:

$$
\begin{aligned}
E[\mu] = {} & P[\mu_{\text{easy}}] \times E[\mu_{\text{easy}}] \\
& + P[\mu_{\text{hard}}] \times E[\mu_{\text{hard}}]
\end{aligned} \tag{9.3}
$$

This problem fits the standard probability model for *repeated Bernoulli trials with multiple results* (discussed in Appendix B). For this type of problem, we organize our samples by how many strike each region. Thus we might find that m_1 samples strike region 1, m_2 samples strike region 2, and so on. The theory tells us that the probability of getting these m_i strikes from n samples from k results with weights w_i is given by Equation B.12:

$$
P[m_1, m_2, \ldots, m_k] = \frac{n!}{m_1! \, m_2! \cdots m_k!} w_1^{m_1} w_2^{m_2} \cdots w_k^{m_k} \tag{9.4}
$$

For any particular input, we can find $E[\mu]$ from Equation 9.4 for all possible outcomes $(m_1, m_2, \ldots, m_k)$ and then weight the results by the corresponding probabilities $P[\text{easy}]$ and $P[\text{hard}]$.

We would like to find a more useful form of Equation 9.3. We begin by filling in the placeholder for the easy case with real values. Let us assume that the quality test requires that all of the n samples have the same value. Then in this easy case, all but one m_i in Equation 9.4 goes to zero (since only one type of event can occur), $n = m_i$, and we get

$$
P[\text{easy}] = w_1^n + w_2^n + \cdots + w_k^n \tag{9.5}
$$

We now turn to the expected value from this result. We know that all n values are the same, but we can't predict which value they will all take on. We can find the expected value as a sum of the individual stripe values, normalized by the weights and taking into account our n samples:

$$E[\text{easy}] = \frac{w_1{}^n I_1 + w_2{}^n I_2 + \cdots + w_k{}^n I_n}{w_1{}^n + w_2{}^n + \cdots + w_k{}^n} \tag{9.6}$$

Substitute these results into Equation 9.3, and recalling $P[\text{hard}] = 1 - P[\text{easy}]$, we find

$$E[\mu] = \mu + \sum_{i=1}^{k} w_i{}^n (I_i - \mu) \tag{9.7}$$

Since the true mean is given by μ, the right-hand term of Equation 9.7 represents an error in our expected value that will usually not be zero; this is the bias.

This bias is introduced because the statistics of the initial sample influence both our test and our calculation of the final value. The problem is somewhat like the situation when a number of unlikely events all happen simultaneously or in quick succession. For example, suppose you're playing a game of cards, and you draw three sevens in a row. You might think that you've experienced something remarkable, compute the (low) probability that you would draw three sevens in a row, and wonder at the unlikely event. This is very human, but a little deceptive. Unlikely events happen all the time; after all, someone almost always wins every lottery drawing. The right way to view the amount of surprise in a situation is to ask yourself *beforehand* if that situation is likely to occur; then you have correctly set yourself up to react if it does come about. In the sampling case, the trick is to ask questions about the samples before they are drawn, not to analyze them afterward.

To remove the bias, we need to eliminate this relationship between the evaluated samples and decisions made on their likelihood. Kirk and Arvo present a modified algorithm, shown in Figure 9.6, that avoids the bias problem.

The basic idea is that we first draw a "pilot" set of samples from some region R contained within X. Those samples are used to estimate the mean of the signal within R only. We then test those samples; if they are sufficiently different, then we will take n_2 samples from the remaining domain $X - R$. Otherwise, we will take n_1 samples from this region. Typically, $n_2 \gg n_1$, so we take many samples when the pilot set is diverse, and only a few when it is more uniform. These new values are then used to estimate the mean in $X - R$. The two means are then added together, weighted by the relative sizes of the two domains.

Kirk and Arvo note that this method will typically take too many or too few samples. In smooth regions, we would like R to be small, so that only a few samples need to be taken to confirm that the signal is easy in this region. When the signal is very complex, we want a large R in order to capture that complexity and trigger the higher-density sampling. Since we don't know the signal, we must take a guess for

UnbiasedEstimateMean(S, R, p, n_1, n_2, T)

$S_p \leftarrow \{X_1, X_2, \ldots, X_p\} \subset R \subset X$	*Draw p samples from region R in X.*
if quality$(S_p) > T$	
then $n \leftarrow n_1$	*Do we need only a few more samples or many?*
else $n \leftarrow n_2$	
endif	
$S_n \leftarrow \{X_1, X_2, \ldots, X_n\} \subset X - R$	*Take more samples from unsampled region of X.*
$\mu_p \leftarrow \overline{S_p} \cdot \|R\|$	*Find means for each sample set.*
$\mu_n \leftarrow \overline{S_n} \cdot \|X - R\|$	
$\mu \leftarrow \mu_p + \mu_n$	*Get the combined mean and return it.*
return(ξ)	
end	

FIGURE 9.6

Unbiased adaptive refinement.

R. If we guess too low, then the initial samples don't contribute much to the final mean, and they become less valuable. If we guess too high, then we take superfluous samples when the region is smooth.

Correcting for bias is an important theoretical point, but it is not clear at present how much it affects practical problems in computer graphics. The cost can be nontrivial, as mentioned above, since we never want to waste even a single sample.

There have not yet been any published analyses indicating how much bias is tolerable in different parts of the rendering process. The best approach is probably a conservative one: we should avoid bias whenever possible.

In the next chapter we will see a variety of techniques that have been proposed for carrying out adaptive sampling. There are many different refinement criteria used to trigger higher-density sampling, and different means for placing samples, but they all boil down to evaluating a coarse distribution of samples to estimate the local bandwidth of the signal, and then taking additional samples in regions where the bandwidth is high.

We mentioned earlier that nonuniform sampling allows us to trade structured aliasing artifacts for noise. Consider that an aliasing problem arises because high frequencies beyond the Nyquist limit overlap with the original spectrum of the signal. These higher frequencies represent periodic sine and cosine signals and they combine to create what appear to be new structures in our reconstructed signal. In other words, the effect of aliasing isn't to simply make the reconstructed signal a poor approximation of the original; it makes the signal wrong in highly structured ways.

For an image, these structures are particularly bad because the human visual system is very good at detecting them. Even in more abstract situations such as shading, some algorithms may be particularly sensitive to structure in the original signal, which can damage the numerical accuracy of the simulation and ultimately cause visual artifacts such as erroneous shadows or highlights. A high-frequency problem (noise) is less likely to cause these large structured problems than a low-frequency problem (structured aliasing). High-frequency foldover is still aliasing, but we distinguish it with the term *noise* because of its unstructured effect on the signal.

9.2.2 Aperiodic Sampling

The point of this section is to show that when samples are taken aperiodically, then we can completely eliminate structured aliasing. Since the resulting sampled signal isn't perfect, the error must go somewhere, and we show that it goes into noise (or unstructured aliasing). By choosing our sampling pattern carefully, we can choose how much of that noise is distributed into different frequencies. Since the human visual system is more tolerant of high- than low-frequency noise, we will typically want to push our sampling errors into the highest frequencies that we can achieve.

The characteristics of aperiodic sampling that distinguish it from periodic sampling are the increased likelihood of sampling all regular structures in the signal, and the transformation of coherent aliasing into incoherent noise. Both of these can be beneficial in some circumstances.

We mentioned above that nonuniform sampling can trade periodic structures (aliases) for noise. We can derive this important result by looking at the Fourier transform of an appropriate aperiodic sequence. The basic theory for this analysis was presented by Leneman in a series of papers in the late 1960s [262–265], which were applied to graphics by Dippé and Wold [124]. This section will give an overview of the derivation of the basic results leading to the spectral characteristics of a signal sampled with a nonuniform pattern. We will follow the developments as described in references [124] and [265].

A few definitions will help us get started. An *impulse process* may be considered a train of pulses characterized by some statistical parameters (note that the term *process* is used here as roughly a synonym for sequence). For example, we will focus on the impulse process $s(t)$ given by

$$s(t) = \sum_{t=-\infty}^{\infty} \alpha_n \delta(t_n) \tag{9.8}$$

where the values $\{t_n\}$ are not uniform. This creates a series of impulses that are not spaced at equal intervals.

If one or more of these pulses is missing, we call it a *skip process*. If the amplitudes α_n are unequal, then it is called a *weighted process*. We will limit our attention in this book to processes where all $\alpha_n = 1$. Initially we will assume there are no skips; we will relax this requirement later on.

It is difficult to directly take the Fourier transform of a class of statistical signals, because we would have to choose a single instance of the parameters to create a single, specific signal. This would defeat our intention to retain the statistical nature of the signal in the transform. It is better to try to work with the collection of all signals specified by a set of parameters, called the *ensemble*. Studying properties of the ensemble tells us what to expect statistically from signals that belong to it.

A basic tool for studying statistical signals is the *autocorrelation*. The autocorrelation of a signal f is written $R_f(t)$ (or sometimes $C(t)$). The autocorrelation tells us how well a signal overlaps with itself when shifted. The idea is to move the signal left or right by a given amount t, multiply the shifted signal with the original, unshifted signal, and then find the expected value of the result. For example, suppose the signal is a constant. Then the autocorrelation is also a constant: for every shift of the signal, it lines up with itself perfectly. A sine wave of period 2π has an autocorrelation of 1 for $t = 0$, but a value of 0 at $t = \pi$, when the shifted signal exactly cancels the original. We can write the autocorrelation for any shift t as the expected value of the signal multiplied by its shifted version:

$$R_f(t) = E[f(t + \tau)f(t)] \tag{9.9}$$

We note that the *cross-correlation* of two signals f and g is defined similarly:

$$R_{fg}(t) = E[f(t + \tau)g(t)] \tag{9.10}$$

The Fourier transform of the autocorrelation is called the *power spectral density* of the function (PSD, or *spectral density*). We will represent the PSD of a function f as $\Psi_f(\omega)$. Intuitively, the PSD expresses the Fourier transform of the ensemble of signals, though each individual instance may vary.

The autocorrelation of $s(t)$ in Equation 9.8 is given by Leneman [265]:

$$R_s(t) = \beta(\delta(t) + \beta) \tag{9.11}$$

where β is the average number of impulses per unit interval of time. The PSD for s is given by

$$\Psi_s(\omega) = \mathcal{F}\{R_s(t)\} = \beta[1 + 2\pi\beta\delta(\omega)] \tag{9.12}$$

Equation 9.12 tells us that the transform of our nonuniform pulse train is a flat spectrum of noise of constant amplitude β, with a single spike at ω. What happens when we sample a signal with this nonuniform train of impulses?

We can't simply convolve this with the Fourier transform of a signal, because this is a PSD. Dippé and Wold suggested that to do the analysis, we consider a hypothetical class of signals f which is constructed so that we can find its autocorrelation R_f, and thus its PSD Ψ_f. Then the sampling operation is represented by multiplying the autocorrelations, giving us a sampled signal g (here described by its autocorrelation R_g):

$$R_g(t) = R_f(t)R_s(t) \qquad (9.13)$$

This multiplication in the time domain turns into convolution in the frequency domain. We don't know $\Psi_f(\omega)$, but we can use our result for $\Psi_s(\omega)$ from Equation 9.12 above:

$$
\begin{aligned}
\Psi_g(\omega) &= \Psi_f(\omega) * \Psi_s(\omega) \\
&= \Psi_f(\omega) * \beta[1 + 2\pi\beta\delta(\omega)] \\
&= \beta \int \Psi_f(\omega)\, d\omega + 2\pi\beta^2 \Psi_f(\omega) \\
&= \beta k_p + (2\pi\beta^2)\Psi_f(\omega) \qquad (9.14)
\end{aligned}
$$

Equation 9.14 is very important: it shows that our sampled signal is *completely free of aliasing*!

Equation 9.14 says that the result of sampling a signal f with an impulse train $s(t)$ is a signal whose PSD consists of a flat sea of noise of amplitude βk_p, and a single copy of the PSD of the signal, scaled by $2\pi\beta^2$.

The most significant point of the discussion so far is that Equation 9.14 contains only one copy of the transform of the signal. Recall that when we sampled with a uniform impulse train, we created endless copies of the original spectrum in the sampled signal. We called these aliases, and we needed to design and apply filters that would remove these aliases without introducing new artifacts or removing useful information. On the other hand, when we sample with a set of nonuniform impulses, we get no aliasing at all. Instead, we get a sea of noise surrounding a single copy of the PSD of the image. Most images are not appropriate for this analysis, but the results encourage us to find practical methods for eliminating aliasing by using a judicial choice of the sampling pattern [124].

Dippé and Wold give a practical example of this analysis for a sampling pattern where the impulses are at time t_k, given by

$$t_{k+1} = t_k + d_k \qquad (9.15)$$

where the d_k are increments that are generated by an exponential distribution. We will also impose a *minimum-distance constraint*, which we will find useful in later chapters. We require impulses to be separated by a minimum distance d_0:

$$
d_k \sim p(d_k) = \begin{cases} \alpha e^{-\alpha(d_k - d_0)} & d_k > d_0 \\ 0 & \text{otherwise} \end{cases} \qquad (9.16)
$$

where $\sim$ indicates that d_k is drawn from the distribution given by $p(d_k)$. The average distance between samples is given by the expected value of d_k:

$$E[d_k] = \alpha/(1 + \alpha d_0) \qquad (9.17)$$

When $d_0 = 0$, then this is uniformly distributed random sampling with an average density $\beta = \alpha$. When $\alpha \to \infty$, the pattern becomes a uniform pattern with sampling rate $\beta = 1/d_0$. The resulting power spectrum for this pattern [124] is

$$
\psi_s(\omega) =
\begin{cases}
\beta \left[1 - \dfrac{2\alpha\omega \sin(d_0\omega) + 2\alpha^2 \cos(d_0\omega) - 2\alpha^2}{2\alpha\omega \sin(d_0\omega) - 2\alpha^2 \cos(d_0\omega) + \omega^2 + 2\alpha^2} \right] & \omega \neq 0 \\[4mm]
2\pi\beta^2\delta(\omega) & \omega = 0
\end{cases}
\tag{9.18}
$$

Figure 9.7 shows plots of Equation 9.18 for different values of $d_0\alpha$. Notice that by increasing $d_0\alpha$, we can reduce the amount of low-frequency noise in the pattern and transfer that energy to higher frequencies.

We now turn to *jittered* sampling. We will discuss this in more detail later, but the basic idea is that we generate a series of regular impulses, and then move each one left or right from its original position [27]. We can write a jittered impulse train as

$$
s(t) = \sum_n \delta(nT + u_n)
\tag{9.19}
$$

where the u_n are independent, uniformly distributed values drawn from the distribution $p(u_k)$.

Leneman [265] uses the symbol $\gamma(\omega)$ to stand for the Fourier transform of $p(u_k)$ defined in Equation 9.16. Dippé and Wold [124] show that for this type of sampling pattern, the PSD is given by

$$
\Psi_s(\omega) = \beta \left[1 - |\gamma(\omega)|^2 \right] + 2\pi\beta^2 |\gamma(\omega)|^2 \sum_{k=-\infty}^{\infty} \delta(\omega - k2\pi\beta)
\tag{9.20}
$$

The term on the left is flat noise, as we saw in Equation 9.14. But on the right we see an endless number of impulses; this will lead to endless copies of the signal spectrum if we sample with this pattern, so it appears that we're back to aliasing.

But all is not lost. Notice that the delta functions are modulated by the jitter transform $|\gamma(\omega)|^2$. If we choose the distribution pattern carefully, then we can make this function go to zero exactly where the impulses appear. If we use a rectangular distribution for $p(u_k)$, then its Fourier transform will be a sinc function. By matching the width of the box to the interval $2\pi\beta$, we can cancel out the impulses. Specifically, if $p(u_k)$ is a box over the interval $[-1/2\beta, 1/2\beta]$:

$$
p(u_k) =
\begin{cases}
1 & -1/2\beta \leq u_k \leq 1/2\beta \\
0 & \text{otherwise}
\end{cases}
\tag{9.21}
$$

then

$$
\gamma(\omega) = \text{sinc}(\omega/2\beta)
\tag{9.22}
$$

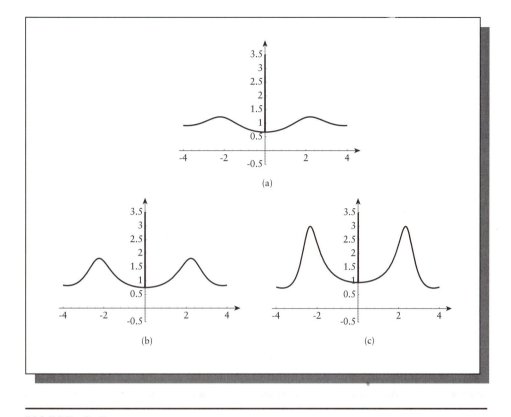

FIGURE 9.7

Equation 9.18 plotted for (a) $d_0\alpha = 0.2$, (b) $d_0\alpha = 0.5$, and (c) $d_0\alpha = 0.9$.

so the resulting sampling spectrum is

$$\Psi_s(\omega) = \beta \left[1 - \mathrm{sinc}^2(\omega/2\beta)\right] + 2\pi\beta^2\delta(\omega) \tag{9.23}$$

This PSD is shown in Figure 9.8. Note that the periodic impulses are exactly canceled out.

Thus sampling with jitter distributed according to a $p(u_k)$ such as that in Equation 9.21 gives us a sampling pattern that completely avoids aliasing! Because they avoid aliasing, nonuniform sampling patterns have proven to be very useful in practical rendering systems.

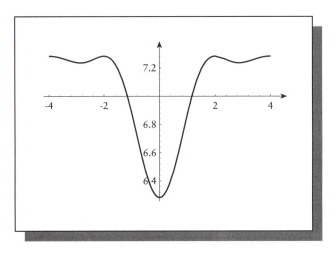

FIGURE 9.8

A plot of Equation 9.23.

9.2.3 Sampling Pattern Comparison

One way to compare the quality of different sampling patterns is by computing the power spectral distribution of the ensemble specified by a given·process. Another approach was suggested by Chen and Allebach [81], who compare patterns based on the mean-squared error between the sampled signal and an original. Since the error depends both on the sample locations and the signal, if we want to compare the patterns alone, the dependence on the signal must somehow be factored out. They do this by considering the maximum of the mean-squared error over a class of signals.

Chen and Allebach call each pattern a *point set*, and notate it as X_i. The general approach is similar to what we have seen before; the reconstructed function is a linear combination of the N samples and a reconstruction filter ϕ:

$$\widehat{f}(x) = \sum_{i=0}^{N} b_i \phi(x - x_i) \tag{9.24}$$

In matrix form, we can write

$$\mathbf{f} = \mathbf{\Phi b} \tag{9.25}$$

or, in tableau,

$$
\begin{bmatrix} f(x_0) \\ f(x_1) \\ \vdots \\ f(x_N) \end{bmatrix} = \begin{bmatrix} \phi(x_1 - x_1) & \phi(x_2 - x_1) & \cdots & \phi(x_N - x_1) \\ \phi(x_2 - x_1) & & & \vdots \\ \vdots & & & \vdots \\ \phi(x_N - x_1) & \cdots & \cdots & \phi(x_N - x_N) \end{bmatrix} \begin{bmatrix} b_0 \\ b_1 \\ \vdots \\ b_N \end{bmatrix} \tag{9.26}
$$

Each point set has a corresponding *point set matrix*, $\boldsymbol{\Phi}_i$. Each element l, m of matrix $\boldsymbol{\Phi}$ is defined by

$$
\Phi_{l,m} = \Phi(|x_m - x_l|) \tag{9.27}
$$

where $|x_m - x_l|$ is the distance between the two sample locations m and l, and the function ϕ is the reconstruction filter, as in Equation 9.25. Note that the point set matrix is in one-to-one correspondence with the point set.

For example, when $\boldsymbol{\Phi}$ is the 2D separable sinc function,

$$
\Phi_{l,m} = \mathrm{sinc}[\mathbf{U}(x_l - x_m)] \, \mathrm{sinc}[\mathbf{V}(y_l - y_m)] \tag{9.28}
$$

When $\mathbf{U}$ and $\mathbf{V}$ are orthogonal vectors, and the samples are uniformly spaced, then Equation 9.25 coincides with the uniform reconstruction theorem.

Chen and Allebach proposed that the quality of the point set matrix (and thus the point sets themselves) may be measured by the mean square average of the quality of a signal sampled with that point set over many signals of the same energy. They present a minimax argument for ranking two matrices [81]. Suppose we have a function Λ which accepts a matrix as an argument and returns the largest eigenvalue in the matrix. Then matrix $\boldsymbol{\Phi}_A$ is preferred over matrix $\boldsymbol{\Phi}_B$ if $\Lambda(\boldsymbol{\Phi}_A) \leq \Lambda(\boldsymbol{\Phi}_B)$. This argument may be extended to sort any number of matrices by preference.

They note that for large matrices, it may be prohibitively expensive to compute the eigenvalues. They offer two other "goodness criteria" that approximate the eigenvalue measurement. The first says that matrix $\boldsymbol{\Phi}_A$ is preferred over matrix $\boldsymbol{\Phi}_B$ if $||\boldsymbol{\Phi}_A||^2 \leq ||\boldsymbol{\Phi}_B||^2$. Here, $||\boldsymbol{\Phi}_A||$ is the Euclidean norm of the matrix:

$$
||\boldsymbol{\Phi}_A|| = \sum_{l=0}^{N} \sum_{m=0}^{N} (\Phi_{lm})^2 \tag{9.29}
$$

The other alternative measurement is that matrix $\boldsymbol{\Phi}_A$ is preferred over matrix $\boldsymbol{\Phi}_B$ if $Q(\boldsymbol{\Phi}_A) \leq Q(\boldsymbol{\Phi}_B)$. Here the function Q is given by

$$
Q(\boldsymbol{\Phi}) = \max_i Q_i
$$
$$
Q_i = \sum_{k \neq i} |\Phi_{ik}| \tag{9.30}
$$

Chen and Allebach found that the rankings produced by the two approximate goodness measures were roughly similar to the more expensive eigenvalue measure.

One way to understand these measures is to think about how they classify some well-understood matrices. For example, suppose matrix Φ_A is the identity matrix, and matrix Φ_B is a matrix of all 1s. The identity matrix corresponds to completely uniform samples spaced at multiples of the Nyquist interval, using the definition of Φ in 9.28. The matrix of all 1s corresponds to all the samples superimposed on each other in one place (there is 0 distance between any two of them). In these extreme examples the measures all prefer the uniform matrix A to the degenerate single-point matrix B.

9.3   Informed Sampling

Now that we have freed our samples from an underlying grid, how might we distribute them to our best advantage? There are two popular techniques for placing samples to reduce the number needed for a good estimate of the signal. They are both based on our knowing something about the characteristics of the signal before we begin. This may seem an unreasonable demand; after all, if we knew much about the signal before sampling, then we might not need to sample it at all. This is true, but we are usually in a situation between perfect ignorance and perfect wisdom, and have some general but incomplete knowledge of the signal that we can use to our advantage.

The two methods are based on ideas very similar to the placement of sample points for Monte Carlo integration in Chapter 7, so we will use the same terminology as in that chapter. The first method is called *stratified sampling*. The idea here is to break up the domain into disjoint regions, and then place one sample into each region. This prevents our samples from all clumping together in one place and missing big pieces of the domain. The second method is called *importance sampling*, and basically tries to direct our sampling process to take more samples in regions where the signal has a large value (and thus makes an important contribution to our estimate), while conserving samples where the signal is small (and therefore less important).

9.4   Stratified Sampling

The method of *stratification* is based on the realization that if we simply take samples of a signal at random places in a domain, we could be very unlucky and the first n samples might all land in the same region, causing them to clump together, as in Figure 9.9.

If the samples are really placed "at random," with uniformly distributed random numbers, then eventually we expect them to cover the domain uniformly. The

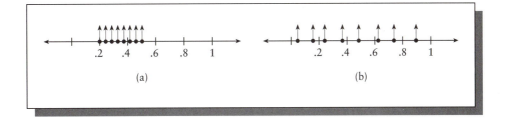

FIGURE 9.9

(a) The first eight samples are all clumped together. (b) The first eight samples are rather well distributed.

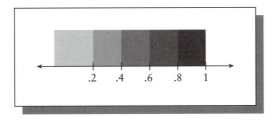

FIGURE 9.10

A domain broken up into strata.

problem is that we want a pretty uniform distribution right away, so that our first few samples give us a good estimate of what's happening everywhere in the domain.

To this end, we break the domain into *strata*, or regions that fill the domain without gaps or overlaps, as in Figure 9.10. The strata need not all be the same size or shape.

Mathematically, we are breaking up our signal into a sum of distinct, independent signals. Suppose we have a 1D signal $f(t)$ over the interval $[0, 1]$, and we break up the domain into four equal-sized intervals, as in Figure 9.11. Each of these intervals then will receive one sample. We are effectively decomposing f into four functions, each defined over an interval of width $1/4$:

$$f(t) = \sum_{i=0}^{3} f(t) b_{1/4}\left(\frac{2i+1}{8}\right) \qquad (9.31)$$

where $b_{1/4}(t)$ is a box of width $1/4$ centered at t.

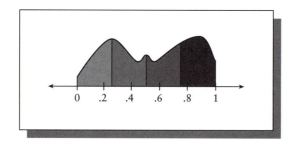

FIGURE 9.11

A signal in the interval [0,1] broken into four equal strata.

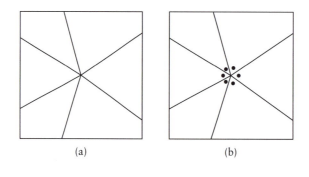

(a)　　　　　　　　(b)

FIGURE 9.12

A poor choice of strata can allow samples to clump together. (a) A stratification of a square. (b) An unlucky sample placement that defeats this stratification.

When a domain has been stratified, our *base* (or starting) sampling will usually take one sample within each stratum. The samples can still clump together locally, as in Figure 9.9, but they can't all land in roughly the same area unless the strata are poorly designed and allow this to happen. An example of a poor decimation of a 2D domain is shown in Figure 9.12, where the strata form wedges that all meet at a common vertex. In this example all of our samples could still end up near the center. Thus it isn't enough just to stratify the domain; the stratification must be designed to enforce a roughly uniform distribution of points.

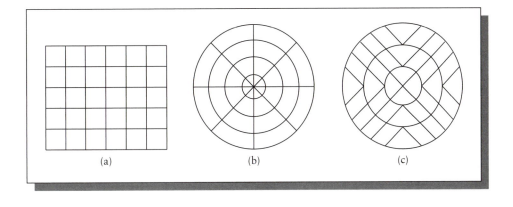

FIGURE 9.13

(a) A common stratification for a square domain. (b) A common stratification for a circular domain. (c) An alternate circular stratification due to Shirley [402].

Stratification for square and circular domains may be based on rectangular and polar coordinate systems, as shown in Figure 9.13. This figure also shows a circular stratification due to Shirley [402].

The big advantage of stratified sampling as presented so far over purely random sampling is that we are guaranteed that the samples are not all clumped together in one place. The big disadvantage is that we must decide, before sampling, the number of strata and their shapes. This can be a difficult decision, particularly when we want to start with a sparse sampling density and gradually increase it.

The method of *adaptive stratified sampling* has been developed to ameliorate this problem. The method depends on an auxiliary data structure that is maintained during sampling, so we will defer a complete description until Chapter 10 when we survey practical sampling techniques. The basic idea is that we can start with an initial stratification of a domain, which may be as sparse as desired. If we want to take one more sample, then we can choose a stratum and split it, as in Figure 9.14.

The sample we have already evaluated will fall into one of the the two newly created strata, so we can generate a sample in the other stratum and evaluate it. The process may be repeated as many times as necessary to fulfill the refinement criteria. Important issues in this algorithm involve choosing which stratum to split, and how to split it.

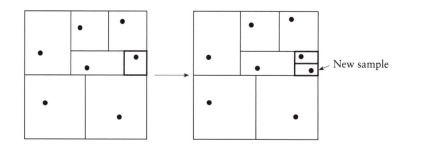

FIGURE 9.14

Splitting a stratum.

9.4.1 Importance Sampling

Another way to make our samples count is try to make sure that each one represents a useful quantity of information. We could define information in a formal sense as in information theory [19], but that would take us rather far afield, and there is instead an intuitive definition that works well.

Consider the 1D signal shown in Figure 9.15(a). In the range $[t_1, t_2]$, the value of the signal varies, but in general it is much smaller than the values in the interval $[t_3, t_4]$.

Suppose the signal of Figure 9.15(a) represents energy (such as the light energy striking a point on an image plane or object surface), and we want to sample the signal with N samples.

We assert that the best distribution of N samples would be one where each sample represents an equal amount of energy. If we have a plot of the signal, as in Figure 9.15(a), then we can break it up into a series of abutting rectangles, where the height of each rectangle is the value of the function at its center, and its width is such that the total area of each rectangle is the same, as in Figure 9.15(b). Placing the samples in such a way that each one represents the same amount of energy is called *importance sampling*. The term may be thought of as indicating that each sample has the same importance, or that when measured linearly along the t axis in the figure, there are more samples per unit area where the signal has a large value, and therefore there are more samples in "important" parts of the signal.

It can legitimately be claimed that regions where the signal is 0 are every bit as important as where it is not. But since every sample is expensive, we want every sample to contribute as much as possible to our knowledge of the integral. Consider a signal over the domain $[0, 1]$ that is zero in the left half $[0, .5]$ and a linear ramp

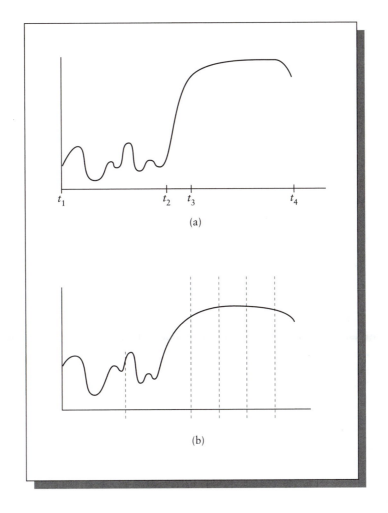

FIGURE 9.15

(a) A 1D signal. (b) The signal divided into N regions of equal energy.

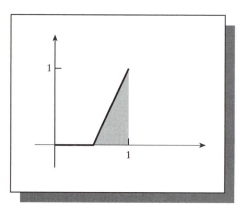

FIGURE 9.16

A half-flat, half-ramp signal.

from 0 to 1 in the right half $[.5, 1]$, as in Figure 9.16. The integral of this signal is 0.25. Now suppose that although this is a trival signal, it's actually the result of some very expensive simulation and every sample comes at great cost. If we take a whole bunch of samples in the left half, they are all going to be 0 and will not contribute to the integral. It's important to look at the left half, of course, but if we know that it's 0 (or even just small compared to the right half), then most of the contribution to the integral will come from the right half. We are better served by placing samples in the "important" regions when we want the best answers as quickly as possible.

Note that in importance sampling the signal has been divided up into equal areas, not equal parametric intervals.

As with stratified sampling, this approach may seem difficult to implement because it requires knowing the function in advance before we can decide where the samples should be placed. This time it's even harder to get information, though, because instead of dividing up the domain of the signal (which we usually have some knowledge of), we need to divide up the integral of the signal (which is just what we're trying to find).

If that's all we knew about the signal, then importance sampling might not get us very far. But in computer graphics we almost never seek just the integral of a signal; there is almost always another function applied to that signal to modulate it. For example, on the image plane there's the pixel-based reconstruction filter on top of each sample, and when the signal is an illumination signal at a point, the reflectance function of the object at that point is applied to the illumination. As these examples illustrate, the signal $s(t)$ is usually modulated by some filter function $f(t)$ to produce a composite signal $s(t) f(t)$. And in general, we know (or can get access to) $f(t)$ even when $s(t)$ is completely mysterious.

The most common way to implement importance sampling in computer graphics is to use the filter function $f(t)$ as an initial guess to the composite $s(t) f(t)$. That is, we use the filter function to control the sample density over the domain. The intuition is that if the signal is bounded over the support of the filter, then the product of the signal and filter will lie below the filter curve scaled by some constant. In other words, the hope is that the filtered signal will have about the same shape as the filter. Figure 9.17 illustrates this idea.

This approach is very attractive for both image-plane sampling and illumination-sphere sampling. In both cases we know the filter function, and we can preprocess it into a sum table [111]. Using a sum table, we can quickly find the total volume under any rectangular region of the filter's domain.

To illustrate its use, suppose the filter $f[n]$ is defined in 1D (or is one component of a separable 2D filter). Then we precompute the sum table $F[n]$:

$$F[n] = \sum_{i=1}^{n} f[n] \qquad (9.32)$$

Suppose the filter table has N entries. To divide the filter into two regions of equal energy, we find the point n_2 where $F[n_2] = F[N]/2$. Similarly, to divide any region $[a, b]$ into two equal-energy regions, we split at the point n_a where $F[n_a] = (F[b] - F[a])/2$.

Although this model of using the filter to approximate the signal for the purpose of importance sampling can work well, the model can break down, as Figure 9.18 shows. If the signal is too large in some areas, then the filter must be scaled so much that the difference between the scaled filter's minimum and maximum values is very small compared to the filtered signal's average value.

It is not unusual for our signals to exhibit this kind of behavior. Consider when we want to estimate the illumination function falling on some point on an object's surface in space. In theory, even a small object far away can reflect a tremendous amount of light toward the point receiving the illumination; think of the sun glinting off of an automobile's outside rear-view mirror on a sunny day. In general, we cannot predict from where bright light will arrive; after all, that is the problem we're trying to solve when estimating illumination.

9.4.2 Importance and Stratified Sampling

Stratified sampling and importance sampling can be combined to make a technique more powerful than either one alone. The basic idea is to build strata that represent equal-energy portions of the signal.

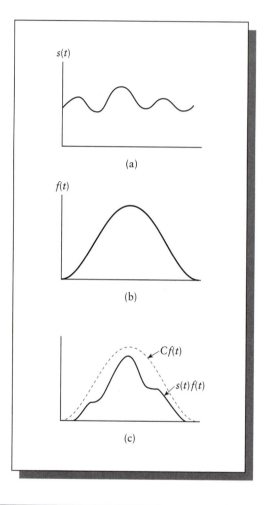

(a)

(b)

(c)

FIGURE 9.17

(a) A signal $s(t)$. (b) A filter $f(t)$. (c) The product $s(t)f(t)$ lies under the scaled filter $Cf(t)$.

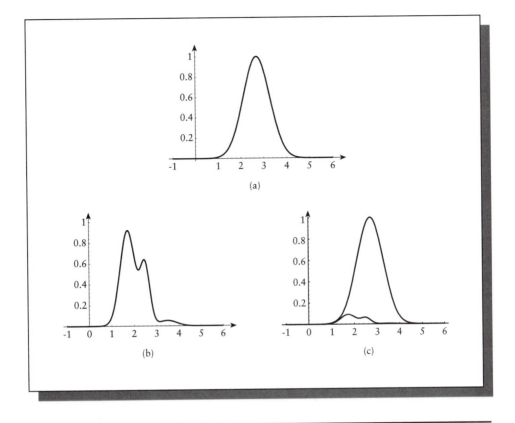

FIGURE 9.18

(a) A signal $s(t)$. (b) A filter $f(t)$. (c) The product $s(t)f(t)$ does not lie under the scaled filter $Cf(t)$ for a useful value of C.

Generating points that conform to different filter functions can be challenging. Shirley [400] summarizes how to sample differently shaped domains with uniformly distributed random variables. Some of the most useful transformations are given in Table 9.1. The complete list may be found in [400], along with a description of the technique for generating additional transformations.

Target space	Density	Domain	Transformation
Disk of radius R	$p(r, \theta) = \dfrac{1}{\pi R^2}$	$\theta \in [0, 2\pi]$ $r \in [0, R]$	$\theta = 2\pi u$ $r = R\sqrt{v}$
Triangle with vertices a_0, a_1, a_2	$p(a) = \dfrac{1}{\text{area}}$	$s \in [0, 1]$ $t \in [0, 1 - s]$	$s = 1 - \sqrt{1 - u}$ $t = (1 - s)v$ $a = a_0 + s(a_1 - a_0) + t(a_2 - a_0)$
Surface of unit sphere	$p(\theta, \phi) = \dfrac{1}{4\pi}$	$\theta \in [0, 2\pi]$ $\phi \in [0, 2\pi]$	$\theta = \cos^{-1}(1 - 2u)$ $\phi = 2\pi v$
Sector on surface of unit sphere	$p(\theta, \phi) = \dfrac{1}{(\phi_2 - \phi_1)[\cos(\theta_1) - \cos(\theta_2)]}$	$\theta \in [\theta_1, \theta_2]$ $\phi \in [\phi_1, \phi_2]$	$\theta = \cos^{-1}(g)$ $g = \cos(\theta_1) + u(\cos(\theta_2) - \cos(\theta_1))$ $\phi = \phi_1 + v(\phi_2 - \phi_1)$

TABLE 9.1

Transformations from the uniform unit random variables (u, v) to various domains. *Source:* Data from Shirley in *Graphics Gems III*, table 1, p. 81.

9.5 Interlude: The Duality of Aliasing and Noise

There is an interesting duality between aliasing and noise in an undersampled signal: beyond a certain point, reducing either of these comes at the expense of the other. To see this, we will take a detour from our main development and discuss *uncertainty*, which will lead to the noise-aliasing duality. This section is not essential to the rest of the book and may be skipped without harm.

We will begin by deriving a famous principle of physics known as the *Heisenberg uncertainty principle*. It states that any pair of physical quantities coupled in a particular way demonstrate a reciprocal relationship with regard to the precision of their measurement. In other words, past some point of accuracy, the better we know one value, the less certain we can be of the other.

One example is given by the position and momentum of a particle. We can measure both position and momentum with increasing precision until some fundamental limit is reached. From there on, the uncertainly principle takes over. If we refine our measurement of the particle's precision, we must necessarily become less sure of its momentum, and vice versa. This has nothing to do with the quality of our apparatus or the care we take when measuring; the product of the uncertainties is inherent in the structure of our universe. Another example is given by the time and energy of an event in spacetime; these observations are related by the Fourier transform, and thus they are coupled in the same way as position and momentum. If we imagine that in a rendering system we have little bundles of energy traveling around on the backs of photons, carrying some given amount of energy from one place to another, then at some fundamental limit we will be unable to specify when those photons depart from and arrive at their source and destination. This value is far smaller than anything normally used in practice in computer graphics, but it does exist.

We can derive the uncertainty principle by a purely theoretical development using the tools of the Fourier transform. We start with a few identities and definitions that will make the derivation flow more smoothly, following the development in Bracewell [61]. In this section, f refers to $f(t)$, and f' refers to its first derivative, $f' = df(t)/dt$. Similarly, F refers to $F(\omega) = \mathcal{F}\{f(t)\}$, and F' is defined as $F' = dF(\omega)/d\omega$. All integrals in this section have infinite limits.

We start by combining the differentiation property of Fourier transforms with Parseval's theorem to find an identity for $\langle f' | f' \rangle$.

$$\begin{aligned} \langle f' | f' \rangle &= \langle 2j\pi\omega F | 2j\pi\omega F \rangle \\ &= 4\pi^2 \langle \omega F | \omega F \rangle \end{aligned} \tag{9.33}$$

We next define the *centered variance* of any function $g(t)$ to be

$$\sigma_c(g)^2 = \frac{\langle tg | tg \rangle}{\langle g | g \rangle} \tag{9.34}$$

This definition is a simplification of the general definition of the variance that also takes into account the first two *moments* of the function and its *centroid*. The centroid of a function $g(x)$ is defined as that value of x for which the the value of g times the total area of g is equal to the first moment of g. In symbols, the centroid x_c is

$$x_c = \frac{\int xg(x)\,dx}{\int g(x)\,dx} \tag{9.35}$$

(For more details on the centroid and various other measures related to the Fourier transform, see [61, pp. 135–156].)

We note the following identity, which is the integration by parts over an infinite integral:

$$\left| \int tf'\,dt \right| = \left| \int f\,dt \right|$$
$$\langle t | f' \rangle = \langle 1 | f \rangle \tag{9.36}$$

Last, we will use a particular form of the *Cauchy-Schwarz inequality*. We will derive this inequality by supposing we have two functions f and g, and some real number ϵ. Then

$$0 < \langle f + \epsilon g | f + \epsilon g \rangle \tag{9.37}$$

unless $g = \epsilon f$, in which case we need to use any $\epsilon' \neq \epsilon$. We can expand out the braket to get a quadratic in ϵ:

$$
\begin{aligned}
0 &< \int \overline{(f + \epsilon g)}(f + \epsilon g) \, dt \\
&< \int (f\bar{f} + \epsilon(g\bar{f} + f\bar{g}) + \epsilon^2 g\bar{g}) \, dt \\
&< \langle f | f \rangle + \epsilon(\langle f | g \rangle + \langle g | f \rangle) + \epsilon^2 \langle g | g \rangle
\end{aligned}
\tag{9.38}
$$

So we get a quadratic $a + b\epsilon + c\epsilon^2$. From the quadratic formula, we know that for this quantity to be greater than zero requires $b^2 - 4ac \leq 0$, so

$$(\langle f | g \rangle + \langle g | f \rangle)^2 \leq 4 \langle f | f \rangle \langle g | g \rangle \tag{9.39}$$

We are now ready to derive the uncertainty relation. We assume that we have a signal f with Fourier transform F, both of which have their centroid at 0. Then by the definition of Equation 9.34, we write

$$
\begin{aligned}
(\Delta t)^2 &= \frac{\langle tf | tf \rangle}{\langle f | f \rangle} \\
(\Delta \omega)^2 &= \frac{\langle \omega F | \omega F \rangle}{\langle F | F \rangle}
\end{aligned}
\tag{9.40}
$$

These are the *uncertainties* in the two signals. The precision of our knowledge of any value $f(t)$ is represented by Δt at that t, similarly our precision of the value of $F(\omega)$ is given by $\Delta \omega$. We want to find a lower limit on their product, so we write the product and expand:

$$
\begin{aligned}
(\Delta t)^2 (\Delta \omega)^2 &= \frac{\langle tf | tf \rangle \langle \omega F | \omega F \rangle}{\langle f | f \rangle \langle F | F \rangle} \\
&= \frac{\langle tf | tf \rangle \langle f' | f' \rangle}{4\pi^2 \langle f | f \rangle \langle F | F \rangle} \\
&= \frac{\langle tf | tf \rangle \langle f' | f' \rangle}{4\pi^2 \langle f | f \rangle^2}
\end{aligned}
\tag{9.41}
$$

where we have used Equation 9.33 and then Parseval's theorem. Continuing, we apply Equation 9.39:

$$(\Delta t)^2 (\Delta \omega)^2 \geq \frac{1}{4\pi^2 \langle f | f \rangle^2} \frac{1}{4} (\langle tf | f' \rangle + \langle f' | tf \rangle)^2$$

$$= \frac{1}{16\pi^2 \langle f| f\rangle^2} \left(\int t\overline{f}f'\, dt + \int tf\overline{f'}\, dt \right)^2$$

$$= \frac{1}{16\pi^2 \langle f| f\rangle^2} \left(\int t(\overline{f}f' + f\overline{f'})\, dt \right)^2$$

$$= \frac{1}{16\pi^2 \langle f| f\rangle^2} \left(\int t\frac{d}{dt}\left(f\overline{f'}\right) dt \right)^2$$

$$= \frac{1}{16\pi^2 \langle f| f\rangle^2} \left(\int f\overline{f'}\, dt \right)^2 \tag{9.42}$$

where we applied Equation 9.36. Simplifying this last expression, we find

$$(\Delta t)^2 (\Delta \omega)^2 \geq \frac{1}{16\pi^2 \langle f| f\rangle^2} \langle f| f\rangle^2$$

$$= \frac{1}{16\pi^2}$$

$$= \left(\frac{1}{4\pi} \right)^2 \tag{9.43}$$

By taking the square root of both sides, we find

$$(\Delta t)(\Delta \omega) \geq \frac{1}{4\pi} \tag{9.44}$$

This is the unitless form of Heisenberg's uncertainty relation. When we use it in an application, we need to apply the appropriate units (and any necessary scaling factors). It tells us that the product of the uncertainty in any two parameters related by a Fourier transform can be no less than $1/4\pi$, no matter how good our equipment is or how carefully we measure. Notice that we made no physical assumptions in our derivation; this is a straightforward result of the inherent uncertainty in any system.

For example, consider the conjugate pair of measurements for time and energy. In 1900, Planck formulated a theory that energy is bundled up into small, indivisible packets called *quanta*, and that each quantum had an associated oscillation of a given frequency. When a system absorbs or emits energy, it does so in discrete steps, corresponding to a single quantum. Planck's relation expresses the relationship between ΔE, the change in energy of the system, and $\Delta \omega$, the change in the vibrational state of the system, as

$$\Delta E = h\Delta \omega \tag{9.45}$$

where the constant $h \approx 6.62 \times 10^{-27}$ erg-second. The value of h is one of the fundamental constants of our universe, similar to the speed of light or the charge on an electron. It is one of the constants that describes the structure of the universe we know.

If we solve for $\Delta\omega$ and plug it into Equation 9.44, we find

$$\Delta t \Delta E \geq h/4\pi \tag{9.46}$$

which is precisely Heisenberg's uncertainty principle for time (measured in seconds) and energy (measured in ergs). It tells us that for any physical phenomenon, we can theoretically determine the time of that phenomenon with as much accuracy as we desire, but beyond a certain limit our concurrent knowledge of the energy in that event will become worse and worse, so the product of the uncertainties never goes below $h/4\pi$.

If we measure the location x of a particle, and its momentum $p = mv$ (m stands for mass, v for velocity), then we write Δx for the uncertainty in position and Δp for the uncertainty in momentum, yielding

$$\Delta x \Delta p \geq h/4\pi \tag{9.47}$$

which is a fundamental limit on how well we can know both the location and momentum of a particle simultaneously.

Many clever experiments have been devised and carried out to test the uncertainty principle in practice; it has not yet been disproven.

As promised at the start of this section, aliasing and noise in an undersampled signal are related by the uncertainty in just the same way as the coupled terms discussed above. We will follow the analysis in Resnikoff [358].

Consider a continuous-time 1D signal f with finite power, but infinite energy. That is, its energy

$$E = \int f^2(t)\,dt \tag{9.48}$$

is not finite, but its power

$$P = \lim_{T\to\infty} \frac{1}{T} \int_{T/2}^{T/2} f^2(t)\,dt \tag{9.49}$$

is finite. For these signals, we will focus attention on the autocorrelation function (which we will write as $C(t)$ in this section) and its Fourier transform, the power spectral density (PSD) $P(\omega)$.

If a signal's PSD is flat within some interval $[\omega_0, \omega_1]$, it is called *white noise* in that interval. Suppose that the PSD of f is a constant over all frequencies; then we know that the autocorrelation function $C(t)$ of f must be a scaled impulse, since $C(t)$ and $P(\omega)$ are a Fourier pair. That is,

$$\lim_{T\to\infty} \frac{1}{2T} \int_{T}^{T} f(u+t)f(u)\,du = 0 \tag{9.50}$$

for $t \neq 0$. Equation 9.50 tells us that f is completely uncorrelated with itself for all possible shifts u, except for the trivial shift $u = 0$, when the signal is perfectly aligned with itself and is perfectly correlated. If a signal is completely uncorrelated with itself, then it has no short- or long-term periodicity or structure; in other words, it is random, or noisy. This observation gives us a measure for the amount of noisiness in a signal; the closer the signal's power spectral density is to a constant, the more noisy it is; larger nonlinearities correspond to less noisy signals.

Suppose we now have a sampled signal $s[n]$. We know that if s contains aliases, then these correspond to large-scale patterns, which means that we will find that the autocorrelation function will have very broad support. In other words, if there are large patterns, then large shifts of the signal will cause it to align with itself to a significant degree, and this will be reflected by a large value in the autocorrelation. The wider the support of the autocorrelation function, the narrower the support of the power spectral density.

To summarize the above discussion, we have noted that when $P(\omega)$ is broad, the signal is noisy. When $C(t)$ is broad, the signal has aliasing. Because the two functions are related by the Fourier transform, as one becomes more broad, the other becomes more narrow.

Using the definitions from above, a measure of the support of the autocorrelation function is given by

$$(\Delta t)^2 = \frac{\int_{-\infty}^{\infty} t^2 C^2(t)\, dt}{\int_{-\infty}^{\infty} C^2(t)\, dt} \tag{9.51}$$

and the support of the autocorrelation function is given by

$$(\Delta \omega)^2 = \frac{\int_{-\infty}^{\infty} \omega^2 P^2(\omega)\, d\omega}{\int_{-\infty}^{\infty} P^2(\omega)\, d\omega} \tag{9.52}$$

Then following the same arguments as before, we find

$$\Delta t\, \Delta w \geq \frac{1}{4\pi} \tag{9.53}$$

Equation 9.53 tells us that when we have a signal with frequencies above the Nyquist rate, we can force either the aliasing or the noise in our reconstructed signal to be as low as we want, but that below a certain limit, further reductions in aliasing will correspond to an increase in noise, and vice versa. We cannot reconstruct an undersampled signal and simultaneously reduce both aliasing and noise indefinitely. At some point, reducing the aliasing will increase the noise, and vice versa. This just says that the extra energy in the signal has to go somewhere, which means either structured or unstructured (aliasing or noise) artifacts.

9.6   Nonuniform Reconstruction

The theory of reconstruction from nonuniform samples is not as complete as the theory that covers uniform samples.

The basics of the theory were laid down in Yen [497]. Since then there have been a variety of approaches which vary in speed, precision, and efficiency. A survey of reconstruction methods published through 1986 is given in Sections V and VI of Marvasti [283]; a thorough up-to-date summary is available in Feichtinger and Gröchenig [143]. One of the biggest difficulties in nonuniform reconstruction is that for a given bandlimited signal $f(t)$ that has been sampled at a finite number of arbitrary sample points t_i, the reconstruction process does not necessarily produce a unique result [244]. This means that in general some extra information has to be introduced into the algorithm. This information is typically either provided by the system or assumed by the nature of the reconstruction method.

Each algorithm for nonuniform reconstruction uses a different set of introduced information, making the results and descriptions somewhat different.

Since there is no unified theory available for this field right now, we will take a pragmatic approach in this book and present several different reconstruction methods in survey form in the next chapter.

9.7   Further Reading

The basic theory behind nonuniform sampling was developed by Yen in a classic paper in 1956 [497]. This work was followed by Leneman [262–265]. Most of this theoretical work is quickly surveyed and put to use for rendering by Dippé and Wold [124] and by Cook [101]. One of the first discussions of jitter for time sampling was presented by Balakrishnan [27]. An extensive discussion of nonuniform sampling and reconstruction from a particular point of view is offered by Marvasti in his book [283].

Resnikoff offers a discussion of the uncertainty principle from an information-theory point of view in [358]. An alternative and highly readable derivation of this principle is offered by Hamming [185].

9.8   Exercises

Exercise 9.1

Find the true mean of the signal $3x^2 + 2x$ over the interval $[0, 4]$. Implement the algorithms of Figure 9.4 with $T = 0.01$ and $n = 10$, and Figure 9.6 with $T = 0.01$, $p = 10$, $n_1 = 20$, $n_2 = 30$. Run your algorithms several times using different seed values for the random number generators. Provide and explain your results.

Exercise 9.2

Using the metric of Equation 9.30, rank the 8×8 uniform sampling matrices over the interval $[0, 1]$ for the following reconstruction filters $\Phi(x)$.

(a) $\text{sinc}(x)$

(b) e^{-x^2}

(c) $|.5 - x|$

Exercise 9.3

We said that sometimes the reconstruction filter is used as an estimate of the importance function for sampling. Suppose we have a signal $f(x) = x^2$ and a reconstruction filter $h(x) = e^{-x^2}$ over the domain $[0, 3]$. Write a Monte Carlo program to compute an integral using importance sampling. Find the value of the integral, and plot the error as a function of the number of samples for 1 to 100 samples using the following importance functions.

(a) $g(x) = 1$

(b) $g(x) = e^{-x^2}$

(c) $g(x) = 5e^{-x^2}$

Interpret your results; was using the filter a good choice?

10

SURVEY OF SAMPLING AND RECONSTRUCTION TECHNIQUES

10.1 Introduction

In this chapter we will survey the sampling and reconstruction schemes developed in recent years for computer graphics applications. The theory of perfect sampling and reconstruction of bandlimited signals presented in previous chapters is only a starting point for practical methods.

The techniques described in this chapter are usually appropriate for any number of dimensions, though the emphasis will be on 2D signals. Most of these methods were originally presented in terms of sampling the image plane, so in the literature there is much discussion of "the image" rather than the signal, and "pixels" rather than new samples of the reconstructed signal.

In this chapter I will refer to the 2D signal being evaluated as the signal (or function) $f(u, v)$. This is meant to encompass any 2D distribution, such as an illumination sphere (where (u, v) refer to direction angles (θ, ϕ)) or the image plane (where (u, v) refer to a screen location (x, y)). The general plan will be to eventually build up a set of n samples $s_n = f(p_n)$ at the locations given by the p_n. When all the samples have been evaluated, they are used to reconstruct a new function $\hat{f}(u,v)$, which is then typically resampled at a new set of *resample* locations $\hat{p}_n$ giving new resample values $\hat{s}_n = \hat{f}(\hat{p}_n)$. This is summarized in Equation 10.1.

$$f(x,y) \overset{\text{sampling}}{\longrightarrow} s_n = f(p_n) \overset{\text{reconstruction}}{\longrightarrow} \hat{f}(x,y) \overset{\text{resampling}}{\longrightarrow} \hat{s}_n = \hat{f}(p_n) \qquad (10.1)$$

The most important property of 3D image synthesis that we must keep in mind when rendering is that we cannot guarantee that our input signal is bandlimited. In fact, it usually will not be. Boundary edges, texture discontinuities, and noncontinuous shading functions will all introduce high frequencies into the signal.

Early polygon-rendering systems were able to prefilter the input data so that it was bandlimited before sampling [109, 325], and thus the sampling theory of the previous chapters could be pretty much implemented in a straightforward way. But modern databases now contain complex geometry, quickly varying surface textures and shading models, and even volumetric components such as smoke and fog. When these models are combined with sophisticated rendering techniques that model motion blur, depth of field, and the propagation of light by multiple objects, the task of prefiltering appears insurmountable. Thus the perfect sampling and reconstruction theorems cannot be used directly, though the ideas behind them will still prove useful.

Because databases are so complex that analytic techniques (like prefiltering) are very difficult to apply, most modern rendering is done by sampling the signal with many point samples and ultimately deriving a new set of samples for further computation or display, as in Equation 10.1. Most of these systems are guided by the following principle:

The Sampler's Credo: *Every sample is precious.*

Most rendering systems spend the bulk of their time valuating samples, which can involve ray tracing, evaluating shading functions, and physical simulation such as calculating motion and deformations. These are very expensive operations, so we want to minimize the number of samples we evaluate and get the maximum benefit from each one.

As rendering and modeling methods get more sophisticated, we seem to be on a trend that makes analytic solutions ever more remote and the cost of sample evaluation ever more expensive. A modern rendering system is as conservative as possible when it comes to taking more samples, always taking the fewest number possible to get the required quality of estimate of the signal.

The techniques in this chapter are designed to try to find the minimum number of samples required to estimate a signal with some specified degree of certainty. Some published reports address just one step of Equation 10.1; others present a set of coordinated techniques that handle all three operations.

There are some general principles that are common to most of these published methods. First, the signal is sampled as though it had a Nyquist rate comparable to the frequency of the expected reconstruction samples. For example, if the signal is energy falling on the image plane, then the initial sampling density is typically on the order of one sample per pixel or per group of pixels. The values of these samples are then examined, and in regions where the signal appears to have a very high bandwidth, more samples are created and evaluated. This is called *adaptive refinement*, and may be repeated until either the samples are judged to represent a good local estimate of the signal, or some recursion limit is reached. Then the sample values are used to reconstruct a signal approximating the input, and this is resampled to derive new sample values. These new samples may be placed into pixel locations in a frame buffer or used as input to a shading algorithm.

10.2 General Outline of Signal Estimation

This section will describe the components of Equation 10.1 in a bit more detail. An expanded block diagram is shown in Figure 10.1.

10.3 Initial Sampling Patterns

The first step in evaluating a signal is to create an *initial sampling pattern* (also called the *base pattern*), which specifies a set of sample locations. We call it the initial pattern because later steps in the sampling process may create additional patterns with new samples to increase the sampling density in some places.

The density of the initial pattern is typically derived from the expected density of the resampling pattern. Each sample in the initial pattern is typically meant to serve as an initial estimate for one or more resamples. The sample pattern may only specify a pair of coordinates in the 2D domain of the signal being sampled, or it may have any number of associated parameters, such as time, or lens position when sampling the image plane.

The expected frequency content of the signal also influences the initial pattern. If the signal is expected to contain significant high-frequency information, the density of the initial pattern may be increased. Estimating the global frequency content of the signal before any samples have been drawn at all is usually difficult and often impractical; many systems don't even bother to try and always use the same initial sampling pattern without attempting to first characterize the signal at all.

Typically the density of the initial sampling pattern is constant across the parameter space. Intuitively, the initial sampling pattern represents an attempt to get a broad picture of the signal, including places where the value and derivatives of the

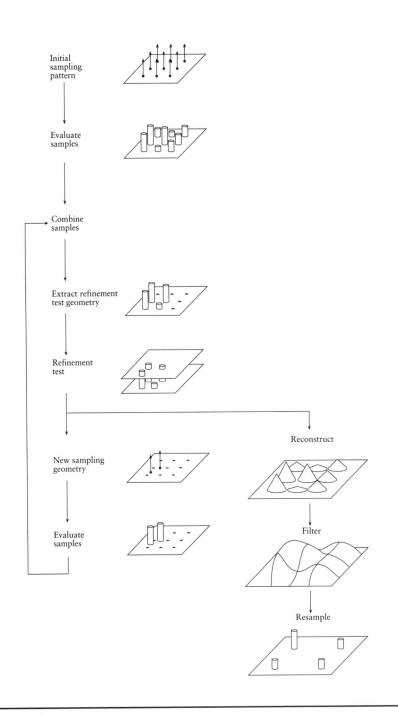

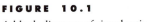

FIGURE 10.1

A block diagram of signal estimation.

signal are high and low. This gives us a general overview of the signal and directs the next step.

To improve on the initial estimate, many techniques then enter into a loop called adaptive refinement. This step is motivated by the observation that in computer graphics many signals contain large areas where the value is constant or only slowly changing. In these regions there are no sharp edges or changes in value, so the signal is bandlimited with a very low upper frequency. This suggests that in this neighborhood we may get a good estimate of the signal with just a small number of samples, perhaps even as few as the ones in the initial estimate. On the other hand, some regions of the signal will be complex in some way and require a closer examination to determine what is happening. In these regions of the image there are many high frequencies, so we want to increase our sampling rate in order to cut down on aliasing.

To determine where more samples are needed, typically some number of nearby samples are examined. These samples make up the *refinement test geometry*. These samples are then evaluated with respect to some *refinement test*, which typically estimates (implicitly or explicitly) the local bandwidth of the signal in this region. If the test suggests that the bandwidth in this area is higher than the current sampling rate, the algorithm will generate new samples at locations given by the *new sampling geometry*. This process of examination and increased sampling repeats until the criteria are satisfied. Typically the refinement criteria include a cutoff test to prevent runaway sampling in pathological cases, and impose an upper limit on sampling in general.

When the signal is sampled to some degree of confidence or quality, we typically want to *reconstruct* it. We may wish to *filter* the signal if necessary before it is *resampled* to yield a new set of sample values. Typical uses for the resamples include evaluation in a reflection function or storage as pixel values in a frame buffer.

We will now look at the various approaches to each of these steps.

10.4 Uniform and Nonuniform Sampling

There are two types of sampling patterns: *uniform* (also called *regular* or *periodic*) and *nonuniform*. Some nonuniform patterns are *random* (or *stochastic*) and are generated on demand by algorithms that use random numbers as part of the pattern-generation process. In general, early algorithms tended to be uniform, while more recent techniques are nonuniform.

The attraction of uniform sampling is that if we assume our signal is bandlimited (that is, $F(\omega) = 0$ for all $\omega > \omega_F$), then we can apply the uniform sampling and reconstruction theory of previous chapters to guide our sampling process. This assumption is unlikely to be true in general, because there are many high-frequency components in graphics signals, as discussed earlier. But if we assume that the energy in most signals used in graphics decreases with increasing frequency, then as we increase the sampling rate we decrease the aliasing error.

One of the best ways to get an intuition for the effects of aliasing is to consider what happens to an image when it is undersampled. When an image is sampled with a regular pattern that is too low, a variety of *aliasing structures* are visible in the result. We use the term "structure" because the artifacts due to aliasing often take the form of clearly visible patterns.

For example, consider Figure 10.2, based on an example from Mitchell and Netravali [310]. Here a regular square grid has been used for the geometry of the sample points. Notice that as the frequency goes up, the quality of the sampling decreases. On the right side of the figure is a very clear set of concentric rings. These rings are the result of sampling error, or aliasing.

Another example, from Cook [101], is shown in Figure 10.3. The image function here is a row of narrow white triangles on a black background. The figure shows the structure of the triangles and the result of sampling with one sample in the center of each pixel. The resulting image is badly aliased, but the error is so strongly structured that it appears to be a perfectly reasonable pattern. Even if the sampling density is increased to four uniform samples per pixel, we still suffer badly from aliasing, yet the final image contains obvious structure.

Error is inevitable when we try to evaluate any signal by point sampling. The problem is that our functions are typically not bandlimited, so the sampling theory guarantees us that we can never take enough samples to capture the complete signal. From a practical standpoint, we can never be sure that we have sampled all the fine structure in a signal, even inadequately. Fine detail in graphics signals can come from many sources, including geometry, shading, texturing, and motion. It is unclear that we will ever have techniques guaranteed to give us accurate and useful upper limits on the local bandwidth, and without them we must resort to guessing the appropriate sample rate. Whenever we guess too low, the result will be an incorrect estimate of the function. Whenever we guess too high, we waste time.

When we sample with a regular pattern, structure in the signal combines with structure in the pattern to create new structure in the samples; this is the source of the structures we saw in the figures above. This is visible in everyday life: when two mesh screens are placed over one another, a set of rich moiré patterns emerge, particularly when one screen is moved over the other.

The heart of the problem is that the two patterns, one each inherent in the signal and created by the sampling geometry, are combining with each other to create new patterns. As we mentioned above, these patterns are often visible in images. Without an upper limit on the local bandwidth of the signal, we cannot avoid aliasing; and if the sampling geometry is regular, we always run the risk of introducing new, extraneous structures into our reconstructed signals. If extra structures are appearing because of interference between two patterns, it may seem possible to eliminate the structures by changing one of the patterns enough so that

(a)   (b)

FIGURE 10.2

(a) A series of concentric rings sampled on a dense uniform grid. (b) The signal sampled on a uniform 128×128 grid.

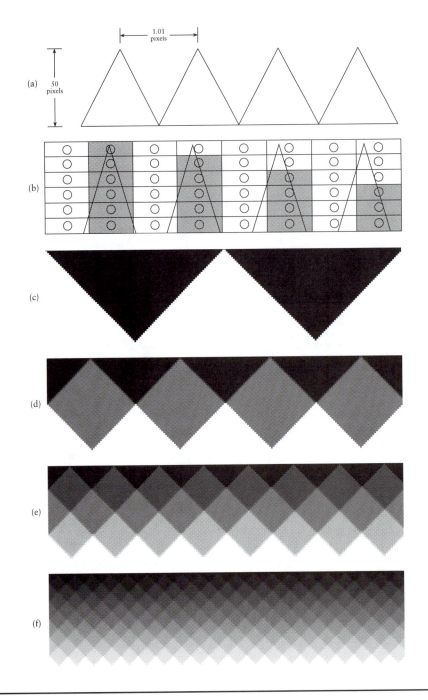

FIGURE 10.3

(a) The geometry of a test pattern. (b) Aliasing caused by regular sampling. (c) One sample per pixel. (d) Two samples per pixel. (e) Three samples per pixel. (f) Four samples per pixel. Based on Cook in *ACM Transactions on Graphics*, fig. 12a–f, p. 66.

there cannot be any regular interference. We can't change the signal (and probably wouldn't want to if we could), but we can change the sampling pattern.

This observation is the driving principle behind the variety of nonuniform sampling techniques described below. As we saw in Chapter 9, nonuniform sampling tends to introduce uncorrelated noise into a signal. If our sampling rate is too low, our reconstructed signal will still contain errors, but they will be of a noisy form that is less objectionable to the visual system than the structural errors that result from uniform sampling.

10.5 Initial Sampling

There are two principal approaches to creating an initial sampling geometry: uniform and nonuniform. Most methods fit into one of these categories; some are hybrids. We will focus our discussion on generating samples of a 2D signal; some generalizations to higher dimensions will be discussed near the end of the chapter. We will take these in turn.

In this chapter we will illustrate the creation of some patterns with short pseudocode algorithms, inspired by Shirley [397]. We posit a function randomInterval(a,b) that produces a uniformly distributed random number on the interval $[a, b]$. Three common intervals have their own shorthand, summarized in Equation 10.2.

$$\text{unit}() \triangleq \text{randomInterval}(0, 1)$$
$$\text{symmetric}(a) \triangleq \text{randomInterval}(-a, a)$$
$$\text{range}(a) \triangleq \text{randomInterval}(0, a) \tag{10.2}$$

The function randomInteger(a,b), where $a, b \in \mathcal{Z}$, returns a uniformly distributed random integer in the range $[a, b]$. We also define a Boolean function flip() that returns true or false with equal probability.

10.5.1 Uniform Sampling

Uniform sampling patterns may be described with respect to a *lattice*. A 2D lattice is a set of points generated by combining two basis vectors in all possible ways. Figure 10.4 shows two examples. The most common uniform sampling pattern in computer graphics is the rectangular lattice.

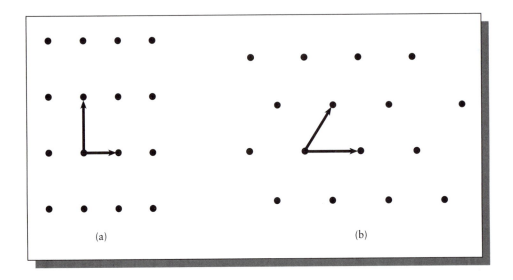

(a)   (b)

FIGURE   10.4

(a) A rectangular lattice and its basis vectors. (b) A triangular lattice and its basis vectors.

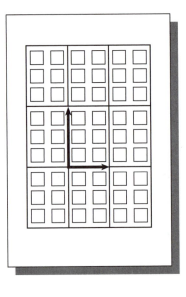

FIGURE   10.5

Supersampling cells. Each contains 2×3 pixels.

```
for r ← 0 to h − 1
    for c ← 0 to w − 1
        k ← (rw) + c
        x_k ← (1 + 2c)/(2w)
        y_k ← (1 + 2r)/(2h)
    endfor
endfor
```

FIGURE 10.6

Regular sampling aligned to resample grid.

10.5.2 Rectangular Lattice

The *rectangular* (or *square*) *lattice* is created by two perpendicular vectors, as shown in Figure 10.5.

This pattern is used extensively for sampling the image plane. This is probably because this pattern matches the resample locations, which are pixel centers in a frame buffer. When used for image sampling, it is common to think of the frame buffer as grouped into rectangular *cells*, each one enclosing $m \times n$ pixels [6, 64, 196, 228, 361, 436, 477, 491]. Sometimes the cells are 1×1, so the lattice geometry and the pixels coincide.

The locations of a regular lattice on a grid of resolution $w \times h$ may be found from the code in Figure 10.6. Here we have used the convention that places the center of pixel (x, y) at $(x + 0.5, y + 0.5)$ [208].

This sampling lattice may be displaced with respect to the pixel centers. If the lattice is the same size as the pixels but is translated by a half-pixel in both directions, the lattice points will fall on pixel corners, as in Figure 10.7 [477, 491]. This causes the pattern to enlarge by one sample in dimension. The code in 2D is shown in Figure 10.8.

10.5.3 Hexagonal Lattice

The *hexagonal lattice* is shown in Figure 10.9. This is called a hexagonal lattice because each sample has six nearest neighbors. This sampling pattern has occasionally been used in computer graphics [124], but it is common in image processing [130, 345].

The code for a hexagonal lattice corresponding to Figure 10.9 is given in Figure 10.10. Here we assume that the hexagon has a height of 2 units, so each edge is of length $2/\sqrt{3}$.

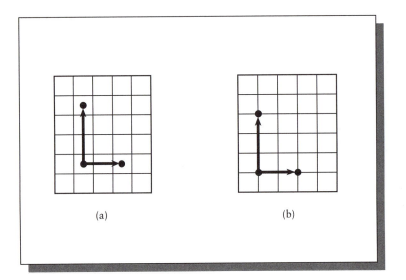

(a)   (b)

FIGURE 10.7

(a) The lattice points fall on pixel centers. (b) The lattice points fall on pixel corners.

```
for r ← 0 to h
    for c ← 0 to w
        k ← (r(w + 1)) + c
        xₖ ← c/w
        yₖ ← r/h
    endfor
endfor
```

FIGURE 10.8

Regular sampling displaced one-half pixel to resample grid.

The hexagonal lattice has several attractive qualities. The *density* of this lattice is higher than the square lattice, so there are more samples from this lattice in any given area. If we are sampling a signal whose spectrum lies within a circle, the hexagonal lattice requires 13.4% fewer samples to represent the signal accurately than a rectangular lattice [130].

In fact, the hexagonal lattice is the densest possible lattice in 2D. To see this, consider a signal with a circular Fourier transform. How densely can we fill the

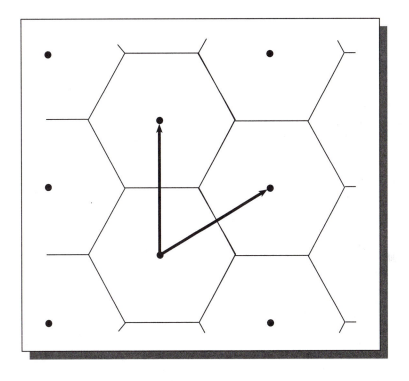

FIGURE 10.9

A hexagonal lattice.

```
for r ← 0 to h − 1
    for c ← 0 to w − 1
        k ← (rw) + c
        x_k ← (3c)/√3
        y_k ← 2(r + (c mod 2))
    endfor
endfor
```

FIGURE 10.10

Hexagonal (or triangular) sampling.

plane with copies of this circular spectrum? The hexagonal arrangement is the densest tiling of the plane with circles.

The hexagonal lattice is also more *isotropic* than the square lattice, so there is more uniform sampling in each direction. For example, the nearest neighbors to any sample in a square lattice may be found in only two directions; in the hexagonal lattice there are neighbors in three directions.

The hexagonal lattice does have some drawbacks. One possible inconvenience from a programming point of view is that the sample points do not fall on integer coordinates. Another, somewhat more serious problem is that the hexagon is not a *reptile*. A reptile is a shape that can be decomposed into smaller copies of itself without overlapping or gaps, as we saw in Figure 6.5. Reptiles are easily used for adaptive supersampling; nonreptiles are harder.

10.5.4   Triangular Lattice

Related to the hexagonal lattice is the *isosceles triangular lattice*, shown in Figure 10.11.

Although it has been used in graphics [405], this lattice is rarely used. One inconvenience is that sample points do not fall on integer locations, a trait shared with the hexagonal lattice. Another problem is that we must keep track of the sense of each triangle (upward- or downward-pointing).

10.5.5   Diamond Lattice

The *diamond* (or *quincunx*) *lattice* is shown in Figure 10.12. This pattern has only been used for image-plane sampling [59], where it is shown in Figure 10.13 with respect to a set of pixels.

This pattern is only recognizable as a diamond when compared to a rectangular resample pattern; otherwise it is simply a rotated square lattice. The diamond lattice is interesting because it matches the directional sensitivity of the human eye, as discussed in Chapter 1. It is denser in directions in which the eye is sensitive. The initial sampling pattern with this lattice may also be defined by cells that cover many pixels [59].

10.5.6   Comparison of Subdivided Hexagonal and Square Lattices

It is interesting to observe how the number and density of samples varies for square and hexagonal lattices as they are subdivided. Figure 10.14 shows how the two types of lattices may be subdivided to make similar lattices of a higher density. Each level

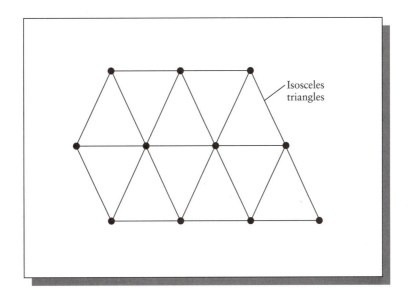

FIGURE 10.11
A triangular lattice.

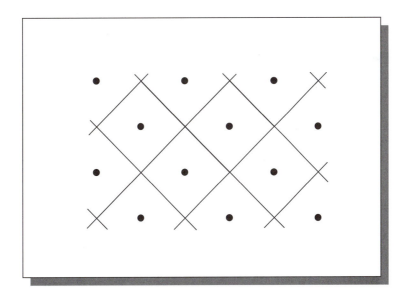

FIGURE 10.12
A diamond lattice.

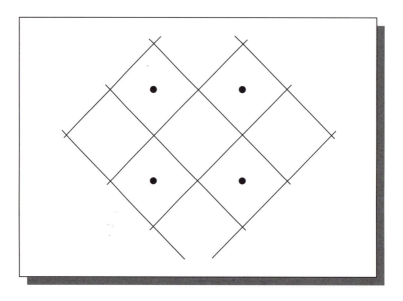

FIGURE 10.13

A diamond pattern over a set of pixels.

of subdivision is called a *generation*; the first level is called generation 0, the next generation 1, and so on. We tile the hexagonal lattice with triangles for uniformity.

We will use g to represent the generation number, and s_g to represent the number of samples involved in generation g. The value d_g is the number of new samples taken to move from generation $g - 1$ to g, so $d_g = s_g - s_{g-1}$. Example values for different generations are shown in Table 10.1, where we use the notation

$$a^+ = \sum_{i=1}^{a} i = 1 + 2 + \cdots + a = (a/2)(a+1) \tag{10.3}$$

The incremental number of samples in each generation for the square grid is given by

$$\begin{aligned} d_\square(g) &= \left(1 + 2^g\right)^2 - \left(1 + 2^{g-1}\right)^2 \\ &= 2^{g-1} \left[\left(1 + 2^{g-1}\right)\left(1 + 2^g\right)\right] \end{aligned} \tag{10.4}$$

and for the triangular grid by

$$\begin{aligned} d_\triangle(g) &= \left(1 + 2^g\right)^+ - \left(1 + 2^{g-1}\right)^+ \\ &= 3\left(2^{g-1}\right)^+ \end{aligned} \tag{10.5}$$

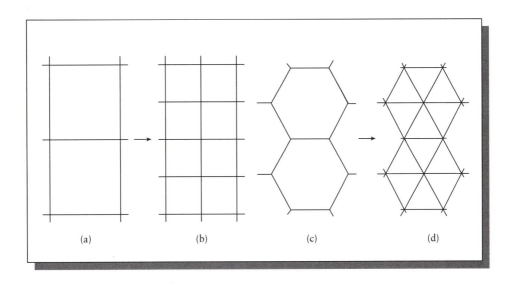

FIGURE 10.14

(a) A square lattice. (b) The square lattice subdivided. (c) A hexagonal lattice. (d) The hexagonal lattice subdivided.

Gener-	Total	New samples		Total samples		Samples per tile	
ation	tiles	Square	Hex	Square	Hex		
0	1	4	3	4	3	4.00	3.00
1	4	5	3	9	6	2.25	1.50
2	16	16	9	25	15	1.56	0.94
3	64	56	30	81	45	1.27	0.70
4	266	208	108	289	153	1.13	0.60
g	4^g	$d_\square(g)$	$d_\triangle(g)$	$(1+2^g)^2$	$(1+2^g)^+$	$(1+2^g)^2/4^g$	$(1+2^g)^+/4^g$

TABLE 10.1

Lattice densities.

We can see that for any given level of subdivision, the triangular grid requires fewer samples overall than the square grid and produces fewer samples per tile. This is advantageous in situations where we want a roughly uniform coverage of the domain with the least number of tiles. This advantage must be balanced against the different shapes of the grids; often a square lattice is just the right shape for a 2D signal in computer graphics.

10.5.7 Nonuniform Sampling

In general, the phrase *nonuniform sampling* refers to any sampling technique that produces a sampling pattern that is not periodic.

The sampling techniques discussed in Chapter 8 are all candidates for nonuniform sampling of a signal. There are two primary types of nonuniform sampling: *patterned* and *random* (or, more specifically, *quasi-random*).

Patterned nonuniform samples are used when a known nonuniform distribution of samples is desired. They are typically used to sample 2D signals with a known, but awkward, parameterization. For example, the surface of a sphere may be parameterized by a 2D function corresponding to spherical angles, but equally spaced samples in this parameter space do not correspond to equally spaced samples on the sphere.

Because generating most types of nonuniform sample geometries is often a time-consuming process, some algorithms create the samples before rendering begins, and then save them in a file. The sample locations may then be retrieved and used immediately as needed. Because of this, the line between random and deterministic nonuniform patterns becomes blurred when rendering with these techniques. Other methods, which generate samples on the fly as needed, are closer to a random process.

10.5.8 Poisson Sampling

The simplest random pattern consists of a series of samples that have no relationship to each other and none between their coordinate values. To generate random samples in $\mathcal{R}^n$, we simply pick n uniformly distributed random numbers and use them as the sample location. This is called *Poisson* (or *random*) *sampling*, and is illustrated by the pseudocode in Figure 10.15.

10.5.9 N-Rooks Sampling

A technique called *N-rooks sampling* is useful for sampling a signal that has been stratified in an $N \times N$ grid [397, 402]. An example is shown in Figure 10.16.

```
for i ← 0 to N − 1
    x_i ← unit()
    y_i ← unit()
endfor
```

FIGURE 10.15

Poisson (or random) sampling.

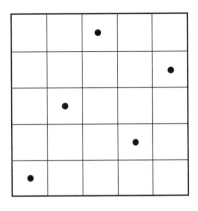

FIGURE 10.16

An N-rooks sampling pattern.

In this pattern, one sample is taken in each row and each column. The name is inspired by the chess piece called the rook, which can only move along rows and columns of the board in an L-shaped pattern—two squares in one direction and one square orthogonal to it. If the grid is thought of as a chessboard and the samples are rooks, then no rook can capture another (i.e., land on its square) in one move, since no two samples are in the same row or column.

To make an N-rooks pattern, begin by placing samples along the main diagonal of the grid, and then randomly permute (or shuffle) the columns. The code for an $N \times N$ grid is shown in Figure 10.17. Here the function permute() shuffles its arguments into a new, random order.

```
for i ← 0 to N
    x_i ← i/(N − 1)
    y_i ← i/(N − 1)
    endfor
permute(x_i)
```

FIGURE   10.17

N-rooks sampling code.

```
for r ← 0 to h − 1
    for c ← 0 to w − 1
        k ← (rw) + c
        x_k ← (1 + 2c + symmetric(1/2w))/(2w)
        y_k ← (1 + 2r + symmetric(1/2h))/(2h)
        endfor
    endfor
```

FIGURE   10.18

Regular sampling aligned to resample grid.

10.5.10 Jitter Distribution

A sampling pattern may be perturbed by the addition of *jitter*. Jitter, or random displacement, may be applied to any pattern based on stratified sampling by moving each sample to a random position within its piece of the domain. So it is easy to add jitter to any of the uniform patterns, or the N-rooks pattern, simply by adding an appropriate amount of random displacement to each sample (taking care that the displacement keeps the sample within its domain).

The code in Figure 10.18 shows how to create a jittered regular square grid by adding noise to Figure 10.6. The noise is enough to move the sample as much as halfway toward either neighbor horizontally and vertically.

An example of this algorithm is shown in Figure 10.19, along with the magnitude of its Fourier transform.

The hexagonal lattice may also be jittered, though the geometry is slightly more complex. Figure 10.20 shows a hexagon divided into twelve equivalent regions.

We can jitter a sample in the hexagon's center by generating a random displacement in the region marked I, perhaps reflecting it about the y axis into the region F, and then rotating it by some integer multiple of $60° = \pi/3$. To pick a random point within I, we first pick an angle $\theta \in [\pi/3, \pi/2]$ and then a distance d from

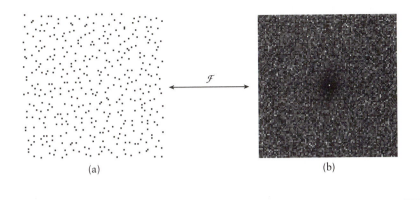

FIGURE 10.19

(a) A jittered rectangular lattice. (b) The magnitude Fourier transform of (a).

the center; a little trig shows that the maximum value for d as a function of θ is $d_{\max} = 1/(2\cos\theta)$. The pseudocode is shown in Figure 10.21.

10.5.11 Poisson-Disk Pattern

A *Poisson-disk distribution* is a random pattern that satisfies the *Poisson-disk criterion*: no two samples are closer together than some distance r_p. The name of this pattern is inspired by the idea of surrounding each random sample by a disk of the given radius, such that no two disks overlap. We also usually want the samples to be as close together as the disks allow.

10.5.12 Precomputed Poisson-Disk Patterns

A theoretically proper way to create a Poisson-disk pattern is to generate a large number of random patterns with Poisson statistics and use only those that satisfy the Poisson-disk criterion [307].

This is not a very efficient way to generate such a pattern, so a variety of alternatives have been devised. One popular approach is to build a small pattern (sometimes called a *prototype* or *tile*) that satisfies the Poisson-disk criterion and then save that pattern in a table. For convenience, we will assume that the tile has unit parameterization; that is, it spans the domain $[0, 0]$ to $(1, 1)$ [101, 124]. The table may then be replicated with rotations and reflections to cover the sampling domain, as discussed below.

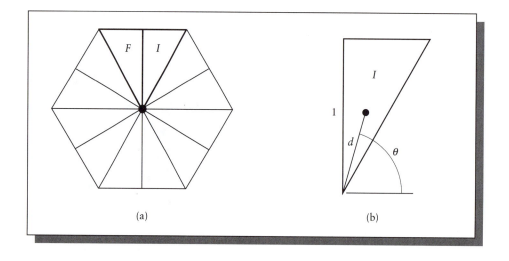

(a)   (b)

FIGURE 10.20

A hexagon broken up into twelve equivalent regions. (a) The initial (I) and flipped (F) regions.
(b) Finding a point within I.

for $r \leftarrow 0$ to $h - 1$ for $c \leftarrow 0$ to $w - 1$	*Scan all rows and columns.*
$\theta \leftarrow$ randomInterval$(\pi/3, \pi/2)$ $d \leftarrow$ range$(1/(2\cos\theta))$ $\Delta x \leftarrow d\cos\theta$ $\Delta y \leftarrow d\sin\theta$	*Pick a random point in the primary region.*

if flip() then
    $\Delta x \leftarrow -\Delta x$
  endif
	Perhaps flip it into region F.

$\phi \leftarrow (\pi/3) *$ randomInteger$(0, 5)$	*Pick one of six sides to rotate into.*
$\Delta x' \leftarrow \Delta x \cos\phi + \Delta y \sin\phi$ $\Delta y' \leftarrow -\Delta x \sin\phi + \Delta y \cos\phi$	*Rotate the jitter vector.*
$k \leftarrow (rw) + c$ $x_k \leftarrow (3c)/\sqrt{3} + \Delta x'$ $y_k \leftarrow 2(r + (c \bmod 2)) + \Delta y'$	*Add the jitter into the hexagon center.*
endfor endfor	

FIGURE 10.21

Jittering a hexagonal lattice.

```
i ← 0
while i < N
    xᵢ ← unit()                              Throw a dart.
    yᵢ ← unit()
    reject ← false
    for k ← 0 to i − 1                       Check the distance to all other samples.
        d ← (xᵢ − xₖ)² + (yᵢ − yₖ)²
        if d < (2rₚ)² then
            reject ← true                    This one is too close—forget it.
            break
        endif
    endfor
    if not reject then
        i ← i + 1                            Append this one to the pattern.
    endif
endwhile
```

FIGURE 10.22

Building a Poisson-disk pattern by dart throwing.

One approach to building the pattern is called *dart-throwing* [101, 124, 307]. In this technique, randomly distributed samples are generated one by one and added into an accumulating pattern. Each new sample is compared against all the previously accepted samples; if the distance to its nearest neighbor is equal to or greater than the Poisson-disk distance r_p, that sample is accepted and added into the pattern. The pseudocode for this technique is shown in Figure 10.22. An example of the result of this algorithm is shown in Figure 10.23.

If the tile is large with respect to the eventual resampling frequency, then we can postulate that most of the aliasing errors will turn into noise, and only those structures that are very large in the image will turn into correlated aliasing errors in the sampled signal. If this assumption is valid, then we can evaluate the intersample distances in the dart-throwing algorithm as though the sample tile was actually a torus: the left and right sides are sewn together, as well as the top and bottom. This is so that the minimum-distance criterion is still satisfied when two tiles are placed side by side.

Dart-throwing is an expensive simulation algorithm and is only practical for small numbers of samples. It is also possible for the simulation to leave large holes in the

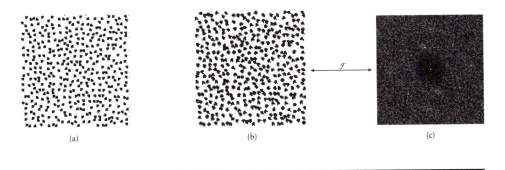

FIGURE 10.23
(a) A pattern built by dart throwing, showing the local disks. (b) The pattern in (a) without the disks. (c) The magnitude of the Fourier transform of (b).

sampling pattern even after testing many candidates. Another problem with dart throwing is that the input to the simulation is the radius of the minimum-separation disk, so it is difficult to generate patterns with a predetermined number of samples.

10.5.13 Multiple-Scale Poisson-Disk Patterns

In the overview discussed at the start of this chapter, the method of adaptive refinement was mentioned as a common technique for increasing the sampling rate locally in regions of high bandwidth. A number of different approaches will be discussed later in this chapter, but it is useful right now to mention that most of them are based on either subdivision or the use of an entirely new higher density sampling pattern.

We will look at two techniques for building patterns that may be used for increasing the sampling density locally while maintaining the statistical characteristics of the samples. Both are based on building a sample tile with the desired characteristics and then replicating that tile across the sampling domain. In particular, we can build a pattern by drawing sequential samples one by one, in predetermined order, from a precomputed list of sample positions. The list is built so that when sample n is drawn, the list of samples s_0 to s_{n-1} satisfy the Poisson-disk criterion. The radius used in the test decreases with increasing n. So by taking more samples from the list, the effective sampling rate goes up, while retaining a Poisson-disk characteristic. The complete list forms a tile that should be reflected and rotated to cover the sampling domain, as with other precomputed patterns.

Both methods are variations on dart throwing, and are somewhat similar. We call the approach suggested by Mitchell [308] the *best candidate* algorithm. It takes as input two values: the number of desired samples N and a quality parameter q.

```
x₀ ← unit()                          Plant the initial sample.
y₀ ← unit()
for i ← 1 to N
  d_max ← 1
  for c ← 1 to iq
    u ← unit()                       Make a candidate.
    v ← unit()
    d_c ← 1
    for k ← 0 to i − 1
      d ← (x_j − u)² + (y_j − v)²    Get distance to nearest existing sample.
      d_c ← min(d_c, d)
    endfor
    if d_c > d_max then
      x_i ← u
      y_i ← v                        Take this if it's the best so far.
      d_min ← d_c
    endif
  endfor
endfor
```

FIGURE 10.24

The best candidate algorithm.

The algorithm begins by placing a single sample at some random position in the tile; this is sample 1. The algorithm then iterates a placement procedure $N - 1$ times. In iteration i, the placement procedure creates iq uniformly distributed samples in the tile. These new samples are compared to the existing ones, and the sample farthest from all the others is added into the pattern. Since the number of samples is scaled by i, there is a constant ratio of candidates to existing samples. This algorithm is given in pseudocode in Figure 10.24.

As the value of q is increased, a larger number of candidates is generated each time around the loop. This is useful because the algorithm selects the best candidate in each iteration. The more candidates that are tested, the better our chance of finding one near the optimal position. This technique may be accelerated by using standard techniques for spatial search such as grids and quadtrees [373, 374].

By keeping a table identifying the samples in the order of their creation, we can use the first N samples to get an approximate Poisson-disk estimate for different sampling densities. An example of this algorithm is shown in Figure 10.25.

Figure 10.25 shows an interesting phenomenon: the Fourier transform of the sampling pattern has a very specific structure. In the Fourier transform, there's a spike at DC (in the center), then a ring of low magnitude, and then, beyond a certain distance from the center, the higher frequencies start to assert themselves in a noisy way. As we add more samples to our pattern, the low-magnitude ring around the center spike becomes larger. This is to be expected, since we know that multiplying a signal by this sampling pattern corresponds to convolving with the sampling pattern's Fourier transform; with a wide ring around the center of the transform, nearby transforms will not overlap in the convolution. Distant samples will contribute some energy, though, because the magnitude of the transform comes back up outside of the center ring. But because this extra energy is noisy, it will not be strongly correlated with the sampling pattern, and the visual system will be inclined to tolerate it as noise, rather than interpret it as structured pattern. So we want this inner ring to be as large as possible (to keep interaction between local neighbors down, and thus reduce the introduction of small-scale patterns); the closer-packed the samples are in the signal domain, the larger the ring in the Fourier domain. This "spike-and-ring" pattern is a characteristic of Poisson-disk-like sampling patterns.

A similar approach to creating a multiple-scale sampling tile, presented by McCool and Fiume [294], is called the *decreasing radius algorithm*. The user specifies N, the number of samples desired in the final tile, a magnification parameter m, a disk-reduction fraction f, and a quality parameter q. The algorithm begins by placing one point at random within the tile and setting the Poisson-disk radius r_p to a large number (e.g., the width of the tile). Then an iteration is started that loops N times. To find sample i, a new loop is entered that creates and tests new uniformly distributed candidate points in the tile. This loop repeats until one of the candidates satisfies the Poisson-disk criterion, or imq candidates have been tried. The value of m is used to adjust the number of candidates created as the number of samples already placed increases. If a new sample satisfies the Poisson-disk criteria, that sample is added to the pattern. Otherwise, the disk radius is decreased by the fraction f and the candidates are tried again. The process is summarized in pseudocode in Figure 10.26.

One way to visualize this algorithm is as a series of cones, as in Figure 10.27. Each time a sample is placed, it establishes the central axis of a right circular cone perpendicular to the plane of the tile. The angle of the cones is controlled by f. The algorithm sweeps the tile plane downward in equal steps toward the plane that contains the apex of all the cones (i.e., the point samples themselves). Each time the plane is moved, the algorithm tries to insert a new cone with initial radius equal to the radius of all other cones at that level. If no such cones can be fit, the plane is swept downward again.

Examples of this algorithm similar to those for the best candidate algorithm

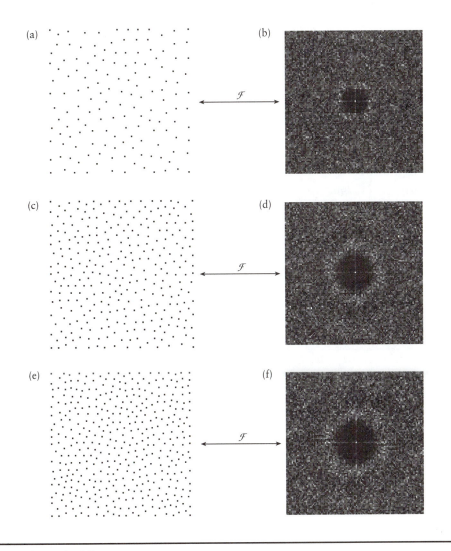

FIGURE 10.25

The best candidate algorithm for $N = 400$ and $q = 10$. (a) The first 150 samples. (b) The magnitude Fourier transform of (a). (c) The first 300 samples. (d) The magnitude Fourier transform of (c). (e) The first 400 samples. (f) The magnitude Fourier transform of (e).

```
x₀ ← unit()
y₀ ← unit()                                    Plant the first sample and set radius.
rₚ ← 1
for i ← 1 to N
  placed ← false
  while not placed
    s ← 0
    d_min ← 1
    while s < imq
      u ← unit()
                                               Throw a dart.
      v ← unit()
      for j ← 0 to i − 1
        d ← (xⱼ − u)² + (yⱼ − v)²
        if d < d_min then
                                               Find the nearest existing sample.
          d_min ← d
        endif
      endfor
      if d_min > rₚ then
        placed ← true
        xᵢ ← u                                 It's a good one—save it.
        yᵢ ← v
      endif
      s ← s + 1
    endwhile
    rₚ ← rₚ * f
  endwhile
endfor
```

FIGURE 10.26

The decreasing radius algorithm.

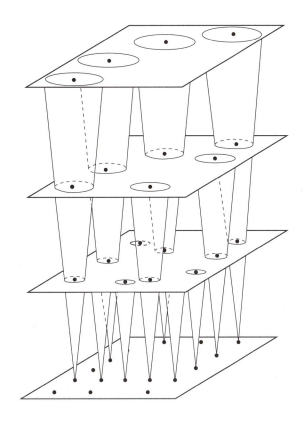

FIGURE 10.27

The geometry of the decreasing radius algorithm.

are shown in Figure 10.28. This algorithm also may be sped up by space-search techniques.

The best candidate and decreasing radius algorithms share much in common, but there are differences. The best candidate algorithm is guaranteed to place a new sample every iteration. There is no guarantee that the pattern satisfies the Poisson-disk criterion at any level, since it simply chooses the best candidate. For the same reason, the nearest-distance value for a sequence of candidates may not be monotonic, which means the pattern may not be increasingly dense overall. The latter problem may be solved by sorting the points after they have been built [294].

The decreasing radius algorithm is guaranteed to satisfy the Poisson constraint, but it requires three user parameters rather than one. The magnification parameter

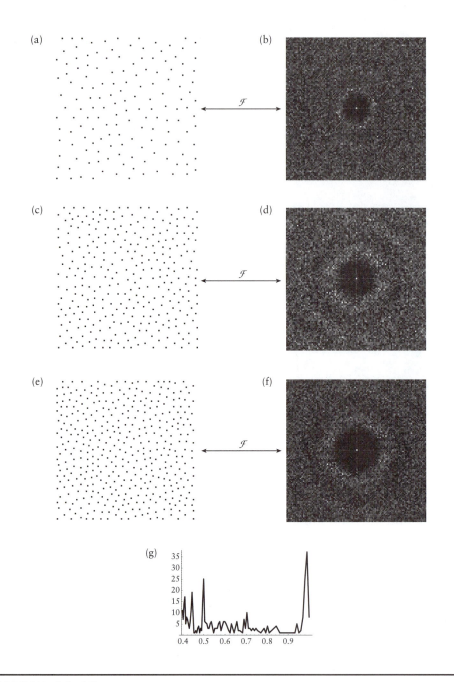

FIGURE 10.28

The decreasing radius algorithm for $N = 400$, $q = 10$, $m = 1$, and $f = 0.99$. (a) The first 150 samples. (b) The magnitude Fourier transform of (a). (c) The first 300 samples. (d) The magnitude Fourier transform of (c). (e) The first 400 samples. (f) The magnitude Fourier transform of (e). (g) The number of points placed as a function of r for (e).

m is actually a generalization of the best candidate algorithm's scheme; setting $m = 1$ causes these two steps to be the same. The quality parameter q is also the same in both algorithms. That leaves the cone angle f, the amount by which the cone is decreased at each step. This should be a value only slightly less than one. Larger values will cause the algorithm to run more slowly, and will tend to produce denser patterns at each level.

Both algorithms will always terminate with the desired number of samples. The best candidate algorithm has the advantage that the candidate selection test may be generalized to create patterns of any sort, not just Poisson-disk. The decreasing radius algorithm will generate a better Poisson-disk pattern, but it requires the evaluation function to be univariate and monotonically easier to satisfy with decreasing values of r_p. The best candidate method is the more general of the two and is better for satisfying arbitrary distributions; the decreasing radius method is tuned to Poisson-disk patterns and is preferable for that case.

10.5.14 Sampling Tiles

The techniques in the last section precompute some small pattern or tile which is then replicated across the domain. The precomputed tile approach is attractive because it allows us to generate patterns that meet almost any criteria, without paying the generation cost at run-time.

The drawback to the tile approach is that simple replication of the tile introduces the periodic sampling we want to avoid [124]. Figure 10.29(a) shows a nonuniform 2D tile, and in Figure 10.29(b) that tile has been replicated by translation to cover the domain. The tile has a width w and contains n samples s_i. If we consider each sample separately, then the operation of replicating the tile creates a uniform, square grid that is w units on a side, with an origin at s_i, as in Figure 10.29(c). So we end up with n different square grids, each slightly displaced to the others. Below we will see a reconstruction method for this type of pattern.

Because the repeated tile in effect creates multiple grids, we have created a pattern that is stochastic locally but periodic globally. The periodicity will come back to haunt us as large-scale structured aliasing artifacts in the signal. To avoid this problem, we can try introducing transformations to the tile each time it is placed. Suppose that the tile is square, as in Figure 10.30(a). Then there are eight possible linear transformations of the tile, corresponding to the eight symmetry transformations that preserve the square. These are the four right-angle rotations (0, 90, 180, and 270°), each of which can be combined with a reflection, as in Figure 10.30(b).

We can break up the grids created by simple translation by applying one of these transformations at random to each tile as it is laid down. It is often necessary, however, to be able to go back to a region of the domain after it has been sampled (when refining adaptively, for example). Rather than store an arbitrarily sized table

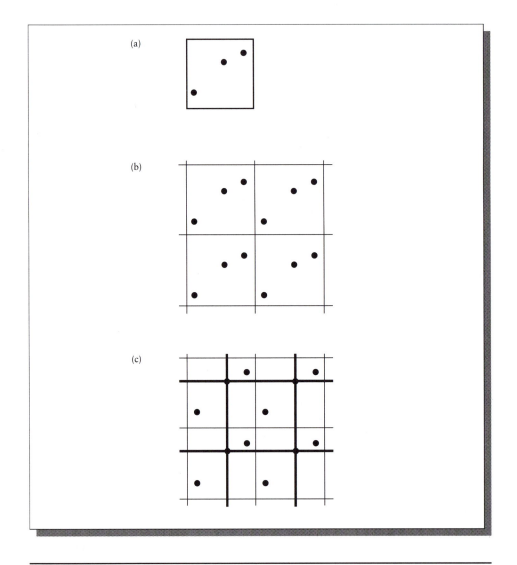

FIGURE   10.29

(a) A single nonuniform tile. (b) The tile of (a) covering the plane by translation. (c) One of the square grids induced by step (b).

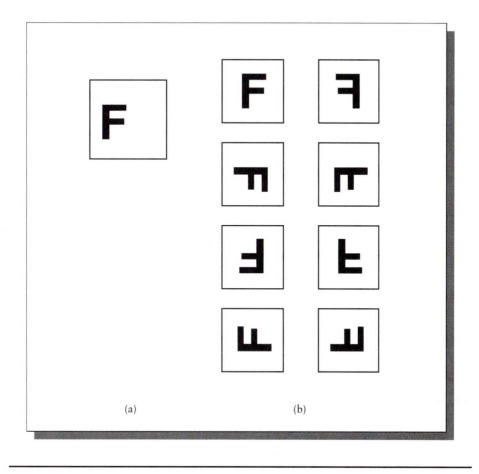

(a)   (b)

FIGURE 10.30

(a) A square tile. (b) The eight linear transformations of (a).

of transformations, we assign the numbers 0 through 7 arbitrarily to the eight transformations, and specify the appropriate operation to be applied as the value of a function T mapping the (x, y) plane to the integer range [0–7]. It is important that this function be aperiodic over the domain being tiled; we don't care if it repeats outside of that domain. These functions can be built from the standard noise functions used for creating textures [272, 338].

Another alternative is to apply a continuous transformation to the tile, where the parameters of the transformation are also drawn from an underlying function. If

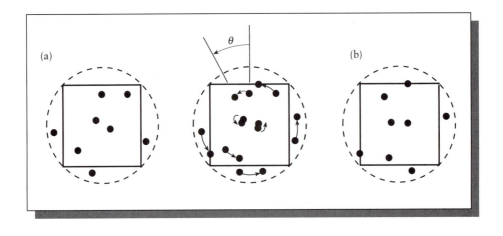

FIGURE   10.31

(a) The initial square tile and the samples in its circumscribing circle. (b) A rotation of the tile by θ produces a new pattern.

the basic tile is a square, we might produce enough samples in the stored pattern to fill the circle circumscribing that square, as in Figure 10.31(a). Then the underlying parameter specifies an angle θ by which the pattern should be rotated about the center of the square, as in Figure 10.31(b). The samples are clipped to the square before they are used. Any of these methods can introduce error in our sampling pattern by bringing samples too close together on the boundaries of transformed tiles.

10.5.15   Dynamic Poisson-Disk Patterns

The above methods for generating Poisson-disk patterns require an expensive prerendering step and the storage of tables. Another class of techniques has been developed that creates approximate patterns during rendering time; we call these *dynamic* or *on-demand* pattern-generation techniques.

Point-Diffusion

Mitchell's *point-diffusion algorithm* [307] adapts the technique of *error diffusion* used by dithering algorithms [445] to guide the creation of approximate Poisson-disk patterns. The algorithm scans a rectangular grid that has a frequency of about four times the desired sampling density along each axis, and selects about one sample out of sixteen. The underlying grid can be hidden by jittering each chosen sample. As with dithering algorithms, the scan should proceed boustrophedonically (in opposite directions on successive lines). A "diffusion value" D is computed for each point as a combination of the values of D stored at its neighbors.

For a point at (m, n), the diffusion values D are gathered from above and adjacent pixels to compute a temporary value T:

$$T = R + \frac{4D_{m-1,n} + D_{m-1,n-1} + 2D_{m,n-1} + D_{m+1,n-1}}{8} \qquad (10.6)$$

where R is a uniform noise source in the range $[3/64, 5/64]$. The value T is then used to decide whether a sample point should be selected; if so, the variable S is set to 1:

$$S = \begin{cases} 0 & \text{if } T < 0.5 \\ 1 & \text{otherwise} \end{cases} \qquad (10.7)$$

The new diffusion value stored at this sampling point is then computed as

$$D_{m,n} = T - S \qquad (10.8)$$

for the values of T and S computed at this point.

The values in Equation 10.6 were chosen experimentally to create a pattern with the desired Fourier characteristics, and to be inexpensive to evaluate (only shifts are necessary if all values are integers).

If this value exceeds a threshold, that sample is selected for evaluation, and the value associated with that sample is decreased by one. The algorithm is described in pseudocode in Figure 10.32. The function `evaluate()` is called to evaluate the signal at the given location. A bit of noise is added to the value of D to suppress orderly patterns; the range of noise is chosen to cause about one grid point in sixteen to be selected.

An example of the pattern generated by this algorithm and its Fourier transform are given in Figure 10.33. As Figure 10.33(c) shows, it is important to scan boustrophedonically to avoid directional artifacts in the pattern.

Hexagonal Jittering

Another type of dynamic, approximate Poisson-disk pattern may be generated by a direct application of jittering. The jittered-lattice techniques described in the previous section can be generated on demand by perturbing samples as they are created, but the methods as described do not satisfy the Poisson-disk criterion. It isn't too hard to modify them to do so.

Recall from above that the densest regular packing of samples in the place corresponds to a hexagonal lattice, so this is a reasonable place to start. We can produce

$i \leftarrow 0$

$\text{for } r \leftarrow 0 \text{ to } h - 1$ *Scan the high-resolution grid.*

   $\text{for } c \leftarrow 0 \text{ to } w - 1$

      $D_{r,c} \leftarrow D_{c-1,r-1} + 2D_{c,r} + D_{c+1,r-1}$ *Get Ds from above.*

      $\text{if } r \bmod 2 = 0$

         $\text{then } D_{r,c} \leftarrow D_{r,c} + 4D_{c-1,r}$

         $\text{else } D_{r,c} \leftarrow D_{r,c} + 4D_{c+1,r}$ *Get D from left or right as appropriate.*

      endif

      $D_{r,c} \leftarrow (D_{r,c}/8) + \text{symmetric}\,(1/16 + 1/64)$ *Average neighbors and add noise.*

      $\text{if } D_{r,c} > 0.5 \text{ then}$

         $D_{r,c} \leftarrow D_{r,c} - 1$

         $\text{evaluate}\,(D_{r,c})$ *Above threshold—evaluate this sample.*

      endif

   endfor

  endfor

FIGURE 10.32

The point-diffusion algorithm, scanning from left to right.

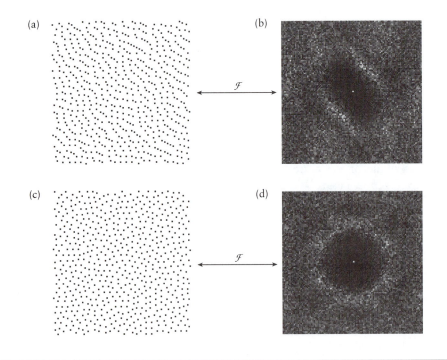

FIGURE 10.33

(a) A pattern generated by the point-diffusion algorithm scanning from left to right. (b) The magnitude Fourier transform of (a). (c) The point-diffusion algorithm with a boustrephendonic scanning. (d) The magnitude Fourier transform of (c).

```
for r ← 0 to h − 1                                    Scan all rows and columns.
   for c ← 0 to w − 1
─────────────────────────────────────────────────────────────────────────────
      θ ← randomInterval(π,)
─────────────────────────────────────────────────────────────────────────────
      d ← range((1 − 2r_p)/(2 cos θ))                 New value for d.
─────────────────────────────────────────────────────────────────────────────
      Δx ← d cos θ
                                                      Pick a random point in the primary region.
      Δy ← d sin θ
─────────────────────────────────────────────────────────────────────────────
      if flip() then
         Δx ← −Δx                                     Perhaps flip it into region F.
      endif
─────────────────────────────────────────────────────────────────────────────
      φ ← (π/3)∗ randomInteger(0,5)                   Pick one of six sides to rotate into.
─────────────────────────────────────────────────────────────────────────────
      Δx' ← Δx cos φ + Δy sin φ
                                                      Find the jitter vector.
      Δy' ← −Δx sin φ + Δy cos φ
─────────────────────────────────────────────────────────────────────────────
      k ← (rw) + c
      x_k ← (3c)/√3 + Δx'                             Add the jitter into the hexagon center.
      y_k ← 2(r + (c mod 2)) + Δy'
   endfor
endfor
```

FIGURE 10.34

Jittered hexagon approximation to a Poisson-disk pattern.

samples that satisfy the Poisson-disk constraint by making sure that they never get closer than r_p to the outer perimeter of the hexagon. This is easily done by decreasing the value of d in Figure 10.21. The new maximum value of d is given by

$$d_{\max} = (1 − 2r_p)/(2 \cos \theta) \tag{10.9}$$

In order to have room to move the sample point, the distance from the center of each hexagon to the midpoint of a side must be at least r_p. We can now write the pseudocode for a jittered hexagon approximation to a Poisson-disk pattern in Figure 10.34; the only change to Figure 10.21 is the calculation of d.

A result of this approach, and its Fourier transform, is shown in Figure 10.35.

10.5.16 Importance Sampling

In general, the samples we evaluate will make different contributions to the estimated signal. For example, we may use image samples to estimate the incident

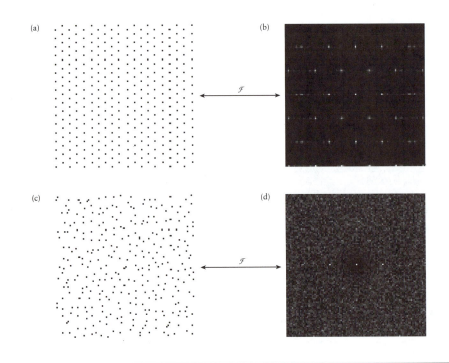

FIGURE 10.35

(a) A regular hexagonal lattice. (b) The magnitude Fourier transform of (a). (c) A jittered hexagonal lattice. (d) The magnitude Fourier transform of (c).

light on a surface, for the purpose of determining how much light is leaving that surface in a particular direction. Each incident direction will then be weighted by some reflectance function when it is taken into account. Thus we might say that some samples are more *important* than others, in the sense that they make a larger contribution to the final value.

There are two general approaches to handling the different contributions of different samples. One approach is to distribute the samples with a uniform density and then weight each one appropriately, shown schematically in Figure 10.36(a). The other method is to distribute the samples in such a way that they fall more densely in regions that we know carry a larger weight. This latter approach is called *importance sampling* [182], and it has been an important part of most nonuniform sampling techniques in computer graphics [101, 234]. This approach is shown schematically in Figure 10.36(b).

Importance sampling is a useful technique in practice because it puts most of

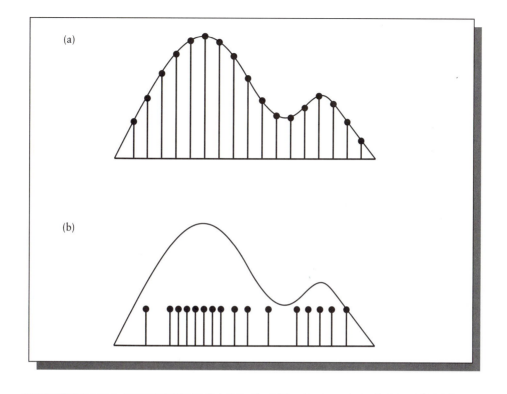

FIGURE 10.36

Two ways to accommodate a nonflat function. (a) Equal distribution of samples, unequal weighting. (b) Unequal distribution of samples, equal weighting.

the samples where they will be most influential. This helps reduce the number of samples needed, since we won't be taking many samples in regions of the signal that are unimportant.

In practice, to apply importance sampling to a signal, we need to know the *filter* with which the signal will be modified. There are then two approaches to using this information.

Intuitively, in the first approach we divide the filter into regions of equal area (or volume) and cast an equal number of samples into each region. This is shown in Figure 10.37. The samples may be distributed uniformly or quasi-randomly within each region; if they are jittered, the size of the jitter must be adjusted to the size of the region.

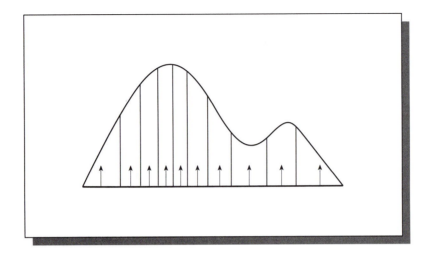

FIGURE 10.37

Importance sampling by dividing a filter into regions of equal volume.

In the second approach, we divide the domain of the filter into equal pieces, and then try to place samples so that the relative density of samples between regions of the filter is proportional to the relative areas or volumes of those regions. This is shown schematically in Figure 10.38. This second approach requires more bookkeeping and seems to be rarely used in practice.

One practical implementation of importance sampling begins with carrying out the equal-volume segmentation of the filter discussed above, followed by taking an equal number of samples in each region [101]. This requires a preprocessing subdivision step, and also means we must decide how many regions to subdivide the signal into before we start sampling. An advantage of this approach is that we are guaranteed to sample all the regions of the signal; a disadvantage is that we cannot smoothly increase the sampling density. The method may be improved to support adaptive sampling by subdividing each region on demand [234].

Another approach is to generate uniformly distributed points in a canonical space (such as the unit interval or unit square), and then deform that space to match the desired density. This approach is discussed in some detail in [400], where Shirley shows the warping to match a separable 2D triangular function. This function may be expressed with the center at the origin as the product of two 1D functions:

$$w(x, y) = w(x)w(y) = (1 - |x|)(1 - |y|) \tag{10.10}$$

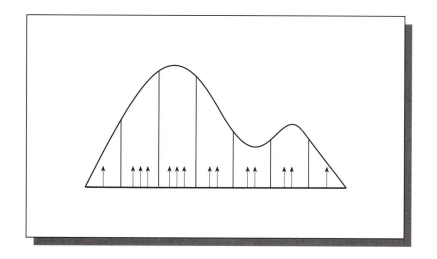

FIGURE 10.38

Dividing a filter into equal-sized regions.

We can write the *distribution function* $W(x)$ associated $w(x)$ as the probability that $w(x) < x$ for each value of x [331]. Since $w(x)$ is the density of points at x, the distribution function is just the integral of w from its lower limit (here -1) to x:

$$W(x) = \int_{-1}^{x} (1 - |\tau|) \, d\tau = \frac{1}{2} + x - \frac{1}{2}x|x| \qquad (10.11)$$

The values of $W(x)$ can be precomputed and stored in a sum table [111].

To make a set of samples (x, y) that match the distribution $w(x, y)$, we generate pairs of uniformly distributed values (u, v), and find $(x, y) = (W^{-1}(u), W^{-1}(v))$ where W^{-1} is the inverse of W, given by

$$W^{-1}(a) = \begin{cases} -1 + \sqrt{2a} & a < 0.5 \\ 1 - \sqrt{2(1 - a)} & \text{otherwise} \end{cases} \qquad (10.12)$$

The multiple-scale templates discussed earlier may also be used to perform importance sampling, using a method described by McCool [294]. The basic idea is to realize that the order in which points were added to the pattern roughly corresponds to the density of the pattern when they were created. So if a sample was added late in the pattern's development, it probably represents a high-density sample and is nearer to at least one other sample than earlier samples. We can use this observation to

$f_{\min} \leftarrow \min(f)$	*Get filter bounds for normalization.*
$f_{\max} \leftarrow \max(f)$	
for $i \leftarrow 1$ to N	*For each sample, find local and*
$\quad r_i \leftarrow i/n$	*filter value.*
$\quad c_i \leftarrow (f(s_i) - f_{\min})/(f_{\max} - f_{\min})$	
$\quad$ if $r_i \leq c_i$ then	
$\quad\quad$ evaluate s_i	*We're below the filter, so use this sample.*
$\quad$ endif	
endfor	

FIGURE 10.39

Importance-sampling a multiple-scale pattern.

choose samples from the template, selecting many of them in regions where the filter has a large value and ignoring those where the filter is small.

To use this idea, we scan through the samples one by one. For each sample, we estimate its local density simply by its index, which tells us when it was added to the pattern. We normalize this index by dividing by the total number of samples n. We then evaluate the filter function at this sample location, and again normalize (effectively scaling and shifting the function so that it runs from 0 to 1). If the sample density is less than the filter density, then that sample is selected and evaluated. Pseudocode for this algorithm is given in Figure 10.39. An example of the result for a particular filter is shown in Figure 10.40.

A graphical look at this technique is shown in Figure 10.41 using the distribution of points as in Figure 10.27. As the filter value becomes larger, it dips into denser regions of the pattern and includes more samples.

10.5.17 Multidimensional Patterns

Most of the patterns we have looked at are 2D in the domain of the signal. When the signal is a 3D scene and the samples determine visibility, they are projecting a 3D function to 2D. In general, the patterns used in graphics project from $\mathcal{R}^m$ to $\mathcal{R}^n$, where $m \geq n$.

An important projection is the one from a 3D scene onto a 2D surface (e.g., a viewing plane or an illumination hemisphere). In a distribution ray tracer, the 3D scene is augmented with a number of other parameters. For example, we might associate a time with each sample and a particular angle to be used for possible reflections off surfaces. These two additional parameters join the three spatial ones,

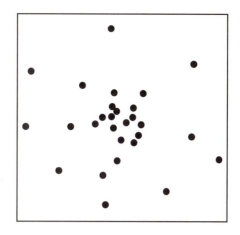

FIGURE 10.40

A Poisson-disk pattern weighted by $\exp(-5(x^2+y^2))$. Redrawn from McCool and Fiume in *Proc. Graphics Interface '92*, fig. 16, p. 102.

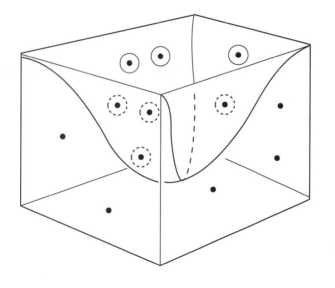

FIGURE 10.41

An illustration of importance sampling of a variable-scale pattern. The filter is the volume scooping downward in the figure; samples inside the filter are circled.

so our samples are actually 5D. When all samples have been evaluated, we still have a 2D function $f(x, y)$ giving the intensity of the signal as a function of spatial coordinates.

The two spatial coordinates play a special role: they are the only ones that are conserved through the sampling process. The other parameters of the sample are created but then discarded once the sample has been evaluated. We will call the spatial parameters *direct parameters* of the sample, and all others *indirect parameters*. We will use the letters x and y to refer to the the direct parameters of a sample, and we will put them at the start of any list of dimensions associated with a sample. Some dimensions involved in sampling are coupled because together they represent a single domain (e.g., x, y on the screen or u, v texture coordinates on a surface), while others are independent (e.g., the time parameter). This topic has been discussed at length by Mitchell [308]; the discussion in this section is based on that presentation.

The most direct way to sample d dimensions is to generate n samples, each of which has associated parameters

$$s_i = \{x_i, y_i, u_i, t_i, \ldots\} \tag{10.13}$$

where each parameter comes from an independent random variable. We know that stratified sampling often leads to a good estimate of a signal value faster than random sampling, so we can imagine dividing each dimension i into N_i regions. This creates a hypervolume that has N_i cells on a side, for a total of $N_1 \times N_2 \times \cdots \times N_n$ cells in the volume.

If there are d dimensions and we split each one into n cells, then to place one sample in each volume, we need n^d samples. This required number of samples rises very quickly with both the number of dimensions and the number of cells per dimension (in current practice, these numbers are often more than eight and sixteen, respectively).

An alternative is sampling with *incomplete block designs*. In this strategy, we imagine that the hypervolume described above is projected onto each dimension (or coupled pair); we design our sampling pattern so that each cell in the stratified projection domain is sampled at least once. For example, we fill the 3D volume representing (x, y, t) with samples in such a way that if we project the volume onto the (x, y) plane, each 2D cell contains at least one sample, and if we project the volume onto the t axis, each 1D cell contains at least one sample.

A means to accomplish this was suggested by Cook [101]. His application was image sampling. For each pixel, he stratified the (x, y) domain into sixteen regions. The time domain was then stratified into sixteen intervals. Each sample in the (x, y) plane was identified with one of the time intervals by use of a template, like the one in Figure 10.42. The precise time for each sample may be jittered within its interval. This approach can be extended to other indirect parameters, such as reflection angle and location on a lens.

7	11	3	14
4	15	13	9
16	1	8	12
6	10	5	2

FIGURE 10.42

Pattern for associating time intervals with spatial regions. Data from Cook in *ACM Transactions on Graphics*, fig. 8, p. 62.

1	2	3	4
5	6	7	8
9	10	11	12
13	14	15	16

FIGURE 10.43

A bad pattern.

Cook noted that if the placement of samples in the cells is correlated in some regular way, then these artifacts will influence the final estimate of the signal (in an image, we will see aliasing artifacts like those from regular sampling). For example, suppose the time values were assigned to the regions as in Figure 10.43. In the figure, the pixel area is shown swept over time. We have broken the time interval into four quarters, so samples with values 1 through 4 fall into the nearest quarter of the cube.

Suppose a black object is moving downward over a white background in the pixel as in Figure 10.44(a); the object only covers 1/4 of the pixel and moves in quick steps every 1/4 second. This (admittedly pathological) example demonstrates the problem that comes up when the motion is correlated with the sample assignment. Every space-time cell that is sampled contains the object, so the entire pixel will be black. If the object is moving upward as in Figure 10.44(b), every space-time cell that is sampled is empty, which results in the equally incorrect answer of an entirely white pixel. In general, if there are correlations within a pixel, those patterns will tend to be amplified by the regular geometry of the pixel grid, and the resulting errors will be easily noticeable. Mitchell has observed that these correlations may be thought of as hyperplanes in the d-dimensional hypercube.

Another way to distribute samples in the d-dimensional hypercube is with the d-dimensional form of N-rook sampling discussed earlier [397]. Suppose that each parameter is divided into n cells. We make a table of d permutations $\pi_1, \pi_2, \ldots, \pi_d$ of

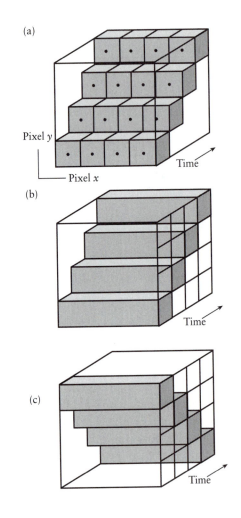

FIGURE 10.44

(a) A sampling pattern in space-time. (b) One bad situation for the pattern. (c) Another bad situation for the pattern.

Permutation	Sample parameters				
	Sample 1	Sample 2	Sample 3	Sample 4	Sample 5
π_x	1	5	3	2	4
π_y	3	2	4	1	5
π_t	4	1	5	2	2

FIGURE 10.45
N-rooks in d dimensions.

the numbers $\{1, 2, \ldots, d\}$; these are just d different ways to list the d integers. Then to place sample i in these d dimensions, assign the first parameter to region $\pi_1(i)$, the second to region $\pi_2(i)$, and so on. An example is shown in Figure 10.45.

Both of the techniques described above work well in the sense that their projections onto the different dimensional axes, planes, or hyperplanes fit our criteria of filling each interval at least once. But except for the way templates are used in the first method, there is no real distinction between direct and indirect parameters. We might ask if we can get an equally good answer with fewer samples by recognizing the basic difference between these two types of parameters.

Mitchell has reported that the distribution of the indirect parameters indeed makes a difference [308]. First, consider just the distribution of the direct parameters. We know that we want this to be as high-frequency a pattern as possible. Now select some circular region of these parameters, and start assigning values of an indirect parameter (say t). We want the distribution of t within this region to have a high-frequency pattern as well. If the region we selected is small, then there will not be many samples, so the values of t must be very different to satisfy the high-frequency requirement. We should thus require that samples that are nearby in the direct parameters be far apart in the indirect parameters. Mitchell also discusses the situation of handling multiple indirect parameters, some of which may be coupled.

A variation on the point-diffusion algorithm may be used to generate these sample values. We begin by stratifying the direct parameters (say x and y) and then scanning the resulting regions. We will place one sample in each direct-parameter region and associate one region from each indirect parameter with each sample. These values may then be jittered.

The scanning algorithm is shown in Figure 10.46 for assigning t values on the basis of (x, y) parameters. We want to assign values to the square marked with a bullet. In this figure, we are scanning top to bottom, left to right. The cells marked S are previously scanned "secondary" (or second-neighbor) cells, and those marked

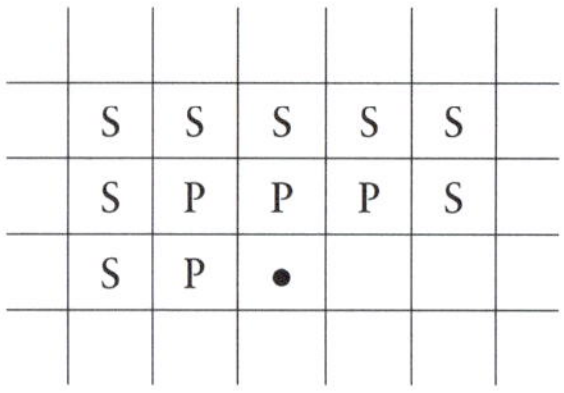

S	S	S	S	S
S	P	P	P	S
S	P	•		

FIGURE 10.46
Sample generation. Data from Mitchell in *Computer Graphics (Proc. Siggraph '91)*, fig. 7, p. 160.

P are "primary" (or first-neighbor) cells; these have already been assigned values of t. An implementation should alternate left-to-right and then right-to-left scanning directions on successive rows.

Mitchell presented a variation of the best-candidate algorithm, which we call the *two-stage best-candidate algorithm*. The process is two passes of the best-candidate procedure, designed to make the best pattern on both a local basis (i.e., with respect to the P cells) and a larger neighborhood (i.e., the S cells). First generate a uniformly distributed samples of t. Find the distance of each of these values of t to each of the four values of t stored at the P cells. Select the b candidates that have the largest minimum distance (i.e., those b values that are the farthest from any of the values stored in the P cells). Now repeat the process with the S cells and select the one candidate that is the farthest from any t in the S cells. Mitchell suggests values of $a = 100$ and $b = 10$.

The two-stage algorithm may be generalized to three or more stages to incorporate additional indirect parameters. It is important to consider these closely because it is not just the projected (or marginal) distribution of each parameter that matters, but also the joint distribution of several parameters taken together. For example, Figure 10.47 shows two 1D parameters attached to eight samples. The projected distributions of each parameter are the same (eight equally spaced points), but their joint distributions are quite different. The distribution on the right is almost perfectly correlated along a line, and hence it badly samples the signal that appears parallel to that line. The figure with fewer correlation samples the pattern better.

So a good distribution of indirect parameters is such that the projected distributions all have most of their energy in high frequencies, and the joint distributions are as weakly correlated as is practical. The two-level sample generation algorithm above may be generalized to n levels for n different sets of parameters.

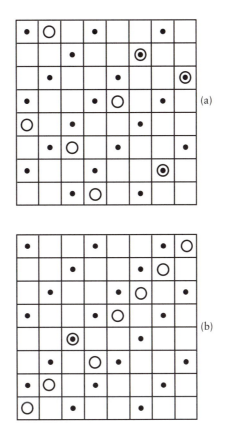

FIGURE 10.47

(a) Uncorrelated joint distribution. (b) A linearly correlated joint distribution. The projected distributions are good in both cases, but the joint distribution in (b) is not very good. The big circles represent sample locations, and the small black disks are places where the signal is 1. Redrawn from Mitchell in *Computer Graphics (Proc. Siggraph '91)*, fig. 1, p. 158.

10.5.18 Discussion

There are several ways to characterize the quality of the sampling patterns described above. Unfortunately, at the moment there is no final word on which pattern is best in all respects.

One way to judge the pattern is to visually examine an average Fourier transform derived from many examples of each class and judge it with respect to an ideal frequency distribution. Examination of the figures in the preceding sections shows that all of the patterns have a DC spike, a small clear zone around the spike, and then a sea of noise, which is roughly the "blue-noise" spectrum. Since we would like the clear zone to be as large as possible, one characterization is to rate the different methods on the radius at which the frequency response starts to become significant.

Dippé and Wold advocate an analytic approach based on the *power signal-to-noise ratio* (SNR) [124]. This measure is proportional to the average number of samples per unit region of the pattern, and to the *flat field response noise spectrum* (FFRNS), which is the noise part of the flat field response scaled by the sampling rate of the pattern. Recall that the flat field response is the result of sampling a flat (or uniform) signal with a given pattern. Dippé and Wold analyzed the FFRNS for Poisson and jitter patterns. They found that low-frequency noise is reduced more by jittered patterns than by Poisson-disk patterns, and felt that this produced perceptually better results when these patterns were used for sampling images. This approach has the advantage of providing a quantitative measure of sampling response, but the FFRNS can be difficult to interpret.

Recall that when discussing Monte Carlo in Chapter 7, we mentioned that *discrepancy* was one way to measure how well a set of points are distributed over a domain.

Intuitively, discrepancy measures the difference between the number of samples we expect in a given area and the number we actually find there. For example, recall that our prototype sampling tile is a unit square. Within any region R of area $A(R)$, we can count the number of samples n within the region. If there are N samples uniformly distributed on the square, then we would expect the ratio of n/N (giving the percentage of points within the region) to be about the same as $A(R)$ (the percentage of area of the unit square occupied by R).

One definition of discrepancy due to Zaremba [397] is based on using rectangular regions with one corner at the origin and one corner at (a, b), as in Figure 10.48. Then the discrepancy $\Delta(x, y)$ is defined as the least upper bound of the difference between the estimated area ratio and the counted sample ratio:

$$\Delta(x, y) = \sup |n/N - ab| \qquad (10.14)$$

A slightly more general definition due to Stroud allows the origin of the box to appear at any point (c, d), as in Figure 10.49. The definition is then

$$\Delta(x, y) = \sup |n/N - (a - c)(b - d)| \qquad (10.15)$$

Shirley has pointed out [397] that we can define a *generalized discrepancy* that takes into account regions of different shapes and sizes. Below, we will see discrepancy based on disks and triangular and quadrilateral portions of a square.

There is a surprising connection between the distribution of sample locations in the pattern and the quality of the estimated signal. Mitchell [309] has pointed out

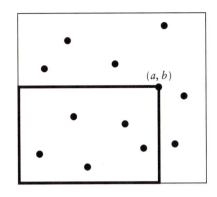

FIGURE 10.48

Calculating discrepancy for a box from $(0,0)$ to (a,b).

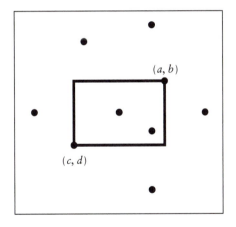

FIGURE 10.49

Calculating discrepancy for a box from (c,d) to (a,b).

Process	Two-dimensional discrepancies		
	16 points	256 points	1,600 points
Zaremba	0.0358	0.00255	0.000438
Jittered	0.0489	0.00633	0.00160
Dart-throwing	0.0490	0.00799	0.00254
N-rooks	0.0461	0.0101	0.00391
Poisson	0.0932	0.0233	0.00932

TABLE 10.2

Two-dimensional discrepancies. *Source:* Data from Mitchell, *Third Eurographics Workshop on Rendering*, table 1, p. 64.

a theorem for 1D signals that says, roughly, if a given set of samples $x_1, \ldots, x_N$ in the unit square have discrepancy D and their variance is bounded by V, then the difference between the average value of the evaluated samples and the real integrated value of the function is bounded by the product VD. In symbols,

$$\left| \frac{1}{N} \sum_{i=1}^{N} f(x_i) - \int_0^1 f(t) \, dt \right| \leq VD \tag{10.16}$$

This result suggests that if we keep the number of samples in our pattern fixed, then as we lower the discrepancy on our sampling pattern, we improve our estimate of the signal by decreasing the error.

Both Shirley [400] and Mitchell [309] present some numerical results that evaluated discrepancy for a variety of patterns and the magnitude of error in a variety of 2D images sampled by those patterns. We present those results below; our comments follow those of the authors.

Table 10.2 shows the discrepancy measured for five different types of patterns, using three different numbers of samples. For the pseudorandom processes, the reported value represents the average of 100 trials. The data is plotted in Figure 10.50.

The data from Table 10.2 is useful because of the wide range of densities it spans; assume it represents the asymptotic behavior of the pattern as the number of samples increases. Recall that our main interest is for relatively low sampling densities, since we want to take as few samples as we can. But sometimes large numbers of samples are necessary, and in any case understanding the long-term behavior of a pattern can help us characterize it.

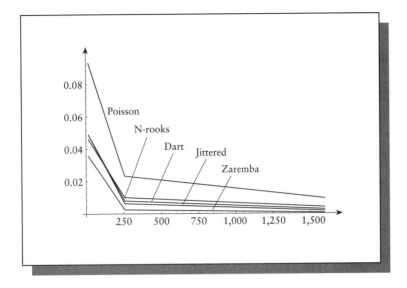

The 2D discrepancy data from Table 10.2.

The pattern that shows the worst asymptotic behavior is the Poisson (or purely random) pattern, which improves only with the square root of the sample size. The Zaremba process improves most dramatically, with the other techniques falling between these two.

An alternative measure of discrepancy uses circular regions, or disks, rather than the axis-aligned rectangles used above. This shape seems to offer a more isotropic measure of discrepancy. The data measured by Mitchell for disks is shown in Table 10.3 and plotted in Figure 10.51.

Again we see that Poisson patterns fare rather poorly. It is interesting that dart-throwing and jittered patterns outperform Zaremba's pattern.

One of the characteristics we want from a pattern is its ability to capture edges of all orientations. That is, do we get at least one sample on both sides of every edge, whatever its orientation? To test this quality, Mitchell created a set of 10,000 random lines in the unit square [309]. He measured discrepancy using the region above each line. The data measured by Mitchell for disks is shown in Table 10.4 and plotted in Figure 10.52.

Zaremba's pattern again performs the best, though jittered and dart-throwing patterns come in a close second.

	Random-disk discrepancies		
Process	16 points	256 points	1,600 points
Dart-throwing	0.0840	0.0120	0.00368
Jittered	0.0994	0.0165	0.00394
Zaremba	0.0855	0.0160	0.00511
Poisson	0.104	0.0239	0.00993
N-rooks	0.0908	0.0224	0.0104

TABLE 10.3

Two-dimensional disk discrepancies. *Source:* Data from Mitchell, *Third Eurographics Workshop on Rendering*, table 3, p. 65.

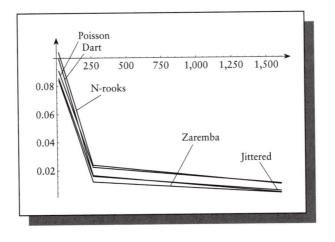

FIGURE 10.51

The 2D discrepancy data for circular regions from Table 10.3.

The discrepancy values given above are useful in quantifying one characteristic of a sampling pattern, namely how uniformly the points are distributed in the tile. They also offer some experimental support for the jittered and dart-throwing patterns, which have justifications from the signal-processing point of view.

But discrepancy does not describe the quality of an image generated with that pattern. For example, Mitchell notes that the Zaremba pattern leads to moiré

Process	Random-edge discrepancies		
	16 points	256 points	1,600 points
Zaremba	0.0504	0.00478	0.00111
Jittered	0.0538	0.00595	0.00146
Dart-throwing	0.0613	0.00767	0.00241
N-rooks	0.0637	0.0123	0.00488
Poisson	0.0924	0.0224	0.00866

TABLE 10.4

Two-dimensional edge discrepancies. *Source:* Data from Mitchell, *Third Eurographics Workshop on Rendering*, table 4, p. 66.

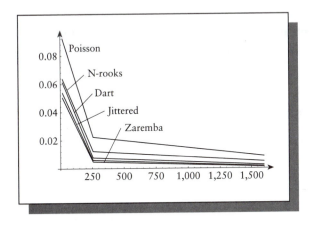

FIGURE 10.52

The 2D discrepancy data for edges from Table 10.4.

Process	Checkerboard	Angled checkerboard	Sine
N-rooks	0.0208	0.0231	0.0517
Jittered	0.0260	0.0258	0.0486
Dart-throwing	0.0271	0.0270	0.0423
Regular	0.0315	0.0252	0.0172
Poisson	0.0359	0.0355	0.0679

TABLE 10.5

Average pixel errors for different patterns. *Source:* Data from Shirley in *Proc. Eurographics '91*, table 3, p. 189.

patterns, and jittered sampling produces images that are grainier than dart-throwing patterns. We conclude that discrepancy is one measure for checking the quality of a proposed sampling pattern, but it is not the primary criterion to be used when choosing a pattern.

In [400] Shirley measured discrepancies for a variety of sampling patterns; the values closely match those given above. But Shirley also applied these patterns to a set of images and evaluated the average pixel error with respect to a high-quality reference image. A measure of pixel error such as this does not tell us anything about the distribution of the error; we cannot tell if the error is uniformly distributed throughout the image in the form of noise, or organized into highly structured artifacts. This is a difficult issue in any case, because the presence of structured aliasing errors depends as much on the underlying continuous image as the sampling pattern that can beat (that is, periodically interact) with it. But pixel errors do give us some idea of how close the final image is to the original in an absolute sense.

We summarize Shirley's measurements in Table 10.5. Three scenes were evaluated. One was a checkerboard receding into the distance, where one axis of the board was aligned with the x-axis of the image plane; thus each scan line cut across a single row of squares. The second was an angled checkerboard rotated 45° to the first, resulting in sighting down diagonals toward the horizon. The third pattern was a sine wave $(\sin(r^2))$, where r is the distance of a pixel to the image origin; this is a set of smoothly varying rings that become thinner and more tightly packed as they spread from the origin. We give Shirley's results for reconstruction with a triangular filter. The message is mixed, but it appears that for this measurement of quality and these images, the jittered and dart-throwing patterns are the best overall performers.

10.6 Refinement

After the initial sampling is completed, you may decide that certain regions of the domain need closer examination. This decision may depend on a variety of factors, but it is usually based on the idea of increasing the local sampling frequency in regions of high local bandwidth. Estimation of the local bandwidth is usually done implicitly, rather than by calculating a Fourier or wavelet transform. In general, the values of some samples in a neighborhood are tested against some criteria. Some additional geometric and structural information about the scene and the image may be included in the test, if it is available. Based on the results of those tests, some new sample locations may be generated in that region and then evaluated. Typically the tests are then repeated on the new samples, and the process repeats until the tests are satisfied or some upper limit on the number of repetitions has been reached.

The general idea is usually based on the expectation that the signal will eventually be reconstructed from the sampled data. When the data is uniform, or homogeneous, in a given region, then we assume that we have completely characterized the signal in that region. For example, a simple reconstruction will use the mean value in a region as the value for all points in the region. Thus, the approach will be to make sure that all the samples in a given region are "similar" in some specified way, so we can feel that we have captured what is happening in a region of the signal. If a region is nonuniform, or heterogeneous, then we will typically want to refine our regions until each subregion is uniform.

In this section we will survey several refinement methods that have been proposed in the literature. In general, each method first performs a *sample selection*, which identifies which samples participate in the test. Then a *refinement test* is applied to those samples, which normally involves several criteria.

Typically when the test is satisfied, that success indicates that the samples represent a good estimate of the signal in that neighborhood. We sometimes see two slightly different approaches in the literature, the *pessimistic* and the *optimistic*. The names are assigned based on the pessimist's idea that more samples should always be taken unless one is explicitly told to stop; the optimist assumes that the samples gathered so far are enough and only takes more if necessary. The *pessimistic approach* assumes that the initial estimate is incomplete. This means we should take ever more samples until the test is satisfied. From this point of view, we say the test implements *stopping criteria*, since the default is to take more samples. The *optimistic approach* assumes that the samples being tested are a good estimate, and more samples are taken only if the test fails; in this case the test implements *refinement criteria*. Both cases boil down to the same thing, but the discussion is slightly different depending on our point of view. For consistency, in this book we will adopt the optimistic approach. We will present all the tests so that they report *acceptance*: if the test fails, it indicates that more sampling is necessary.

Many of the tests are described in the literature with respect to "pixels." Typically these authors are implicitly using the fact that when an image is resampled onto a pixel grid, the values near the center of pixels usually get weighted more than those farther away from the center. In other words, they know that the low-pass filter step (carried out by convolution) and resampling are going to be rolled together, so they can implicitly carry out importance sampling and consider the centers of pixels to be more important than the edges. If this approach is taken, we must be extra careful about reconstruction. We will return to this in the reconstruction section below. In general, if we know the resampling locations at the time of the original sampling, this information can be used to our benefit. Since adaptive refinement of sampled signals is appropriate for applications other than estimating image intensity at the image plane, we will refer to *resample locations* rather than pixels.

Some of the tests select the samples to be used based on how they are expected to be arranged. For example, it is not uncommon to examine the four corners of a pixel or the centers of neighboring pixels. Such tests only make sense in their original form if the samples fall in the expected locations. Most of these special cases are based on image sampling where square pixels are expected; they are gathered together below in one section.

When the refinement test fails and more samples are needed, we must decide where they should go. Some algorithms generate new samples on the fly, usually on the basis of some subdivision scheme among the samples used in the test. Others use more samples from a precomputed pattern such as those presented earlier. We will show the different choices used by different algorithms.

It is also worth noting that when one region needs refinement, an adjacent region will often also need more samples. If the regions overlap, then some of the new samples created for the first region may be useful in the second, if the test and new-sample geometries coincide.

10.6.1 Sample Intensity

Many tests are defined in the literature in terms of the *intensities* of sample points. This is appropriate when the signal is any multidimensional vector quantity, though the term evokes a gray-scale image. Because the idea of intensity comparison is so useful in describing refinement tests, we pause for a moment to interpret this term for different situations.

We assume for the discussion of refinement tests that the value of each sample s is an n-dimensional vector: $s \in \mathcal{R}^n$. This may stand for any abstract quantity. It is particularly useful when the sample represents a color in some color system. Different color systems use different values of n. If a system evaluates the image color as a full spectrum, n might be 30 or more, one for each wavelength. If the system represents colors with RGB or XYZ descriptions, n would be 3. For a black-and-white gray-scale image n would be 1. If the system evaluates each spectral wavelength independently, n would be 1, but it would have an associated wavelength attached to it.

Comparison among these different color representations is traditionally handled in a rather cavalier fashion. Two RGB colors A and B are frequently compared using either the $\mathcal{L}^\infty$ norm or the $\mathcal{L}^2$ norm:

$$\mathcal{L}^\infty(A, B) = \max(|A_r - B_r|, |A_g - B_g|, |A_b - B_b|)$$
$$\mathcal{L}^2(A, B) = \sqrt{(A_r - B_r)^2 + (A_g - B_g)^2 + (A_b - B_b)^2} \qquad (10.17)$$

although a comparison in $L^*a^*b^*$ or $L^*u^*v^*$ color space is probably more appropriate. Alternatively, the color components may be compared against different thresholds, or the difference may be found in some other color space. The correct interpretation of terms like "similar" and "different" when applied to two or more sample values depends on the context, which provides an interpretation of sample values.

From here on, when we mention "intensity," and discuss whether two or more "intensities" are "similar" or "different," we mean these terms to stand for any of these interpretations, depending on what is appropriate in context for that signal. The thresholds for similarity are also dependent on this context.

10.7   Refinement Tests

We distinguish refinement tests into five general categories. The categories are distinguished by the type of information used in the test. The five types of tests are *intensity comparison, contrast, object-based, ray-tree comparison*, and *intensity statistics*. These different types of tests are discussed in order below.

Each type of test typically involves several samples. We will refer to the collection of samples used in any test as the *study set* S of samples for that test, containing n samples $\{s_0, s_1, \ldots, s_{n-1}\}$ with corresponding values $\{v_0, v_1, \ldots, v_{n-1}\}$. In any set S, we define the minimum and maximum values to be $S_{\min}$ and $S_{\max}$. Notice that more than one sample can have a value corresponding to the minimum and maximum. We also define the mean of all the samples $\overline{S}$ as

$$\overline{S} = \frac{1}{n} \sum_{i=1}^{n} v_i \qquad (10.18)$$

10.7.1   Intensity Comparison Refinement Test

The simplest form of adaptive refinement test compares the intensity of the samples in the study set.

```
if Smax − Smin > ε
   then fail
   else succeed
   endif
```

FIGURE 10.53

Adaptive sampling from Whitted [477].

Intensity Difference

In the first paper on adaptive point-sampling, Whitted stated that when considering four samples that form a small square in the sampling domain, "If the intensities calculated at the four points have nearly equal values and no small object lies in the region between them, the algorithm assumes that the average of the four values is a good approximation of the intensity over the entire region" [477]. We will return to the "small object" idea below. Pseudocode for the intensity clause of this simple algorithm is shown in Figure 10.53.

The value of ϵ in Figure 10.53 is user-defined. Whitted offers no advice in its selection, and indeed in different contexts different values will be most appropriate. When this method is used at the image plane for sampling an image function, a common rule of thumb is that if you are going to display on a frame buffer with eight bits of RGB color specification, then $\epsilon \approx 1/2^8 = 1/256$ is in the right ballpark. Note that the number of bits used here is the depth of the color value, not the color identifier. So if a frame buffer is eight bits deep but each entry points to a colormap entry with twelve bits per color component, we would choose $\epsilon \approx 1/2^{12} = 1/4096$.

Intensity Groups

A similar test is used in Jansen and van Wijk [228]. In this test, the min and max of a set of values are compared against a reference value t; again, if the difference is too large, the test fails and the sample set should be refined. This method is shown in Figure 10.54.

Jansen and van Wijk present this method in the context of a recursive refinement algorithm that subdivides a region of a domain over and over. They state that although the value of ϵ may be held a constant, computation time may be saved if ϵ is increased as the recursion level increases. This makes the first steps of the recursion more important than later steps. When there are many regions to be refined at once, this will help enforce a breadth-first refinement of the domain, where most regions are subdivided a bit before some regions become highly refined. They reported good

```
if (|S_max − t| > ε) or  (|S_min − t| > ε)
  then fail
  else succeed
endif
```

FIGURE 10.54

Jansen and van Wijk's test.

results using the sequence of $(0.0, 0.05, 0.15)$ for ϵ to generate smooth-shaded ray-cast images.

10.7.2 Contrast Refinement Test

Mitchell has pointed out [307] that *contrast* is a good predictor of the response of the eye to variations in light intensity. One definition of contrast for a study set S is defined by

$$C = \frac{S_{\max} - S_{\min}}{S_{\max} + S_{\min}} \tag{10.19}$$

(other definitions are given in Section 3.3.3). This is a good heuristic to use for evaluating image functions intended for viewing by human observers. When contrast is used in a system that samples in red, green, and blue, Mitchell observed that three different contrast values may be used for each of these color bands. This allows the system to give more weight to the green component of the signal, to which the eye is sensitive, less to the red, and still less to the blue. He reported good results with red, green, and blue contrasts set to $(0.4, 0.3, 0.6)$, respectively.

This type of ratio test is not appropriate when pixel values are all zero or very small. The uniformity condition is easily tested and indeed must be tested for or one will divide by 0. When pixel values are small in magnitude, the test can be overly sensitive. If $S_{\max} = .1$ and $S_{\min} = .3$, then $C = 1/3$, which is the same result if $S_{\max} = .01$ and $S_{\min} = .03$. We probably want to trigger sampling in the former case but not the latter. One way to distinguish these is to multiply the contrast by the mean, using $C' = C\overline{S}$ rather than C. This would give $C' \approx 6/1,000$ in the former case and $C' \approx 6/100$ in the latter case.

When we are sampling the image plane, contrast then seems like a reasonable metric to control refinement, though it is of less value for other functions such as illumination signals.

```
if obj₁ ≠ obj₂
  then fail
  else succeed
  endif
```

FIGURE 10.55
The Roth test.

10.7.3 Object-Based Refinement Test

Rather than examine just the intensity values of samples, we can use additional information carried by the samples that is unique to a computer graphics environment. In particular, for image and illumination signals, every sample may be characterized as a ray that strikes some particular object (we assume the scene is enclosed in a bounding "background" object that can be uniquely identified; a ray that passes out of the scene may be assumed to strike this object). This conceptual characterization holds true whether or not the samples are in fact evaluated by ray-tracing methods. We will call the object number associated with a given sample the "object tag" for that sample.

Object-Difference Test

Roth suggested locating edges adaptively by comparing the object tags for adjacent samples [361]. New samples are created and evaluated between the two samples, and the process iterates until the distance between the two differing samples is below some threshold. This simple algorithm is outlined in Figure 10.55.

The primary advantage of this approach is that it does not require any user-specified thresholds (except a recursion limit). The primary disadvantage is that it is *only* sensitive to changes in object tag. If a single object has varying characteristics (due to texture, high-curvature geometry, or surface finish), then this approach will not capture the effect of those variations on the signal.

Four-Level Test

This idea was pushed a step farther by Argence [12], who noted that sometimes a single object is broken up into many smaller patches during the modeling or rendering phases. Many systems distinguish an "object number," which is consistent for an entire continuous surface, from a "patch number," which starts at one for each

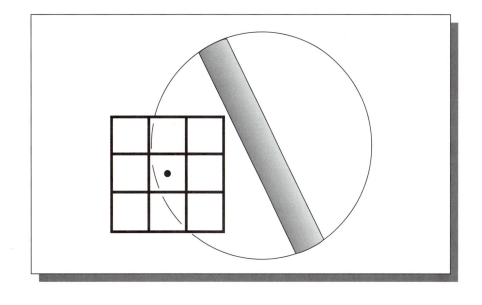

FIGURE 10.56

A problem with minimal bounding spheres for hit detection.

surface and enumerates the derived patches. Thus, an object/patch pair acts like a major and minor identifier. Argence requires that patch numbers also be the same for the refinement test to pass.

Two more criteria are included in this test. The first is a check that the object pointed to by the object tag and patch number is illuminated by the same light sources. If the point visible from one sample is not illuminated by the same set of lights as a neighboring sample, then there is a change in illumination and shadow between those samples, and Argence finds this phenomenon worthy of refinement.

There is also a test for small objects. This type of test was first suggested by Whitted [477], who enclosed each object in a sphere with a radius chosen to guarantee that the sphere covered at least one screen pixel. If an eye ray intersected that bounding sphere but did not hit the object, then the four subsquares sharing that ray as a common vertex were subdivided to "look" for the object. Roth has pointed out [361] that this approach has a problem for long, skinny objects, as illustrated in Figure 10.56. A ray may hit the bounding sphere, but none of the squares around it intersect with the projection of the object. Thus the refinement algorithm will never find the object, no matter how far it refines.

```
if (obj₁ ≠ obj₂)
  or (patch₁ ≠ patch₂)
  or (lighting₁ ≠ lighting₂)
  or (small-object-detected)
  then fail
  else succeed
  endif
```

FIGURE 10.57

The Argence test.

Argence includes a similar test, but only builds and uses the minimal sphere if the object's projection is smaller than one intersample distance (e.g., a pixel width). This removes the problem demonstrated by Figure 10.56, but it also means that the long shape shown in that figure could be completely missed by the algorithm. Pseudocode for the Argence method is shown in Figure 10.57.

The "small object test" was extended and made more robust by Thomas et al. [436]. They suggested that refinement should occur near edges in the function being sampled. When the function is the image, important classes of edges are the boundaries of objects, as mentioned above for Roth's method. Thomas et al. place *covers* around each object to help detect edges. A cover is a unique pair of surfaces associated with each object. One surface encloses the object, the other is enclosed by the object. The thickness of the covers is chosen to guarantee that at least one sample point will pierce each cover. Using covers projected to the image plane, you can determine if there is an object boundary between any given pair of pixels. Then an algorithm similar to Figure 10.55 may be used to trigger refinement in those regions. Like Roth's method, this technique is good for finding boundaries but will not detect other phenomena that can cause high-frequency information in the signal.

Object-Count Test

A similar approach for image functions was described by Hashimoto et al. [196]. Using projections of silhouette edges onto the image plane, they are able to identify the number of different objects in a given region. If there are more than two objects in the region, refinement is triggered, as in Figure 10.58.

```
if #objects > 2
  then fail
  else succeed
```

FIGURE 10.58
Hashimoto's test.

FIGURE 10.59
All the samples have the same value.

Mean-Distance Test

To catch high-frequency information caused by texture, van Walsum et al. proposed texture-space measures associated with each set of samples [450]. They note that we typically know a lot of information about textures, particularly those stored in tables or images, and that this information may be used to improve our sampling quality. For example, Figure 10.59 shows samples of a black-and-white texture that are all white. There is no way to know, simply from looking at the sample values, that the texture is in fact not entirely white.

We are lucky when dealing with textures because we can gather a complete picture of what is happening between these texture samples. They proposed three criteria to use for refinement. The first is *uniformity*: the texture values between two samples are examined for variation; more than a certain amount is grounds for refinement. The *distance* criterion measures whether the texture locations represented by two samples are farther away than some threshold. The third measure, called the *filter* criterion, estimates whether a prefiltered local average of the texture is close to the texture value attached to that sample. These three tests may be used together or independently, with the appropriate values for each threshold. van Walsum et al. report their results for a variety of thresholds for some test images; the uniformity criterion seemed to be the best performer for the high-frequency texture they studied.

Cook's Test

Cook switches to a higher level of refinement in a region if any object moves more than eight pixels horizontally or vertically throughout the duration of that frame [101].

10.7.4 Ray-Tree Comparison Refinement Test

In a ray-tracing environment, each sample may be represented by a *ray tree*, which gives a complete object-intersection history encountered by a screen sample representing a ray of light (ray tracing is discussed in detail in Chapter 19). The trees of neighboring samples can be compared for similar structure or content.

The method of Argence described above [12] can use this mechanism to compare lighting. Recall that subdivision is called for if two samples fall on the same patch of the same surface, but the illumination on the intersected points is different. One way to check this latter condition is by examining the ray tree associated with each sample.

The refinement test used by Akimoto et al. [6] tests the entire ray tree against a number of criteria. Like Jansen and van Wijk, Akimoto et al. know where the resamples will be located in the domain. The goal is to determine not if more samples need to be taken, but rather which of the already placed samples should be evaluated. They distinguish four levels of evaluation for each sample, based on its neighbors. The classifications are shown in Figure 10.60.

In level 1, the ray trees associated with the selected neighbors are structurally different. Thus, we cannot say anything about the similarity of the samples or assume anything about the new samples; they must be fully evaluated. In level 2, the trees are structurally similar, but the lighting information is different. This is similar to the test used by Argence, but it includes lighting information through the entire ray tree, not just the top level. In this case the new sample inherits the common ray tree of its neighbors, but the shadow information is recomputed. In the third case, the trees are equivalent and the shadow information is the same, but some of the

Level	Test	Action
1	Trees unequal.	Ray-trace the sample.
2	Trees equal but shadows differ.	Ray-trace only the necessary samples.
3	Trees equal and shadows equal but textures present or excessive intensity difference.	Recompute shading information for samples.
4	Trees and shadows equal, no textures present, and intensities sufficiently similar.	Interpolate sample value.

FIGURE 10.60

The four refinement levels for ray-tree refinement.

```
if (max(|v_i - S̄|) > ε)
   then fail
   else succeed
```

FIGURE 10.61

Adaptive sampling from Akimoto et al. [6].

surfaces have a texture upon them, or the values of the samples exceed a threshold. Akimoto et al. compare the largest distance of each intensity from the mean, as in Figure 10.61. In this case the new sample can again inherit the ray tree of its neighbors, but the shading at each node needs to be recomputed. The advantage here is that the visibility problem does not need to be solved again. The fourth case identifies when the neighbors are sufficiently similar that the new sample may be estimated from its neighbors by interpolation.

The intensity comparison tests described in this section are summarized in Table 10.6.

10.7.5 Intensity Statistics Refinement Test

Several researchers have investigated refinement tests based on statistical measures of the values of samples in a neighborhood. These are typically based on the "intensity" values of the samples.

Name of test	Test	Parameters	Reference
Intensity difference	$S_{\max} - S_{\min} > \Delta I$	ΔI	[477]
Intensity groups	$(|S_{\max} - t| > \Delta I)$ or $(|S_{\min} - t| > \Delta I)$	ΔI	[228]
Object difference	$\text{obj}_1 \neq \text{obj}_2$	—	[361]
Four-level	$(\text{obj}_1 \neq \text{obj}_2)$ or $(\text{patch}_1 \neq \text{patch}_2)$ or $(\text{lighting}_1 \neq \text{lighting}_2)$ or `(small-object-detected)`	—	[12]
Object count	$\#\text{objects} > n$	$n =$`number of objects`	[196]
Mean distance	$\max(|v_i - \overline{S}|) > \Delta I$	ΔI	[6]

TABLE 10.6
Intensity difference tests.

SNR Test

Dippé and Wold [124] proposed computing the *signal-to-noise ratio* (SNR) of a set of samples. One conceptual model of the SNR of a signal is that it measures the degradation of a perfect signal over an imperfect communications line. The line introduces noise into the otherwise accurate signal; the SNR measures the extent of this degradation. They note that the quality of the SNR estimate can depend on the number of samples used in its computation; if there are only a few samples, the confidence in the estimated SNR is low.

Dippé and Wold observed that *root-mean-square signal-to-noise ratio* (RMS SNR) is equal to the square root of the sampling rate times a constant, which is based on the spectrum of the signal and the filter used to reconstruct the signal. It is usually the case in graphics that we don't know the spectrum of the signal we're sampling, but we usually need to assume it can contain very high frequencies.

Variance Test

Lee et al. [261] suggested using the *variance* of a study set to estimate its accuracy. The basic idea is that as the variance diminishes, the samples are more consistent, and it is increasingly likely that the samples are a good estimator of the signal.

The variance after N samples is estimated by σ_N, which is found from

$$\sigma_N{}^2 = \frac{1}{N} \sum_{i=1}^{N} (S_i - \overline{S})^2 \tag{10.20}$$

where $\overline{S}$ is the mean of the samples:

$$\overline{S} = \frac{1}{N} \sum_{i=1}^{N} S_i \tag{10.21}$$

To test the quality of a sample set, we ask if the variance σ_N of the set is below some threshold T. Now recall that σ_N is just an estimate of the true variance of the signal, so it is necessarily imprecise. So we introduce a slightly less precise test, and check to see if the *probability* that the variance is less than T is within some probability tolerance β.

The test is set up by defining a real number $\chi_\beta^2 \in \mathcal{R}$ so that

$$\text{prob} \left[\frac{N \sigma_N{}^2}{\text{var}(S)} < \chi_\beta^2(N-1) \right] = \beta \tag{10.22}$$

In words, the test succeeds if the estimated variance is probably less than the constant, where "probably" means the test has a chance of β of being right.

To implement this we need a value for χ_β^2. Normally this value is obtained by looking it up based on β and $(N-1)$ in a table of statistical values, though chi-square values are often easily available using symbolic mathematics programs. The choice of T and β can be made based on the maximum number of samples we are willing to take. Suppose M is the highest variance we expect in the scene, and we want to take a maximum of Z samples. Then we want the variance test to succeed after Z samples when the maximum variance has just been reached; this happens when

$$T = \frac{M}{\chi_\beta^2(Z-1)} \tag{10.23}$$

Lee et al. suggest precomputing a table of values for $T\chi_\beta^2(N-1)$ for $N = 1, 2, \ldots, Z$. They set the maximum variance to $M = 1/128$ based on their frame buffer's color resolution, and $Z = 96$ based on desired run time. Then $\beta = 0.05$ and $T = 0.000105$.

To implement the test after N samples, first compute $\sigma_N{}^2$ using Equation 10.20, and then evaluate

$$G = \frac{\sigma_N{}^2}{\chi_\beta^2} \tag{10.24}$$

If $G < T$, where T is the variance threshold, then stop sampling. Otherwise draw another sample and repeat the test. The probability of stopping too early is

$$\frac{\text{var}(S)}{N} > T \tag{10.25}$$

which by construction is less than β.

Confidence Test

Purgathofer presents a test based on a *confidence interval* [351]. To test for refinement, we estimate the likelihood that the mean of the current samples is within a certain tolerance of the accurate mean of the signal in that neighborhood. The user supplies the tolerance $2t$ and probability α; for example, 99% certainty corresponds to $\alpha = .01$. The probability P that the current mean of n samples is within w on either side of the accurate mean is given by the t test with $(n-1)$ degrees of freedom. Refinement is triggered if the desired probability P is less than the estimated probability p:

$$p \le P \tag{10.26}$$

or equivalently,

$$t_{1-\alpha, n-1} \frac{\sigma}{\sqrt{n}} \le w \tag{10.27}$$

where σ is the standard deviation for this group of samples, from Equation 10.20.

Purgathofer reinforces Dippé and Wold by stressing that when there are only a few samples (i.e., n is small), then the test of Equation 10.27 will give inaccurate results. We must always begin with "enough" samples to make the test meaningful before it can be used. To determine how many samples are enough, Purgathofer gives an elegant argument for the worst case: an asymmetric bimodal distribution.

Suppose that we are sampling an image in a square pixel, and a vertical edge divides that image into two unequal pieces, the left one larger and filled black, the right one smaller and white, as in Figure 10.62. The black signal has value 0, the white signal value 1. We assume that the box has area 1, and the left half has area d; the right then has area $1 - d$.

Suppose we have terrible luck and every sample we evaluate lands on the white region; our reported value will then be 1, rather than d. The test will be valid as long as we can get at least one value from both domains, so we want to know the probability that we will hit one of each domain after n samples. We generate n independent random samples u_i. The probability of each one landing in the smaller zone is $(1 - d)$, and because they are independent, the probability that they will all land in that zone is

$$(1 - d)^n \tag{10.28}$$

FIGURE 10.62

A pixel split into a black left and white right.

d	α							
	0.025	0.050	0.075	0.100	0.125	0.150	0.175	0.200
0.004	402	435	474	519	575	647	748	921
0.025	64	69	75	83	91	103	119	146
0.050	32	34	37	41	45	51	59	72
0.075	21	23	25	27	30	34	39	48
0.100	16	17	19	20	22	25	29	36
0.125	13	14	15	16	18	20	23	28
0.150	10	11	12	13	15	16	19	23
0.175	9	10	10	11	12	14	16	20
0.200	8	8	9	10	11	12	14	17

TABLE 10.7

Values of n given d and α.

We want this probability to be less than our desired $(1 - \alpha)$, so $(1 - d)^n \leq 1 - \alpha$, or

$$n \geq \frac{\log(1 - \alpha)}{\log(1 - d)} \tag{10.29}$$

The value of n for values of $0.8 \leq \alpha \leq 0.99$ and $0.01 \leq d \leq 0.2$ is shown in Figure 10.63. Some values of n are tabulated in Table 10.7.

Notice how quickly n grows as the confidence increases and the interval decreases. Figure 10.64 shows the value of n for different choices of α when $d = 1/256 \approx 0.004$.

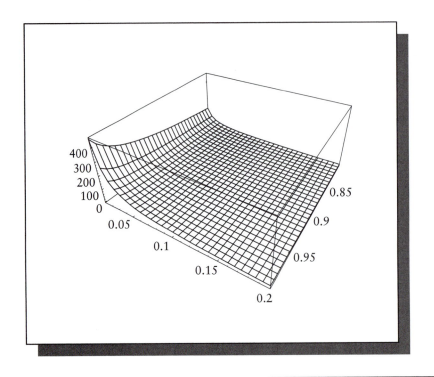

FIGURE 10.63

The value of n versus α and d from Equation 10.29.

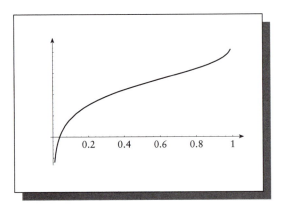

FIGURE 10.64

Values for n when $d = 1/255 \approx 0.004$. This is a log-linear scale; the horizontal axis is linear in α, the vertical is logarithmic in n. The lower-left value is for $\alpha = 0.01$, $n = 3$; the upper-right value is $\alpha = 0.99$, $n = 149$.

Notice that if we take eight samples in a pixel, we can only estimate that the mean of these samples will be within $1/256$ of the true mean with 0.03% certainty.

Purgathofer remarks that this worst-case analysis is necessarily pessimistic, and that we can almost always get away with fewer samples. Stratified sampling, for example, is particularly effective for making sure that much of the domain gets sampled; in the black-white example above, if our eight samples were distributed evenly in the domain, we couldn't help but hit both regions. Stratified sampling doesn't help on all signals, but by using it we can often get away with a smaller study sample than Equation 10.29 would require.

t Test

Painter and Sloan [328] also use a confidence test, based on the number of samples n, their variance $v = \sigma^2$, and a desired confidence level $(1 - \alpha)$. They also use the t test and compare it to a threshold T:

$$t_{\alpha/2v} < T \tag{10.30}$$

Sequential Analysis Test

The theory of *sequential analysis* is used by Maillot et al. [280] to guide their sampling. They refer to a test developed by Wald called the *sequential probability ratio test*, or SPRT. The test requires a measure of homogeneity, or smoothness, of a region. They suggest that the range of intensity values S_i with respect to their mean $\overline{S}$ is a good measure of homogeneity. The test may be phrased in terms of random samples within the neighborhood represented by this study set. If we pick a random sample location y in this neighborhood, we would like to find the probability p that the sample's value $f(y)$ is within ϵ of the mean $\overline{S}$. In symbols,

$$p = P(|f(y) - \overline{S}| < \epsilon) \tag{10.31}$$

If ϵ is small and p is small (say less than some threshold p_0), that suggests that the region contains a lot of variation, and requires refinement. If p is large (say above a threshold p_1), then the region is heterogeneous and only a few samples are required.

To use this test requires an estimate of $\overline{S}$. Since this value is unknown, in practice Maillot et al. use the mean of the first few samples evaluated in the neighborhood. The test then proceeds to determine if the signal if *homogeneous*, and thus smooth, or *inhomogeneous*, and thus requiring refinement. If neither answer can be stated clearly, new samples are drawn until one of the two decisions is accepted or an upper limit is reached. Maillot et al. note that using the first few samples introduces some bias, but they did not analyze the result of that bias.

The test runs by first taking a pilot sample set and determining the mean $\overline{S}$ from it. Then for each sample we decide if it is within the interval of half-width ϵ around

Name of test	Test	Parameters	Reference
SNR	$\text{SNR} > T$	$T = \text{maximum SNR}$	[124]
Variance	$\overline{S}^2/\chi_\beta^2(N-1) < T$	T	[261]
Confidence	$t_{1-\alpha,n-1}\frac{\sigma}{\sqrt{n}} \leq w$	w, α	[351]
t test	$t_{\alpha/2v} < T$	T	[328]
Sequential analysis	$P(|f(y) - \overline{S}| < \epsilon) \leq p_T$	ϵ, p_T	[280]

TABLE 10.8
Intensity statistics tests.

that mean. If a large percentage of the points is within the mean, then the region is assumed to be homogeneous, and sampling can stop. If a large percentage is outside the mean, the region is heterogeneous and again sampling may stop because it is assumed that the current set of samples is representative. If the percentage is between these two extremes then more samples are drawn. Maillot reports that p_0 and p_1 should be chosen based on the perceptual qualities of the human visual system to distinguish homogeneous regions, and on the fact that good results have been obtained with $p_0 = 0.7$ and $p_1 = 0.9$ [279].

Summary

Table 10.8 summarizes the tests in this section. They all perform reasonably well in practice for basic anti-aliasing, but they all are based on user-set parameters that may be difficult to select.

10.8   Refinement Sample Geometry

One set of techniques is based on refining the estimate of a signal based on increasing the local density of a fixed sampling pattern. We call this "predictable" geometry, since we can state the location of every potential sample before the sampling process even begins. These techniques merely evaluate samples at predefined locations.

An alternative set of methods is based on "unpredictable" geometry. These are generally the result of random processes that place samples in arbitrary locations.

Between these two extremes are those nonuniform patterns that are derived from one or more stored templates. Theoretically, we could enumerate all possible sample locations derived from these templates. These are usually meant to increase the efficiency of unpredictable sampling. In practice, it is easier to classify template methods with the unpredictable patterns, since the geometry is closer to that of the unpredictable patterns than that of the predictable ones.

10.9 Refinement Geometry

The refinement test typically only indicates when more samples are needed in a neighborhood; it does not indicate where those samples ought to go. In this section we review various proposals for the placement of new samples.

10.9.1 Linear Bisection

One class of refinement methods restricts attention to the straight line between two samples. Both of the methods we will examine work on a square grid that is used for image sampling and is therefore identified with the pixel grid. The methods look for borders between homogeneous regions along a line between either pixel centers or pixel corners.

The *linear bisection* looks for single edges that occur between two objects seen by adjacent samples [361]. The approach examines the object represented by each sample. The algorithm assumes that if two horizontally or vertically adjacent samples represent different objects, then exactly one edge intersects the line between the samples, and that edge is shared by those two objects. Figure 10.65 shows examples of situations that satisfy and violate this assumption.

The linear bisection algorithm iterates until the edge is trapped to within some fraction of the distance between the samples. The error in the algorithm when its assumptions are fulfilled is the amount by which the area measures are off. If we assume that all edges are linear, then a worst case is shown in Figure 10.66, where an edge passes through two pixels almost parallel to the line between their centers. The bisection routine will trap the edge near the line between the pixels and assign the left one a color of black and the right one white, though both should be almost the same shade of gray.

This technique was used by Roth, who associated samples with pixel centers [361]. He does not give details on how to reconstruct the signal from this information, though its use for line drawing is mentioned. Roth used the object-difference test for refinement.

Wyvill and Sharp use this method when samples are associated with pixel corners, which allows them to use a central-star reconstruction technique [491]. This is illustrated in Figure 10.67.

They reconstruct and resample the signal in one step by assuming that the resample grid is composed of squares with their vertices at the samples. The center of

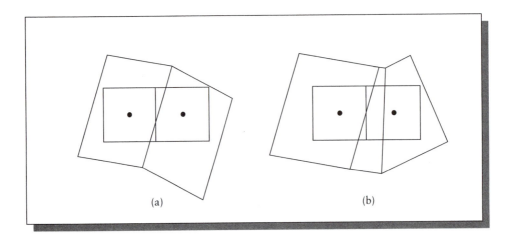

FIGURE   10.65

(a) The assumption made by the linear bisection algorithm is satisfied here; the objects in the samples are separated by one shared edge. (b) The assumption is violated by this nonlinear edge.

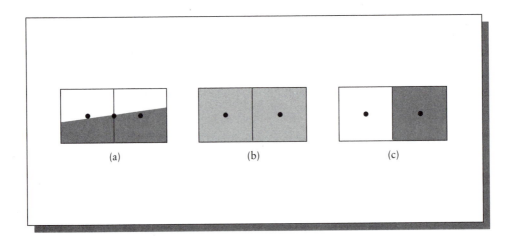

FIGURE   10.66

A worst case for linear bisection. (a) The edge is almost perpendicular to the vertical edge between the pixels. (b) The correct answer is a light shade in both pixels, which are each about half-covered. (c) The result of linear bisection, which assumes the edge is oriented vertically.

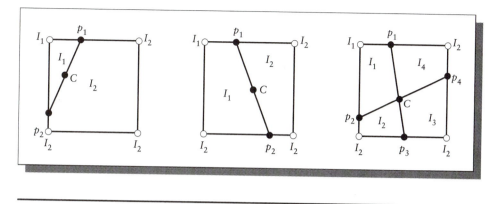

FIGURE 10.67

Corner refinement and star reconstruction.

gravity C is found by averaging all points p_i on the sides of the square where edges have been inferred; because of the assumptions there is at most one such point on each edge. Then a star is drawn from C to each point p_i; these are assumed to be the boundaries of the colored regions. The signal is reconstructed to have a flat value across the pixel, with a value given by the estimated mean $\overline{S}$. This mean is estimated by summing the product of the intensity I_i of each region with its weight w_i, equal to its area:

$$\overline{S} \approx \sum_i w_i I_i \qquad (10.32)$$

The signal is then resampled at the pixel center, yielding the estimated mean for use as the pixel value.

A similar subdivision method is used by Hashimoto et al. [196]. They begin by projecting the silhouette edges of all objects onto the image plane. The plane is initially subdivided into a number of large cells, each enclosing many samples ultimately intended to be pixel centers. If there are more than two *regions* in a cell, the cell is subdivided at its midpoint into four subcells; here a region is a contiguous area due to any single object, or the background.

When a square region contains no more than two regions, subdivision stops and a few samples are evaluated. The samples chosen are those on the corner of the cell and two pairs that straddle the expected location of the edge, as shown in Figure 10.68. This algorithm needs to use the projected edges both to estimate the number of objects in a cell and to determine which samples straddle the edge on the cell boundaries.

The refinement test used by Hashimoto et al. is based on object count within a

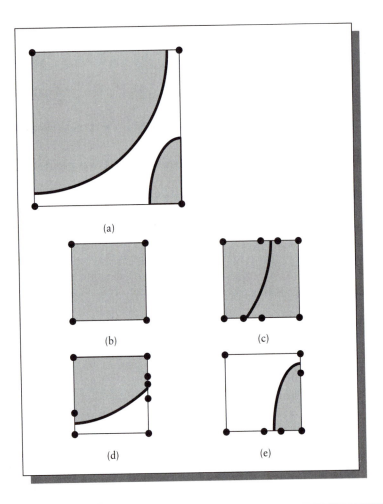

FIGURE 10.68

Samples to be evaluated are marked in black. (a) The initial cell. It contains more than two regions, so it is subdivided. (b) The upper-left cell contains only one region, so only the corners are selected. (c) The upper-right cell contains two regions, so the edge is captured between samples. (d) The lower-left cell also contains two regions and captures an edge. Note that the lower-left corner serves as one of the two samples that trap the edge. (e) The lower-right cell contains too many regions; this cell will be subdivided further. Redrawn from Hashimoto et al. in *New Advances in Computer Graphics*, fig. 4, p. 554.

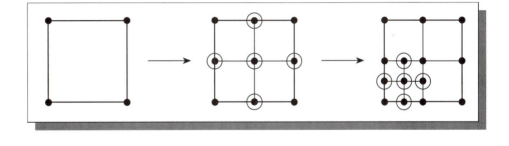

FIGURE 10.69

Sample selection geometry and recursion from Whitted [477].

region, coupled with linear bisection along the edges of the smallest cells to trap the known discontinuity between objects.

10.9.2 Area Bisection

An area bisection test was proposed by Whitted [477] to refine complex regions enclosed by four first-level samples; these were identified with pixel corners. The refinement test is applied to these four corners of each box. If more samples are needed, the square is subdivided into four equal quadrants, five new samples are placed and evaluated, and the test is reapplied to each new subsquare, as in Figure 10.69. This form of binary subdivision can in theory repeat forever in some special cases (such as a fractal dust cloud), but in practice it is usually halted at some large (but arbitrary) number of recursions.

Two different forms of isosceles triangular subdivision have been studied by Shu and Liu [405]. They have looked at subdivision based on right isosceles triangles and symmetrical isosceles triangles, as shown in Figure 10.70.

Each stage of subdivision introduces three new samples, located on the edges of the old cell. Each new sample is shared by two of the larger cells. They present an analysis that suggests that a triangular cell subdivision will usually require less samples to produce an image of equal quality to a square cell. This is to be expected given the more directionally isotropic properties of the hexagonal lattice, as discussed earlier.

The method described by Jansen and van Wijk [228] starts with large cells, each of which encloses many final elements (these are identified with pixels). A sample is then placed in the center of the lower-left element of each cell and evaluated. The entire cell is assigned a single constant intensity from that sample; all points within

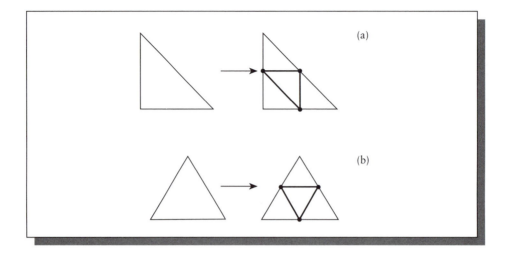

FIGURE 10.70

(a) Right triangular subdivision. (b) Centered isosceles triangular subdivision.

the cell return that value until the cell is subdivided and a new lower-left corner is established. When all cells have been evaluated with an initial sample, a scanning process starts at the bottom-left cell and proceeds left-right, bottom-up. Each cell encountered is subdivided into four equal square subcells. In each subcell on the top row and right column, a new sample is placed in the center of the lower-left pixel. This sample is not evaluated, but is rather assigned the value of the parent cell. Figure 10.71 shows the geometry.

Each of these four subcells is then examined. The position of each subcell specifies which samples are used in the refinement test. On the basis of the result of that test, the value of the sample in the lower-left corner of that cell is either left unchanged (so it inherits the value of its parent), or it is explicitly evaluated. For the three cells in the upper row and right column, the test compares the current value of the cell with the values of three neighboring cells.

The samples used in the refinement test are determined for the four subcells as follows, using the naming of Figure 10.72. The lower-left cell is unchanged. For the upper-right cell, the cells marked A are selected. For the upper-left cell, the cells marked B are selected. For the lower-right cell, the cells marked C are selected. The samples in the selected cells are passed to the refinement test and compared against the value of the parent cell. If the test fails for any of the three subcells, the sample in the lower-left corner of that subcell is evaluated. Otherwise that sample is unchanged

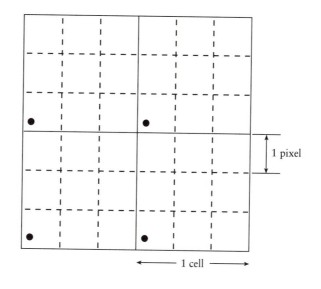

FIGURE 10.71

Initial sampling and subdivision from Jansen and van Wijk [228].

and thus inherits the value of the parent cell. Recall that the value in any cell is the color of its lower-left sample, so if the upper-right sample in a subcell is examined but that cell has not been explicitly sampled, the value of the lower-left corner of the parent cell is used. When a complete scan has finished, another scan may begin. This technique is also used by Bronsvoort et al. [64].

The adaptive refinement presented by Bouville et al. is based on increasing the sampling density of a diamond pattern [59]. Figure 10.73 shows the approach. A square grid is laid down and a diamond sampling pattern (marked P) is used in the first level. Where refinement is called for, the edges and centers of the diamonds (marked S) are evaluated. The process may be repeated recursively. This is very similar to the square adaptive procedure due to Whitted described above, except that it is oriented at 45° to the underlying square resampling grid. In this example, the initial lattice samples form a checkerboard pattern on the underlying pixel grid; after refinement, diamond samples land on pixel centers or corners.

A similar approach is described by Akimoto et al. [6]. They also assume an underlying square resampling grid. The grid is subdivided into supercells containing many elements from the underlying grid, and the corners of these cells are evaluated. They use an intensity difference test to determine if refinement is required. They

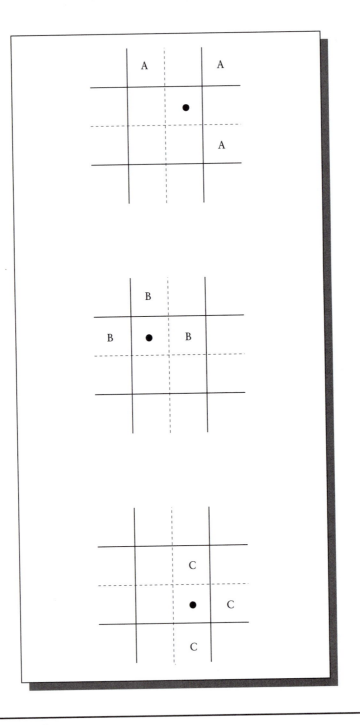

FIGURE 10.72

Sample selection geometry and recursion from Jansen and van Wijk [228].

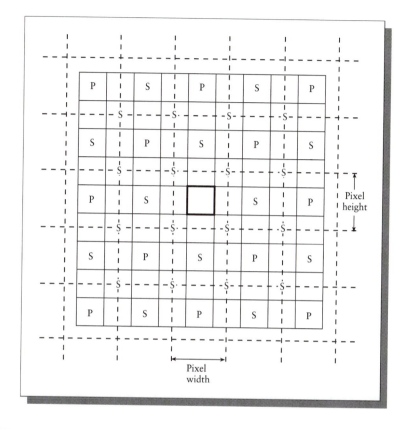

FIGURE 10.73

Diamond pattern sampling. Redrawn from Bouville et al. in *Proc. Eurographics '91*, fig. 7, p. 175.

note that when the supercells are aligned to the resampling grid, then features at an angle to the grid are likely to be missed, as in Figure 10.74.

To suppress this problem, they alternate between square and diamond patterns (with respect to the underlying resampling grid). They begin with the square (oriented) supercells and determine which need refinement. Before proceeding with the refinement, though, the value at the center of each square is found (either by explicitly creating and evaluating a sample, or by estimating from the corner values). This now converts the original square grid into a higher-resolution diamond pattern, as in Figure 10.75.

The refinement of the diamond pattern leads to another square pattern, and the

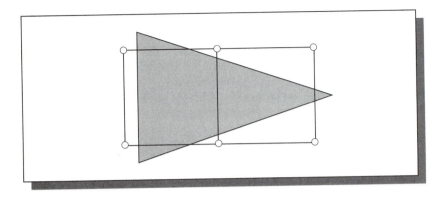

FIGURE   10.74

The "bow tie" between these two checkerboard squares is missed when the supercell is oriented with the underlying sampling grid; the result is breakup of the pattern in the image.

two patterns alternate as needed until the subdivision limit is reached or no cells are flagged for subdivision.

10.9.3   Nonuniform Geometry

When sampling is nonuniform, the bisection techniques discussed above are not appropriate for adaptive refinement. Rather than precisely searching some small region for a desired feature, nonuniform refinement generally involves producing more samples in the region, such that some relevant statistics of the sampling pattern are preserved. In particular, it is often desirable to maintain some sort of Poisson-disk pattern or approximation.

10.9.4   Multiple-Level Sampling

A *multiple-level sampling algorithm* precomputes a number of sampling patterns at different densities. Typically the lowest-density pattern is used to generate and evaluate samples. Then refinement tests are applied to the samples; in regions where a higher sampling density is required, the next-denser pattern is applied in that region. This process may recur until the highest-density template has been used. If an algorithm has n templates, we call it an *n-level strategy*.

Suppose the templates are ordered in a list $\{T_1, T_2, \ldots, T_n\}$, such that T_1 is the lowest-density version and T_n is the highest. Each template may be generated in-

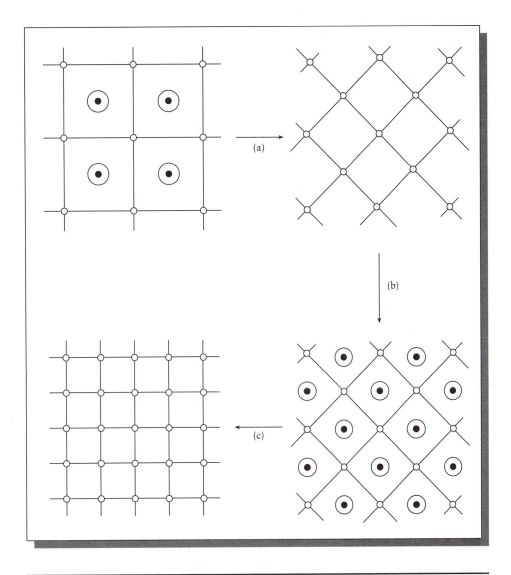

FIGURE 10.75

The refinement process of Akimoto et al. [6]. (a) The original square grid is built and tested for refinement. (b) The cell centers are estimated and the diamond grid is tested. (c) The process repeats.

dependently to possess the desired statistics for that density. But the construction process may take into account the intended use, so that each partial sum of k templates $\{T_1, T_2, \ldots, T_k\}, k \leq n$, will also possess the correct statistics. We say that a set of templates satisfying this condition is *cumulatively compatible*. If a set of templates is cumulatively compatible, then all the samples in templates 0 to k taken in the region together form a statistically desired set. Otherwise, at step k we must decide how to handle the samples from templates 0 to $k - 1$. Some choices include discarding them (this is very undesirable; remember the Sampler's Credo), reconstructing each set separately and somehow combining the results, or reconstructing all the samples together despite their statistics.

Cook proposed a two-level strategy for distribution ray tracing [101]. In his application, the function being sampled was an image, so the regions were pixels. The first pass created sixteen samples per pixel; a second template contained sixty-four samples per pixel. This wasn't strictly a two-pass method since either one sampling density or the other was selected before sampling began, based on motion estimates within the pixel.

A similar two-level strategy was used by Mitchell [307]. His initial *base pattern* has a density of about one sample per pixel. The refinement test looks at a cluster of eight or nine of these samples. If the test indicates refinement is needed, then a second-level pattern is used in that area, with a density of about four or nine samples per pixel. Mitchell notes that for a distribution ray tracer, higher densities at both levels may be necessary.

Dippé and Wold [124] use several independent sets of samples in their error estimator. Presumably these are uncorrelated sampling patterns of roughly the same density. They mention that when refinement is called for, more samples need to be generated in the region, but they do not discuss the geometry of these new samples, nor the disposition of the sets.

10.9.5 Tree-Based Sampling

Another class of algorithms uses a tree-based data structure to organize the samples taken so far and guide the placement of new samples.

Kajiya presented a number of ways to use trees for adaptive sampling [234]. The first is called *sequential uniform sampling*. The idea is that at any time in the refinement process, the sampling pattern consists of a number of regions, with a single sample in each region. Any region may be refined by splitting it in two; the existing sample will land in one of the two subregions, and a new sample may then be placed in the other, empty subregion.

We can describe this hierarchy of regions with a tree. Each internal node represents a split region; each leaf node is a region with a single sample, as in Figure 10.76. The procedure for splitting a node is summarized in Figure 10.77.

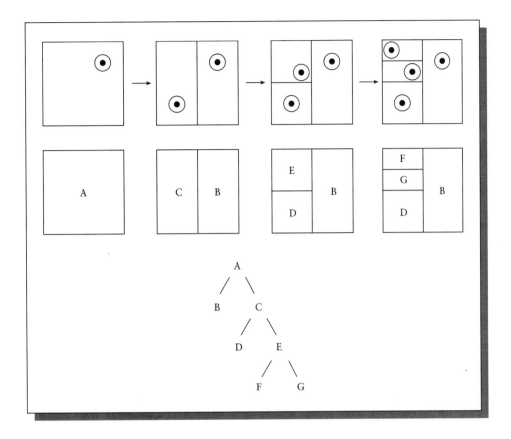

FIGURE 10.76

A refinement tree and its associated domain.

There are several ways to go about choosing which node should be split at any time. To get the most uniform distribution of samples, the tree can be scanned breadth-first, so that all nodes at any given level are split before any nodes below that level are split. Kajiya notes that if the nodes are examined in strict tree-traversal order (say prefix or infix order), then the result is very orderly. A better way to go for breadth-first splitting is to choose the nodes in random order, as shown in Figure 10.78.

This approach will search out the domain spanned by the root region, but not in any predetermined order.

The splitting operation of Figure 10.78 may be generalized to n-dimensional

```
Refine Node(node)
if node is not a leaf
  then
    Choose a subnode
    Assign a child to subnode        If inside tree, descend to a leaf.
    Refine Node(subnode)
    return
  endif
Split node
Put old sample in its region        Split the leaf and take a new sample.
Evaluate new sample in other region
```

FIGURE 10.77

Node refinement.

```
Choose a Subnode(node)
if left-child is a leaf
  then return(left-child)               If left child is a leaf, take it.
  endif
if right-child is a leaf
  then return(right-child)              If right child is a leaf, take it.
  endif
if level(left-child) < level(right-child) and is-balanced(left-child)
  then return(left-child)               Select left if shallower and balanced.
  endif
if level(right-child) < level(left-child) and is-balanced(right-child)
  then return(right-child)              Select right if shallower and balanced.
  endif
if uniform()<0.5
  then return(left-child)
  else return(right-child)             Return either child at random.
  endif
```

FIGURE 10.78

Random order breadth-first refinement.

distributions by replacing the binary tree with a *k-d tree* [36]. In a k-d tree, each level corresponds to subdivision along a given dimension. For example, the first level might split along the x axis, then the second level along y, the third along z, and so on. This approach generalizes to any interpretations of the dimensions, not just those representing space.

Since we have knowledge of the regions represented by each sample, we can use that information to speed up our process of estimating the local signal using a process called *hierarchical integration*. We can build our approximation of the signal as a piecewise-continuous function, where the pieces are given by the sampling regions and the values are given by the corresponding sample values in those regions. By weighting each sample with its associated area, Kajiya points out, we will often get a better estimate of the signal more quickly than if we work simply with the many point samples and ignore their associated areas. Use of this technique will probably influence the selection and use of the test used for refinement.

This method may be made more powerful by adding an adaptive element, resulting in *adaptive hierarchical integration*. Kajiya points out that the refinement test may be driven by factors other than just uniformity; we will see some examples below. The test may make use of information stored in the sampling tree either for other reasons or specifically to improve sampling quality. The different criteria end up controlling our descent in the tree, influencing our choice of the region we finally split. Suppose we have n different tests, each of which has an output ϕ_i; this is the probability that we should choose the left subnode (so $\phi = 1$ is a sure choice for the left node, $\phi = 0$ is a sure choice for the right, and $\phi = 0.5$ means that the choice will be random). We can weight these different probabilities with a scalar $w_i \geq 0$ for each test; to make things easier, we assume the weights add to 1:

$$\sum_{i=1}^{n} w_i = 1 \qquad (10.33)$$

We can form a final choice ϕ from the sum of the choices:

$$\phi = \sum_{i=1}^{n} w_i \phi_i \qquad (10.34)$$

Most of the tests discussed above were designed to produce binary results: the output is simply whether a region needs refinement or not. With the test just described, we can allow more range in our result, expressing just how much an area needs refinement. Kajiya tried out five different strategies:

- The constant threshold ($\phi = c$).

- The random threshold ($\phi = 0.5$).

- The difference of integrals associated with the subnodes.

- Statistics based on the samples below the subnode.

- User knowledge of the function (ϕ comes from a lookup table).

Finally, we can choose the splitting plane to be somewhere other than the midpoint of the range. Specifically, we can choose to subdivide where we think it likely that we will have equal amounts of signal on both sides. This is a form of importance sampling with *dynamic stratification*; we make up the regions as we go. Finding the right place to split is usually not obvious. Kajiya points out that if the filter we will eventually use is known in advance, then we can try splitting so that we have equal integrals under the filter in each of the two subregions. This approach isn't perfect, since it's really the product of the filter and the signal that we want to balance, but it's a starting point. If the filter is stored in a sum-table as described by Crow [111], then finding the midpoint of the filter in any region is simplified. Shirley and Wang [401] point out that using the filter as the sampling has some theoretical justification for the types of signals we usually encounter in computer graphics.

In one dimension, suppose that the left and right ends of the interval have values $F(x_l)$ and $F(x_r)$ in the sum table; we need only search this interval (by bisection or other means) to find that point x_m where $F(x_m) = [F(x_l) + F(x_r)]/2$.

Painter and Sloan [328] also organize the samples into a tree. The domain is originally one large region with one sample. When the neighborhood is refined, the region is subdivided and the existing sample is associated with the subregion it falls in; the other regions are then sampled in turn. The tree structure is used to guide the adaptive sampling process by storing some additional information at each node. The subdivision tests and sampling structures are closely coupled in this technique.

Central to their approach is the idea of a *target reconstruction density*. When sampling an image, this is the density of the pixel resampling grid, so they refer to this density as the *pixel level*. They note that the goal of the sampling process is to produce the most accurate answer at the target level, so they use two different strategies when sampling, one for nodes representing regions above (larger than) the target density, and another below. Above the target density, they try to sample so that no large regions of the domain are unsampled, and to locate large-scale features that will need closer attention. At resolutions above the target density (i.e., nodes below the target level), they want only to increase their confidence in the estimate of the mean for the target-level parent of that node.

To guide the sampling process, they save several pieces of information at each node:

- The area of the region represented by this node.

- The mean of all samples at and below this node.

- The number of samples at and below this node.

- The *internal variance*: the variance of the samples at and below this node.

■ The *external variance*: the variance of the mean estimates at this node and all its sibling nodes (i.e., all first-generation children of this node's parent).

The internal variance estimates the local complexity of the signal represented by this node, while the external variance gives us a measure of the complexity in this part of the subtree. The information at each node is used to give it a *priority*; when a new sample is to be taken, it will go into the highest-priority node (ties are broken randomly).

Each node at the target level (and each leaf above that level) is given a priority formed by the product of external variance and area. Each internal node above that level inherits a priority formed by the maximum of its children's priorities. Leaf nodes below the target level are assigned priorities so that of all children of a given node, the child with the highest mean variance has the highest priority.

A leaf node is removed from further refinement, or "closed off," if the confidence level there meets the desired threshold. An internal node is closed off if both of its children are closed off. When a node is closed off, its sampling is complete, and no further samples will be taken in that node's subtree.

10.9.6 Multiple-Scale Template Refinement

The multiple-scale patterns mentioned earlier may be used directly for finding new sample locations when refining a region. They may be considered a variant of the multiple-level approach. We can think of the creation of a multiple-scale pattern as the construction of a set of cumulatively compatible templates. Thought of this way, the first sample in the pattern defines template T_1, the second sample is template T_2, and so on. This is not a particularly useful point of view, since each template adds only one new sample.

The most straightforward approach is to place the template over the region to be sampled, and then evaluate samples from the template one after the other until the refinement test is satisfied. The selections may be taken directly from the template [308], or as modulated by a filter [294].

10.10 Interpolation and Reconstruction

In Chapter 5 we identified the errors that arise when a bandlimited signal is not sampled quickly enough, and copies of the spectrum fold onto the baseband (or central copy). This is usually called *aliasing*. When the signal is correctly sampled but incorrectly reconstructed, the errors may look like aliasing errors, but in this book we call them *reconstruction errors*. (Other common names for reconstruction errors are *post-aliasing* errors [310] and, for 2D images, *rasterization* [109].)

Typically in computer graphics we reconstruct in order to resample at a lower rate, which usually requires a low-pass filter after the reconstruction filter, as discussed in Chapter 5. The central issues in practical reconstruction are the choices of these filters. The reconstruction filter transforms the discrete-time signal into a continuous-time signal, and the low-pass filter bandlimits that signal so that no frequencies remain that are above the Nyquist rate of the resampling pulses.

In computer graphics practice it is common to see the reconstruction and low-pass filters combined into one. When the samples are nonuniform, this can be difficult to implement, so the two steps are executed sequentially. When filtering isn't necessary, we often reconstruct and resample in one step, by convolving the signal with the reconstruction filter only at the points where we wish to resample. This is usually less work than reconstructing the entire signal in the frequency domain, since that would require a forward and inverse Fourier transform step.

The theory of reconstruction for uniformly sampled signals was discussed in detail in Chapter 8 and that for nonuniform samples in Chapter 9. Adaptive subdivision on a regular grid is an interesting case that is somewhere between the two. From a sampling point of view, adaptive subdivision on a grid (such as the square subdivision method of Whitted) is properly viewed as a variant of uniform sampling, since there is a regular pattern to the sample geometry, though not all the sample locations have been evaluated. When reconstructing, it is better to think of the result of this operation as a nonuniform set of samples, since we cannot use the regular filters that expect a value at each filter location.

Graphics algorithms typically have not employed the nonuniform reconstruction methods of Chapter 9, but instead have relied on simpler, local approximations to the signal. In this section we will review some of the published algorithms for reconstructing from a nonuniform set of samples.

We will usually take the point of view that we have a set of samples that has not been processed in any way (except that the samples have been evaluated), and we want a new value of the signal at some particular *reconstruction point* (this is the resample point, but this term emphasizes that we are reconstructing and filtering the signal before sampling again on a sample-by-sample basis). This location is usually associated with a neighborhood, and only samples within that neighborhood are involved in the reconstruction. When rendering images, the resample point is often the pixel center, and the neighborhood is the surrounding pixel or a 3×3 grid of pixels. For other types of signals, the neighborhood is usually implied by the radius of the reconstruction filter. Although this filter sometimes has an infinite width in theory, in practice it is always zero beyond some distance, and we ignore all samples beyond that distance from the reconstruction point. We will call the location of the reconstruction point P, its value P_v and the neighborhood N; each of the n samples in the neighborhood has a location s_p and a value s_v.

We will assume our original signal is $f(t)$ and it has a Fourier transform $F(\omega)$. Unless otherwise stated, we will also assume that $f(t)$ is bandlimited, that is, $F(\omega) = 0$

for all $|\omega| \geq \omega_0 = \pi/T$. The function is sampled at sample locations t_n. If the samples are uniform, then $t_n = nT$; otherwise the index n only serves to identify the sequencing of the samples.

10.10.1 Functional Techniques

Functional techniques are based on transforming the input data in some way, typically into another domain. They are not directly useful in computer graphics because they are impractical for large numbers of samples, but we will review two approaches that give the flavor of the approach.

A functional reconstruction of nonuniform samples has been presented by Kim and Bose [244]. They build a frequency-space representation of the signal which contains uniformly spaced frequency samples. This representation takes the form of a matrix, which is then processed by the inverse discrete Fourier transform to recover the original signal. They have found that this is always possible in 1D, but that in 2D the transformation matrix does not always exist. They present the necessary conditions for the existence of the 2D matrix, and discuss a block algorithm to make the matrix computations more efficient.

Wingham has taken an approach whereby the signal is expanded in a series form [483]. The linear algebra method of singular value decomposition is used to identify the eigenvalues and eigenvectors of the signal. These measures provide a way to reconstruct the large-scale structure of the signal, and offer tolerance to noise in the signal.

Although functional methods are capable of extracting a lot of useful information from the signal, they typically require processing of the entire signal at every stage. For a typical computer graphics image with a million or more samples, this is very expensive; even for an illumination hemisphere of several hundred samples and carefully designed implementations, the costs are probably prohibitive. The examples used by Kim and Bose reconstruct the signal from only nine sample points, and Wingham presents his results on a signal with eight samples.

10.10.2 Warping

The family of *warping* techniques is based on a simple idea: if we can map the nonuniform samples onto a uniform grid with an invertible mapping, we can reconstruct on the uniform grid using traditional methods, and then invert the mapping to get the result in the original space. We will summarize the work of Clark et al. [92] as a representative sample of this approach.

We begin by recalling the 1D uniform sampling theorem from Equation 8.13. If $f(t)$ is a function with Fourier transform $F(\omega)$ such that $F(\omega) = 0$ for $\omega \geq \omega_0 = \pi/T$, and is sampled at the points $t_n = nT$, then $f(t)$ can be exactly reconstructed from

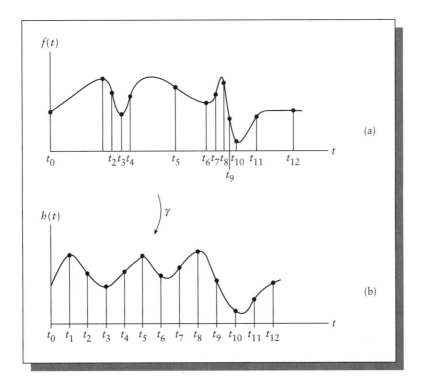

FIGURE 10.79

(a) A function $f(t)$ sampled nonuniformly at locations $\{t_n\}$. (b) The warped function $h(\tau)$.

its samples from

$$f(t) = \sum_n f(nT) \operatorname{sinc} \left[\frac{\omega_0}{\pi} (t - nT) \right] \tag{10.35}$$

We now consider the nonuniform sample sequence $\{t_n\}$ applied to $f(t)$, as in Figure 10.79(a). We would like to warp the t axis so that all the samples are uniformly spaced with interval T. Suppose we had a warping function $\gamma(t)$ that gave us a new axis, τ. Then the image of $f(t)$ on that axis, which we call $h(\tau)$, would be uniformly sampled, as in Figure 10.79(b).

If we can carry out this mapping (and $h(\tau)$ is bandlimited), then we can use the techniques of uniform reconstruction on $h(\tau)$. If the mapping function γ is invertible, then we can recover our original function $f(t) = h(\gamma(t))$.

We can state this observation as the *1D nonuniform sampling theorem*:

The 1D Nonuniform Sampling Theorem: A signal $f(t)$ is sampled nonuniformly at points $t = t_n$. If a one-to-one continuous mapping $\gamma(t)$ exists such that $nT = \gamma(t_n)$, and if $h(\tau) = f(\gamma^{-1}(\tau))$ is bandlimited to $\omega_0 = \pi/T$, then $f(t)$ may be reconstructed from

$$f(t) = \sum f(t_n) \operatorname{sinc}\left[\frac{\omega_0}{\pi}\left(\gamma(t) - nT\right)\right] \tag{10.36}$$

This theorem requires that $h(\tau)$ be bandlimited, but it says nothing about the original signal $f(t)$. In fact, it is rather surprising that $f(t)$ need not be bandlimited for the reconstruction to proceed successfully.

There is an alternative way to write Equation 10.36 that can give some different insights into the problem. Consider a signal that is very smooth in some places and changes quickly in others. It seems reasonable that if we only can take a predetermined number of samples, they ought not to be distributed uniformly, but rather should be clustered densely near the busy parts of the signal, and scattered more sparsely where the signal is smooth. In other words, the density of samples in some interval of the signal should match the amount of high-frequency information in that interval (this is importance sampling reappearing).

To estimate the local high-frequency content, we assume that at every point on $f(t)$ we have an associated bandwidth estimate $B(t)$. Then we know that if we have at least $2B(t)$ samples per unit time in that interval, we can exactly reconstruct the signal. Said in reverse, we can find the desired spacing between samples from the implicit relation

$$t_n = \frac{n}{2B(t_n)} \tag{10.37}$$

Equation 10.37 gives us an implicit relation on the spacing of the samples so that they capture all the high-frequency information and the signal may be reconstructed. Our reconstruction formula is then

$$f(t) = \sum_n f(t_n) \operatorname{sinc}\left[2B(t)t - n\right] \tag{10.38}$$

The instantaneous sampling rate at some point in the signal is given by $d\gamma(t)/dt$, the derivative of the warping function, so

$$d\gamma(t)/dt = (2\pi/\omega_0)B(t) \tag{10.39}$$

Integrating both sides, we find

$$\gamma(t) = k + \int_0^t (2\pi/\omega_0)B(r)\,dr \tag{10.40}$$

If the local bandwidth $B(t)$ is roughly constant in some interval around t, then we can simplify Equation 10.40 to

$$\gamma(t) = (2\pi/\omega_0)B(t)t \tag{10.41}$$

When this approximation holds, we see that Equations 10.36 and 10.38 are equivalent.

The reconstruction formula of Equation 10.38 represents convolution of the sample points $f(t_n)$ with the inverse Fourier transform of time-varying low-pass filter with cutoff frequency $\omega_F = 4\pi B(t)$. Determining $B(t)$ is difficult because it is intended to be a local measure, and Fourier transforms require the entire signal to be used. One way to estimate the local bandwidth is to use a wavelet transformation. Alternatively we can just take a short-term Fourier transform and hope that it is a reasonable local estimate. But since we never use infinite-width signals or filters in practice, if we window the signal and take a transform of that local region, we are only increasing the severity of an error we regularly commit and are content to tolerate.

The essential step of this method is to find the warping function $\gamma(t)$ that satisfies our invertibility and bandlimiting conditions for a given set of samples $\{t_n\}$. In one dimension this seems like a plausible task; it is much harder in general in 2D. This is due to one of the classic problems in generalizing problems of this type: in 1D we know how to sort without ambiguity, but in 2D we do not. We may try several heuristics to "juggle" a set of samples into some uniform lattice, but no algorithms are known that will preserve connectivity and adjacency for all nonuniform sample geometries.

The situation is different if the sampling pattern is always the same, or is one of a small number of known patterns. It may then be possible to precompute a warping function γ_i for each pattern i. This process may require significant expense and a priori information about the sampling pattern. When the warping functions have been constructed, they may be stored and then used directly in the reconstruction formulas above when that pattern is encountered. This approach is reasonable in any number of dimensions for which the warping functions can be computed.

This discussion may be generalized theoretically into two dimensions. Suppose that we have a 2D function $f(\mathbf{x})$ which has been sampled at some set of 2D points $\{\mathbf{x}_s\}$. We assume we have a continuous, one-to-one mapping γ:

$$\boldsymbol{\xi} = \gamma(\mathbf{x})$$
$$\boldsymbol{\xi}_w = \gamma(\mathbf{x}_s) \tag{10.42}$$

where the former equation represents the transformation of any point $\mathbf{x}$, and the latter is defined only for sample points $\mathbf{x}_s$. We can also assume another function h defined by

$$h(\boldsymbol{\xi}) = f(\gamma^{-1}(\boldsymbol{\xi})) \tag{10.43}$$

If h is bandlimited, then we can write the sampled signal after passing through a low-pass filter g as

$$h(\xi) = \sum_{x_i} h(\xi_s)g(\xi - \xi_s) \qquad (10.44)$$

We can now write f as

$$f(\mathbf{x}) = \sum_{\{\mathbf{x}_s\}} f(\mathbf{x}_s)g(\gamma(\mathbf{x}) - \gamma(\mathbf{x}_s)) \qquad (10.45)$$

As before, we can state this in a theorem, this time as the *2D nonuniform sampling theorem:*

> **The 2D Nonuniform Sampling Theorem:** A signal $f(\mathbf{x})$ is sampled nonuniformly at points $\mathbf{x} = \mathbf{x}_n$. If a one-to-one continuous mapping $\gamma(\mathbf{x})$ exists such that $a\mathbf{U} + b\mathbf{V} = \gamma(\mathbf{x}_n)$ for two linearly independent vectors $\mathbf{U}$ and $\mathbf{V}$, and if $h(\boldsymbol{\tau}) = f(\gamma^{-1}(\boldsymbol{\tau}))$ is bandlimited to $|\omega_0| = \pi/\min(|\mathbf{U}|,|\mathbf{V}|)$, then $f(\mathbf{t})$ may be reconstructed from
>
> $$f(\mathbf{x}) = \sum_{\{\mathbf{x}_s\}} f(\mathbf{x}_s)g(\gamma(\mathbf{x}) - \gamma(\mathbf{x}_s)) \qquad (10.46)$$
>
> where g is the inverse Fourier transform of an ideal 2D low-pass filter.

Again, this theorem states nothing about the spectral properties of the original function that was sampled and that we are reconstructing; only the projection of the signal through the warping function γ is required to be bandlimited.

This warping approach has been studied for computer graphics by Heckbert [206]. He examined a number of different filter designs for texture and image processing. In particular, he found that rather than warping the signal and then processing, you can sometimes apply the inverse warp to the reconstruction filter and then apply it direction.

Another approach to the warping process has been taken by Wolberg [485], who studied the requirements of nonuniform reconstruction for applying complex transformations to images.

10.10.3 Iteration

The methods based on *iteration* generally work by guessing an estimate of the signal, plugging that into the known samples of the function, and using the error to derive a new approximation. We will summarize the work of Sauer and Allebach [376] as a representative sample of this class; other examples of this method include [330], [281], and [142]. Sauer and Allebach actually present three variations on the same theme; we begin by describing the basic method and then describe the two variations.

We suppose our signal $f(t)$ has been sampled nonuniformly. Based on the samples, we make a guess of the function and call the guess $f_1(t)$. We then apply a pair of operators $\mathcal{P}$ and $\mathcal{Q}$ to find a new approximation $f_2(t)$:

$$f_{k+1} = \mathcal{T} f_k = \mathcal{P} \mathcal{Q} f_k \tag{10.47}$$

where we have used a composite operator $\mathcal{T}$ to represent the sequence $\mathcal{P}\mathcal{Q}$. Applying Equation 10.47 over and over gives us a sequence of estimates f_k for the original signal.

If our samples of $f(t)$ are sufficient to uniquely determine the signal, and the algorithm is convergent, then eventually we reach a fixed point where our estimates match the signal:

$$\lim_{k \to \infty} \mathcal{T} f_k = f \tag{10.48}$$

One way to view this type of algorithm is to think of $\mathcal{P}$ and $\mathcal{Q}$ as *projecting* their arguments into particular spaces. When these spaces are different for $\mathcal{P}$ and $\mathcal{Q}$, the representation of each estimate f_k bounces back and forth between the two representations. Typically these are signal space and frequency space, so each step of improvement involves modifying the signal and its spectrum. This process is called *alternating nonlinear projections onto convex sets*, and there is a substantial body of mathematical literature addressing the subject in general [499]. Implicitly, $\mathcal{P}$ and $\mathcal{Q}$ include forward and inverse Fourier transforms.

In Sauer and Allebach [376], the signal-space operator is called the *sampling operator*, and is denoted $\mathcal{S}$. This operator identifies how to evaluate our estimate at any point. The geometry behind $\mathcal{S}$ is shown in Figure 10.80.

We start by determining a scalar ϵ by searching all pairs of samples $\mathbf{x}_i$ and finding the nearest neighbors; ϵ is set to half that distance. To find the value of the operator $\mathcal{S}$ on a function $g(\mathbf{x})$ at any point $\mathbf{x}$ in 2D, we find the nearest sample $\mathbf{x}_i$ to $\mathbf{x}$, form a *ball* of radius ϵ around $\mathbf{x}_i$, and integrate $g(\mathbf{x})$ over that ball. In 1D, a *ball* is an interval, in 2D it is a circle, in 3D a sphere, and so on. We assume that the definition of ϵ results in a value small enough that $g(\mathbf{x})$ is almost the same as $g(\mathbf{x}_i)$ for each point $\mathbf{x}$ in the ball around $\mathbf{x}_i$.

In symbols, we write the sampling operator $\mathcal{S}$ on a vector-valued function $g(\mathbf{x})$ as

$$\mathcal{S}g = \begin{cases} \dfrac{1}{\pi\epsilon^2} \displaystyle\int_{B_{\epsilon,i}} g(\mathbf{x})\, d\mathbf{x} & \text{for } \|\mathbf{x} - \mathbf{x}_i\| < \epsilon \\ 0 & \text{otherwise} \end{cases} \tag{10.49}$$

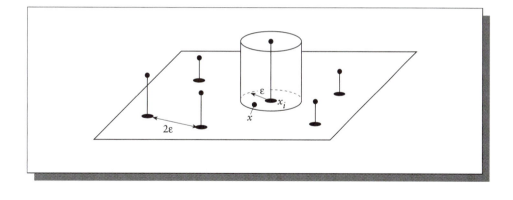

FIGURE   10.80

The circular regions of integration of the operator $\mathcal{S}$.

where $B_{\epsilon,i}$ is a ball of radius ϵ centered at $\mathbf{x}_i$, and

$$0 < \epsilon < \frac{1}{2} \min_{i,k} \| \mathbf{x}_i - \mathbf{x}_k \|, \qquad i \neq k \qquad (10.50)$$

If we evaluate $\mathcal{S}(f - f_k)$ at each sample point, we find the amount of error between estimate k and the original signal.

The frequency-space operator is called $\mathcal{P}_2$, and it is simply a perfect low-pass filter. Operating on a spectrum G, the operator $\mathcal{P}_2$ passes G for all frequencies ω within some finite interval Γ centered at the origin, and sets the others to 0. In symbols,

$$\mathcal{P}_2 G = \begin{cases} G(\omega) & \omega \in \Gamma \\ 0 & \text{otherwise} \end{cases} \qquad (10.51)$$

The basic technique is to find the error in our estimate f_k by finding $\mathcal{S}(f - f_k)$, scaling that by some amount $\lambda \in \mathcal{R}$ and adding that correction term back into f_k. The resulting "corrected" signal is then low-pass filtered, resulting in the new estimate. We can write this iteration algorithm for f_{k+1} as

$$f_{k+1} = \mathcal{T} f_k = \mathcal{P}_2 \left[f_k + \lambda \mathcal{S}(f - f_k) \right] \qquad (10.52)$$

Note that $\mathcal{P}_2$ may be implemented by a frequency-space box if it is surrounded by a Fourier transform, or as a signal-space convolution. It can be proven that when $0 < \lambda < 2$, the algorithm of Equation 10.47 will converge.

Equation 10.47 can be written in a slightly different form that will make it easier to compare it with the variations below. We write an operator $\mathcal{A}_1$ operating on a signal g as

$$\mathcal{A}_1 g = g(\mathbf{x}) + \mathcal{S}\left[f(\mathbf{x}) - g(\mathbf{x})\right] \tag{10.53}$$

Then the iteration becomes

$$f_k = \mathcal{T} f_k = \mathcal{P}_2\left[1 + \lambda\left(\mathcal{A}_1 - 1\right)\right] f_k \tag{10.54}$$

Three variations on this algorithm are also given in Sauer and Allebach [376]. We call the technique of Equations 10.47 and 10.54 method 1. Method 2 is similar, but approximates the signal as a triangular mesh over a number of sample points. This signal is then refined by alternating projection in signal and frequency spaces, as before.

In method 2 the frequency-space operator $\mathcal{P}_2$ is unchanged, but $\mathcal{A}_1$ is replaced by $\mathcal{A}_2 = \mathcal{R}\mathcal{S}$, the product of a new operator $\mathcal{R}$ and the sampling operator $\mathcal{S}$ from above. The basic idea is to treat the sample points as the vertices of triangles. The signal at any point p may then be found by evaluating the plane equation of the appropriate triangle at that point:

$$\mathcal{R}g(p) = ap_x + bp_y + cp_z + d \tag{10.55}$$

for a plane with normal (a, b, c) and constant offset d. So $\mathcal{A}_2(f - f_k) = \mathcal{R}\mathcal{S}(f - f_k)$ is a collection of triangular facets. The iteration equation may be written

$$f_{k+1} = \mathcal{T} f_k = \mathcal{P}_2\left[f_k + \lambda\mathcal{A}_2(f - f_k)\right] \tag{10.56}$$

In method 3, an additional constraint is introduced to compensate for the fact that the farther a point is from a sample point, the less we know about what the signal should be. Thus, the error at these points is weighted less. A distance function is introduced and a new operator $\mathcal{A}_3$ is used to include its effect.

Although the convergence condition mentioned above is rigorous, Sauer and Allebach note that it is often useful to start the method with a much more aggressive degree of overrelaxation. If successive iterations begin to diverge, they decrease the value of λ and perform that iteration again. In their paper they compare the three methods above against each other and the thin-plate spline method of Franke [149].

Although iterative techniques are theoretically appealing, they suffer the drawback of requiring a great deal of computation. If the signal is an image, then at every iteration we must either compute a forward and inverse Fourier transform, or convolve with a very large approximated sinc function. When pictures have thousands of samples on a side, this calculation time can become prohibitive. We have presented them here because they are theoretically interesting, provide good results, and may be practical in situations where only a few samples are involved.

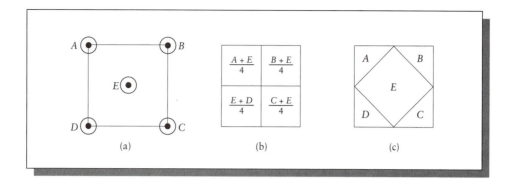

FIGURE 10.81

Subdivision in Whitted's method. (a) The initial sampling at corners and center. (b) The four squares defined by this sampling pattern. (c) A visual expression of the weights of the samples.

10.10.4 Piecewise-Continuous Reconstruction

The most straightforward reconstruction is to assume that the neighborhood is *tiled* by regions (that is, the regions fully cover the neighborhood with no gaps over overlaps). The regions R are built from the samples, so each region i has the value R_i.

Whitted's Method

Whitted's reconstruction method [477] essentially builds rectangular regions in the neighborhood, and then box-filters the resulting signal to form a single flat reconstructed surface over the neighborhood. Whitted does not provide the details of the area subdivision technique, but one reasonable interpretation proceeds as follows [156].

Initially, the four corners and center of a square with unit area neighborhood are evaluated, as in Figure 10.81(a). After these first five samples are evaluated, all further decimations of the neighborhood will be based on squares defined by two diagonally opposite corners. We will consider the signal in each of these square regions to be constant, with intensity given by the average of the sample values on the corners. Thus after the first step, we have the four corners A, B, C, and D, and the center E. As shown in Figure 10.81(b), each corner-center pair defines one subsquare with total area 1/4 and intensity given by the average of the samples. So

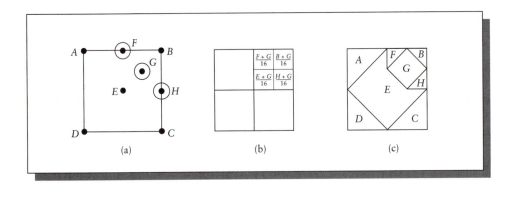

FIGURE 10.82

One level of subdivision. (a) The new sampling points F, G, and H. (b) The evaluation of the subpixels. (c) A visual expression of the new weights of the samples.

our first estimate for the value of this neighborhood is

$$P_v = \frac{1}{4}\left(\frac{A+E}{2} + \frac{B+E}{2} + \frac{C+E}{2} + \frac{D+E}{2}\right) \tag{10.57}$$

A visualization of these weights is shown in Figure 10.81(c), where the size of the area associated with each sample is equal to its weight (these areas are meant only to communicate the size of the weight, and are probably not the best shapes for real areas associated with each sample; Voronoi regions are better and are discussed below).

Suppose that the upper-right corner needs refining. We take new samples F, G, and H, as shown in Figure 10.82(a). Then the 1/4 total contribution due to that square is now distributed among the five samples there, using the same basic weighting as in Equation 10.57. Thus the term $(B+E)/2$ is replaced by a new expression

$$\frac{B+E}{2} \rightarrow \frac{1}{4}\left(\frac{E+G}{2} + \frac{F+G}{2} + \frac{B+G}{2} + \frac{H+G}{2}\right) \tag{10.58}$$

and diagrammed in Figure 10.82(b).

We will follow the process through two more steps to clarify the subdivision and show how some samples may be shared among regions. If we refine the lower-right corner of the square defined by points G and H, then the term $(H+G)/2$ in

$$P_v = \tfrac{1}{4}\left(\boxed{\tfrac{A+E}{2}} + \boxed{\tfrac{B+E}{2}} + \tfrac{C+E}{2} + \tfrac{D+E}{2}\right)$$

$$\tfrac{1}{4}\left(\tfrac{E+G}{2} + \tfrac{F+G}{2} + \tfrac{B+G}{2} + \boxed{\tfrac{H+G}{2}}\right)$$

$$\tfrac{1}{4}\left(\tfrac{G+K}{2} + \tfrac{L+K}{2} + \tfrac{H+K}{2} + \tfrac{J+K}{2}\right)$$

$$\tfrac{1}{4}\left(\tfrac{A+R}{2} + \tfrac{F+R}{2} + \tfrac{E+R}{2} + \tfrac{Q+R}{2}\right)$$

FIGURE 10.83

Assigning weights to a subdivided square.

Equation 10.58 becomes a new expression in the new samples J, K, and L:

$$\frac{H+G}{2} \rightarrow \frac{1}{4}\left(\frac{G+K}{2} + \frac{L+K}{2} + \frac{H+K}{2} + \frac{J+K}{2}\right) \tag{10.59}$$

Finally, we will refine the upper-left subsquare defined by points A and E in the original neighborhood, and create new samples Q and R. We already have sample F from the previous subdivision. The term $(A+E)/2$ in Equation 10.57 becomes

$$\frac{A+E}{2} \rightarrow \frac{1}{4}\left(\frac{A+R}{2} + \frac{F+R}{2} + \frac{E+R}{2} + \frac{Q+R}{2}\right) \tag{10.60}$$

If this is the end of refinement, then we can express the final value P_v for the neighborhood by combining Equations 10.57 through 10.60. A little algebra confirms that the weights add up to 1.0. This process is illustrated in Figure 10.83.

Wyvill and Sharp's Method

Another piecewise-linear tiling was presented by Wyvill and Sharp [491]. If a square neighborhood has samples only on its edges, they assume that all the edges in the signal are linear and radiate from the center of gravity of the samples on the square's sides and corners. They assume that a maximum of one edge can pass through each square side. Since every edge must enter and then exit, there will be 0, 2, or 4 points on the square edges, as shown in Figure 10.84.

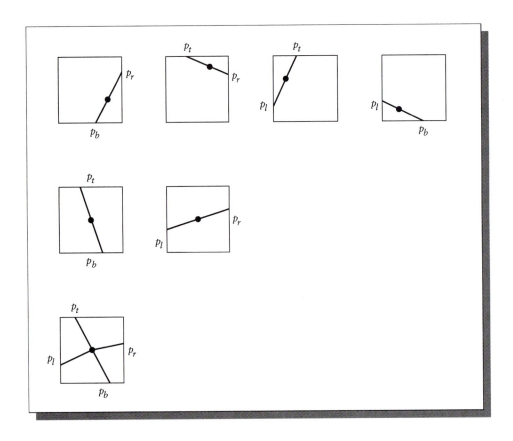

FIGURE 10.84

If edges are linear and only one edge may pass through each square side, then there will be 0, 2, or 4 intersections of signal edges and the square sides. Here we show the intersections, their center of gravity, and the radial pattern associated with the configuration.

They assume that the color of each patch within the square is constant, so one can take the value at the corner and weight it by its associated area. Figure 10.85 gives the formulas for this reconstruction, using the notation of Figure 10.86.

To illustrate, suppose that we have a vertical edge that intercepts the top and bottom of the pixel, at p_t and p_b, respectively. Then from the seventh line of Figure 10.85, we compute

$$\alpha = \frac{1}{2}(1 - p_r)(1 - p_t) \tag{10.61}$$

p_l	p_t	p_r	p_b	α	αC	$(1-\alpha)C$
0	0	0	0	•		
0	0	0	1	•		
0	0	1	0	•		
0	0	1	1	$\alpha = \frac{1}{2}(1 - p_b)p_r$	LR	UL
0	1	0	0	•		
0	1	0	1	$\alpha = p_t + \frac{1}{2}(p_b - p_t)$	LL	UR
0	1	1	0	$\alpha = \frac{1}{2}(1 - p_r)(1 - p_t)$	UR	LL
0	1	1	1	•		
1	0	0	0	•		
1	0	0	1	$\alpha = \frac{1}{2}p_b p_l$	LL	UR
1	0	1	0	$\alpha = p_l + \frac{1}{2}(p_r - p_l)$	LL	UR
1	0	1	1	•		
1	1	0	0	$\alpha = \frac{1}{2}p_t(1 - p_l)$	UL	LR
1	1	0	1	•		
1	1	1	0	•		
1	1	1	1	$(UL/2)[(1 - p_l)c_x + p_t(1 - c_y)]$ $+ (UR/2)[(1 - p_t)(1 - c_y) + (1 - p_r)(1 - c_x)]$ $+ (LR/2)[p_r(1 - c_x) + (1 - p_b)c_y]$ $+ (LL/2)[p_b c_y + p_l c_x]$ $c_x = (p_t + p_b)/2$ $c_y = (p_r + p_l)/2$		

FIGURE 10.85

Central-star reconstruction. For all but the last row, the value for α is applied to the two corners indicated. A bullet indicates a disallowed configuration.

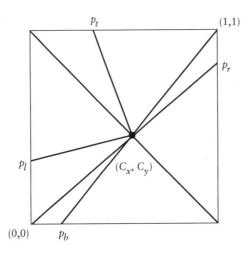

FIGURE   10.86

The notation for the reconstruction scheme. The square has origin (0,0) in the lower left and (1,1) in the upper right. Each intercept has a value from 0 to 1. The values of the corners are weighted by the corresponding area.

and compute the color C from $C = (\alpha\, UR) + ((1 - \alpha)\, LL)$, where we have chosen arbitrarily to use UR for the right color and LL for the left color; the colors at UL and LR respectively would have done as well.

The most important assumption in this method is that the internal edges are linear, there is only one per edge, and they may be modeled by the star-radiating pattern. Figure 10.87 shows three interpretations of the same data: two opposite corners are white, the other two are black, and the four transition points are in the center of each edge. If white is given value 1 and black 0, we can sensibly make estimates of 0.25, 0.75, or 0.5 for the final value. When pixels are simple, the reconstruction discussed here is probably reasonable, but when a situation is sufficiently hard, a more powerful reconstructor should be used instead.

Painter   and   Sloan's   Method

Painter and Sloan [328] use a piecewise-constant reconstruction based on a stored tree of samples. If the samples were generated using a k-d tree, then there is an associated data structure of k-dimensional boxes, where each box has one sample.

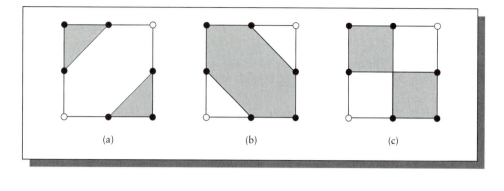

FIGURE 10.87

The same configuration of corner colors and edge intercepts can lead to three different values for the neighborhood. (a) $C = 0.25$. (b) $C = 0.75$. (c) $C = 0.5$.

In 2D, these boxes are just rectangles in the plane. They assume that the entire rectangle has a single uniform color given by its representative sample.

This makes it particularly easy to apply the low-pass filter prior to resampling. Figure 10.88(a) shows a roughly Gaussian filter placed over a region of the plane tiled with rectangles. The filter's total response can be broken down into a sum of responses, one per rectangle, as shown in Figure 10.88(b). We can write this symbolically as the result of a filter function $f(x, y)$ over a signal $s(x, y)$ defined in a 2D neighborhood N:

$$P_v(x, y) = \int_N f(x - u, y - v) s(x, y) \, du \, dv$$
$$= \sum_{i=1}^{t} r_i \int_{A(i)} f(x - u, y - v) \, du \, dv \qquad (10.62)$$

where in the second line we have replaced the signal $s(x, y)$ as a sum of t rectangles with area $A(i)$ and value r_i. Since the rectangles are disjoint, each integral is independent of the others.

The advantage of this observation is that we have efficient tools for finding the integral of a tabled function over any rectangular region. Some filters (e.g., polynomial functions) may be simple enough that we can do the integration analytically. Otherwise, we can convert the filter into a sum table [111], so that four table lookups, three adds, and a divide will give us the integral under any rectangular region. Each rectangle R_i needs to be clipped to the sum table boundary T before access, which is simply a box-box intersection. If we have a routine sum-table(f) that represents

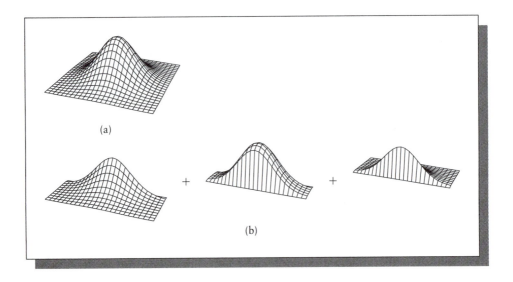

FIGURE 10.88

(a) A filter $f(x, y)$ over a domain tiled with rectangles. (b) That filter's response is the sum of its response to each rectangle.

the filter function $f(x, y)$, then we can write the total response as

$$P_v(x, y) = \sum_i r_i \; \texttt{sum-table}(f)(R_i \cap T) \qquad (10.63)$$

If the filter is separable, then it can be stored as two 1D sum tables rather than one 2D sum table, reducing the storage costs from $O(N^2)$ to $O(N)$, where N is the number of samples we have used per dimension to digitize the filter.

For image reconstruction, Painter and Sloan recommend a Laczos windowed sinc filter with a 7×7 pixel support [185].

Although piecewise-constant rectangles provide a nice mathematical structure to the image, and permit efficient calculation of filtered values, higher-order interpolation methods are likely to yield more accurate values. This is worth investigating since a better reconstruction scheme may allow us to reduce the number of samples we need to evaluate. Painter and Sloan suggest using the sample locations to produce a Delaunay triangulation of the plane [346].

We can apply the same piecewise-constant technique applied above to rectangles for these triangles, or use a higher-order interpolation scheme. Two good candidates are the algorithms by Cendes and Wong [79] and Salesin et al. [372]; the

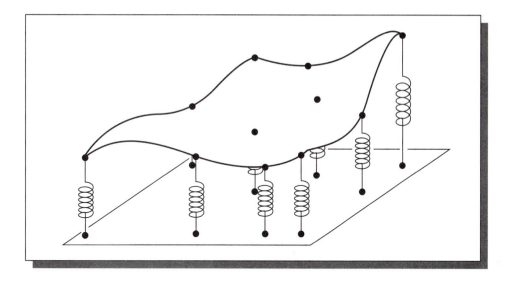

FIGURE 10.89

Uncertain and certain samples are modeled by loose and stiff springs, respectively, and a thin plate is built to accommodate those springs.

latter is particularly powerful because it can handle discontinuities of the signal over triangle edges. The convolution step is a bit more difficult with triangles than rectangles because sum tables are only efficient for rectangular regions; efficient discrete convolution over triangular regions is still an open problem.

Thin-Plate Splines

Franke reconstructs a univariate function from nonuniform sample points by fitting a thin plate through the data [149]. The plate is defined by a set of splines, and is everywhere continuous in its first derivative.

A similar reconstruction method has been suggested by Metaxas and Milios [299]. At every sample point a spring is placed; the rest length of the spring is defined by the value of the sample at that point, and its stiffness is related to the confidence associated with that value. So if we have some sample whose values we are uncertain of, those values would be represented by relatively loose springs, while those values we are confident about would be represented by stiff springs, as in Figure 10.89.

The surface v is created to minimize the total potential energy in the sheet. This is the sum of two energy factors: the deformation in the sheet, and the accommodation to the given data represented by springs each of which has an associated rest length and stiffness. The sheet minimizes the potential energy of deformation E_p, given by

$$E_p(v) = \frac{1}{2} \int_A (v_{xx}^2 + 2v_{xy}^2 + v_{yy}^2) \, dx \, dy \qquad (10.64)$$

The region A is the area over which we will build this piece of the sheet, and the subscripts on v are partial derivatives. To accommodate the springs, we introduce a constraint function $C(v) = 0$; the energy cost in matching the constraint is E_{con}, given by

$$E_{con}(v) = \int_A \beta(x, y)[C(v(x, y))]^2 \, dx \, dy \qquad (10.65)$$

where $\beta(x, y) > 0$. Since we have a finite number of springs, we can write this as a summation

$$E_{con}(v) = \frac{1}{2} \sum_A \beta(x_i, y_i)[v(x_i, y_i) - c(x_i, y_i)]^2 \qquad (10.66)$$

where $c(x_i, y_i)$ is the value of sample i, and $\beta(x_i, y_i)$ is our confidence in that value (or, conversely, the amount of noise we think is in that value). The total potential energy is the sum of these two energies:

$$E_v = E_p(v) + E_{con}(v) \qquad (10.67)$$

Metaxas and Milios solve this problem with a finite-elements approach, breaking the signal domain into a finite number of squares and solving for a solution over each square that is C^0 and C^1 continuous with the adjacent square.

This approach is different from the preceding methods in a number of ways. Most significantly, it has the ability to accommodate noisy data. It also has an interesting continuity condition: as defined, it produces a result that is continuous in value and in first derivative everywhere on the surface. This can be both an advantage and a problem.

The effect of enforcing this continuity is that abrupt changes in the signal will be smoothed out. A disadvantage of this is that if the neighborhood is large, then sharp edges and corners will be lost. This can be a problem if the technique is used in the image plane, where we typically want sharp boundaries between objects to remain sharp in the image. On the other hand, if the signal needs to be low-pass-filtered prior to resampling, this technique produces a result very similar to that operation. An analytic description of the frequency-space properties of this algorithm has not been carried out, so it is difficult to say just what sort of low-pass filtering is performed, and where the transition band is located.

Metaxas and Milios recognize the challenge of discontinuities and propose a method to automatically detect them and break the continuity constraint at those places during surface fitting. They estimate the bending moment of the sheet and consider any bend that is too large to effectively mean there is a big change in signal value, implying the presence of an edge. They note that the edges are not very well detected, and that when used for images, there is interference of colors around object edges.

We can get additional insight into the utility of thin-plate spline methods from observations due to Sauer and Allebach [376]. They measured the signal-to-error ratio against known test data for iterative methods and a thin-plate spline method. They found that their iterative method had a better signal-to-error ratio after only three iterations, and that after forty iterations the improvement over splines is generally between 4.5 and 33.5 dB. The result seems to be that iterative methods produce results of equal quality to spline methods after only a few iterations, and that iterative techniques continue to improve after that, while the spline solution, once determined, remains fixed.

10.10.5 Local Filtering

Another approach to nonuniform reconstruction is essentially the same idea that is used when we want to resample a uniformly sampled signal, which is to simply apply a reconstruction filter (or a combined reconstruction/low-pass filter) directly to the sampled data, centered over the desired reconstruction location. Exactly how a filter is applied to nonuniform sample geometry varies from algorithm to algorithm.

A good survey of filter characteristics with regard to image quality is given in Mitchell and Netravali [310]. The following discussion follows their presentation and uses their images to demonstrate filter behavior.

There are several criteria we want our reconstruction filters to achieve. Of course, we want their frequency-space response to be such that they do not attenuate the baseband (central copy of the signal spectra) too much, and that they allow only a little energy from spectral replicas of the baseband to pass through. The ideal box filter matches these two constraints perfectly, though it is not realizable in practice because it has an infinite impulse response.

Most filters used in graphics are *space-invariant*, meaning that their shape and size do not change with respect to the domain being filtered. The alternative is a *space-variant* filter, such as the elliptically weighted average filter developed by Greene and Heckbert [168]. They also present a good summary of different filter types for texture-mapping applications.

After discussing some filter characteristics, we will survey some filters that have been proposed in the literature.

Filter Criteria

It may be surprising to note that when a picture is reconstructed with a practical implementation of the theoretically ideal low-pass filter, the result is often not a satisfactory image. An example is shown in Figure 10.90(a) (color plate), where we have enlarged an image by convolving with a very wide sinc filter. Notice the distracting *ringing* around the edges. This ringing is a combined result of the truncated reconstruction filter and the fact that our image function is effectively windowed by a box filter; the image is 0 outside of its square boundaries. This sudden discontinuity in intensity introduces some high frequencies into the signal that show up in the reconstruction. So it is insufficient to apply even a good approximation of the sinc to an image and expect a good-looking result; practical reconstruction requires a closer look at the filters and their effect on the image.

A useful set of criteria for characterizing a filter include *sample-frequency ripple*, *anisotropic effects*, *ringing*, *blurring*, and *reconstruction error* or *post-aliasing*. These are discussed in turn, following the presentation by Mitchell and Netravali [310].

Sample-frequency ripple occurs when the DC component of the signal aliases and is included in the reconstructed signal. The name comes from the fact that this component shows up in the spectrum at multiples of the sampling frequency. The visual artifact is shown in Figure 10.90(b). To remove this from the signal, we would like our filter to be zero at all multiples of the sampling frequency; then DC components at those frequencies will be canceled out.

Anisotropic effects are visible when the filter has unequal response in different spatial directions. A particularly common example of this type of problem is when a separable filter is used on a square resampling grid, and the underlying square pixels show through. An example appears in Figure 10.90(c).

Ringing occurs when an edge turns into a rippling set of lighter and darker bands, as shown earlier in Figure 10.90(a). This is a result of alternating positive and negative lobes in the filter response, which serve to increase and decrease the signal in the neighborhood of an edge. Ringing can be useful for edge sharpening when it is carefully controlled.

If the filter attenuates the baseband too much in the higher frequencies, then sharp edges become blurry, as in Figure 10.90(d).

If the filter allows too much of the spectrum beyond the Nyquist rate to survive in the reconstructed image, we get post-aliasing, as in Figure 10.90(e).

In practice we cannot satisfy all of these criteria at once, but rather must make some trade-offs and get good behavior in some categories at the expense of inferior quality in others.

Mitchell and Netravali point out that if each sample contains not just its value but also the derivatives of the signal at that point, then reconstruction may proceed more accurately or more quickly with a given number of samples. This information is usually difficult to obtain in rendering systems.

Flat-Field Response

Pavicic [335] has suggested that one characterization of a good filter is that when the original signal is flat (i.e., all samples have the same value), then the reconstructed function should also be flat. That is, if all the sample values are 1.0, then the convolution sum h of the sampled signal s and the filter f in Equation 10.68 should be as close as possible to 1.0 for all values of x and y.

$$h(x, y) = \sum_{i=-\infty}^{\infty} \sum_{k=-\infty}^{\infty} s(i, k) f(i - x, k - y) \tag{10.68}$$

This problem is very similar to the flat-field display response studied in Chapter 3. There we were given the display function (which was also radially symmetrical) and we sought the proper intersample spacing to achieve a flat field. Here we have the opposite problem, where we are given the spacing but seek a reconstruction filter that achieves a flat field when evaluated at all points within the field.

To measure the quality of the field, Pavicic proposed a test situation where all samples have height 1 on a square lattice of side 1. His measurement involved finding the volume of the difference between a flat sheet of height 1 and the filter response f over the square. We call the absolute error at each point $e(x, y)$:

$$e(x, y) = |f(x, y) - 1| \tag{10.69}$$

Pavicic integrates this error over the sample square to get a single volume measure ϵ_v:

$$\epsilon_v = \iint e(x, y) \, dx \, dy \tag{10.70}$$

Max [284] also finds the maximum difference in contrast, ϵ_c, over the reconstructed signal $h = f * s$:

$$\epsilon_c = \max_{0 \le x, y \le 1} h(x, y) - \min_{0 \le x, y \le 1} h(x, y) \tag{10.71}$$

He has also used the RMS error ϵ_{RMS} of $e(x, y)$ over a dense set of n points inside the square:

$$\epsilon_{RMS} = \sqrt{\frac{1}{n} \sum_i \sum_k e^2(i, k)} \tag{10.72}$$

We will use these measures below to compare filters.

Normalization

It is important to *normalize* our filters, which requires dividing their response by their total volume; this makes their response to a flat-field input of 1 equal to 1. This is particularly easy if the filter is radially symmetric. The cylindrical-shell method from vector calculus says that if we have a radially symmetric filter defined by $f(r)$ evaluated in an interval $[0, b]$ where $f(r) \geq 0$ for all $r \in [0, b]$, then the volume obtained by rotating this around the Z axis is

$$V = 2\pi \int_0^b r f(r) \, dr \qquad (10.73)$$

If the filter is given piecewise, the integrals may be done over smaller intervals and summed together.

Noise Sensitivity

In the physical sciences, unwanted *noise* can influence the samples of a signal in several ways. Many techniques have been developed to deal with various types of noise during reconstruction. We don't have the same kind of explicit problem with noise in computer graphics, since in theory we can compute with arbitrary accuracy. In fact, there is always a limit on the precision with which we carry out any of our calculations, and there is quantization error on top of that. A careful characterization of the errors we introduce depends on the precise algorithms used, the program that implements them, and the computer that the program runs on. But if we use a nonuniform sampling process, then we are deliberately introducing high-frequency noise into our samples to avoid regular aliasing artifacts. An important problem in reconstruction from nonuniform samples is to filter out this high-frequency noise before we resample the signal.

One form of high-frequency noise is known as *shot noise*, which occurs when a few samples out of many have a significantly different value than the others. Such samples are sometimes called *rogues* or *outlyers*.

The technique of Metaxas and Milios discussed above is tolerant of some noise, but we need to identify the rogues and give them large spring constants or the algorithm will attempt to match those samples, and perhaps even deduce the presence of an edge. This is not a problem unique to their algorithm; robust tolerance of noise is a difficult problem.

Lee and Redner [260] have suggested using a class of nonlinear filters called *alpha filters* to eliminate rogues. These filters may be used in conjunction with other reconstruction techniques. The basic idea is that in any neighborhood, we gather together the n samples s_i and sort them into increasing order. We then discard samples from both ends of the sorted list, starting with s_1 and s_n, then removing s_2 and s_{n-1}, and so on. The number of samples to remove is given as a percentage α of the number of samples n.

The *alpha-trimmed mean* s_α for the n samples $\{s_1, s_2, \ldots, s_n\}$ is defined by

$$
s_\alpha = \begin{cases}
\dfrac{1}{n - 2\lfloor \alpha n \rfloor} \displaystyle\sum_{i=\lfloor \alpha n \rfloor + 1}^{n - \lfloor \alpha n \rfloor} s_i & n,\ \text{odd} \\[3em]
\dfrac{1}{n - 2\lfloor \alpha(n-1) \rfloor} \displaystyle\sum_{i=\lfloor \alpha(n-1) \rfloor + 1}^{n - \lfloor \alpha(n-1) \rfloor} s_i & n,\ \text{even}
\end{cases}
\tag{10.74}
$$

Note that when $\alpha = 0$, no values are trimmed from the summation, and the result is the sum of all the samples; this is equivalent to a box filter. When $\alpha = 0.5$, then we get back the median value of the set of samples. The filter is also dependent on its width w, which is the radius of a circle about the pixel center; samples falling within this circle are included in the filter.

Lee and Redner discuss the use of alpha-trimmed means in a variety of disciplines, and stress its utility for removing rogue values while preserving edges. They note that the filter is usually much too large for typical image-synthesis applications if samples are assumed to be distributed with a density of about one per pixel. Either we should work with a much higher sampling density, or create interpolated values near a pixel center derived from the pixel's neighbors.

They also note that repeated application of the filter with different values for the parameters (α, w) usually gives results that are superior to a single application. For a relatively smooth ray-traced scene (no textures and mostly diffuse objects) with eight samples per pixel, they reported good results from the two-pass combination $[(0.5, 1.0), (0.4, 1.0)]$. For an image with more high-frequency content, the two-pass combination $[(0.5, 0.5), (0.4, 0.25)]$ worked well. They do not give suggestions for automatically picking values of α and w from the samples themselves, but it seems that as the image becomes more complex, a good approach is to use a filter with a radius on the order of half the intersample spacing and a relatively high value of α (near 0.5), to remove most of the pops. A second pass with a smaller radius and smaller α removes the less dramatic rogues without overly softening the edges.

Alpha-trimmed mean filters are useful when the sampling density is roughly uniform in the neighborhood being sampled. They are not appropriate in regions of extreme variation of sampling density. If the filter sits over a region where there are many samples clumped together, they will tend to overwhelm the samples in the more sparsely sampled part of the region, leading to an incorrect average (this is true even when $\alpha = 0$). The second discussion on multistage filtering below addresses that issue.

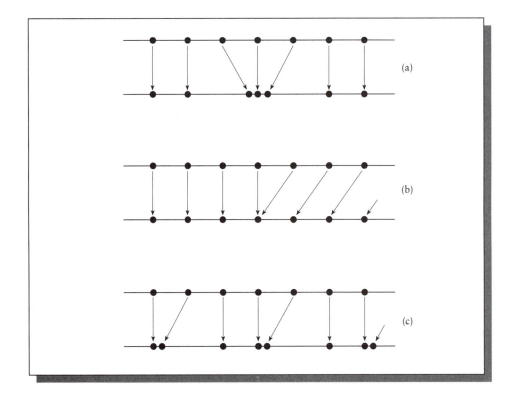

FIGURE 10.91

The three types of sample patterns studied by Yen [497]. (a) Migration of a finite number of points. (b) A single gap in the distribution. (c) Recurrent nonuniform sampling. Redrawn from Yen in *IRE Transactions on Circuit Theory*, figs. 1–3, pp. 252–253.

10.10.6 Yen's Method

Yen [497] studied reconstruction from three types of nonuniform sampling patterns. These are illustrated in Figure 10.91.

The first type of pattern occurs when a finite number of samples move from a regular pattern to slightly different locations, as in Figure 10.91(a). The second pattern occurs when a single discrepancy occurs in the pattern; for example, all samples beyond a certain point are shifted by a constant value with respect to all samples before that point, as in Figure 10.91(b). This could be caused by a one-time mechanical failure in a sampling instrument, for example.

Most important to our study is the pattern Yen called *recurrent nonuniform sampling* which is the case when the sampling pattern is formed by a repeated cluster of N nonuniformly spaced samples, as in Figure 10.91(c).

Yen showed how to reconstruct the function f from these samples, when it is bandlimited to a maximum frequency of ω_{max} and the clusters are spaced in intervals $N/w\omega_{max}$. He introduced a minimum-energy constraint to obtain a unique interpolating function. The idea is that one can think of the sampling pattern as N separate uniform patterns, each with an intersample spacing of $N/w\omega_{max}$. We can thus write the total sampling sequence as the sum of N subsequences τ_{pm}, each of which is an infinite set of periodic samples:

$$f(t) = \sum_{p=1}^{N} \tau_{pm} = \sum_{p=1}^{N} \sum_{m=-\infty}^{\infty} t_p + m \frac{N}{2\omega_{max}} \tag{10.75}$$

Then the reconstructed function $f(t)$ is given by

$$f(t) = \sum_{p=1}^{N} \sum_{m=-\infty}^{\infty} f(\tau_{pm}) \Psi_{pm}(t) \tag{10.76}$$

where

$$\Psi_{pm}(t) = \frac{\prod_{q=1}^{N} \sin\left(\frac{2\pi W}{N}\right) (t - t_q)}{\prod_{q=1 \neq p}^{N} \sin\left(\frac{2\pi W}{N}\right) (t_p - t_q)} \frac{(-1)^{mN}}{\frac{2\pi W}{N} \left(t - t_p - \frac{mN}{2W}\right)} \tag{10.77}$$

Jerri [231] notes that this technique is theoretically superior to alternatives such as low-pass filtering and spline interpolation, but Sankur and Gerhardt [375] report that it can be difficult or impractical to implement. Yen provides some reasons for this difficulty in his original paper. When the samples are closely bunched, the distances $t_p - t_q$ become small. Since these values are in the denominator of Equation 10.77, it causes the values of the reconstruction formula at that point to become very large.

When the signal values are amplified by a large value, any errors in the values are correspondingly amplified. Thus the values of bunched-up samples must be of increasingly higher precision as the bunching becomes more dense. Yen also notes that derivatives can be important in the reconstruction process, and that they can also impose precision requirements on the sample values.

Pavicic

Pavicic investigated the flat-field response of several different radially symmetric filters and found their volume errors ϵ_v.

Radius	Height
0.00	1.000
0.25	0.788
0.50	0.558
0.75	0.149
1.00	0.000

FIGURE 10.92
Coefficients for a nonuniform cubic B-spline filter.

He found his best filter by direct calculation; it is given by a nonuniform cubic B-spline with the coefficients in Figure 10.92. This filter has a volume $V = 0.60$. The flat-field response of this filter is given in Figure 10.93.

Cook's Filter

Cook proposed reconstruction with a difference of Gaussians [101]. This radially symmetric filter is given as a function of r, the distance from the pixel center. The filter is drawn from a family of one-parameter filters based on w, the filter width. For image reconstruction, Cook sets $w = 1.5$. The filter is given by

$$f(r) = \begin{cases} e^{-r^2} - e^{-w^2} & r < w \\ 0 & \text{otherwise} \end{cases} \tag{10.78}$$

and is shown in Figure 10.94. The volume of this filter is given by

$$V = \pi \left[1 - e^{-w^2}(1 + w^2) \right] \tag{10.79}$$

We can think of Equation 10.78 as a Gaussian bump that has been shifted downward by a constant and then windowed by a box. Thus, the filter does not blend away smoothly. Its derivative is

$$\frac{df}{dr} = -2re^{-r^2} \tag{10.80}$$

so when the filter reaches 0 at $r = w$, it has a derivative of $-2we^{-w^2}$.

Because of the abrupt clipping created by the box, the filter will pass some high frequencies, and this is evident in the Fourier transform of the filter shown in Figure 10.94(b).

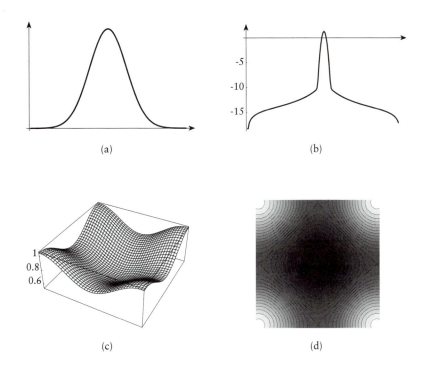

FIGURE 10.93

The Pavicic filter. (a) Filter curve. (b) Fourier transform of (a). (c) 3D plot of flat-field response. (d) Contour plot of (c).

Cook mentions two ways to apply the filter. In the first, we evaluate the filter value at each sample location and use that to weight the sample. The second method is appropriate when the samples have been jittered on a regular grid and the jitter distance is small compared to the filter width. Then the filter may be converted into a 2D table of values, which is placed over the desired reconstruction point. Each sample is weighted by the nearest stored filter value.

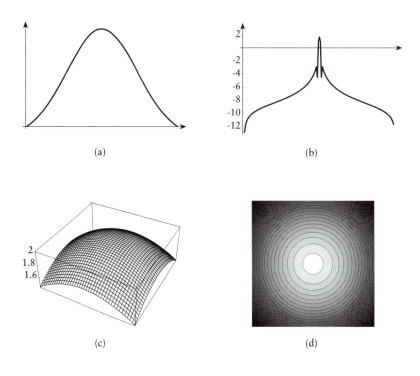

FIGURE   10.94

Cook's difference of Gaussians filter. (a) Filter curve. (b) Fourier transform of (a). (c) 3D plot of flat-field response. (d) Contour plot of (c).

Bouville et al.

In Bouville et al. [59] the sampling geometry is expected to be a diamond lattice, and the resampling pattern is a rectangular lattice. In this way they distinguish the reconstruction filter from the following low-pass filter. In the paper they provide coefficients for filters of various sizes. The coefficients for the reconstruction filter are given in Figure 10.95. Note that the filter is vertically and horizontally symmetrical about the origin and designed for a diamond lattice; the entries of 0 correspond to sample locations that are not expected to have values.

$$\begin{bmatrix} 0 & 20 & 0 & 19 & 0 & 20 & 0 \\ 20 & 0 & -89 & 0 & -89 & 0 & 20 \\ 0 & -89 & 0 & 375 & 0 & -89 & 0 \\ 19 & 0 & 375 & 0 & 375 & 0 & 19 \\ 0 & -89 & 0 & 375 & 0 & -89 & 0 \\ 20 & 0 & -89 & 0 & -89 & 0 & 20 \\ 0 & 20 & 0 & 19 & 0 & 20 & 0 \end{bmatrix}$$

FIGURE 10.95

The coefficients of the 7×7 reconstruction filter. *Source:* Data from Bouville et al. in *Proc. Eurographics '91*.

Dippé and Wold

Dippé and Wold [124] suggest the use of a one-parameter family of radially symmetric raised cosine filters $f(r)$. The filter parameter is w, which specifies the width. The filter is given by

$$f(r) = \begin{cases} \frac{1}{w} \left[\cos\left(\frac{2\pi}{w} r\right) + 1 \right] & r < w \\ 0 & \text{otherwise} \end{cases} \tag{10.81}$$

The volume of this filter is simply

$$V = \pi w \tag{10.82}$$

Dippé and Wold [124] discuss how to choose w in Equation 10.81 on the basis of the local sampling density. Suppose that e_{tot} is the estimated RMS error in the signal within a filter of width w_0, and we desire to reconstruct with an RMS error bounded by e_b. Then the reconstruction filter width W is given by

$$w = w_0 \left(\frac{e_{tot}}{e_b} \right)^2 \tag{10.83}$$

The response for this filter is given in Figure 10.96.

They also present a discussion of another filter, based on an assumption that the signal is statistically stationary. Unfortunately, most signals in computer graphics (with the notable exception of noise textures) are not stationary, so the analysis is not directly applicable.

Max

Max [284] has noted that for image reconstruction, it is desirable to have the sum of the filters be C^1 smooth in the area between the samples, and observed that

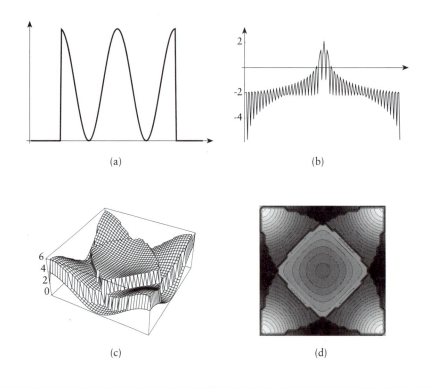

FIGURE 10.96

The Dippé and Wold filter for $w = 1$. (a) Filter curve. (b) Fourier transform of (a). (c) 3D plot of flat-field response. (d) Contour plot of (c).

the Pavicic filter described above does not fit that criterion. He proposed a class of radially symmetric two-parameter filters $f(r)$ based on a defining curve $g(r)$ that satisfies the following criteria (the notation g' refers to the derivative of g with respect to r):

1 $g(r)$ is a nonuniform quadratic spline.

2 $g(r)$ is downward sloping in $[0, s]$ and upward sloping in $[s, t]$, where $s, t \in \mathcal{R}$ and $0 \leq s \leq t$.

3 $g(s) = g(t)$.

4 $g'(s) = g'(t)$.

5 $g(0) = 1$, $g'(0) = 0$, $g(t) = 0$, $g'(t) = 0$.

Conditions 1 and 2 set the general nature of the curve, which is defined in two parts, $[0, s]$ and $[s, t]$. Conditions 3 and 4 guarantee that the two parts meet with C^0 and C^1 continuity, and the remaining conditions ensure that the curve starts at one and drops to 0, with a flat derivative at both ends.

Max's filter $g(r)$ meeting these criteria is given by

$$
g(r) = \begin{cases} 1 - \dfrac{r^2}{st} & 0 \leq r \leq s \\[2ex] \dfrac{(t-r)^2}{t(t-s)} & s \leq r \leq t \\[2ex] 0 & t \geq r \end{cases} \tag{10.84}
$$

This curve is plotted in Figure 10.97.

To normalize the filter, we need to know its volume V, which is given by

$$
V(s,t) = 2\pi \left(\frac{s^2}{2} - \frac{s^4}{4st} + \frac{t^4}{12t(t-s)} - \frac{s^2 t^2}{2t(t-s)} + \frac{2s^3 t}{3t(t-s)} - \frac{s^4}{4t(t-s)} \right) \tag{10.85}
$$

We define the two-parameter filter family $f(r) = (1/V)g(r)$, where each filter has unit volume.

Max analyzed his filter using the same setup as Pavicic: four identical filters were placed at the corners of a square, and the field between them was analyzed for deviance from a perfectly flat sheet of height 1. Max searched for three different criteria: smallest contrast (maximum height minus minimum height), smallest value of V as defined by Pavicic, and smallest RMS error between the summed field and 1. The smallest value for each of these criteria, and the values of s and t where it was achieved, are given in Figure 10.98.

Note that the error value of $\epsilon_v = 0.210$ is much lower than Pavicic's minimum of $\epsilon_v = 0.60$. The response of this filter is shown in Figure 10.97.

Mitchell and Netravali

Mitchell and Netravali [310] have developed a set of two-parameter filters appropriate for many reconstruction tasks.

The filters $f(r)$ are based on two parameters, B and C, and are defined for the

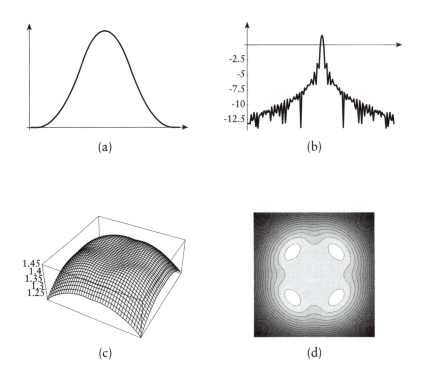

FIGURE   10.97

The Max filter with $s = 0.4810$ and $t = 1.3712$. (a) Filter curve. (b) Fourier transform of (a). (c) 3D plot of flat-field response. (d) Contour plot of (c).

range $|r| < 2$. The filters are given by

$$
f(r) = \frac{1}{6}
\begin{cases}
\begin{aligned}
&(12 - 9B - 6C)|r|^3 \\
&\quad + (-18 + 12B + 6C)|r|^2 + (6 - 2B)
\end{aligned} & |r| < 1 \\[2ex]
\begin{aligned}
&(-B - 6C)|r|^3 + (6B + 30C)|r|^2 \\
&\quad + (-12B - 48C)|r| + (8B + 24C)
\end{aligned} & 1 \le r \le 2 \\[2ex]
0 & \text{otherwise}
\end{cases}
\tag{10.86}
$$

The volume of this filter is given by

$$
V = 2\pi \frac{9 + 5B - 4C}{60}
\tag{10.87}
$$

Equation 10.86 includes several well-known filters. The value $(B, C) = (1, 0)$

Criterion	value	s	t
ϵ_v	0.885	0.4848	1.3778
ϵ_{RMS}	0.245	0.4810	1.3712
ϵ_v	0.210	0.4792	1.3682

FIGURE 10.98
Results for the Max filter.

is the cubic B-spline, $(0, C)$ is the one-parameter family of cardinal cubic splines, $(0.0.5)$ is the Catmull-Rom cubic spline, and $(B, 0)$ contains the tensioned B-splines discussed by Duff [131].

Mitchell and Netravali attempted to characterize this 2D space of splines by an informal experiment. They selected an image for reconstruction, and on a single monitor showed a blurry, ringing, anisotropic, high-quality reconstructed image. In the center was shown an image reconstructed with the filter of Equation 10.86 for some values of B and C, and subjects were asked to choose which reference image the center picture was most similar to. Their results are shown in Figure 10.99.

The dotted line $2C + B = 1$ in Figure 10.99 represents a line where an analysis suggests good splines can be found; notice that it contains the cubic B-spline $(1, 0)$ and the Catmull-Rom spline $(0, 0.5)$. Mitchell and Netravali suggest that the best trade-off may be found at $(1/3, 1/3)$, which is plotted in Figure 10.100.

The frequency response of the filters in Equation 10.86 is given by

$$F(\omega) = \frac{3 - 3B}{(\pi\omega)^2} \left[\text{sinc}^2(\omega) - \text{sinc}(2\omega)\right]$$
$$+ \frac{2C}{(\pi\omega)^2} \left[-3 \; \text{sinc}^2(2\omega) + 2 \; \text{sinc}(2\omega) + \text{sinc}(4\omega)\right]$$
$$+ B \; \text{sinc}^4(\omega) \tag{10.88}$$

The response of the (1/3,1/3) filter is plotted in Figure 10.100.

10.10.7 Multistep Reconstruction

All the reconstruction techniques discussed above place a copy of the appropriate filter over the resampling point and generate an interpolated value at that point. There is no preprocessing of the samples once they have been evaluated.

This process works well when the sampling density under the filter is roughly

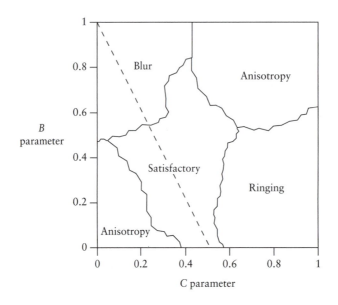

FIGURE 10.99

(B, C) filter space. Note that the B parameter is on the vertical axis and the C parameter on the horizontal. Redrawn from Mitchell and Netravali in *Computer Graphics (Proc. Siggraph '88)*, fig. 13, p. 224.

uniform. Then we can estimate the local sampling rate at the resample point, choose a filter of the appropriate width, and reconstruct. But when the sampling density under the filter is far from uniform, artifacts can appear in the reconstructed signal. We refer to the artifacts caused by variant sampling density in an image as *grain noise* [307].

If the sampling density is nearly uniform, we can suppress the artifacts by using a *weighted-average filter* [101]. In one dimension, we write the reconstructed signal $r(x)$ as the product of the samples $s(x)$ and the reconstruction filter $f(x)$, divided by the weights applied to the samples:

$$r(x) = \frac{\sum_n f(x - x_n)s(x_n)}{\sum_n f(x - x_n)} \tag{10.89}$$

But as Mitchell points out [307], this filter does not handle extreme variations

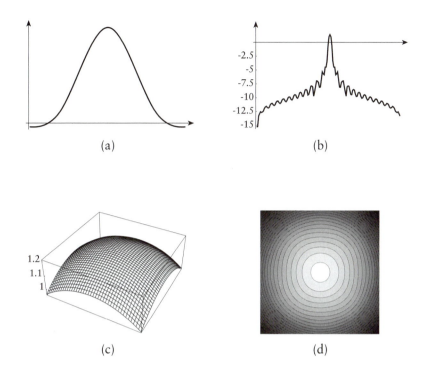

FIGURE 10.100

The Mitchell-Netravali cubic filter $(1/3, 1/3)$. (a) Filter curve. (b) Fourier transform of (a). (c) 3D plot of flat-field response. (d) Contour plot of (c).

in local sample density. Figure 10.101 (color plate) shows this filter applied to a straight edge between a black region and a white one; the filter reconstructs a bumpy transition rather than a smooth one.

This behavior comes about because the goal of adaptive nonuniform sampling is to gather information, and not to present that information in a way that is appropriate for reconstruction. When an adaptive, nonuniform sampling technique is used to sample the edge of Figure 10.101(a), samples of the signal are drawn until we can deduce the relative areas of the two regions. This deduction is made on the basis of the sample values and their locations, particularly where they group together. A

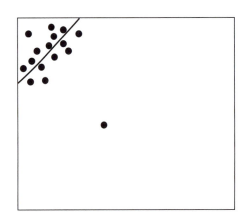

FIGURE 10.102

Sample clumping at an edge.

dense set of black samples is likely to represent a black region of the image, but it is no more black than another region containing only one sample.

Figure 10.102 shows one possible result of adaptively sampling an edge between a white region (with value 1) and a black region (with value 0) in a rectangular cell of edge length 1. We suppose that the initial sampling pattern placed two samples in this cell, and one each fell on the black and white regions. Suppose that a refinement algorithm was then invoked, and samples were drawn densely near the edge, where about half landed on the black side and half on the white side. Together, the sample values and locations do a pretty good job of representing the signal in this cell.

Suppose we now filter this cell for reconstruction, using a box filter. The white region occupies the upper-left triangle of a square about $1/3$ on a side, so the white area is about $1/18 \approx 0.056$. But because our samples are almost evenly distributed in the two regions, we will get an average of about 0.5, which is about an order of magnitude of error (quantized to eight bits, this is a value of about 127 rather than the more accurate 14). We would get qualitatively similar results using the reconstruction filters described above.

To handle this problem, Mitchell has proposed a *multistage filter* [307]. The filter is actually several box filters applied successively. Suppose that we want to reconstruct for new sample geometry on a 2D square grid with intersample distance d.

The multistage filter begins by scanning the grid, taking steps $d/4$ in both x and y. At each step, a box filter with total width $d/4$ is applied to the signal; all the

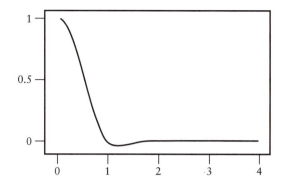

FIGURE 10.104

The multistage filter spectrum. Redrawn from Mitchell in *Computer Graphics (Proc. Siggraph '87)*, p. 68.

samples in this filter are averaged together and the result deposited back into that sample location.

Next the image is scanned again, this time in increments of $d/2$ in both directions, and with a box filter with side lengths $d/2$. Mitchell applies this filter twice. Finally, the grid is scanned with step d and a box filter d units on a side is used at each step. The filtered value is used as the final value for that sample, with the result of Figure 10.103 (color plate) for the step function. Each of these filters is normalized before application by dividing by the number of samples under it.

The multistage filter works well even when the sampling rate is very nonuniform under any of the filters. This is because locally dense clusters of samples do not get the opportunity to overwhelm sparse samples by virtue of sheer numbers. The box-filter passes first average together the samples in regions that are very small with respect to the final sampling density. Even if there is great variance of sampling rate in the first-pass cells, each contributes only 1/16 to the final sample values, so a few errors at this stage don't influence the final value too much. The next stages have the effect of smoothing the signal at the next level of granularity, since there can still be some clumping in one corner of a cell and not much information in another. Finally everything in a tile around the file sample is averaged.

This intuitive explanation is supported by a theoretical argument based on multiple convolution by box filters. The multistage filter may be written as the convolution of four boxes, which is equivalent to a piecewise cubic filter. This filter is shown in Figure 10.104. The topic of multiple convolution with box functions has been studied extensively by Heckbert [204].

Name	$f(r)$	Volume	Width
Pavicic	B-spline	0.60	1
Cook	$\begin{cases} e^{-r^2} - e^{-w^2} & r < w \\ 0 & \text{otherwise} \end{cases}$	$\pi \left[1 - e^{-w^2}(1 + w^2) \right]$	w
Dippé	$\dfrac{1}{w} \left[\cos\left(\dfrac{2\pi}{w} r \right) + 1 \right]$	πw	w
Max	$\begin{cases} 1 - \dfrac{r^2}{st} & 0 \le r \le s \\[2mm] \dfrac{(t-r)^2}{t(t-s)} & s \le r \le t \\[2mm] 0 & \text{otherwise} \end{cases}$	$2\pi \left(\dfrac{s^2}{2} - \dfrac{s^4}{4st} \right.$ $+ \dfrac{t^4}{12t(t-s)} - \dfrac{s^2 t^2}{2t(t-s)}$ $\left. + \dfrac{2s^3 t}{3t(t-s)} - \dfrac{s^4}{4t(t-s)} \right)$	t
Mitchell	$\dfrac{1}{6} \begin{cases} (12 - 9B - 6C)r^3 \\ + (-18 + 12B + 6C)r^2 \quad r < 1 \\ + (6 - 2B) \\ (-B - 6C)r^3 \\ + (6B + 30C)r^2 \qquad 1 \le r \le 2 \\ + (-12B - 48C)r \\ + (8B + 24C) \\ 0 \qquad\qquad\qquad \text{otherwise} \end{cases}$	$2\pi \dfrac{9 + 5B - 4C}{60}$	2
Multistage	?	?	variable

FIGURE 10.105
A summary of the reconstruction filters in this section.

Summary

A summary of the above filters is given in Figure 10.105. It would be very useful to be able to state at this point what the "best" filter is for all uses, and then recommend that filter for rendering programs. Unfortunately, this is almost impossible. As we saw earlier, all filter designs impose trade-offs among several different criteria, which are often mutually antagonistic. My purpose here has been to present a small collection of generally useful filters, but no one is best for all uses.

Having given that caveat, some guidance may be useful: I recommend the two filters at the bottom of Figure 10.105. The cubic filter of Mitchell and Netravali is probably the most extensively reported in graphics for image reconstruction, and it has good performance characteristics. The multistage algorithm handles variation in sampling density with a series of box filters; it's therefore relatively easy to implement and fast to execute.

Filters are complex and subtle, and a lot is known about both analog and digital filter design. Computer graphics has not used much of the classical digital filter repertoire, such as the filters discussed by Hamming [185]. This is probably because we are often interested in the reconstruction of nonuniform samples, which has not been a big issue in most of the image processing literature. The great body of work in audio filters is also not appropriate for graphics work, because, as Mitchell and Netravali pointed out [310], those 1D filters often produce sonically acceptable artifacts that are visually unacceptable. Once again the point is that whether or not a filter is "good" depends very strongly on the application. In this engineering discipline, nothing substitutes for experience, measurement, and careful observation.

When selecting a reconstruction or low-pass filter, you need to balance off implementation and running time with performance issues. We often use fast (and somewhat sloppy) filters when reconstructing the illumination signal at a point, and put more attention on the image signal. This approach, while attractive in terms of performance, can seriously compromise the numerical accuracy of the rendered image. When it's important to have a correct simulation of a real scene, it's not enough to simply gather illumination carefully. The image needs to be processed properly during the shading step, which often requires reconstruction, filtering, and resampling. The filters described in this chapter can be used for that task as well.

10.11 Further Reading

A survey of filters and filtering techniques for image processing may be found in Pratt [345]. Multidimensional filtering is discussed by Dudgeon and Mersereau [130]. Efficient filtering methods often require sophisticated data structures for quick access to the relevant samples; a thorough discussion of data structures may be found in the two-volume set by Samet [373, 374]. A variety of work on nonuniform reconstruction is summarized in Marvasti's book [283], though it is difficult to obtain. A thorough discussion of various extensions to the sampling theorem is presented by Jerri [231].

The aliasing problem was first addressed in computer graphics by Crow in 1977 [108]. A good discussion of practical anti-aliasing methods as of 1981 is given in a later paper by Crow [109]. Stochastic sampling was introduced to computer graphics by Cook in a classic 1986 paper [101], but see the follow-up letters by Pavlidis [336] and Wold and Pépard [486]. A survey of digital signal-processing methods for computer graphics is presented by Wolberg in his book [485], which includes many filter discussions and some source code for the FFT and various interpolation methods. Heckbert [206] also discusses nonuniform reconstruction and filtering.

Many methods have been developed to avoid noise that may have crept into a signal being sampled. If the noise itself is of interest, Shapiro and Silverman have presented a means to sample that noise without aliasing [394]. This may be useful in characterizing the amount of noise in a signal prior to a step where it is removed. Cheung and Marks [87] have shown that under specific conditions, some samples may be disposed of from a sample set, effectively lowering the sample rate without introducing aliasing.

Although the reconstruction problem is often phrased (as here) as though getting final sample values into the frame were the ultimate goal, those sample values when finally displayed are essentially filtered by the display device. This issue has been addressed in the graphics community in a letter by Pavlidis [336] and a paper by Kajiya and Ullner [238].

Most of the papers referenced in this chapter contain a discussion of the various signal-processing issues they address. For a good overview of some practical issues in signal processing in a rendering system, see Shirley and Wang's paper [401].

10.12 Exercises

Exercise 10.1

Give a geometric proof of the hexagonal jittering formula in Equation 10.9.

Exercise 10.2

To sample a square domain using triangular sampling, the domain must be placed inside a triangle. Find the largest square than can fit inside an equilateral triangle. Give a formula for the number of samples inside the square as a function of the uniform subdivision level g of the triangle.

Exercise 10.3

Implement the algorithm of Figure 10.22 to build a jittered sample pattern of samples within a unit square. Compute the largest possible value of the radius r_p assuming hexagonal packing of $N = 50$ samples.

(a) Using a radius $r_p/2$, run the algorithm five times with different starting seeds to generate $N = 50$ samples, and count how many samples are tested until fifty have been accepted. Plot a graph of number of samples accepted as a function of the number generated.

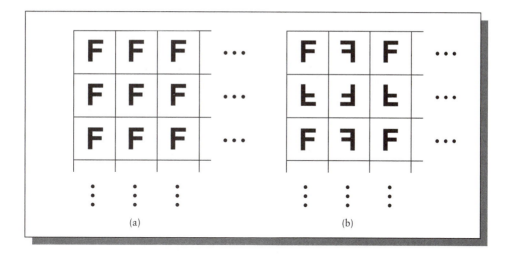

FIGURE 10.106

(a) Filling the plane by translating a single tile. (b) Filling the plane by flipping tiles across common borders.

(b) Repeat (a) for a radius of $3r_p/4$.

(c) Repeat (a) for a radius of $7r_p/8$.

(d) Interpret your results for parts (a), (b), and (c). Is this a fair implementation of rejection sampling? Is this a good way to develop a dense pattern?

Exercise 10.4

Using one of your patterns from Exercise 3, create a sampling grid 10×10 squares on a side by translating your tile ninety-nine times, as in Figure 10.106(a).

(a) Plot the log magnitude of the Fourier transform of your original tile. Interpret the distribution of energy represented by this transform.

(b) Plot the log magnitude of the Fourier transform of the larger tiled domain. Interpret the distribution of energy represented by this transform.

(c) Create a different 10×10 domain by reflecting the tile across each border, as in Figure 10.106. Plot the log magnitude of the Fourier transform of this domain, and interpret the distribution of energy represented by this transform.

(d) Create a different 10×10 domain by choosing a random orientation of the tile in each cell, selecting from the eight possible transformations of a square.

Plot the log magnitude of the Fourier transform of this domain, and interpret the distribution of energy represented by this transform.

Exercise 10.5

Discuss the advantages and disadvantages of controlling sampling on the image plane based purely on the relationships of the intensities of the samples. Can this ever lead to wasteful computation? Can it ever neglect computation that should occur?

Exercise 10.6

Create a nonuniform sampling pattern by jittering a 32×32 grid of points in a unit square, and use this pattern to sample a 20×20 black-and-white checkerboard in the square. Reconstruct the signal using the following filters, and then resample the result on a 32×32 grid.

  (a) Nearest neighbor.
  (b) Abutting box filters.
  (c) Gaussians with a height of 1 and value 0.001 at radius $1/64$.
  (d) Gaussians with a height of 1 and value 0.5 at radius $1/64$.

Compare the quality of the images produced by the different filters.

[1] Edwin A. Abbott. *Flatland*. Dover Publications, Mineola, NY, 1952.

[2] Ralph H. Abraham and Christopher D. Shaw. *Dynamics: The Geometry of Behavior*. Addison-Wesley, Reading, MA, 1992.

[3] Forman S. Acton. *Numerical Methods That Work*. Harper & Row, New York, 1970.

[4] Miguel P. N. Águas and Stefan Müller. Mesh redistribution in radiosity. In Michael Cohen, Claude Puech, and François Sillion, editors, *Fourth Eurographics Workshop on Rendering*, pp. 327–336. Elsevier, Amsterdam, 1993.

[5] Ali N. Akansu and Richard A. Haddad. *Multiresolution Signal Decomposition*. Academic Press, San Diego, 1992.

[6] Taka-aki Akimoto, Kenji Mase, Akihiko Hashimoto, and Yasuhito Suenaga. Pixel selected ray tracing. In W. Hansmann, F. R. A. Hopgood, and W. Straßer, editors, *Proc. Eurographics '89*, pp. 39–50. North-Holland, Amsterdam, 1989.

[7] B. Alpert, G. Beylkin, R. Coifman, and V. Rokhlin. Wavelet-like bases for the fast solution of second-kind integral equations. *SIAM Journal on Scientific Computing*, 14(1):159–184, January 1993.

[8] Bradley K. Alpert. A class of bases in L^2 for the sparse representation of integral operators. *SIAM Journal of Mathematical Analysis*, 24(1):246–262, January 1993.

[9] John Amanatides. Ray tracing with cones. *Computer Graphics (Proc. Siggraph '84)*, 18(3):129–135, July 1984.

[10] Michael A. Andreottola. Color hard-copy devices. In H. John Durrett, editor, *Color and the Computer*, chapter 12, pp. 241–254. Academic Press, San Diego, 1987.

[11] Arthur Appel. Some techniques for shading machine renderings of solids. *AFIPS 1968 Spring Joint Computer Conference*, 32:37–45, 1968.

[12] J. Argence. Antialiasing for ray tracing using CSG modeling. In Tosiyasu Kunii, editor, *New Trends in Computer Graphics (Proc. CG International '88)*, pp. 199–208. Springer-Verlag, New York, 1988.

[13] James Arvo. Backward ray tracing. In Andrew S. Glassner, editor, *Siggraph '86 Developments in Ray Tracing course notes*. ACM Siggraph, New York, August 1986.

[14] James Arvo. Linear operators and integral equations in global illumination. In Paul Heckbert, editor, *Siggraph 1993 Global Illumination course notes*, chapter 2. ACM Siggraph, New York, August 1993.

[15] James Arvo. Transfer equations in global illumination. In Paul Heckbert, editor, *Siggraph 1993 Global Illumination course notes*, chapter 1. ACM Siggraph, New York, August 1993.

[16] James Arvo and David Kirk. Fast ray tracing by ray classification. *Computer Graphics (Proc. Siggraph '87)*, 21(4):55–64, July 1987. Also in *Tutorial: Computer Graphics: Image Synthesis*, pp. 196–205. Computer Society Press, Washington, DC, 1988.

[17] James Arvo and David Kirk. A survey of ray tracing acceleration techniques. In Andrew S. Glassner, editor, *An Introduction to Ray Tracing*, pp. 201–262. Academic Press, San Diego, 1989.

[18] Frédérik Asensio. A hierarchical ray-casting algorithm for radiosity shadows. In Alan Chalmers, Derek Paddon, and François Sillion, editors, *Third Eurographics Workshop on Rendering*, pp. 179–188. Elsevier, Amsterdam, 1992.

[19] Robert B. Ash. *Information Theory*. Dover Publications, Mineola, NY, 1965.

[20] P. R. Atherton, K. Weiler, and D. Greenberg. Polygon shadow generation. *Computer Graphics (Proc. Siggraph '78)*, 12(3):275–281, August 1978.

[21] Kendall Atkinson. An automatic program for linear Fredholm integral equations of the second kind. *ACM Transactions on Mathematical Software*, 2(2):154–171, June 1987.

[22] Kendall E. Atkinson. *A Survey of Numerical Methods for the Solution of Fredholm Integrals of the Second Kind*. SIAM, Philadelphia, 1976.

[23] Larry Aupperle and Pat Hanrahan. A hierarchical illumination algorithm for surfaces with glossy reflection. *Computer Graphics (Proc. Siggraph '93)*, 27(3):155–162, August 1993.

[24] Larry Aupperle and Pat Hanrahan. Importance and discrete three point transport. In Michael Cohen, Claude Puech, and François Sillion, editors, *Fourth Eurographics Workshop on Rendering*, pp. 85–94. Elsevier, Amsterdam, 1993.

[25] Ezekiel Bahar and Swapan Chakrabarti. Full-wave theory applied to computer-aided graphics for 3D objects. *IEEE Computer Graphics & Applications*, 7(7):46–60, July 1987.

[26] Christopher T. H. Baker. *The Numerical Treatment of Integral Equations*. Clarendon Press, Oxford, England, 1977.

[27] A. V. Balakrishnan. On the problem of time jitter in sampling. *IRE Transactions on Information Theory*, IT-8(3):226–236, April 1962.

[28] Thomas F. Banchoff. *Beyond the Third Dimension*. Scientific American Library, New York, 1990.

[29] Hujun Bao and Qunsheng Peng. A progressive radiosity algorithm for scenes containing curved surfaces. In R. J. Hubbold and R. Juan, editors, *Proc. Eurographics '93*, pp. 399–408. North-Holland, Amsterdam, 1993.

[30] Jack Barth, Doug Kirby, Ken Smith, and Mike Wilkins. *Roadside America*. A Fireside Book, New York, 1986.

[31] Rui Manuel Bastos, António Augusto de Sousa, and Fernando Nunes Ferreira. Reconstruction of illumination functions using bicubic hermite interpolation. In Michael Cohen, Claude Puech, and François Sillion, editors, *Fourth Eurographics Workshop on Rendering*, pp. 317–326. Elsevier, Amsterdam, 1993.

[32] Daniel R. Baum, Stephen Mann, Kevin P. Smith, and James M. Winget. Making radiosity usable: Automatic preprocessing and meshing techniques for the generation of accurate radiosity solutions. *Computer Graphics (Proc. Siggraph '91)*, 25(4):51–60, July 1991.

[33] Daniel R. Baum, Holly E. Rushmeier, and James M. Winget. Improving radiosity solutions through the use of analytically determined form-factors. *Computer Graphics (Proc. Siggraph '89)*, 23(3):325–334, July 1989.

[34] Daniel R. Baum and James M. Winget. Real time radiosity through parallel processing and hardware acceleration. *Computer Graphics (Proc. 1990 Symposium on Interactive 3D Graphics)*, 24(2):67–75, March 1990.

[35] Barry G. Becker and Nelson L. Max. Smooth transitions between bump rendering algorithms. *Computer Graphics (Proc. Siggraph '93)*, 27(3):183–190, August 1993.

[36] J. L. Bentley and J. H. Friedman. Data structures for range searching. *ACM Computing Surveys*, 11(4):397–409, April 1979.

[37] Jeffrey C. Beran-Koehn and Mark J. Pavicic. A cubic tetrahedral adaption of the hemi-cube algorithm. In James Arvo, editor, *Graphics Gems II*, pp. 299–302. Academic Press, San Diego, 1991.

[38] Jeffrey C. Beran-Koehn and Mark J. Pavicic. Delta form-factor calculation for the cubic tetrahedral algorithm. In David Kirk, editor, *Graphics Gems III*, pp. 324–328. Academic Press, San Diego, 1992.

[39] Sterling K. Berberian. *Introduction to Hilbert Space*. Oxford University Press, New York, 1961.

[40] G. D. Bergland. A guided tour of the fast Fourier transform. *IEEE Spectrum*, 6:41–52, July 1969.

[41] William H. Beyer. *CRC Standard Mathematical Tables*. CRC Press, Boca Raton, FL, 26th ed., 1984.

[42] G. Beylkin, R. Coifman, and V. Rokhlin. Fast wavelet transforms and numerical algorithms I. *Communications on Pure and Applied Mathematics*, 44:141–183, 1991.

[43] N. Bhate and A. Tokuta. Photorealistic volume rendering of media with directional scattering. In Alan Chalmers, Derek Paddon, and François Sillion, editors, *Third Eurographics Workshop on Rendering*, pp. 227–245. Elsevier, Amsterdam, 1992.

[44] Buming Bian, Norman Wittels, and Donald S. Fussel. Non-uniform patch luminance for global illumination. In Kellogg Booth and Alain Fournier, editors, *Proc. Graphics Interface '92*, pp. 310–318. Canadian Information Processing Society, Toronto, 1992.

[45] Philippe Blasi, Bertran Le Saëc, and Christophe Schlick. A rendering algorithm for discrete volume density objects. In R. J. Hubbold and R. Juan, editors, *Proc. Eurographics '93*, pp. 201–207. North-Holland, Amsterdam, 1993.

[46] James F. Blinn. Models of light reflection for computer synthesized pictures. *Computer Graphics (Proc. Siggraph '77)*, 11(2):192–198, July 1977.

[47] James F. Blinn. Simulation of wrinkled surfaces. *Computer Graphics (Proc. Siggraph '78)*, 12(3):286–292, August 1978.

[48] James F. Blinn. A generalization of algebraic surface drawing. *ACM Transactions on Graphics*, 1(3):235–256, July 1982.

[49] James F. Blinn. Light reflection functions for simulation of clouds and dusty surfaces. *Computer Graphics (Proc. Siggraph '82)*, 16(3):21–29, July 1982.

[50] James F. Blinn. Dirty pixels. *IEEE Computer Graphics & Applications*, 9(4):100–105, July 1989.

[51] James F. Blinn and Martin E. Newell. Texture and reflection in computer generated images. *Communications of the ACM*, 19(10):542–547, October 1976.

[52] Edward A. Boettner and J. Reimer Wolter. Transmission of the ocular media. *Investigative Ophthalmology*, 1(6):776–783, December 1962.

[53] Craig F. Bohren and Donald R. Huffman. *Absorption and Scattering of Light by Small Particles*. John Wiley & Sons, New York, 1983.

[54] A. I. Borisenko and I. E. Tarapov. *Vector and Tensor Analysis with Applications*. Dover Publications, Mineola, NY, 1968. Translated from the Russian by Richard A. Silverman.

[55] Max Born and Emil Wolf. *Principles of Optics*. Pergamon Press, Tarrytown, NY, 2nd rev. ed., 1964.

[56] Kadi Bouatouch and Pierre Tellier. A two-pass physics-based global lighting model. In Kellogg Booth and Alain Fournier, editors, *Proc. Graphics Interface '92*, pp. 319–328. Canadian Information Processing Society, Toronto, 1992.

[57] Christian Bouville, Kadi Bouatouch, Pierre Tellier, and Xavier Pueyo. A theoretical analysis of global illumination models. In K. Bouatouch and C. Bouville, editors, *Eurographics Workshop on Photosimulation, Realism and Physics in Computer Graphics*, pp. 53–66. Elsevier, Amsterdam, 1990.

[58] Christian Bouville, Jean-Luc Dubois, Isabelle Marchal, and M. L. Viaud. Monte Carlo integration applied to an illumination model. In David A. Duce and Pierre Jancene, editors, *Proc. Eurographics '88*, pp. 483–498. North-Holland, Amsterdam, 1988.

[59] Christian Bouville, Pierre Tellier, and Kadi Bouatouch. Low sampling densities using a psychovisual approach. In Frits H. Post and Wilhelm Barth, editors, *Proc. Eurographics '91*, pp. 167–182. North-Holland, Amsterdam, 1991.

[60] William E. Boyce and Richard C. DiPrima. *Elementary Differential Equations*. John Wiley & Sons, New York, 3rd ed., 1977.

[61] Ronald N. Bracewell. *The Fourier Transform and Its Applications*. McGraw-Hill, New York, 2nd rev. ed., 1986.

[62] David H. Brainard. Calibration of a computer controlled monitor. *Color Research and Application*, 14(1):23–34, February 1989.

[63] William L. Briggs. *A Multigrid Tutorial*. SIAM, Philadelphia, 1987.

[64] Willem F. Bronsvoort, Jarke J. van Wijk, and Frederik W. Jansen. Two methods for improving the efficiency of ray casting in solid modeling. *Computer-Aided Design*, 16(1):110–116, January 1984.

[65] Frederick P. Brooks, Jr. Grasping reality through illusion—interactive graphics serving science. In *Proceedings of CHI '88*, pp. 1–11. ACM, New York, 1988. (Special issue of the SIGCHI bulletin).

[66] Earle B. Brown. *Modern Optics*. Reinhold Publishing, New York, 1965.

[67] Jichun Bu and Ed F. Deprettere. A VLSI system architecture for high-speed radiative transfer 3D synthesis. *Visual Computer*, 5(6):121–133, June 1989.

[68] Chris Buckalew and Donald Fussell. Illumination networks: Fast realistic rendering with general reflectance functions. *Computer Graphics (Proc. Siggraph '89)*, 23(3):89–98, July 1989.

[69] Phong Bui-Tuong. Illumination for computer generated pictures. *Communications of the ACM*, 18(6):311–317, June 1975.

[70] Dionys Burger. *Sphereland*. Apollo Editions, New York, 1965. Translated by Cornelie J. Rheinboldt.

[71] Brian Cabral, Nelson Max, and Rebecca Springmeyer. Bidirectional reflection functions from surface bump maps. *Computer Graphics (Proc. Siggraph '87)*, 21(4):273–281, July 1987.

[72] Kathleen Cain. *Luna: Myth & Mystery*. Johnson Books, Boulder, CO, 1991.

[73] A. T. Campbell III and Donald S. Fussell. Adaptive mesh generation for global diffuse illumination. *Computer Graphics (Proc. Siggraph '90)*, 24(4):155–164, August 1990.

[74] Ingrid Carlbom. Filter design for volume reconstruction and visualization. In Gregory M. Nielson and Dan Bergeron, editors, *Proceedings of Visualization '93*, pp. 54–61. IEEE Computer Society Press, Los Alamitos, CA, 1993.

[75] Kenneth M. Case and Paul F. Zweifel. *Linear Transport Theory*. Addison-Wesley, Reading, MA, 1967.

[76] E. D. Cashwell and C. J. Everett. *A Practical Manual on the Monte Carlo Method for Random Walk Problems*. Pergamon Press, Tarrytown, NY, 1959.

[77] Kenneth R. Castleman. *Digital Image Processing*. Prentice-Hall, Englewood Cliffs, NJ, 1979.

[78] Edwin Catmull. A tutorial on compensation tables. *Computer Graphics (Proc. Siggraph '79)*, 13(2):1–13, July 1979.

[79] Zoltan J. Cendes and Steven H. Wong. C^1 quadratic interpolation over arbitrary point sets. *IEEE Computer Graphics & Applications*, 7(11):8–16, November 1987.

[80] Sudeb Chattopadhyay and Akira Fujimoto. Bi-directional ray tracing. In Tosiyasu Kunii, editor, *Computer Graphics 1987 (Proc. CG International '87)*, pp. 335–343. Springer-Verlag, New York, 1987.

[81] David Shi Chen and Jan P. Allebach. Analysis of error in reconstruction of two-dimensional signals from irregularly spaced samples. *IEEE Transactions on Acoustics, Speech, and Signal Processing*, 35(2):173–180, February 1987.

[82] Hong Chen and En-Hua Wu. An adapted solution of progressive radiosity and ray-tracing methods for non-diffuse environments. In T. S. Chua and T. L. Kunii, editors, *Computer Graphics Around the World (Proc. CG International '90)*, pp. 477–490. Springer-Verlag, New York, 1990.

[83] Hong Chen and En-Hua Wu. An efficient radiosity solution for bump texture generation. *Computer Graphics (Proc. Siggraph '90)*, 24(4):125–134, August 1990.

[84] Hong Chen and En-Hua Wu. Radiosity for furry surfaces. In Frits H. Post and Wilhelm Barth, editors, *Proc. Eurographics '91*, pp. 447–457. North-Holland, Amsterdam, 1991.

[85] Shenchang Eric Chen. Incremental radiosity: An extension of progressive radiosity to an interactive image synthesis system. *Computer Graphics (Proc. Siggraph '90)*, 24(4):135–144, August 1990.

[86] Shenchang Eric Chen, Holly E. Rushmeier, Gavin Miller, and Douglass Turner. A progresive multi-pass method for global illumination. *Computer Graphics (Proc. Siggraph '91)*, 25(4):165–174, July 1991.

[87] Kwan F. Cheung and Robert J. Marks II. Imaging sampling below the Nyquist density without aliasing. *Journal of the Optical Society of America*, 7(1):92–104, January 1990.

[88] K. Chiu, M. Herf, P. Shirley, S. Swamy, C. Wang, and K. Zimmerman. Spatially nonuniform scaling functions for high contrast images. *Proc. Graphics Interface '93*, pp. 245–253, Canadian Information Processing Society, Toronto, 1993.

[89] Per Christensen, David Salesin, and Tony DeRose. A continuous adjoint formulation for radiance transport. In Michael Cohen, Claude Puech, and

François Sillion, editors, *Fourth Eurographics Workshop on Rendering*, pp. 95–104. Elsevier, Amsterdam, 1993.

[90] C. K. Chui. *Wavelet Analysis and Its Applications*. Academic Press, San Diego, 1992.

[91] CIE Technical Committee 3.1. An analytic model for describing the influence of lighting parameters upon visual performance. Technical report CIE 19/2.1, International Commission on Illumination, 1981.

[92] James J. Clark, Matthew R. Palmer, and Peter D. Lawrence. A transformation method for the reconstruction of functions from nonuniformly spaced samples. *IEEE Transactions on Acoustics, Speech, and Signal Processing*, 33(4):1151–1165, October 1985.

[93] James Alan Cochran. *The Analysis of Linear Integral Equations*. McGraw-Hill, New York, 1972.

[94] Mac A. Cody. The fast wavelet transform. *Dr. Dobb's Journal*, pp. 16–28, 101–103, April 1992.

[95] Michael Cohen, Shenchang Eric Chen, John R. Wallace, and Donald P. Greenberg. A progressive refinement approach to fast radiosity image generation. *Computer Graphics (Proc. Siggraph '88)*, 22(4):75–84, August 1988.

[96] Michael Cohen and Donald P. Greenberg. The hemi-cube: A radiosity solution for complex environments. *Computer Graphics (Proc. Siggraph '85)*, 19(3):31–40, July 1985. Also in *Tutorial: Computer Graphics: Image Synthesis*, Computer Society Press, Washington, DC, 1988.

[97] Michael Cohen, Donald P. Greenberg, Dave S. Immel, and Philip J. Brock. An efficient radiosity approach for realistic image synthesis. *IEEE Computer Graphics & Applications*, 6(3):26–35, March 1986.

[98] Michael F. Cohen. Is image synthesis a solved problem? In Alan Chalmers, Derek Paddon, and François Sillion, editors, *Third Eurographics Workshop on Rendering*, pp. 161–167. Elsevier, Amsterdam, 1992.

[99] Michael F. Cohen and John R. Wallace. *Radiosity and Realistic Image Synthesis*. Academic Press, San Diego, 1993.

[100] Robert L. Cook. Shade trees. *Computer Graphics (Proc. Siggraph '84)*, 18(4):223–231, July 1984.

[101] Robert L. Cook. Stochastic sampling in computer graphics. *ACM Transactions on Graphics*, 5(1):51–72, January 1986.

[102] Robert L. Cook, Thomas Porter, and Loren Carpenter. Distributed ray tracing. *Computer Graphics (Proc. Siggraph '84)*, 18(3):137–145, July 1984.

[103] Robert L. Cook and Kenneth E. Torrance. A reflectance model for computer graphics. *ACM Transactions on Graphics*, 1(1):7–24, January 1982.

[104] James W. Cooley and John W. Tukey. An algorithm for the machine calculation of complex Fourier series. *Mathematics of Computation*, 19(90):297–301, April 1965.

[105] R. R. Coveyou, V. R. Cain, and K. J. Yost. Adjoint and importance in Monte Carlo application. *Nuclear Science and Engineering*, 27:219–234, 1967.

[106] Roger A. Crawfis and Nelson Max. Texture splats for 3D scalar and vector field visualization. In Gregory M. Nielson and Dan Bergeron, editors, *Proceedings of Visualization '93*, pp. 261–268. IEEE Computer Society Press, Los Alamitos, CA, 1993.

[107] Frank Crow. Personal communication, January 1994.

[108] Franklin C. Crow. The aliasing problem in computer-generated shaded images. *Communications of the ACM*, 20(11):799–805, November 1977.

[109] Franklin C. Crow. A comparison of antialiasing techniques. *IEEE Computer Graphics & Applications*, 1(1):40–48, January 1981.

[110] Franklin C. Crow. A more flexible image generation environment. *Computer Graphics (Proc. Siggraph '82)*, 16(3):9–18, July 1982.

[111] Franklin C. Crow. Summed-area tables for texture mapping. *Computer Graphics (Proc. Siggraph '84)*, 18(3):207–212, July 1984.

[112] Christine A. Curcio, Kenneth R. Sloan, Robert E. Kalina, and Anita E. Hendrickson. Human photoreceptor topography. *The Journal of Comparative Neurology*, 292:497–523, 1990.

[113] Leonardo da Vinci. *The Notebooks of Leonardo da Vinci*. Dover Publications, Mineola, NY, 1970. Reprint of the 1883 edition; translated by Jean Paul Richter.

[114] Norm Dadoun, David G. Kirkpatrick, and John P. Walsh. The geometry of beam tracing. In Joseph O'Rourke, editor, *Proc. of the Symp. on Computational Geometry*, pp. 55–61. ACM Press, New York, 1985.

[115] I. Daubechies. *Ten Lectures on Wavelets*. SIAM, Philadelphia, 1992.

[116] B. Davison and J. B. Sykes. *Neutron Transport Theory*. Oxford University Press, New York, 1957.

[117] Hugh Davson, editor. *The Eye: The Visual Process*, volume 2. Academic Press, San Diego, 1962.

[118] Hugh Davson, editor. *The Eye: Visual Optics and the Optical Space Sense*, volume 4. Academic Press, San Diego, 1962.

[119] Mark de Berg. *Efficient Algorithms for Ray Shooting and Hidden Surface Removal*. Ph.D. thesis, Rijksuniversiteit te Utrecht, The Netherlands, March 1992.

[120] L. M. Delves and J. L. Mohamed. *Computational Methods for Integral Equations*. Cambridge University Press, New York, 1985.

[121] V. F. Dem'yanov and V. N. Molozemov. *Introduction to Minimax*. Dover Publications, Mineola, NY, 1990.

[122] H. H. Denman, W. Heller, and W. J. Pangonis. *Angular Scattering Functions of Spheres*. Wayne State University Press, Detroit, MI, 1966.

[123] Russell L. DeValois and Karen K. DeValois. *Spatial Vision*. Oxford University Press, New York, 1988.

[124] Mark A. Z. Dippé and Erling Henry Wold. Antialiasing through stochastic sampling. *Computer Graphics (Proc. Siggraph '85)*, 19(3):69–78, July 1985.

[125] George Drettakis and Eugene Fiume. Concrete computation of global illumination using structured sampling. In Alan Chalmers, Derek Paddon, and François Sillion, editors, *Third Eurographics Workshop on Rendering*, pp. 189–201. Elsevier, Amsterdam, 1992.

[126] George Drettakis and Eugene Fiume. Accurate and consistent reconstruction of illumination functions using structured sampling. In R. J. Hubbold and R. Juan, editors, *Proc. Eurographics '93*, pp. 385–398. North-Holland, Amsterdam, 1993.

[127] George Drettakis, Eugene Fiume, and Alain Fournier. Tightly-coupled multiprocessing for a global illumination algorithm. In Carlo E. Vandoni and David A. Duce, editors, *Proc. Eurographics '90*, pp. 387–98. North-Holland, Amsterdam, 1990.

[128] Steven M. Drucker and Peter Schröder. Fast radiosity using a data parallel architecture. In Alan Chalmers, Derek Paddon, and François Sillion, editors, *Third Eurographics Workshop on Rendering*, pp. 247–258. Amsterdam, Elsevier, 1992.

[129] James J. Duderstadt and William R. Martin. *Transport Theory*. John Wiley & Sons, New York, 1979.

[130] Dan E. Dudgeon and Russell M. Merserau. *Multidimensional Digital Signal Processing*. Prentice-Hall, Englewood Cliffs, NJ, 1984.

[131] Tom Duff. Splines in animation and modeling. In *Siggraph '86 State of the Art in Image Synthesis course notes*. ACM Siggraph, New York, 1986.

[132] D. R. Duncan. The colour of pigment mixtures. *Proceedings of the Physical Society*, pp. 380–390, 1940.

[133] H. John Durrett. *Color and the Computer*. Academic Press, San Diego, 1987.

[134] E. R. G. Eckert and E. M. Sparrow. Radiative heat exchange between surfaces with specular reflection. *International Journal of Heat and Mass Transfer*, 3:42–54, 1961.

[135] Will Eisner. *Comics & Sequential Art*. Poorhouse Press, Tamarac, FL, 1985.

[136] A. F. Emery, O. Johansson, M. Lobo, and A. Abrous. A comparative study of methods for computing the diffuse radiation viewfactors for complex structures. *Journal of Heat Transfer*, 113:413–422, May 1991.

[137] Bruno Ernst. *Adventures with Impossible Figures*. Tarquin Publications, Norfolk, England, 1986.

[138] E. Esselink. About the order of Appel's algorithm. Technical report computing science note KE5-1, Department of Computer Science, University of Groningen, The Netherlands, 1989.

[139] D. Farnsworth. A temporal factor in colour discrimination. In *Visual Problems in Color, II (National Phys. Lab. Symposium)*, number 8, p. 429. Her Majesty's Stationery Office, London, 1958.

[140] R. Farrell. Determination of configuration factors of irregular shape. *Journal of Heat Transfer*, pp. 311–313, May 1976.

[141] Martin Feda and Werner Purgathofer. Accelerating radiosity by overshooting. In Alan Chalmers, Derek Paddon, and François Sillion, editors, *Third Eurographics Workshop on Rendering*, pp. 21–32. Elsevier, Amsterdam, 1992.

[142] Hans G. Feichtinger and Karlheinz Gröchenig. Iterative reconstruction of multivariate band-limited functions from irregular sampling values. *SIAM J. Math. Anal.*, 23(1):244–261, January 1992.

[143] Hans G. Feichtinger and Karlheinz Gröchenig. Theory and practice of irregular sampling. In John J. Benedetto and Michael W. Frazier, editors, *Wavelets: Mathematics and Applications*, chapter 8. CRC Press, Boca Raton, FL, 1994.

[144] Richard P. Feynman. *QED*. Princeton University Press, Princeton, NJ, 1985.

[145] Kenneth Paul Fishkin. *Applying Color Science to Computer Graphics*. Master's thesis, University of California, Berkeley, December 1983.

[146] Karen Fitzgerald. Don't move that CRT! *IEEE Spectrum*, p. 16, December 1989.

[147] James D. Foley, Andries van Dam, Steven K. Feiner, and John F. Hughes. *Computer Graphics: Principles and Practice*. Addison-Wesley, Reading, MA, 2nd ed., 1990.

[148] Grant R. Fowles. *Introduction to Modern Optics*. Dover Publications, Mineola, NY, 2nd ed., 1975.

[149] R. W. Franke. Smooth interpolation of scattered data by local thin plate splines. *Comp. Math. Appl.*, 8(4):273–181, 1982.

[150] Akira Fujimoto, Takayuki Tanaka, and Kansei Iwata. ARTS: Accelerated ray-tracing system. *IEEE Computer Graphics & Applications*, 6(4):16–26, April 1986. Also in *Tutorial: Computer Graphics: Image Synthesis*, pp. 148–158, Computer Society Press, Washington, DC, 1988.

[151] Robert A. Gabel and Richard A. Roberts. *Signals and Linear Systems*. John Wiley & Sons, New York, 2nd ed., 1980.

[152] David W. George, François X. Sillion, and Donald P. Greenberg. Radiosity redistribution for dynamic environments. *IEEE Computer Graphics & Applications*, 10(7):26–34, July 1990.

[153] Andrew S. Glassner. Space subdivision for fast ray tracing. *IEEE Computer Graphics & Applications*, 4(10):15–22, October 1984. Also in *Tutorial: Computer Graphics: Image Synthesis*, pp. 160–167. Computer Society Press, Washington, DC, 1988.

[154] Andrew S. Glassner. Spacetime ray tracing for animation. *IEEE Computer Graphics & Applications*, 8(3):60–70, March 1988.

[155] Andrew S. Glassner. How to derive a spectrum from an *rgb* triplet. *IEEE Computer Graphics & Applications*, 9(7):95–99, July 1989.

[156] Andrew S. Glassner. An overview of ray tracing. In Andrew S. Glassner, editor, *An Introduction to Ray Tracing*, pp. 1–32. Academic Press, San Diego, 1989.

[157] Andrew S. Glassner. Some ideas for future work. In Andrew S. Glassner, editor, *Siggraph '90 Advanced Topics in Ray Tracing course notes*, chapter 7. ACM Siggraph, New York, 1990.

[158] Andrew S. Glassner. Dynamic stratification. In Michael Cohen, Claude Puech, and François Sillion, editors, *Fourth Eurographics Workshop on Rendering*, pp. 1–14. Elsevier, Amsterdam, 1993.

[159] Andrew S. Glassner. *3D Computer Graphics: A Handbook for Artists and Designers*. Design Books, New York, 2nd ed., 1994.

[160] Andrew S. Glassner, Kenneth P. Fishkin, David H. Marimont, and Maureen C. Stone. Rendering within constraints. Technical report ISTL-CGI-1993-07-01, Information Sciences and Technologies Lab, Xerox PARC, 1993. (To appear in *ACM Transactions on Graphics*).

[161] James Gleick. *Chaos: Making a New Science*. Penguin Books, New York, 1987.

[162] Michael A. Golberg. A survey of numerical methods for integral equations. In Michael A. Golberg, editor, *Solution Methods for Integral Equations*, chapter 1. Plenum Press, New York, 1978.

[163] Jeffrey Goldsmith and John Salmon. Automatic creation of object hierarchies for ray tracing. *IEEE Computer Graphics & Applications*, 7(5):14–20, May 1987.

[164] E. H. Gombrich. *Art and Illusion: A Study in the Psychology of Pictorial Representation*. Pantheon Books, New York, 1960. Bollingen series XXXV 5.

[165] Cindy M. Goral, Kenneth E. Torrance, Donald P. Greenberg, and Bennett Battaile. Modelling the interaction of light between diffuse surfaces. *Computer Graphics (Proc. Siggraph '84)*, 18(3):213–222, July 1984.

[166] Steven Gortler, Michael F. Cohen, and Philipp Slusallek. Radiosity and relaxation methods. *IEEE Computer Graphics & Applications*, 14(6):48–58, November 1994.

[167] Steven J. Gortler, Peter Schröder, Michael Cohen, and Pat Hanrahan. Wavelet radiosity. *Computer Graphics (Proc. Siggraph '93)*, 27(3):221–230, August 1993.

[168] Ned Greene and Paul S. Heckbert. Creating raster Omnimax images from multiple perspective views using the elliptical weighted average filter. *IEEE Computer Graphics & Applications*, 6(6):21–27, June 1986.

[169] Ned Greene, Michael Kass, and Gavin Miller. Hierarchical z-buffer visibility. *Computer Graphics (Proc. Siggraph '93)*, 27(3):231–238, August 1993.

[170] Robert Greenler. *Rainbows, Halos, and Glories*. Cambridge University Press, New York, 1980.

[171] R. L. Gregory. *The Intelligent Eye*. Macmillan, New York, 1970.

[172] Günterh Greiner, Wolfgang Heidrich, and Philipp Slusallek. Blockwise refinement—A new method for solving the radiosity problem. In Michael Cohen, Claude Puech, and François Sillion, editors, *Fourth Eurographics Workshop on Rendering*, pp. 233–245. Elsevier, Amsterdam, 1993.

[173] D. F. Griffiths and G. A. Watson, editors. *Numerical Analysis 1987*, volume 170 of *Pitman Research Notes in Mathematics*. Longman Scientific and Technical, Harlow, Essex, England, 1988.

[174] Branko Grünbaum and G. C. Shephard. *Tilings and Patterns*. W H Freeman, New York, 1987.

[175] Chet S. Haase and Gary W. Meyer. Modeling pigmented materials for realistic image synthesis. *ACM Transactions on Graphics*, 11(4):305–335, October 1992.

[176] Wolfgang Hackbusch. Error analysis of the nonlinear multigrid method of the second kind. *Aplikace Matematiky*, 26(1):18–29, 1981.

[177] Eric Haines. Essential ray tracing algorithms. In Andrew S. Glassner, editor, *An Introduction to Ray Tracing*, pp. 33–78. Academic Press, San Diego, 1989.

[178] Eric Haines. Shaft culling for efficent ray-traced radiosity. In Andrew S. Glassner, editor, *Siggraph 1991 Frontiers in Rendering course notes*, chapter 2. ACM Siggraph, New York, July 1991.

[179] Kenneth Haines and Debby Haines. Computer graphics for holography. *IEEE Computer Graphics & Applications*, 12(1):37–46, January 1992.

[180] David E. Hall and Holly E. Rushmeier. An improved explicit radiosity method for calculating non-lambertian reflections. Technical report GIT-GVU–91–16, Graphics, Visualization & Usability Center, Georgia Institute of Technology, Atlanta, September 1991.

[181] Roy Hall. *Illumination and Color in Computer Generated Imagery*. Springer-Verlag, New York, 1989.

[182] John H. Halton. A retrospective and prospective survey of the Monte Carlo method. *SIAM Review*, 12(1):1–73, January 1970.

[183] J. M. Hammersley and D. C. Handscomb. *Monte Carlo Methods*. Methuen & Co., London, 1964.

[184] R. W. Hamming. *Coding and Information Theory*. Prentice-Hall, Englewood Cliffs, NJ, 2nd ed., 1986.

[185] R. W. Hamming. *Digital Filters*. Prentice-Hall, Englewood Cliffs, NJ, 3rd ed., 1989.

[186] Pat Hanrahan. A survey of ray-surface intersection algorithms. In Andrew S. Glassner, editor, *An Introduction to Ray Tracing*, pp. 79–120. Academic Press, San Diego, 1989.

[187] Pat Hanrahan. Three-pass affine transforms for volume rendering. *Computer Graphics (Proc. San Diego Workshop on Volume Visualization)*, 24(5):71–90, November 1990.

[188] Pat Hanrahan. Rendering concepts. In Michael F. Cohen and John R. Wallace, *Radiosity and Realistic Image Synthesis*. Academic Press, San Diego, 1993.

[189] Pat Hanrahan and Paul Haeberli. Direct WYSIWYG painting and texturing on 3D shapes. *Computer Graphics (Proc. Siggraph '90)*, 24(4):215–223, August 1990.

[190] Pat Hanrahan and Wolfgang Krueger. Reflection from layered surfaces due to subsurface scattering. *Computer Graphics (Proc. Siggraph '93)*, 27(3):165–174, August 1993.

[191] Pat Hanrahan and David Salzman. A rapid hierarchical radiosity algorithm for unoccluded environments. In K. Bouatouch and C. Bouville, editors, *Eurographics Workshop on Photosimulation, Realism and Physics in Computer Graphics*, pp. 151–171. Elsevier, Amsterdam, 1990.

[192] Pat Hanrahan, David Salzman, and Larry Aupperle. A rapid hierarchical radiosity algorithm. *Computer Graphics (Proc. Siggraph '91)*, 25(4):197–206, July 1991.

[193] A. J. Hanson and P. A. Heng. Illuminating the fourth dimension. *IEEE Computer Graphics & Applications*, 12(4):54–62, July 1992.

[194] Andrew J. Hanson and Robert A. Cross. Interactive visualization methods for four dimensions. In Gregory M. Nielson and Dan Bergeron, editors, *Proceedings of Visualization '93*, pp. 196–203. IEEE Computer Society Press, Los Alamitos, CA, 1993.

[195] John C. Hart and Thomas A. DeFanti. Efficient antialiased rendering of 3-D linear fractals. *Computer Graphics (Proc. Siggraph '91)*, 25(4):91–100, July 1991.

[196] Akihiko Hashimoto, Taka aki Akimoto, Kenji Mase, and Yasuhito Suenaga. Vista ray-tracing: High speed ray tracing using perspective projection image. In Rae A. Earnshaw and Brian Wyvill, editors, *New Advances in Computer Graphics (Proc. CG International '89)*, pp. 549–561. Springer-Verlag, New York, 1989.

[197] Xiao D. He, Patrick O. Heynen, Richard L. Phillips, Kenneth E. Torrance, David H. Salesin, and Donald P. Greenberg. A fast and accurate light reflection model. *Computer Graphics (Proc. Siggraph '92)*, 26(2):253–254, July 1992.

[198] Xiao D. He, Kenneth E. Torrance, François X. Sillion, and Donald P. Greenberg. A comprehensive physical model for light reflection. *Computer Graphics (Proc. Siggraph '91)*, 25(4):175–186, July 1991.

[199] Donald Hearn and M. Pauline Baker. *Computer Graphics*. Prentice-Hall, Englewood Cliffs, NJ, 2nd ed., 1986.

[200] Eugene Hecht. *Schaum's Outline of Theory and Problems of Optics*. McGraw-Hill, New York, 1975.

[201] Eugene Hecht and Alfred Zajac. *Optics*. Addison-Wesley, Reading, MA, 1974.

[202] Paul Heckbert. *Simulating Global Illumination Using Adaptive Meshing*. Ph.D. thesis, University of California, Berkeley, January 1991.

[203] Paul Heckbert. Finite element methods for radiosity. In Paul Heckbert, editor, *Siggraph 1993 Global Illumination course notes*, chapter 2. ACM Siggraph, New York, August 1993.

[204] Paul S. Heckbert. Filtering by repeated integration. *Computer Graphics (Proc. Siggraph '86)*, 20(4):315–321, August 1986.

[205] Paul S. Heckbert. Survey of texture mapping. *IEEE Computer Graphics & Applications*, 6(11):56–67, November 1986. Also in *Tutorial: Computer Graphics: Image Synthesis*, pp. 321–332. Computer Society Press, Washington, DC, 1988.

[206] Paul S. Heckbert. *Fundamentals of Texture Mapping and Image Warping*. Master's thesis, Dept. of Electrical Engineering and Computer Science, University of California, Berkeley, June 1989.

[207] Paul S. Heckbert. Adaptive radiosity textures for bidirectional ray tracing. *Computer Graphics (Proc. Siggraph '90)*, 24(4):145–154, August 1990.

[208] Paul S. Heckbert. What are the coordinates of a pixel? In Andrew S. Glassner, editor, *Graphics Gems*, pp. 246–248. Academic Press, San Diego, 1990.

[209] Paul S. Heckbert. Writing a ray tracer. In Andrew S. Glassner, editor, *An Introduction to Ray Tracing*, pp. 263–294. Academic Press, San Diego, 1990.

[210] Paul S. Heckbert. Discontinuity meshing for radiosity. In Alan Chalmers, Derek Paddon, and François Sillion, editors, *Third Eurographics Workshop on Rendering*, pp. 203–216. Elsevier, Amsterdam, 1992.

[211] Paul S. Heckbert and Pat Hanrahan. Beam tracing polygonal objects. *Computer Graphics (Proc. Siggraph '84)*, 18(3):119–127, July 1984.

[212] K. Ho-Le. Finite element mesh generation methods: A review and classification. *Computer-Aided Design*, 20(1):27–38, January/February 1986.

[213] Guido Hoheisel. *Integral Equations*. Frederick Ungar, New York, 1968. Translated by A. Mary Tropper.

[214] Hugues Hoppe, Tony DeRose, Tom Duchamp, John McDonald, and Werner Stuetzle. Mesh optimization. *Computer Graphics (Proc. Siggraph '93)*, 27(3):19–26, August 1993.

[215] John R. Howell. *A Catalog of Radiation Configuration Factors*. McGraw-Hill, New York, 1982.

[216] Ping-Kang Hsiung and Robert H. P. Dunn. Visualizing relativistic effects in spacetime. In *Proc. Supercomputing '89*, pp. 597–606. ACM Press, New York, 1989.

[217] Ping-Kang Hsiung, Robert H. Thibadeau, Christopher B. Cox, Robert H. P. Dunn, Michael Wu, and Paul Andrew Olbrich. Wide-band relativistic doppler effect visualization. In *Visualization '90: Proc. First IEEE Conference on Visualization*, pp. 83–92. IEEE Computer Society Press, Los Alamitos, CA, 1990.

[218] Thomas S. Huang. The subjective effect of two-dimensional pictorial noise. *IEEE Transactions on Information Theory*, pp. 43–53, January 1965.

[219] R. W. G. Hunt. *The Reproduction of Color*. Fountain Press, Surrey, England, 4th ed., 1988.

[220] R. S. Hunter. *The Measurement of Appearance*. John Wiley & Sons, New York, 1975.

[221] IES. Nomenclature and definitions for illuminating engineering. Technical report ANSI/IES RP-16-1986, New York, 1986.

[222] IES Computer Committee. IES standard file format for electronic transfer of photometric data and related information. Technical report IES LM-63-1991, New York, 1991.

[223] Yasuhiko Ikebe. The Galerkin method for the numerical solution of Fredholm integral equations of the second kind. *SIAM Review*, 14(3):465–491, July 1972.

[224] David S. Immel, Michael Cohen, and Donald P. Greenberg. A radiosity method for non-diffuse environments. *Computer Graphics (Proc. Siggraph '86)*, 20(4):133–142, August 1986.

[225] Masa Inakage. Volume tracing of atmospheric environments. *The Visual Computer*, 7:104–113, 1991.

[226] E. Atlee Jackson. *Perspectives of Nonlinear Dynamics I*. Cambridge University Press, Cambridge, England, 1990.

[227] E. Atlee Jackson. *Perspectives of Nonlinear Dynamics II*. Cambridge University Press, Cambridge, England, 1990.

[228] Frederik W. Jansen and Jarke J. van Wijk. Fast previewing techniques in raster graphics. In P. J. W. ten Hagen, editor, *Proc. Eurographics '83*, pp. 195–202. North-Holland, Amsterdam, 1983.

[229] Björn Jawerth and Wim Sweldens. An overview of wavelet based multiresolution analysis. Submitted to *SIAM Review*, January 1993.

[230] Francis A. Jenkins and Harvey E. White. *Fundamentals of Optics*. McGraw-Hill, New York, 1957.

[231] Abdul J. Jerri. The Shannon sampling theorem—its various extensions and applications: A tutorial review. *Proceedings of the IEEE*, 65(11):1565–1596, November 1977.

[232] D. B. Judd and G. Wyszecki. *Color in Business, Science and Industry*. John Wiley & Sons, New York, 3rd ed., 1975.

[233] James T. Kajiya. Anisotropic reflection models. *Computer Graphics (Proc. Siggraph '85)*, 19(3):15–21, July 1985.

[234] James T. Kajiya. The rendering equation. *Computer Graphics (Proc. Siggraph '86)*, 20(4):143–150, August 1986.

[235] James T. Kajiya. Radiometry and photometry for computer graphics. In Andrew S. Glassner, editor, *Siggraph 1990 Advanced Topics in Ray Tracing course notes*, chapter 2. ACM Siggraph, New York, August 1990.

[236] James T. Kajiya and Brian P. Von Herzen. Ray tracing volume densities. *Computer Graphics (Proc. Siggraph '84)*, 18(3):165–174, July 1984.

[237] James T. Kajiya and Timothy L. Kay. Rendering fur with three dimensional textures. *Computer Graphics (Proc. Siggraph '89)*, 23(3):271–280, July 1989.

[238] James T. Kajiya and Michael Ullner. Filtering high quality text for display on raster scan devices. *Computer Graphics (Proc. Siggraph '81)*, 15(3):7–15, August 1981.

[239] Malvin H. Kalos and Paula A. Whitlock. *Monte Carlo Methods: Volume I: Basics*. John Wiley & Sons, New York, 1986.

[240] Ram P. Kanwal. *Linear Integral Equations: Theory and Technique*. Academic Press, San Diego, 1971.

[241] Michael R. Kaplan. Space-tracing, a constant time ray-tracer. In *Siggraph '85 State of the Art in Image Synthesis course notes*. ACM Siggraph, New York, July 1985.

[242] John K. Kawai, James S. Painter, and Michael F. Cohen. Radioptimization—goal based rendering. *Computer Graphics (Proc. Siggraph '93)*, 27(3):147–154, August 1993.

[243] Timothy L. Kay and James T. Kajiya. Ray tracing complex scenes. *Computer Graphics (Proc. Siggraph '84)*, 18(3):269–278, July 1984.

[244] S. P. Kim and N. K. Bose. Reconstruction of 2-D bandlimited discrete signals from nonuniform samples. *IEEE Proceedings*, 137, Pt. F(3):197–204, June 1990.

[245] David Kirk and James Arvo. The ray tracing kernel. In Michael Gigante, editor, *Proc. Ausgraph '88*, pp. 75–82. Australasian Computer Graphics Association, 1988. Also in *Siggraph '90 Advanced Topics in Ray Tracing course notes*. ACM Siggraph, New York, 1990.

[246] David Kirk and James Arvo. Unbiased sampling techniques for image synthesis. *Computer Graphics (Proc. Siggraph '91)*, 25(4), July 1991.

[247] R. Victor Klassen. Modeling the effect of the atmosphere on light. *ACM Transactions on Graphics*, 6(3):215–237, July 1987.

[248] Peter Dale Kochevar. *Computer Graphics on Massively Parallel Machines*. Ph.D. thesis, Cornell University, Ithaca, NY, August 1989.

[249] Arjan J. F. Kok. Grouping of patches in progressive radiosity. In Michael Cohen, Claude Puech, and François Sillion, editors, *Fourth Eurographics Workshop on Rendering*, pp. 221–231. Elsevier, Amsterdam, 1993.

[250] Arjan J. F. Kok, Celal Yilmaz, and Laurens J. J. Bierens. A two-pass radiosity method for Bézier patches. In K. Bouatouch and C. Bouville, editors, *Eurographics Workshop on Photosimulation, Realism and Physics in Computer Graphics*, pp. 117–126. Elsevier, Amsterdam, 1990.

[251] J. Kondo. *Integral Equations*. Clarendon Press, Oxford, England, 1991.

[252] Bart Kosko. *Fuzzy Thinking*. Hyperion Books, New York, 1992.

[253] Bart Kosko. *Neural Networks and Fuzzy Systems*. Prentice-Hall, Englewood Cliffs, NJ, 1992.

[254] Rainer Kress. *Linear Integral Equations*. Springer-Verlag, New York, 1989.

[255] P. Kubelka and F. Munk. Ein beitrag zur optik der farbanstriche. *Zurich Tech. Physik*, 12:543, 1931.

[256] Paul Kubelka. New contributions to the optics of intensely light-scattering materials (Part I). *Journal of the Optical Society of America*, 38:448, 1948.

[257] Edi Lanners. *Illusions*. Holt, Rinehart, and Winston, Orlando, FL, 1977. Translated by Heinz Norden.

[258] David Laur and Pat Hanrahan. Hierarchical splatting: A progressive refinement algorithm for volume rendering. *Computer Graphics (Proc. Siggraph '91)*, 25(4):285–288, July 1991.

[259] Bertrand Le Saec and Christophe Schlick. A progressive ray-tracing-based radiosity with general reflectance functions. In K. Bouatouch and C. Bouville, editors, *Eurographics Workshop on Photosimulation, Realism and Physics in Computer Graphics*, pp. 103–116. Elsevier, Amsterdam, 1990.

[260] Mark E. Lee and Richard A. Redner. A note on the use of nonlinear filtering in computer graphics. *IEEE Computer Graphics & Applications*, 10(5):23–29, May 1990.

[261] Mark E. Lee, Richard A. Redner, and Samuel P. Uselton. Statistically optimized sampling for distributed ray tracing. *Computer Graphics (Proc. Siggraph '85)*, 19(3):61–67, July 1985.

[262] Oscar A. Z. Leneman. Random sampling of random processes: Impulse processes. *Information and Control*, 9:347–363, 1966.

[263] Oscar A. Z. Leneman. Random sampling of random processes: Optimum linear interpolation. *Journal of the Franklin Institute*, 281(4):302–314, April 1966.

[264] Oscar A. Z. Leneman. Statistical properties of random pulse trains. *1966 IEEE International Convention Record*, 6:167–172, March 1966.

[265] Oscar A. Z. Leneman. The spectral analysis of impulse processes. *Information and Control*, 12:236–258, 1968.

[266] Jaquiline Lenoble. *Radiative Transfer in Scattering and Absorbing Atmospheres: Standard Computational Procedures*. A. Deepak Publishing, 1985.

[267] Humboldt W. Leverenz. *An Introduction to Luminescence of Solids*. Dover Publications, Mineola, NY, 1968.

[268] Marc Levoy. Efficient ray tracing of volume data. *ACM Transactions on Graphics*, 9(3):245–261, July 1990.

[269] Marc Levoy. A hybrid ray tracer for rendering polygon and volume data. *IEEE Computer Graphics & Applications*, 10(3):33–40, March 1990.

[270] L. Lewin. *Dilogarithm and Associated Functions*. Macdonald, London, 1958.

[271] Harry R. Lewis and Christos H. Papadimitriou. *Elements of the Theory of Computation*. Prentice-Hall, Englewood Cliffs, NJ, 1981.

[272] J. P. Lewis. Algorithms for solid noise synthesis. *Computer Graphics (Proc. Siggraph '89)*, 23(3):263–270, July 1989.

[273] Robert R. Lewis. Making shaders more physically plausible. In Michael Cohen, Claude Puech, and François Sillion, editors, *Fourth Eurographics Workshop on Rendering*, pp. 47–62. Elsevier, Amsterdam, 1993.

[274] Dani Lischinski, Filippo Tampieri, and Donald P. Greenberg. Combining hierarchical radiosity and discontinuity meshing. *Computer Graphics (Proc. Siggraph '93)*, 27(3):199–208, August 1993.

[275] Dani Lischniski, Filippo Tampieri, and Donald P. Greenberg. Discontinuity meshing for accurate radiosity. *IEEE Computer Graphics & Applications*, 12(6):25–39, November 1992.

[276] Richard L. Longini. *Introductory Quantum Mechanics for the Solid State*. Wiley-Interscience, New York, 1970.

[277] M. Luckiesh. *Visual Illusions*. Dover, Mineola, NY, 1965. (Reprint of the 1922 edition).

[278] David MacDonald. *Space Subdivision Algorithms for Ray Tracing*. Master's thesis, University of Waterloo, Waterloo, Ontario, 1988.

[279] J.-L. Maillot. Personal communication, January 1993.

[280] J.-L. Maillot, L. Carraro, and B. Peroche. Progressive ray tracing. In Alan Chalmers, Derek Paddon, and François Sillion, editors, *Third Eurographics Workshop on Rendering*, pp. 9–20. Elsevier, Amsterdam, 1992.

[281] Farokh Marvasti, Mostafa Analoui, and Mohsen Gamshadzahi. Recovery of signals from nonuniform samples using iterative methods. *IEEE Transactions on Signal Processing*, 39(4):872–878, April 1991.

[282] Farokh Marvasti and Tsung Jen Lee. Analysis and recovery of sample-and-hold and linearly interpolated signals with irregular samples. *IEEE Transactions on Signal Processing*, 40(8):1884–1891, August 1992.

[283] Farokh A. Marvasti. *A Unified Approach to Zero-Crossings and Nonuniform Sampling*. Nonuniform Press, Oak Fork, IL, 1987.

[284] Nelson Max. An optimal filter for image reconstruction. In James Arvo, editor, *Graphics Gems II*, pp. 101–104. Academic Press, San Diego, 1991.

[285] Nelson Max and Roy Troutman. Optimal hemicube sampling. In Michael Cohen, Claude Puech, and François Sillion, editors, *Fourth Eurographics Workshop on Rendering*, pp. 185–200. Elsevier, Amsterdam, 1993.

[286] Nelson L. Max. Atmospheric illumination and shadows. *Computer Graphics (Proc. Siggraph '86)*, 20(4):117–124, August 1986.

[287] Nelson L. Max. Unified sun and sky illumination for shadows under trees. *CGVIP: Graphical Models and Image Processing*, 53(3):223–230, May 1991.

[288] Nelson L. Max and Michael J. Allison. Linear radiosity approximation using vertex-to-vertex form factors. In James Arvo, editor, *Graphics Gems II*, pp. 318–323. Academic Press, San Diego, 1991.

[289] Gregory M. Maxwell, Michael J. Bailey, and Victor W. Goldschmidt. Calculations of the radiation configuration factor using ray casting. *Computer-Aided Design*, 18(9):371–379, September 1986.

[290] David F. McAllister. *Stereo Computer Graphics and Other True 3D Technologies*. Princeton University Press, Princeton, NJ, 1993.

[291] C. S. McCamy, H. Marcus, and J. G. Davidson. A color-rendition chart. *Journal of Applied Photographic Engineering*, 2(3):95–99, summer 1976.

[292] E. J. McCartney. *Optics of the Atmosphere*. John Wiley & Sons, New York, 1976.

[293] Scott McCloud. *Understanding Comics*. Kitchen Sink Press, Princeton, WI, 1993.

[294] Michael McCool and Eugene Fiume. Hierarchical Poisson disk sampling distributions. In Kellogg Booth and Alain Fournier, editors, *Proc. Graphics Interface '92*, pp. 94–105. Canadian Information Processing Society, Toronto, 1992.

[295] Donald A. McQuarrie. *Quantum Chemistry*. University Science Books, Mill Valley, CA, 1983.

[296] Aden Meinel and Marjorie Meinel. *Sunsets, Twilights, and Evening Skies*. Cambridge University Press, New York, 1983.

[297] Louis K. Meisel. *Photo-Realism*. Harry N. Abrams, New York, 1985.

[298] Robin M. Merrifield. Visual parameters for color CRTs. In H. John Durrett, editor, *Color and the Computer*, chapter 4, pp. 63–82. Academic Press, San Diego, 1987.

[299] Dimitris Metaxas and Evangelos Milios. Color image reconstruction from nonuniform sparse samples using a thin plate model. In Carlo E. Vandoni and David A. Duce, editors, *Proc. Eurographics '90*, pp. 75–86. North-Holland, Amsterdam, 1990.

[300] Gary W. Meyer. Wavelength selection for synthetic image generation. *Computer Vision, Graphics, and Image Processing*, 41:57–79, 1988.

[301] Gary W. Meyer, Holly E. Rushmeier, Michael F. Cohen, Donald P. Greenberg, and Kenneth E. Torrance. An experimental evaluation of computer graphics imagery. *ACM Transactions on Graphics*, 5(1):30–50, January 1986.

[302] Yves Meyer. *Wavelets: Algorithms and Applications*. SIAM, Philadelphia, 1993. Translated and revised by Robert D. Ryan.

[303] Solomon Mikhlin. *Multidimensional Singular Equations and Integral Equations*. Pergamon Press, Tarrytown, NY, 1962. Translated by W. J. A. Whyte and edited by I. N. Sneddon.

[304] Gavin Miller. From wire-frames to furry animals. *Proc. Graphics Interface '88*, pp. 138–145, Canadian Information Processing Society, Toronto, 1988.

[305] M. Minnaert. *The Nature of Light & Colour in the Open Air*. Dover Publications, Mineola, NY, 1954.

[306] Charles W. Misner, Kip S. Thorne, and John Archibald Wheeler. *Gravitation*. W H Freeman, New York, 1970.

[307] Don P. Mitchell. Generating antialiased images at low sampling densities. *Computer Graphics (Proc. Siggraph '87)*, 21(4):65–72, July 1987.

[308] Don P. Mitchell. Spectrally optimal sampling for distribution ray tracing. *Computer Graphics (Proc. Siggraph '91)*, 25(4):157–164, July 1991.

[309] Don P. Mitchell. Ray tracing and irregularities of distribution. In Alan Chalmers, Derek Paddon, and François Sillion, editors, *Third Eurographics Workshop on Rendering*, pp. 61–69. Elsevier, Amsterdam, 1992.

[310] Don P. Mitchell and Arun N. Netravali. Reconstruction filters in computer graphics. *Computer Graphics (Proc. Siggraph '88)*, 22(4):221–228, July 1988.

[311] K. D. Möller. *Optics*. University Science Books, Mill Valley, CA, 1988.

[312] Parry Moon. *The Scientific Basis of Illumination Engineering*. McGraw-Hill, New York, 1936.

[313] Parry Moon. On interreflections. *Journal of the Optical Society of America*, 30(5):195–205, May 1940.

[314] Hans P. Moravec. 3D graphics and the wave theory. *Computer Graphics (Proc. Siggraph '81)*, 15(3):289–296, August 1981.

[315] N. I. Muskhelishvili. *Singular Integral Equations*. Wolters-Noordhoff, Groningen, The Netherlands, 1953. Translated by J. R. M. Radok.

[316] S. Hamid Nawab and Thomas F. Quatieri. Short-time Fourier transform. In Jae S. Lim and Alan V. Oppenheim, editors, *Advanced Topics in Signal Processing*, pp. 289–337. Prentice-Hall, Englewood Cliffs, NJ, 1988.

[317] László Neumann and Atilla Neumann. Efficient radiosity methods for non-separable reflectance models. In K. Bouatouch and C. Bouville, editors, *Eurographics Workshop on Photosimulation, Realism and Physics in Computer Graphics*, pp. 83–102. Elsevier, Amsterdam, 1990.

[318] F. E. Nicodemus, J. C. Richmond, J. J. Hsia, I. W. Ginsberg, and T. Limperis. Geometrical considerations and nomenclature for reflectance. Technical report 160, National Bureau of Standards, October 1977. Also in Lawrence B. Wolff, Steven A. Shafer, and Glenn E. Healey, editors, *Physics-Based Vision, Principles and Practice: Radiometry*, pp. 94–145. Jones and Bartlett, Boston, 1992.

[319] Harald Niederreiter. Quasi-Monte Carlo methods and pseudo-random numbers. *Bulletin of the American Mathematical Society*, 84(6), 1978.

[320] Tomoyuki Nishita, Yashuhiro Miyawaki, and Eihachiro Nakamae. A shading model for atmospheric scattering considering luminous intensity distribution of light sources. *Computer Graphics (Proc. Siggraph '87)*, 21(4):303–310, July 1987.

[321] Tomoyuki Nishita and Eihachiro Nakamae. Continuous tone representation of three-dimensional objects taking account of shadows and interreflection. *Computer Graphics (Proc. Siggraph '85)*, 19(3):23–30, July 1985.

[322] Tomoyuki Nishita and Eihachiro Nakamae. A new radiosity approach using area sampling for parametric patches. In R. J. Hubbold and R. Juan, editors, *Proc. Eurographics '93*, pp. 385–398. North-Holland, Amsterdam, 1993.

[323] Tomoyuki Nishita, Takao Sirai, Katsumi Tadamura, and Eihachiro Nakamae. Display of the earth taking into account atmospheric scattering. *Computer Graphics (Proc. Siggraph '93)*, 27(3):175–182, August 1993.

[324] Ben Noble. A bibliography on "Methods for solving integral equations". Technical report 1177, Mathematics Research Center, University of Wisconsin, Madison, September 1971.

[325] Alan Norton, Alyn P. Rockwood, and Philip T. Skolmoski. Clamping: A method of antialiasing textured surfaces by bandwidth limiting in object space. *Computer Graphics (Proc. Siggraph '82)*, 16(3):1–8, July 1982.

[326] Alan V. Oppenheim and Ronald W. Schafer. *Digital Signal Processing*. Prentice-Hall, Englewood Cliffs, NJ, 1975.

[327] Alan V. Oppenheim and Alan S. Willsky with Ian T. Young. *Signals and Systems*. Prentice-Hall, Englewood Cliffs, NJ, 1983.

[328] James Painter and Kenneth Sloan. Antialiased ray tracing by adaptive progressive refinement. *Computer Graphics (Proc. Siggraph '89)*, 23(3):281–288, July 1989.

[329] Edward D. Palik. *Handbook of Optical Constants of Solids*. Academic Press, New York, 1985.

[330] A. Papoulis. A new algorithm in spectral analysis and band-limited extrapolation. *IEEE Trans. Circuits Syst.*, CAS-22:735–742, September 1975.

[331] Athanasios Papoulis. *Probability, Random Variables, and Stochastic Processes*. McGraw-Hill, New York, 1965.

[332] S. N. Pattanaik. *Computational Methods for Global Illumination and Visualisation of Complex 3D Environments*. Ph.D. thesis, Birla Institute of Technology & Science, Pilani, India, February 1993.

[333] S. N. Pattanaik and S. P. Mudur. Computation of global illumination by Monte Carlo simulation of the particle model of light. In Alan Chalmers, Derek Paddon, and François Sillion, editors, *Third Eurographics Workshop on Rendering*, pp. 71–83. Elsevier, Amsterdam, 1992.

[334] S. N. Pattanaik and S. P. Mudur. The potential equation and importance in illumination computations. *Computer Graphics Forum*, 12(2):131–136, 1993.

[335] Mark J. Pavicic. Convenient anti-aliasing filters that minimize "bumpy" sampling. In Andrew S. Glassner, editor, *Graphics Gems*, pp. 144–146. Academic Press, San Diego, 1990.

[336] Theo Pavlidis. Comments on "Stochastic sampling in computer graphics". Letter to the editor, *ACM Transactions on Graphics*, 9(2):233-236, April 1990.

[337] Mark S. Peercy. Linear color representations for full spectral rendering. *Computer Graphics (Proc. Siggraph '93)*, 27(3):191–198, August 1993.

[338] Ken Perlin. An image synthesizer. *Computer Graphics (Proc. Siggraph '85)*, 19(3):287–296, July 1985.

[339] Ken Perlin and Eric M. Hoffert. Hypertexture. *Computer Graphics (Proc. Siggraph '89)*, 23(3):253–262, July 1989.

[340] Roger Tory Peterson. *The Birds*. Time, Inc., Alexandria, VA, 1964. Life Nature Library.

[341] Georg Pietrek. Fast calculation of accurate form factors. In Michael Cohen, Claude Puech, and François Sillion, editors, *Fourth Eurographics Workshop on Rendering*, pp. 201–220. Elsevier, Amsterdam, 1993.

[342] G. C. Pomraning. *The Equations of Radiation Hydrodynamics*. Pergamon Press, Tarrytown, NY, 1973.

[343] David Porter and David G. Stirling. *Integral Equations: A Practical Treatment, from Spectral Theory to Applications*. Cambridge University Press, New York, 1990.

[344] Pierre Poulin and Alain Fournier. A model for anisotropic reflection. *Computer Graphics (Proc. Siggraph '90)*, 24(4):273–282, August 1990.

[345] William K. Pratt. *Digital Image Processing*. John Wiley & Sons, New York, 2nd ed., 1991.

[346] Franco P. Prearata and Michael Ian Shamos. *Computational Geometry: An Introduction*. Springer-Verlag, New York, 1985.

[347] Rudolph W. Preisendorfer. *Radiative Transfer on Discrete Spaces*. Pergamon Press, Tarrytown, NY, 1965.

[348] William H. Press, Saul A. Teukolsky, William T. Vetterling, and Brian P. Flannery. *Numerical Recipes in C, 2nd ed.* Cambridge University Press, New York, 1992.

[349] Claude Puech, François Sillion, and Christophe Vedel. Improving interaction with radiosity-based lighting simulation programs. *Computer Graphics (Proc. 1990 Symposium on Interactive 3D Graphics)*, 24(2):51–57, March 1990.

[350] Xavier Pueyo. Diffuse interreflections. Techniques for form-factor computation: A survey. *Visual Computer*, 7(7):200–201, July 1991.

[351] Werner Purgathofer. A statistical method for adaptive stochastic sampling. In Aristides A. G. Requicha, editor, *Proc. Eurographics '86*, pp. 145–152. North-Holland, Amsterdam, 1986.

[352] Werner Purgathofer and Michael Zeiller. Fast radiosity by parallelization. In K. Bouatouch and C. Bouville, editors, *Eurographics Workshop on Photosimulation, Realism and Physics in Computer Graphics*, pp. 173–183. Elsevier, Amsterdam, 1990.

[353] Anthony Ralston and Philip Rabinowitz. *A First Course in Numerical Analysis*. McGraw-Hill, New York, 2nd ed., 1978.

[354] Maria G. Raso and Alain Fournier. A piecewise polynomial approach to shading using spectral distributions. In Brian Wyvill, editor, *Proc. Graphics*

Interface '91, pp. 40–46. Canadian Information Processing Society, Toronto, 1991.

[355] Mark S. Rea, editor. *Lighting Handbook Reference and Application*. IES, New York, 8th ed., 1993.

[356] Rodney J. Recker, David W. George, and Donald P. Greenberg. Acceleration techniques for progressive refinement radiosity. *Computer Graphics (Proc. 1990 Symposium on Interactive 3D Graphics)*, 24(2):59–66, March 1990.

[357] Christopher E. Reid and Thomas B. Passin. *Signal Processing in* C. John Wiley & Sons, New York, 1992.

[358] Howard L. Resnikoff. *The Illusion of Reality*. Springer-Verlag, New York, 1989.

[359] Olivier Rioul and Martin Vetterli. Wavelets and signal processing. *IEEE SP Magazine*, pp. 14–38, October 1991.

[360] Hazel Rossotti. *Colour: Why the World Isn't Grey*. Princeton University Press, Princeton, NJ, 1983.

[361] Scott D. Roth. Ray casting for modeling solids. *Computer Graphics and Image Processing*, 18(2):109–144, February 1982.

[362] H. L. Royden. *Real Analysis*. Macmillan, New York, 2nd ed., 1968.

[363] Steven M. Rubin and Turner Whitted. A 3-dimensional representation for fast rendering of complex scenes. *Computer Graphics (Proc. Siggraph '80)*, 14(3):110–116, August 1980.

[364] Rudy Rucker. *The Fourth Dimension*. Houghton Mifflin, Boston, 1984.

[365] Walter Rudin. *Real and Complex Analysis*. McGraw-Hill, New York, 2nd ed., 1974.

[366] Holly Rushmeier, Charles Patterson, and Aravindan Veerasamy. Geometric simplification for indirect illumination calculations. In *Proc. Graphics Interface '93*, pp. 227–236. Canadian Information Processing Society, Toronto, 1993.

[367] Holly E. Rushmeier. Radiosity methods for volume rendering. Technical report GIT-GVU–91–01, Graphics, Visualization & Usability Center, Georgia Institute of Technology, Atlanta, 1991.

[368] Holly E. Rushmeier, Daniel R. Baum, and David E. Hall. Accelerating the hemi-cube algorithm for calculating radiation form factors. In *5th AIAA/ASME Themophysics and Heat Transfer Conference*, pp. 1044–1047, 1990.

[369] Holly E. Rushmeier and Kenneth E. Torrance. The zonal method for calculating light intensities in the presence of a participating medium. *Computer Graphics (Proc. Siggraph '87)*, 21(4):293–302, July 1987.

[370] Holly E. Rushmeier and Kenneth E. Torrance. Extending the radiosity method to include specularly reflecting and translucent materials. *ACM Transactions on Graphics*, 9(1):1–27, January 1990.

[371] Georgios Sakas and Mattias Gerth. Sampling and anti-aliasing of discrete 3-D volume density textures. In Frits H. Post and Wilhelm Barth, editors, *Proc. Eurographics '91*, pp. 87–102. North-Holland, Amsterdam, 1991.

[372] David Salesin, Dani Lischinski, and Tony DeRose. Reconstructing illumination functions with selected discontinuities. In Alan Chalmers, Derek Paddon, and François Sillion, editors, *Third Eurographics Workshop on Rendering*, pp. 99–112. Elsevier, Amsterdam, 1992.

[373] Hanen Samet. *Applications of Spatial Data Structures*. Addison-Wesley, Reading, MA, 1990.

[374] Hanen Samet. *Design and Analysis of Spatial Data Structures*. Addison-Wesley, Reading, MA, 1990.

[375] B. Sankur and L. Gerhardt. Reconstruction of signals from nonuniform samples. In *IEEE International Conference on Communications*, pp. 15.13–15.18, June 1973.

[376] Ken D. Sauer and Jan P. Allebach. Iterative reconstruction of band-limited images from nonuniformly spaced samples. *IEEE Transactions on Circuits and Systems*, 34(12):1497–1506, December 1987.

[377] Mateu Sbert. An integral geometry based method for fast form-factor computation. In R. J. Hubbold and R. Juan, editors, *Proc. Eurographics '93*, pp. 409–420. North-Holland, Amsterdam, 1993.

[378] H. M. Schey. *Div, Grad, Curl, and All That*. W. W. Norton, New York, 1973.

[379] H. Schippers. *Multiple Grid Methods for Equations of the Second Kind with Applications in Fluid Mechanics*. Mathematisch Centrum, Amsterdam, 1983. Mathematical Centre tracts 163.

[380] Christophe Schlick. *Divers Éléments pour une synthèse d'images réalistes*. Ph.D. thesis, Université Bordeaux 1, November 1992.

[381] Christophe Schlick. A customizable reflectance model for everyday rendering. In Michael Cohen, Claude Puech, and François Sillion, editors, *Fourth Eurographics Workshop on Rendering*, pp. 73–84. Elsevier, Amsterdam, 1993.

[382] Chris Schoeneman, Julie Dorsey, Brian Smits, James Arvo, and Donald Greenberg. Painting with light. *Computer Graphics (Proc. Siggraph '93)*, 27(3):143–146, August 1993.

[383] Peter Schröder. Numerical integration for radiosity in the presence of singularities. In Michael Cohen, Claude Puech, and François Sillion, editors, *Fourth Eurographics Workshop on Rendering*, pp. 123–134. Elsevier, Amsterdam, 1993.

[384] Peter Schröder, Steven J. Gortler, Michael F. Cohen, and Pat Hanrahan. Wavelet projections for radiosity. In Michael Cohen, Claude Puech, and François Sillion, editors, *Fourth Eurographics Workshop on Rendering*, pp. 105–114. Elsevier, Amsterdam, 1993.

[385] Peter Schröder and Pat Hanrahan. A closed form expression for the form factor between two polygons. Research report CS-TR-404-93, Department of Computer Science, Princeton University, Princeton, NJ, January 1993.

[386] Peter Schröder and Pat Hanrahan. On the form factor between two polygons. *Computer Graphics (Proc. Siggraph '93)*, 27(3):163–164, August 1993.

[387] Sven Schuierer. Delaunay triangulations and the radiosity approach. In W. Hansmann, F. R. A. Hopgood, and W. Straßer, editors, *Proc. Eurographics '89*, pp. 345–353. North-Holland, Amsterdam, 1989.

[388] Bernard F. Schutz. *A First Course in General Relativity*. Cambridge University Press, New York, 1990.

[389] Robert Sekuler and Randolph Blake. *Perception*. Alfred A. Knopf, New York, 1985.

[390] Carlo H. Séquin and Eliot K. Smyrl. Parameterized ray tracing. *Computer Graphics (Proc. Siggraph '89)*, 23(3):307–314, July 1989.

[391] Min-Zhi Shao and Norman I. Badler. Analysis and acceleration of progressive refinement radiosity method. In Michael Cohen, Claude Puech, and François Sillion, editors, *Fourth Eurographics Workshop on Rendering*, pp. 247–258. Elsevier, Amsterdam, 1993.

[392] Min-Zhi Shao, Qun-Sheng Peng, and You-Dong Liang. A new radiosity approach by procedural refinements for realistic image synthesis. *Computer Graphics (Proc. Siggraph '88)*, 22(4):93–101, August 1988.

[393] Ping-Ping Shao, Qun-Sheng Peng, and You-Dong Liang. Form-factors for general environments. In David A. Duce and Pierre Jancene, editors, *Proc. Eurographics '88*, pp. 499–510. North-Holland, Amsterdam, 1988.

[394] Harold R. Shapiro and Richard A. Silverman. Alias-free sampling of random noise. *Journal of the Society for Industrial and Applied Mathematics*, 8(2):225–248, 1960.

[395] Peter Shirley. Physically based lighting calculations for computer graphics: A modern perspective. In K. Bouatouch and C. Bouville, editors, *Eurographics Workshop on Photosimulation, Realism and Physics in Computer Graphics*, pp. 67–81. Elsevier, Amsterdam, 1990.

[396] Peter Shirley. A ray tracing method for illumination calculation in diffuse-specular scenes. In *Proc. Graphics Interface '90*, pp. 205–212. Canadian Information Processing Society, Toronto, 1990.

[397] Peter Shirley. Discrepancy as a quality measure for sample distributions. In Frits H. Post and Wilhelm Barth, editors, *Proc. Eurographics '91*, pp. 183–194. North-Holland, Amsterdam, 1991.

[398] Peter Shirley. Radiosity via ray tracing. In James Arvo, editor, *Graphics Gems II*, pp. 306–310. Academic Press, San Diego, 1991.

[399] Peter Shirley. A ray tracing framework for global illumination systems. In Brian Wyvill, editor, *Proc. Graphics Interface '91*, pp. 117–128. Canadian Information Processing Society, Toronto, 1991.

[400] Peter Shirley. Nonuniform random point sets via warping. In David Kirk, editor, *Graphics Gems III*, pp. 80–83. Academic Press, San Diego, 1992.

[401] Peter Shirley and Changyaw Wang. Distribution ray tracing: Theory and practice. In Alan Chalmers, Derek Paddon, and François Sillion, editors, *Third Eurographics Workshop on Rendering*, pp. 33–43. Elsevier, Amsterdam, 1992.

[402] Peter S. Shirley. *Physically Based Lighting Calculations for Computer Graphics*. Ph.D. thesis, University of Illinois at Urbana-Champaign, 1991.

[403] Leonard Shlain. *Art and Physics*. William Morrow, New York, 1992.

[404] Ken Shoemake. Animating rotations with quaternion curves. *Computer Graphics (Proc. Siggraph '85)*, 19(3):245–254, July 1985.

[405] Renben Shu and Alan Liu. A fast ray casting algorithm using adaptive isotriangular subdivision. In Gregory M. Nielson and Larry Rosenblum, editors, *Proc. Visualization '91*. IEEE Computer Society, Los Alamitos, CA, 1991.

[406] Robert Siegel and John R. Howell. *Thermal Radiation Heat Transfer*. Hemisphere Publishing, Bristol, PA, 3rd ed., 1992.

[407] François Sillion. Detection of shadow boundaries for adaptive meshing in radiosity. In James Arvo, editor, *Graphics Gems II*, pp. 311–315. Academic Press, San Diego, 1991.

[408] François Sillion and Claude Puech. A general two-pass method integrating specular and diffuse reflection. *Computer Graphics (Proc. Siggraph '89)*, 23(3):335–344, July 1989.

[409] François Sillion and Claude Puech. *Radiosity and Global Illumination*. Morgan Kaufmann, San Francisco, 1994.

[410] François X. Sillion, James R. Arvo, Stephen H. Westin, and Donald P. Greenberg. A global illumination solution for general reflectance distributions. *Computer Graphics (Proc. Siggraph '91)*, 25(4):187–196, July 1991.

[411] Louis D. Silverstein. Human factors for color display systems: Concepts, methods, and research. In H. John Durrett, editor, *Color and the Computer*, chapter 2, pp. 27–62. Academic Press, San Diego, 1987.

[412] Sandra Sinclair. *How Animals See*. Croom Helm Ltd., Beckenham, Kent, England, 1985.

[413] I. H. Sloan. Superconvergence. In Michael A. Golberg, editor, *Numerical Solution of Integral Equations*, chapter 2. Plenum Press, New York, 1990.

[414] Brian E. Smits, James R. Arvo, and David H. Salesin. An importance driven radiosity algorithm. *Computer Graphics (Proc. Siggraph '92)*, 26(4):273–282, July 1992.

[415] Jerome Spanier and Ely M. Gelbard. *Monte Carlo Principles and Neutron Transport Problems*. Addison-Wesley, Reading, MA, 1969.

[416] E. M. Sparrow. A new and simpler formulation for radiative angle factors. *Journal of Heat Transfer*, pp. 81–88, May 1963.

[417] E. M. Sparrow and R. D. Cess. *Radiation Heat Transfer*. Wadsworth, Belmont, CA, 1966.

[418] Stephen N. Spencer. The hemisphere radiosity method: A tale of two algorithms. In K. Bouatouch and C. Bouville, editors, *Eurographics Workshop on Photosimulation, Realism and Physics in Computer Graphics*, pp. 127–135. Elsevier, Amsterdam, 1990.

[419] David J. Statt. Method for the reproduction of color images based on viewer adaptation. U.S. patent 5,276,779, January 1994.

[420] Maureen C. Stone, William B. Cowan, and John C. Beatty. Color gamut mapping and the printing of digital color images. *ACM Transactions on Graphics*, 7(3):249–292, October 1988.

[421] Gilbert Strang. *Linear Algebra and Its Applications*. Academic Press, San Diego, 2nd ed., 1980.

[422] Gilbert Strang. Wavelets and dilation equations: A brief introduction. *SIAM Review*, 31(4):614–627, December 1989.

[423] Gilbert Strang. Wavelet transforms versus Fourier transforms. *Bulletin Am. Math. Soc.*, April 1993.

[424] Paul S. Strauss. A realistic lighting model for computer animators. *IEEE Computer Graphics & Applications*, 10(11):56–64, November 1990.

[425] K. R. Stromberg. *An Introduction to Classical Real Analysis*. Wadsworth International, Belmont, CA, 1981.

[426] Wolfgang Stürzlinger. Radiosity with Voronoi diagrams. In Alan Chalmers, Derek Paddon, and François Sillion, editors, *Third Eurographics Workshop on Rendering*, pp. 169–177. Elsevier, Amsterdam, 1992.

[427] Anthony Sudbery. *Quantum Mechanics and the Particles of Nature: An Outline for Mathematicians*. Cambridge University Press, New York, 1986.

[428] Jizhou Sun, L. Q. Zou, and R. L. Grimsdale. The determination of form-factors by lookup table. *Computer Graphics Forum*, 12(4):191–198, 1993.

[429] Wim Sweldens and Robert Piessens. Quadrature formulae for the calculation of the wavelet decomposition. Available via anonymous ftp from Yale wavelet server.

[430] Katsumi Tadamura, Eihachiro Nakamae, Kazufumi Kaneda, Masashi Baba, Hideo Yamashita, and Tomoyuki Nishita. Modeling of skylight and rendering of outdoor scenes. In R. J. Hubbold and R. Juan, editors, *Proc. Eurographics '93*, pp. 189–200. North-Holland, Amsterdam, 1993.

[431] J. H. Tait. *An Introduction to Neutron Transport Theory*. Elsevier, New York, 1964.

[432] Barry N. Taylor. The international system of units (SI). Technical report NIST special publication 330, 1991 edition, U.S. Government Printing Office, Washington, DC, August 1991.

[433] M. M. Taylor. Visual discrimination and orientation. *Journal of the Optical Society of America*, pp. 763–765, June 1963.

[434] Group TC4-16. Recommended file format for electronic transfer of luminaire photometric data. Technical report CIE 102-1003, International Commission on Illumination, 1993. ISBN 3-900-734-40-2.

[435] Seth Teller and Pat Hanrahan. Global visibility algorithms for illumination computations. *Computer Graphics (Proc. Siggraph '93)*, 27(3):239–246, August 1993.

[436] D. Thomas, Arun N. Netravali, and D. S. Fox. Anti-aliased ray tracing with covers. *Computer Graphics Forum*, 8(4):325–336, December 1989.

[437] Spencer Thomas. Dispersive refraction in ray tracing. *Visual Computer*, 2(1):3–8, January 1986.

[438] Georgi P. Tolstov and Richard A. Silverman (translator). *Fourier Series*. Dover, Mineola, NY, 1962.

[439] K. E. Torrance and E. M. Sparrow. Theory for off-specular reflection from roughened surfaces. *Journal of the Optical Society of America*, 57(9):1104–1114, 1967.

[440] Roy Troutman and Nelson L. Max. Radiosity algorithms using higher order finite element methods. *Computer Graphics (Proc. Siggraph '93)*, 27(3):209–212, August 1993.

[441] Jack Tumblin and Holly Rushmeier. Tone reproduction for realistic computer generated images. Technical report GIT-GVU–91–13, Graphics, Visualization & Usability Center, Georgia Institute of Technology, Atlanta, July 1991.

[442] Jack Tumblin and Holly Rushmeier. Tone reproduction for realistic images. *IEEE Computer Graphics & Applications*, 13(6):42–48, November 1993.

[443] Greg Turk. Re-tiling polygonal surfaces. *Computer Graphics (Proc. Siggraph '92)*, 26(4):55–64, July 1992.

[444] G. P. A. Turner. *Introduction to Paint Chemistry*. Chapman and Hall, New York, 1967.

[445] R. Ulichney. *Digital Halftoning*. MIT Press, Cambridge, MA, 1987.

[446] Steve Upstill. *The RenderMan Companion*. Addison-Wesley, Reading, MA, 1989.

[447] Barbara Upton and John Upton. *Photography*. Little, Brown, Boston, 2nd ed., 1981.

[448] H. T. M. van der Voort, H. J. Noordmans, J. M. Messerli, and A. W. M. Smeulders. Physically realistic volume visualization for interactive image analysis. In Michael Cohen, Claude Puech, and François Sillion, editors, *Fourth Eurographics Workshop on Rendering*, pp. 295–306. Elsevier, Amsterdam, 1993.

[449] Marc van Kreveld. *New Results on Data Structures in Computational Geometry*. Ph.D. thesis, Rijksuniversiteit te Utrecht, The Netherlands, June 1992.

[450] Theo van Walsum, Peter R. van Nieuwenhuizen, and Frederik W. Jansen. Refinement criteria for adaptive stochastic ray tracing of textures. In Frits H. Post and Wilhelm Barth, editors, *Proc. Eurographics '91*, pp. 155–166. North-Holland, Amsterdam, 1991.

[451] Christopher G. Van Wyk, Jr. *A Geometry-Based Insulation Model for Computer-Aided Design*. Ph.D. thesis, University of Michigan, Ann Arbor, 1988.

[452] Amitabh Varshney and Jan F. Prins. An environment-projection approach to radiosity for mesh-connected computers. In Alan Chalmers, Derek Paddon, and François Sillion, editors, *Third Eurographics Workshop on Rendering*, pp. 271–281. Elsevier, Amsterdam, 1992.

[453] Christophe Vedel. Improved storage and reconstruction of light intensities on surfaces. In Alan Chalmers, Derek Paddon, and François Sillion, editors, *Third Eurographics Workshop on Rendering*, pp. 113–121. Elsevier, Amsterdam, 1992.

[454] J. Vilaplana and X. Pueyo. Exploiting coherence for clipping and view transformations in radiosity algorithms. In K. Bouatouch and C. Bouville, editors, *Eurographics Workshop on Photosimulation, Realism and Physics in Computer Graphics*, pp. 137–150. Elsevier, Amsterdam, 1990.

[455] Josep Vilaplana. Parallel radiosity solutions based on partial result messages. In Alan Chalmers, Derek Paddon, and François Sillion, editors, *Third Eurographics Workshop on Rendering*, pp. 217–226. Elsevier, Amsterdam, 1992.

[456] Susan J. Voigt. Bibliography on the numerical solution of integral and differential equations and related topics. Technical report 2423, Applied Mathematics Laboratory, Naval Ship Research & Development Center, Washington, DC, November 1967.

[457] Michael J. Vrhel, Ron Gershon, and Lawrence S. Iwan. Measurement and analysis of object reflectance spectra. *Color Research & Applications*, 19(1):4–9, February 1994.

[458] M. Vygodsky. *Mathematical Handbook—Higher Mathematics*. Mir Publishers, Moscow, 1975. Translated by George Yankovsky.

[459] John R. Wallace. Trends in radiosity for image synthesis. In K. Bouatouch and C. Bouville, editors, *Eurographics Workshop on Photosimulation, Realism and Physics in Computer Graphics*, pp. 1–14. Elsevier, Amsterdam, 1990.

[460] John R. Wallace, Michael F. Cohen, and Donald P. Greenberg. A two-pass solution to the rendering equation: A synthesis of ray tracing and radiosity methods. *Computer Graphics (Proc. Siggraph '87)*, 21(4):311–320, July 1987.

[461] John R. Wallace, Kells A. Elmquist, and Eric A. Haines. A ray tracing algorithm for progressive radiosity. *Computer Graphics (Proc. Siggraph '89)*, 23(3):315–324, July 1989.

[462] George N. Walton. Algorithms for calculating radiation view factors between plane convex polygons with obstructions. *Fundamentals and Applications of Radiation Heat Transfer, HTD* Vol. 72:45–52, August 1987.

[463] Brian Wandell. *Foundations of Vision: Behavior, Neuroscience, and Computation*. Sinauer Press, Sutherland, MA, 1994.

[464] Changyaw Wang, Peter Shirley, and Kurt Zimmerman. Monte Carlo techniques for direct lighting calculations. *ACM Transactions on Graphics*. In press.

[465] Franklin F. Y. Wang. *Introduction to Solid State Electronics*. North-Holland, Amsterdam, 1980.

[466] Sidney W. Wang and Arie E. Kaufman. Volume sampled voxelization of geometric primitives. In Gregory M. Nielson and Dan Bergeron, editors, *Proceedings of Visualization '93*, pp. 78–84. IEEE Computer Society Press, Los Alamitos, CA, 1993.

[467] Greg Ward. Personal communication, 1994.

[468] Greg Ward. A contrast-based scalefactor for luminance display. In Paul Heckbert, editor, *Graphics Gems IV*, pp. 391–397. Academic Press, San Diego, 1994.

[469] Gregory J. Ward. Measuring and modeling anisotropic reflection. *Computer Graphics (Proc. Siggraph '92)*, 26(4):265–272, July 1992.

[470] Gregory J. Ward, Francis M. Rubinstein, and Robert D. Clear. A ray tracing solution for diffuse interreflection. *Computer Graphics (Proc. Siggraph '88)*, 22(4):85–92, August 1988.

[471] Tony T. Warnock. Computational investigation of low-discrepancy point sets. In S. K. Zaremba, editor, *Applications of Number Theory to Numerical Analysis*, pp. 319–343. Academic Press, San Diego, 1972.

[472] G. S. Wasserman. *Color Vision: An Historical Perspective*. John Wiley & Sons, New York, 1978.

[473] Alan Watt and Mark Watt. *Advanced Animation and Rendering Techniques: Theory and Practice*. Addison-Wesley and ACM Press, Reading, MA, 1992.

[474] H. G. Wells. The time machine. In *Seven Science Fiction Novels of H. G. Wells*. Dover Publications, Mineola, NY, 1955.

[475] Stephen H. Westin, James R. Arvo, and Kenneth E. Torrance. Predicting reflectance functions from complex surfaces. *Computer Graphics (Proc. Siggraph '92)*, 26(4):255–264, July 1992.

[476] Lee Westover. Footprint evaluation for volume rendering. *Computer Graphics (Proc. Siggraph '90)*, 24(4):367–376, August 1990.

[477] Turner Whitted. An improved illumination model for shaded display. *Communications of the ACM*, 23(6):343–349, June 1980. Also in *Tutorial: Computer Graphics: Image Synthesis*. Computer Society Press, Washington, DC, 1988. Abstract in *Computer Graphics (Proc. Siggraph '79)*, no. 2, p. 14.

[478] Charles S. Williams and Orville A. Becklund. *Optics: A Short Course for Scientists & Engineers*. Wiley-Interscience, New York, 1972.

[479] David R. Williams and Robert Collier. Consequences of spatial sampling by a human photoreceptor mosaic. *Science*, 221:385–387, July 1983.

[480] Lance Williams. Pyramidal parametrics. *Computer Graphics (Proc. Siggraph '83)*, 17(3):1–11, July 1983.

[481] M. M. R. Williams. *Mathematical Methods in Particle Transport Theory*. Butterworth-Heinemann, Stoneham, MA, 1971.

[482] G. Milton Wing. *An Introduction to Transport Theory*. John Wiley & Sons, New York, 1962.

[483] Duncan J. Wingham. The reconstruction of a band-limited function and its Fourier transform from a finite number of samples at arbitrary locations by singular value decomposition. *IEEE Transactions on Signal Processing*, 40(3):559–570, March 1992.

[484] Andrew Witkin and Michael Kass. Reaction-diffusion textures. *Computer Graphics (Proc. Siggraph '91)*, 25(4):299–308, July 1991.

[485] George Wolberg. *Digital Image Warping*. IEEE Computer Society Press, Los Alamitos, CA, 1990.

[486] Erling Wold and Kim Pépard. Comments on "Stochastic sampling in computer graphics". Letter to the editor, *ACM Transactions on Graphics*, 9(2):237-243, April 1990.

[487] Lawrence B. Wolff and David J. Kurlander. Ray tracing with polarization parameters. *IEEE Computer Graphics & Applications*, 10(11):44–55, November 1990.

[488] Elizabeth A. Wood. *Crystals and Light: An Introduction to Optical Crystallography*. Dover Publications., Mineola, NY, 2nd rev. ed., 1964.

[489] Günter Wyszecki and W. S. Stiles. *Color Science: Concepts and Methods, Quantitative Data and Formulae.* John Wiley & Sons, New York, 2nd ed., 1982.

[490] Geoff Wyvill and Craig McNaughton. Optical models. In T. S. Chua and T. L. Kunii, editors, *Computer Graphics Around the World (Proc. CG International '90),* pp. 83–93. Springer-Verlag, New York, 1990.

[491] Geoff Wyvill and P. Sharp. Fast antialiasing of ray traced images. In Tosiyasu Kunii, editor, *New Trends in Computer Graphics (Proc. CG International '88),* pp. 579–587. Springer-Verlag, New York, 1988.

[492] H. P. Xu, Q. S. Peng, and Y. D. Liang. Accelerated radiosity method for complex environments. *Computers and Graphics,* 11(1):65–71, 1990.

[493] Jin-Chao Xu and Wei-Chang Shann. Galerkin-wavelet methods for two-point boundary value problems. Submitted to *Bulletin Am. Math. Soc.,* July 1993.

[494] S. Yakowitz, J. E. Krimmel, and F. Szidarovszky. Weighted Monte Carlo integration. *SIAM Journal of Numerical Analysis,* 15(6):1289–1300, December 1978.

[495] Yoshiyuki Yamashita. Computer graphics of black holes: The extension of ray-tracings to 4-dimensional curved space-time. *Transactions of the Information Processing Society of Japan,* 30(5):642–651, 1989. (In Japanese).

[496] John I. Yellot, Jr. Spectral consequences of photoreceptor sampling in the rhesus retina. *Science,* 221:382–385, July 1983.

[497] J. L. Yen. On nonuniform sampling of bandwidth-limited signals. *IRE Transactions on Circuit Theory,* CT-3:251–257, December 1956.

[498] Shigeki Yokoi, Kosuke Kurashige, and Junichiro Toriwaki. Rendering gems with asterism or chatoyancy. *Visual Computer,* 2(9):307–312, September 1986.

[499] D. C. Youla and H. Webb. Generalized image restoration by the method of alternating orthogonal projections. *IEEE Transactions on Circuits and Systems,* CAS-25:694–702, September 1978.

[500] Nicholas Young. *An Introduction to Hilbert Space.* Cambridge University Press, New York, 1988.

[501] Ying Yuan, Tosiyasu L. Kunii, Naota Inamato, and Lining Sun. Gemstone fire: Adaptive dispersive ray tracing of polyhedrons. *Visual Computer,* 4(11):259–270, November 1988.

[502] S. Zaremba. The mathematical basis of Monte Carlo and quasi-Monte Carlo methods. *SIAM Review,* 10:303–314, 1968.

[503] Harold R. Zatz. Galerkin radiosity: A higher order solution method for global illumination. In *Computer Graphics, Annual Conference Series, 1003*, pp. 213–220. ACM Siggraph, New York, 1993.

[504] Yong Zhou and Qunsheng Peng. The super-plane buffer: An efficient form-factor evaluation algorithm for progressive radiosity. *Computers and Graphics*, 16(2):151–158, 1992.

[505] Yining Zhu, Qunsheng Peng, and Youdong Liang. PERIS: A programming environment for realistic image synthesis. *Computers and Graphics*, 12(3/4):299–307, 1988.

[506] Giuseppe Zibordi and Kenneth J. Voss. Geometrical and spectral distribution of sky radiance: Comparison between simulations and field measurements. *Remote Sensing of the Environment*, 27:343–358, 1989.

INDEX